CONGO
JOURNEY

By the same author

Joseph Conrad and Charles Darwin: The influence of scientific thought on Conrad's fiction

Into the Heart of Borneo

In Trouble Again

CONGO JOURNEY

Redmond O'Hanlon

HAMISH HAMILTON · LONDON

To my wife, Belinda

HAMISH HAMILTON LTD
Published by the Penguin Group
Penguin Books Ltd, 27 Wrights Lane, London w8 5tz, England
Penguin Books USA Inc., 375 Hudson Street, New York, New York 10014, USA
Penguin Books Australia Ltd, Ringwood, Victoria, Australia
Penguin Books Canada Ltd, 10 Alcorn Avenue, Toronto, Ontario, Canada m4v 3b2
Penguin Books (NZ) Ltd, 182–190 Wairau Road, Auckland 10, New Zealand

Penguin Books Ltd, Registered Offices: Harmondsworth, Middlesex, England

First published 1996
1 3 5 7 9 10 8 6 4 2

Grateful acknowledgement is made to James Fenton for permission
to quote lines from his poem 'The Wild Ones', from *The Memory of
War and Children in Exile: Poems 1968–93*, published by
the Salamander Press

Set in 11.25/13.5pt Monotype Garamond
Typeset by Rowland Phototypesetting Ltd, Bury St Edmunds, Suffolk
Printed in England by Clays Ltd, St Ives plc

A CIP catalogue record for this book is available from the British Library

Hardback ISBN 0–241–12768–8
Trade Paperback ISBN 0–241–13374–2

Acknowledgements

The author wishes to thank Andrew Franklin; Galen Strawson; Simon Stockton; John Stanbury; Pat Kavanagh; Peter Carson; Jonathan Kingdon; James Fenton; Bill Buford; Ursula Doyle and *Granta*; Ferdinand Mount and the *TLS*; Linda Hopkins; Rosie Boycott; Andrew Kidd; Alexandra Pringle; Jon Riley; Fred Bayliss; Max Peterson; Will Self; David Warrell; Jacques Meunier; Mark Harvey Smith; Chris Shaffer; Charles O. Warren; Ian Glasby; Tim Gravestock; Keith Taylor; Louis Muzzu; Ossebei Douniam; Yvette Leroy and Assitou Ndinga.

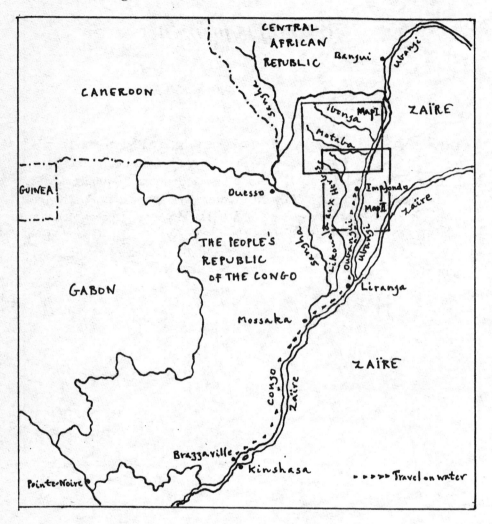

The first journey

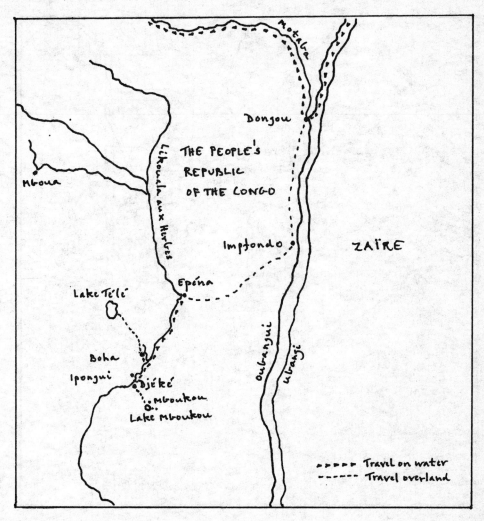

The second journey

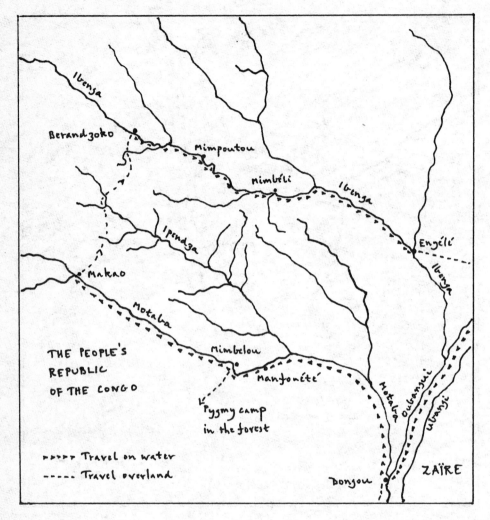

BOOK I

I

In her hut in Poto-Poto, the poor quarter of Brazzaville, the féticheuse, smiling at us, knelt on the floor, drew out a handful of cowrie shells from the cloth bag at her waist, and cast them across the raffia mat.

Lary Shaffer and I, despite ourselves, leaned forward on our wooden stools, studying the meaningless pattern; the shells, obviously much handled, shone like old ivory in the glow of the paraffin lamp. The féticheuse stopped smiling.

'One of you', she said slowly in French, 'is very ill, *right now.*'

The rain seemed to clatter with increased urgency on the corrugated-iron roof. I had the absurd feeling that the other objects in the little breeze-block room – a pile of laundry in a red plastic bucket, a rough double-bed (its mosquito-net suspended from a hook on a cross-beam) – were watching us. It's simply that we're not yet acclimatized, I told myself, we've only been in the Congo for two days: a thought which immediately made the humidity and the heat doubly oppressive.

Lary, still staring at the floor, wiped the blisters of sweat from his forehead and the bridge of his nose. His hand, I noticed, was shaking.

'It's me,' he said, stumbling over his words. 'It's me. I'm the one who's ill. Nine years ago I was in a wheelchair. I have this thing called multiple sclerosis. I forced myself to walk again. One yard one day. Two yards the next. My sight came back. And then last year I cycled across America. Thirty-three days. West to east. Coast to coast. It's okay.'

'A wheelchair?' I said, unable to keep the panic out of my voice.

'I swim forty-five minutes a day. A mile and a quarter. I'm fit. I'm all right. You can see I'm fit. And anyway – I thought I'd rather die in Africa than strip paint in my house in Cornelia Street all summer. There's no problem. There's no worry. No need at all.'

'Please!' said the féticheuse, tossing her head right back and pressing her palms into her eyes. 'You must be quiet. If you talk one to the other I cannot see. And if I cannot see I cannot help you.' And then, 'Here, take these,' she said, opening her eyes, reaching forward, gathering up the shells and giving us three each. 'Hold these against a banknote and breathe your desires into them.'

With my free hand I drew two 1000 CFA (two pound) notes out of my leg-pocket, gave one to Lary, and crumpled the other over the shells in my cupped palm.

'Now,' she said, 'who is responsible for all this?'

'I am,' I said, puffing out my chest.

'Then tell me – what is it that you really want? What is it that you want most when you are quiet inside? – and don't bother me with anything else, don't tell me the story you prepared for your wives.'

'I hope to go on a great journey through the far northern forests', I said, liking the sound of the words, 'by dugout to the headwaters of the Motaba where we'll abandon the boats, walk east through the swamp jungle and across the watershed to the Ibenga, take a chance on finding another canoe, and then, if we're lucky, paddle down to the Likouala aux Herbes and walk to the hidden lake, Lake Télé, where Mokélé-mbembé, the Congo dinosaur, is said to live.'

'No! No! No!' sang the féticheuse.

'What's wrong? You think the army won't let us go? You think we'll never get out of Brazzaville?'

'You are not an educated man,' she said, exasperated, rattling the shells in her hand like dice in a box. 'You don't speak your desires. You think them. *I see everything.*'

She snatched my shells and the banknote and threw them hard across the mat; the note spun down like a sycamore seed.

'Your children love you,' she intoned, glancing with contempt at the scatter. 'Your wife loves you.'

I thought: I'll double her fee.

'If you stay for two months,' she said, already turning to Lary, 'the spirits of the forest will not harm you. But if you stay for two months and one day, you will die.'

'But I'm staying for six months!'

'Then you will die,' she said, fixing her attention on Lary with indecent haste and closing her eyes.

He held his shells and 1000 CFA note in the approved manner and bowed his head. A drop of sweat fell from the end of his nose to the floor. His lips moved.

I realized, with a twinge of disquiet, that the subconscious of this all-American frontiersman (who had personally built three houses for himself at different stages of his life) was fully engaged with something in the room. Lary Shaffer, the emphatically rational Professor of Psychology at the State University of New York at Plattsburgh, was not responding as I thought a scientist should; this specialist in animal behaviour, who had been film-cameraman to the Nobel-laureate Niko Tinbergen at Oxford and written his doctoral thesis on the predation of crabs by Lesser black-backed gulls – this man, I decided, had momentarily lost touch with his own view of the world. But then it dawned on me how presumptuous I'd been: you haven't seen him since you were at university together twenty years ago, I thought, you hardly know him. Or maybe, I comforted myself, it's just that in a mere two days of heat and anxiety and far too much whisky, Africa has got to us.

The féticheuse took Lary's cowries and banknote from him, laid the note carefully at her side, added his shells to her own, spread them across the mat with a gentle roll of her wrists, stared at their pattern – and began to rock backward and forward like a deserted child.

'You think too much,' she said, her voice rising in pitch, becoming start-lingly high. 'You have too many worries for one man to bear. You have great problems with your wives. You have led a life broken in many places. Each time you have mended yourself and begun again.'

Lary opened his eyes wide.

'That's right,' he said. 'My mother and then my father died; I got ill; my marriage unravelled; my wife went to live in California with an African American; and the night before I flew out of New York to London to join Redmond and come here I had a phone call – the voice said, "Hi, Daddy, I'm your daughter. It's my birthday. I'm twenty-one. I'm allowed to speak to you." I didn't know. I have a daughter that I've never seen. My only child. I never played with her. I never saw her grow up. Twenty-one years ago I had a row with my girlfriend – we said terrible things to each other and we parted and I went to Oxford and that was that; she never told me.'

We were silent, staring at the floor. The cowrie shell by my boots lay on its tortoise-shaped back, the long slender opening of its underside exposed. It was easy to see, I thought blankly, why a cowrie worn round a woman's neck was supposed to ensure conception and ease childbirth. I wondered how it had got here: it was a genuine money cowrie, *Cypraea moneta* from the Maldive Islands in the Indian Ocean, perhaps brought to Egypt by an Arab dhow in the thirteenth century, traded along the north coast by Arab merchants, south across the Sahara in a saddle-bag slung on a camel, and then on from one small kingdom to another until it reached Central Africa. Or maybe it arrived in a European slave ship: a stray statistic whined in my skull like a mosquito: in 1520 the Portuguese were paying 6370 cowries for one man or woman. '6370,' sang the mosquito, '6370 . . .'

With a convulsive gesture, Lary pushed both hands up over his head as if trying to scalp himself. A startled gecko moved fast across the wall beside him and stopped, its toes as delicate as ivy tendrils.

He gave me a small, wry smile. 'And now,' he said, 'I'm in the sucking Congo.'

The féticheuse retrieved her cowries and the two notes, put them in her bag, and got to her feet. We stood up. 'You are full of courage,' she said to Lary, drawing aside the plastic-strip curtain that served as a door to the outer room. 'You have made yourself strong. You are a brave man. You are a good man.' She touched his arm and smiled at him, a smile that lit up her tired eyes and transformed her, for a moment, into a young girl.

2

———————————

At a central table in the outer room, by the light of an oil-lamp, the féti-cheuse's two teenage sons were studying their homework.

'Well done,' said Lary in English, in a professional, proprietorial way, his sense of normality temporarily restored. 'You keep it up. You learn all you can.'

The younger gave him a dazzling grin. 'Thank you, sir,' he said, 'and good morning.'

'It's good night,' said Lary.

A fridge and a cooker stood against the back wall, flanking the entrance to another room. By the standards of Poto-Poto the féticheuse was rich.

I gave her 5000 CFA and we stepped out into the rain and the deep wet sand of the road. A stray goat, soaked and miserable, sheltering under the narrow eaves, flicked its ears and tail as we passed.

Nicolas Ngouakala, our two-days-old friend the taxi-driver, sad-faced, in his fifties, was waiting at the corner in his decrepit Nissan.

'That was quick,' he said in French, as we concertinaed the broken springs of the back seat.

'It didn't feel quick,' said Lary, running the right sleeve of his blue heavy-duty cotton shirt along his receding hair-line, squeezing the sweat out of his moustache with the flat of his index finger. 'I was in there for months.'

'Then that's *good*,' said Nicolas, starting the engine and turning on the headlights. 'That just shows you. She's very powerful. She's the best féticheuse in Brazzaville.'

'So what does she do for you?' I said.

'She treats my family,' said Nicolas, swerving to avoid three damp chickens roosting among the rubbish at the side of the road. 'I have six children and my little boy is ill with malaria. There's a new type of malaria here. It's dangerous. In Brazzaville it kills lots of people every week. My wife – she works in the hospital. She was sent to Moscow and trained to be a nurse. She gets medicines at the hospital. But we go to the féticheuse too, to make

7

certain. The féticheuse cures everyone. She's powerful. She's good for other things, too.'

'What kind of things?'

'Family problems. Private matters,' he said, as the car undulated through the potholes and its lights swung up over the low mud or breeze-block huts with their corrugated-iron roofs, the occasional banana or mango or palm tree, and back down to the rubbish-strewn sand. 'It's like this – I have a daughter, my eldest daughter, and I love her very much. But she wanted to marry a man I didn't like at all. He was a great dancer, but he was also a thief. Everyone knew. Besides, we are Batéké and he was a Vili from the coast. The other drivers, they were laughing at me. So I went to the féticheuse.'

'And she blew him away,' said Lary, enthusiastic.

'No, no. For that you go to a sorcerer. The féticheuse – she just put a spell on them. But it's very important to tell the young people. They have to know about it.'

'Shrivelled him up,' said Lary, relaxing back into his seat with admiration. 'Dick like a drawing-pin.'

We all laughed.

'What's the difference between a sorcerer and a féticheur?' I said, as the car emerged onto a made-up road, someone mended the main Brazzaville dynamo, and all the street-lights came on. 'Do you visit a sorcerer?'

'I'm a peaceful man. I don't need a sorcerer. They are more powerful. But also more expensive. You can be in Paris and your enemy goes to a sorcerer and the sorcerer puts your photo in a bowl and he takes a machete. "You want to kill this man?" "Yes." Boom!'

'I see,' said Lary, less enthusiastic.

'But most powerful of all are the kings,' said Nicolas, as we lurched over a one-track railway-line, up a small hill and into a wide avenue of the old French Quarter. 'Our Makoko, for instance, he lives in a palace full of sculptures and all his furnishings are red. He has an ancient throne, the same throne his forefather sat on when he made the treaty with de Brazza and the French, when he made the country that in 1960 became the Marxist-Leninist People's Republic of the Congo. He can see everything. He's very powerful. If he says no one must go to the forest, to the plantation today, no one goes. He's so powerful he has two sacred animals – the leopard and the lion. If he plants a palm seed in the morning that palm will be big and bearing fruit by the evening. The King's successor, he can eat one food and not the other – it's a long training.'

'What did you make of that?' I said, as we entered our anonymous room high up in the M'Bamou Palace Hotel.

Lary lay down on his bed and closed his eyes. 'Which particular piece', he mumbled, 'of this unremitting 100-volt culture-shock did you have in mind?'

'The féticheuse,' I said, pouring us each a triple whisky. 'Didn't you think she had a good line?'

'How do you mean?'

'It's simple. When two or three people are gathered together in Brazzaville – one of them will be sick.'

'I don't know. I don't know any more. And come to that – what's all this about the Congo dinosaur? Dinky the dino! You don't actually believe all that bullshit, do you? I'm a serious biologist. I can't go chasing dinosaurs. I'll lose my job.'

'Of course not. But there must be *something* odd about Lake Télé. It's a pygmy story. And the pygmies are reliable – it was persistent Bambuti pygmy descriptions that set Johnston on to his search for the forest giraffe, the okapi. 1901. It's not that long ago.'

'Okapi,' said Lary, taking a swig. 'Dinky.'

'All right,' I said, ruffled, unzipping the document wallet in the top flap of my pack and taking out a sheaf of photocopies I had made in Oxford, 'then listen to this – it's from a bizarre book by a biochemist at the University of Chicago, Roy Mackal, *A Living Dinosaur? In Search of Mokélé-mbembe* (1987) – it's not the book itself that's interesting, it's an appendix. It's by one of the Congo's leading biologists, Marcellin Agnagna. He spent seven years studying science in Cuba and three years reading for his doctorate – on crocodile growth-rates – at Montpellier. Say what you like, he's serious. He's head of the Ministry for the Conservation of Fauna and Flora. He can't afford to lose his job, either. Listen – it's startling. Mackal himself never reached Lake Télé' ('That figures,' said Lary, unlacing his calf-length leather-and-canvas boots) 'but Marcellin Agnagna later made another attempt. In 1983, he writes here, he stayed for a week at the village of Boha in the Likouala swamp-forest, "the inhabitants of which 'own' Lake Télé, one of the reported habitats of Mokele-mbembe, where 'disruptions . . . caused morale problems among expedition participants'" ('I know how they feel,' said Lary, kicking the boots off). "However, on April 26 the expedition then set out on foot, accompanied by seven villagers from Boha who were to act as guides in the forest. The trail through the forest proved to be quite difficult and it was usually necessary to cut through the foliage to allow passage. It being the dry season, water was scarce, and it became necessary to drink from muddy pools.

'"The 60-kilometre trek to Lake Tele was completed in two days, and it was with some emotion that we finally looked across this little sea, located right in the heart of the equatorial forest of Central Africa. The lake is oval in shape, about 5 kilometres by 4 kilometres. A base camp was established at the water's edge, and one of the Boha villagers caught a large turtle which served as dinner that first night. Two days of intensive observing of the lake produced no sightings of the supposed Mokele-mbembe, although there were frequent observations of a large turtle, with a shell reaching 2 metres in length.

'"On May 1 1983, the author decided to film the fauna in the low-canopy forest surrounding the lake. This forest is a habitat for many mammalian and bird species. The author and two Boha villagers, Jean-Charles Dinkoum-bou and Issac Manzamoyi, set out early in the morning. At approximately 2.30 p.m., the author was filming a troop of monkeys. One of the villagers, Dinkoumbou, fell into a pool of muddy water, and went to the edge of the lake to wash himself. About 5 minutes later, we heard his shouts to come quickly. We joined him by the lake, and he pointed to what he was observing, which was at first obscured by the heavy foliage. We were then able to observe a strange animal, with a wide back, a long neck, and a small head. The emotion and alarm at this sudden, unexpected event disrupted the author's attempt to film the animal with a Minolta XL-42 movie camera."' ('Surprise, surprise,' said Lary.) '"The film had been almost totally exposed already, and the author unfortunately began filming in the macro pos-ition."'('Of course he did,' said Lary.)

'"By the time this was realized, the film had been totally exposed, as determined by subsequent processing in a French laboratory."' ('Douche-bags,' said Lary. 'Quiet,' I said.)

'"The animal was located at about 300 metres from the edge of the lake, and we were able to advance about 60 metres in the shallow water, placing us at a distance of about 240 metres from the animal, which had become aware of our presence and was looking around as if to determine the source of the noise. Dinkoumbou continued to shout with fear. The frontal part of the animal was brown, while the back part of the neck appeared black and shone in the sunlight. The animal partly submerged, and remained visible for 20 minutes with only the neck and head above the water. It then submerged completely, at which point we trekked rapidly through the forest back to the base camp, located 2 kilometres away. We then went out on the lake in a small dugout with video equipment to the spot where we had observed the animal. However, no further sightings of the animal took place.

'"It can be said with certainty that the animal we saw was Mokele-mbembe, that it was quite alive, and, furthermore, that it is known to many inhabitants of the Likouala region. Its total length from head to back visible about the waterline was estimated at 5 metres."'

'Look,' said Lary, sitting up and pouring himself another whisky, 'I'm perfectly prepared to believe that *every* law of nature is suspended in this goddam country. Will that do?'

'No.'

'Well, when we were in the plane and the lights of Brazzaville and Kinshasa came up in the dark with the black river between them, and the pilot starting circling, and there I was sitting with that sucking plastic bag on my knees containing more film than I've ever carried in my life, and over the Tannoy the pilot announces that he thinks he just ought to remind passengers unwise enough to be disembarking in Brazzaville that anyone caught taking photographs in the city goes straight to prison and is never seen again, and I said, "What do you estimate they'll actually do to me?" and you said, "Oh, nothing much, Lary, they'll just tap you about with the odd swagger-stick," and when we got across the tarmac and into that brown cage of a shed with the naked light-bulbs sure as hell there were enough soldiers to start a medium-sized war and they were all carrying swagger-sticks and Kalashnikovs and hand-grenades and Christ knows what and taking people apart in booths and robbing them stupid, I suppose you thought that was funny?'

'It was funny. Ish.'

'It wasn't a bit funny. And but for Madame Leroy meeting us, you and me and all these army packs and kit-bags and suspicious-looking bundles would have lasted exactly eleven-and-a-half minutes in the People's Republic of the Congo. I timed it. I thought then − if you're going to suspend the laws of nature, this airport is a good place to start.'

'I asked her to meet us. I wrote to her. Madame Leroy is supposed to be the President's front woman. We're safe with her. Besides, she rears gorillas.'

'I expect she does. If you say so. And takes in orphaned Martians and keeps Dinky in the backyard. But I've been doing some reading, too' − he reached into his right-hand shirt-pocket, pulled out two crumpled paperback pages and smoothed them out on his knee. 'She won't be able to help you with this one, will she? The latest warning from *Africa on a Shoestring*: "Depending on your nationality and where you apply for your visa, you may be given only 5 days, though 15 days is the usual with a fixed date of entry. It will be hard going to get through the country in that time. Two Australians who recently got their visa in Kinshasa were given five days, but on arrival in Brazzaville by ferry they were refused entry and no reason was forthcoming . . ."'

'We've got fifteen days.'

'Yeah. So listen: "*Visa extensions are not available.*" And just in case you're planning to go in there without permission perhaps you should get this, too: "There are police checkpoints every 25 to 30 kilometres in the countryside where you will be stopped and asked for your passport and vaccination certificates." Now we all know what that means – the white American capitalist spy Lary Shaffer will be cut in half with a burst of Kalashnikov fire and some bastard will nick his boots.'

'Spy? What are you talking about?'

'That's right: "Avoid discussing politics with strangers in this country. There are many plain-clothes policemen in the towns and cities." You can bet your ass this room is bugged. There's probably no money for anything useful but I expect the Russians fund the police and the army. It may have escaped your notice, Redso, but this is a Communist state. This was the base from which the Russians and Cubans won the war in Angola. 350,000 Africans dead. The CIA and South Africa bankrolled Unita. They don't like Americans here.'

'That's part of the point. This is the most difficult equatorial African country to get into, the least visited, the least explored, the most interesting. In the swamp-forest we'll see gorillas, chimps, guenons, Forest elephants, Swamp antelope, pythons, three species of crocodile – and a sauropod dinosaur.'

'They'll kick us out. We'll see that shithole of an airport again in precisely thirteen days from now. The once-weekly flight to Brussels. Home to Platts-burgh! Chris. The kindest, sharpest, sexiest girl in the United States of America. A carwash or two.'

'Carwash?'

'Sex in the shower.'

'Don't torture yourself. It's a great mistake.'

'It's *this* that's a great mistake.' He gestured at the olive-drab packs. 'I figure that if the soldiers aren't going to torture me I may as well torture myself. On the other hand' (he poured himself another whisky) 'I reckon that as I haven't caught one of those gut nematodes yet, those roundworms long as grass-snakes, I may as well celebrate.'

'Is that your real fear? Parasites?'

'I'd classify that as one of some sixty-three secondary worries. My primary fear is uncharacteristic. It's irrational. It's called the Gaboon viper. I just *know* those suckers are waiting for me out there. They're six feet long, wide, sluggish and perfectly camouflaged. They dislike being stepped on, very much. They can rear up to half their length. Their fangs deliver fifteen drops a shot. Four drops are enough to kill you. I went to see them at the zoo. A bad move. There were supposed to be a pair in a glass cage twelve feet square. At first I thought it must be empty. I swear it took me five minutes to spot them – all you could see were four tiny horns poking up above the leaves. You see, I can't feel my feet, and I don't always know where I'm putting them. But you can't explain that to a Gaboon viper. So I figured I'd buy the tallest pair of boots in L. L. Bean.'

'Everything depends on tomorrow. Everything. Jean Ngatsiebe, the Cabinet Secretary to the Ministry of Scientific Research, and Dr Serge Pangou, his adviser from Marien Ngouabi University, are coming to dinner. We'll wear our suits. We're going to be a scientific expedition. We've got to get them to give us a *laissez-passer*. I've worked on this for a year.'

'I know. I know. When I think of the money and effort it's cost you to get here, I could cry.'

'So could I.'

'And I can't think of a single reason why they should want to let you in.'

'Neither can I.'

'And what about this jerk who says he's seen Dinky? Nanyanya?'

'He's not a jerk and his name's Agnagna. When he's written up his latest Forest elephant survey he's coming with us. We leave in two weeks.'

'Straight back to Brussels. London. Kennedy airport. Plattsburgh. My girl.'

'Don't play those games. You'll drive yourself insane.'

'This whole project is insane. Sorcerers and dinosaurs, for Chrissake. What is it you *really* want to see?'

'The pygmies. But there's something else. As irrational as your Gaboon viper. Before the war my father was an Anglican missionary in Abyssinia. He wrote a book on the Coptic Church. He got out when the Italians invaded, taking the royal Bible, the Emperor's Bible, with him, for safe keeping, and he gave it back when Haile Selassie went into exile and came to live in Bath. Anyway, he had a wonderful collection of books on Africa in his big dark study in the Wiltshire vicarage where I grew up. The study was out of bounds, but when he was visiting his parishioners, or at choir practice, or evensong or bell-ringing or the PCC meeting, I'd creep in and take a volume of Bannerman's *Birds of Tropical West Africa* down from the second shelf on the right behind the door, and lay it out over the papers on his table. I'd sit in his chair, which looked out down the grass bank, past the sundial, across the lawn where a Green woodpecker came to forage for ants, out to the yew, the bushes where we played jungles, the huge copper beech, the conker tree, and beyond that was a stream where I'd catch minnows in Lucozade bottles baited with bread, and the water came over the tops of my wellington boots . . .'

'Yeah. That's great,' said Lary, lying back on the pillow and closing his eyes. 'Well, my father was a glove-leather salesman in Gloversville – and we had a little piece of Africa in the house for a while, too. He'd been in the military police in Cairo. "I'll show you something special," he said to me one day. He had this little yellow stone in his hand, about half the size of a boiled sweet. "I'm kind of ashamed of it now," he said, "I brought this down from the top of the Great Pyramid. I've looked at it lots of times and thought of the men who carried it up there in the first place." I loved him. He probably threw it out when he got Alzheimer's. My mother died of cancer and I was there when she had a cerebral haemorrhage and they carried her out with her skull full of blood. "Can I kiss her one last time?" he said. He would have been an ideal companion for you. He never complained about *anything*.'

'Maybe you won't need to complain. Maybe it'll be a piece of cake.'

'Oh yeah. With lots of broken glass. And a touch of arsenic.'

'I want to see a Pennant-winged nightjar.'

'A what?'

'I must have been eleven or twelve. There's a drawing in volume three of Bannerman of a Pennant-winged nightjar trailing its twenty-eight-inch plumes across the moon. I thought it was the oddest, the most desirable bird in the air. I still do. And that night, surrounded by dissecting kit, alum, and packets of porridge oats to soak up the mess, sitting at the kitchen table and all night furtively skinning a badger which became so like a Giant panda that he was banished to an outhouse, I would have given several boxes of rabbit-skins for half a chance to stuff a Pennant-winged nightjar. I still would.'

'Strange but true,' muttered Lary, with a profound sigh. 'He's left his family, risked everything, spent his last penny and come all this way . . . to see . . . a bird . . .' And he began to snore.

Suddenly feeling as homesick as a seven-year-old sent away to boarding school, I comforted myself, not with a tear-blotched copy of the *Eagle*, but with the photocopies of Mackal. Even here, high up in a concrete-block hotel, looking out at the lights of the Elf oil-company tower, it was easy to believe that the land of the Congo forest had remained stable for sixty-five million years or almost (pushing it a bit) to agree with Mackal that

In a region known as the Likouala, just north of the equator, lie some of the most formidable jungle swamps on the face of the globe . . . 140,000 square kilometres (55,000 square miles) of mostly unexplored swamp and rain-forest. To be sure, the French, during their colonial rule, made excursions up the major rivers. And a few intrepid European explorers also penetrated the area, bringing back intriguing tales of terrible pygmies and amazing animal life.

I could not, off-hand, remember any nineteenth-century travellers who had described the humorous and gentle pygmies as remotely terrible; and it was a pity that the French had not actually had the decency to limit themselves

14

to excursions up the major rivers. But surely the animal life would indeed be amazing – even if we confined ourselves to those direct descendants of the great reptiles which were undeniably still about the place, those flying dinosaurs, the birds.

3

'Just look at this!' called Lary, squatting in a corner of the hotel car park, in the early morning heat, under a grey sky. He looked absurdly happy as I walked up to him, running his stubby fingers down a piece of old iron serving as a post in the fence.

'You don't see this in England or the States any more,' he said, enchanted, 'it's not a T-rail. It's a figure-eight in cross-section. Long ago this shape was easier to roll in the mills – I suspect it came out here in one of the earliest rail-building efforts. What a superb bit of track! This should be in a museum! It's very heavy, very serious, obviously a high-quality attempt from the beginning. What do you think? 120 to 130 pounds per yard? It may be a little lighter. Perhaps 100 to 120? Eh?'

'I really don't know,' I said, bending down, scrutinizing a length of railway-track for the first time in my life. 'I read it up in Plattsburgh,' said Lary. 'I've always liked railways. Ever since I was a kid. My grandfather – I loved him, too. He was one hell of a guy. He worked on trains all his life. He began as a guard ticket-collector. He made it – all the way up to Controller. I guess this is early 1920s. French. The Belgians built a line from Kinshasa to Matadi in the 1890s and the French followed with a rival route from Brazzaville to the coast, at Pointe-Noire, from 1921 to 1934. 318 miles of single track – and they pushed right through the Mayombe forest. The French had to mount man-hunts to get enough workers. Malaria and accidents killed between fifteen and twenty-three thousand Africans, depending on whose estimate you believe. *Fifteen per cent of the workforce.*'

Nicolas arrived, pooping his horn, and we set off to visit Madame Leroy and her gorillas. The Heads of State of Rwanda and Gabon and President Mobutu of Zaïre were in town, visiting the Leader, Colonel Denis Sassou-Nguesso, so all the main thoroughfares were shut, and Nicholas took us on a tour of the backroads of the city. We caught a glimpse of the fishermen still out on Malebo Pool, two to each dugout, standing up with their long paddles, silhouetted against the reflected light of the great expanse of water; and then we were enclosed in long streets of brightly placarded shops, stalls selling arm-thick lengths of manioc wrapped in light-brown leaves, pyramids of doughnuts, oranges, bananas, pineapples and cans of Coke. By the morgue we pushed our way slowly through an excited crowd, the men in jeans and tee-shirts and gym-shoes, the women in purple and yellow and red wrap-around dresses, many printed with the President's name, so that the sibilant DENIS SASSOU-NGUESSO curved voluptuously across their breasts and buttocks, their broad backs. Several small boys were pulling miniature cars and lorries made of bent spring-clips and painted cardboard on strings behind them, turning round intently to watch the wire wheels plough tracks through the sand; and all the little girls wore their hair in the latest fashion, twirled out from their heads in spikes like wireless antennae.

Men banged on the roof of the Nissan and shouted greetings and jokes through the open windows in Batéké; Nicolas shouted back; it was obviously some kind of fiesta. A Pied crow, perched on top of a telegraph pole, its white collar and breast glowing as if it were itself a source of light in the black surround of its head and chest and back and tail, looked down at us with mild interest, raised a black foot and scratched its black chin.

Once clear of the crowd, Nicolas relapsed into his habitual melancholia. 'A young man was killed in a fight,' he announced, and then, as we entered a slightly richer quarter of low houses set behind walls of fretwork breeze-blocks, 'Modern Life – this is the problem,' he said, raising his right hand from the driving-wheel, palm upwards, fingers spread, pointing at a Toyota truck which was coming the other way, in from the country and loaded with sacks of manioc flour – on which perched at least ten people, twenty cooking-pots, one chair and a trussed white goat. 'That's what I blame. That's where the problem lies. In the village where I grew up none of this would have happened. Our life – it was lived all together. My father had two wives and I had four brothers and five sisters. The young men went hunting and whatever they caught they shared with everyone. Food was free. Manioc was free. There were no diseases. The central house was the school and also the palace of justice, the court. That is where the old men talked over the problems of the village and where they taught the children our stories, the history of our people, how to live. Life in the village when I was a child – that was the only true Communism, the real life in common. The air was fresh. There were no lorries. There was no money. Fish was free. And the féticheur – if you broke a leg he would break a chicken's leg and both legs would heal at the same time. I saw it with my own eyes. In the city, nowadays, that is no longer possible. I have never heard of it.'

There was a sudden onslaught of sound, the noise of the air bursting apart, and a shape like a double-barbed spear-point shot low overhead, a jet fighter, a darker streak of grey in the grey sky. All the way down the street the Pied crows scrambled from their telegraph poles, rose, circled, croaked a black and white protest, and, having seen off the intruder to their own satisfaction, resumed their posts, swearing.

'That,' said Lary in a small voice, mournful as Nicolas, 'was a Russian MIG.'

'We're near the airport,' said Nicolas, 'the aeroplanes – they are protecting the President.'

We came to a wider street with a made-up road, the odd two-storey house, and a huge billboard proclaiming the Heroes of the People in four gigantic portraits side by side: MARX, ENGELS, LENIN, MARIEN NGOUABI.

'Douche-bags,' said Lary, with deep feeling.

Nicolas drew up by a tall spiked gate in a head-high green concrete and fretwork wall. 'If you don't mind,' he said, 'I'll stay in the car.'

'No, no,' I said, peeling the back of my sweat-soaked shirt and trousers off the plastic seat-cover, 'you come in with us.'

'Gorillas are dangerous,' said Nicolas flatly, winding up his window.

On the veranda of the large whitewashed bungalow, its windows criss-crossed with steel lattice, a young man in jeans and a denim jacket sprawled in a wicker chair. A small chimpanzee, wearing a nappy, clung to his chest.

'Hi,' he said, somnolent with motherhood. 'Yvette is expecting you. I'm Mark Attwater, and this is Max. He's a young Pygmy chimp.'

Max, hearing his name, detached a long black right arm from the hugging position and, with the delicate fingers of a dark-brown hand, tousled Mark's hair.

'This is the first Pygmy chimp I've seen,' said Mark, easing Max's thumb out of his ear. 'They're very rare. They live only in Zaïre, south of the river. He was brought in by the Forest Service. Someone was trying to sell him as a pet in the market. It's the babies we get – almost always gorillas. The hunter in the forests kills the mother, cuts her into steaks, smokes the meat, and takes the baby back to his village for the children to play with – and they knock it about until it dies. Very occasionally one is rescued, usually by the paramilitaries of the Ministry of Water and Forests, and they send it to us – by truck if it's from the Mayombe forest in the west (they call that the south here) or by Air Congo, the little internal airline, or by river-steamer, if it's from the great forest in the north. But it's hopeless. They arrive with machete wounds or lead shot in their back, dehydrated with dysentery, their stomachs full of earth they've scraped up in the village because they're starving, hookworms, fungus, parasites of all kinds. They're psychologically delicate, too, gorillas are sensitive, full of emotion – they've watched their mothers die in front of them, they're traumatized, and if they don't die of disease, they die of grief. They just lose the will to live, they refuse to eat. Twenty-seven baby gorillas have arrived in the last two years and only four are still alive.'

'And Pygmy chimps?' said Lary, sitting down heavily on the veranda step. 'Do they die of grief?'

'Not yet,' said Mark, putting one arm round Max and stroking his back with the other. 'I'm treating him for parasites, but otherwise he's in good shape. He seems much more intelligent even than a Common chimpanzee, an ordinary chimp of his age, much more social. Very little's known about Pygmy chimps. But now there are two teams, American and Japanese, trying to study their behaviour in Zaïre.'

'You're a zoologist?' said Lary, brightening.

'No, but I'd like to be. I'm not just a nursemaid, you know. I was a keeper at Howlett's, John Aspinall's zoo in Kent, and I'm here to set up and direct his gorilla orphanage in the grounds of Brazzaville Zoo. We'll have a proper vet, all the facilities, lots of money, everything. We'll establish a breeding colony and then release them somewhere safe – a big island in the middle of the Congo river, somewhere like that.'

Mark stood up. 'We must find Yvette. This is the one day of the week when she has enough staff to let Magne out of his cage. He's her three-and-a-half-year-old gorilla. He's lively.' He paused, extracting Max's right foot from his shirt-pocket. 'See – Pygmy chimps have a web between their second and third toes' (Max studied the little flap of skin, too, as if he'd never noticed it before) 'they weigh 20 per cent less than Common chimps, their hair is blacker, their faces are rounder, their ears are smaller and they don't go bald.'

'Very sensible,' said Lary, running a hand over his remaining hair.

Mark opened a steel-grilled glass door and we entered a large room full of couches and cushions; children's toys were strewn across the floor, wooden building bricks, red rubber rings, a chewed-up rag doll. A Bantu girl in a red dress lay on a bed in the corner, watching a television on the shelf opposite her; a very small, very still gorilla snuggled against her stomach.

'Albertine Ndokila,' said Mark, introducing us. 'She looks after Kambala, one very sick, very sad gorilla, eighteen months old.'

The inner door swung open and Madame Yvette Leroy swept into the room, a gorilla clinging to either side of her red blouse, a little black face pressed against each large breast, a pair of dark-grey legs wrapped back and front round the waist-band of her white skirt.

'Quick!' she said. 'Bring some chairs! The guards are about to release Magne in the garden. He's lively!'

'He's lively,' said Lary.

'I stay here with Max,' said Mark with a knowing smile, lying back on a couch.

We carried our wicker armchairs out into the garden. Yvette knelt on the grass, crouched forward, one arm protectively round each of her charges.

'Sit quietly,' she said, 'stay in your chairs and – whatever you do – don't look into his eyes. Gorillas *never* stare at each other. It's a threat.'

'Bonzo,' said Lary in English. 'Gentle giants. Fubsy babies.'

There was the sound of a bolt being drawn back, the clang of a cage door, a short, sharp, barking scream, a rumbling noise on the concrete, and round the corner of the bungalow came Magne on all-fours, in a hunched, scooting gallop.

Big and grey, Magne slapped Yvette on the back, detached her two screaming infants, roughed them up a bit, banged his chest, tore at the grass, and, with a sideways glance, moved towards the newcomers, us.

'That Bonzo', said Lary, 'has a hornet up his arse.'

'Jean!' shouted Yvette. 'Take the Englishman's glasses!'

The brown hair on top of Magne's head, his low black brow, his close-set, small, deep-brown eyes, his wide, flat, black nose, dissolved into a blur. I stared into the fuzz, trying to remake his features.

'Nice Bonzo,' said Lary. 'Good dog. Go bite Redso. Rabbits.'

'He's jealous,' said Yvette, still out of breath from her blow on the back. 'He's jealous of my two new babies. Come here, Magne! Come to Mama!'

I thought: knuckle-walking, that's what it's called, technically, the way they move – but when you're a three-and-a-half-year-old and you've just been separated from your mother Yvette; when you've been supplanted by two infants from out of town, from God knows where; when you've been parted from the biggest, softest, most desirable breasts you've ever laid your muzzle on; and when you've been penned up all week in a cage with no trace of even an average pair to be found in it anywhere, then really it should be called knuckle-sprinting, knuckle-galloping, the knuckle launch, the flying knuckle, the airborne knuckle-duster . . . and at that moment Magne's actual knuckles arrived on my thighs, followed by his big black man-like feet as his hands moved up to grip my shoulders.

'Good boy,' I said, stupid with the weight, the solidity of him, the rank musk of his bristly chest-hair. I put both hands up and pushed with all my strength against the surge of muscle; without effort he pressed closer, brought his shiny black wrinkled face close up to mine and opened his mouth. I was conscious of two upper canines, as big as marlin spikes, a pink cavern and tongue, grinders, spit, a smell as sweet as cow's breath, and then he bit my ears, carefully, first one side and then the other, growling maniacally the while, a growl which varied in pitch and tempo, as though he were engaged in a very fast, very aggrieved conversation with himself.

Satisfied that he had improved my manners, taught me not to stare, Magne paused and looked about his kingdom.

Lary was lying back in his chair, helpless with laughter. 'Go bite Redso!' he howled. 'Go bite Redso!'

Magne, intelligent, sensitive, a thinking man's gorilla, jumped off my lap, took two sideways galloping paces, and bit Lary in the stomach.

Back in the taxi, Lary pulled up his shirt and inspected the red patch on his diaphragm.

'Strange but true,' he said. 'Gentle giants. Fubsy babies. Teeth like that – and he didn't even break the skin.'

Lary inspected my ears. 'They're red,' he pronounced, disappointed. 'I was *sure* they'd come off. I thought we could dry them and send them to your wife.'

'We should stick to pussy-cats.'

Lary said, 'Nothing bigger than a gerbil.'

Jean Ngatsiebe, Cabinet Secretary to the Ministry of Scientific Research, overweight, domineering, dressed in a perfectly tailored Parisian suit, a man of the world, put his enormous fist on the white tablecloth.

'Mr O'Hanlon, I hear you have written a book on Darwin,' he said in French. 'Is that so?' (I nodded.) 'Good. Then you can tell me, if you will – in your opinion, do you think that you and I are the same species?'

Dr Serge Pangou, his adviser from the university, bearded, wearing a suit which, like mine and Lary's, might have fitted him ten years ago, embarrassed, looked into the night beyond the large plate-glass window of the hotel dining-room, at the lights round the swimming-pool.

Lary's eyes bulged.

'I'm sure of it,' I said, taken aback. 'Our ancestors evolved in Africa around 100,000 years ago. Maybe not far from here.'

Jean Ngatsiebe put his black hand next to my pink one.

'You're sure?'

'Of course he's sure,' said Lary, butting in, 'skin colour is a very superficial affair. A matter of a mere ten genes or so in tens of thousands.'

'Good. Then that's settled. I, too, am an admirer of Darwin. I believe everything that Darwin says. At first I was sceptical, but now I am convinced – because Darwin's fish diet is certainly whitening my skin.'

He turned his hand palm upwards.

'I may be wrong,' I said, 'but I don't remember Darwin prescribing a diet for anything.'

'You mustn't bother about Redmond,' said Lary quickly, with a forced smile, 'he's always arguing. Darwin's his thing. Of course Darwin worried about his diet. He was a sick man.'

'Whereas I am in the best of health,' said Jean Ngatsiebe, ordering another bottle of white wine.

We talked about the appalling price of French cars; about the dastardly way the French had kept their factories in France, so that when the Marxist-Leninist revolution happened there were no means of production for a decent Communist to seize; about the ozone conference in London, and how the People's Republic of the Congo actually contributed ozone to the atmosphere, whereas the hypocritical industrial countries had long ago cut down all their own forests and were even now fouling the upper air; and 'So what is it, exactly,' said Jean Ngatsiebe over the cognac, 'that you wish to do in my country? I do not understand. Why are you here?'

'We want to see the birds and mammals and reptiles in the jungles of the north,' I said, 'and to visit Lake Télé.'

Jean Ngatsiebe was silent.

'I am fascinated by the People's Republic of the Congo,' I said lamely, and then, without thinking, 'I've been writing to Marcellin Agnagna at the Ministry for the Conservation of Water and Forests. He says he'll come with us.'

'Two different Ministries?' said Ngatsiebe, displeased. 'You write to two different Ministries?'

'Jopop!' said Dr Serge Pangou. 'But I know him!'

'Jopop?' said Jean Ngatsiebe, with distaste.

'I was at university with him in Havana. Jopop! He knew all the songs of Otis Redding. He was always dancing with the girls of Cuba. He's a pharmacist.'

'A pharmacist?' said Lary.

'Well, that's his training. But he went on to study crocodile growth-rates at Montpellier. He wants to be a crocodile farmer. And he says he's seen the sauropod dinosaur.'

'So you don't believe it?' said Lary, turning to face Serge Pangou. 'You don't believe it exists?'

Serge Pangou's happy student memories ghosted back into his past; his face reverted to middle age. He said quietly, 'It is only white men who laugh at Mokélé-mbembé. We Africans know there is something there. If you ever reach Lake Télé – and I consider that impossible, for reasons I am not at liberty to discuss – you will certainly hear strange sounds. You will hear calls that no man has ever been able to explain.' He put his head back and shut his eyes. 'Ooooooooooh,' he lilted, *sotto voce*, a high-pitched, thin, ululating cry. 'Ooooooooooh woooooooooooh.'

The diners at the neighbouring table, an anxious Frenchman and two relaxed Congolese, looked up sharply from their T-bone steaks.

With his right hand Serge Pangou jiggled the brandy round in his glass, making a little whirlpool of spirit, sniffing at the fumes. 'The tracks of Mokélé-mbembé have been photographed. We have reliable reports of turtles with shells over two metres in diameter, of giant Monitor lizards. Enormous pythons gather to mate at Lake Télé. Even the trees round the shore are of exceptional size. Besides, the pygmies who live in the swamp-forest have never been to school – but if you ask them to make you a picture of Mokélé-mbembé they will pick up a stick and draw you a perfect sauropod dinosaur in the mud. So how do you explain that?'

'Yes – how do you explain that?' said Jean Ngatsiebe, leaning forward, bearing down on Lary across the table, looking into his eyes. 'How do you explain that, Dr Shaffer of New York?'

'No idea,' said Lary, his stubby fingers, with surprising strength, busy bending a hotel spoon into a semi-circle. 'But have either of you actually been to this lake?'

'Certainly not,' said Jean Ngatsiebe, insulted, 'I run a Government Ministry.'

'No, I haven't,' said Serge Pangou, 'I am a professor at the university. I teach classes. Lake Télé is far away from here, in the interior. To make an expedition on that scale, why – apart from anything else – it would cost me more than my year's salary.'

'So, Mr O'Hanlon,' said Jean Ngatsiebe, his voice full of hostility, 'you have come to investigate some kind of dinosaur? To make fun of us? To mock the African?'

'Of course not,' I said. 'I'm interested in the wisdom of old men. I always have been. I want to learn about the history of the many different Bantu groups who live in the far interior. I want to learn about the history of your people.'

Jean Ngatsiebe leant back in his chair. He smiled for the first time. 'Then I may be able to help you,' he said, placing his huge hand briefly on my shoulder. 'My father was himself what used to be known among us as a Big Man. He was a great provider, a great sorcerer. Everyone respected him. He knew all the plants of the forest. He would lay special leaves along the forest paths round our village – and the next morning hundreds of poisonous snakes would be lying on them, dead.'

'Look,' I said, growing desperate, 'I am a Darwinian Marxist with a deep interest in sorcery.'

'In that case,' said Jean Ngatsiebe, with a violent bark of laughter, slapping his thigh, 'I will give you a six-month visa for your travels in my country. You may collect it from my office tomorrow morning. Dr Serge Pangou will call for you at nine o'clock.'

Outside on the hotel steps, released from the air-conditioning, we were enveloped in the sweaty humidity of the night, the odd, sweetish smell of the darkness, a compound of sand, laterite soil, palms and mangoes breathing out the heat of the day, with perhaps just a hint of garbage.

Drunk, we all embraced by the black Mercedes, and Serge Pangou whispered in my ear, in perfect English, 'Jean Ngatsiebe is not a man of science, he is a relation of the President.'

4

Lary and I waited on a brown, termite-eaten sofa, in an otherwise empty room, inside the one-storey backstreet building of the Ministry of Scientific Research; light slanted down from the slats of a small window set above the door and lay in stripes across the brown mould-patches on the concrete walls. Lary looked uneasy. 'This is just the kind of place,' he whispered in my ear, 'if this was not such a' – he raised his voice – 'well-ordered, just, enlightened, Marxist, visitor-friendly country' – he resumed his whisper – 'where we might disappear for ever. This place – it *stinks* of fear.'

We sat in silence, sweating in our heavy suits. A column of tiny ants stretched like a length of brown thread out from a crack at the base of the wall opposite us, split into two at our feet, mounted the right front leg of the sofa, re-formed somewhere in the torn stuffing, and, via the left front leg, returned to base at the apex of the triangle.

The door opened; we jumped up; two men, their cheeks scarred with vertical lines as though someone had run a comb through their flesh, came in carrying an enormous typewriter: they laid it in front of us without a word, and left. We sat down again.

'Search me,' said Lary, running a finger round inside his shirt-collar. He leaned forward and cocked his head over the roller. 'It's ticking,' he said, 'it's a bomb.'

There was a knock at the door. We sprang off the sofa as if someone had fired a Luger through the keyhole.

A girl in a bright-green wraparound announced, 'Dr Jean-Joseph Akouala, Director of Scientific and Technical Cooperation, will see you now. Follow me,' and she led us down a narrow passage.

Dr Akouala, large and friendly, received us in his office, which contained a small table, three chairs and a wall of empty bookshelves; a sheaf of papers, tied up with red string, lay on the topmost shelf, and an office date-pad, two years old, sat alone on its little wooden stand in the centre of the table. 'Why are you here?' he said, smiling. I explained. He wrote out our names on his pad, tore off the scrap of paper and pushed it down inside the breast-pocket of his suit. 'Excellent,' he said, 'we will now attend the meeting of the Ministry Committee.'

We retraced our steps, past the waiting-room (where the ants, I felt sure, would by now be marching in step through the metallic halls and stairways of the typewriter), and were ushered into the Committee Room.

Jean Ngatsiebe rose from his long table (complete with leather desk-set) and introduced us to his personal assistant (a thin young man with a galvanic twitch in his left eyebrow) and to Marc Ampion, Assistant to the Director of Science and Technology, in his late twenties and lightly cut with vertical scars to the cheeks and forehead. Serge Pangou was sitting next to him. There's no need to be romantic about it, I said to myself, but Serge Pangou and this Marc Ampion are obviously genuine scientists – they have that slight absence, the manner of men with real interests outside themselves, an inner distance from the concerns of family, the earning of money.

Dr Akouala took his place behind the table, we sat on the chairs waiting in front of it, and the interview began.

'The Advisory Committee to the Cabinet Secretary of the Ministry of Scientific Research of the People's Republic of the Congo', said Jean Ngatsiebe, 'would like to know exactly why you are here.'

I explained. A long discussion in Lingala took place, and then Serge Pangou turned to me. 'You will need antivenin,' he said, 'serums for two very common and very dangerous snakes of the forest floor, the Forest cobra and the Gaboon viper. You have some from London, of course?'

'No,' I said, floundering, 'in my experience you meet very few snakes. I didn't bother.'

'In general,' said Serge Pangou quietly, 'you should always bother. And in my experience it only takes one snake to kill a man. In my experience – please correct me if I'm wrong – only sea-snakes hunt in packs.'

'Snakes in the sea?' said Jean Ngatsiebe, his voice booming round the high, bare, windowless walls. 'Packs?' He tapped his gold Sheaffer pen on the table-top. 'Do not let us waste time in argument, Comrades. We have important matters to settle.'

'I have morphine', I said, 'in spring-loaded syrettes. The SAS use it – when your legs are blown off you take one out of your belt-kit fast and roll on it. So you don't scream and give away your position.'

'SAS?' said Jean Ngatsiebe. 'An airline?'

'Correct,' said Lary, nervously. 'They're Scandinavian.'

'How does that help?' said Serge Pangou, intrigued. 'Does it counteract venom shock?'

'No,' I said, 'you die happy.'

Everyone laughed except Lary.

'We must be serious,' said Jean Ngatsiebe, 'this is an Official Committee. I am warning you, Mr O'Hanlon, and you, Dr Shaffer of New York – the northern province is not fully under the control of my Government. We have reports of bands of poachers, armed with automatic weapons from the Sudan, who hunt elephant in our forests, and they kill our people, too. One day we will liquidate them all – but for the moment the People's Army is fully occupied dealing with incursions from Zaïre. However, you will take four soldiers with Kalashnikovs. Once in the jungle two will march at the front of your column, two at the back. You will capture or kill any poachers you meet.'

'Er – I don't think that's part of our job,' said Lary quickly, interrupting, sweat gathered on his nose again. 'We're supposed to be, you know, non-aggressive.'

'We can't have soldiers with us,' I said, alarmed. 'We want to see the Forest elephants and monkeys and monkey-eating eagles and chimpanzees and gorillas. Soldiers – they'll make too much noise.'

'Gorillas!' shouted Ngatsiebe, on his feet, his arm in the air. 'They're giants! They're nine feet tall! They attack without warning. They rip your head off. You must shoot!' He raised an imaginary Sten-gun to the hip. 'Ta-ta-ta-ta!'

Serge Pangou winked at me. Jean Ngatsiebe sat down. 'Very well,' he said, disappointed. 'No soldiers. There is nothing else I can do for you. This meeting of the People's Committee of the Ministry of Scientific Research is hereby dismissed. Comrade Ampion will prepare the necessary documents.'

I stood up, half-airborne with relief. The Committee began to file out in order of seniority: Dr Jean-Joseph Akouala, Dr Serge Pangou, Marc Ampion. Lary and I followed.

'Bonzo,' I heard Lary mutter under his breath, 'go bite Redso.' And his shoulders shook.

'Behave yourself!' I hissed at the back of his neck.

'You two! You will stay behind!' boomed Jean Ngatsiebe. 'You will be seated. This is a Ministry of the People's Republic.'

For a moment that froze my legs I thought I was back in school – about to be savaged across the buttocks by some mad headmaster.

Marc Ampion closed the door behind him. The Personal Assistant chewed on a pencil and twitched about the eyebrow. We sat down.

'You saw the typewriter?' said Jean Ngatsiebe, picking up a black leather briefcase from beside his chair, placing it square on the table in front of him, fiddling with the combination locks and clicking the lid open. I thought: he's got a very big pistol in there. 'Dr Shaffer of New York – you saw the typewriter?'

'I saw the typewriter,' said Lary. 'It was a very fine typewriter.'

'It's a rotten typewriter. It was made in the United States of America. It's broken.'

'I'm sorry,' said Lary, rightly assuming responsibility for his country and its typewriters.

'The Ministry needs new typewriters.'

'I expect it does,' said Lary.

I realized what the important matters we had to settle might be – and just why Serge Pangou thought that a journey to the Likouala might cost more than his year's salary.

'Naturally,' said Jean Ngatsiebe, 'you will want to make a contribution.'

'Of course,' I said, 'it's only fair. It's a privilege to be allowed into your country.'

Lary studied his boots.

Jean Ngatsiebe smiled, closed his briefcase, spun the code-wheels of the locks and replaced it on the floor. 'How much would you like to contribute?'

'£250?' I said.

Jean Ngatsiebe leaned back in his chair and laughed.

'£500?'

Jean Ngatsiebe looked at the right-hand wall and hummed a tune to himself.

'£1000?' I said, breathing hard.

Jean Ngatsiebe became sharply attentive.

'You have that in French francs?'

'No.'

'Dollars?'

'No.'

'Okay. CFA will have to do. You will bring them here tomorrow, in a plain envelope, not addressed to me, and you will give them to my personal assistant. You can trust him *absolutely*. And on no account will you mention a word of this to anyone, and especially not to your friend Pangou. Understood?'

Serge Pangou himself was waiting outside. 'Come on,' he said, motioning us into a little red Fiat, 'I'm going to book you into a sensible place to stay.' I got in the front, Lary in the back, and we puttered off down the street. 'You can't afford to waste your money in that ridiculous hotel. That's for people who are frightened of Africa – for oilmen up from the coast or aid agency personnel or businessmen trying to buy mining rights or sell us Japanese trucks – those sort of people. I know why you're there – you thought it would impress us, the locals, that we'd think you were rich and so let you into our country. Well, believe me, brothers' – he banged the steering-wheel for emphasis, and grinned – 'we're not fooled, no rich man in his right mind would be seen dead in suits like yours.'

We turned out into the main road, behind a Berliet army lorry full of soldiers sitting quietly in two rows under the canvas, dressed in black fatigues, their automatic rifles held upright between their knees.

'Crack troops,' said Serge, 'part of the Presidential Guard.'

We forked left up a hill and into a quarter of two-storey colonial houses with tall pitched roofs and shuttered windows, desirable, cool, airy-looking houses set in peaceful gardens with lawns and palm trees and bougainvillaeas.

'Besides,' said Serge, 'I wanted to have a word with you, and here it's always better to talk in a car. I like you. And Dr Shaffer – Lary – you at least are a scientist. Maybe you have real work ahead of you. Perhaps you will make further contributions to science. Your life in North America – with all that equipment, all the latest machines – you must not throw all that away. For me, I'm happy, I study the medicinal plants of the Congo. By African standards I have a great collection. I love my herbarium. It pleases me. But of course we can't afford to subscribe to the learned journals. I can't read what they think in other lands. There is no money to go to conferences and meet people like myself, not even for symposia in Cuba or Russia. Not even at my old university, in Havana. When I'm dead – it's okay, I've come to terms with it, I'm not bitter any more – I know very well that only my family will remember my name. But for you, Lary, it is different. Do not get killed. Do not throw it all away. It is not safe at Lake Télé. I could see you thought it was a joke – the soldiers. Well, it wasn't. I can't say any more – you know I can't say any more – *but you should have agreed to the soldiers.*'

We pulled off the road onto a wide verge of scuffed grass and dried mud alongside a whitewashed wall, topped with spikes. 'And there again,' said Serge, one hand on the wheel, turning to me. 'Even in the northern forests you need to be fit. And you, Redmond, are not in good shape. Although you, Lary' – he addressed the driving-mirror – 'are clearly an athlete. You have legs like a football champion's. And your eyes are clear.'

'I'm a cyclist,' said Lary, embarrassed, 'and I drink too much.'

'We all drink too much,' said Serge. He paused, staring through the dusty windscreen at a half-open ironwork gate: above it the stems of a bougainvillaea twisted across an iron pergola, an aerial thicket of glaucous green leaves and purple-pink flowers. 'Just take my advice,' he said, lowering his voice as if someone was watching us, 'I swear I'm not joking. Going to Lake Télé – it's dangerous. Don't do it.' He clapped both hands on the steering-wheel. 'Out you get. I must go and teach. The hotel's through that gate. They're expecting you. If I don't see you again – good luck, and remember, this is the most beautiful country in the world.' And with that he reversed the little red car and drove off up the empty road.

Inside the gate a concrete path led to the right down to a sprawl of a bungalow, its windows heavily barred, the reception desk enclosed in a hut built on the front. A girl behind a ticket-window, a bougainvillaea flower pink in her black hair, wrote down our names, took a key off a hook and met us inside the main door. She unlocked a room off the central corridor.

'It's the only one we have free,' she said with an inviting smile.

I glanced inside – a wardrobe against the right-hand wall, a table with lamp and chair to the left, a large bed, a frosted window the length of the opposite wall, a bathroom off the far corner.

'Fine,' I said, 'we'll take it.'

The girl left and I sat down on the edge of the bed, suddenly very tired, and I wished we had a fridge, and a bottle of whisky.

'Er ... you Englishmen,' came an odd voice from the doorway.

I looked up.

'You're all the same,' said Lary, not crossing the threshold, his head half-poked into the room.

'What?'

'I know that in your culture, of course, it's all perfectly normal,' he said, his eyes big, his shoulders raised, his arms pressed into his sides. 'I don't want you to think I'm being judgemental, Redso, or anything. It's okay by me, in a general way, you know. For other people, I mean.'

'What the hell are you talking about?'

'You Englishmen,' he repeated, his mouth askew as if someone was trying to strangle him. 'It's not a criticism. I'm well aware that a case could be made. You could argue that it's me – that it's my culture that's aberrant.'

I thought: keep calm, gibbering is the first sign, he's having a fit, it's hours since we had a drink of water, the heat has got to him, his brain is dehydrated.

'Water,' I said.

'Yes,' he said, backing out into the corridor, not taking his eyes off me, 'don't get me wrong – as an idea I can live with it. I know that fundamentally you're all the same. Without exception. But it's goddam different when it actually goes right ahead and happens in front of you. I just don't think we're ready for this, if you don't mind. It's just not my thing – *sleeping in a bed with another man.*'

'Don't be absurd,' I said. 'It's cheaper,' I choked. 'We can't afford two rooms,' I spluttered. 'And anyway they don't have two rooms.' I sat back on the bed. 'We'll sleep wrapped up,' I howled. 'IN OUR TARPAULINS!'

'That's okay then,' said Lary, his voice still dry with the horror, and he came gingerly into the room.

5

I paid the bill at the M'Bamou Palace, we found Nicolas parked in his usual patch by the doughnut-stall across the road, and together we managed to stow and rope the five kit-bags and four backpacks into and onto the Nissan. 'You're making a big mistake,' said Lary, obviously still shaken by the thought of the double-bed, not quite restored to his normal self-contained good humour, 'you should not be leaving this central location.' He squeezed himself into the back-seat beside two olive-drab kit-bags. 'And anyway, what the hell's in all these things?'

'Presents, mostly,' I said, getting in the front. Nicolas started the engine and we pulled out into the traffic. 'Two thousand pounds-worth of medicines for the people upriver – antibiotics, quinine and Fansidar for malaria, dressings, bandages, antiseptic creams, everything you need for minor wounds, all the stuff I should have had in Borneo and South America. And some repeats – Oxford pipes and Balkan Sobranie tobacco for the Chiefs, Swiss Army knives, Maglite torches and English batteries for the people with us, Birmingham machetes that last a lifetime. I've brought a pair of binoculars in a case for Marcellin Agnagna, a belt-kit with water-bottles, a hat. Of course, it still doesn't mean they'll be pleased to see us.'

'Quite,' said Lary. 'But we're in the nineteenth century, aren't we? You love all that, don't you? You should have been born 150 years ago. Bearers and paddlers and those white Brit hats like a bra-cup stuck on your head. I know. And a sedan-chair or whatever you call them with punkah-wallahs and tiffin-boys and under-pig-stickers and things.'

'I'm not sure. I'm not quite so keen on the nineteenth century as I used to be, not round here – up on the west coast, according to Mary Kingsley, 80 per cent of white men died or were invalided home to die in their first year. But it's true I'm never ill. I've never caught malaria.' And, remembering our evening with the féticheuse, I immediately regretted the boast.

Lary was quiet as the Nissan made its way uphill, moving so slowly that our own cloud of black diesel exhaust swelled in through the open windows, and then he said, 'Are we going anywhere near the Ebola river?'

'Why? Yes. Quite close. It's east of our route up the Oubangui.'

'That's my other fear,' he said, leaning forward between the backs of the front seats, 'that and the thought that mosquitoes may carry HIV. All the literature in the scientific journals just says there's no evidence they do. No one says they can't or don't. When I told the tropical diseases guy at Platts-burgh that I was going to the Congo he just said, well, sure, why waste time? Why not jump in an open sewer and start drinking?'

'What's in the Ebola river? The sixty-foot python? The one that swallows dugouts whole?'

'It's not funny. It's called the Ebola virus. Another of God's little jokes. A filovirus – a thread virus. Another one he *really* worked on. Seven days plus, I'd say. And if this one breaks out we're also in deep trouble. It's just for *Homo sapiens*. It's adapted to take advantage of our caring for the dead. It's in there at the funeral service.'

'Never heard of it.'

'It erupted simultaneously in fifty-five villages along the Ebola river. Sep-tember 1976. You get a headache. You get a fever. Your immune system gives up. Your cells fill with the replicating virus and sprout threads like hairs. You haemorrhage and clot at the same time. Your skin goes pulpy. Your gut fills with blood. You leak blood from your eyes, nose, mouth and anus. You die and your body melts, liquefies, turns to slime. When someone picks you up to bury you they get it, too. No vaccine. No cure.'

'That's the hospital,' said Nicholas in French, right on cue, nodding towards a big white building set back from the road. 'The Russians built it for us. My wife, she works there. She's worked there ever since she came back from her training in Moscow – when she got back, she said to me, Nicolas, she said, you'll never believe it, but when they have a baby, white women – they scream just like black women!'

We turned right and bumped down the road to Les Bougainvillées. 'Mind you,' said Nicolas, helping us to stack the bags inside the gate, 'black women also scream *before* they go in there. That hospital, it looks good from the outside. But no one wants to be taken there. You go in to have a baby, and that's it, or you go in with one illness and come out with ten. Thirty people a week die of malaria in there, but others come out and you think they're fine and then they just waste away in front of you. They get other fevers, worse fevers, that's what my wife says. We nurse our children at home. We go to the féticheuse, like I said. But poor people – sometimes they have no choice.'

We had just lugged everything into the forlorn little room and changed out of our suits when there was a loud knock on the half-open door: a very tall, fit-looking man stood in the doorway; he was perhaps in his mid-thirties, with a sharp chin, a slightly hooked nose and the darkest skin-tone I had ever seen. His face was velvet-black, the kind of black which, as you look at it, appears to absorb all the surrounding light. 'Marcellin Agnagna!' he said in a high-pitched shout. 'I'm hungry! I have a taxi! We must eat!'

I grabbed Serle and Morel's *Birds of West Africa* and Haltenorth and Diller's *Mammals of Africa* from the side-pocket of my pack, locked the door, and we followed him up the path. In his wake the tang of aftershave overwhelmed the smell of fish-frying from the hotel kitchen; his white shirt was dazzling in the heat; his blue jeans were freshly laundered. In one smooth, athletic movement, a double flash of white trainers, he disappeared into the back of the taxi. I got awkwardly into the front, turned round, and was surprised to see that he was not alone: a young girl, her pupils dilated with admiration and desire, was massaging the back of his neck with one hand and his right inside leg just above the knee with the other; her breasts so stretched her meagre white tee-shirt that its hem barely reached her navel; her red cotton dress curled half-way up her slim back thighs.

Lary, his mind on some previous train of thought, got into the back beside Marcellin, noticed the girl and extended an arm to shake hands: 'Madame Agnagna?'

'She's not my wife!' shouted Marcellin, pushing Lary's hand away. 'And she doesn't speak English!'

'Is your wife joining us?' said Lary, fuddled with embarrassment.

'Of course not!' Marcellin yelled into Lary's ear. 'She's pregnant!'

'Pregnant?'

'She's having a baby!' explained Marcellin, slightly louder. 'I have one daughter already! And now my wife – she is pregnant again!'

'Congratulations,' said Lary, bemused, his eardrum probably beginning to malfunction. 'Well done. Congratulations.'

Marcellin sat up. The girl withdrew her hands as if he had slapped her. 'Look!' he shouted, his chin jutting forward. 'Let's get one thing straight, shall we? Right at the start. This is not England! This is not small-town America! This is Africa! My wife is pregnant. So we can't have sex. So here is Louise, who finds it hard to stop having sex. Okay?'

Marcellin directed the driver out of town to a café with a terrace overlooking a little tributary of the Congo river. In the middle of the tributary was a sandbank, and in the middle of the sandbank was a hippopotamus, and under the middle of the hippopotamus was his extraordinarily long, thin, tremblingly erect penis.

'Muh muh muh,' said the hippopotamus.

'That's right,' said Marcellin. 'See? He needs sex too. Only his wife's not pregnant. The army shot her and ate her.'

'Of course,' said Lary.

'But now he's safe. This place belongs to a high-ranking officer. He realized people were coming out here just to watch the hippo – so he renamed the place L'Hippopotame and now he employs a boy to feed it bales of grass, to keep it here.'

The hippo, looking up at us, saw Marcellin's girl, and, deciding at length that there was nothing he could do about it, like any sensible man he subsided into the river for a cold bath. He lay half-submerged, his stubby tail hidden, the skin of his grey back rumpled into three vertical folds, his little ears laid back, the pouches for his huge lower canines sticking up on either side of his muzzle, and he watched us with his right eye, a brown lens beneath an eyebrow set on top of his head like a giant snail, a snail about to glisten its way towards his rump. There was a hint of pink about his cheek – the 'sweated blood' of the hippo, in fact a secretion which keeps his skin moist and prevents his every wound from turning septic, even in the filthiest of his pools and wallows. It was odd to think that his forest relative, the Pygmy hippo (much smaller, but still a large animal, the size of a wild boar) was almost unstudied in the wild: it lives in family parties of male, female and calf, but as for the rest of its social life – there's not a whisper of gossip to enlighten us.

We ordered fish and Primus, the Congo beer, and I opened William Serle and Gerard J. Morel's *A Field Guide to the Birds of West Africa* (1977) at the plate of the Crowned eagle, an immensely powerful eagle given to dropping out of trees onto forest antelope and ripping them to bits with its feet.

'Have you seen it?'

'Of course I've seen it,' said Marcellin, shedding his bluster, concentrating on the picture, speaking at European volume. 'I've watched it sitting quietly near a troop of monkeys, facing the other way, whistling softly. The monkeys can't help themselves. They're mesmerized. They make pathetic chattering noises and all together they move towards it until wham!' – Marcellin clapped his hands together – 'He's got one.'

'Smart,' said Lary.

'Or he hunts by flying at the monkeys, round the tree trunks, between the branches – the monkeys drop to the floor of the forest, he dives on one – wham! He never misses. The pygmies, they say the leopard hunts with him. The leopard, he waits for the monkeys to hit the ground and – zap!'

'Best not to be a monkey,' said Lary, finishing his glass of beer. 'Horrid life.'

I showed Marcellin the grey-wash plate in Serle and Morel, number 26, where an overstuffed museum specimen of the Pennant-winged nightjar sits on the ground, lined up with five other equally lifeless species of nightjar, and Marcellin, not surprisingly, shook his head at them. My Pennant-winged nightjar, I told myself – it didn't look like that, either.

'These pygmies,' said Lary, 'are they friendly?'

'Of course they're friendly. In any case, most of them live like slaves behind the villages along the river-banks. But it's true – some are still out in the forest. Those ones, they're difficult to reach.'

'We must find them,' I said, feeling like Stanley.

'We may find them, we may not,' said Marcellin, looking out across the river at a small cliff of red earth where a track had been half cut in the hill, at the straggle of palm trees and scrub, a line of empty sheds. 'But they say there's a Frenchman in the north. He's sixty years old. He was a journalist in Paris. He came out here to write an article on the pygmies – all about the pygmies who live just like our early Stone Age ancestors lived 100,000, maybe 250,000, years ago. Well, so they do, but he fell in love with a pygmy girl and he married her and he stayed up there. He's their Chief. They hunt Forest elephant for the meat and the ivory, and in their part of the forest they kill intruders with poisoned arrows. So now the Frenchman is rich. But his money is no good to him. He thinks he's king of the pygmies. But really they have him prisoner. When the moon is full he howls like a dog. All night. That's what they say.'

Lary, lost in a private dream, was rocking his empty beer glass to and fro between his hands on the table-top, staring at the swinging needle of reflected light as if it were some inner pointer, loaded with meaning. Louise, her needs more immediate, gazed at Marcellin in the heat, moved her thighs rapidly apart and together for a moment, and giggled.

'Let's go to the rapids,' said Marcellin, prolonging her distress. 'We'll find a taxi. Just to look at all that excited water, Redmond – it's an aphrodisiac.'

We stood on a big grey boulder, hypnotized by the start of the cataracts which Stanley described in *Through the Dark Continent* (1879). After making his way for 1235 miles down the Congo, surviving thirty-three pitched and running battles with the peoples on its banks, Stanley looked out on

the wildest stretch of river that I have ever seen. Take a strip of sea blown over by a hurricane, four miles in length and half a mile in breadth, and a pretty accurate conception of its leaping waves may be obtained. Some of the troughs were 100 yards in length, and from one to the other the mad river plunged. There was first a rush down into the bottom of an immense trough, and then, by its sheer force, the enormous volume would lift itself upward steeply until, gathering itself into a ridge, it suddenly hurled itself twenty or thirty feet straight upward, before rolling down into another trough. If I looked up or down along this angry scene, every interval of fifty or 100 yards of it was marked by wave-towers – their collapse into foam and spray, the mad clash of watery hills, bounding mounds and heaving billows, while the base of either bank, consisting of a long line of piled boulders of massive size, was buried in the tempestuous surf. The roar was tremendous and deafening. I can only compare it to the thunder of an express train through a rock tunnel. To speak to my neighbour, I had to bawl in his ear.

It was appalling to think that even after such a journey Stanley still had the energy to attempt to shoot the sets of rapids, warp the heavy dugouts past the whirlpools, drag them overland on brushwood trails he made around waterfalls – for five months and a mere 180 miles. In the process he lost Frank Pocock, his friend and right-hand man, just twenty-seven years old, the son of a fisherman in Kent, and Kalulu, a slave boy presented to him by an Arab trader during his search for Livingstone, whom he had taken back to London and treated like an adopted son. Both drowned in the rapids, together with seven of his Zanzibaris.

Back on the road, Marcellin gestured out across the brown and white water. 'A French stuntman came here fifteen years ago. He'd just gone over Niagara Falls in a wooden barrel, so he thought our rapids would be easy. He put on a pair of waterwings and jumped in off that rock. Lots of reporters waited downriver.'

'What happened?' said Lary.

'No trace of him yet,' said Marcellin with pride, and gave his girl a squeeze.

'That island,' said Lary, pointing to a large forested outcrop in the middle of the river, 'what's it called?'

'Devil Island,' said Marcellin, waving down a taxi. 'It's haunted. No one ever goes there.'

'I must tell Aspinall,' said Lary to me, as we got in. 'That's just the place to put Bonzo.'

On Marcellin's instructions we stopped outside a shack with rooms for hire. He disentangled himself from Louise and leaned forward. 'You'll pay me my Government salary. Thirty pounds a day.'

'But I've already agreed to pay Ngatsiebe £1000,' I said, with reflex annoyance.

'Was that all? You got a bargain. He must have liked you both.'

'It's bribery,' said Lary. 'It's corruption.'

'It's Africa,' said Marcellin. 'How else is he to make up his salary? Those jobs don't last long. They're just a political favour. In and out every four years. Even I can't count on my salary, as a government employee. Some months I'm paid, some months I'm not. At least with you, Redmond, I know I'll get my money.'

'How do you know?' I said, stupidly.

'Because you'll pay me every franc in advance,' said Marcellin, getting out of the car. Louise followed him, hoiked a puff of his white shirt out of the back of his jeans, slid her arm inside around his waist, and disappeared with him into the hotel.

'What is it about Lake Télé?' I said, as we wrapped up in our crackly army tarpaulins, after a supper of fried fish at a café table in the little hotel garden. 'Why does everyone say it's dangerous? Why does Pangou think we're going to be killed? Why can't he tell us about it?'

'No idea,' said Lary, arranging the bottle of Johnny Walker Black Label, the plastic tooth-mug and the Penguin edition of Mark Twain's *Roughing It* on his bedside chair. 'But if you take my advice – and it's not my business – I wouldn't ask that Marcellin Agnagna about it. It's just an instinct, it's just a hunch I have, but if you let on to that creep that your real aim is Lake Télé, that that's your primary objective and that you intend to work your way round to it from the north – he won't go with you, he'll find some excuse. He's frightened of something. Tell him at the last possible moment. That's my advice.'

'What do you mean – not your business?'

'It's not my problem,' said Lary, with an enormous grin. He turned his back on me, propped himself up on his elbow, and, with his left hand, poured himself a long gurgle of whisky. 'If you're going up the Motaba almost to its source, walking right across the watershed and then expecting to find a dugout in the middle of nowhere waiting just for you' – he took a big gulp from the tooth-mug – 'a dugout, I guess, with a personalized greeting card from God stuck on it – you know the kind of thing – "Dear Redso, every hair on your head is numbered and of course there's a mansion up here with your name beneath the doorbell-pushbutton but, in the mean-time, here's a celestial canoe, old boy, just because you're such a jolly good chap, such a pukkah English pig-sticking pervert, oh yes, Redso, and I nearly forgot, I'm sending jobs with wings to drop in a few supplies and lift you out when you break a leg" – you won't get anywhere near Lake Télé inside three months.'

'Jobs with wings?'

'Angels.'

'Of course we'll find a canoe.'

'Yep. Everybody knows. East of the Motaba, you can hardly hear yourself speak for flapping wings. It's neon-lit with flashing haloes.'

'Jesus.'

'Quite. But I have to get back. My students will be waiting. I'm telling you now – three months is all I can spare. And I feel I've had three years of this already.'

'I'm sorry. It'll be different, the moment we start travelling.'

'You know what I'll do? If I ever see Heathrow again?'

'No.'

'I'll get down on my knees like the Pope – and I'll kiss the sucking tarmac. And then I'll start right in on those nice men from Customs.'

6

In the morning Nicolas drove us to the bank in the centre of the city and I changed my entire remaining savings into small-denomination notes. We carried the two big brown parcels into the marble lavatory of the bank, locked ourselves in the only cubicle, placed the parcels on the lavatory-seat cover and laid aside £1000 in CFA for Jean Ngatsiebe, £3000 for Marcellin; I took out the sheaf of transparent plastic sealable bags I had ready in my back-pocket, eight Tubigrip cylinder-bandages (four for fractured shins, four for ruptured thighs) from my leg-pockets; we divided and packed the rest of the CFA into the plastic bags; we took off our boots and socks; we dropped our trousers and stepped out of them; someone rattled the door, hard.

I looked at Lary. Lary looked at me. 'That's one cheap lock,' he said.

'Quiet,' I whispered.

The man outside, hearing voices, took a moral stance and gave the door a twenty-pounder kick.

In one of those moments of mystical certainty I knew it was Ngatsiebe out there. He'd followed us to the only bank; he was out there with a pistol in each enormous hand; he had a machete between his teeth.

'Locked in a toilet with an Englishman,' said Lary, aghast.

'Robbed,' I said. 'No money. Deported.'

'Naked,' said Lary.

The man outside kicked the cubicle again; the soles of his shoes squeaked as he turned on the wet tiles; he slammed the outer door.

'Quite right,' said Lary. 'I don't blame him. He's gone to call the soldiers.'

We sweated; we fumbled the large tubular bandages up into position on our thighs; we scrabbled the small tubular bandages over our shins; we stuffed the clammy plastic bags down inside them; we put on our trousers and socks; we panicked like schoolchildren over our bootlaces; we pocketed the loose cash for Marcellin's salary and Jean Ngatsiebe's bribe; we burst out of the doors and, too fast, down the stairs to the street.

'Steady,' said Lary, as we reached the waiting taxi, dived inside and banged the rusty doors behind us.

'You okay?' said Nicolas. 'You robbed the bank?'

At the Ministry of Scientific Research we found Ngatsiebe's lieutenant and slipped him a bulky brown envelope in return for a letter to Marc Ampion, and in an outbuilding of the university, part of the old colonial library, set in a quiet park, we found Marc Ampion himself sitting behind a table in a high room with a big window. He took the official letter; we sat down on a bench against the right-hand wall, to await the final prize, a Ministry pass, a *laissez-passer* to the otherwise forbidden forests.

'What do you study?' said Lary, as Marc Ampion began to fill in two large stencilled forms. 'What's your field? Your research?'

He looked up with a shy smile; wrinkles spread out from the corners of his mouth and, on either cheek, changed the five vertical lines of scarification into irregular curves. 'I teach at the university. And I also have my official duties for the Ministry, here, in this room. But whenever I can, you could say, Dr Shaffer – if you exclude the micro-organisms – that I study the most numerous of all the living creatures in Africa, the termites. They are very important. We have to study them because they destroy our grasslands. They eat up our timber. That is what I shall say in my dissertation. But, in reality, I like to watch them because they are so old. They were here already, in our country, at least one hundred million years ago. The termites of that date are almost the same as the termites of today. Yes, you yourself could think of them living underground here, in their passageways and chambers, at the same temperature, in the same darkness, for one hundred million years. There are over fifty different species in the Congo – and I think that perhaps I may have found one that is new to science. But it is difficult to be sure. The Central Committee does its best, of course. But our facilities are not good. Our microscope was made in Germany. It, too, is very old. Perhaps you, Dr Shaffer, could help me?'

'Of course I'll help,' said Lary, leaning forward, his eyes bright. 'Send your paper to me and I'll get some termite guy to read it.'

'That is very kind,' said Marc Ampion, pushing the completed documents across the table. 'At present I am engaged in repeating the breeding experiments of Professor S. H. Skaife. I agree that the saliva of the Black-mound termite blackens everything it touches and that the young queen has a pure white abdomen. I have confirmed that the workers apply their lips to the queen for the sake of the fatty exudations given off from her distended skin. I have seen that she comes to be dark brown in colour. I have also noted that when she grows old and is no longer so fertile the workers crowd in upon her by day and by night and move their mouth-parts over her abdomen. It is correct that she grows thinner and thinner until only her shrivelled skin is left. It is true that the workers lick her to death.'

Secure in our final permission to go, but with ten days to wait until the steamer returned from upriver, we settled into a routine – or rather the methodical Lary showed me how a life with a routine might be constructed. We would wake to the alarm at six, take a shower, strap on half the cash (the rest taped into the top map-pocket of the bergens), drink our coffee and crumble our croissants at a café table in the garden of Les Bougainvillées, in the only fresh part of the day, under the awning, under the grey sky, watching a pair of Grey-headed sparrows cheep-cheep-cheeping about their nest beneath the roof of the bungalow, familiar and busy and craning their necks to look round at us, just like the sparrows in Oxford. Then we would walk (at a cyclist's pace, it seemed to me, in the enveloping heat) until Lary decided that he had had his morning's quota of exercise, when we would return to the gateway-pergola of the garden, read, eat fried Congo-river fish for lunch, take a siesta, wash one set of sweat-soaked clothes in the basin, hang them to dry on the wardrobe, change, walk downtown to eat, drink a litre of cheap red Spanish wine each (£8 per ten-gallon drum), wrap up in our tarpaulins and fall asleep.

On that first morning of our new life we set off to Marcellin's office, up the quiet, privileged road that was rapidly becoming our home street; we passed the gigantic False cotton tree on our right, the steel telegraph poles, the watching Pied crows, and we turned left at the main thoroughfare with its intermittent cargo of mopeds, Toyota and Nissan trucks, Berliet army lorries, mini-van buses, green taxis and bicycles. We crossed over to gain the shade of the wide, tree-lined avenue opposite, where, talking hard, we only just avoided an unmarked, four-foot-wide drain-inspection shaft, its top flush with the pavement, its bottom a black mutter of water fifteen feet below. 'Sonofabitch,' said Lary. 'In Plattsburgh 20,000 people would sue the road department. They should fence this off. They should go get themselves a simple sonofabitching man-hole cover.' We passed L'Hippocampe, a North Vietnamese restaurant in a covered courtyard whose entrance was guarded by a young soldier with a Kalashnikov slung across his chest. 'Don't look at him like that,' said Lary, out of the corner of his mouth, his eyes on the path, 'he's dying to pull us in. It's crazy – carrying all this cash. I have this queasy feeling. It's just below the pelvis. You can say what you like – I just *know* some foaming mobster of a soldier is going to saw me off at the legs.' So we looked across the road – straight into the eyes of a young soldier with a Kalashnikov slung across his chest, guarding the entrance to a football field.

The Ministry for the Conservation of Fauna and Protected Areas lay down to the left, behind the zoo, and its *chef de service*, Marcellin Agnagna, sat at a table in one of an L-shaped row of offices. Wearing a pink striped shirt, white trousers and smart brown shoes, he was writing in biro on a block of foolscap, a blue diary open in front of him. Otherwise the hot little room was almost empty – just a pinboard of photographs on the right-hand wall, and an issue of *The Journal of Cryptozoology* by Marcellin's left elbow.

'I am preparing the official report of my Forest elephant survey,' he said, looking up. 'I went with Mike Fay, a great biologist. He lives in the Central African Republic and he works for the Worldwide Fund for Nature. He knows more about Forest elephants than any man on earth. And he walks fast in the forest, with little steps. He's fit. He never gets ill. But he needs his tea – if we don't keep stopping and making a fire and boiling up his tea he can't work, he can't move!'

'So how was your survey conducted?' said Lary, relaxing, propping himself against the wall, his hands at the small of his back. 'How do you get a sample?'

'We mark out 100-metre squares in the jungle with white cotton thread, and then we count the piles of shit in each square. Mike Fay says there's a 25 per cent margin of error, but no one can think of a better method, not even in Cambridge. *Loxodonta africana cyclotis* does not wait to be counted. Only a pygmy can walk up to a Forest elephant undetected.'

'I see,' said Lary, as if he was at a seminar. 'So how do you know you're not counting the same nomadic group over and over?'

'We don't. We record the rough age of the droppings, which helps. You get a feeling. We estimate that the total Forest elephant population in the Congo has been reduced by 50 per cent in the last ten years. And there's real evidence of that on the ground – in the drier areas of the northern forests you see elephant boulevards, wide trackways they've trampled through the jungle, maybe for several thousand years. Only now the great trails are half hidden – invasive species, shrubs, young trees have grown up, sometimes twenty feet high. You suddenly come across thick belts of secondary vegetation. It's the Muslims, it's the traders from Sudan and the Central African Republic – they lend the pygmies high-powered rifles, they pay them a few packets of cigarettes and they come back later to collect the ivory. No one can guard a jungle border. It's not possible.'

'You're sure that's the main problem?' said Lary. 'It's not logging, land-clearance, population pressure?'

'You'll understand when you get there, my friend. The huge swamp-forest between the Oubangui and Sangha rivers – it's the last untouched jungle in Africa. The population density is a mere 0.9 per square kilometre – and even they are confined to the banks of the rivers. They fish, they work in their plantations, but they never venture far into the swamp-forest. You'll see why that is, too, when you get there.'

'Why?' said Lary, straightening up.

'It is hard, Dr Shaffer. You may be in water up to your waist. You'll be attacked by bees. There'll be leopards round the camp at night. You'll get ulcers on your legs. You'll develop body fungus. You must take care with vipers and cobras. And along the waterways – the tsetse flies are truly terrible.'

'Thanks,' said Lary, hunching his shoulders.

'For the Forest elephant it's a natural protection. They like the bottomlands with plenty of water-holes, that's what Mike Fay says. And I like to think of them safe in there, under my own protection. The locals say the elephants leave the swamp-jungle in the rainy season and move up to the terra firma forest. That's when they get shot. I don't know. Maybe we'll find out. In any case, my Director, Assitou Ndinga – he is pleased I have the opportunity to make this journey with you. I will be able to inform the Chiefs and the Vice-Presidents of the People's Party Committees in the villages of the far interior that our laws have changed. We now consider that the hereditary Chiefs, rather than the Government of the People's Republic of the Congo, are once more to be the direct guardians of their traditional areas of the forest – it is now their job to help us stop the poaching, by warfare, if necessary. We'll be an official expedition.'

'Right,' said Lary, appalled.

'Besides,' said Marcellin, standing up and moving towards the door, our audience at an end, 'it's safer for us that way. I think, on balance, that a Government expedition is slightly less likely to be speared, or cut with machetes, or shot.'

Glancing at the pinboard of pictures, mostly colour portraits of Marcellin in the forest, presumably taken by Mike Fay, a black and white photograph in the bottom right-hand corner caught my eye: an enormous gorilla stared up at me, slumped against a hut wall, a bullet-hole in his chest.

'Marcellin, what's this?'

'It's an old rogue male. He wandered out of the forest one day and moved into a house in the small town of Impfondo. He terrorized the people. The army shot him.'

A taxi drew up outside. A young man in brown military shirt and trousers, black boots and a green beret got out of the passenger seat. The driver, plainly disgruntled, stayed at his wheel and shouted through the window at Marcellin. The young man laughed, opened the boot, heaved two dead African civets out by their front legs, dropped them in front of us and slammed the lid back down. The taxi drove off.

The civets' short black legs and thickly furred tails lay limp on the concrete pavement; their grey bodies, as big as spaniels, were covered in black spots and lines; their eyes were dead and black, their muzzles short, their ears small and rounded. I bent forward to take a closer look, and was at once wrapped in a smell so glutinous I could feel it sticking to my face: a mix of stoat, fermented urine, half-rotted faeces humping with maggots, and a mild suggestion that someone had just thrust my nose between the unlicked testicles of a pig. It was impossible to imagine, I thought, burying my face in the crook of my shirt-sleeve, that the oil scooped out from the civet's anal gland was the base of perfumes, however it might be refined, or that King Solomon was already sending to Africa for it thirty centuries ago.

'Those taxi-drivers,' said Marcellin, laughing as I backed away, 'they don't like us. We can commandeer a car any time we like. My guard here confiscated these civets at the port – they eat them and you can sell the skins. But that poor taxi-driver – his cab'll stink for a month.'

'Lary,' I said, as we walked downtown that evening for supper, 'why do you think Marcellin's a creep?'

'I'm sorry,' he said, quickening his pace across the railway-track, 'it's just a prejudice I have. I know it's not fashionable, but I can't help it, perhaps it's genetic – I believe in trust, fidelity, call it what you like. I just don't think he should cheat on his wife. What's the point of marriage, all those promises, if you don't intend to honour your partner? Jesus. And she's *pregnant*.'

'Maybe it's different here.'

'Well, yeah, I don't go along with all that either. I don't agree it's okay to cut a young girl's clitoris out simply because you're a Muslim or a Seventh Day freakshow or a Born Again butthole or whatever. I really don't.'

In Poto-Poto we stopped to watch two boys in tee-shirts, shorts and flip-flops, tense with concentration in a sand-floored compound, sitting astride the ends of a short bench, a rectangle of hardwood between them. Thirty-two scoops, each one like the mud-lined cup of a thrush's nest, had been hollowed into the board, and varying numbers of small green malachite balls lay like eggs in each cup – the boys, in turn, redistributed the balls with their right hands at unnerving speed from cup to cup. Lary decided that the rules were too complex to decipher without several years of field observation, and that asking for information directly would be as unthinkable as talking to a pair of grandmasters at a chess tournament, so we walked on up to Le Soir au Village through the deep-sand street, alongside the open drains of stagnant water, tin cans, plucked chicken-feathers, stray pieces of cardboard, corrugated iron, and one decapitated plastic doll.

'Here's your reserve of malaria,' said Lary. 'This is one long wriggling network for mosquito larvae, ready-made, perfect, one short whine from puddle to host and back again.'

'But where are the mosquitoes? I don't understand it. You see more mosquitoes in Oxford. I've only been bitten five times. I've been counting.'

'I expect it's fair to guess,' said Lary gloomily, as we entered the little reed-thatch and breeze-block restaurant and took our seats at an empty table, 'that the difference in infection-rates is statistically significant.'

'Nicolas says this is the only restaurant in Brazzaville that serves real African food.'

'That figures,' he said, equally gloomily, staring at the menu-blackboard on the right-hand wall which bore the inscription: 'Crocodile and saka-saka'.

'Sonofabitch,' he said. 'What's saka-saka?'

'Search me.'

So we ordered crocodile and saka-saka.

'And four bottles of beer,' said Lary.

'Max,' said Lary, pouring his Primus into a glass.

'Max?'

'That Pygmy chimp at Madame Leroy's. The way he looked at me. I can't get him out of my mind. I'd never seen one before. The bonobo. You know about them?'

'No,' I said reluctantly, 'I'm pig-ignorant.'

'Of course you are,' said Lary, cheering up, emptying his glass and starting on the second bottle. 'They weren't discovered until 1928 – and I guess *all* your knowledge of anything stops at about 1900. Pith helmets. The Khyber Pass. Right? Well, there are *living* guys working on Pygmy chimps at my own university, the State University of New York, *at this very moment*, Alison and Noel Badrian. It's an extraordinary story: we share ninety-eight per cent of our genetic material with Pygmy chimpanzees. Our haemoglobin is identical to theirs in all 287 units. Their dome-shaped skulls are exactly the same as those of *Australopithecus*, our earliest ancestor. And it seems that the human and chimpanzee lineage may have split as recently as 4.3 million years ago' ('On a Sunday morning at ten o'clock, still in bed, in the missionary position,' I said, but Lary ignored me) 'and not, as we used to flatter ourselves, twenty million years ago. It looks as though our Pygmy chimp ancestors were cut off from Max's ancestors in the second African mountain-building, volcano-spewing, Rift Valley-forming period around six million years ago. Our great-to-the-nth grandparent Pygmy chimps were isolated in rainforests deprived of rain by the new mountains to the west. So the trees dwindled away to scrub and savanna. Max's lot stayed happy just where they were, south of the Zaïre river, unaware that their relatives had got a bum deal. We didn't leave the forests. The forests left us. So Max in the jungle went his own way, even in the most stable part of the most stable continent on earth. Or maybe he didn't change his behaviour, maybe their culture was always like that, maybe that used to be our culture, too.' He waved a mosquito away from his face and refilled his glass from the second bottle. 'No, I guess things really are different with them.'

'What things? What's worrying you? What's the matter?'

'Marriage,' said Lary, not looking at me, beginning to bend a spoon. 'I guess they really do have a different kind of society. I'm sorry I got emotional back there – you know, about fidelity, all that stuff.'

'What are you talking about?'

'They're so close to us genetically. But they use sex in different ways. Well, different from most of us.'

'Tell me about it,' I said soothingly, feeling like a psychiatrist, wishing I had a cigar to smoke, 'take your time.'

Lary looked up sharply. He said, 'You'd make a snot-bad shrink.'

'What?'

'Don't even *think* of it. First off – you'd turn everyone's problems into jokes, to protect yourself. Second off – I bet you've never kept a secret in your life. I can tell.'

'Of course I keep secrets,' I said, unable to remember a single success. 'You can trust me. Absolutely.'

'Absolute prime-time bags of broccoli,' said Lary. He grinned. 'You'd make a snot-bad son of a bastard of a lousy shrink. But I've thought about this, over and over. Morality, it must have evolved, it must be an evolved behaviour as Darwin says in *The Descent of Man* – it's obvious, guys who stuck together, who helped each other, who weren't selfish – they'd wipe it with any rival society, any bunch of warriors where it was every man for himself, however tough those mean guys were as individuals.'

'Of course they would.'

'Pygmy chimps are peaceful, they've got it right. They don't occasionally murder each other like ordinary chimps, they don't suddenly snatch some low-ranking female's baby and eat it. They're not cannibals. It's the *women* who bond with each other. The women run the society.'

'Pygmy chimps. The PCs. The politically correct. Societies run by women. Always a good idea. I saw it with the Iban in Borneo. More sex. Less competition. More fun. More sleep.'

'Nope,' said Lary, without a trace of a smile. 'Don't turn it into one of your comedies. They just use sex differently. The females have evolved

47

enormous clitorides. The clitoris hangs down like a bent index finger, crooked forward. They rub them together. In the jargon it's called G-G rubbing. Genito-genital rubbing.' ('Frottage,' I said.) 'One female walks up to another and stares into her eyes. The recipient of this gaze lies on her back. The soliciting female mounts. They rub their clitorides together. They pant. They scream with orgasm.'

'Jesus.'

'Pygmy chimps build snug little nests in the trees and sleep in them alone. They get up at five-thirty. And from five-thirty to nine-thirty they make love an average of 1.7 times an hour with different partners, females, males, juveniles, all mixed up. When a mother has finished G-G rubbing with another female her male infant will cling to her female partner – who waits while he grasps her hips and inserts his tiny penis into her and bangs away with it like the bill on a woodpecker. She doesn't seem to mind. Other juveniles come and touch the female's buttocks and wait their turn. She just looks a bit bored. You have to agree – it's a very advanced sex education.'

'Keep your voice down,' I said, as the crocodile, the saka-saka, and a wrist-thick tube of cold glaucous manioc arrived. 'You'll have us thrown out. You ought to be locked up. They should put you away.'

'Pygmy chimps *specialize* in peaceful co-existence,' he said, ordering more beer, oblivious of the ambush lurking on his plate. 'Unlike ordinary chimps – where the males bond into gangs – Pygmy chimps live together all the time. It's only the adolescent females who leave their own group and seek out another – so any one group is composed of mothers and sons and incoming girls, the mothers all G-G-rubbing friends and every man a mummy's boy. But the men have to perform. If a woman presents herself and the guy refuses she just *yells* her outrage – and all the other women rush to her aid and chase him up a non-fruiting tree. So the men have got wise. They've learned. Most of the time they copulate without ejaculating. They make damn sure they don't get caught with a limp dick. And the incoming girls, the adolescents, the most sexually active females (who like to make love lying on their backs) – they're infertile. So the birth-rate is very low. The primary function of almost all that sex is just to give everyone pleasure and keep the society together.'

'What about you?' I said, working my jaw on a length of crocodile muscle (fishy, fibrous as a good steak). 'Is that the kind of research you wish you'd done? The possible sex-lives of our ancestors?'

'Nope. Bernd Heinrich's my hero. *Bumblebee Economics*,' said Lary, also working his jaw, a stray piece of saka-saka (like spinach) very green on his ginger-brown moustache. 'One of the great books of all time. Heinrich designed these incredibly elegant experiments – he discovered that bumble-bees warm themselves up for a flight with their wings declutched. They exercise their flight muscles to pull their temperature up above the environ-ment, mechanically connect the wings to the muscles again – and away they go. They're not warm-blooded like a mammal, they're partially warm-blooded, like the dinosaurs probably were. They can store heat in their thorax – there's a heat-valve between the thorax and the abdomen – but they have to work out the cost of each flight, how far away the nectar is, how many flowers held nectar on their last visit. They're burning fuel to carry fuel. Will the out-trip be too far? If they run short, they land and walk the rest of the way. And sometimes, late in the day, if a bumble-bee has misjudged the economics of a flight – in those circumstances it'll lay up on some bit of plant and wait for sunrise. They're a northern species, a tundra bee that's expanded its range south, and they've come into competition with the honey-bee, a tropical species that's extended its range north. The bumble-bee workers in their little colonies store queens, not honey – the original colony dies off at the end of the summer, the fertilized queens disperse, each one finds a disused mouse-hole where she over-winters in a torpid state and emerges in the spring. They hit the flowers early in the morning when it's still too cold for the honeybee to fly, switching to low-yield flowers once the honeybees arrive, to get the best deal, working out the pay-offs. It's a lovely story. Just a lovely story. If I'd done that work I could die happy. I could just look round the room and say, "I made all those intricate discoveries about the life of the bumble-bee and sure as hell I'm going to go right ahead and die happy."'

'Isn't it just as important – what you do – the teaching?'

'You mean those huge foundation classes? The new students? The idea of a university? All that? Or the biology for nurses? The straight zoology?'

'All of it.'

'I didn't think so. Not before I came here,' he said, pushing the remains of his manioc to the edge of the plate, focusing on it for the first time. 'Now I'm not so sure. My students don't know how lucky they are. They think the world consists of a loop from Plattsburgh to New York. If I ever get out of here I'll goddam tell them otherwise.'

He prodded the manioc with his fork (it tasted like half-set putty, marinated in Jeyes' Fluid for a week) and, contemplative, moved his tongue back and forth under his top lip, against his front teeth, where another piece had obviously stuck. He said, 'What the hell is this stuff?'

'Manioc. We lived on it in South America. Only there it usually came in wood-chipping and sawdust form. The Portuguese brought it over in the sixteenth century to feed to their slaves. The tuber's full of cyanide – you have to soak it, grate it, squeeze out the poison in a press of some kind, drive off any remaining moisture by roasting it in pans over a fire, and then you make the flour. Don't you like it?'

'Like it?' said Lary. 'I could barf up my guts.'

7

We admired the fitness of the platoons of soldiers, carrying their Kalashnikovs, who would run past Les Bougainvillées at the double, in formation,
in full kit, in the heat of the day, singing; we took walks down past the great
windowless concrete block of the prison that smelt like a sewage farm; we
dined on soup and sausage at the North Vietnamese restaurant; we ate
Congo-river fish and drank our cheap red wine and made lists of stores we
thought we might need, and eventually I got a hangover.

It was worse than any hangover I had ever had (but then so was the red
wine). Returning from one of our forced walks, as we passed the shuttered
Iranian embassy with its two black dogs which leaped silently against the
high chicken-wire perimeter fence, as we made our way home past breeze-
block walls with broken beer-bottles cemented into their tops, I realized that
it hurt just to touch the hair on my head. The final steps down to Les
Bougainvillées set off a slap-slap of pain inside my skull, like water in a
bucket. The back of my neck locked rigid. My intestines seemed to uncoil and
move beneath my stomach like a sidewinder. Contorted on the lavatory-seat, I
decided that this was the worst diarrhoea I had ever had (but then so was
the sausage). I said aloud, 'You'd better lie down'; but my body spun itself
round and threw up so violently into the diarrhoea-filled pan that I thought
the lining of my throat and oesophagus might rip loose and hang from my
mouth like an inverted sock.

'Christ,' said Lary, as I regained the room, 'you'd better lie down.' His
head detached itself from his shoulders and loomed over me. 'Christ,' it said.
I closed my eyes. I was eight years old, flying my grandmother to America
on the contraption I had built of planks and tins and bits of bicycle in the
little copse above the front lawn, behind the high stone wall, where I kept
my bantams; I was paddling with my father in his two-seater canvas canoe
on a Wiltshire stream; I was dumb with fear, sitting in the back seat of his
Riley, half-way across a desolate Salisbury Plain, being taken away to a
prep-school in Dorset; but the involuntary memories kept snapping, the
images broke up and disappeared into a nausea of yawning, deep groaning
yawns that felt as if they must unhinge my jaw.

'If you ask me,' said Lary, from a long way off, 'that's no hangover.'

Hours later, or so it seemed, I was back on a family holiday in the west of Ireland, on top of Croagh Patrick, in a sudden blizzard, only my mother and father and elder brother had abandoned me, and I lay in the gathering snow, just beside the cairn, wearing nothing but my scratchy grey school shorts.

'They've left me,' I said. 'I'm cold.'

'But it's 90 degrees in here,' said Lary from the bottom of the mountain.

'Please. Get me some clothes.'

I began to shake as the cold icicled from the base of my neck down my vertebrae, but the shivering dispersed the gasping nausea. And Lary was the right man to have with you on a mountain. He'd think of something. He'd work it out. He'd bring my pack up on a donkey.

There was a rattling noise in my inner ear, the sound of hooves on the scree, and Lary emptied my spare trousers, shirts and pants, a sweater and two blankets over me. He covered the corpse with a tarpaulin.

'Your pack's a mess,' he said, kneeling down by my head. 'Why don't you have a system? It's all just shoved in any old how. Crammed into plastic bags. It's truly horrible. First off, you should differentiate between the main load-bearing sack and the side-pockets. Second off, you should put the maps flat in the map-pocket, properly folded. They're precious. We're going to need them. And why's the whole thing stuffed with socks?'

'The SAS major in Hereford said that's what you do. You s-stuff the c-crannies with s-socks.'

'You could breed rats in there,' said Lary.

He paused, and I felt my mind shaken like a web with a wasp in it – but the buzzing came from one of the market stalls we had visited that week; the wasp was caught in the coils of a long strip of dirty red cloth, a rope of twisted cloth which had been made into a triple noose and fastened round the neck of a foot-high sculpture of a standing man. He was wearing a raffia kilt. His mouth was wide open and his eyes shut. He had been dead some time. It was a sorcerer's doll; I knew it would never have been offered for sale to Ibrahim Mahamat, nicknamed Chinois (because of his slightly slanted eyes) if it had not been proved to have lost its smoke-blackened power. I picked it up. The rope-cloth had been knotted nine times. Its neck had been freshly scraped – you invite your enemy round, slip the wood-dust into his palm-wine, watch him drink it, tell him what you've done, and wait for him to lapse into terminal depression and hang himself. Victim number ten had obviously had access to a stronger sorcerer; this defeated and exhausted doll had been discarded. Another bout of shivering seized me; my teeth chattered like a Lewis gun.

'Here it is,' said Lary in a distended voice. 'Found it. Right at the bottom. John Hatt, *The Tropical Traveller*. Enlarged and updated. I should hope so. Let me see. Page ninety-five.' There was a silence. Then, *'Just as I thought,'* he said. '"The areas of the world with extremely high risks of malaria are nearly all in low-lying tropical Africa . . . Remember that however careful you have been about taking the tablets, *there is no guaranteed prophylactic against malaria* . . . Usually only falciparum malaria will kill you . . . It is important to realize that the symptoms of falciparum malaria may not always follow the classic symptoms of vivax malaria, which include a cold stage, then shivering, then a hot stage, followed by profuse sweating as the temperature falls (the entire cycle takes about twenty-four hours and is repeated every other day). Instead, falciparum malaria usually starts with flu-like symptoms, including fever and headache. Vomiting and diarrhoea may be the more obvious symptoms.'

'J-Jesus.'

'So there's nothing to worry about,' said Lary, 'you've got the only strain of malaria that kills you.'

'I'm a named p-patient,' I said, trying to take control of my jaw muscles, 'there's a new drug in the medicine p-pack. It's called Lariam.'

'You made that up,' said Lary.

'I don't know what a named patient is. It s-sounds s-sinister.'

'Too damn right it is,' said Lary, going to the medical backpack. 'I just can't wait for my turn. Couldn't we get the hell out of here? Before I get this thing? Go home?'

'Professor D-David Warrell at the T-Tropical Diseases Research Unit in Oxford gave it to me. He says it may make you dizzy.'

'Dizzy!' said Lary, crackling through the heavy-duty plastic bags.

It sounded as if he was walking in his big boots, very slowly, over a ploughed field in the frost.

'Here you are,' he said, handing me three big white pills and a refilled black water-bottle. 'Three more in six hours' time. Side-effects unknown. Slight dizziness suspected.'

'I'm cold.'

Lary appeared with a bundle of his own spare dry clothes under his right arm and pulled back the tarpaulin with his left. 'Christ!' he said, dropping the trousers and shirts on top of me, 'That's one mother of a sweat you're having. There's water *actually running off* the inside of this thing. It's *soaking* in here.' He shook the tarpaulin, spread the clothes, and replaced it. 'And you told me to keep one set of clothes dry at all times. I might just as well go chuck them in the river.' He put two more water-bottles beside the bed.

'You're a h-hero.'

'I sure am. I'd call a doctor. But I guess he'd kill you. Look – it's evening.

53

I'm off for a sausage. Okay? Don't go for a run. Don't move. I'll be back.'
And he shut the door.

So I lay still, eight years old, on top of the wide slabs of Bath stone, covered in lichen, the secret way along the top of the vicarage kitchen-garden wall. It was summer, and there were greengages and the odd peach on the fruit-trees immediately beneath me to my right, trained against the yellow wall, its ancient masonry pitted with the nail-holes of generations of gardeners. Behind me was the big house with its high windows and grey slate roof, the little courtyard of wash-house and coal-shed, the well under the big flagstone, the apple-store where we kept our bicycles. In front of me, set in the corner of the wall, stood the gazebo, the garden-house with a big stone ball fixed to the apex of the roof, with its two rooms, one above the other, the top one (reached up a flight of stone steps) full of warm straw, the bottom full of chickens who had the run of the glebe, the church field on the other side of the wall, Rhode Island red buffalo that I would hunt, when no one was looking, on my imaginary horse with my real bow-and-arrow. To my left, directly below me, our Large white sow was asleep in her sty, built against the wall; beyond her the field sloped down to the river and the duck-house, where, every morning when I let him out, Percy the Aylesbury drake would put his head down, stretch his neck forward, waggle his tail from side to side, spread the webs on his feet like a Flying frog – and slide down the mud chute into the water, his line of Khaki Campbell ducks behind him.

I lay on the wall with my father's binoculars and my very own *The Observer's Book of Birds* beside me, knowing nothing, at the time, of bleak statistics, and convinced that as Savernake Forest was near enough for family picnics, and as my father had told me that a roller had been seen there in 1888, then any day soon another one was bound to land somewhere along the lines of apple trees down the centre path (I was not sure where exactly, but certainly in plain view, and I was ready). I'd know it when I saw it, he said (it was too special to have its picture in my book), I'd know it not by its shape like a crow and its light-brown back but because the rest of it was made of different blues, as bright as all the blues in the sky in summer, that's what he said. And if a roller was sure to come then so was a bee-eater (it was not in my book either) because one had been shot at Bishopstrow near Warminster in May 1866, and Warminster was not far away and a bee-eater was brown and blue and green and black and all kinds of colours and the most beautiful bird in the air, he said, and I began to shiver with excitement because you couldn't miss it and it loved bees, of course, and it wasn't a bit worried by the stings and our garden was full of bees; in one minute it would come and tweak the bumblebees out of their bee-tunnels in the foxglove flowers.

The wall began to pitch up and down, so I opened my eyes: the floor of a bedroom I did not recognize rose up in irregular waves and hit the ceiling; so I shut my eyes again, and several years later an oncoming wave swept me up Derry Hill on my first motorbike, a two-stroke 150cc BSA Bantam, right to the top, where I dismounted at Reg Way's cottage.

Reg Way (the keeper of a small estate with an absentee landlord), my childhood hero, came out to greet me, wearing his work-clothes – a brown tweed cap, a brown tweed suit and waistcoat, a khaki shirt and tie, brown leather gaiters and brown hob-nailed boots. As a young man in the First World War, an under-age volunteer in the Wiltshire Yeomanry, he had been caught by a burst of German machine-gun fire down the side of his trench; when the attack was beaten off six hours later, stretcher-bearers took him unconscious to the field hospital where his left arm was amputated above the elbow, the four mangled fingers of his right hand lopped off, and various pieces of metal and lead, too deep to remove, left in his upper body.

In constant pain (so my mother said), Reg Way spoke slowly, walked slowly, smiled slowly, did not believe in God (an education in itself) and was the kindest man I had ever met. In the hallway of his cottage he took off his jacket and waistcoat, inserted the stump of his left upper arm into the funnel-shaped leather mount of his hook (held in place by a double bandolier of straps across his chest), replaced his jacket and waistcoat, reached up to the oak gun-rack, and, with his palm and thumb, took down the double-barrelled .410 Webley and Scott sidelock hammergun which he was teaching me to use. Ten years old again, I cradled it in the crook of my left arm, barrels pointing at the floor. From the small cardboard box in the hall-table drawer he filled the right-hand pocket of my thornproof (two sizes too big, for growing into) with the slim, magical, light-brown, uncrimped, number-five-shot (for rabbits) four-long Eley cartridges with their shiny brass ends. For himself he picked out the hammerless-ejector Damascus-barrelled Holland and Holland twelve-bore, adapted, like his eight-, sixteen- and twenty-eight-bores, with a steel bracket on the fore-end to fit the leather wrist of his hook.

He stuffed his straight pipe with Wills Cut Golden Bar, tamped down the tobacco with his thumb, lit it with his silver lighter, slipped the tin and lighter into his jacket pocket, and we walked down past his netted blackcurrant, gooseberry and raspberry bushes, his wigwams of runner-beans, to the old goods-waggon where he kept his dogs (he was the best gundog-trainer in the county). He unbolted the creosoted black plank door and out sprang Hubert, a brushed-shiny, neurotically happy Golden cocker spaniel.

'You're a bit mad, aren't you?' he said, stooping down and patting the dog five times on top of the head with the flat of his thumb. 'And a bit hard in the mouth, too, when all's said and done.' Hubert gulped, wagged his docked tail, slobbered, shook his long fluffy ears with a clap like wood-pigeons' wings, and bounded off to look for pheasants in the runner-beans.

'He's good in water,' said Reg, giving a sharp whistle and letting us through the garden gate into the field. 'But they're too small, cockers, they can really only manage half a day's work. You mustn't push them too hard. They get exhausted. They just stand there shivering.'

We walked along the track and turned left past the thick hedge with the spreading brambles, down to the stream and the withy bed, up past the wet bit with the clumps of reed-grass where you sometimes found a snipe, and Hubert, retrieving all the smells he could, eventually came to heel.

We passed through the stone archway beneath the railway embankment and up the hedge of Angel's field; a cock yellow-hammer, bright as a parrakeet, perched on top of a blackthorn bush, sang his territorial song: *a-little-bit-of-bread-and-no-cheese*.

Inside the outer ditch and the broad earthwork (topped with pollard oaks) of the medieval wood boundary there was a small rectangle of bank enclosing a shallow pit full of nettles – the ruins, said Reg, of the wood-reeve's cottage; and the surrounding scatter of ancient rowan trees (he called them rune trees) were always planted, he said, in the old days, to blind the evil eye.

We walked up the ride through the ash plantation with its boot-high purple mist of bluebells; we checked an empty pheasant-pen and two wooden feeding-hoppers full of barley; we inspected a line of wire between two elm-suckers where Reg habitually pegged out the bodies of the stoats, weasels, Grey squirrels, moles, jays, magpies and crows he had trapped or shot; and we wandered up through the hazel-coppice, the ground thick with faintly onion-smelling ramson leaves, where butterflies, Speckled woods, intent on their mating flights, jinked and spiralled in the shade.

We lingered in Reg's favourite retreat, in the grove of huge oaks, some of them stag-headed, their upper branches dead, beneath which, in winter, we would wait for woodpigeon coming in to roost (they made their first touch-down on the bare oak-twigs, an easy landing, and then flopped, wings spread, onto the branches of the young Sitka spruce in the adjacent plantation, waddling up inside, out of sight in warm cover, for a final purring coo and a soft sleep). Rooks would flock in at twilight, followed, in the gloaming, by pairs of crows, and, last of all, in deep dusk, by the high-pitched cacophony, the *nee-ack nee-ack* of thousands of jackdaws, wheeling, at sunset, like charred flecks above a bonfire.

In a clearing at the centre of the stand of hornbeam we visited the big pheasant-pen (where a baby Forest elephant was short-sightedly hoovering up barley with its trunk) and made our way towards the top of the wood and the almost plant-free ground beneath the thick canopy of 120-foot-high Douglas firs, where, even at midday, the light was dim. Reg Way, seeing something ahead of us, stopped, took the pipe out of his mouth, tapped it quietly against his leg and pushed it stem-first into his breast-pocket. Hubert crept against his boots.

'Young Redmond,' he whispered in my ear, 'be as quiet as you can. Watch your feet on the fir-cones. As you know, this wood has always been full of dangerous pygmies – they shoot you with poisoned arrows. But this is worse. Much worse.'

Very slowly, he raised his gun to his right shoulder, placing his leather forearm in the steel bracket, his hook protruding, his palm on the neck of the stock, his thumb resting along the trigger-guard.

'Use the choke barrel,' he said. 'Throw the pattern further. Remember – it's the rear trigger. You take the man on the right. But don't get too close. *They've got Kalashnikovs.*'

I could just make them out, twenty or thirty men lying in wait beneath the firs, their turbaned faces black in the centre, ghostly white round the edge, like a moonlit warren of rabbit burrows on the Downs.

'They're poachers,' said Reg Way, in his soft Wiltshire burr. 'They're from the Sudan . . .'

Hubert whimpered. And then the fever came back.

8

The next morning I woke cured, temporarily over-charged with mental energy, euphoric. I took a cold shower (the only kind of shower you could take) without waking the irregularly snoring Lary, put on my sweat-damp clothes, and was just cutting up our pre-breakfast pineapple on the tiles when the characteristic sound of a Gloucester Old Spot sow with a full farrow of twelve piglets, one to each teat, stopped; half a minute later Lary lurched into the room, sat down on the edge of the bath, put his elbows on his knees and held his head in his hands. He looked very tired indeed.

'I am well aware', he said, looking down at me, 'that men under stress argue about the most absurd things, fight about the last bottle of tomato ketchup, murder each other over tooth-brushes – but do you really have to do that? Do we really have to eat that pineapple straight from the sucking shit-stained bathroom floor? Don't you think your budget would stretch to a paper plate?'

'Anything you like,' I said. 'Wedgwood. Ming. You name it. It's okay. I'm cured. Did you give me the rest of the pills?'

'Of course I did. I set the alarm-clock. Not that I needed to – how was I supposed to sleep with you banging your teeth together and steaming like a kettle all night?'

'I don't remember. I don't remember anything much.'

'I said to myself: okay, so it's 65 per cent certain he's going to die. I'll go to the US embassy. I'll go to the US embassy and get a body-bag. This is the worst night of my life. No doubt about it. Panic is a bad strategy, Shaffer. Get some sleep. But you turned like a lathe and made these awful groaning noises and clacked your jaws fit to smash every filling in your mouth. That was okay. I could take that. But then you stopped moving altogether. It was so quiet I put the light on. Christ – your eyes are *open*. You are lying with your head up on the pillow and the sweat running off your face and you are *smiling*. I try to talk to you. I wave a hand in front of your face. No reaction. Scares me to death. Then you begin to burble in this eerie little voice I can hardly catch. You think there are birds in here – and bees on roller-skates, as far as I can gather. Much later you begin yelling: "There are dangerous pygmies! Let's find the dangerous pygmies!" Then something gets to you. You go silent. You won't take your eyes off the wardrobe. You give me the creeping horrors so bad I actually get out of bed and take a look inside the goddam thing for myself. I think, right, that's it, don't panic, his mind's really gone, it's cerebral malaria, it's in the meninges, it's got to the lining round his brain. I shout: "You've gone and died on me – before we've got upriver, before we've seen anything. How could you go and die in a doss-house? Where's the sense in that?" You sit up. You bend your arms in front of you. I think: he's holding a gun. And then you fall back and scream and hold your stomach and thrash about with your legs and you shout for your mother.'

'My mother? Don't be ridiculous.'

'Yeah. Horrible. Towards morning you got quite lucid. You put on your normal voice and you wanted to know why it was that young soldiers, when their arms are blown off or their stomachs shot out – why they always cry for their mothers. "Mama! Mama!" they scream, just before they die. "Mummy! Mummy!"'

We were silent; then he said, 'I loved my mother too, you know. In fact, she only ever did one thing wrong, in my opinion. Although I can't deny it, no matter what, it didn't make a blind bit of difference, she'd do it whenever she'd saved the money.'

'What did she do?'

'She'd send me clothes', said Lary, 'that I wouldn't wear to a rabbit round-up.'

After breakfast (which I couldn't eat) Marcellin arrived and we took a taxi down to the main market to buy stores. In the press of the narrow alleyways, between the little wooden stalls roofed with tarpaulins or corrugated iron and selling bolts of cloth, flip-flops, hides of goat-leather, meat in skins of flies, tins of condensed milk, Coca-Cola, bottles of Fanta and Primus, pine-apples, papayas, oranges, sacks of manioc flour, zinc and plastic buckets, enamel basins and smoked fish dappled with flies, Lary forgot his exhaustion. He stood transported, pole-axed with interest in front of an assemblage of ironmongery – hammers, nails, screws, scissors, bits of wire and lumps of metal whose use was not apparent.

The stallholder, sitting cross-legged at the back of the table itself, under a purple awning, said, 'Me, I'm an Arab from Chad. You, sir – what race are you? What race? What race?'

'What a mind-busting idea!' said Lary. 'They sell *generic* bicycle gears! They sell *all-purpose* spokes!'

A legless man, sitting in a low tricycle with a luggage-box at the back, jerked into view at the near corner and, alternately pushing and pulling at levers set to either side of his seat, worked his way past us over the sand. He carried a cargo of cooking-oil, in plastic bottles.

'That', said Lary, following him, 'is an arm-paddle wheelchair with trailer attached. It's constructed from motorbike, pram and bicycle components. It's ingenious! *That is one hell of a piece of welding!'*

And so, with Lary happy, awarding one of his personal Nobel Prizes to the discoverer of the chemical formula of Lariam, and the other to the inventor of the arm-paddle wheelchair, we bought sacks of rice (because it would be twice as expensive upriver in Impfondo, said Marcellin); manioc flour (a better quality in Brazzaville); two five-gallon plastic drums of cheap red wine and five bottles of Johnny Walker Red Label (for the Chiefs — so he said — and the Vice-Presidents of the People's Party Committees in the villages of the interior); twenty-five cartons of cigarettes (for the pygmies); tins of sardines, brown sugar, powdered milk, tea and coffee (because Impfondo might not have any); packets of salt, flaked onions and chicken-flavoured stock-cubes (essential, apparently, to mask the taste of the Giant Gambian rat); soap in big red bars (for clothes) and soap in small white bars (for armpits); knives, forks, spoons, aluminium plates, machetes and disposable lighters; and one small blue camping-gas cooking-stove with retractable legs (because Marcellin couldn't resist it).

'Marcellin,' I said, the euphoria wearing off, feeling weak and giddy as we lugged the booty into the hotel and filled every one of the spare kit-bags, 'I've had malaria.'

'Of course you've had malaria,' said Marcellin, without the slightest interest, hiding the stove deep inside the rice sack. 'This is Africa. You'll get it again upriver. You'll both get it. We all will.'

'But,' said Lary, 'there's no more Lariam.'

Marcellin retied the neck of the sack, felt round the waist for any tell-tale metallic bulge, and, satisfied, turned to go. 'I'll be here at six tomorrow morning. Make sure you're ready. If we miss the steamer, it's another two weeks' wait, maybe more. And I start counting off my salary, Redmond, from tomorrow, whatever happens. Okay? Understood?'

'Understood,' I said, sitting on the manioc sack.

Marcellin paused in the doorway. 'The steamer calls at Mossaka, where the Sangha river joins the Congo. It is a bad area for sleeping sickness. Everyone knows. We just do not have the money to eradicate the tsetse fly. But I have an agent in Mossaka, a dealer in crocodile skins. If he is still alive, we will see him. He wrote to me by the last boat. There is a cholera outbreak at Mossaka. Many people are already dead. Perhaps we will get that, too, and then – just for the chance to earn thirty pounds a day – I will never see my daughter, Vanessa Sweet Grace, again.'

We heard him slam the outer door.

By five the next morning Lary had rewrapped, redistributed and repacked the stores. At six Marcellin and Nicolas arrived – yes, they had been to the dock: there was a chalk notice on the gate-blackboard: the steamer was delayed upriver; perhaps it would come next week. Two mornings later, much to Lary's surprise ('All we do here is wait to die') Nicolas called to take us to the port: the boat had berthed the previous evening.

Under the grey sky, in the heavy gathering heat of the early morning, people fanned out from the high, steel-grilled gates of the dock-shed, down the pavements, across the wide road, up against the warehouse opposite. Women waiting to return upriver stood talking, gesticulating, laughing, shouting, trying to corral their children, guarding their piles of newly bought possessions, their plastic chairs and formica-topped tables, old iron bedsteads, wickerwork baskets, cooking-pots, stoves, foam-mattress strips, corrugated-iron sheets. Marcellin was nowhere to be seen.

We dumped the bergens and kit-bags onto the tarmac. A Berliet troop-carrier, its air-brakes whistling, slewed to a halt beside us. The soldiers, in their black fatigues, jumped down as if going into battle. Nicolas grabbed a couple of porters (dressed in red overalls with circlets of plaited red cloth on their heads), loaded them with three kit-bags apiece – one on the head, one in each hand – and we followed close behind the soldiers, the invisible shock-wave in front of them parting the crowd right up to the steel entrance.

'That's the only way,' said Nicolas, pleased with himself, dropping a pack on the olive-drab pile. 'It's against the law to touch a soldier.'

The queue re-formed around us. The guard on the gate, swinging it open to let the soldiers pass, repadlocked the chains at head- and ankle-height, restoring the one-man-wide slit.

'It's my elder brother!' said Nicolas.

'It's that mournful little twisted-Nickers, the fly in my palm-wine, the dog-turd in my doughnut!' (or something of the sort) said the guard in Batéké. They yelled and laughed at each other, through the grille, above the noise of the crowd, in their ancient, semi-private language.

'Have you noticed', Lary said to me, in English, 'that we're the only honkies going on this trip?'

Nicolas turned to us. 'My brother says, Redmond, that he will let you through to clear your papers with Security. And now – I have to go! It is sad! You are the most sympathetic men I have ever had in my taxi!' (He hugged us.) 'You went to my féticheuse!' (He lowered his voice.) 'At all times, you must remember her advice. There are *wicked* men in the north. You must take care. And, as from today' – he drew a finger across his throat – 'you must forget all about the monster in Lake Télé.' He hunched up his shoulders, put his arms tight down his flanks, moved sideways, and slipped into the crowd.

'I don't like this,' said Lary. 'I don't like it one bit. Where's Marcellin?'

'No idea.'

'He's saying goodbye to that girl. Or maybe – maybe it was a mistake, paying him all that money in advance. Perhaps he's going to keep the cash? Have done with us?'

'You guard the baggage.'

'How do I do that?'

'Sit on it.'

Nicolas's brother let me through the gap in the gate, shook my hand, laughed, slapped me on the back, and pointed me into the dim interior. To the right, at the end of the warehouse-sized hall, a crowd pressed up against a brown metal grille.

Someone sidled out of the shadows and tugged at my sleeve. A very thin young man, in blue jeans and a white tee-shirt, stood at my elbow. 'William Ipemba,' he said. 'Secret agent.'

'How do you do?' I said, nonplussed.

'Very well,' said William Ipemba. 'You need help?'

'I expect so.'

He took my arm and towed me into the semi-circular crush of subdued, anxious-looking men and women, each one holding an identity card.

'We ought to wait in the queue,' I said. 'We ought to wait our turn.'

'There is no queue,' said William Ipemba, dragging me up to the grille. Behind it a row of officials sat at a long table, examining papers, tickets, identity cards, checking lists, sweating, exchanging shouts with their suppli-cants through the bars.

William Ipemba took my boat-ticket and passport, leafed the one inside the other and, with a backflip of the wrist, sent them spinning under the grille, across the table (scattering other people's papers as they went) into the lap of a clerk on the end of the row. The clerk, middle-aged, tired (he had not slept well – perhaps he never slept well), was holding his spectacles in one hand and rubbing his eyes with the other. He replaced his spectacles and looked up, annoyed. We pushed our way down to him.

He scrutinized me, and my passport, with distaste.

He said, 'You are a big problem.'

'I know,' I said, attempting a smile. 'I always have been. All my life.'

'This is not funny,' he said, leaning back in his chair and handing my passport to an office boy, who disappeared with it through a door to the right.

'No,' I said, the smile jammed half-open.

'Security!'

A guard opened a narrow steel gate against the wall and beckoned us inside.

'The foreigner will see the Chief of the Port Police,' he said. 'Ipemba, William – you will wait here.' He ushered me into a side-room and knocked twice at a black door. 'Enter!' came an uninviting shout. The guard pushed me in and shut the door at my back.

The Chief of the People's Port Police was wide and squat and wore a Sten-gun. He sat facing me, my passport open on his desk. The small, sparse rectangular office was lit by a single, barred window high on the wall behind him.

'You have nothing,' he said. 'Nothing but an entry visa.'

I leaned forward, repossessed my passport, turned two pages, unfolded the precious taped-in document from the Ministry of Scientific Research and laid it in front of him. 'Look – here is my permission to journey in your country. I have the full authority of the Ministry of Scientific Research. Jean Ngatsiebe himself has signed it.'

The Chief of the People's Port Police stood up. I revised my initial impression: he was still wide and wearing a Sten-gun, but only his top-half was squat: his legs had towered him way above six feet. He unslung his Sten-gun; he cocked it with a two-tone hollow metallic click; he clattered it down on his papers, the stub of a barrel towards me. I took a step backwards. He ripped the stencilled form out of my passport and came round the desk at me; he held the document under my chin, cupped in the palm of his left hand; with the back of his right hand he gave it an explosive crack. I took a jump backwards.

'Ngatsiebe?' he shouted, closing the gap, his face six inches from mine. 'Who is this Ngatsiebe?'

His breath smelt of black coffee. I thought: he's manic with caffeine.

'Jean Ngatsiebe is Secretary to the Cabinet for the Ministry of Scientific Research.'

'Ministry of nothing! Ministry for nothing of the least importance! This is a piece of lavatory paper!' (He rubbed the form between his fingers.) 'It's not even quality lavatory paper!' (He took a deep breath.) 'You are lucky, my friend, because me – I'm only a policeman. But soon you will meet *the army*. Now get out – and come back with a proper visa.' (He looked at his gold watch.) 'You have five hours – and it takes ten days! It takes ten days minimum!'

He sat down, pushed the Sten-gun to the edge of the desk, handed me the passport and the paper, half-pulled an in-tray of identity cards towards him, and paused. He looked up.

'Why are you here? What are you doing?'

'I'm going.'

'No, no. Why are you really in the Congo? Oil? Timber? Diamonds? Or are you, for instance' – he smiled – 'just pretending to be incompetent? Perhaps you are working for the CIA? The Americans? Perhaps you are paid by the Government of Zaïre?'

I explained; and as I did so I realized that I was weak and dizzy; that I had not eaten for three days; that the light from the high barred window made a vertically striped trapezium on the right-hand wall; that a mosquito was resting in the middle of the third yellow patch from the left; that its shadow whiskered out its curved legs and upturned antennae and straight proboscis to absurd proportions; and that everything was hopeless.

'Gorillas?' said the Chief of the People's Port Police. 'Birds? *Birds?*' He waved an official hand, exasperated.

'We must go to Immigration,' said William Ipemba. 'But I warn you – our Government does not encourage visitors. It is not easy.'

I gave him 10,000 CFA. William Ipemba at once lost his slight stoop; he hauled me through the crush of pectoral muscles and biceps and thrusting breasts and jamming buttocks with a sweaty, brutal dedication. Outside, Lary sat on the bags, encircled, two deep, by small boys, who stared at him, soundlessly. The outgoing stream of people whirled me past; Lary, wild about the eyes, shouted, 'Redso! I need you here! If someone heists a bag . . .' But the conclusion was lost in the crowd.

Immigration was a two-storey building next to the white marble-fronted town hall, in the square opposite the entrance to the main Brazzaville barracks. As the taxi drove off William Ipemba took a small brown plastic wallet from the back-pocket of his jeans.

'You must never talk in a taxi,' he said. 'But it's not true.'

'What's not true?'

'I'm not really a secret agent. But I *want* to be a secret agent.'

'That's okay,' I said. 'I won't tell anyone. I won't blow your cover.'

He unfolded the sole content of the wallet, a tattered clipping from an American magazine, an advertisement extolling 'The Texas School for Operatives . . . ninety per cent of our graduates are now in full-time employment . . . fifty simple lessons by post . . . qualified tutors . . . instruction in state-of-the-art surveillance techniques . . . you too can be . . . send only $1000 to register . . .'

'Perhaps you shouldn't believe it,' I said, as gently as I could. 'Can't you stay here? Isn't there more scope?'

'But I've been saving for three years already!' he said, replacing the bright hope with shaking fingers. 'In this country – they only take the best students, from the university. You need the highest grades – it's even harder than joining the army. It's the best job there is.' He regained his stoop, slouching into Immigration, a place of concrete walls and floors, waiting people, and narrow passageways ventilated only by the occasional one-breeze-block-size hole to the outer world. 'You don't know what you're talking about,' he said, over his shoulder. 'Why – when you get promoted, you can send money home, you can keep one official wife, and, perhaps, later on, *two more that you really like.*'

We squeezed up to a counter in the largest of the narrow rooms. On the powerless side, our side, it was worn as smooth as one of Ibrahim Mahamat's nineteenth-century wooden fetish-statues in the market. 'There is no hope for you,' said the young girl facing me, with an incredulous laugh. 'None whatever.' William Ipemba, whom she obviously knew, pleaded; she ripped a square from her official note-pad and scrawled: 'This is to certify that William Ipemba and his client called here. Anita.'

We took a taxi back to the port. The crowd had grown even larger; the gates were set further apart, at two-person width; the opposing streams of people were moving faster; Lary's light-blue denim shirt, I noticed, as I was swept past him and his incomprehensible shout, was now dark with sweat. 'So what is *this?*' said the Chief of the People's Port Police, taking a rabbit-chop at the chit in his palm; the square of paper, transformed into a V, butterflied down and settled on the floor; he put his boot on it. 'Out! You need a visa! It takes ten days! You have four hours left! You have wasted one hour! Ten days minimum! Out! Out!'

Outside, Marcellin had arrived; his air of authority had created a little beach of calm around Lary on his island of kit-bags and bergens, a shoulder-width shore in the conflicting currents of people. William Ipemba, respectful, stooping, explained our problem.

'Redmond!' shouted Marcellin, his voice at its highest pitch. 'All this time – what the hell have you been doing?'

'I thought the Ministry permission was enough,' I said, feeling like a schoolboy. 'I paid £1000 for it.'

'More than enough,' said Lary, sweating.

'Idiots!' shouted Marcellin. 'Idiots!'

The depth of his anger was comforting; he cared; Marcellin would do something; I felt very hungry indeed.

'William Ipemba,' said Marcellin, 'you will stay here. You will help Dr

Shaffer guard every piece of this official Government expedition equipment.'

I thought of eggs, bacon, chips and beans; I thought of a British Rail sandwich; I even thought of a length of manioc. 'This is no time to eat,' said Marcellin, back in the concrete passageways of Immigration. He let himself into offices marked private, he was charming to everybody, his laugh was almost genuine, he knew everybody. Clean-shaven, in his long-sleeved white cotton shirt, his pressed jeans, his washed-white trainers, he really was a *chef de service*. Blearily, in the waiting-room passages, propped against one wall or another, I decided that the air was so thick with sweat that every breath was as good as a soup-spoon of beef and onion, and I congratulated myself, once again, on picking companions made of the right stuff: when in doubt, go for the man who sees dinosaurs. 'I have informed this taxi-driver', said Marcellin, as we careered across the city, 'that you will pay him exactly double his normal fare, because he will drive at exactly double his normal speed.' I clung to the hand-hold above the door. At Les Bougainvillées we collected a hotel receipt and my return ticket; back at the port we forced Lary to unbutton the breast-pocket of his shirt and hand over his passport, inoculation documents and return ticket (he gave it a frantic goodbye kiss). In the centre of the city we found a photo-copying shop (whose manager insisted on trimming each piece of paper with a pair of nail-scissors); in the photographic studios across the road, which boasted one of the two cameras in Brazzaville that takes your passport photograph, the camera had been stolen that morning, so we drove to the rival establishment, a shack in Poto-Poto; and in the poor quarter, down behind the railway-line, off a courtyard, in a building with no sign as to its present function (it had perhaps once been a pig-shed), in the fourth concrete stall on the right (perhaps they had once been farrowing pens) sat a very old woman at a very small table, and in the middle of the table lay one book of the stamps required for the visas of long-stay visitors to the People's Republic of the Congo.

We returned to the backroom at Immigration; for the first time one of the officers looked up at me from his crowded desk and smiled; but where was the photograph of Shaffer, Lawrence? Marcellin took a taxi to the port – to get his brother to guard the bags and Lary to the one remaining passport camera. I sent William Ipemba out to buy a crate of beer. Everyone smiled. The officer picked up a red metal date-stamper: I watched it hover for a moment above my papers: clunk! and a big square wooden stamp-press: bang! and a small round wooden stamp-press: bang! (at a higher pitch). We opened the bottles. Lary arrived. 'Redso,' he gasped. *'my return ticket...'*

The Chief of the People's Port Police did not smile, but then neither did he unsling his Sten-gun. He stood up and addressed himself to Marcellin:

'You are a strong man,' he said, studying Marcellin's face with deliberate intensity, as if committing it to memory. 'Such a thing has never happened before . . .' It was fifty-nine minutes past eleven. The boat was due to leave at twelve.

9

Marcellin, his brother Manou (perhaps in his early twenties, thin, shy, wearing a wide-brimmed brown bush hat), Lary and I carried the kit-bags and bergens, in relays, through the gate, across the hall, down the sloping concrete apron of the quay, over the narrow wooden gangplanks – and onto the iron pontoons of the dock, to which the steamer itself was moored.

'What are all these people doing?' said Lary, as we picked our way between families preparing to camp out on the rust-filthy pontoon decks, untying their foam mattresses, positioning suitcases and plastic bags, staking claims. Lary paused, still shell-shocked by the crush, the heat or the noise, a kit-bag in each hand, steadying himself, in his big boots, to step over a pile of cooking-pots. 'What's up? What are they waiting for?'

'Doing?' said Marcellin. 'They are going with us. Upriver.'

'On what? Where?'

'On these barges! Where do you think? These are poor people. Traders. Village people. Third-class passengers. They will sleep in the open for two weeks, maybe three. Some of them will die. One or two very young children will roll over in their sleep and disappear down the gaps, into the river. It always happens. There are 3000 people here, maybe more.'

'No handrails,' muttered Lary. 'Even at the edges, there are no handrails.'

'Second-class passengers,' said Marcellin, leading the way, his dark-blue pack on his back, 'they live over there.' He waved dismissively at a white two-decker houseboat with a flat roof, a barge I had assumed to be separately moored at the dockside, a dockside, a rapidly forming town, which, I now realized, was coming with us. Looking at the houseboat's rows of dark-brown cabin doors, at the vertical white external struts supporting its verandas, I failed to notice a steel hawser stretched taut at ankle-height in front of me, tripped, dropped both kit-bags, and fell against the back of a man standing to my left. I involuntarily clutched at his jacket, a jacket which had once, perhaps, been part of a dark suit. He turned with a quick, violent twist, jabbing out with his elbows, clenching his fists. Righting myself, I looked up – into his old and angry eyes. Some disease of the epidermis, or some genetic misfortune, had grown pocket-tops of skin down his cheeks; they flapped slightly as he moved; his neck was wattled like a turkey's. I backed off, too surprised to speak, picked up the kit-bags, and hurried after Marcellin's dark-blue bobbing pack.

'Second-class,' Marcellin was saying as I came up behind him, 'four or six bunks to a cabin. That's where little Manou will go. Whereas we, Redmond, we will travel like kings, like real Chiefs, like *bosses* – I made you buy the best, you know, first-class. Our tickets will mean three meals a day, in a *dining-room*. We will not have to bargain for our food from women on the barges, or from fishermen over the side. And there are only two beds in each cabin. Well, it was necessary. If you want to travel with all this equipment – you must have a cabin with a door that locks.'

We reached the steamer, the *Impfondo* (in big red letters under the bridge); Marcellin paused at the base of a stairwell and half-turned to look at me: 'Besides, you and Lary will share one cabin – and the other, if I'm very lucky, perhaps the second berth will not be taken. Perhaps I will be able – how would you say it? – perhaps I will be able to live with a girl' – he switched into English – '*from the lower decks.*'

Two stairwells up, on the starboard side, the Purser (small, fussy, foxy, in late middle-age and a man, I told myself, with a ruling secret) opened the second and third cabins along in a row of five, handed us the keys, and withdrew to his centre of interest, back down the companionway. Each cabin contained two narrow beds, a wardrobe, a tiny basin.

'It's magnificent,' I said. 'It's luxurious.'

'If you say so,' said Lary.

'First-class,' said Marcellin.

Manou, slight and shy, smiling to himself, his face half-hidden under his big hat, ran his finger round the rim of the basin.

Lary and I stowed the bergens and kit-bags in and against the wardrobe in our cabin, locked the cabin door, and we all walked forward beneath the bridge. Leaning over the rail, we watched the town setting itself up on the iron barges: mothers bathing their toddlers from plastic buckets, mortar-and-pestling manioc leaves, mixing fou-fou into manioc paste; pounding palm kernels into palm oil. Directly below us an old man was making a fishing net, tying knots with his right hand, holding the top line taut between his left index finger and right big toe. People were still flowing aboard, bundles on their heads, and, the best places taken, decanting themselves down into the holds of the two barges on the port side.

To starboard, on the great river draining an area the size of India, islands of reed and water-hyacinth floated perpetually past from the far interior, islands which the French used to call Portuguese concessions, a numbing progress of vegetation on its way to the rapids and the sea. Through the binoculars I resolved an upturned black and white chair with a sagging seat into a drowned, piebald goat, its legs stiff and straight, black in the reflected light, its white belly bloated in the heat.

Twenty-four kilometres away, across Malebo Pool, we could see the towers of Kinshasa, murky under the grey sky, a city, Marcellin told us, of disorder, corruption, armed gangsters (most of them, he said, soldiers and policemen), the capital of a country whose copper and cobalt, well managed, could have made every citizen rich, but whose wealth had been stolen by the biggest gangster of them all, the son of a hotel cook, educated by capitalist mission-aries, the self-styled Mobutu Sese Seko Koko Ngbendu Wa Za Banga, 'The all-powerful soldier who, because of endurance and an implacable determi-nation to succeed, will go from triumph to triumph leaving fire in his wake', a man, said Marcellin, who also called himself the Helmsman, the Redeemer, the Messiah, and who, under the protection of the Christians in North America, had stolen five billion dollars from his people. I had a rare moment, feeling morally superior, standing on the Communist side of the river.

With Marcellin and Manou we walked ashore (down the slimy stairwells, along the slippery iron barges, the whole vast landscape to our right, the 450 square kilometres of the pool, sultry, oppressive in the grey heat, waiting for a storm that never seemed to break). Outside the gates, in the café at the end of the dock road, we drank beer and fish soup and ate bread and sausage (several times each). As we wandered back, Lary noticed three men working their way through the crowd: over their left arms they carried long transparent plastic sheets of brightly coloured pills, orange, blue and red; a pair of scissors on a string dangled from each belt; almost every woman appeared to be buying selections of the different colours, in whatever length she could afford.

'Those men get rich,' said Marcellin. 'They are from Zaïre. In the Congo it is illegal to sell antibiotics like that – you must go to a qualified pharmacist. But the police, they have given up. It is hopeless. Every mother wants those pills for her children. They use them for every illness, in every kind of dose. These are ignorant people. And anyway, there are no instructions. There is no pharmacological investigation. The factories are in Zaïre. Maybe those pills are just palm oil in coloured gelatin coats, maybe they really are anti-biotics. Who knows? The Zaïrois – they damage us in every way they can.'

Marcellin spotted Louise in the crowd and disappeared round the back of the warehouse with her, to say goodbye. Manou, not to be outdone, pretended that he, too, had seen a girlfriend, and set off in a semi-purposeful line towards the beer-stall.

'Tuberculosis,' said Lary, as we sweated back through the gates. 'It figures.

Antibiotic-resistant strains. Give the bacillus just a little dose with those random capsules. Don't kill it off. Give it time to think. Let it adapt. Help it spread.'

Safe in our rank and musty cabin, so hot it made you gasp for breath, Lary tried to turn on the air-conditioner. 'It's broken,' he announced, delighted, unpopping his Leatherman tool from its little case at his belt.

With the Philips screwdriver he detached the imitation-wood front panel; with his three sizes of ordinary screwdrivers he took substantive-looking parts to pieces; he performed intimate and serious internal operations with the pliers; he may even have used the file, but he did not, as far as I could judge, employ the ruler, the knife or the can-opener.

'It's been fixed on stop,' he said, in that loud voice that professional plumbers use.

The machine reassembled, we knelt on the floor in front of it. Lary turned the knob. There was a preparatory hum, it began to shake, and then it banged like a Howitzer, it clanked like a goods-yard, it whined like an approaching jet. A cat's breath of warm air, scented with fish, yawned itself out of the left-hand ventilator.

'I've done it!' shouted Lary.

'Of course you have,' I said, my fingers in my ears.

Lary turned it off.

'There's something wrong,' he said, full of reproach. 'There is something wrong with this air-conditioner.'

'If you say so,' I said, soothingly, lying down on my bed. 'But there's nothing wrong with the beds.'

'I've read about that,' said Lary, sheathing his Leatherman like a poniard. 'In a place like this you should turn your mattress. Then the body-lice have to start over and make their way back up.'

'Don't do that,' I said, too late.

Lary had the bottom right-hand corner of his mattress half out of its box-base. There came the sound of finger-nails on wood, the acrid smell of a deep-litter chicken-shed; cockroaches, the size of shrews, cascaded over the lip of the box, fell to the floor, righted themselves, and scuttered to safety in all directions across the linoleum.

'There's *hundreds* in there,' said Lary, dropping the mattress, sticking out his right boot and killing one on the floor.

'It's best to leave them,' I said. 'They've got stink glands on their backs. They only smell when disturbed. Besides, they're indestructible. Not even radiation bothers them. When the bomb falls, the cockroaches clear up.'

'Yeah, yeah. And they're older than Mokélé-mbembé. I know. Fossil

71

cockroaches just like this one' – he picked it up between index finger and thumb – 'are abundant in Carboniferous strata, 300 million years ago, seventy-five million years before the sauropod dinosaurs show up. But it still doesn't mean I want them in my bed.' Its antennae, palps and six spiky legs hung limp; dark-brown all over, it had a pretty orange-yellow band across its head and thorax. 'If I took this sucker back to Plattsburgh,' said Lary, simple to compound eye with it, 'I could charge admission.' He dropped it on the floor, spread his tarpaulin and lay cautiously down on his bed.

'Mad Frank Buckland,' I said, 'the man who shocked everyone by eating crocodile.' ('They were right,' said Lary.) 'Buckland says in his *Curiosities of Natural History* (1857) that a gentleman coming home by ship from India was much annoyed by cockroaches: "they actually at night, when he was asleep, came and devoured the little rims of white skin at the roots of the finger-nails."'

Lary said, 'That man you fell against on the barge . . .'

'Yes?'

'He worried me all morning.'

'How come?'

'He was standing right next to me. The weirdest freak I ever saw.'

'So?'

'All those little boys, the ones sitting round me and the bags . . .'

'What about them?'

'Well – it was *me* they were staring at.'

He turned off his torch. The night was full of noise: the background pounding of the steamer's generator; the jangling blast of competing cassette-players; shouting and laughter.

'Just remember,' I said, turning over to face the wall, 'when you sleep with that pillow you sleep with every person that pillow has ever slept with.'

There was a silence in the cabin, followed by a pulling, a crackling, a smoothing. Lary was readjusting his tarpaulin.

'Control!' shouted a soldier, going down the line of cabins, banging on the doors with the butt of his Kalashnikov. 'Control!' In the grey dawn we jostled ashore with the three to four thousand other inhabitants of the extended *Impfondo*. 'They search the empty ship and all the rubbish on the barges', said Marcellin, at my elbow, 'for criminals and spies and enemies of the state' – he dropped his voice – 'in other words, for young men with lots of courage and no money.'

We queued to cross a gangplank and show our papers to the waiting soldiers, made our way up the concrete slope, through the dock building – and we drank coffee and fish soup and Primus and ate bread in the café at the end of the dock road, and waited. Marcellin's wife, young, beautiful, pregnant, carrying the two-and-a-half-year-old Vanessa Sweet Grace in her arms, arrived to see him off. The child fixed her pudgy fingers in Marcellin's shirt-front and burbled her adoration. Lary and I walked on down the quay; we sat under a big *Fromager*, a Red silk-cotton tree, its tall, narrow crown perhaps 120 feet above our heads, its silvery, scaly bark at our backs, a short buttress to either side of us, and a crushed Coke can as yet unscavenged at our feet.

'I composed a poem last night,' I said. 'It's in French.'

'I'm sorry to hear it,' said Lary.

> J'ai mangé du fou-fou
> Et j'ai eu
> Le palu
> C'est tout.'

('I've eaten manioc flour and I've had malaria. That's it.')

'I see,' said Lary, non-committal. 'Don't you think it needs a little R and D?'

'R and D?'

'Research and Development – you know, a bit more detail?'

'It's perfect as it is,' I said, huffy. 'It's rounded.'

'Rounded,' said Lary.

Big red ants had materialized out of the dust, around the rim of the Coke can.

'You should have left those binoculars in the cabin,' said Lary. 'They're obvious military kit. You look like a spy.'

'But we might see a bird.'

'There aren't any birds.'

Three hours later, with everyone back on board, two manoeuvrable tugs on tow-lines, and one big engine-block of a tug, the *Sounda*, lashed to the *Impfondo* level with our cabin, all the diesels opened up together, full astern. The whole sprawling township shuddered; the sledgehammering volume of noise emptied the brain. Lary and I, leaning on the rail of the fan-deck, watched the brown surface of the river back and fill and turn white. We were on the move.

10

Out in Malebo Pool the Captain set his engines on slow ahead. Standing under the bridge, Lary, Marcellin and I watched a flotilla of ten small white tugs come out from the shore, form into a line, tie up down the port side of the barges and cut their engines. They were timber-tugs, said Marcellin, they were hitching a lift upriver to collect their log-rafts, mostly limba, a softwood, and okoume, a hardwood, both species of mahogany, but in general the forests of the Congo were difficult to exploit – in swamp-forest it was impossible, and what with the Congo rapids, the cost of transport by rail to the coast, it was all very difficult. Still, it was a good job to have, working on those boats, it was steady, well paid, and besides, because it was regular you could have a wife in every village where you stayed the night.

Further up, by wide flat sandbanks covered with reed-grass, grey boats were waiting, plank-built, high-sided, upturned at the prow, squared off at the stern, some with flimsy roofs on gunwale struts and each one with an outboard motor – *baleinières*, said Marcellin, as they swung into the vacant berths between the tugs, whale-boats; they, too, were going to ride upriver with us – they would peel off to collect village produce, manioc, smoked fish, oranges, mandarins, baskets of lemons, and float back down to Brazzaville, steering with their outboards.

We entered the channel to the north of the chain of sandbanks, M'Bamou Island, which divides the eastern end of Malebo Pool; the rounded hills of the Batéké plateau edged close enough for us to see the straggled bushes and dry grass, the savanna-scrub on their slopes; we passed beneath the white sandstone outcrop which Frank Pocock, homesick for his Kentish village, asked Stanley to name Dover Cliffs; and, with all engines on full power, we moved slowly up the fast deep waters of Le Couloir, 125 miles long and a mile or so wide, the gorge which marks the course of the once backward-cutting headwaters of a coastal river, a river which, perhaps as recently as sixty-five million years ago, inched a trough back through the uplifted rim of the Congo basin and cascaded the waters of its vast inland lake down and out to the sea.

*

The Purser skipped up behind us, striking an empty Primus beer-bottle with a table-knife.

'A meal!' said Marcellin.

The small semi-circular dining-room was just aft of the galley, and its windows would have looked out on the fan-deck if brown curtains had not been drawn across every one of them; it smelt of old meat, and cockroaches. Our fellow privileged travellers were already seated: a white nun in a blue nurse's uniform, a crucifix round her neck; a tense young man in a brown cotton African (collarless) suit; and a man in his forties with squashy jowls and a big paunch, his bulk wrapped in a long white robe and tied with a tasselled cord. We drew the steel chairs up to the remaining places at the formica-topped table, sat down, and introduced ourselves. The young man worked for the boat company; the fat man was a dealer in crocodile-skins; and the nun was returning from a visit to her family in Spain, in Galicia, where she had many brothers – her father and mother could not afford to feed them all, so she had become a nun, and she wrote to them every week and she saw them once every five years and her heart ached, and yes, if God willed, she would spend the rest of her life working in the mission hospital at Mossaka. But from the moment the Purser brought in the plates of oxtail, the bowl of potatoes, the jug of watery gravy, eye-contact was broken, conversation stopped. In the land of the tsetse fly, the bearer of sleeping sickness and nagana, the killer of cattle, oxtail-on-the bone was obviously a delicacy demanding concentration of the senses, silence.

Outside again, two decks down, we followed Marcellin, who, fired by all that meat, had begun a serious hunt for a mistress. We squeezed past newly set-up stalls selling candles, tins of sardines, batteries, torches, steel-wool scouring pads, Bic biros, envelopes, assorted pills, tee-shirts, flip-flops, cigarettes, used cassette-tapes and onions in plastic buckets. We kept Marcellin's white shirt in view past a crowd of men at the bow of the *Impfondo* who were waiting to buy a ladleful of fish soup or a manioc-paste doughnut from two huge women (each with a slightly thinner assistant) – Lary paused to inspect their stoves (old diesel drums with holes cut at their bases for log fires and with metal grilles fixed just beneath their rims) – and when we looked up Marcellin had disappeared. So we sat on a packing-case at the edge of the first barge, and waited.

At every fold in the slow-moving hills a stream supported a meagre twist of gallery forest, and by its outlet to the great river the huts of a fishing village would shelter beside a few giant Cotton trees, a few trees with high horizontally spreading branches like Cedars of Lebanon, oil-palms and fan-palms. Through the binoculars we sometimes saw women working in the plantations, among the wispy manioc shrubs which grew on the lower slopes;

and up ahead, hanging in the current upstream, paddling their dugouts standing up, were their menfolk. They thrust towards the floating city as we passed, and grabbed the fender of a timber-tug, the gunwale of a whale-boat, a rope thrown from the lower deck of the steamer or, most precarious of all, the side of another already tethered dugout emptied of its crew and cargo and slewing, bucking, lashing its tail, frantic in the slipwaves from several thousand tons of kinetic energy.

The moment they tied up, bargaining began with the merchants on the steamer and the barges. The fishermen handed or threw up or carried aboard stacks of smoked fish, blackened carp-shaped fish clamped between the elliptical open-wickerwork basket-tops whose purpose had been a mystery to us in Brazzaville dock; big fresh whiskery catfish; and zinc bowls full of little fish like whitebait. The booty would disappear into a pushing, shouting, gesticulating chaos of people. It was a relief to contemplate the young mother whose patch we sat beside: her hair was plaited back from her forehead in tight lines and tied at the back, her breasts were loose in her blue cotton shirt, her wraparound (a design of yellow knights riding yellow chargers across a black background) stretched from her supple waist to her calf muscles. She paid out the string on the handle of an old powdered-milk can, lowering it into the gap between the barges, drew it up and filled a white enamel pail with brown river water. She undressed her timid little girl (yellow frock over the head), took a bar of white soap, washed her all over, and rubbed her down with a red tea-towel. She cupped out a handful of palm oil from a blue plastic jerry-can and worked it slowly into the little girl's skin, attentive to every crease and to the spaces between the toes. Satisfied, she lit a stove in an empty paint can and began to boil up a saucepan of drinking water. The child, lustrous, wearing nothing but a tin bracelet on her tiny left wrist, sat down heavily in the middle of her washing-puddle and, absorbed, with her right index finger she began to draw secret watery toddler symbols on the iron deck.

Lary and I made our way back, through the heat from the oil-drum stoves, the pounding diesels (the engine-room fenced off with chicken-wire), the smell of frying manioc, boiling fish, and now, all pervasively, the stench of latrines.

On the fan-deck the eight white wooden chairs, slatted chairs with quarter-reclined backs and broad flat arms – 'Colonial chairs,' said Lary – had been pulled into a circle by young men in cotton trousers, white shirts and trainers: they sat forward, cards spread in their left hands, gambling like gangsters and listening to a cassette-player (vibrating at full volume) as a stretched tape slurred out the rhythms of pop songs from Zaïre. A solitary Black kite hung off the stern, quartering the wake for garbage, its pointed wings tilting and flattening in the conflicting air-currents, the hot bright air, the bouncing light of the open river temporarily displaced by the still fiercer heat, the thick shimmer from the big black funnels of the *Impfondo* and the *Sounda*. The kite rode the turbulence with ease, dipping down across the surface of the water and again rising over the ship, its tail appearing forked as it narrowed, square as it extended. 'Hi, darling,' said Lary, addressing the bird directly, 'no wonder you're lonesome. Poor baby – the only garbage out back is one long trail of shit. Sweetheart, I hate to have to break the news, but this is a non-disposing society. Paint cans, Coke cans, old bicycle spokes, manioc leaves, rags, fish bones – you can't have them, baby, they're in the soup. They get used . . .'

'Redmond!' came a familiar high-pitched shout. 'Where did you get to? Come and buy us a beer!'

Marcellin, triumphant, was holding the hand of a young girl; she was markedly like Louise, but on a smaller scale: she wore a thin white tee-shirt with wide black transverse stripes and her small breasts (with surprisingly long nipples) poked out the cotton between the third and fourth stripes down; beneath the hem of her tee-shirt, above the belt of her tight blue jeans, her little navel peeked at Marcellin's left thigh. She held her head down and looked up at Lary.

'Are you rich?' she said.

Lary, flustered, said, 'I'm a teacher.'

'Oh,' she said, sorry for him.

'She's tiny, isn't she?' said Marcellin to me in English, grinning like a small boy with a knickerbocker glory. 'I found her on the last barge, right at the front. It's just her mother and a baby brother up there. Her father's at Dongou, way up the Oubangui. They're very poor. I like her. Do you like her? Do you like her nipples?'

'I like her nipples very much.'

'Good,' said Marcellin decisively, reverting to French, 'then you can buy us a beer. Her name's Marie. We'll go to the bar.'

'A bar?'

'Of course there's a bar.'

As we jostled down the stairwell to the lower deck there was a long broken scream, shouting, beneath us, from outside. We pushed up to the rail: six empty dugouts were tied to the *Impfondo* in a quarter-fan, their painters attached to a single loop of cable, their sterns swinging free. An overloaded dugout was attempting to dock alongside the outermost hull: the bow-paddler, a teenage boy in red nylon shorts, pigeon-chested, his shoulders thin, had somehow lost his paddle overboard. He was half-kneeling, his left hand on the gunwale, his right lunging for the paddle – just out of reach, spinning, disappearing, gathering speed in the current. The canoe rocked; the fisherman at the stern dug his own paddle into the water, trying to propel the boat forward against the wake of the *Impfondo* and the force of the current; the men and women around us yelled instructions; in the dugout, an old woman, naked to the waist, sitting amidships behind a humped pile of belongings – pots, pans, buckets, a yellow cushion, a net, a foam-mattress, a stack of smoked fish – held a baby to her wrinkled breasts and screamed.

The stern of the furthest canoe in the fan swung out and clipped the bow where the boy crouched: still clutching the gunwale with his left hand, he pitched into the water. The dugout rolled over. The long narrow upturned hull glistened wet in the sunlight; the adze-marks, the hundreds of hours of patient work, were clearly visible on the burnt-black wood.

The foam-mattress, the baby and the grandmother, the yellow cushion and the fisherman surfaced, in that order. The upturned hull jarred against the sterns of the inner dugouts, smacked into the steel side of the *Impfondo*, and was sucked beneath the ship. The grandmother, her lungs obviously in prime condition, held the baby's head above water, and screamed.

Two young men in an approaching dugout, loaded with fish, abandoned their own attempt to dock (and so any chance of trade for another two or three weeks) and, with a virtuoso display of balance and control (their bare feet splayed on the gunwales, triangular slabs of contracting muscle outlined on their shoulders) they pulled the grandmother, the baby and the fisherman from the water. Everyone cheered. The young men waved, dropping back in the current, heading for the distant shore.

I trained my binoculars on the boy – he was moving downriver at speed, well ahead of the chopped-up sections of dugout splintered by the steamer's screws, the paddle still just out of reach. I thought: maybe he's not quite right in the head? Or perhaps that paddle was a last present from his dead father? Or maybe he borrowed it from a sorcerer?

And then, as he was swept past the only remaining dugout that might have saved him, I realized that he and the paddle were simply caught in the same current, midstream, in the deep fast waters of Le Couloir. A long way back, beyond resolution by the naked eye, his black head bobbed in and out of focus in the white light, the glare of the river – and disappeared.

'He's gone!' I shouted. 'Tell the Captain! He's gone!'

Marcellin put his free arm hard round my shoulders and pulled me against him like an errant child. 'Quiet,' he said. 'You're the only person who saw it. You and the Captain are the only people on this ship who possess binoculars. You're a foreigner. Why should anyone believe you? The story goes like this: everyone lost overboard is picked up by fishermen. Okay?'

'But he's gone! I saw his head – it disappeared!'

'That's enough,' said Marcellin sharply, releasing his grip. 'You keep calm.

There's nothing to be done. This ship never turns back. It can't. You can't turn round with three or four thousand people on barges in this current. It can't be done.'

'But he's drowned!'

'So he's drowned,' said Marcellin, looking out across the water at a village on the opposite bank. 'This is the best-governed country in Africa, our people are the best educated. There's no war, no famine. But it's still Africa. Where we're going – you'll hear wailing women all day long. If you make a fuss like that every time someone dies, my friend, you won't last. You'll be wasting my time. We won't complete our mission.'

'The rescue launch!' said Lary.

'There is no rescue launch.'

'Why not?' said Lary, incredulous, fingering his moustache.

'Who would pay? Who'd find the money?'

'The Government, of course. Taxes.'

'Government!' said Marcellin, shrugging his big shoulders. 'Taxes!' He smiled at Lary. 'Let's not upset Marie. Okay? Let's go to the bar.'

I I

————————

The bar was small and hot. Rolled-up sleeping-mats, jerry-cans and baskets were slung from the iron beams, tied with rope or knotted rags. A soldier sat slumped at one of the formica-topped tables, his head on his arms, his beret lying at the end of a carefully arranged line of empty Primus bottles. The rest of his table and all its chairs were unoccupied – even asleep, soldiers were plainly dangerous – so we joined him. Marie held Marcellin's right arm tight as a lifebelt. The young barman brought us each a Primus and, on Marcellin's instructions, turned up the volume of the big chrome cassette-player on the bar-top.

Marcellin said, 'Let's dance.'

'Wait a minute,' said Lary. 'That grandmother – what the hell was she doing in a dugout? And the baby, for Chrissake, why didn't they stay at home? The fishermen, I can understand that, it's one hell of a way to go to market but I can see why every one of them has to risk his life once a fortnight. But a grandmother. And a baby. It's unforgivable.'

Marcellin took a weary swig at his beer. 'How else can she get upriver? Maybe the baby's father is in Liranga or Mossaka or Impfondo. There's no road. This is the only way. It would take months in a pirogue, hugging the bank. The little aeroplane from Brazzaville to Impfondo – that's for rich people. And besides, the airline has no money. Sometimes there's fuel and it flies. Sometimes there isn't and it doesn't.'

Marcellin got to his feet; Marie, still holding his arm, moved out with him on to the four feet of open space that served as a dance-floor, half-closed her eyes, arched her back and swayed her little buttocks in time with the music.

'Go find yourself a woman!' shouted Marcellin to Lary. 'Let's dance!'

'This place is a hell-hole,' said Lary to me, getting up, leaving his beer unfinished. I paid for the drinks and followed him out. 'No war. No famine,' said Lary, as we climbed the clammy stairwell. 'I'm sorry, I can't get that boy out of my head.'

We leaned on the rail of the fan-deck and stared at the left bank of the river, at Zaïre. A road twisted down through the scrub hills to a complex of buildings over which towered two enormous beehive-shaped kilns, smoking in the still air; through the binoculars I could see the timber-rafts at the wharf, the line of derricks, the big articulated lorries parked by the piles of logs and planks on the quay. 'That's a serious effort,' said Lary. 'Charcoal-burners and sawmill combined. At least someone has some work.' He rubbed his right hand across his eyes. 'Borneo and the Amazon logged out today,' he said. 'Africa tomorrow.'

A kingfisher, as big as a pigeon, with a fluffy head and a massive black bill, flew low across the water past the stern of the steamer, making straight for the opposite shore; its flight was heavy, irregular, its back and wings and tail a slaty-grey flashing with points of white.

'A Giant kingfisher!' I said. 'Our first African Giant kingfisher!'

'Sure,' said Lary, his shoulders loosening. 'But that's where I'd like to be' – he pointed at two Lesser black-backed gulls who had joined the kite in our slipstream – 'back in England on Walney Island. Studying those gulls. Young again. Full of plans.'

'What sort of plans?'

'I set up my own film company, Biograph. I shot a lot of natural history footage. I had a Bell and Howell, an editor, I knew I could do it. I wanted to be the next D. W. Griffith. Hook-nose Dave. It didn't seem *that* fantastic. Not at the time. And while I waited for the call from Hollywood there were those gulls to think about – I lived with my first wife Beth in a rough little coastguard cottage, just off a mixed breeding colony of 50,000 pairs of Lesser black-backs and Herring gulls. They feed on anything. They scavenge at rubbish-tips, plunge-dive for fish at sea, follow the plough, prey on the broods of other birds, even heist each other's eggs and young. And because they regurgitate, and feed their partners at the nest and discard anything indigestible, there's junk all over the place – fish bones, mussel shells, starfish, chicken bones, Baltic tellin, Dog whelks, rubber bands, butter wrappers, condoms. But now and then we'd locate these Herring gull nests surrounded by great piles of really quite big carapaces of the Edible crab, *Cancer pagurus*. Where were the gulls finding crabs like that? Rejects from fishing boats? Unlikely. So we'd gotten ourselves a problem. We couldn't figure it out.

'But one day we were taking time off with Niko and Lies Tinbergen, walking along the low-tide beach that surrounded the colony, when Lies bent down to dig up a round flat stone – just right for skipping out over the water. It was buried under a low dome of sand. Only it wasn't a stone, it was a crab.

'Once alerted, we found domes all down the beach – some mere cracks in the sand you could only spot when a metre away, some big enough to cast a shadow and visible at fifteen metres. Several had been pecked out by gulls. There were even natural experiments strewn around – air bubbles trapped under wet sand that the gulls had also had a go at, dummy domes. So Beth and I built a raft from driftwood, big enough to take a four-by-four-foot canvas hide, and we anchored it over a crab-rich section of beach that was exposed for several hours at each low tide. We'd swim out as the tide began to fall, take the hide out of a box we'd bolted to the deck of the raft, set it up, get inside and wait. After a few days the gulls came and searched for crab-domes right in front of us – some would walk back and forth along the receding waterline, others would fly past low, gliding, turning their heads from side to side, scanning the beach. When a gull did find a crab there'd be a tug of war – the crab has its legs spread like tree-roots in the tightly packed sand – female Herring gulls occasionally gave up the struggle and even a big male might take five minutes to pull a crab free . . .'

'But if you're a crab – why hang about on a beach? Why wait to have your guts pecked out? Your legs snapped off?'

'Solving that took forever,' he said, leaning over the rail, looking down at the steamer's wake, his weight on his forearms, his hands together, the tips of his thumbs and fingers touching in a characteristic gesture of concentration. 'First off we collected and measured crab carapaces from the colony. Second off we marked out a rectangular section of beach, 200 metres wide, extending from the high to the low waterline, and defined it with yellow plastic gallon-bottles anchored on short ropes to concrete blocks at fifty-metre intervals – from which the position of any crab found within that area could be measured by triangulation. We searched at every daylight low tide during spring and early summer: we triangulated, sexed, measured, marked and reburied each crab we found.

'Our first prediction – that the more beach exposed at low tide, the greater the number of crabs we'd find buried in it – was wrong. The critical factor turned out to be the *time* of high tide. On most days we found only a few crab-domes, but then in each tidal cycle there would be two days when the beach was riddled with them. Whenever high tide was around four in the morning. Why? Any ideas? Can you guess?'

'Of course not,' I said, suddenly aware that a medium-sized crab (or something very like it) was beginning to dig itself in beneath the oxtail in my stomach.

'Well – to begin to answer that you have to know that mature crabs spend the winter offshore, beyond the twenty-fathom line: in spring they move inshore, take shelter under rocks in shallow water, and cast their carapaces. That allows for their annual growth spurt of five millimetres. For up to forty-eight hours they're soft, and that's the only chance the male gets to insert his spermatophore, his bag of sperm, into the female. From October through December they migrate offshore again – sometimes eight miles offshore – and the females spawn in deep water, each one extruding from 460,000 to three million eggs: these eggs stick to their swimmerets. In July through August the females move inshore again, the eggs hatch and the crab larvae join the floating mass of coastal plankton, a rich food supply. Anyway you can see the point – the post-larval crabs are confined all year to the shallow water where they were hatched or to rocks between the tide marks, larger crabs live just below the low tide-line, bigger ones slightly further out – and they're not sexually mature until they're five if they're male and eight if they're female. So there are plenty of candidates for stranding. But why the peaks? Answer: once I really *imagined* it – being a crab, that is – I realized I'd be nocturnal, that I'd only really feel safe creeping about sideways in the dark, that when sunrise came and the big fish woke up and the shit hit the fan, then sure as hell I'd get my butt down and work sand over my head and disappear. And that was it. That was the answer. Crab-dome peaks always occurred when the time of high tide correlated with the time of sunrise.'

'A classic piece of animal behaviour research,' I said, holding my own abdomen, not at all sure that I wasn't about to extrude from 460,000 to three million eggs myself, 'but I think I'd better find the bog.'

All three white-painted iron lavatories were locked (a Herring gull began to peck out my stomach) but there was movement from within the cubicle to the left, the sound of a lever being repeatedly pulled, a valve lifting and falling in a dry cistern, the door opened – and out pushed the fat crocodile-skin dealer, sweating. We pretended not to see each other. I stepped over the sill, locked the door, retched at the stench, realized I was squashing turds beneath my boots, decided not to look, found the lavatory paper in my leg-pocket, dropped my trousers, added to the mound topping the bowl, rattled the flush lever – and opened the door, sweating. The Purser stood in front of me, smiling. 'Good day,' he said. In his left hand he held a big blue plastic bucket. On his right hand he wore a black rubber glove, a hole in the index finger.

That night, under the Southern Cross, Marcellin, Marie, Lary and I sat in the colonial chairs, drinking whisky from our plastic mugs, the steamer's lights reflected in the water alongside us, the deck-plates juddering to the engines. The two searchlights, mounted port and starboard on the roof of the bridge, probed the river ahead, and, apparently at random, panned rapidly back and forth along the near bank, plucking the occasional straggle of huts from the darkness, making white tracery of a dead tree, searching for the way-marks, the decrepit wooden boards nailed to poles that were once reliable pointers to the channel.

'It's that oxtail,' said Lary, as I handed out a couple of codeine-phosphate diarrhoea-blockers apiece and poured everyone a second quarter-mug of Johnny Walker. 'Why we should have to eat the arse-end of some animal in a pre-war reject French tin when this whole boat is flapping with fresh fish ... And the way that Purser grins when he serves it up! You can bet your butt he wouldn't touch that stuff himself – not if it was the last thing between him and his little old bones under a cactus bush. Nope. He wouldn't.'

'Meat like that is a luxury,' said Marcellin. 'The Company provides it. First-class. Besides, the Purser has a family. He buys all the fish he can and stores it wherever he can and then he'll sell it in Impfondo. He needs money. He has a family.'

'Most everyone has a family.'

'No, no, my friend – not your kind of family, with two children and a car and a dog and a house full of machines. I mean an African family. It's hopeless. It's the cause of all our problems. Lary Shaffer, I've heard you talk about corruption. You call it corruption but that is not the case. The true explanation is this: the African family. I myself – I have a wife and two children just like you do in the West; but my mother, she has fifteen children, six from my own father and nine from Kossima, the husband she took when my father left her in Impfondo and moved to Brazzaville. I am the eldest son. I went with him. I studied hard. We were poor. We had no electricity. I did my homework under a street-lamp – and when it rained I put a sheet of polythene over my book and my head. I sat for my secondary studies exam, my *brevet*, my BEMG, in 1966, when I was fifteen, and I did well, I did brilliantly! – I went to the best school in Africa, the Lycée Savorgnan de Brazza in Brazzaville. I was taught by famous Frenchmen, terrible strict men who cared about you, who really made you learn things; I got my *baccalauréat* in natural science – and I won a scholarship to Cuba, to Havana, to university! I got away! I escaped!'

'Well done!' said Lary, excited at the prospect himself. 'Well done! Good for you!'

'We learned Spanish for a whole year at the Havana-Vedado Language School, Cuba. And then I studied pharmacology for a year at the real university, changing to biology, specializing in vertebrate biology. I even carried out a project of research – "The evaluation of nutritional states in pre-school children for the prevention of malnutrition diseases" – and I got my diploma in animal biology. I studied the immobilization of mammals using anaesthetic drugs – and I got a diploma in veterinary medicine. I won a scholarship to go to France! To the Montpellier International Centre of Advanced Tropical

Agronomic Studies and Forestry Studies, and I presented a scientific paper on the conception and management of a zoological park, a protected area. And I am still working for my doctorate on the biology of crocodiles, *Crocodylus cataphractus* and *Crocodylus niloticus*, with the Natural History Museum of Paris. So I'm telling you, it's obvious, isn't it? *I do not deserve to be poor.* I am a scientist. I am highly educated. I speak French, Spanish and English. Yet I return home – and what happens? I have become a Big Man! The head of the family! Now I don't want to be a Big Man or the head of anybody's family, but that makes no difference – the moment I get my job in the Ministry of Water and Forests and earn some money and rent a house, then any one of my mother's fifteen children and their wives and their relations by marriage, any one of my father's new family, all those cousins, they can all just turn up and sit on my new chairs and eat all the food in my fridge before I come home from work – and then it's Dr Marcellin this and Dr Marcellin that and do look at the holes in my shoes I need some new trainers and if only I had a big leather briefcase from that shop where the American ambassador goes I'd be sure to get a job in an office – you wouldn't believe it! One of them wanted me to buy him a taxi! A taxi! So I thought – why bother? Why bother to work or be successful or try harder when you're expected to share out everything you have? But my uncle, the customary head of the family, he was the worst, really bad. He was terrible.'

'What did he do?' I said, beginning to understand why Mobutu needed all those billions. 'What did he want?'

Marcellin ignored the question, turning instead to Marie, giving her his whole attention. 'I outwitted them,' he said, his right hand on the arm-rest of her chair.

'But they were right,' she said, in a breast-soft voice. 'You *are* a Big Man.'

'I fooled them. I stopped it. I moved to a really small house with three tiny rooms – and in the first of those rooms, by the door to the compound and the street, I dug a shallow pit, and in that shallow pit I put two crocodiles.' (Marie gasped.) 'They trust no one but me. I promise you – they can tell if you're frightened. They're fierce!'

'But your wife,' said Marie, 'do they trust your wife?'

'No!' shouted Marcellin, committing himself. 'They hate her! They snap at her!'

Marie laughed, dropped her empty whisky mug on the deck, drew her legs up on to the chair, and hugged herself around the knees.

'They snap! They lash their tails! At mealtimes she has to stand right back and *throw* their fish to them! Besides,' he said, getting to his feet, scooping Marie up in his arms, sitting down again and placing her sideways on his lap, 'when a man owns crocodiles it *means* something.'

'What does it mean?' I said, over-eager.

'You'll find out,' said Marcellin languidly, his right hand on Marie's left breast. 'There's a village in the forest, Makao. That's where you'll find out. Whereas for you, Marie, my crocodiles – they wouldn't snap at you. I think they'd start here' – with his free hand he eased off her left sandal – 'it's toes – the first nibble – it's always at your toes' (she sighed), 'they have all these teeth, you see, rows and rows of teeth, with lots and lots of others waiting to replace them, pushing up hard from underneath . . .'

'It's time to go,' said Lary to me sharply, gathering up the plastic mugs; and we walked forward to our cabin along the companionway, stepping over sleeping bodies as we went.

Settled in our bunks in the airless heat, Lary said, 'I think I do have a dream, as it happens. Plans, you know, fresh plans, like Walney Island and the filming, the gulls, the crabs, happiness, problems to solve, D. W. Griffith, that sort of thing.'

'What sort of thing?'

'Well – if I ever make it out of all this – my ambitions are to marry Chris, and then go find a truck.'

'A truck?'

'Yeah. One of those old Dodge Power Wagons. Late 1940s are best. They're like rubber-tyred tanks. The engines are not all that large, it's true, but they're geared low and they make these growling noises as they lumber along the roads. I don't suppose I'd be lucky enough to find one with the back bit of the body, the pick-up box, still on it, not straight off. They're rare, those pick-up boxes. The trucks largely outlasted them: most all the early Dodge Power Wagons I've seen have had some other thing codged on the back as a replacement for a rusted-and-gone box. And it doesn't end there, of course, because you then have new priorities – headlights, I suspect, a glove-box door, a speedometer cable. You have to go find other Wagons like your own that are being parted out, Wagons that are at the end of their days on some farm or forestry outfit with all of their parts for sale. And I know what you're thinking – why go looking for Dodge trucks when there's the house to work at? Well, that's 100 per cent correct. I've got to jack up the house and build new main support beams under it. This will not be easy. The cellar is full of upright posts holding the house up. I shall have to fabricate the new beams on site by glue-and-screw laminating two by eight timber to make eight by eights, twenty-five foot long, remove the posts one at a time and gently Stonehenge each of the five new beams into position . . .'

I fell asleep as he talked and I dreamed of Wiltshire stone circles, of measuring in Neolithic yards upright posts with heads on them, and that I had become a member of the Imbangala, the sixteenth-century army that terrorized the savanna to the south of us, an army of men cut off from their lineages and societies by the children they had eaten and the oaths they had taken in the initiation ceremony that bound them to their leader; I dreamed that I was sitting too close to a fire in a fortified camp, the war chief at its centre, surrounded by his wives, and that, like everyone else, I was ready to break out to the west and make my fortune with two discoveries – the densely populated kingdom of Ndongo and the waiting ships of the overseas slave-trade.

12

Early the next morning we passed yellow sandstone cliffs streaked with white and black, and the occasional sandbar strewn with black boulders – perhaps the remnants of shales and mudstones laid down in ancient swamps – and resting, I knew, on thick sedimentary strata which were still almost horizontal, undisturbed, rocks that had remained stable for at least 1500 million years. And we passed, too, the *Colonel Ebeya*, a Zaïrean steamer-township like ours, but more luxurious: every barge was a covered two-decker. On the *Impfondo* (flying the red flag from her mainmast, from the mast of every timber-tug and whale-boat) the traders and fishermen and soldiers on the starboard side lined the rails and raised clenched fists, exchanging shouted insults with the capitalists as they swept by, bound downriver for Kinshasa.

Marcellin, Lary and I picked our way forward to visit Marie. Among the usual clamps of smoked fish and the big, round-headed catfish coming aboard were three species we had not seen before: a rust-brown torpedo-shaped fish with a long down-turned muzzle, perhaps the Elephant-snout fish, a deep-water bottom-feeder; a carp-like fish with a narrow oval body and rose-bud lips; and a four-foot-long fish like a pike with silver scales and raggedly spaced Dracula teeth, which Marcellin said was *Le capitaine*, the most feared fish in the river, notorious for biting chunks from passing crocodiles and testicles from swimming men.

The heat gathered; mothers spread their remaining Brazzaville-bought baguettes out to dry on every possible flattish surface, rigged awnings from plastic sheets to protect their smaller children from the sun, and began the long preparation of fish soup and saka-saka (manioc-leaf spinach, said Marcellin).

An albino, sitting below us in one of the open holds, his back against the side, raised for a moment his bloodshot eyes, his pale and gritty face, and gave Lary a covert smile.

'For them it is terrible,' Marcellin shouted over his shoulder in English, stepping across a baby-width gap to the next barge. 'They must work hard, they must earn a lot of money – far more money than you'd think – just to have a woman for one night!'

'Poor sonofabitch,' said Lary from behind me. 'Out here you need every spot of pigment you can get. Fewer than 10 per cent of those guys make it beyond thirty. Did you see his face? Those pre-malignant lesions?'

Collapsed in our bunks, half-way through our early afternoon 95-degrees-heat-exhaustion siesta, we were woken by a hammering knock on the cabin door.

'We've been buzzed!' came Marcellin's shout from outside. 'Quick! Quick! We've been buzzed!'

'Buzzed?' said Lary, opening the door, letting in the blinding light. 'Buzzed?'

'The Zaïrois! A Zaïrean military helicopter! It flew right over us, really low, like that' – he skimmed the flat of his right hand over his left – 'We thought we'd be machine-gunned. The Captain – he has radioed for more soldiers. The Marines are coming.'

'Oh God,' said Lary.

And an hour or so later, as we watched from below the bridge, a timber-tug and a speedboat from the Marxist-Leninist bank joined the *Impfondo*. Twenty-five Marines began to search the ship and the barges (for fifth columnists? Spies? Weapons? 'For beer,' said Marcellin); and an hour or so after that, from the second barge up on the port side, there came a bang and a scream loud enough to be heard above the thumping of the diesels.

Marcellin, squaring his shoulders, straightening his back, becoming an official of the People's Republic, ordering us to stay where we were, ran down to investigate – and returned just as four Marines, a fifth holding a saline drip, carried one of their number to the speedboat, yanked the outboard to life and set off downriver.

'Drunk,' said Marcellin. 'Shot himself in the leg. He was standing up, bending forward. The bullet travelled down his thigh, re-entered via the calf-muscle, came out at his ankle and ricocheted overboard. I saw him lying on the deck. He was screaming – he lay screaming in a pool of blood. The medic injected him with morphine. He had a lot of blood, a great deal of blood. Kalashnikovs – they're powerful. Myself, I don't think he'll live.'

That evening the Captain ran the town-ship into the bank for the night, looping steel hawsers round two giant trees. The next morning, waking just after dawn, the mist already dispersing, the ship on the move, we saw why: the river had opened out to around three miles wide; the whole lashed-together convoy, guided by marker-buoys, swung ponderously from side to side between the oncoming sandbanks. High in the clear air above us, the rays of the rising sun catching their grey undersides, their bright scarlet tails, a flock of African grey parrots flew fast and straight to the northern shore.

Through the binoculars I watched thick-set little plovers scuttle along the margins of the sandbars, darting patterns of black and white and grey: a black head (with a white stripe above the eye), a white stomach and breast (with a black band) and a grey back – they would run in a straight line, probe in the sand, scratch backwards with one foot after another like a dog making a gesture of burying its droppings, burst into jerky flight, land again and repeat the process. They were, I decided, Crocodile birds (so called because Herodotus, on his travels in Egypt in 459 BC, claimed to have seen them toothpick scraps from the jaws of basking crocodiles).

'Lary! Redmond!' called Marcellin from the stairwell.

'Here comes Poe,' said Lary, opening his eyes wide like a clown in a circus, 'and his raven, like Barnaby Rudge/Two-fifths of him genius and three-fifths of him fudge.'

Marcellin shouted from the end of the companionway: 'We're going to talk to the Captain! Come on! I've made an appointment!'

'An appointment?' said Lary.

'The Captain', said Marcellin, leading us up the forbidden steps to the bridge-deck, 'is a *very* important man.'

Eugène Manguélé knew it: forty-one years old, fit, strong, broad-shouldered, his presence was commanding. Dressed in a white heavy-cotton shirt with breast-pockets, blue trousers and new Adidas trainers, he was standing behind the helmsman (an anxious young man sitting upright and forward in a high armchair with both hands on the wheel). The Captain scanned the great river ahead, the sandbars, the forested islands, the faraway banks and inlets (or perhaps they, too, were mazes of islands, coalesced by distance). He raised his ancient Zeiss binoculars (their black coating worn away to the brass where his thumbs supported the tubes) and studied an oncoming timber-tug pushing its bow-raft of logs. He was relaxed and digni-fied; he looked like a man who rarely smiled and never laughed. Obviously used to supplicants, he eventually put down his binoculars on the console (two levers with black knobs, a bank of switches, dials) and turned to us with a regal nod. Yes, it was a long training to become a captain; nowadays there was a school for sailors, but there was nothing like that in his time, not in 1967 when he began, back then there was no nonsense about theory – no, it was repairing engines, tapping rivets, getting your hands dirty. He was a straightforward, practical man himself and he'd enjoyed it, the two years apprenticed to a steamer captain, getting to know the river, the three years working with the captain of a timber-tug, the long succession of small commands, and then this, the big one, the top of his profession. And now he had two wives and ten children, all in the best of health. Problems? With his wives? Certainly not – he divided all his money equally. He was fair. His household was peaceful. I meant problems with the river? Of course, all the time, the river kept changing its channels, the French charts, the Belgian charts, white men's charts, they were useless, useless! All that mattered was a feel for the job, experience, you had to know the ways of the water in the fog, the snags, the obstacles. Mokélé-mbembé? Yes, yes, it was well known. It was a mistake to think that white men from Europe knew all about Africa – they never had and they never would. No, he had not seen the monster himself but other captains had, and sometimes at night he had heard loud, bizarre, blood-curdling cries. Besides, there were mysterious places on the waters, especially in the Sangha – particularly near a certain abandoned village – where if you tried to tie up your boat for the night it would release itself and make off downriver. But now, if we'd excuse him, he had work to do.

On the empty flat roof of the steamer aft of the bridge, beside the yellow and black-banded funnel, the Captain's cook was squatting in his flip-flops and with his machete hacking off the hindleg of a dead, newly bought De Brazza's monkey. The monkey's face, unwounded, lay towards us: dark-green fur and ear-tufts grew on top of its head, above a chestnut brow, soft brown eyes, green bushy side-whiskers and a long, white moustache and beard, which began half-way up its nose and hung down to its chest.

Outside our cabins I decided that the time had come to give Marcellin his presents: a pair of binoculars (hidden in the medicine kit-bag), a briar pipe from Savory's in Oxford, a tin of Balkan Sobranie, a machete in its scabbard, a floppy jungle-hat, a webbing belt and two attachable water-bottles.

'Thank you,' said Marcellin with his biggest smile, placing the hat on his head, the binoculars round his neck, the pipe and tobacco in his pocket. 'But don't expect anyone else to say thank you' – he snapped on the belt-kit – 'because this is Africa. There is no word for thank you in Lingala. Here you give someone a present because they've earned it, or because they're part of your family, or because you expect something from them.'

'Quite right,' I said.

Lary and I found a spare patch of deck against the mess-cabin and settled down to read – Lary with *Our Mutual Friend* ('D. W. Griffith said Dickens wrote film-scripts') and I with André Gide's *Travels in the Congo* (1927). Marcellin joined us, still wearing his hat, binoculars and belt-kit, but with a Walkman clipped to the webbing and earphones under the hat. 'This was Mike Fay's present to me!' he yelled above the music which only he could hear. He patted the cassette-player with his left hand and raised his right in a fist salute. 'But the Bob Marley tape – I bought it myself! He's the message! A hero! A revolutionary!'

There was a long ululating wail from the deck below, screams, a rhythmic chanting.

'Marcellin!' I said, shaking his shoulder. 'What's that?'

'What's that?' yelled Marcellin; then he pushed his headphones back from his ears and listened.

'I forgot to tell you,' he said. 'A baby died this afternoon. The mother gave it unboiled water to drink. Diarrhoea. It's a boy. The mother cries out for her husband – but he is in Impfondo. The father is in Impfondo. The father does not know that his son is dead.'

We were silent.

'Go on,' said Marcellin, readjusting his headphones. 'Go and pay your respects.'

The baby was lying on a mattress, face up, wrapped in a white sheet. Two benches flanked the little body: on one the mother sat, rocking from side to side, held by two friends, her eyes shut; on the other six women sang their sad songs and beat time with gourd-rattles full of seeds.

13

The *Sounda*, two whale-boats and a tug broke away; on the bank ahead a short-wave wireless-mast, huts, a few breeze-block buildings came into view; long manoeuvrings took place as barges were shuffled off, timber-tugs repositioned, pirogues paddled to shore; we had arrived at the port of Mossaka.

We walked up the deep-sand main street to visit Marcellin's friend, the crocodile-skin dealer. Small, thin, anxious to please, he was waiting by the gate of his cactus-hedge compound and led us round the corner to a breeze-block shed, talking to Marcellin in French. 'People are sick,' he whispered. 'People here are sick, sick, sick. Even some of the shopkeepers – they've left. There is cholera' – he unlocked the door – 'and the sleeping sickness. For business – it's bad. Very bad.'

Light from the doorway filled the windowless room, illuminating the concrete-wash walls, a big blue petrol drum, a paddle, enamel bowls and, on a raised wooden platform, thick bundles of skins rolled underside-out and tied with liana ropes, their square white scales dappled with brown, black and yellow patches. They were salted, well cured; the stale air was only mildly suggestive of rot and fish.

The dealer stood staring at his stock, his head on one side; he chewed his lower lip. 'This is all I have,' he said. The two men talked in Lingala and something was decided. Marcellin turned to me, gesturing at the crocodile-skins as if he now owned them: 'The Nile crocodile, the African slender-snouted, the Congo dwarf crocodile – they're all here. We'll see them upriver. We'll hunt them at night. But the Congo dwarf, Redmond, he's the most interesting, *Osteolaemus tetraspis* – he never goes near the open rivers, he makes his nest under roots, you fish for him with a stick – he clamps his teeth on a stick and he growls. To get at him, you have to chop down the tree!'

We said goodbye to the dealer, wandered down the street, and sat at a café table drinking Primus. 'I like crocodiles,' said Marcellin, taking off his floppy hat, running his hands round the rim, 'I really do. They're the right kind of animal for a man with my ancestors. I had a chance, once, to work with them properly, to farm them. I joined up with two Belgians, one a financier, the other a technician, and we established a crocodile farm upriver, at Liranga. Well, it's the story of this country – the technician made off with all the money and he sold all the crocodiles and *then* he put in for a licence from my Ministry! The financier was discouraged, you understand, and now he imports cars.'

Marcellin placed the hat back on his head, the rim set out like the roundel of a topee. 'Me, I'm young enough to start again,' he said, as if he didn't quite believe it. 'Apart from my legs.'

'Your legs?' said Lary, sympathetic.

Marcellin rolled up his jeans. Wet sores, pink on black, speckled his shins.

'They're ulcers,' he said, pushing the denim down again over the faintly dribbling raised edges of the wounds. 'They're just tropical ulcers. They come from walking in the forest. You'll both get them. But mine – they never seem to heal.'

'No problem,' I said, feeling useful. 'I'll give you a course of Floxapen. That's what it's for – lesions of the skin.'

'And my tooth,' said Marcellin, producing a little piece of metal from his shirt-pocket. 'A cap came off. It must be all the beef. I'm not used to it.'

'Neither am I,' said Lary, getting up and peering inside Marcellin's mouth, feeling useful. 'I'll give you a course of dentistry. We've got a tooth-kit. That's what it's for – fillings.'

The next morning the Captain waited while the dead baby was carried ashore and buried.

Lary made Marcellin sit in a chair on the fan-deck as he fiddled about with the tooth-kit, mixing pastes with a plastic spatula on a plastic plate. I stood at the rail with my binoculars – a small blue swallow, with a white chin-spot and a squared-off, white-fringed tail, was making short sweeps, from its perch on the steamer's stern-cable, out across the slack brown surface of the river through the rising and falling clouds of mosquitoes. Turning to Serle and Morel, I saw that his intent, alert little self had been named, sensibly enough, the White-throated blue swallow. And further off the stern a pair of much larger swallows were hawking flies; Mosque swallows, long-winged, blue-black on top, rufous below, their flight was so like that of a kestrel that at any moment I expected them to swing up and hover.

'Just remember,' said Lary, poking inside Marcellin's mouth with a plastic rod and the spatula (Marcellin's eyes signalled severe alarm), 'the two basic rules of life – first off, don't sweat the small stuff. Second off, it's all small stuff.'

Lary pushed, with some vigour, the thumb and index finger of both his hands further into Marcellin's mouth (Marcellin's eyes signalled panic). 'Done,' said Lary, stepping back, pleased with himself.

Marcellin gurgled, shut his mouth, put a hand to his throat, opened his mouth, coughed, choked, and spat out the paste and the filling.

'Sonofabitch,' said Lary.

In the afternoon the mourners returned, the convoy was rehawsered; we set off upriver, past the confluence with the Likouala and the Sangha (or so our chart said, but the profusion of forested islands and blind inlets and sandbanks and conflicting currents made it impossible to tell). And the next morning we were woken by an outsize soldier banging on the cabin door with the butt of his Kalashnikov. 'Control!' he boomed at Lary, through the window, and moved off down the companionway.

'Jesus,' said Lary as we laced up our boots, 'if we're going to prison I'll need this book' – he stuffed the Penguin edition of *Martin Chuzzlewit*, its covers torn, its back broken, into the right-hand pocket of his jeans. 'I feel like Mark Tapley: "A touch of fever and ague caught on these rivers, I dare say; but bless you, *that's* nothing. It's only a seasoning; and we must all be seasoned, one way or another." It'll comfort me, before I die.'

From the top deck we looked out on a village of wattle-and-daub huts with corrugated-iron roofs, which a wrinkled old man, squashed along beside us on the lower deck, chewing on an empty pipe, said was called Liranga. And as we joined the queue to go ashore down the central aisle of the barges, watching everyone ahead pass slowly up the laterite bank and present their papers, beneath an ancient mango tree, to the waiting soldiers of the People's Militia (their uniforms were ragged, their manner more officious than regular soldiers), 'Redso,' said Lary, 'I'm very grateful for all this new experience, I really am, don't get me wrong' – his face was flushed, he'd worked himself up – 'but I'd just like you to know, in case it had escaped your notice, it may surprise you to know that in the United States of America, where I used to live about 200 years ago, you can get all the way from Plattsburgh, New York State, to Burlington, Vermont, *without one single cocksucking roadblock*. In fact – and I know you won't believe it – you could probably go from New York to San Francisco without one single douche-bag of a psychopath of a soldier offering to ram a Kalashnikov up your butt and blow your turds out your ears if you don't give him one dollar and seventy-five cents. At current exchange rates.'

'Trouble?' said Marcellin, pushing his way forward from behind us. 'Trouble? What's up?'

'Nothing,' said Lary. 'Nothing at all.'

*

95

While the soldiers searched the now-empty ship and barges, Marcellin took us on a walk through the village. 'It's full of fishermen,' he said. 'It's rich. It's two kilometres long.'

The main street, an avenue of oil-palms, ran along beside the river. Small trees clustered by the bank, each one holding to the slope with prop-roots, roots which curled out from just above the base of their light-grey trunks like downturned fingers, and their branches sprouted upwards at an angle of forty-five degrees, just beneath the shallow domes of their crowns, like the spokes of an umbrella.

'Marcellin,' I said, 'tell us about the trees. All their names.'

'Too difficult,' said Marcellin, striding along in his trainers, avoiding oncoming children, goats and puddles. 'Only Mike Fay and the pygmies know all the names of all the trees in the forest. But this is the oil-palm' – he waved at the avenue of straight-stemmed palms with their scruffy green and brown fronds, several hung with weaver nests – 'we couldn't live without it. That's where the money comes from – you get an orange oil from the flesh of the nut and kernel oil from the seeds. But you'll see all that upriver. You cook with it, and you sell it' – he grinned – 'to white men, for making soap, and margarine. You collect the sap by making cuts with your machete near the growing-point of the stem, or down at the base' – he pointed to V-shaped scars on the nearest tree – 'all you have to do is hang a bucket or a gourd up there and that's palm-wine, ready-made. But if the palm is branched, of course, no one must touch it, you leave it alone, it belongs to the sorcerer.'

'What's this?' said Lary, looking up at the massive, black, straight trunk of the tree we had seen from the steamer in every village on the bank, its branches, way above the surrounding palms, spreading like a Cedar of Lebanon.

'That,' said Marcellin, 'is the Canthium. Don't even brush against it. The bark – it's covered in biting ants. And when that tree flowers it stinks. It stinks of dead people. It is fertilized by flies – its pollen is carried by flies. But the Canthium matters. It's important. The sorcerer, he can make special objects from its wood, and also the walking-stick, the staff of the Chief, the mark of his office.'

'And that?' I said, pointing at one of the trees with prop-roots.

'Those – they grow wherever you make a clearing, and along the rivers. From their wood you make floats for fishing nets: *Parasolier, Musanga cecropiodes, Kombo-Kombo* in Lingala – and you Englishmen, Redmond, you call it the Umbrella tree.'

We admired the neatly laid-out compounds, with their orange and lemon, avocado and almond and breadfruit trees, and one False cotton tree, an emergent giant, leafless above the surrounding palms, its puffs of flowers a brilliant white against the grey sky. And eventually we came to a long red-brick wall, decayed, sprouting ferns (Victorian brickwork, said Lary, a bad design, the flat copings were all wrong); a simple church with a squat bell-tower; and a low building fronted by a porch with three arches (one bricked up), its corrugated-iron roof half-collapsed, wooden scaffolding supporting its end-wall. It must have been, I realized, the place where Gide stayed in 1925, on his way upriver to Bangui:

> After passing through a fine avenue of palm-trees one comes to a brick church, beside the long, low building where we are to put up. A black 'catechist' opened the doors for us, and, as all the rooms are at our disposal, we shall be very comfortable. It is frightfully hot, damp, and thundery – stifling. Fortunately the dining-room is very airy. I rose from my after-lunch siesta streaming; then went out walking. The path began by leading through some big orchards of banana trees, with very wide leaves, quite different from those I have seen hitherto; it then grew narrower and plunged into the forest. One could easily walk for miles in this way, enticed on by a fresh surprise at every twenty steps. But the night began to fall. A terrific storm was brewing, and delight gave way to fear.

We pushed open the door of the mission house: a termite-mound reared up to our right; the rest of the floor was thick with bat-droppings.

The following afternoon the steamer edged between forested islands, the water changed colour to a lighter shade of brown, and we entered the Oubangui – wide, shallow, striped with sandbars. Pied kingfishers hung off the spits of sand: in the round frame of the field-glasses I watched them hovering, wings beating hard, their white breasts and stomachs hanging almost vertically, their black and white heads, their black bills (half as long as their bodies) pointing down at the slack of water. They would dip in the air, move to a new station and hover again; or take a sharply angled dive, re-emerge with a white splash of water and fish, and fly off to the nearest perch on the trapped flotsam of bleached wood.

On one sandbank twelve birds like terns sat huddled together, all facing downstream: African skimmers, their wings hung loosely at their sides as though they were stupefied by the heat. The upper mandibles of their heavy orange bills were much shorter and smaller than the lower, an arrangement which gave them a permanent smile (and which enables them to fish by flying a downbeat above the surface of calm water, ploughing it with open beaks).

The cargoes coming aboard grew richer, more various. Nile crocodiles lay tethered to capstans and struts, their jaws bound shut with lianas, their grey bodies restrained by loops of liana tied just in front of their back legs. Small black Forest crocodiles lay trussed in alleyways. Big Central African flagshell turtles were piled among the bags and mattresses in liana baskets: they had withdrawn their heads and flippers into their lightweight leathery shells and sealed them away beneath their plastrons – their undersides – with strong hinged flaps of shell: flaps which are one of the very few characteristics that distinguish them from their ancestors, the turtles which appear in the fossil record 200 million years ago, contemporaries of the earliest dinosaurs.

That evening we moored at the little village of Njoundou, so that the crew could mend one of the engines (it sounded as if they were assaulting it with a sledgehammer), and by the time Marcellin, Lary and I got ashore it was dark: everyone, every household, seemed to be getting drunk on the *Impfondo* merchants' crates of beer. Speckled toads croaked all along the river-bank, and little fireflies (one small green light apiece), the size of earwigs, flicked and flashed in the Umbrella trees.

The next day (the engine repaired), as the sun dispersed the grey river-mist, the Purser covered the fan-deck with part of his store of smoked fish, his smoked, chopped-up monkeys, and one small, very dead turtle with a yellow and black-brown carapace. The dismembered monkeys, said Marcellin, were Agile mangabeys, large monkeys, tree-living baboons, fond of river-banks and restricted to the dense forests of the Congo; the turtle was rare, perhaps some kind of African mud-turtle. As the fish, the monkeys and the turtle reached a critical temperature, maggots squirmed out of the carcasses, plopped to the deck and rippled slowly towards us.

Off the stern a hornbill was crossing the river, its flight undulating, buoyant – four deep flaps followed by a glide – its plumage black in front and white behind, the great bill and casque curving down, the long white tail seemingly cut in half (by a band of black feathers), the wings set forward – the Brown-cheeked hornbill, said Serle and Morel, a true forest hornbill. And high in a thermal over a sandbank, two great birds were soaring, on black, broad, ragged wings, their heads and breasts white, their white tails so short that they appeared to be part of the deep wings' trailing edges – our first African fish eagles. As I watched them through the binoculars the higher eagle dived at his mate, brought his feet forward and up as he passed her and, for a moment, locked his talons into hers: they cartwheeled downwards, in a whirl of black wings, parted, and resumed their calm, wide, upward spirals. Even Gide, I decided, sometimes got things wrong – 'it must be confessed', he wrote in his diary on 22 September 1925, 'that the ascent of the Ubangui is hopelessly monotonous'.

In the early afternoon we passed a long low stretch of forest with occasional flat-topped or spherical-crowned trees emerging above the canopy – *Symphonia*, said Marcellin, their trunks were cylindrical, greyish-yellow, they had stilt-roots, they lived in swamp-forest, the kind of forest that we were bound for, the forest that runs ulcers up your legs, the forest that was dark, full of roots, water and rot.

And two hours later we reached Impfondo.

BOOK II

14

Outside our cabins Marcellin swung his small blue pack on to his shoulders, Lary and I struggled into our bergens, and Manou appeared. He smiled his shy smile at Lary.

'Where've you been?' said Lary, delighted. 'We've missed you! You been hiding? You swim up here?'

Manou took a kit-bag in each hand.

Marcellin said, 'I told him to keep out of the way. He's my brother, Redmond, you'd say half-brother, I didn't want him creeping about, making himself useful. It's demeaning. The question is this: do you want him or not? You'll take him with us? Yes or no?'

'Of course we'll take him.'

'Thank you,' said Manou, looking me in the eye for the first time. 'This kindness – I will never forget it. I have a wife and son.'

'Wife!' said Marcellin, with a laugh.

'I have a wife and son,' repeated Manou. 'They love me.'

'I'm sure they do,' said Lary, and we made our slow way down and along the line of barges.

On the ramp of the wharf a soldier inspected our papers – and pocketed our passports.

'It's okay,' said Marcellin. 'I know all the soldiers, all the officers. Trust me.'

'Trust my aunt,' muttered Lary, reaching for the soldier's pocket.

'Don't touch!' shouted Marcellin, grabbing Lary's wrist.

The soldier smiled.

'Lary, Redmond,' said Marcellin, pointing to the low yellow-painted wall of the dock building, 'pile the packs over there. Sit on them. Guard them. Impfondo is full of thieves. And you, Manou – you ferry out the rest of the bags. I'll be back. Here' – he threw Manou the cabin keys – 'be quick about it. I must see Joseph. I must get the truck.' And he disappeared into the crowd.

'Truck?' said Lary, intoning the magic word. 'Truck?'

'It's a Dodge,' I said. 'It's a red Dodge Power Wagon. Circa 1940.'

'Land Cruiser!' said Manou, straightening his back. 'Toyota Land Cruiser! Yellow! Every truck here must come up on the barges. They're from Japan. They're special. Dr Marcellin – he enjoys it. He drives about Impfondo like a Big Man. The Land Cruiser – it belongs to the Department of Water and Forests. It belongs to the People's Republic. When Dr Marcellin is here, Joseph, he has to walk. When Dr Marcellin is not here, Joseph is a Big Man. He is a Guard of the Water and Forests. He arrests the poachers, he confiscates their ivory, the people buy licences for their guns from him, he imports the bushmeat from Zaïre, he is a taxi – he makes lots of money, lots of money for his family. Whereas me, I'm poor.'

'But now you have a job,' said Lary, as we dumped the packs against the wall. 'You'd better snag those kit-bags.'

'No hurry,' said Manou, tilting his wide-brimmed hat back, lighting a cigarette. 'Dr Marcellin, he will want to drive Marie to her home, he will wish to show her the Land Cruiser.' And he walked slowly off towards the steamer, a young man who seemed to vanish even as you looked at him, to occupy no space around himself.

'It's sad,' said Lary, neurotically checking the empty breast-pocket where he kept his passport. 'I like that kid. He should come to Plattsburgh. He's bright. I can tell.'

A little swallow was criss-crossing the air fifty feet above us, the crowd, the sweat, the noise. Its delicate tail was deeply forked, its white breast lined with black speckles, its head chestnut, its wings grey beneath, dark blue above. It should have been named, I thought, the Untroubled, the Perfectly happy whizz-diving swallow, and not, as Serle and Morel boringly told us, the Lesser striped; and it appeared to be hunting the same insects as the pair of another species, the Absolutely ordinary, comforting European house martin.

'Lary,' I said, 'do you realize we've seen *four* species of swallows and martins already? Without even trying! But I'm sorry, I'm really sorry we missed the African river martin – that's the strangest of them all, confined to the Congo and Oubangui rivers with a few on the Gabon coast. It's all black with a big round head and red eyes. It hovers, it runs like a pratincole, it nests in burrows, it tunnels into the flat sandbars in the middle of the rivers. It's bizarre.'

'Look,' said Lary, swotting a small green fly on his cheek, 'I realize that for you the real journey is only just beginning. But for me that boat trip was the most extraordinary, and also the grimmest experience of my life. The dead baby, the people drowned, all for nothing. And pratincole, what's that? A rude word. Birds, sure I like to see them around. But when they're that size, they're off my map, they're just too small, they're LBJs.'

'LBJs?'

'Little Brown Jobs.'

'But those are blue! And the African sand martin – that's black!'

'Correction,' said Lary. 'Little Blue Jobs. Little Black Jobs.'

Lary, Manou and I sat on the bags on the flatbed of the Toyota, Marcellin climbed into the driving seat, and Joseph (a worried man, his movements not quite coordinated, his lower lip sagging) got into the cab beside him. We drove up a mud chute, the elephant-grass, to either side, standing higher than a man on a horse, and onto a tarmac road ('Built by the Brazilians,' said Manou. 'From nowhere to nowhere,' said Lary.) The road ran north along the river, past wattle-and-daub thatched huts to our left, breeze-block huts, a huge compound with mown lawns, a modern church to our right (the American Protestant Mission, said Manou), a bar, a petrol pump – and the Hôtel du Parti, a two-storey concrete building with external stairs and a balcony, set back from the road.

Marcellin and Joseph took the Toyota to search for the *patron* of the hotel (he might be at home, said Joseph, or in the bar, dancing, or attending to his fish-traps) and Manou joined us where we sat, as usual, on the bergens, on the concrete. Madame Langlois owned the bar, said Manou, and also a little store where you could buy tee-shirts and jeans and dresses. Her husband died. He loved Impfondo. He lived in a house the French built, a house for *colons*, a beautiful house with a high roof and lots of air and space and shutters on the windows, down by the river. Most of the white people, they ran away after Independence, when Impfondo became Marxist, full of Communists who really meant it, hard-line Communists, and all the shops were robbed, but no one harmed Madame Langlois and her husband because everyone knew they really loved Impfondo, they belonged. It was a proper town, you see, it was laid out like a big village with mud streets, but it had an airstrip, a hospital, two good bars, two restaurants, a barracks for the soldiers, a bank, a market.

After dark Marcellin returned without Joseph but with the *patron*; Manou set off for his mother's house carrying his small gym-bag; the *patron* tottered to his nightwatchman's shed, found the keys and a torch, fell up the step, and led us down the concrete corridor and into our separate concrete rooms. 'Lock the packs in!' said Marcellin. 'We're off! To a restaurant! To Yvette's!'

The Toyota lights, bucking and slewing above the deeply rutted mud road, picked out a cactus hedge, palm trees, a neatly swept sand courtyard and two reed-thatched huts, one with split-bamboo slatted walls, the restaurant.

'Did you notice your bed?' whispered Lary, as we sat down at the only free table. 'We've got sheets. Real sheets!'

A tall, big-boned, flat-chested woman in her thirties entered the hut and stood for a moment beneath one of the two naked overhead electric light-bulbs, scanning the tables. Every man in the restaurant looked at her, every woman pretended not to notice; her movements were sinuous, her face alert, knowing, intelligent.

Marcellin sat forward, his breathing quickened, his chest seemed to expand beneath his tee-shirt. 'Florence!' he shouted.

Florence strode over like a model on the catwalk, pulled out the remaining chair at our table, tugged down the hem of her white blouse, smoothed the sides of her red wraparound patterned with big yellow-petalled, black-corolla'd flowers, and joined us.

'I've been thinking about you,' said Marcellin in French, 'I've been dreaming about you. Every night.'

'Here we go,' said Lary.

'She has a job!' said Marcellin with a lover's pride. 'She works in the bank!'

Marcellin, taking Florence home, dropped us off at the Hôtel du Parti. The town generator stopped, the lights went out; Lary and I, full of monkey stew and cheap red wine, groped our way down the pitted concrete corridor and into our separate rooms. I took my torch from the bergen, undressed to my shirt and pants and climbed into bed. The sheets opened with a noise like that of an old, dry, over-used handkerchief when you pull it apart; under my cheek the pillow crackled with something that felt like mud on a football shirt. I turned the torch back on: someone, long ago (only a faint acidic whiff remained in the air) had been very sick indeed. Feeling queasy myself, I got out of bed, unpacked a tarpaulin, spread it over the sheets, filled a water-bottle from the bucket in a corner of the shower-room (the taps didn't work and neither did the shower), dropped in a double dose of Puritabs, and, waiting for the pills to dissolve, took out my precious pygmy notebook from the top flap-pocket of the bergen.

I liked the idea (very much) that the first writing about pygmies was engraved in stone around 2500 BC (1000 years before Stonehenge was built) on the walls of the tomb of Herkhuf, nomarch of Elephantine, at Aswan. Herkhuf was the ruler of a nome, a province, and a great explorer and trader, a leader of caravans. In the second year of the reign of the Pharaoh Pepi II (Nefrikare), who was then a child of eight, Herkhuf returned from a journey in Nubia where he had reached the province of Yam, and sent word that he had a dancing pygmy as a present for the king. The eight-year-old replied, delighted (and Herkhuf was so delighted with the reply that he had it inscribed in his waiting tomb):

I have noted the contents of your letter to me, your King. I learn from it that you have penetrated with your troops into the land of Iman.

In your letter you also state that you are preparing to bring with you many choice gifts, which Hator, the goddess of Iman, has prepared for the person of Nefrikare.

I further learn from your letter that you are bringing a pygmy with you, who dances the dance of the Gods in the Land of Legend, a dwarf apparently like the one whom the treasure-keeper of the Gods, Baured, brought from Punt in the days of Aosis. You also inform my majesty that never was anything to equal him in value, brought home before by any servant of my majesty.

You have the pygmy in your retinue whom you have brought from the Land of Legend, so that he may dance the dance of the Gods, and thereby fill the heart of King Nefrikare with joy.

When you bring him to the ship, choose reliable men to keep watch on both sides of the vessel, lest perchance he may fall into the water, and when he sleeps at night tell off ten stout fellows to sleep alongside him.

My majesty yearns mightily to see this pygmy.

See that you bring the pygmy alive, hale and sound to my palace, and then my majesty will confer on you far higher awards than those given by the treasurer of the Gods in the days of Aosis. From this gauge how great is the yearning of my majesty to see this pygmy.

Egyptologists said that no one knows where the land of Yam or Iman was, that the pygmy might not have been a real pygmy but rather any old dwarf (although the word used is *deneg*, whereas the usual term for a dwarf in the hieroglyphic texts is *nemu*) – still, it seemed to me that Herkhuf and Pepi would have known the difference between a pygmy and a dwarf, even if the Egyptologists did not.

But the first European to see a pygmy is generally thought to have been Georg Schweinfurth, the German botanist and explorer who in *The Heart of Africa* (1873) describes how his Nubian boatmen on the Nile were as fascinated by the pygmies as young Pepi had been:

they would declare that we were on the route which would lead us, like the cranes, to fight with the Pygmies; ever and again they would speak of Cyclops, of Automoli, or of 'Pygmies', but by whatever name they called them, they seemed never to weary of recurring to them as the theme of their talk. Some there were who averred that with their own eyes they had seen this people of immortal myth; and these – men as they were whose acquaintance might have been coveted by Herodotus and envied by Aristotle – were none other than my own servants.

Staying by the palace of King Munza of the Monbuttoo (whose territory spread across the easternmost tributaries of the Uele river) he eventually met his first pygmy:

After a few mornings my attention was arrested by a shouting in the camp, and I learned that Mohammed had surprised one of the Pygmies in attendance upon the king, and was conveying him, in spite of a strenuous resistance, straight to my tent. I looked up, and *there*, sure enough, was the strange little creature, perched upon Mohammed's right shoulder, nervously hugging his head, and casting glances of alarm in every direction. Mohammed soon deposited him in the seat of honour. A royal interpreter was stationed at his side. Thus, at last, was I able veritably to feast my eyes upon a living embodiment of the myths of some thousand years! ... in a couple of hours the Pygmy had been measured, sketched, feasted, presented with a variety of gifts, and subjected to a minute catechism of searching questions.

His name was Adimokoo. He was the head of a small colony, which was located about half a league from the royal residence. With his own lips I heard him assert that the name of his nation was Akka ...

But really (as Schweinfurth himself acknowledged) the honour of being the first European to meet a pygmy belongs to Paul du Chaillu, the French-American explorer of the forest far away to the west, in present-day Gabon. The son of the French manager of a West African coastal trading-post, du Chaillu went to America, became an American citizen and returned with a grant from the Boston Society of Natural History for an expedition inland. In his magnificent first book, *Explorations and Adventures in Equatorial Africa* (1861), he describes, amongst much else, his discovery of the gorilla. In his second, much less well-known *A Journey to Ashango-Land* (1867) there is a by-the-way account of his 1865 finding

in traversing one of the tracts of wild forest through which runs the highway of the country ... a cluster of most extraordinary diminutive huts, which I should have passed by, thinking them to be some kind of fetich-houses, if I had not been told that we might meet in this district with villages of a tribe of dwarf negroes ... From the loose and exaggerated descriptions I had heard on my former journey, I had given no credence to the report of the existence of these dwarf tribes, and had not thought the subject worthy of mention in my former narrative. The sight of these extraordinary dwellings filled me with curiosity ... I rushed forward, hoping to find some at least of their tenants inside, but they had fled on our approach into the neighbouring jungle. The huts were of a low oval shape, like a gipsy tent; the highest part – that nearest the entrance – was about four feet from the ground: the greatest breadth was about four feet also. On each side were three or four sticks for the man and woman to sleep upon. The huts were made of flexible branches of trees, arched over and fixed into the ground at each end, the longest branches being in the middle, and the others successively shorter, the whole being covered with large leaves. When I entered the huts, I found in each the remains of a fire in the middle of the floor.

Du Chaillu eventually met his dwarf-people and, from his Ashango guides, was the first to report something of their way of life:

The Ashangos like the presence of this curious people near their villages because the Obongo [pygmy] men are very expert and nimble in trapping wild animals and fish in the streams, the surplus of which, after supplying their own wants, they sell to their neighbours in exchange for plantains, and also for iron implements, cooking utensils, water jars, and all manufactured articles of which they stand in need.... They are eminently a migratory people, moving from place to place whenever game becomes scarce. But they do not wander very far; that is, the Obongos who live within the Ashango territory do not go out of that territory ... Obongos are said to live very far to the east, as far, in fact, as the Ashangos have any knowledge.

Very far to the east ... Like Pepi II, yearning mightily to see a pygmy, I fell asleep.

15

Marcellin arrived early in the morning, tired, pleased with himself, and drove us to Yvette's.

Lary, red-eyed, toying with his fish soup, said, 'That was the worst night of my life.' He pushed his plate of manioc chunks aside. 'There were turds all over the floor. There was vomit on my pillow. The smell! I'd rather sleep outside. Fact is – I'd rather sleep in a snake-pit.'

Marcellin grinned. 'The *patron* himself – he told me he couldn't bear to go in there. I had a look. It's true. That is not a place you could take Florence! But there's an annexe. First-class. There's a woman paid by the Government. She's paid just to clean those rooms. We'll take two. One for you and Redmond. One for me and Florence.'

'Oh no,' I said, seeing it all. 'We must get upriver.'

'Three nights!' said Marcellin, with one of his rare, genuinely happy laughs. 'You give me three nights with Florence and I'll work to get us out of here. I'll work, as you say in England, like a black. I'll work like the blacks who made France, who dug the canals, who made the roads, the blacks who saved France in two World Wars!'

'Done,' I said.

Back at the hotel Marcellin found the *patron* and we carried our bags across the grass to a single-storey building with a high, overhanging, corrugated-iron roof supported on five concrete pillars front and rear. Each room contained a double-bed with a mosquito-net suspended from a hook in the ceiling, a little desk, a chair, a chest of drawers, and, in the bathroom at the back, a hole in the floor as a lavatory and a square lip of concrete with a drainage grille and a bucket as a shower.

'I've been thinking,' said Lary, with sudden emphasis, as we stowed the bags against the right-hand wall. 'Why bother to go way up through the northern forests when all you really want to do is check out Lake Télé? Why not just go west? Get it over with?'

'I don't know,' I said, caught off-guard. 'I just have this feeling, I have an idea that once we've moved through those villages, found the pygmies in the forest, seen gorillas and chimps and guenons and elephants, when we've caught a glimpse of how people think – we'll *know* what's in Lake Télé before we even get there.'

'I see,' said Lary, pushing his bergen under the bed. 'So we needn't go. Right?'

We drove to the police station, a bungalow surrounded by elephant-grass, where the Chief of the Frontier Police at Impfondo, spare, severe, sitting behind his desk, ready to spring, stamped, dated and handed back our passports. We officially presented ourselves to the Regional Governor (fat and happy, reigning benignly over voluptuous secretaries and rotting armchairs). And in the long, low market of wooden stalls where women sold fresh and smoked fish and crocodile pieces and bargained over small piles of green plantains, pineapples, peppers and bowls of chopped manioc leaves, we bought pineapples and lengths of manioc for our stay in Impfondo, and an extra sack of fou-fou, manioc-flour, for the journey to come.

At Marcellin's insistence we called at the chemist's shop (opposite the little bank) where he announced that without condoms for his own use, and without hypodermic syringes, sterilizing pads and ampoules of penicillin for our unprotected bearers who would certainly catch syphilis and gonorrhoea, the journey would be impossible (and so I added to the medical stores). In a house at the other end of town, up the road beside the great brown river, we bought two boxes of double-o twelve-bore cartridges, for shooting bushpig, said Marcellin, each red carton illustrated with possible targets: an antelope, a buffalo, a lion – and an elephant.

Back at the hotel, Marcellin was equally adamant that we pay a visit to the adjoining compound, across the mud road on the upriver side, the Roman Catholic Mission. As I had already made the elementary, the unforgivable mistake of those about to enter the Congo forest, he said, climbing out of the Toyota, placing his hat on his head like a judge passing sentence, as I had already put the lives of all my companions in danger by failing to bring antivenin even against the bites, the injections of the most common snakes of the jungle floor (they were everywhere), the Gaboon viper and the Forest cobra, then we would have to go and humiliate ourselves in front of the Christians. We would have to beg for a medicine that only the White Fathers possessed.

The laurel-hedged compound enclosed a modern church and two colonial houses with steeply pitched roofs and greywash walls, against one of which we found a large, bearded monk, dressed in a dirty white robe with a knotted rope round his stomach and sandals on his feet, keeping goal. It was very hot, he was bulky, he sweated, his pupil-strikers were good – they dribbled, they passed, they yelled – but the monk was a wise old man in these matters:

the chalked goal-posts were suspiciously close together, and at each shot, as the black and white ball came curling in across the dust, the monk spread his legs wide beneath his robe and caught it in the cloth. 'Try harder!' he shouted, as the little boys scissored and feinted and slammed and power-headed. 'Harder!'

Between incoming balls Marcellin explained what he wanted, the monk rearranged the teams, and we followed him into the house nearest the gate. His study was full of cardboard boxes with their top flaps cut off, on the desk to the right of the door, on the table in the middle of the room, on the shelves along the walls, boxes full of candle-ends, pencil-stubs, blue caps of spent Bic biros, string, rubber bands, chalk; propped between these boxes, piled on top of them, were bundles of papers, the odd missal, a rosary, a crucifix on a wooden plinth, a pair of sandals (with both straps broken) and a framed colour-print of the Virgin Mary with droopy eyes.

'English?' said the monk, rummaging in a drawer. 'Yes?'

'Correct,' said Marcellin, 'and the other one – he is American.'

'Hah!' said the monk, addressing the objects in the drawer, all of which seemed to be wrapped in tissue-paper. 'I come from Bayeux. My parents both come from Bayeux. My great-great-grandfather lived in Bayeux. We are all from Bayeux!' (He found what he was looking for – something wrapped in tissue-paper, flattish, six inches long – and he beat time with it like a teacher with a ruler.) 'And what is in Bayeux? Yes! The tapestry! The defeat of the English! The battle of Hastings! The victory of the French!'

Lary laughed.

'And why do you laugh? America – Land of the Free. Nonsense! Who are the really free? Who made your statue? Who gave you your Statue of Liberty? Hah! Tell me that!'

'The French!' shouted Lary, to his credit.

'Hah!' said the monk, calming down and handing the wrapped object to Marcellin.

'Give him 5000 CFA,' Marcellin said to me.

At that moment something else in the room caught my eye, a statue, about two feet tall, on the left-hand shelf above our heads. Once seen, its presence seemed to fill the room: the white, cowrie-shell eyes bore down on us from the rough, blackened wood of the face; the mouth, fringed with human teeth, was open wide in one long soundless scream: its back and chest and groin were stuck full of nails, hundreds of them.

'What's that?' I said, handing over the money.

'I call him Saint Sebastian,' said the monk, with an odd little smile. 'He's a Kongo fetish. A *nkisi*. A nail fetish. When you are afraid because you have to go on a journey or when you really want some one thing, good or bad, the sorcerer lets you see the fetish and he takes your nail and with it he pierces the fetish.'

'But what's it doing in here?'

'Hah!' said the monk, flapping his arms, shooing us out like chickens. 'One must get to know the enemy! And now I must teach. I must teach the little devils!'

Marcellin, looking at his watch, walked fast up the track towards the long school bungalow, the high wireless mast, the playing-field.

'What's the hurry?' I said, catching up with him.

'A surprise!' said Marcellin.

'And what was in that tissue-paper?'

'Here,' said Marcellin, handing it to me (I unrolled a length of compressed charcoal). 'Put it in the medicine pack. When we live in the forest we must know exactly where it is *at all times*.'

'But what do you do with it?'

'You place it on the snake-bite, right over the puncture-wounds – and it draws out the venom, it pulls out all the poison.'

'Magic,' said Lary.

Marcellin turned left and led us through the press of mud tracks, huts, palm trees, cactus hedges, Umbrella trees and elephant-grass to his mother's house. A cement-wash bungalow, it had spawned a palm-thatch hut off to its far side, a long line of a hut that was still growing, a new section of posts and lateral slats awaiting only its mud in-fill. Marcellin's mother came out to welcome us; it was impossible to reconcile her small, thin, slightly stooping figure with the image I had formed of a mother of fifteen children: she waited on us, treating Marcellin as a visiting potentate, and we drank milky-white palm-wine and ate fish soup and bushpig and saka-saka at the family table in the front room with its dresser and sofa and two armchairs. And after the almost silent meal Marcellin's stepfather joined us from the backroom and Manou slipped in from outside; it was obvious that the rest of the family had been banished to the long hut. Marcellin's stepfather, wide-shouldered, big, treated Marcellin with a surly respect, answering his questions with monosyllables; Manou sat on the sofa, revolving in his hands a coil of thick bronze wire, the ancient currency of central Africa. I caught myself thinking: this house is bewitched – and I immediately rephrased it: there is a deep family problem here that needs to be discussed. Lary and I thanked our hosts and left.

On the way back we called in at the little store to buy Coca-Cola and Fanta to drink in the hotel and – Lary was emphatic – two more bottles of whisky. The shop was shutting and no, said the man behind the counter, we could not take soft drinks home, he had to account for the bottles, bottles were valuable, we must drain them there and then – so I had a Coca-Cola and Lary, for want of a Fanta, a bottle of something labelled Gintonic. 'Alcoholic?' said Lary. 'Tonic!' said the shopkeeper. 'It's late! Hurry! Drink it down!'

In the broad-leaved grasses by the squat tree in the hotel compound (a tree whose trunk was composed of hundreds of thin stems) two swallowtails were fluttering; the large black wings of one species flashed a band of bright green; the other, a few feet away, was almost identical in size and shape (and with the same little spatulate tails jutting at 45 degrees from the base of each hindwing) but it was semi-camouflaged in the speckled shade, its wings a dapple of yellow blotches on dark brown.

A purposeful streak of violet and white, perhaps a sunbird, passed us at head level.

'Lary – what was that?'

'Whash?' said Lary, stumbling on the step to the annexe.

'Did you see it?'

'No,' said Lary, leaning against the door of our room. 'And my legsh don't work.'

I unlocked the door. Lary collapsed on the bed. He mumbled to himself. He began to snore.

Slurred speech, I thought, the loss of feeling in his legs. It's multiple sclerosis. We're finished.

A big purple fly followed us in: it made remarkably little noise as it zig-zagged about the room; its buzzing was restrained; it was obviously a parasite; it was plainly the kind of bloodsucker that lands on your back undetected and creeps towards your neck. I tried to swot it against the bare wall, and missed. I forced myself to go to the bergen, find John G. Williams's *A Field Guide to the Butterflies of Africa* and look up the swallowtails – there they both were, plate two; they were the male and female of the same species, the Green-patch swallowtail, a butterfly with two types of female, one the form I'd seen outside and one coloured like the male. But even that discovery seemed unexciting, the plates began to lose their colour, the life drained out of them.

There was a knock at the door. Marcellin came in, newly showered, wearing a clean white shirt. 'Florence – she is waiting for me!' He perched on the edge of the bed. 'She is not like a young girl. My Florence, she knows what to do – she makes love in the grand manner!'

'Lary is ill,' I said, sitting down heavily on the upright chair. 'He's had another attack. It's his multiple sclerosis. We're finished.'

'Ill?' said Marcellin, looking at Lary. 'He's drunk!'

'Drunk?' I said slowly. 'Marcellin – what's in that Gintonic stuff? The man in the shop – he said it was just tonic, tonic water.'

'Tonic?' said Marcellin with a shriek of laughter, his teeth a brilliant white. 'It's 80 per cent proof!'

At midnight I was woken by a banging on the window-slats. I switched on my torch and opened the door. A young man in the uniform of the People's Militia fell to his knees. He smelt of beer and sweat.

'Nzé!' he shouted, pulling off his Cuban Army peaked cap. 'I'm Marcellin's brother!' He turned his head slowly from side to side, like a hornbill. By the light of the torch I could see that his right eye was scanning my face and that his left eye was focused on the moon. 'I live in Dongou! We share an uncle. I'm a cook. You must take me with you. *You must try my sauces!*'

16

Three days later, early in the morning, we took the long straight narrow stretch of new Brazilian road which ran north through the forest, just west of the course of the Oubangui river, to Dongou. And in Dongou, outside the offices of the District Commissar, Lary and I left Manou and Nzé lolling half-asleep in the back of the Land Cruiser on the bergens and kit-bags and sacks of fou-fou wedged around a 40-horsepower Yamaha outboard-motor (the only one of any kind for hire in Impfondo), and we followed Joseph and Marcellin up the steps of the old colonial building.

Black and red moulds grew across the white façade, along the lintels of the tall, rectangular, glassless windows, above the high central archway. In the atrium, open to the weather, defunct political billboards were stacked against the walls. The Commissar's office lay off to the right, a small room ventilated with an overhead fan and cantilevered corrugated-iron shutters; a hen scratched at the dust and tocked to her chicks in the garden outside. The Commissar was middle-aged but fresh-faced, energetic; yes, he said, looking up from his neatly arranged piles of papers, some tied with red string, he would do all he could to help us, Marcellin was an old friend of his, but we must understand, he was busy – very busy – it was not easy, converting the Chiefs of his district to Lenin's ways, it was almost impossible to introduce the idea of collective farms to the villages; the young men were on his side but the Chiefs, no; perhaps it would take another generation, maybe two. All the same, it was a great trust, an honour to institute the Marxist reforms the Party required, and yes, he knew a *pinacier*, a boatman who would take us up the Motaba river; but we must remember that the law did not reach that far, not yet; we must not expect him to help us, it was dangerous; and, at the moment, he was sad to say, his Military Zone had no money for petrol. But yes, of course he would stamp our passports and papers and he would give us something extra, too, his personal blessing – because he had heard that we had come from England and from America just to look at the birds of his country and to help Dr Marcellin Agnagna to kill the poachers from Zaïre. Long ago he, the Political Commissar, had been a schoolteacher, at Ouesso, and at Ouesso there was a great tree, and on the fruits of that tree big white birds came to feed, and no matter how often you tried to shoot those birds – no matter what bullets you used – you would miss, because the tree protected everything in it and everyone around it. It had been a privilege to live by such a tree, and since those days he, too, had been fond of birds. He understood.

We found the boatman in his compound by the river and left the baggage and the outboard-motor with him; we drove to the other end of the sprawling settlement of tumbledown huts, stray goats, chickens, hillocks grazed to the hard red earth, to share our sardines, corned beef and fried manioc doughnuts with Nzé's gentle, pretty, pregnant wife, beside their tiny hut, its roof a mix of reed-thatch, assorted planks, logs, twisted pieces of corrugated iron and one dustbin-lid.

We filled the boatman's petrol-drum at the town pump; we drove back down to the river-bank and manhandled the drum into the big plank-sided dugout; we said goodbye to Joseph (and Lary, I noticed, gave the bonnet of the truck a surreptitious, farewell pat); we stowed the kit amidships and helped the boatman to rig the outboard on the stern-frame of the canoe. Manou took his place as our nominal bow look-out; Lary and I leaned back against the bergens; Marcellin, in front of us, poled the boat out from the shore, and Nzé, much excited, aft of the baggage, still in the uniform of a soldier of the People's Militia, stood up and yelled heroic valedictions to the children who had gathered on the bank. The boatman, large, jovial, wearing a brown baseball cap, a blue shirt and green check trousers, started the engine at the second pull.

Almost at once the Motaba grew wild, deserted, its black open water no more than fifty yards across, fringed by the light-purple spikes of water-hyacinth in flower and backed by the low trees of riverside swamp-forest, raffia palms, cascades of lianas. We passed an inlet covered in water-lilies, their white flowers half-closed against the heat, their large oval leaves with upturned serrated edges a bright green on top and, where they tipped up against their neighbours, red-brown underneath. As the small waves of our wake slapped into them, the red-brown edge of one lily-pad metamorphosed into the red-brown body of a lily-trotter, a strip of white and gold sunlight resolved into its neck and collar, and the complete bird detached itself from its low nest of floating waterweed. So it's a male, I thought, as he unfurled his extraordinarily long legs and spindly toes, because only males incubate the eggs and look after the young (he will carry them from danger, held between his body and wings, two under each arm with just their toes showing beneath his coverts). He high-stepped away across the lily-pads, his wings held vertically up above his back for a moment, watched us from a leaf as we passed, circled back, scuttled furtively to the nest, fluffed up his feathers, lowered himself on to the eggs and disappeared into the vegetation.

'I'm not the complaining kind,' said Lary, taking off his hat and flicking the sweat from his forehead, 'but now that we're actually on the move I don't mind telling you that Dongou is the filthiest, most one-horse noisome town I've ever set my eyes on, believe me.'

The outboard-motor misfired once, twice and stopped.

Back at the Dongou landing-place, we stowed the paddles and carried the bags up the bank to the small guest-hut, in the half-light. Lary and I laid out our tarpaulins on the sand floor in silence. Even Nzé, head cocked on one side, making his first attempt to assemble the camping-stove, was silent. The boatman sent one of his younger brothers down to spend the night in the dugout, a guard for the petrol-drum. Marcellin and I took our torches and walked up the muddy track towards the town, to visit a shop run by a Muslim, said Marcellin, a Muslim who sold some mysterious potion that Marcellin had forgotten to pack. In the little shop, lit by a single kerosene lantern suspended from the middle of the ceiling, we bought packets of green tea, tins of sardines, coffee, candles – and a bottle of spray-on aftershave.

Marcellin held up the green bottle and, one eye shut, sighted through it at the hanging lantern. 'Upriver, Redmond, there are many beautiful women. You'll see – when I smell of this they'll come to me. They'll come to me like butterflies. Like butterflies to a flower.'

After a supper of fou-fou and sardines we stretched out on the sand; Lary, exasperated by the whining of mosquitoes in his ear, the sharp silence as they sucked, got up, went to his bergen, found his head-net, put it on and lay down again; looking like a bank-robber in a stocking-mask, he fell asleep at once, and began to snore.

The boatman woke us at three in the morning. His brother would look after the useless outboard; he, the boatman, had fixed up his own eight-horsepower Yamaha; it worked well; we must leave at once.

By four the little engine was pushing us upriver, in the dark, through the mist; by five-thirty it grew light enough to see the islets of vegetation floating past the gunwales; by six the rising sun had dispersed the mist, caught the fresh purple of the water-hyacinths, the yellow and white of the opening lilies, the red and purple-spotted flowers of orchids in the margin of the reed-beds – and the brown back of a bird swimming low in the water like a grebe, skulking beneath the overhanging reeds, its black tail splayed on the surface of the water, its long neck jerking backward and forward as it swam, its red bill stabbing the air: the African finfoot. Not quite a grebe or a duck or a darter or a cormorant or a rail, it shares parts of its structure and some of its habits with all of them, but is more primitive, a living fossil of a bird that retains a claw on its wing even as an adult, the kind of bird that you could easily imagine paddling (low in the water, neck pumping back and forth) past a foraging Mokélé-mbembé, sixty-seven million years ago.

'He's afraid of us now,' said Marcellin, picking up the single-barrelled shotgun and pretending to shoot, 'but that little bird can boom like a big drum! He can bellow like a bull!'

Round the next bend three huge black hornbills, the Black-casqued, were flapping and gliding from right to left across the river, their bills apparently curved downward by the weight of their ivory outgrowths, their wings reaching forward as if put on back-to-front – and the whoosh of their ragged primaries was loud enough to be heard above the putter of the motor.

'Women, Florence,' said Marcellin, apropos nothing in particular, turning round to look at us, 'they *like* it when you go into the forest. They *want* you to risk your life. As long as you come back. Otherwise me, I wouldn't bother. What's the point? But if I return, if I see Impfondo again ... Sometimes, in bed, she's like a Parisienne. A duchess from Paris. And sometimes she's like a leopard. And you know, when she has her orgasm – she whinnies like a horse.'

Lary said, 'Risk your life?'

'The Cuvette,' said Marcellin. 'It was in the Cuvette. Joseph told me about it. Two of my guards. I didn't know them, their names meant nothing to me. But technically I was their boss. They were my responsibility. They were shot as they made camp in the forest. Joseph said the back of their heads – there was nothing left. The poachers, they got close.'

On the occasional wide sweep of the river with its crescent of reed-bed, when our enclosed world momentarily opened out, we could see the emergent giant trees above the forest canopy and, sometimes, the branched spire of a liana projecting vertically above them, perhaps the crown of a climbing palm. Ahead of us, every 400 yards or so, a finfoot splashed for cover; and Giant kingfishers, as big as crows, would watch us intently from their fishing perches, their crests ruffled up as though the mere sight of us made their hair stand on end, until, with a single *kek* of alarm, they flew off low upriver to another overhanging branch, doubling back only as we reached the invisible boundary of each private kingdom. And above the shallows by the reed-beds scarlet dragonflies hovered and zig-zagged, intermittently twitching down the tips of their abdomens, breaking the slow-moving surface of the water.

'Great guys,' said Lary. 'They're dapping. Laying eggs. The larvae hatch out in the mud and do most everything with their butts. They've got gills in there, and a rectal water-pump. When there's trouble they blast away on a jet of water. And in my opinion, Redso' – he raised both eyebrows – 'that's a trick we're going to need.'

Marcellin put on his headphones and leant back against a kit-bag; Manou, in the bow, and Nzé, behind the bergens, appeared to be asleep; the boatman, one hand on the tiller of the little motor, his peaked cap pulled low on his forehead, stared at the winding central channel where the river ran deep, at its bright white flashes of ripples, at its irregular cargo of weed-clumps, pads of hyacinth, broken branches.

A big black and white moth of a bird sailed out above the canopy to our left, hung over our heads for a moment, and curved back out of sight – the Vulturine fish eagle, an eagle with a passion for palm nuts, the only mainly vegetarian bird of prey in the world; and just beyond an eddy to our right the pointed head of a dark-brown water-snake metamorphosed into a long bill, grew a body like a cormorant, slapped the water with black, white-streaked wings, took off, spread its black tail into a fan, kinked its neck, and, with surprisingly rapid wing-beats, banked past the tops of the raffia palms and disappeared. The African darter, said Serle and Morel: 'breeds in colonies in trees, generally in company with Cormorant and Heron species. Nest a platform of sticks. Eggs 3–5, chalky-white with a green tinge.'

'It sure is odd,' said Lary, turning round and pulling his old Nikon camera out of the side-pocket of his bergen. 'All this. The whole business. There's no history of travelling in my family – apart from the one trip.'

'What trip?'

'The one that all post-Columbus Americans have taken – the journey that made them Americans. I've been thinking about it. As far as I'm concerned, it's all oral history. I got most of it from my grandmother. And I guess that's how most everybody round here gets their history.'

'I expect so. If the grandmother lives long enough.'

'We're Palatine Germans, from Bavaria.' (He took a long lens out of its black leather tube and twist-clicked it on to the camera body.) '1708 we went to England. Religious refugees. The Brits looked after us well. They made a refugee camp in the East End of London. But we were Bavarians, of course, we worked hard, and the local people were very poor and they objected, they couldn't compete. So the Government sent us to America to produce supplies for the navy. Pitch and oakum. We were indentured servants. The Brits said, "You go to America for ever and we'll look after you in a big camp on the upper Hudson river." A lot died on the way over, the lower decks were awash. It was a terrible voyage, rough and cold. Gerhard Schaefer's daughter was born on the trip, and he had a son already, Johan, a teenager. Well, it turned out that the northern pines were White pines, no good for pitch – for that you need the pitch pines in the south, the Yellow pines of southern Carolina. So they spent their days squashing oak-bark to make into oakum, loose fibres you use with pitch for caulking the seams of ships, for plugging leaks. Anyway, in 1711 Gerhard got the chance to go fight the French and Indians in Quebec. He walked north, joined the British army and got killed. So that left Johan, in his late teens, his sister and mother – when they were released from naval supplies they built a log-cabin and made a little family farm in central New York State. There was a German enclave there – there's still a Palatine Bridge over the Mohawk river.'

On our own river we flushed a Purple heron from a reed-bed to our left; Lary took its portrait as it veered away into a side-stream, its russet neck held in a downward bulge, its grey wings hardly coordinated, its long legs trailing.

'We stayed until my great-grandad moved out to Gloversville. Around 1870. Martin Luther Shaffer. My great-grandmother, Frances, she spelt his name wrong in the family Bible when she married him and that's how it's remained to this day. I knew her, she was Dutch, the first non-German in the family. She died in 1956. 103 years old. She remembered Lincoln being assassinated; she saw the railway arrive; the first cars; electricity. She saw *gaslight* come and go. Imagine that! But I don't suppose it impressed her. They were gentle and kind, the Shaffers. They were hard-working people who never got excited about anything much. It just didn't occur to them to say "Sod this pitch lark." I guess I have a stolid ancestry. "Things could be worse" – that's what they used to say.'

Another Purple heron stood in the reeds, but it was twice the size it ought to be – about five feet tall – and for one mad moment I thought it might spear the canoe. It held its black and yellow bill straight as we passed, its rufous-chestnut head still, its long curve of a neck (fronted with black and white feathers cascading into plumes) motionless.

Lary grabbed the bird book.

'LBJ,' I said. 'Little Brown Job.'

'Biggest sucker I ever saw,' muttered Lary, turning to the plate of flamingos, pelicans, herons and egrets. 'Goliath heron. Damn right. And then some.'

Every three to four hours wooden floats or a cluster of poles and sticks by the bank would mark a net or a wickerwork-basket fish-trap, the first sign of an approaching village, followed, perhaps, by the odd fisherman paddling a small canoe – at which point Nzé would wake up, and he and the boatman, city-dwellers from Dongou, would engage the fisherman in a shouted conversation of news and insults, banter and gossip which, I was sure, like the contact calls of the Goliath heron, could be heard from two kilometres away in every direction.

A line of oil-palms, a strip of sand with a few drawn-up canoes, a huddle of waving children, and the jungle would close in again. No wind moved the fronds of the raffia palms, the tops of the big bushes with red flowers borne on a single spike and leaves like a Horse chestnut, the heads of the reeds beside us. But in the late afternoon there was a crashing and shaking in the under-canopy to our left: a man stood high up in a fork of a tree – only he had a tail.

Our first monkey, an Eastern pied colobus, the guereza, big and grubby-looking, sat down on the right-hand branch and stared at us. His black face was framed with a white beard and side-whiskers; plumes of white fur wisped out from his shoulders, his ribs and his upper thighs. His black tail, hanging straight down below the branch, blossomed into a long tuft, a brush of yellowish white. He watched us, chin out, and rolled his lips one against the other.

Through the binoculars I searched the tree for other members of the troop – and as I began to scrutinize a gap in the lianas low and to the right, the circle of my vision filled with an onrush of barred brown and white underwings, huge yellow feet, the twisting splay of a long tail: and the eagle was gone.

'The Monkey eagle! The Crowned eagle!'

'Yup,' said Lary, taking his hat off and running a hand over his bald patch. 'Biggest sucking eagle I ever saw.'

'They kill antelopes!'

'Yup,' said Lary.

Two bends later, in a tree like an oak but hung with red fruits, six Pied colobus were feeding – and at least four monkeys of a different species were foraging with them, their fur looking black against the light, with no hint of a plume, their tails long and thin. And right above us, very still on the dead branch of a straggly tree, screened from behind by lianas, perched a Crowned eagle, his crest slightly raised, his bill hooked, his yellow eyes fixed on us as if to say, 'Monkeys, what monkeys?'

Well after dark, navigating by torchlight, we turned into a tiny creek full of duckweed and carried the baggage up to the village of Manfouété where, said the boatman, he had two wives, both younger than his three wives in Dongou.

17

The boatman, his buttocks wobbling slightly as he walked, led us off to the left at the top of the slipway, to the big school-hut at the edge of the village; he bid us goodnight and retired, presumably, to his own compound, to the comfort of his two young wives.

Marcellin shone his torch over the mud walls: the school hut was big, palm-thatched and dirt-floored; it contained three rough bench-desks, one long log and two termite mounds. The entrance had no door, the walls no windows.

'This is my first visit to Manfouété,' said Marcellin, his voice quieter than I had ever heard it, almost a whisper. 'There is something wrong with this village.'

'Dr Marcellin,' said Manou, 'perhaps we should leave?'

'By night? You know the river? You know where the boatman lives? You can steal his motor?'

Manou was silent.

'You're a *petit*!' said Marcellin, untying his pack, pulling out his blue tent.

'You're pitching a tent?' said Lary. 'In here?'

'Of course,' said Marcellin, clattering out the aluminium poles. 'It's the only protection against the mosquitoes, against chiggers: the fleas – they lay their eggs under your toe-nails. When they grow in your flesh you must dig them out with a knife. It hurts! You can't walk!'

'Chicken-fucker,' muttered Lary, bent over his bergen.

'What's that?' said Marcellin.

'He's hungry,' I said. 'He wants a chicken.'

'Tomorrow,' said Marcellin, 'when the village wakes up. There'll be chickens and pineapples and palm-wine. And lots of pygmies for Redmond to play with – and dancing and *women*. Women for everyone!'

'Chicken-fucker,' repeated Lary under his moustache, laying out the canvas of our tiny two-man tent.

'Tomorrow!' said Marcellin. 'Chickens!'

I untied the cords on the bergen full of presents (trade-goods, I said to myself, with nineteenth-century satisfaction); I presented Nzé and

Manou with pocket-knives, machetes, mosquito-nets, two army tarpaulins each, Maglite torches, batteries, and one Petzl head-torch to share between them.

Nzé squatted down and, moving his head from side to side, inspected his small pile of kit with professional disdain, as if he had been expecting a Land Rover, at least. Manou opened his Swiss Army knife, felt the blade, closed it, stroked the red handle, and slipped it into the pocket of his once-white cotton trousers. He picked up his Maglite (black, medium-sized) twisted it on and pointed the beam at the smoke-blackened thatch of the roof, at the axe-hewn rafter above his head, at a big brown Wolf-spider running along the wood (it scrabbled to cover between the dry, layered leaves).

'I'll make a prediction,' Lary said to me in English, knocking in the tent-pegs with the flat of his machete. 'In fact I suggest to you right now, in some confidence, that that kid does not have a cupboard at home bung-full of cuddly toys. He is a stranger to the plastic building brick. He is unaware of the long-jib crane you make from Meccano. And unlike someone I know, he has never lined up his tin soldiers across the yard. Those are the first presents that Manou has ever received.'

Nzé, disgruntled, strapped on the head-torch, took a tin-opener and a can of pilchards from the sack of stores, knelt down and tried to clamp the opener to the rim of the can. As he turned his head to focus his right eye on the lid, the line of light from the lamp (centre-top on his forehead) moved across the floor to his left and rose one yard up the mud wall; changing to his left eye, intending to catch the can by surprise, he flicked his head the other way – the yellow circle passed flat across the mud floor and came to rest two-and-a-half yards up the wall to his right. Nzé, swinging and dipping his head faster and faster, made an attempt on the speed of light; and in the resulting chaos of shadows it did indeed look as if his head was growing bigger and bigger, swelling its mass according to Einstein's equation – until Manou, quiet, thoughtful, lodged two of our candles in the ground, one to either side of the can of pilchards, and lit them.

Nzé, exasperated, snatched off the head-torch and dropped it at Manou's feet. Manou, without a word, bent down, took off his hat, strapped on the still-shining lamp and, arms outstretched like the wings of an aeroplane, followed the target of light all the way round the bare rectangle of the hut.

'That kid,' said Lary. 'He's got imagination.'

After a supper of cold fou-fou and pilchards Nzé and Manou rigged up their mosquito-nets along the wall to the right of the open entrance; Marcellin crawled into his tent, tying the flaps behind him; Lary and I followed suit.

We wrapped ourselves in our tarpaulins in the close, blue, stuffy interior, ventilated only by two small squares of mosquito-netting let into the inner canvas sides.

'I'm not complaining,' said Lary, knotting two shirts into a pillow, 'but this mud floor – it's hard as cement.'

'I expect we'll get used to it,' I said, wondering how I'd turn over without dislocating a hip. 'Anyway, we've seen a Pied colobus – and a Crowned eagle.'

'Yup,' said Lary, lying back and staring at the blue slope of ceiling two feet above his head. 'I like the whole colobus concept – their tails, their faces, their white whiskers just like yours, Redso – but it's their social life I really go for: very little work's been done on them but we do know they're fundamentally non-aggressive – in the Red colobus the female has a permanently swollen perineum and the male seems to mimic it with bulbous bits round his anus. They walk along the branches with their tails sticking up, displaying to each other. It's as if men and women both had breasts and went about topless and everyone half-fancied everyone else. It makes fighting impossible – there are no reports of bite-scars on colobus skins. They play-wrestle, they hug each other all the time, the females look after each other's babies. It's perfect.'

At first light, as we sat on the kit-bags spooning our breakfast fou-fou and pilchards out of our mess-tins, a small man, furtive as a young rat, slipped into the hut. He stood in front of Marcellin, running his right hand over the scrubby beard on his jaw-line. He wore a torn checked shirt, orange trousers and flip-flops.

'Comrade Dr Marcellin Agnagna, I am the Vice-President of the People's Village Committee of Manfouété,' he said in French. Marcellin remained seated. The Vice-President lowered his head, looked at his flip-flops. 'The boatman has told me about your mission. I will inform the Hereditary Chief. The forest is to be ours again. We may kill the poachers from Zaïre and also from the Sudan. You have come with two white men who wish to find the pygmies in the forest. You are an official representative of the Government. You are a Big Man in a real Ministry. You can trust me, Comrade. I have important things to tell you. It is urgent.' He took his hand off his chin and, as if he held a machete, chopped at the air. 'I wish to make a full report. There are problems . . .'

'Koko!' came a tremendous shout from outside, followed by a battering-ram of a thump on the mud wall. For a moment the hut went dark as the entrance filled; a huge man towered in front of us. 'Koko!' he said, striking a desk-top with the base of his fist. We stood up as if he owned us.

He was perhaps seven feet tall and he looked taller because he wore a Russian tank-driver's hat, complete with ear-flaps.

'The Commandant!' he said. 'The People's Militia! The village of Man-fouété!' He slapped the breast-pocket of his combat-fatigues. 'Koko!'

'The clown,' said Lary, which was brave of him.

'It's Lingala,' said Marcellin in English, shaking the Commandant's hand. 'It means "Can I come in? Hello! Is anyone at home?"'

'Comrade Agnagna! I know all about you! The boatman – he has given me my orders. From the Chief of the Army, the Hero of the People, Colonel Denis Sassou-Nguesso!'

The Commandant snapped the heels of his combat boots together and saluted. Marcellin, startled, sat down.

'Count on me! We will kill the poachers. A pleasure! But first – you have a present for me? We must drink. We must drink together. You will stay here, in my village. You will show my pygmies to these whites. We will introduce them! I have many pygmies!'

Marcellin put both hands to the back of his neck, as if he had just slipped a disc. He said to me, 'Have you any drink? Is there any whisky left?'

Caught unprepared, my legs carried me straight to Lary's bergen: from the back pocket in the inner bag I tugged out the last of our Johnny Walker Red Label, cocooned in its black sock. In the early morning light from the doorway, the bottle, newly emergent, shone like amber.

'Johnny Walker!' said the Commandant, seizing it. 'Red Label!'

He unscrewed the top and took a long swig. Bubbles rose in the upturned bottle. 'Whisky!' he shouted, between gulps. 'In here!'

Three big men wearing fatigues and carrying machetes processed into the hut. The Commandant took a gargantuan pull at the bottle and passed it to his Lieutenant, who took a deep breath and a deeper draught and passed it to the Sergeant, who took a respectful nip and passed it to the Corporal, who finished it.

'Dear God,' said Lary.

'Pygmies!' said the Commandant. 'Follow me! Bring the white men!'

Lary grabbed the Polaroid camera and a bag of film and we followed the Commandant and his officers. They strode like conquerors up the narrow path ahead of Marcellin and his men, Nzé and Manou, who walked one behind the other, their heads down, their shoulders hunched, as if roped together at the neck.

'A railway-line!' said Lary, stopping, parting the grass to his right, kicking at the soil.

'Come on,' I said. 'This may be it – our one chance to find a group of pygmies in the forest.'

'Narrow-gauge,' said Lary. He pushed his hat to the back of his head like a cowboy at a gold-strike. 'It sure is narrow-gauge.'

'We'll admire it later.'

'But what's it doing here?'

'Search me.'

We entered a long wide clearing: the wattle-and-daub huts were large, rectangular, thickly palm-thatched. The Commandant halted, clapped his hands, shouted – and a small man in torn grey shorts came running from an open-slatted cooking-hut to our left. He paused in front of us: his eyes bright, his body muscled, his legs short, his feet bare. The Commandant shouted something, issued instructions, raised his arm, pointed, and his subordinate turned and ran steadily up the street, over the dried mud, the scuffed grass.

'My pygmy!' said the Commandant. 'Dancing! The pygmies – they will dance for us!' He took off his hat, flicked it across his right knee, and replaced it. His head was shaved bald.

The main street divided into a fan of pathways twisting away between smaller compounds; the Commandant led us down a track to the left, into young secondary forest (Umbrella trees, small bushes, straggly shrubs).

'I don't like it,' said Lary, behind me. 'Where are the children? They're frightened. Why aren't we being followed by crowds of children?'

'No idea,' I said, as the Commandant took a turn to his right: a marker-post stood at the fork in the path, and as he passed he stroked its side with his palm, a quick little compulsive gesture at odds with his flamboyant confidence. Drawing level myself, I inspected it: three cut saplings had been thrust into the ground and supported, at chest-height, a decayed wickerwork basket shaped like a rib-cage and draped with shards of rotted flesh.

The thin path led down to a village, but a village like no other we had seen: little rectangular huts, flimsy, dilapidated shelters, some of them with their roofs half-collapsed, their cross-poles sticking out, ringed a rough clearing. The Commandant's servant was fussing everyone into the central space: young women wearing nothing but raffia skirts (strips of palm-leaf, like dried-brown couch-grass, cut off just above the knee); older women, their breasts flat hanging triangles, babies clinging to their backs; young men with raffia skirts slung over their cotton trousers. They were perhaps four-and-a-half to five feet tall, their skin brown rather than black, their noses flat and broad, their eyes set far apart.

From a nearby hut the Commandant's henchmen rolled out two drums, tapered barrels of hollowed-out tree-trunk, the stretched skins bound on with liana-twine; they propped one drum on the side of the other, frog-marched a young pygmy into the playing position, and rejoined the Commandant outside the circle. 'Dance!' he yelled. 'Dance!' Two small hunting-dogs (with yellow-brown coats and upcurved tails) scuttled for cover between the shelters.

The drummer, legs awkwardly astride the top drum, beat out a slow, simple rhythm; the pygmies shuffled round the circle, swaying half-heartedly; the women began a high-pitched, desultory song. No one looked at us; no one smiled.

'Let's get out of here,' said Lary, beside me. 'It's grotesque.'

'Take their pictures with the Polaroid,' I said, misjudging things. 'Maybe they'll like us. Maybe they'll help us.'

'Redso, I hate to be a party to this,' said Lary, slotting in a film. 'Commander Coco – he's dangerous. He's psychotic.'

As we left, half an hour later, the Commandant was clapping his hands, mustering the little people round him, stealing every one of the precious photographs for himself.

Just inside the doorway of the hut the Vice-President sat tapping his fingers on a desk-top. 'Comrade Agnagna!' he said, jumping up, taking Marcellin by the elbow. 'We must talk. Quick! We must walk in the forest.'

'Nzé, Manou,' said Marcellin, allowing himself to be steered towards the path at the back of the hut, 'you guard the packs.'

'When in doubt,' said Lary, 'think engineering.' So we went for a comfort-inspection of the little railway-line; and on the way back we came to a high ruined shed with real clay-brick pillars, and in front of it, on its side, lay a heavy steel cylinder with gearing, an axle and a broken wheel attached to one end.

'It's an ancient centrifuge,' said Lary, running his hand over its smooth flank. 'There must have been a works here. It's bizarre. Oil-nuts? A processing plant? It's off the wall!'

Back at the hut, Marcellin was waiting. 'Redmond!' he said. 'I have heard a rare bird. We must find it!'

He looked agitated, strapping on his army belt complete with his machete in its sheath, his two water-bottles and the Sony Walkman. 'Manou, you will stay inside with the packs. Lary, you will drag out a school-desk and sit at it, reading a book. You will not show fear. Nzé, you, too, will sit at a desk, but you will oil the gun, in plain view. You will sit with a box of cartridges at your side. If there is trouble, you will fire in the air!'

'With all due respect,' said Lary, tugging at his moustache, 'what the hell's going on?'

'Birdwatching!' said Marcellin, pulling my arm. 'We must find the bird!' And he led me up the path beside the hut.

A hundred yards or so beyond an abandoned plantation we came to a little clearing, and in the centre of the clearing was a well-kept grave with a headstone. 'NDOSSA, RAPHAEL,' it said, '1910–1975.' Beneath the headstone was a saucepan capped with its lid, and in front of the saucepan an empty Ballantine's gin bottle.

'He must have been a Big Man,' said Marcellin, sitting on a log at the foot of the grave.

'Why the saucepan?' I said, joining him.

'He must have been a hunter, a powerful man. He kept the pot full. And the gin bottle – a mark of respect. And to keep his spirit happy, to keep him happy in the world of spirits.'

'Cooeee! Kweeko!' said something up in a thicket to our right, and I caught a glimpse of a bird the size of a thrush, brown with a white belly. It tipped forward, raised its wings, and repeated the greeting: 'Cooeee! Kweeko!'

'There you are,' said Marcellin, with a sideways grin. 'Told you so. He sang when I was here with the Vice-President. You find him round every village. The most common bird in Africa. The Common garden bulbul. And he sings in English, just for you. "Quick, doctor, quick!" That's what he says.'

Marcellin looked at his feet. 'It's safe. We can talk here. I like to talk by a grave. It's safe.'

'What's up? What's going on?'

'I'm not sure. They speak Mondongo and I don't understand it. I'm as much of a foreigner as you are. Maybe more so. My people used to fight the Mondongo. They hate us.'

'But the Vice-President?'

'He is an educated man. But he is broken, frightened. It is unfortunate. This is not normal. My country is not like this. He tells me there is a leopard sect here. The men are cut down their backs and arms when they are fifteen years old and take an oath to kill each other's enemies. He tells me that the Commandant rules the village. The Commandant – he is violent, mad. The pygmies are his slaves. The schoolmaster was the only man brave enough to stand up to him. These young schoolmasters, straight out of college in Brazzaville – the Government sends each one, all alone, to teach Marx and everything else for two years to a village in the interior. They get no help, they have no visits!'

'What happened?'

'The Commandant was drunk. He took the schoolmaster by night and beat him. The schoolmaster escaped downriver. Or maybe he took the schoolmaster and killed him and buried the body in the forest. It is not clear.'

'So there's no school?'

'We're camping in the school! For two years already there has been no school. The children have no chance, no education. If we escape, I shall make a report.'

'But we're going to find the pygmies in the forest!'

'Not from here. The pygmies here are too frightened to take anyone to the forest. The Vice-President – he says that the Commandant wants our packs. He wants our packs, boots, shirts and trousers. But I think it's okay. His spies will tell him – we have a gun. We have cartridges. We have lots of cartridges! He's had your whisky. He's not used to whisky. And now with his men he drinks palm-wine. When they fall down drunk we make our escape. At first light.'

Back at the hut, opposite the doorway, a small group of pygmies stood in the shade of the great trees. A young mother, with a hesitant smile at Lary, pushed her little girl towards us. The child was five or six years old, very thin, wearing a rolled strip of red cotton round her waist, and her eyelids, cheeks, nose and lips were encrusted with sores, raised, cracked blisters of infection.

'Marcellin,' said Lary, 'what the hell is it?'

'*Pian*,' said Marcellin, squatting down, holding the girl's hand. 'Yaws. It's related to syphilis. But it's nothing to do with having sex. It's carried from wound to wound on the feet of flies. The first signs, the little bumps – they start in the corners of the eyes or the lips, the base of the nostrils, wherever the flies go to suck your moisture. The Bantu, we're free of it – you don't get it if you wash with soap, if you bathe in the river. But pygmies don't have soap – and anyway they never wash.'

'What can we do?' said Lary. 'What's the cure?'

'Simple,' said Marcellin, standing up. 'One shot of Extencilline. Protects you for life. But nobody comes this far. No policemen. No doctors. No nothing.'

'Floxapen,' Lary said to me. 'What about the Floxapen?'

I went to the hut, rustled through the plastic bags in the medical kit and found our last course.

'You're mad to part with this,' said Marcellin, handing the bottle to the mother, miming taking a pill when you wake up, when the sun is directly above the clearing, and when you go to sleep. 'You should look after your own people first. Nzé and Manou – they'll get ulcers. We all will.'

The pygmies withdrew between the trees; Lary resumed his reading of *Our Mutual Friend*; Manou arrived back from the river with our five-gallon container half-full of water; Nzé, looking happy with a bamboo cleaning-rod, a plastic bottle of cooking-oil, a box of cartridges and the ripped-up pieces of a blue cotton tee-shirt in front of him on the desk-top, took another professional squint down the barrel of the shotgun. Marcellin explained his plan. Nzé stopped looking happy; Manou disappeared into the hut; Lary stuffed *Our Mutual Friend* into his pocket. We carried the desks inside.

After nightfall we pulled three logs and two desks across the bottom half of the entrance, drank green tea, ate sardines and fou-fou and went to bed with our boots on, leaving Nzé on guard behind the barricade, clutching the shotgun.

Some hours later Lary shook me awake.

Loud drumming, the waves of sound coming at us just faster than a panic heartbeat, swept through the mud walls of the hut.

'What the hell's that?' said Lary.

'It's drumming.'

'Don't smartarse with me,' said Lary, switching on his torch. There was a big drop of sweat on the end of his nose.

'Sounds ominous,' I said, trying to be helpful, easing myself into a sitting position off the hard mud floor and attempting to rub some feeling back into my arms and legs.

'*I'm sick,*' said Lary. '*I'm just sick of being terrorized night and day.* I've been more frightened in thirty-four days on this trip than in my whole fucking life.' He opened the tent-flap and peered out: an intermittent, flickering light from outside played over the barricade. Nzé crouched behind it, head well down beneath an upturned desk-top, his right hand reaching up to the stock of the shotgun, whose unattended barrel was levelled at the doorway.

'Coco's out there,' said Lary, reversing into the tent. 'He's out there in his hat. I just know he has that hat on his head, a brand of flaming copal in one hand and a machete in the other. He wants our packs. He wants our packs and he is going to light the thatch of this hut. He's going to light the thatch and make us run out – and then he and all his friends are going to hack us to bits with machetes.'

'Nzé will shoot him.'

'It may have escaped your notice, Redmond, but Nzé is a bag of syphilis. And in addition he has one eye permanently fixed on the sky and one on the ground. He can't focus. He couldn't shoot a rabbit in a box.'

'So where would you like to be, now?' (When you have no idea what to do next this is always a soothing question.)

Lary paused. With his right hand he wiped the sweat off his face. 'In Burlington, Vermont, there's a bookstore, Chassman and Bem – and it may surprise you to know this but you can get in there without passing a guard with a gun and you can actually go right ahead and pick a *book* off a shelf and *sit in a chair*, like a human being, and read your book and listen to Mozart and no one comes up to you and shouts in your ear and offers to take his machete and cut you into pork ribbons if you don't give him your last bottle of whisky, one backpack and a pair of trousers.'

I said, 'That's very reassuring.'

'Really? That's all you have to say?'

'Look, Lary. I'm sorry. I don't know what's going on and I don't know what to do. And when I don't know what to do, I go to sleep. Conrad has a name for it.'

'Does he now?' said Lary, looking mean.

'Yeah. It's called do-nothing heroics.'

And I fell asleep.

Five minutes later (or so it felt) Lary pulled at my shoulder. The hut was light, it was dawn. 'For Chrissake,' he whispered, 'something odd is moving in this hut.' The drumming had stopped, but there was the sound of fast breathing – then a sudden clatter, over by the barricade.

Lary, holding his machete, did a half-roll through the tent entrance. Putting on my glasses, I crawled after him.

'A dog!' he shouted. 'A dog!'

A little white dog took a last lick at a mess-tin by Nzé's sleeping head, jumped on to the rim of a desk and scrabbled to safety over the logs, his back leg kicking the shotgun as he went.

The shotgun fell, stock first, on to Nzé's stomach. Nzé sat up, peered at us, and clapped his right arm hard against his side.

'Quick!' yelled Marcellin, thrusting out of his tent. 'Fire! Fire the gun!'

There was a stirring under a tarpaulin in the far corner of the hut. 'I'm here,' said Manou, in a small voice, sticking his head out, coming to the rescue.

We all laughed.

Marcellin looked at his watch. 'It's late. The boatman – he'll be waiting. Quick!'

Bowed down with a bergen on my back and a kit-bag in each hand, a movement in the short grass to the side of the hut caught my eye: six heavy-bodied, purple-red hawkmoths, perhaps Elephant hawkmoths, were hovering over a patch of tiny scarlet flowers, like hummingbirds, sucking in nectar through their long proboscides, their sharp little tails cocked up with pleasure.

18

———————

By the mud slipway the boatman and the Vice-President were waiting; a boy with a long spear stood further out in the shallows. We waded through the duckweed, loaded the packs and took our positions in the dugout. Marcellin, the last in line, turned and shook the Vice-President's hand: 'Albert Ndongo, you are a brave man. I shall inform the Government of the People's Republic.'

'Thank you, Comrade,' said the Vice-President. He was shivering. Malaria, I thought, or the cold mist, or perhaps just spasms of hopeless anxiety.

The boy stabbed at the water with his spear, quick as a heron; he held up a black catfish, wrenching from side to side, transfixed behind the head.

The boatman started the motor; we puttered down the creek and out into the river.

'Jesus,' said Lary, wild-eyed. 'That was the worst night of my whole life.'

'Yeah? How did it rate? On the Impfondo scale?'

'Oh, way off. Way off. Impfondo didn't figure. I was sweat-terrorized. Stomach-numbing fear shitstruck. I'd gladly sleep with my head down the toilet rather than go through that again. I'd no idea it was possible for a man to be so frightened. And you, you fat bastard, you just went straight off to sleep. "Oh, listen to those drums," you said, "that sounds ominous," and then you went to sleep. You snored.'

'I'm sorry.'

'I tried to tell myself that I'd *made* this decision: I would much rather die in some African jungle than strip fucking paint in Cornelia Street all summer. But when it came to it it didn't work at all. *Not at all.* I found I wasn't ready. I just wasn't ready to die. You can say what you like – that mad Sergeant and his cronies were psyching themselves up to burn the thatch. I'm sure of it. The hooch got him before he got to us, that's all.'

I was silent.

'If I ever get home – when next someone says, "Don't worry", I'll say "You've never *seen* me worry. Here in Plattsburgh you don't know what worry is." Maybe it was the green tea, but I was waiting for the other shoe to drop, I really was. I had this fantasy. They work themselves up with palm-wine. They drum all night. They torch the thatch and hack us up with machetes as we run for it. Only I escape. I have the sense to hide near the oil-nut building, in the centrifuge, and not in the jungle where they'd find me right away. And after dark I steal a pirogue and get downriver. There's no food. Everyone's hostile. I've lost everything. But I make it. And I come back with the Marines and blow that fucking Sergeant Pepper inside out.'

'Food!' shouted Nzé from the stern, handing mess-tins full of cold fou-fou and sardines over the baggage.

'Chicken!' said Lary, passing two to Marcellin, in front of us, who stretched forward and gave one to Manou in the bow.

'The next village,' said Marcellin, turning round on his stool. 'Chicken!'

'Barfballs,' said Lary. 'But I'm not complaining.'

'Marcellin,' I said, 'that thing on a post outside the pygmy settlement, the bits of dried meat, what was that?'

'Twins.'

'Twins?'

'It's a catastrophe,' said Marcellin, mashing his sardines into the fou-fou with the flat of his Swiss Army knife. 'To give birth to twins – that's terrible. Me, I don't believe it, but people will say you've slept with a spirit. To have more than one child at a time – that's like the animals! In the old days the sorcerer would kill the mother, throw her babies into the forest, everything she owned would be destroyed, her pots smashed, her clothes ripped, burned. She would never become an ancestor. She would cease to exist. From that day no one would mention her name. Not even her mother.'

'And now?'

'Now only the afterbirths are carried to the edge of the trees. They protect the village. They keep the spirit-father in the forest.'

Two small chestnut ducks, snug on the water ahead, paddled for the bank as we approached, changed their minds, took off in bursts of spray, flew low past a curve of raffia palms and perched half-way up a tree to our right. As we passed beneath them they waggled their tails like Aylesbury drakes, tilted their black heads sideways, and looked down at us with one brown eye apiece.

'Tree ducks,' said Lary, decisively.

'Hartlaub's ducks. They must be. Because that's the only duck living in the jungle. Almost nothing's known about them – no one's ever found a nest.'

'That figures. Not one single sucker's been dumb enough to come out here and take a look.'

'Someone did catch a couple and get them to breed. They made their nest in the bottom of an upright barrel. The chicks had sharp claws and they climbed out up the sides – but there were only two days in their lives when they could manage it. So what do you think? They nest in hollow trees?'

'Sure. They worked it out. Round here, it's the only way to survive. Make a nest no one can find. Go hide in a centrifuge.'

At midday we reached the next village. The boatman ran the dugout ashore, stepped out and spat on the grass.

'He is unhappy,' said Marcellin in English as we walked up the incline towards the huts. 'Here in Mimbélou he has no wives, but the people are Mondongo, he has relatives, they will spy on him. So he can't have sex! He'll lose weight! He'll get sick!'

Five small boys ran towards us, pushed round Lary and fell into step behind him. 'Mondélé! Mondélé!' they chanted.

'Why pick on me?' said Lary.

'It's your face,' said Manou unexpectedly. 'You have a kind face. You come from America.'

We piled the baggage round the trunk of an old mango, a talking-tree, said Marcellin, a tree under whose branches all the major decisions of village life would be taken. The Chief appeared, carrying a wooden three-legged stool in each hand. 'Comrade Agnagna,' he said, placing the stools just wide of the mango's roots, 'we will talk.' Nzé slipped into the nearest hut and returned with a stool of his own; Manou, Lary and I took our seats on the bergens, and the council began. 'I am not a stranger here,' said Marcellin in French. 'But I have lived in Cuba and in France. I have seen distant lands. I am an agent of the Government of the People's Republic.'

'We will talk,' repeated the Chief, quiet and dignified, and the slow discussion moved into Lingala.

Half an hour later the two men stood up. 'The Chief of Mimbélou will help us,' said Marcellin. 'He has decided. Redmond will pay the customary dues. The white men will pay 10,000 CFA and eight gourds of palm-wine. We will take five pygmies. We will repack. We will enter the forest. We will place all the kit-bags and sacks we do not need safe in the hut of the Chief of Mimbélou. We leave in half an hour.'

'Me – I will kill the poachers,' said the old man with a wan smile, shooting the ragged cuffs of his red shirt, hoisting up his brown cotton trousers (a tear across the right knee), and flip-flopping off to his hut.

Three of the Chief's men paddled us, the five pygmies, the four bergens and Marcellin's pack across the river in their fishing canoes, poled us up a long narrow creek, and left us on dry ground. Marcellin, Lary and I filled our army water-bottles from the sluggish little stream and slotted them back in their belt-pouches; Manou and Nzé filled their plastic cooking-oil bottles and tied them to their belts with string; the pygmies cut lengths of liana with their machetes and peeled them into flat strips.

Lary bent down to pick up his bergen.

'No, no,' said Marcellin, touching him on the shoulder. 'We are not bearers. We are *scientists*. We are officers of the Government.'

'But I always carry my own pack,' said Lary, swinging it up by the webbing.

'So do I,' I said, with less conviction.

'Not here,' said Marcellin, detaching Lary's bergen from his back and replacing it on the ground. 'This is Africa. Part of the point of you is to give jobs to the people. My own servants, Nzé and Manou, they will not carry loads. My attendants – they are not bearers.'

'Well, it's not right,' said Lary. 'It's not democratic.'

'Democratic!' said Marcellin, with a genuine laugh. 'Democratic!'

The pygmies were barefoot, wearing cast-off shorts several sizes too big for them (held up with twine); they were all young men, quick in their movements, horribly fit. Disregarding the complicated adjustable strapping of the bergens, they tied lengths of liana to the shoulder harnesses, swung the loads on to their backs and carried the whole sixty pounds suspended from a loop over the top of their heads.

I followed the lead pygmy, half-hypnotized by the speed with which his legs were moving, by the small clumps of hairs on the backs of his calf-muscles, by his bare feet, splayed out at almost 45 degrees from his ankles, pat-patting along the hardly visible trail with such quick, short steps.

Trying to keep up, taking enormous strides, I slid across the dank scatter of leaves on the wet mud or pitched into thorny lianas or the flank of a buttress or tripped on the surface roots which radiated over the path from the boles of the largest trees. In the humid, unmoving air, the sweat began to ooze down my face from the band under my hat, the pale-brown flick-flick of the soles of the pygmy's feet began to blur, and I realized that to stay upright at all I must try and match my steps to his. Getting vaguely into the manic, mincing rhythm I managed to pull a water-bottle from its pouch, take a swig, replace it, wipe my face with my sleeve, and, now and then, risk taking my eyes off the track. We passed through stretches of forest in which the trunks of great trees towered straight up without tapering for sixty feet or more to the canopy above us, when their massive branches spread out almost horizontally until the furthest twigs stopped a few feet short of the neighbouring crowns; lianas looped and sagged and spiralled over them; ferns and epiphytic orchids grew wherever plant debris had lodged in their high forks; and every surface was patched with lichens. But it was not a dense forest. There were many gaps in the high canopy where the sunlight dappled down through the tops of saplings directly to the forest floor, and where, thinly scattered among the straggled shrubs of the understorey, I noticed that great rarity in a jungle, a flower in bloom (a mace of pale red spikes borne on a green stalk three feet high). There were occasional clumped patches of a single species of herb, perhaps an aroid, with stems ten to fifteen feet tall, each one rhubarbing into a gigantic leaf shaped like a flattened spear-point; and, every hour or so, we came across little clearings ringed with abandoned shelters, half-dome frames of bent saplings, some with their leaf cladding still in place, rotted brown and yellow, some skeletal, some charred, burnt black. What had happened, I wondered, trying to keep my thoughts off the pain in my legs as we left clearing number six (roof-leaves still attached) without a falter in the pace or a backward glance. Had the pygmies moved on because someone had died, as Turnbull, living with the Mbuti far away in the forest to the east, in Zaïre, said in *The Forest People* (1961)? Or was it simply time to make a new camp when the infestation of chiggers became unbearable, as the great French anthropologist Serge Bahu-chet, studying the ecology of the Aka in the forest to the north, in the Central African Republic, decided in *Les Pygmées Aka et la Forêt Centrafricaine* (1984)?

An hour later, confused, exhausted, as I was still trying to remember one more piece of information from Bahuchet, anything, there was a sudden overpowering stench, a mix of sweat, woodsmoke, excrement and burning fur. The path broadened, there was a clearing, a log to sit on, a lilting yodel and a thump of blood in my ears, a press of people moving in and out of focus, bare arms, breasts, loincloths, raffia skirts, men shaking my hand, a child running his little fingers across my sweaty forehead. We had arrived.

I took a steam-boiler pull of deep breaths, felt better, and stood up.

'Koko!' came a familiar voice behind me. 'Koko!' said Lary, with a ridiculous grin. 'Is anyone at home? Can I come in?'

The others appeared; only Lary, and the pygmy bearers, looked entirely unaffected by the forced march.

'Just in time,' said Marcellin. 'It's almost dark.'

'There are twenty-four shelters and one lean-to in this clearing,' said Lary.

'Water!' said Manou, collapsing onto my log. 'We need water!'

'The Chief of Mimbélou,' said Marcellin, sitting on a bergen, kneading his calf-muscles, 'he tells me his young pygmies speak Lingala. He allows them to study in his village school. They come top of the class! But then all the pygmies disappear, they go back to the jungle, sometimes for months. It's hopeless.'

Immediately to our right a young woman was sitting on a leaf mat at the entrance to her shelter: one leg folded under her, one extended towards us, she was naked but for a dyed-red raffia skirt and a necklace of tightly rolled red cloth. Her possessions were propped against the slightly projecting porch of arched-over saplings and leaf-thatch: two smoke-blackened gourds stoppered with leaves, and one wickerwork carrying-basket, with back-straps of plaited liana, big as a bergen. From the domed roof of the hut, no more than four feet high, patched with the huge leaves of the herb we'd passed in the forest, smoke seeped into the air and drifted up to join the communal band hanging beneath the great trees round the edge of the clearing.

Noticing my stare, she gave us a dazzling smile. I took off my misted glasses and smeared them cleaner on my shirt-sleeve. Nzé walked over, knelt down in front of her, cocked his head to one side, put his hands on her firm young breasts, and squeezed.

'Stop that!' said Lary, with a convulsive start forward. He jerked up his right arm as if to throw a punch, thought better of it, and took off his hat. 'This place,' he muttered, sitting down on Manou's log, 'I guess it's none of my business.'

Marcellin said to Nzé, wearily, in French, 'Don't do it. I've told you before.'

'But they love it, doctor!' Nzé stood up. 'Everybody knows. It means "You're beautiful."' He planted a sucking kiss on his right palm and then his left. 'It's the only way, doctor! It's the only way to say to a pygmy: "*You have wonderful breasts!*"'

'This is an official expedition,' said Marcellin. (Nzé, with his better eye, gave Lary a wink.) 'Nzé Oumar, I warn you, when you are with me, the leader of this expedition, you will treat these people with respect.'

'I am an official soldier of the People's Militia of Dongou,' said Nzé with a beguiling laugh, wiggling his buttocks like a dancing girl, 'and I tell you, Comrade Doctor, that these pygmies are not people. They live in the forest! They have no rights!'

'That must change,' said Marcellin, straightening his back, raising his voice.

'They don't exist!' yelled Nzé. 'They have no villages! They have no committees! *They have no Vice-Presidents!*' He pulled a packet of cigarettes from his pocket, tapped one on the box and lit up. His fingers were shaking with rage.

'So that's it,' said Marcellin, with a sudden grin. 'You've been at the stores. You're smoking the cigarettes. You're smoking the cigarettes that belong to the pygmies. That's their payment.' Marcellin said something in Lingala to one of the bearers, and to us: 'We must have water. And then we pitch the tents. And then, Redmond, you give out the presents!'

The young woman, laughing at us (everyone seemed to be laughing at us), reached into her hut, found a long stick, jumped up, pushed the thick end for a moment into the smouldering fire in the centre of the clearing, held up a flaming torch, and beckoned to us to follow her.

'Copal,' said Marcellin, as we filed after her under the dark trees. 'It's the resin from the tree. The pygmies collect it. It's valuable. You can sell it.'

'If I was that girl's husband,' said Lary in English, 'I'd put an arrow into Nzé. Right between the eyes.'

'Nzé is not an intellectual,' said Marcellin, stumbling over a root, 'he is not a scientist. He only says what everybody says. The Bantu – they think that pygmies are animals. They really do. But I myself, I don't agree. Me, I think the Bantu have had their revolution, they have freed themselves from slavery, from slavery to the white man. And now the pygmies – they must have their revolution, they must free themselves from slavery, from slavery to the Bantu!'

'I could do with a wash,' said Lary. 'I stink. I could do with a bathe.'

'You're in luck,' I said. 'Turnbull swears the pygmies in the Ituri always make camp by a clear stream. But it's true, he's a romantic. He talks about a "multitude of sounds" in the forest, "most of them as joyful as the brightly coloured birds that chase one another through the trees". I remember that bit.'

'A babbling brook,' said Lary. 'I could do with a babbling brook.' And then, 'Some babble,' he said, as the young woman held her torch over a small black pit, a muddy hole dug in the jungle floor. We lay down in turn, reached in and filled our water-bottles.

An old man, his frizzled hair and sparse, wiry beard grey-white, took Lary by the elbow and led him to the other side of the clearing, to a gap between shelters; with his thin arms he mimed cutting and bending saplings, pushing them into the ground, covering them with leaves: he wanted Lary as a neighbour.

So we pitched our tents, as instructed, and Nzé and Manou rigged their tarpaulins alongside the lean-to, a square roof of sapling-slats and leaves, sloping to the ground on the side towards the jungle, open on the others, and held up by three thin posts. The lean-to was for bachelors, said Marcellin, for the unmarried men who were waiting for a girl to grow up, or who were bad hunters, undesirable in some way, men who couldn't sing or dance or tell stories, or who were not strong like him, Marcellin, but weak, ineffectual – people, he feared, like his nephew, little Manou.

The old man fetched a half-burnt log from the fire inside his hut, three more from the big fire in the centre of the clearing, arranged them on the ground in front of our tent like the spokes of a wheel, piled an armful of sticks on the charred hub, squatted down, and, in two long breaths, presented us with flames. Pulling a leaf from the roof of his hut, he placed it near the fire, sat on it with both legs stretched out in front of him and looked at Lary, hard, like an anthropologist.

Nzé filled our cooking-pot with water and manioc-flour and hung it from a stick over the flames; we pulled up the kit-bags and sat on them; the old man stopped studying Lary, turned his head towards the other side of the clearing, and 'Beya!' he shouted with surprising force, 'Beya!'

A young man appeared from the wispy smoke, the moving shadows, the hubbub of voices – the pygmy I had followed in the forest, but transformed, masterful, wearing a red loincloth, his village tee-shirt and shorts discarded. He was carrying two leaf-bundles tied with liana-strips, and, sitting on the end of Nzé's kit-bag, next to the old man, he laid them on the ground, unwrapped one – it contained small black pieces of meat – and passed the other to Nzé.

Nzé loosened the neck of the leaf-bag and smelt inside. 'Honey!' he said, thrusting in his right hand, withdrawing a scoop, gobbling at his fingers. 'That's enough!' said Marcellin, grabbing the bag and giving it to Lary. Lary dipped in two stubby fingers, licked one – and dumped the honey-pot on my knees. With his left hand he groped in the right pocket of his jeans, found his torch and swivelled it on: a cluster of small black insects struggled feebly on his unlicked fingernail. 'Bees!' said Lary. 'I swallowed a buncha bees!'

'It's okay,' said Marcellin. 'Dark honey – the best! Mopani. The little bees that have no sting, the bees that like us, the bees that drink our sweat!'

'And these leaves?' I said, passing the pot to Manou. 'The herb we saw in the forest, the leaves they use for everything?'

'*Maranflacées.* Gorillas like them. They eat the shoots. Giant phrynium. I only know because Mike Fay told me – and he knows all the names of all the plants in the forest; but there again, that's only because the pygmies taught him.'

'So what's that big red flower on a three-foot stalk?'

Marcellin turned to Beya and talked in Lingala; Beya translated for the old man; a long discussion took place over the manioc and smoked antelope and honey supper in mess-tins and on Giant phrynium leaves; Marcellin, receiving a reply at last, said, 'They don't know. They have no use for it. So it has no name.'

Setting down his empty leaf-plate, wiping his hands on his loincloth, the old man slowly got to his feet and, with great seriousness, as if he had taken some difficult decision, put both hands round Lary's right wrist and stared into his eyes. 'Bakolo,' he said.

'Lary Shaffer,' said Lary, embarrassed, standing up, bending down. 'Pleased to meet you.'

'This old man is head of the group,' said Marcellin. 'Beya told me. And you might also call him their féticheur, the interpreter of messages from the world of spirits. He says that you, Lary, are not like other men, you could be a teacher, like him, because your ancestors, they are proud of you – your spirit-father is close to you.'

Lary disentangled himself from the old man's grip. 'Look – I'll get the kit-bag,' he said, putting a hand up to his forehead, rubbing his eyes. 'I'll get the bag of presents.'

So by the light of the big central fire and five smaller fires dotted round the ring of shelters, Bakolo and Beya (the master of the dance, said Marcellin) distributed the gifts – two packets of cigarettes for each man, a necklace of red, white and blue beads for every woman, loose glass beads (pierced marbles) for the children. Lary, sitting next to me on his bergen and with his right foot edging his half-full mess-tin towards the long (and intently pointing) muzzle of one of the small, floppy-eared, curly-tailed hunting-dogs, said, 'You should have brought something useful – gas lighters, Extencilline.'

Bakolo and a boy, perhaps his grandson, pushed four short Y-shaped poles into the ground in front of us at the corners of a rectangle, placed two cross-pieces on the notches and a layer of trimmed saplings across the middle.

'So what's this?' said Lary, intrigued by construction of any kind. 'A sleeping-platform? A smoking-rack?'

'It's for us,' said Marcellin. 'A bench.' (So we sat on it.) 'Beya says the pygmies go hunting tomorrow. With nets. But the place he has chosen is far away. And for a time the nets have been no good, barren, infertile. So tonight they will dance to persuade the spirits, to ask the spirits of the ancestors to drive game towards the hunters. Maybe a dance for the nets. Maybe something else, a new dance, to amuse the spirits. Who knows? Bakolo, he will decide. And as for you – he says you may sit and watch, or go to your tents and sleep. It's all the same to him. But whatever happens, you must not join in, you must stay still.'

Lary said, 'Thank God for that.'

'I am not well,' said Manou, getting up again, putting a hand over his shoulder, rubbing the top of his spine. 'My back hurts. I am ill. I must go to sleep.'

'I, too, am ill,' said Nzé, digging his elbow into Lary. 'I am ill because I need a woman.'

Children brought leaves and came and sat all round us, some of them still holding their big multicoloured (flecked and whirled) glass beads, the girls in raffia skirts, the boys in loincloths, one little boy wearing nothing at all and staring like a hare at Lary.

The women appeared from their huts, garlands of small green leaves tied round their waists, bunched out over their raffia skirts, rustling like stiff silk as they moved. One young mother carried her toddler slung tight against her side, a broad cloth sash running from her right shoulder, under her left arm, beneath the child's buttocks: he hung on hard to the edge of the sash with one hand, to the skin under her left breast with the other, and peered at Lary.

'You've got a better beard,' I said. 'You've got a better hat. You look like Butch Cassidy.'

'I stink,' said Lary. 'I feel like bullshit.'

A heavily muscled man with a raised scar on his right cheek, perhaps an old hunting wound, his loincloth arranged with a tail hanging down at the back, propped himself on the edge of a log some ten yards in front of us; between his knees he held a small drum, a tapered cylinder with skin both ends, lines of rolled twine stretched tight from one roundel of skin to the other.

The drummer shut his eyes, shook his head, opened his eyes, blew on his hands and began to play.

The women formed a circle, moving slowly one behind the other, picking up the drummer's fast, insistent rhythm only with the complex small steps of their bare feet, a dance that swayed their raffia and leaf skirts from side to side, a rippling undulation that matched the rise and dip of their high melodic song. The children set up a contrapunctual clapping, the men, over by the bachelors' lean-to, a low chant; it was both sophisticated and anarchic: an old woman, a band of cloth running tight beneath her armpits to hold her long breasts flat against her chest and stomach, wearing a cast-off wrap-around as a skirt, shuffled into the centre of the circle and began a private dance, her arms stretched out straight and down in front of her, her hands shaped to the head of an imaginary child.

There was a shout, the screams of running children, over by the far side of the clearing; from the darkness, from a hut set back behind the others, a tall grey figure entered the open space, and in front of it Bakolo walked warily, shaking a gourd rattle, directing its movements. The figure began to whirl, coming closer – by the light of the fire we could see that its feet were bound in barkcloth, that it wore red trousers beneath a skirt of leaves, that the top half of its body was wrapped in barkcloth, that it had no arms, that its eyes were big black empty sockets of bone, that its face was a gorilla skull.

With a violent sideways kick-step the figure spun towards the women; it wound itself down to its ankles and gyrated up again: in front of it, a high-pitched yodel echoing one to the other, the women scattered, regrouped, and strutted forward, stamping, legs apart, heads thrown back, crying out like the Monkey eagle.

The figure broke away, the women followed, and the dance repeated itself, retreating and advancing to the far edge of the clearing, when the spirit finally whirled into the darkness, and disappeared.

Bakolo, his job done, came and sat beside us, his scrawny chest heaving, his hands limp on his knees, the gourd rattle at his feet. The women resumed their circular dance, breaking into a lilting melody, a lullaby, the songs, maybe, that the boy Pharaoh, Pepi II, had so wanted to hear, the little people dancing under the great trees, the music, perhaps, of prehistory.

Beya, disrobed to his red trousers, the master of the dance, slipped out of the shadows between the sitting children and the curled-up dogs (and, I was surprised to see, a chicken, roosting on one leg); his chest and back oiled with sweat, shiny in the firelight, he took his place on the end of the bench next to Bakolo. The old man talked at him, hard, and when he had finished Beya leaned forward and spoke in Lingala to Marcellin, who turned to Lary: 'Bakolo says your spirit-father is close to you, he is proud of you, your father was proud of you when he was here in the forest. For this reason he, Bakolo, has worked hard for us – he has stopped a storm. When you want the rain, he says, it is easy – you take some leaves and throw them in water, and at once there is rain. But it's lots of work to stop a storm, you put leaves in a string round your waist and you think with all you know, with all your strength. It's like a fever in the head.'

'Please thank him,' said Lary, shifting from one thigh to the other. 'Thank him very much, if you don't mind. He wants cigarettes? Right?'

'Certainly not,' said Marcellin, offended on Bakolo's behalf. 'He means it. He's serious.'

On the other end of the bench Nzé, despite the sinuous circle of young breasts and raffia skirts and calf-muscles and bare feet not five yards away, was asleep, one leg tucked up under him, his head dropped forward on his chest, very like the roosting chicken.

'The dance,' I said, 'can they tell us about the dance?'

Marcellin, Bakolo and Beya conferred.

Lary said to me, 'I think I'm going to fall in love with these people.'

'I'm not surprised.'

'It's not what you think,' he said, staring, abstracted, at the dancing women, his elbows on his knees, the tips of his stubby fingers pressed together. 'It's their technology. It's so simple. All the transportation's done in their heads. You have to relocate? Fine. Just forget all your household goods and furniture and accessories, your leaf pots and pans, beds and chairs – and when you get where you're going, make yourself some more, and a house, too, while you're at it. Probably takes them half a day. It was one of the happiest times of my life, when I lived a bit like that, when I built myself a house in a wood, Acorn Bank, making simple things and solving problems, self-sufficiency . . .'

'The dance!' said Marcellin, pleased with himself. 'The name of this dance is Egnomo. Its origin is with the Kabounga pygmies to the north of the Likouala aux Herbes river. Beya walked there, through the forest, and in exchange for the knowledge of this dance he gave the Kabounga pygmies one hunting net.'

'But what does it mean?'

'That information! I have it too! The spirit of the dead, he came to drink palm-wine – but he drank too much, he was trapped, he was caught by the féticheur and carried back to the pygmy camp in the forest to entertain the people with his dancing. That is the way! That is the way I myself, I dealt with death – me, I agree with the pygmies, make death drunk, if you can, make him dance, make him fall down! Lary and Redmond, that is how I saved your lives, that is how I saved us, that is how I trapped the Commandant of the Militia of Manfouété, Simon Mbenga. I made him drunk, I made him dance, I made him fall down!'

'Correct,' said Lary, suddenly attentive. 'I sure as hell appreciate that. Thank you.'

'But this dance,' said Marcellin, lowering his voice, 'it is not to be confused with Ezengi, the Dance of the Dead. Ezengi – you must only dance Ezengi when someone has died, when someone is dead forever.'

The children began to drift away; the old woman left; Marcellin retired to his tent; even a dog uncurled and went off to sleep somewhere else; but the girl that Nzé had admired, and four of her friends, began a new dance, more sensual, more active: Nzé was right, she did have wonderful breasts, but she needed no one to tell her as she danced and sang and yodelled with her eyes on the unmarried men; she was smaller than the rest of the women, confident, happy, her life still full of the future.

Beya, unable to control himself a moment longer, bounded off the bench: tendons taut, muscles bunched, he half-crouched, elbows in, forearms out, palms up, knuckles bent: '*Booossa booossa booossa,*' he shouted. The girls laughed, moved close to him, redoubled their efforts. '*Aweeee-ow aweeee-ow aweeee-ow,*' they sang.

Nzé and the children were still asleep where they sat and stood, as though Zengi, Spirit of the Dead, had borrowed their souls.

'We're in the way,' said Lary. 'We're old. It's time to go.'

*

'What the hell are you muttering?' muttered Lary, as we lay in our tarpaulins, in the tent, in the dark, listening to the dance.

'It's a mnemonic. "On Old Olympus Towering Tops a Finn and German Pick Some Hops." The cranial nerves of the dogfish. Olfactory, Optical ... I've forgotten. Delayed shock, I expect. I can't sleep.'

'Strange but true,' said Lary. 'He can't get to sleep. And, as it happens, just for the record, I *don't* know the goddam cranial nerves of the dogfish.'

I switched on my torch, untied my bergen and pulled the sheaf of notes from the top-flap map-pocket. 'Ezengi – I'm sure that's the spirit Bahuchet talks about – the great forest spirit.'

'The dogfish and I never met. I did theatre studies, if you remember. I only changed to psychology, animal behaviour, because they let you play with more equipment. I'd had it with theatre lighting. In zoology they let you loose with film, and cameras ...'

'I made rough translations of all his stuff about pygmy beliefs. Here we are, I thought so – there are two spirit-fathers of humanity, Zengi, the elder, and Ziakpokpo, the younger.'

'Zengi's death, right? Like Father Time, with a scythe? Only I guess round here he has a machete. You see him. You croak.'

'I don't think so. Zengi commands the hunt. Zengi leads the perfect hunts in eternal life – from a camp in the forest just like this, a camp where the ancestors live, a camp swarming with women and children, all the lost children.'

Lary shut his eyes. 'So it's a gut-wrencher,' he said slowly. 'It's like that terrible story in Kipling. The one where the bereaved father, lost in the middle of a wood, finds himself outside a great house. The house is guarded by spearmen cut out of privet hedge. Inside lives a blind woman with psychic powers – all the locals know about her, but the father doesn't; the beautiful house and garden and wood are full of children playing – you see them waving from upper windows, you hear them laughing behind the fountain, you catch a glimpse of them running through the trees, but they're shy, out of reach. He sits by her fireside with his hand hanging over the arm of his chair – and the ghost of his dead child kisses his palm, a secret sign, part of a code they invented when the boy was alive.'

The drumming and singing outside grew erratic, faltered, and stopped.

'What about God?' he said. 'Do they have a God?'

'He's far away. Inaccessible. He's fixed in the sky with the sun, the moon and the stars – and the only link from sky to earth is thunder.'

'Anything else?'

'It's simple: earth emerged from water, drawn out and made by the sun. It's a thin flat layer with nothing underneath, covered by trees. And in a thin layer of this forest live men and spirits, the shades, the ancestors, the original men who were born at the creation of the world. They're the real owners of the jungle and you must treat them with respect – most of the time they mean well, but they can be dangerous.'

'They get you in the night?'

'Not in camp, not in the village in the forest. That's your private domain, the familiar space you take with you when you move to another camp, make another clearing, and the paths – they're safe, too, lines of ordinary life through the world of the spirits.'

'So what bugs them?'

'The least sign of neglect. You might be too tired to dance the night before a hunt. You might ignore some message sent by the sorcerer.'

'Redso.'

'Yes?'

'I have this problem.'

'Yes?' I said, awaiting some deep confidence. 'Tell me.'

'I just *can't* sleep with my boots higher than my head. I'm easy about this root in the small of my back but I surely can't sleep with my head down this hollow – would you mind? Could we swap sides? Would that be okay?'

'There's another spirit world out there,' I said, as we swapped sides. 'The spectral animals. They go for the children – if your daughter gets a fever, or your baby cries all the time, or your son can't sleep, that's because your wife has upset the spirit of a forest animal, she's crossed a spirit-track without making a gift of leaves.'

'You'd think they'd cut it out,' said Lary, trying to get comfortable. 'You'd predict that a people as sensible as the pygmies would act to minimize their anxiety levels. Or perhaps that's it – when you live this close to death, when your child's got yaws – I guess it helps to spread the fear around. Give yourself a whole bunch of little worries? Protect yourself from panic? Keep your mind off the big one?'

'The most dangerous of all the spirit-animals, the most risky to cross, is the little Golden mole, and as they live in tunnels underground it's difficult to see how you could avoid it . . .'

'So what do you do?'

'You make a fire. You add eight prescribed species of plants and lichens and fumigate your child, pass it through the smoke.'

'That stuff from Conrad, about your going to sleep, "do-nothing heroics" – what did that mean?'

'That? *Typhoon*. It's from *Typhoon*. A young officer in the worst of the storm puts so much energy into fighting his fear that he can't do anything else. He thinks he's unafraid, but he can't move, he's paralysed. It's a form of cowardice.'

'I see,' said Lary, as if some great worry had been resolved. 'That's all right then.' And he fell asleep.

19

The alarm-clock woke us at four in the morning; we ate bits of antelope and cold manioc stodge in the dark – and at dawn the first bees arrived. They settled on our sweat-salty shirts; they crawled down inside at the chest and the back of the neck; they tried to cluster in our armpits; and in a moment or two they were joined by others seemingly conjured from behind every shrub in the understorey, and by the stingless bees or mopani, a quarter their size and black, who came buzzing in close clouds around our faces and made their way into our hair, sucking at the corners of our eyes and mouths, at the mucus in our noses and the wax in our ears. We took off our shirts, hung them as near the fire as possible, cut switches from the miniature trees on the jungle floor (stiffer and better, said Marcellin, than bunches gathered from the broad-leaved ginger and acanthus and arrowroot herbs), and then tried not to let our arms touch our sides (stings in the armpit, said Marcellin, are almost as painful as stings in the crotch).

There was a yell from the trees immediately behind us, a child's shout. Beya grabbed a stick from the pile by the fire – when we caught up with him he was standing beside a little girl and her mother, and all three of them were staring at the ground, at the brown and black decaying leaves between the plank buttresses of a forest giant. As we watched, part of the pattern of leaves took an S-bend towards us, straightened and reared into the air. Lary and I moved back so fast we fell over each other. Beya struck with the stick.

'Forest cobra!' said Marcellin. 'He applies his fangs to your leg. He chews. Your nervous system is no longer in order. You die.'

'But he has no hood,' said Lary, pushing the limp, three-foot-long, brown and black body with the toe of his boot.

'His hood is small. He's slim. He's quick. He climbs trees!'

Lary and I decided that the sting of the African honeybee (he now had three swellings on his back and I had two under my left armpit) was no worse than that of the ordinary English or American honeybee, but no better; and that their foods in a pygmy camp were, in order of preference, the remains of their own honey (on discarded Giant-phrynium-leaf wrappers), the sugar in our tin (emptied before Nzé secured the lid), sweat, scraps of meat and dog faeces. Bees of some refinement, Lary noticed, they had no appetite for chicken droppings.

'Marcellin,' said Lary, as we shook the bees out of our shirts, 'I thought pygmies were hunter-gatherers. Why the chickens?'

'Diseases,' said Marcellin, strapping on his belt-kit. 'In the village it's diseases for men, diseases for chickens. So the *propriétaire*, the owner of a pygmy, he will say to that pygmy, "You and your family, when you go to live in the forest, you will take these chickens, my second-best cockerel and two hens, and they will stay with you and eat the food of the forest – and then if the diseases come and kill all the chickens in the village when you are away, we can start again when you return. We can have new chickens."'

Manou, resting his back, lay in the bachelor's lean-to; Nzé, sitting on our bench, said that he, too, had had enough of the forest for now, thank you, and besides, if all the men were leaving for a hunt it was obvious that he, Nzé Oumar, of the People's Militia, must stay behind to protect all the youngest and prettiest girls in camp.

So Marcellin, Lary and I set off in single file behind Beya, who in his right hand carried a long spear with a barbed iron point, and, suspended on split-vine straps from his bare shoulders, two huge bundles of liana-rope mesh hanging front and rear, a hunting net. The fearsome load had no effect on his habitual pace: I barely had time to notice the occasional spiky red flowers with no name seeming to hang disembodied in the gloom three feet above the jungle floor (waiting to be fertilized by what? Bees, butterflies, thrips?) and, beneath a great buttressed tree, a scatter of fruit like giant puffballs (but they were green), before the sweat began to run into my eyes, my glasses steamed up every time I lowered my head, and it took all my energy to avoid the sudden tangles of lianas with inch-long thorns, the twist of surface roots across the path, and to concentrate on Lary's boots, the tallest, sturdiest pair in L. L. Bean.

An hour later Beya stopped in a clearing, an opening made by the collapse of a massive tree, its surprisingly shallow root-mass (there was no tap-root) jacked out of the ground at right angles, the top of its rough circumference three or four feet above Marcellin's head.

With a start I realized that the clearing was full of people: men and boys sitting silent, impassive, their arms on their knees, their dark-brown skins matching the brown of the fallen leaves, the soft shadows. Their spears were leaning, point-up, against the surrounding trees; their nets, like inverted root-masses, hung from saplings cut off at pygmy head-height and trimmed into posts; and each net was crowned with phrynium leaves.

The women appeared behind us, mothers with toddlers slung to their sides, and the girls who had danced until dawn. The men and boys got up, swung their nets over their shoulders, collected their spears and moved off ahead; the women followed. A young boy, taking three attempts to lift a hunting net on to his head, was the last to leave. He looked out at us as he passed, his eyes big as an antelope's between the knotted dreadlocks of the net, his forehead still with the convex curve of childhood. He walked up the track (marked only by the odd bent-back twig or cut liana) in front of us, staggering slightly under his load. Lary said, 'We should help that kid. I'll carry his net.' 'Quiet,' whispered Marcellin over his shoulder. 'We must now be silent. Besides, for you it would be impossible. It is difficult.' A thought struck him and he swung right round. 'You'd catch yourself in it!' he shouted, delighted with the joke. 'You'd catch yourself!'

The soil grew wetter, the canopy lower, the thickets denser, the thorns more predatory, and eventually everyone halted. Nobody spoke; the men, weaving between the trees, unrolled the nets with surprising speed; with wooden pegs already tied to the mesh the women fastened the bottom lines to the ground and hooked the tops to bushes and shrubs and saplings; a three-foot-high fence of linked nets curved out of sight in both directions. Behind it, two or three yards back, the women sat and waited, half-concealed in the vegetation. Marcellin, Lary and I followed suit: fifteen yards away, on the other side of the net, a spearman stood almost invisible in the shadow of a thicket.

From the middle distance the sound of the beat reached us, a high-pitched yodelling; and ten minutes later a long-legged brown and white dog followed his muzzle out of the thicket, saw the net, realized he had overshot, wagged his long tail apologetically and plunged back in; the beaters shouted sharp instructions to the waiting spearman; a line of leaves flicked fast across in front of us; a woman yelled from somewhere down the nets to our right.

'Mosomé! Mosomé!' sang a little boy, running past us.

'The Bay duiker!' said Marcellin. 'Quick!' and we ran after the little boy – which was not as easy as he made it look: by the time Lary and I had disentangled ourselves from a hanging net of thorn lianas the woman and two hunters were pulling the antelope out of the real net. About three feet long, its coat a dark brown-red (with a black strip from head to tail along the spine), its hindquarters bulky, its back legs longer than its front, in shape it was a tapered cylinder, an antelope evolved for moving low and at speed through thick vegetation. The men rolled it kicking onto its back, the woman held its head stretched out by the ears – elliptical ears that were longer than the two little conical horns set between them; one man gripped its fetlocks; the other, with a small knife, cut away the left front leg, then the right. The antelope made a deep snoring noise and died only when the hunter opened up its chest.

Shocked, I said, 'You'd think they'd spear it first.'

The woman looked up and laughed happily.

'Yup,' said Lary, turning away from the blood on the ground, the division of the meat, the wrapping it in leaves. 'But I guess we were like that once. When our ancestors were hunter-gatherers. Before we took chickens seriously. Before farming arrived in Europe, 10,000 years before present. Not that long ago. I don't think you care for animals, as we might understand it, until you have to look after them, bring them up, treat them as surrogate children.'

Further down the line a small deer was struggling in the net, trying to stab down at the cords with little tusks in its upper jaw. Its body was about the same size as the duiker's, but its legs were much shorter and its yellow-brown coat was spotted and striped with white, like sunlight on the floor of a thicket. I recognized it at once – the Water chevrotain or Mouse deer, not really a deer at all, but midway in form between deer and pigs and much older than either, almost unchanged from its fossils of thirty million years ago, looking much the same lying on the grasses at our feet as it did six million years before grass itself evolved, 29.8 million years before *Homo sapiens sapiens* appeared.

Back in camp, Manou, his shirt off, was sitting on a thin log outside the bachelors' quarters, leaning forward, his elbows on his raised knees, his hands clasped tightly together. Bakolo held him by the left shoulder. A younger man, obviously under instruction, perhaps Bakolo's son, was squatting behind Manou and fiddling about in a dyed-red antelope-skin bag. 'It's okay,' said Manou, as if he was sure it wasn't. 'Bakolo will mend my back.'

From the bag the apprentice took a small knife (with a rusty blade); Bakolo gave the command; the apprentice pinched up a fold of Manou's skin from the base of his back, on the left side, and slit it. Bakolo pulled out a small horn, removed the leaf-stopper, tipped a smear of black ointment on to his finger and rubbed it into the cut. Two inches to the right they repeated the process. Manou's eyes glazed over.

Three small boys came over to watch – and to show us how good they were at bouncing and catching a white rubber ball. (They were Olympic standard.) 'Latex,' said Marcellin. 'They get it from a vine. Latex, me, I think that has been the cause of more suffering round here than anything else. It was not our fault. One day, when I am angry, I will tell you about it.'

Bakolo was supervising cut number eight when the drummer from the night before, the man with the scar on his right cheek, strolled out of the jungle carrying a crossbow in one hand and a monkey in the other.

'May I?' said Lary, taking possession of the crossbow.

The drummer shrugged, smiled, handed me the monkey and sat down on our bench.

'This bow is *heavy*,' said Lary, handling the rough wood as if it was a rare violin. 'I see. The lock is activated by pulling up this long underslung trigger . . .'

(The monkey's yellow-brown fur was warm and soft to the touch, its eyes brown, its fluffy whiskers yellow, its ears blue, its face blue with a white flash between the nostrils and upper lip, its hands and feet black, its long tail russet, its scrotum azure, its penis cobalt. '*Cercopithecus cephus*,' said Marcellin. '*Le Moustac*. The Moustached monkey.')

'. . . and that results in the lifting of this twisted vine bowstring out of its notch. Neat. Very neat. A really steady release . . .'

(The last ten inches of the underside of the Moustached monkey's tail were black-skinned, of the same texture as the palms of its hands and the soles of its feet, with lateral ridges for extra grip round a branch. Blood oozed from a puncture-wound in its stomach.)

'But wait a minute. *There is no groove to direct the bolts*.' Lary put the crossbow to his shoulder and sighted along it. The drummer pulled an arrow from a bag like Bakolo's slung over his shoulder and passed it to Lary.

'But it's not much longer than a pencil,' said Lary, turning it between his fingers. 'And half the diameter. And the flight – it's just one leaf, all in the same plane. How can you shoot with this? How can you shoot straight with a bolt like this?'

The drummer nodded his head and smiled.

Marcellin took Lary's wrist between his finger and thumb. 'You must give it back. It's poisonous. The monkey – he dies in two minutes! You scratch yourself – you die in ten. You suffocate. You can't breathe!'

So we surrendered the arrow, the crossbow and the monkey, and the drummer retired to his shelter.

Bakolo, evidently satisfied at last, put a hand to Manou's forehead. Manou, seeming to wake from a trance, stood up, tottered, turned round and gave us one of his enormous grins. 'That must hurt like hell,' said Lary, inspecting the fifteen small, soot-black and slightly bloody vertical slits across the base of Manou's back and the four cuts to each shoulder-blade. 'In fact I think it's safe to predict, Manou, your complaining days are over.'

Nzé appeared at the other end of the clearing, carrying our two plastic bottles full of water.

'Well done, Nzé!' said Marcellin. 'You went to the water-hole without an order. Well done!'

'Oh no I didn't,' said Nzé, refuting the accusation. 'It was Manou's fault.

I was hiding. Manou – he told the pygmies. He said my cock was sick. He said I was always sick in my cock. So I ran off, doctor. I didn't want to be cut up. Not down there! I don't want scars on my cock!'

Beya, back from the second hunt, and Bakolo, tired from his medical triumph, joined us round our fire for fou-fou and charred duiker (supplied by Beya). 'Lary, Redmond!' said Marcellin. 'Beya, he says a gorilla followed us back from the hunt. He followed us for a long way – Beya found his tracks, right on top of ours. An old male.'

'Why would he do that?' said Lary, spooked.

'Curiosity. They're curious. Besides, he'd never seen white men. He thought, "Aha! There go two spirits of the dead. And they *smell*."'

'I certainly *feel* like a spirit of the dead,' said Lary, picking at the white splodge of fou-fou in his mess-tin.

I said, 'Do they smell? The spirits of the dead?'

Marcellin put it to Beya, who asked Bakolo.

'He tells us,' said Marcellin. 'Bakolo tells us that the spirits of the dead can enter the animals – they can take the form of a leopard or a bushpig or a hornbill or even a fungus. But to see them then, to know them – for that you must be a sorcerer, you must be initiated, that is a great skill, very difficult. On the other hand, spirits take a smell with them, like a shadow, and this smell – it can be recognized by everyone.'

'What kind of smell?'

Marcellin put it to Beya, who asked Bakolo; and the answer rippled back round the semi-circle.

'A smell like no other.'

Late that night, in the tent, the camp outside full of laughter and stories and snatches of song (the second and third hunts had netted seven more antelope), I looked up the Water chevrotain or Mouse deer in Haltenorth and Diller. It has odd habits for a deer: it browses on the leaves of low bushes, as you might expect, and eats seedlings and fallen fruits; it swims and dives well; but it will also climb trees if there is a liana or two to give it a hoofhold and it takes small animals and insects and catches fish in forest streams. And, come to that, the forest duikers (the oldest of all the antelopes, yet with the largest brain to body-weight ratio) are hardly normal, as antelopes go; secretive, they live in thick cover, and little is known about their habits except that both sexes defend their territory, they have one calf a year, eat leaves, fruits, shoots, buds, seeds and bark – and sometimes hunt small birds and rodents and even feed on carrion.

'These pygmies,' said Lary, lying flat out with his boots on and staring at the patch of reflected torchlight on the blue ceiling, 'the Babinga, do they have their own language? What's your Bahuchet got to say about that? Beya and Bakolo – can the Bantu understand them?'

'The Bantu call them Babinga, but their own name for themselves is Bayaka. The usual story goes like this: the pygmies are the original inhabitants of the forest, they've been here since mankind evolved. Around 5000 years ago, when the primitive Bantu farmers and fishermen first moved up the rivers, the pygmies retreated to the forest heartlands. But they gradually developed a symbiosis with the Bantu, trading meat for cultivated roots and fruit, and in the process they became slaves or serfs or vassals, and lost their language. But Bahuchet won't have it. He says that if you discount Turnbull's Mbuti far to the east (quite different) and the Twa way to the south and west (they're *fishermen*), you're left with a group of pygmies in the Oubangui –Sangha, the Aka, living in 100,000 square kilometres of forest – and throughout this whole vast area they understand each other; they may speak different dialects but they understand each other. And when you think that in this same forest there are twenty-two different ethnic groups of *Grands Noirs*, the Bantu that the pygmies consider to be marginal men, freaks living on the very edges of the world of true humanity, and that all *their* languages are mutually incomprehensible . . .'

'That's great,' said Lary, pulling at his moustache. 'That's a distraction.'

'But the pygmy language – it's still part of the Bantu group. So Bahuchet thinks the pygmies split away at some very early stage – moved into the jungle proper. And much later in came the original Bantu, moving south and east. But in the meantime the pygmies had adapted to the great forest, grown smaller, like the duiker and the Mouse deer . . .'

'Great,' said Lary.

'What do you mean, a distraction?'

'I have a recurrent daydream to dispel,' said Lary, rousing himself, unlacing his big boots. 'It'll help me think about something else for a moment or two. I've been torturing myself – you know, what you're not meant to do. I'm with Chris, the best, most sensible, most capable girl in the United States of America, where it seems to me I used to live a very long time ago – and which, as I see now, too late, is *the most desirable country on the whole goddam earth*.'

'Yes?'

'In Burlington, Vermont, there's a Chinese restaurant. The Silver Palace. Now, this restaurant has some of the trappings of an old movie theatre and some of the trappings of a Chinese restaurant. I'm thinking, in particular, of the flock wallpaper. Chris and I are in there together and we're eating the Hunan country chicken, a sort of a deep-fried chicken with glazing you crunch through. After that we have Ben and Jerry's Ice Cream. Ben and Jerry's gone national, you know. There are more cows than people in Vermont. And when we've finished we start over. And then we start over again, only with the addition of a spring roll and fried rice. And at no point in this whole meal does anyone – but anyone – so much as mention the possibility that human beings, anywhere on earth, would actually go ahead and eat something as one hundred per cent noxious and totally barfsome as *manioc.*'

As I fell asleep I wondered if we'd see (on the journey across the watershed? On the walk to Lake Télé?) any of the special animals that Bahuchet lists, the taboo animals that no pygmy mother or father – from the first signs of pregnancy to the child's first steps – must eat. Way out in the forest we'd meet, maybe, one of those animals that you pull from their womb-like retreats with your hands: the Small-scaled tree pangolin (a long-tailed and long-snouted anteater covered in scales like a fir-cone) or the Tree hyrax (very like the common ancestor of the horses, tapirs, rhinoceroses, hippopotamuses and elephants, which is the size of a rabbit, lives in trees, and, on moonlit nights, screams like a baby). Or perhaps we'd flush one of the forbidden animals that live in holes underground, a Giant pangolin or an aardvark? Or catch a glimpse of something altogether too close to the world of ghosts, half-animal, half-bird, the Flying squirrel? Or see or smell any of the forest cats that are, presumably, a real danger to children – the leopard, the Golden cat, or the two common species of genet, the Servaline and the Large-spotted? But most of all I wanted to see one of the final category of proscribed animals (those, like Lary and me, and many monkeys and small antelope, with white, the colour of the spirits, on their faces): the Bongo, the largest known forest antelope, deep chestnut with vertical white stripes on its flanks (and a white chevron between the eyes) living in the densest cover, near water, whose chief delight is to wallow in mud-holes and rub itself on tree-trunks. And it was the Bongo that jumped the nets, jinked brown and white through the back-curved barbs of flying spears, and outran the poison ends of airborne pencils through my dreams.

20

We left as the camp cockerel began to crow and a Speckled tinkerbird, a tiny barbet that seemed to live in the tree above the bare patch of ground that had been our home, went off like a rundown alarm-clock, *tick-tick ticktick-ticktick-tick*. Six hours later, exhausted, we arrived back on the right bank of the Motaba river opposite Mimbélou, Beya gave a hooting call for the fisherman to ferry us across in his dugout, and we made our way up the slipway path to the Chief's hut.

I bought two chickens, three pineapples, a coconut and a bunch of bananas from the Chief's three wives, and paid off our bearers. In front of the Chief – or perhaps simply because they were in the village – the pygmies seemed diminished; even Beya, whose knowledge and prowess in the jungle, I realized, had made me see him as a giant, appeared to have lost his confidence, shrunk in stature, regained his pygmy height. Manou went to fetch water from the river; Nzé, on the dried mud in front of the hut, began to prepare our supper: he flattened the first chicken under his knee and swiped its head off with his machete, while the second, tethered by the leg a yard away, looked on, nonplussed. As we made to follow the Chief, at his insistence, for a stately tour of his village, I noticed a big Bantu with a wisp of a beard detach himself from the circle of onlookers and take all the notes from Beya's hand.

We admired the big cleared sandy compound of the school, the school hut with its rough-hewn desks and benches and a blackboard, and the school garden, fenced with palings, laid out with plots of manioc and pineapples and plantain cuttings.

'The pupils in my village are happy,' said the old man, swatting a big blue biting fly on the side of his neck. 'The schoolmaster is happy. But we have no pens. We have run out of pens. How can our children learn to write – if we have no pens?'

Lary twisted his signet ring, tugged at his moustache – and from the breast-pocket of his shirt he produced two of his three remaining biros and presented them to the Chief of Mimbélou.

In return, the Chief of Mimbélou, round the back of a big hut, introduced us to his younger sister. Hidden behind a raffia-palm-frond screen, she sat on a log under an open shelter, smiling, wrinkled, almost toothless (one incisor in the upper jaw, two in the lower), ladling water, with a gourd-bailer, from half a fuel-drum at her feet up to a wadding of cloth tied round two drainpipes declining past her head.

'It's a still!' said Lary. 'That is one real hillbilly piece of goddam engineering!' He stepped closer. 'Jack Daniels,' he murmured, as if in private prayer. 'Early days.'

Oblivious of the heat, he peered at the top of the big container on its metal stand above the fire. 'One forty-five-gallon gasoline-drum cut in half. Maize-mash. Top sealed on with beeswax. Two galvanized condenser pipes. Three feet long. One-and-a-half-inch diameter. A V-reed in the pipe terminals combines and focuses the alcohol into her jar – and that's all there is! This is the earliest, simplest still . . .'

The Chief spat. 'The schoolmaster, he says this is against the law.'

Marcellin shrugged. 'Laws like that – they apply in the capital.'

Completing our tour, in a shelter by the Chief's hut we handled the ritual mace, a heavy wooden club pointed at one end, carved into a head, neck and outstretched arms at the other; and we stroked the sides of the signalling drum, a section of hollowed-out tree-trunk, shaped like the middle of a dugout, with rounded ends, four legs and two long carrying poles.

And that night, after a supper of chicken and fou-fou, sitting in the Chiefly chairs, we drank palm-wine (sickly sweet) and maize-alcohol (sickly sharp) as Marcellin, the Chief and the boatman talked and joked in Lingala and French. 'This boatman,' said the old Chief, wiping his lips with the back of his hand, bringing the conversation to a close, 'he has a small motor in his boat and a big motor in his trousers.' The Chief withdrew through a plastic curtain to his wives in the inner rooms, and, drunk, we climbed on to our wooden sleeping-platforms. 'Maize-alcohol,' said Lary, as the mosquitoes fed on our faces. 'Single Mimbélou Malt. A Splayside. The Glenstrip-your-epiglottis-right-out. The Glencirrhosis. The Glenskullcracker. The Glendroop. The Glen KO.' And he lost consciousness.

The next day, five hours upriver, around noon, the boatman put in to a break in the jungle on the right bank, a small slipway with one dugout pulled up on the shore. On the mud at the water's edge hundreds of butterflies were feeding: little butterflies like Chalkhill blues, grey-speckled whites – Congo whites – and two species of swallowtail: one, its wings blotched and streaked with iridescent green on black, held them in a V as it sucked; the other, its wings orange-scarlet on brown, flicked them open and shut, flashing half-inch flames across the shine of mud.

Marcellin jumped out and strode up towards a hut on the left (each step of his white trainers marked by a fresh puff of butterflies). 'Why stop here?' said Lary. 'We were on the fly!'

'On the fly?'

'On the move. Getting the hell out. Going well.'

'Dr Marcellin must make a visit,' said Nzé, picking the shotgun off the duckboards and splashing ashore. 'A very important man lives here. A Big Man.'

'Our uncle lives here,' said Manou, uncurling himself from the bow. 'He's famous. And for us your uncle, your mother's brother – he's more important than your father. He's the head of the family.'

'Today we eat well,' said Nzé, as we followed him over the mud.

'What happens here?' I said. 'Why all these butterflies?'

Nzé stopped. 'You really don't know?'

'Know what?'

'This is where the meat is washed.' Nzé grinned. He put his left hand under his right armpit, and, fist clenched, forearm bent to a right-angle, he snapped his right upper arm to his ribs with a sharp clap. 'Here you will have a big surprise. In Makao – a bigger surprise. And for the biggest of all, a surprise big enough to kill us – for that you will go to Lake Télé!'

Marcellin emerged from the hut with a man shaped like a Gurkha; the Gurkha (wearing grey trousers rolled up to the knee, a green army shirt and a wide-brimmed camouflage hat) watched our approach, expressionless.

Nzé slowed his pace and lowered his voice. 'Dr Marcellin – he is a Big Man in a Ministry, all the elephants, they are in his care. But his uncle, our uncle, he is a bigger man. He kills the elephants. He is a famous hunter, he is the biggest poacher in the forest!'

'Nzé,' said Marcellin with quiet menace, 'you will fetch the sardines. Here we eat fou-fou, and sardines.'

Nzé's forehead furrowed in the middle, he opened his mouth, his lips drooped at the corners. 'We'll buy meat – for later?'

'No. We will not buy meat. Here we eat fou-fou, and sardines.' Nzé shuffled back down towards the dugout and the stores.

We shook hands with the uncle; two pygmy boys fetched stools from the hut; a young Bantu woman placed a gourd of palm-wine and six enamel cups in the centre of the circle and withdrew; Nzé, sunk in a meatless despondency, returning with the food sack, filled the mess-tins and an extra bowl with fou-fou and one sardine apiece; and Marcellin and his uncle began to argue.

'I have conducted a survey of Forest elephants,' said Marcellin in French, for our benefit. 'A Government survey. There are very few elephants left.'

The uncle gave us his first smile. The skin on his face was oddly smooth, unwrinkled, his cheeks rounded like the leather panels on a football. He spread his disproportionately large, heavily muscled hands. 'The forest is full of elephants.'

'It's the same small group. They wander through the forest – from here to the Gabon and back again.'

'But I have many large tusks, many points.'

Marcellin switched to Lingala, his voice rose in pitch, he chopped at the air with his right hand – and began to speak in a language we had never heard before, full of plosives and gutturals. Marcellin's uncle, a figure of authority, used to respect, leaned forward on his stool, goaded by some unexpected, outrageous, inexplicable impertinence, and, as you might attempt to discipline a dog, he shook his finger in Marcellin's face.

Nzé, seeing his cousin and his uncle so absorbed, drained his cup, grabbed the gourd from its stand, filled his cup, drained it, and filled it again. Feeling better, his good humour bubbling back up from his stomach, he took shy Manou's cup and filled that, too.

Lary and I held our own cups defensively between our knees, sealed with both hands. 'It's no good looking at me like that,' said Lary. '*You* were the one who gave away the whisky.'

'Nzé,' I said, 'what language are they speaking?'

'Kaka. The language of Makao. Manou and me, we don't understand it. We speak Munoocouto, the language of Impfondo, a proper language.'

A big hut stood opposite us, perhaps a storehouse, its broad palm-thatch roof supported on an outer wall of wattle-and-daub, the entrance to the inner wall a massive wooden double-door; to the left of the storehouse was a latrine hut, a low mud wall beneath an open shelter; and between the two was a large fig tree; and in the fig tree were bouncing, running and hopping blues and yellows and chestnuts: a party of five Blue plantain-eaters, as big as pheasants but absurdly agile. As I watched, a bird ran along a branch, bobbed its blue, black-crested head, fanned its yellow tail and its glossy black wings (displaying its chestnut belly) and, with a couple of flaps, launched into a glide, mewing like a buzzard as it went, and turning itself, as it lost height and its back became visible, into one long shaft of disappearing blue.

'Lary,' said Marcellin, 'you may now take photographs of elephant tusks.' Marcellin and his uncle, their argument apparently settled, stood up, and we followed them into the hut.

The uncle sat on a low stool: an enormous shiny brown tusk curved up to either side of him, the roots by his broad feet, the tips resting against the wall a foot above his head; two more, ringed with black near their bases (perhaps they had been hidden, buried for a time), made a low arch past his ankles. Three pages from a magazine, illustrations of telescopic sights and large-calibre rifles, were nailed to the mud wall above his head. A dark-spotted skin with a black-ringed tail, flanked by two small tusks, was pinned up spreadeagled to his right (a Servaline genet, said Marcellin) and, to his left, nails stretched out the skin of a grey cat with a bushy tail (the kind of Golden cat you find in the forest, said Marcellin).

Lary took the portrait, and two more of Nzé and Manou (who insisted on posing between such potent trophies, such testimonies to their persever-ance and courage); we shook hands, returned to the dugout, found the boatman asleep under an Umbrella tree, woke him up, and set off for Makao.

The river narrowed; the beds of floating grass, water-hyacinth and papyrus grew less extensive; the thick vegetation of well-defined banks replaced the stands of raffia-palm. We passed the occasional Long-tailed cormorant stand-ing on the bare branch of a half-submerged tree, its wings spread to dry, or already swimming for the covering overhang of shrubs and bushes – showing us only its black neck and head, its yellow bill, the bare red skin of its face, its ruby eye. And for the first time I began to notice two tame, quiet little birds of the river-bank: an ash-grey flycatcher, the size of a hedge-sparrow, skulking in the mesh of trailing lianas (Cassin's grey, said Serle and Morel) and a larger species, the White-browed forest flycatcher, who was always preoccupied, on duty, watching ephemerae from a perch on some horizontal branch over the water, making routine flights out through the low-level swarms of hatching flies and back again.

'Red-headed lovebirds!' said Lary, tugging at my sleeve as two small parrots green-blurred across the river, above the trees. Black-collared lovebirds, said Serle and Morel – the only lovebirds with green heads, the only lovebirds of primary rainforest. 'Okay,' said Lary. 'I don't want to screw you over with this nineteenth-century natural history thing of yours – but the fact is that Red-headed lovebirds are *theoretically* interesting, *scientifically* significant. W. C. Dilger did this really elegant, simple experiment: the Red-headed lovebird carries nest material tucked between the feathers of its tail, some other lovebird carries nest material in its bill. Dilger got the two species to interbreed – the hybrids carried some in their bills, some half-tucked into the tails, where it fell out. This suggests there's a large genetic component in their behaviour. Fair enough. But that doesn't mean I go along with your nine-teenth-century guys Francis Galton and Karl Pearson and their twentieth-century followers, Burt in England and Henry Goddard, Stanley Hall and Terman in the States. Burt's father was Galton's GP and young Burt sat on old Galton's knee, so I guess that excuses him. But in my opinion, for what it's worth, I think it's time we all admitted that Terman was an intolerable little racist jerk. That everything to do with intelligence tests is bullshit. That we can all go on learning, all the time. That it's never hopeless. That if you take someone's Intelligence Quotient – a lousy test standardized on white middle-class Americans – if you multiply that by a hundred to get your whole number and then divide by their chronological age, *everyone* will become stupid as they get older. You'll wind up dividing by seventy or eighty. We all become morons!'

'Lary, what's this? What's up?'

'This place. The Congo!' He took his hat off, held it by the brim, turned it round and round between his hands. 'Education. That's all that's needed round here. Good teaching. Not by off-the-wall Marxists and post-breakdown missionaries full of news from the Middle Ages. Sensible teaching, by people like me. And a little engineering. That's all.'

(A pair of heavily built, all-black birds with squared-off tails, the size of thrushes – weavers? drongos? – crossed the river with an irregular dipping flight and disappeared into a thicket of reeds to our left.)

'Mendl meant well. He found one small corner of the story. Not the whole thing, not by any means. Genes are turned on and off by factors in the environment; we can all develop; it all matters. Lots of studies support my case – Skeels's work in the Iowa State orphanage, for example: in the 1930s it was a garbage can for problems, kids were just dumped in there. But two very young girls, nine months old, victims, hopeless, little vegetables – they were too damaged even for the orphanage, so Skeels had them offloaded, stuck in a mental hospital. Now the mental hospital was full of deprived adults, inmates bored out of their skulls – and those inmates fussed over the tinies. Those tinies suddenly had mothers and fathers and aunties and then some, like you wouldn't believe – and in six months they were fine, perfectly normal children. Skeels noticed; he got permission from the State authority to place the worst orphanage cases, those with an IQ around sixty-four, into mental hospitals; and he kept a control group, those with an IQ of eighty-five/eighty-six, in the orphanage. One-and-a-half years later the hospital kids were up around ninety and the orphanage kids had dropped to seventy. Skeels finally concluded his study in the 1960s – he tracked down all his former charges, every single one: those who'd spent their childhoods with all that stimulation in a mental hospital were leading normal middle-class lives; those who'd been dumped in an orphanage were washing dishes, they'd never married, they were at the bottom of society. So genes don't cause everything; the IQ is not a measurement of something innate; the first five years don't matter all that much – it all matters! We can change, develop, keep learning. It all matters!'

'*What's* the matter?' said Marcellin, from behind us, taking off his head-phones.

Lary turned round, still holding his hat in his hands. He said, '*I just do not believe that intelligence tests measure a fixed ability.*'

Marcellin looked hard at Lary, decided, obviously, that the environment had got to him, replaced his headphones, shook his head and shouted, 'Neither do I! Don't panic! It's okay!'

21

Late in the afternoon we came to a pool in the curve of a bend, a break in the trees, three dugouts beached on a slipway of red mud and one broken dugout turned hull-up in the shallows.

'Makao!' said Marcellin with uncharacteristic excitement. 'We're here! This is it!'

The little path led up to a broad laterite street, a line of thatched wattle-and-daub huts to the left, an open space and a school hut to the right. 'Marcellin! Marcellin! Dr Marcellin!' chanted the children; women waved; a girl kneeling outside her hut, rubbing a manioc tuber back and forth on a wooden grating-board, got to her feet and put a hand to her hair; everybody knew him.

'The guest hut!' said Marcellin, sliding off his pack in front of a cement-wash building with a narrow veranda and an overhanging roof of corrugated iron. 'Makao!'

Nzé and Manou laid out their tarpaulins on the mud inside; Marcellin, Lary and I put up our tents on the mud outside; the children watched, the Bantu in ragged tee-shirts and shorts and wraparounds, the pygmies in loin-cloths and raffia skirts. One little boy (a fist-sized swelling on his belly-button) held a miniature crossbow pointing arc-skywards on his shoulder and looked at us with unsmiling dignity, as befits a hunter; a younger child, wearing a pair of blue dungarees several sizes in advance of his years, straps held in place by one shiny brass button to the left, one wooden toggle to the right, kept shadow-close to Lary and stared at his hat.

Makao looked odd, I decided, unfamiliar, something was missing. Fronted by the occasional oil-palm, the great trees of the forest pressed close in on us, they towered straight up behind the parallel lines of huts – there were no compounds, I realized, no gardens.

To our left, nine brown goats with floppy ears lay sprawled on the hot laterite; beyond them we could see the centre of the village, marked by the conical thatch of an open-sided shelter, the talking-house. Directly opposite our tents stood a solitary hut, with no neighbours for a hundred yards to either side. The central patch of darkness in its doorway detached itself and began to walk towards us.

The children watched for a moment, retreated backward in silent disorder, turned, re-formed into a gaggle, and ran off up the street – the goats scrambled upright in kicks of dust, coalesced into a herd, and bobbed along behind them.

'Dokou!' said Marcellin. 'I have wine for you!'

'Red wine?' said the old man, in a voice deep and cracked, lowering himself onto a bench against the veranda wall. He wore black boots, black trousers, an open-necked black shirt; in the open neck of the black shirt a goitre shifted like a bag of giblets; beneath the goitre, tied to a necklace of string, were three little bundles of fur, the shape of House mice, hanging by their necks.

'Wine?' said Lary.

'Dokou,' said Marcellin, sitting down beside the old man and putting a hand on his knee, 'I've carried it all the way from Brazzaville. It's hidden in my pack. It's for you! Cavesco! Red wine from Spain! The best!'

Manou and Nzé dragged another school bench out of the hut and sat on it, expectant.

'Tobacco?' said Dokou, covering Marcellin's hand with both his own and staring into Marcellin's face with intense and bloodshot eyes. 'Tobacco?'

'The white men have a pipe for you, and tobacco from England, from far away.'

'Koko!' said a fat, middle-aged man in dirty white shorts and singlet, slapping the veranda pillar.

Dokou looked up, put his right hand briefly over his eyes, and got to his feet. 'Later,' he said to Marcellin, over his shoulder. 'Tomorrow. In the dark.' And, with surprising vigour, he made off across the street to his hut.

The fat man leaned on the pillar and smiled at Marcellin. 'One day,' he said, 'someone will harm your Dokou. Someone with greater powers. I'll swear to it.'

Marcellin was silent.

'But for now Marcellin Agnagna – tomorrow night, you will come and see me before you see him. I have pains in my back. I need your medicine.' And he, too, turned and left.

'Who was that?' said Lary. 'The Sheriff?'

'The Chief. The head of the largest group of families in Makao, the most important lineage. We must do what he says. We need his pygmies.' Marcellin rose and picked up his pack. (Nzé, head to one side, considered it, as a one-eyed fox might consider a chicken.) 'It's late. We must eat. Tonight – sardines. Tomorrow – saka-saka! Pineapples! Women! Sugarcane!'

We carried the benches inside and placed them in the centre of the hillocky mud floor. Termite passageways curved up the walls like the brown stems of old ivy and disappeared into the wooden beams, the ragged palm-thatch of the roof. Two square window-holes, in the back wall, gave straight on to a giant clump of bamboo. 'I don't know anyone here,' said Manou, folding down on to his tarpaulin as if he'd been shot – hit perhaps by the desolation of the room, or the acid smell of the bat-droppings, or maybe the thought of Dokou's presence so close across the street. 'I've got malaria. I'm not well. I don't *know* a woman at Makao. I've never been so far from everyone I know.'

'Neither have I,' said Lary, with feeling.

Marcellin laughed.

'Leave it to me,' said Nzé, squatting on the floor, unfolding the legs of the camping-stove. 'Manou Jean-Felix Burono, I, Nzé Oumar, swear by the spirit of my grandfather at Dongou, and also on this cooker' – he lit it – 'to find you a young girl for tomorrow night, a girl who won't make you nervous, a girl who's young and shy, a girl with breasts like palm nuts?'

'I miss my wife,' said Manou, picking at the tarpaulin with his right hand. 'Vivie Charlotte. And my son, little Manou, Manou Prince.'

'Perhaps I should send you away,' said Marcellin, his back to Manou, unpacking the last of the sardine tins from the food-sack. 'The boatman leaves tomorrow morning – maybe you should go with him. It's your last chance.

'The path through the forest to Berandzoko – that's hard. Days and days. And it's not marked, you must keep up with the pygmies, if you're slow you're lost, the leopards will have you. And who knows? Maybe at Berandzoko there's no pirogue. They're poachers and farmers, they don't fish. So we might be trapped.'

'Here,' said Lary, spreading Manou's mosquito-net out from a hook in the wall, 'let's get this up properly. And now come and sit by me. Have a barfball. Be my guest.'

The light began to fade; a heat-haze of mosquitoes vacillated in the windows. Nzé stuck two candles in the floor, placed a saucepan of water for coffee on the stove, and we addressed ourselves to the manioc stodge in our mess-tins.

'Marcellin,' said Lary, 'I've been worrying it over. The centrifuge at Manfouété – how did it get there?'

'I know all about that,' said Marcellin, peeling the lid off a tin of sardines. 'It's not a pretty story. The first white men, Frenchmen, they came up those rivers in 1901 – to begin with they contented themselves with making trading stations, they paid for their ivory with the things we needed, axes and hoes and machetes, cloth and salt, beads for the women – and later with spirals of iron and brass wire. But then they wanted latex, rubber. Well, that was different – it's boring, no one wants to collect rubber, there's no point to it. The trees you have to tap grow far apart from each other, deep in the forest. No one bothered. So in 1902 the French on the Ibenga said they'd tax everyone at three francs a year. You had to earn your three francs by giving the French ivory or rubber or meat or by serving as a porter, you had to leave your plantation for weeks at a time, your children might starve. So no one paid the tax. The French, they recruited soldiers and built prisons at the trading stations and took the Chiefs hostage, and women and children too. They beat the Chief Macpo to death with sticks. In revenge, the French agent, Livry, he was killed and eaten. We organized. We went to war. We made our headquarters at Berandzoko. It's fierce that village, believe me – Berandzoko, it wasn't recaptured until 1908! We burnt down the trading stations – and the traitors, the Africans who'd joined the French, we hacked them to pieces with our French machetes!' (Marcellin cut the air with the flat of his hand.) 'Schick! Schick! Schick!'

'Bohmaaa!' yelled Nzé.

Manou looked at the floor.

'And the centrifuge?' said Lary.

'That I do not know,' said Marcellin. 'The centrifuge, that is a mystery.'

Nzé lobbed one palmful of coffee powder, two palmfuls of milk powder and half a slab of brown sugar into the saucepan.

'It's a horrible little story,' said Lary. 'Plain nasty. There's no excuse.'

'Better than the English,' said Marcellin. 'If you're going to be colonized – let it be the French.'

'Why?'

'Because they liked us! They liked us for ourselves. They married our women. They had mistresses, black mistresses, lots of mistresses. They didn't make cricket clubs and snob clubs and bring their white women to Africa and set themselves apart. They even told us we were citizens of France – and that was something, even if they didn't mean it. They liked us, they wanted to live here forever. And besides, they almost understood, they think they believe in reason, the French, but they don't – I tell you, Lary, there are more astrologers than priests in France. And just think how many priests there are! So that's two big groups of Frenchman who believe in magic. And what are priests and astrologers? Eh?' (Marcellin pressed his face within six inches of Lary's. Lary shut his eyes.) 'Can you tell me? No? Sorcerers! They're sorcerers!'

'Okay,' said Lary, opening his eyes. 'That's okay.'

'Me, I don't believe in sorcery. I don't like it, I think that once you start, you can't stop. I'm a scientist. I think more like an Englishman. I know that when we die we go to the ground to rot. But that's not what they think in France, and it's not what they think in Makao.'

Early in the morning I crept out of the tent and round to the back of the guest hut, clutching my precious roll of lavatory paper in its green waterproof bag; behind the bamboo-clump stood one of the multiple-stemmed trees we had seen in Impfondo, its foliage as dark and dense as yew, its lower branches curving right down to the ground. Inside their protective circle, lines of light radiated across the jungle floor like stripes on the flank of a Bongo. It was the safest of childhood dens, I decided, a place where no nightmare could take you unawares.

We finished the fou-fou (and the last of the sugar for the coffee); Nzé strode off whistling, to begin the long and arduous selection process, the all-day interviewing to appoint a mistress for the night; we left Manou in the hut to guard the bergens and set off to the river for a swim and a wash.

Women (barefoot, in bright wraparounds) coming up the red laterite path with plastic or zinc bowls or buckets full of water balanced on their heads, the tendons tight in their long necks, swapped restrained Kaka badinage with Marcellin as they passed; women on the way down with us, their empty vessels in their hands, shrieked with laughter at Marcellin's suggestions and greetings, clucked their tongues, tossed their heads, slapped their long thighs: Marcellin was even more desirable in this far place than he had been in Brazzaville; Marcellin was a Big Man at Makao.

'Can you imagine anything more stupid?' said Lary, walking beside me in his boots from L. L. Bean. 'A dumber way to spend your time? Can you figure out a less energy-cost-effective strategy? To go haul water with a washing-up bowl on your head? To bust your gut? In this heat? Jesus! All they need is one plain old simple home-cooking hydraulic ram. Everyone knows about hydraulic rams. As you're well aware, there's no bozo on earth so sucking dumb he couldn't build a hydraulic ram!'

'Of course,' I said, having no idea what a hydraulic ram might be. 'That's obvious.'

The girl who had stared at Marcellin the evening before, the girl who had put a hand to her hair – she stood in the water by the upturned hull of the broken pirogue, on the side towards the open river, a small pile of washing on the smooth wood to her left, a piece of tar soap to her right, rubbing a white tee-shirt with a rounded, palm-sized stone. She wore a red wraparound hitched up to her waist; the dark water swirled between her naked thighs.

We laid our mould-sticky towels over the side of a beached dugout, stripped to our pants, placed our sweat-clammy shirts and trousers and socks beside the towels, and waded in; the girl glanced at Marcellin, rinsed out the tee-shirt, put her right hand to her left shoulder, unhooked a clasp or pulled a pin – and the wraparound curled off her shoulders to her waist, where she tied it. She ran the block of tar soap gently over her long arms, into her armpits, across the twin ridges and hollows of her collar-bones, the prominent curves of her ribs, and, turning slightly in front of us so that she was back-lit by the reflected light from the river surface, over her deep, low-slung breasts, her erect nipples.

Back at the hut Manou was agitated; he was alone; there was no sign of the usual supplicants for medicines and cigarettes; there was not a child in sight. He was holding a machete.

'The Chief was here!' he said. 'Dr Marcellin, Uncle, he came to warn you – but I told him you'd left me and gone away. You went for a swim!'

'I know,' said Marcellin. 'Put that thing down.'

Manou dropped the machete on the floor.

'It's Dokou! He lives over there!'

'I know,' said Marcellin.

'This morning,' said Manou, showing the whites of his eyes, 'a man died.'

'Let's sit down,' said Marcellin.

We sat on the bench.

'This man!'

'Calm yourself,' said Marcellin. '*We share a mother.* In front of Lary and Redmond – it doesn't matter. They don't belong here. But you are not to shame my family in Makao. Manou, I promise you now, if you show fear outside this hut, I promise you – I'll send you downriver. Everyone will know. They'll say behind your back, for ever, "Marcellin sent Manou away."'

'This man! He died because he went by night, in the spirit way, to the house of Dokou the sorcerer. He went to kill the sister of Dokou the sorcerer. But Dokou – he reacted with more powerful magic. In front of his door in the morning there was blood on the ground. All the people saw it. The man was ill thereafter, and died.'

'So what? Why are you shaking? What's so frightening?'

'Dokou!' said Manou, turning round on the bench and pointing at the open doorway, his arm rigid. 'He lives over there!'

'I know,' said Marcellin.

There was a long, faint, descending wail, followed by a chaos of crying.

'The women!' said Marcellin. 'The funeral!' He stood up, went to his pack, snapped on his full belt-kit of two water-bottles, document bag and the Birmingham machete in its canvas sheath, added his badge of office, the Sony Walkman, hung its headphones and the binoculars round his neck, and placed his floppy hat on his head. 'Come on! We must go. We must pay our respects. And you, too, Manou, you must come. The bags – they'll be safe. No one steals when women are wailing. Samalé will protect us.'

'Samalé?' said Lary. 'The Chief?'

'No,' said Marcellin.

Beside the talking-house in the middle of the village a crowd of women and children parted to let Marcellin through – but everyone, I noticed, even the toddlers, turned their faces away from him – and we stood in front of three big drums: the drum in the centre was perhaps eight feet tall, its top was three or four feet across, its hollowed tree-trunk tapered to a base supported on three squat, outcurving legs; behind it a wooden platform waited. The two flanking drums were smaller, short enough for a tall man to command, but still impressive: the tension in the lattice of liana-ropes that held their drumskins tight, the violence preserved in their knots – it was disturbing to contemplate.

The rising and falling lament came from a hut on the other side of the street, the hut, plainly, in which the dead man lay. Between the hut and the drums a wiry little man (in a red tee-shirt and grey trousers cut off at the knee) danced, with gargoyle-exaggerated steps, before a long line of men and teenage boys. Striking an empty beer-bottle with a clasp-knife, he beat time to his barefoot dusty stamping, his low leaps and swaying turns; the men and boys copied him, half a step behind. The chief drummer, naked to the waist, mounted the platform; his two subordinates stood to their drums; the dancing-master withdrew into the crowd; the men and boys turned to face the drums; the dance began.

Sound-waves – rolling rounded hill-tops, deep valleys of sound – swept across the square, complicated cross-currents, and, from the big drum, subterranean pounding like the onset of an earthquake: and then there was silence. The enlarging circles of sound dissipated into the forest; the vibrations in the hard laterite soil died under our boots. The drummers, square-breasted with muscle, held their heavy drumsticks poised. There came an answering sound from the quarters of the forest, a prolonged, hoarse roar.

'Samalé! Samalé!' yelled a little boy next to me.

The women and children scattered, screaming, running for the huts.

'Quick!' said Marcellin, grabbing Manou by the shoulder. 'Lary! Redmond! In here!' And he bundled us into the nearest hut.

The hut was dark, cramped, crowded, and smelt of woodsmoke. We sat on logs against the front wall and peered out through the slats. The roars ceased; the drumming began again; the line of men formed into a circle and danced slowly round the drums, swaying backwards and forwards, caught in the swell of sound.

'They've barricaded the door!' said Lary. 'Samalé – for Chrissake, what is it?' I looked round, my eyes adjusting to the gloom. It was true: three wooden poles wedged the main door shut; the women and children of the household had retreated to the inner room, pulling a slatted panel across behind them. Manou sat beside it, miserable as a banished dog; we were alone.

'For me, this is not a good death,' said Marcellin. 'This is not a good funeral.'

'Samalé?' insisted Lary. 'The next village? A warrior-cult? *What is all this fear about?*'

'Lary, this is no place for such a discussion,' said Marcellin, his voice barely audible. 'I'll tell you later. I give you my word. Dokou will explain.'

Lary turned away, put his eyes back to the slit on the outside world. A bundle of smoke-blackened gourds, like upended skulls in the half-light, hung from the low rafters above his head. He said slowly, 'I really feel that I have been away from Plattsburgh for many years. That I have not talked to anyone sensible since God was a boy.'

Marcellin, stung, stirred himself. 'When we first arrived, when we walked into this village, you saw a man running? A thin young man in bright-red trousers, running as fast as he could?'

'No,' said Lary. 'As it happens, I didn't.'

'He thought I'd come to arrest him, to kill him, to shoot him!'

'Then no wonder he ran,' said Lary, still staring out of the crack. 'That makes sense.'

'He's a merchant. I know him. I know all about him! This is a poaching village. He comes here to buy ivory. He's from the Sudan. He lends the pygmies guns, he gives them a few packets of cigarettes, he pays their owners 4000 CFA a kilo and he sells in Brazzaville for 10,000 – or he goes to Zaïre. One thousand tusks a year are exported to Zaïre. He thinks he's rich because he has bright-red trousers, new trousers! But really he stays poor. It's the merchants in Brazzaville who make money, the President's wife, so they say, who takes tusks to Belgium in her private jet, the men who sell to Japan.'

Lary said, 'Bye-bye, Forest elephant.'

'The forests of my country are big,' said Marcellin, raising his voice. 'Very big. There are vast stretches of swamp-forest where no one goes, where no one has ever been, no pygmies, no one. The elephants there are safe. They are under my protection.'

Three hours later the drumming stopped, we heard two shots (fired over the grave, said Marcellin), the women released us, and everyone drifted down to the river to cleanse themselves, to wash.

Nzé was sitting on the low wall of the veranda of our hut, playing an instrument that seemed to be a hybrid of the guitar and the harp, its boat-shaped sounding-box held between his knees, its long concave neck, pierced by nine pegs holding the strings taut, curving up above his head. Quiet, absorbed, a different Nzé, his hands moving with certainty, he produced a sad little melody that had no place in the flat hard light, against the concrete-wash wall, in the desolation of the empty guest hut.

'Nzé, where did you get that?' said Marcellin, standing in front of him. 'Where have you been? Did you steal it?'

Nzé stopped playing, looked about in confusion – as if he had no idea where he was – readjusted, and adopted his usual self-defensive grin.

'A girl lent it to me. The most beautiful girl in Makao. "Nzé," she said, "you play like a spirit, you have special powers. I can see that from your eyes. Borrow this. Think of me when you play it. And don't forget – you will spend the night in my hut. The whole night! All of it!"'

'We must buy chickens,' said Marcellin, sitting down.

'The food – I've arranged it,' said Nzé, propping the guitar-harp against the wall. He stood up, shouted across the street, and almost at once a young girl came out of Dokou's hut: in her right hand she carried a bucket and, tucked under her left arm, a chicken.

'I hope *that's* not your girl,' said Marcellin, as she approached.

Nzé said to Lary, by way of explanation, 'You spend the night with her – you'll be dead before the morning.'

'Of course,' said Lary, putting his right hand briefly across his eyes, sitting down on the parapet. 'It makes sense.'

She gave Lary a little smile, handed the bucket to Nzé, the chicken to me, and fled back across the street.

The hen was warm under my arm. It looked like a Rhode Island Red, red-brown all over with yellow legs, just like the chickens that had the run of the glebe field of my childhood; the feathers of her upper back, in the curve at the base of her neck, were firm and silky to the touch; as I stroked her she slid her nictitating membranes, her semi-transparent third lids, horizontally across her eyes.

Nzé put down his bucket, fetched his short length of cord with its wooden peg from the food-sack, took the hen from me and tethered her out on the mud floor of the hut, by the left leg, just inside the entrance.

'Make sure you kill her cleanly,' I said. 'She's beautiful.'

'It's a chicken,' said Nzé.

'Nzé is my brother,' said Manou suddenly. 'You'd say cousin. He can play anything. Whenever he wants – he can make music.'

'Manou,' said Nzé, 'go and fetch some water from the river.' And Manou collected the water-bottles.

Nzé slopped the saka-saka and meat from the bucket into our mess-tins (putting Manou's aside, on the bench). 'Lary,' said Marcellin, as we began to eat, 'you must understand. Of course it means nothing to me, but this is what people really believe. That young girl, she's fifteen years old, the village beauty – but no one will touch her.'

'Why not?'

'Because she's Dokou's new wife! Dokou – the most powerful sorcerer between here and Senegal! He is seventy-eight – an old man, the oldest man in Makao. Why's that? Can you tell me? Why do sorcerers live so long?'

'I give up,' said Lary, scrutinizing the very tough, gristly, grey lumps of meat hiding among the fresh green manioc-leaf saka-saka in his mess-tin.

'They don't rot outwards from the crotch! Go mad! Die screaming, covered in boils!'

'What?'

'They never get ill. They're the only men without sexual infection. They're safe. If they sleep with a woman who is not one of their wives – the whole village will know about it, they'll lose their powers. If an ordinary man sleeps with a sorcerer's wife – he dies. Phut! Dead on penetration!'

'Marcellin,' said Lary, chewing hard, 'what is this stuff?'

'Elephant nose!'

Lary set down his mess-tin. He stood up, lurched slightly, held on to the corner of the hut, retched twice, and was sick onto the ground.

'He's ill,' said Nzé, thoughtfully. 'Perhaps he has malaria.'

Lary wiped his mouth with the back of his hand, reconsidered, took a mould-ball of handkerchief from his pocket, ran it over his moustache and chin, retrieved his mess-tin, flicked its contents into a bush, scuffed mud over the little pile of yellow and green vomit, sat down again and reached for his water-bottle.

'To be sick by suggestion so fast,' I said, 'I didn't know it was possible.'

'It's been coming on,' said Lary, 'for a *very* long time.' He took a couple of deep gulps from the black plastic water-bottle. 'Marcellin,' he said, 'in your estimation, seriously, what's your take on that man's death? How did he die?'

'There's no mystery about the *mechanism*,' said Marcellin, refilling his mess-tin, scooping it into the bucket. 'Dokou's first wife is sixty-one years old. She gave that man a message from Dokou, "I have played with your palm-wine." She told all the village. So suddenly the victim found he had no friends. No one will talk to a man who carries a curse. Misfortune is catching. Misery is infectious. So even his closest friends, his four men friends – they walked right past him on their way to the plantation. For four months they looked the other way, they turned their heads in case the curse caught them in the dark, too. So he discovered that all those years of friendship, all that palm-wine he had gathered in buckets slung from his own trees, and given to his friends – it was all wasted, every drop. People find other reasons, of course. "He did this, he did that, he looked at my wife, he was mean with his axe, I helped him in his garden twice but he only came once to mine," the usual nonsense. The truth is – no friendship can withstand the fear in the dark, the fear at night. He died of loneliness.'

Lary said, 'It's the same at home. No one likes a failure. It's contagious. Chronic reactive depression. Four months. That's about right.'

'You don't have to pick on a failure,' said Marcellin. 'The victim does not have to be a failure.'

'Yes,' said Lary, as Manou returned. 'Shock. Despair. A month or two. Then you'd feel you'd have to go. To make space. To put things right.'

A crowd of men gathered outside the hut, the man who had danced and drummed the dead soul out of the village: they shouted at Marcellin in Kaka, in their insistent, domineering, bass voices. Marcellin translated: they wanted Western medicine for their headaches, their malaria, their boils and tropical ulcers – and for a mysterious itch. The chief drummer, a huge man with a torso like a javelin-thrower, stood over me and scratched his massive fore-arms, mimed with his fingers a ball of wriggling maggots. There were patches of small white-edged flaky scales on his skin. Yes, said Marcellin, translating, he the drummer was an exceptional man, a strong man, so it didn't matter so much, but for weak men and women, people, as it were, added Marcellin, like Manou, people who had a lot of fevers, for them it could be terrible, they couldn't think, they couldn't work, they couldn't even have sex! The itch tormented them every moment of the day, the worms under their skin would not keep still.

From the plastic bag in the bergen of medicines I handed out fifteen glossy white-coated quinine pills apiece; and from their silver-foil sheets I tore off the accompanying courses of Fansidar, for vivax malaria, the so-called benign malaria; I added Paracetemol, vitamins, Savlon, dressings – supplies which had seemed so excessive in Oxford, now shrunk to no more than a gesture. 'That's it,' said Marcellin. 'That's enough. Don't give it all away. We have a journey to make. You must keep some for us. Besides – it's time to see the Chief. The Hereditary Chief of Makao awaits us. You'll make a portrait with the instant camera. You still have film?'

I dug out the Polaroid, a packet of film, a rack of flash-bulbs; Lary took his Nikon; we left Manou and Nzé to defend the bags and walked up through the village, past the sleeping goats, beyond the talking-house, onto a broad path fringed with short jungle grasses and speckled with chickens. They were mostly thin, wiry and light brown, but there was one comforting Rhode Island Red hen. She was picking up beakfuls of fallen seed and proffering them to each of her four chicks in turn, and as I watched she opened her wings, only they were black and fast and twisting away, banking over us, a spread of white barred black, a yellow streak of legs and chick, a slipstream of black-barred tail vanishing between the trees. The chickens scattered, rocking from side to side as they ran for cover.

'The Great sparrowhawk!'

'Bandit country!' said Lary. He unslung the Nikon from his shoulder and held it ready in his right hand. 'Just in case we meet the next size up,' he said. 'Just in case the Great golden eagle decides to drop in and take you for a ride.' He looked thoughtful. 'And talking of that sort of thing – did you clock the muscles on that drummer?' (I did.) 'You did? Then how do you suppose he functions with biceps, triceps, deltoids, pectorals and dorsals like that in one of these goddam poky airless underconstructed huts? Eh? These huts that have uneven floors, no windows, no headroom, no chimneys and roofs that don't even keep the rain out? Where does he put himself? I guess it's just another one of those little secrets that's obvious to everyone but me round here. I guess he just goes home in that working rig of his, like the suit of armour they stuck on Henry VIII, and "Hi, darling!" he says. "I'm back!" And then he takes off his muscles and hangs them on a coathook and turns into a sucking ghost.'

Marcellin stopped on the path; he snatched his hat off and slapped it across his knees; he bent forward, pressed both hands and the hat to his stomach, and howled with laughter, a genuine, high-pitched howl of laughter.

'But that's all there's room for in these huts!' said Lary, mildly offended. 'That's their specification. No wonder this place is stiff with ghosts. They're a simple function of the sucking People's Party Committee Code of Building Practice. Construction so bad it's off the scale. Jesus! They don't even use grade A timber. There's more A1 timber right round this village than you'll find in the whole of New York State. And for nothing! You could build two-storey timber-frame houses with high cool airy rooms that were filled with light! You could have pitched roofs to keep the heat off. You could even have real fun and go build yourself a crow-stepped gable like . . .'

'And this,' announced Marcellin, with a snort of suppressed hilarity, giving me a helpless wink, biting his lip and tugging at his nose, 'this is the hut of the Hereditary Chief of Makao.'

The Chief, in his white singlet, shorts and trainers, sat on a stool under an awning of palm-thatch in front of his hut. Remaining seated, he shook

Marcellin's hand and nodded at the bench in front of him. Marcellin sat down, Lary and I took our places to his left and right and removed our hats. I laid the film and flash-bulbs on the bench beside me. Marcellin, for our benefit, began his speech in French: he was an official representative of the Government, he had the full authority of the People's Party to inform the Chief of Makao that the Central Commitee had changed the People's law: as from this moment the Chief was once again to consider the surrounding forest as his by hereditary right; he was to kill all poachers and intruders; the preservation of the Forest elephant was his responsibility. The Chief, polite but mystified, scratched his left armpit, his chest, stared at the floor, transferred the hand to the small of his back, and replied in Kaka.

As I watched a low-ranking cockerel (he had a dull comb) half-heartedly raking the dust about at the base of a mango tree outside (he was obviously as bored as I was), and as I wondered vaguely why such a geriatric bird had not been eaten, I noticed something grey, bound, at head-height, to the trunk of the tree: a skull. A loop of liana-twine ran through its left eye-socket: another ran over the cranium between the rounded, projecting ridge of the forehead and the sharp, upturned keel of bone at the back of the head: a gorilla skull. The keel, the rear crest of bone, had once been an anchor for the great muscles of the jaw and neck – it was the skull of an old male. How many children had he fathered? How many were still alive? 'A gorilla, an old man,' said Marcellin in English, breaking into my reverie, following the direction of my gaze, 'a leader. He's powerful. He protects the Chief. When the Chief of Makao is asleep – the gorilla gives him protection. The pills? Did you bring the pills?'

'I forgot,' I said, jumping up. 'I'll go back. I'll get them.'

Lary, on his feet simultaneously, said, 'Don't worry. I'll go. That's okay.'

'You're needed here,' I said. 'You've got the Polaroid.' And I stuck it under his arm.

It was dusk; smoke from the fires inside the huts, stoked up in preparation for the dark, rose through the palm-thatch roofs; a pair of bats, as big as blackbirds, with broad, rounded wings, flew erratically between the diffuse little clouds of smoke. They certainly looked like Ur-bats, the original bats, the bats of prehistory, their slow, laboured flapping interspersed with ungainly glides, and indeed perhaps they were a species of Leaf-nosed bat, not much altered from their fossil ancestors of sixty million years ago and probably earlier – seventy to a hundred million years ago – early enough to have been catching insects in the evening over a shallow lake full of dinosaurs.

The primitive Leaf-noses, I thought, as I passed the talking-house (the goats had gone, penned up somewhere, safe from leopards) – they just hadn't had to bother to improve themselves, to get elegant, to evolve scimitar wings like the Giant mastiff bat to the east, a bat which flies straight and fast as an Alpine swift. The slow, unchanged life suited them; they probably fed on the winged phases of ants and termites, sluggish moths, the larger mosquitoes.

Nzé and Manou were lying on their tarpaulins, heads against the left-hand wall, a candle at their feet; the hen, fluffed up for the night, fast asleep, stood on her tethered leg to the right of the entrance.

'Don't you disturb us,' said Nzé, raising his head an inch off his pillow (a spare pair of militia trousers, neatly folded). 'There'll be no sleep tonight. Not where we're going. With a new girl, the first time – you must be *strong*.' (He was at once awake with the thought of it, his eyes, in the candlelight, wide as a bushbaby's.) 'You must be strong like the elephants in the forest – the ones with the big tusks. And then – you must move like a leopard!'

'May the tusks be with you,' I said, getting my torch from the bergen. I found the distalgesics, the DF 118s, and, feeling a sudden lower-gut-liquefying twinge of diarrhoea (salmonella in the manioc? The smoked-hard lumps of elephant-trunk, rotten in the middle?) I grabbed the green bag of lavatory paper and made a dash for the protective retreat of the enclosing tree.

Safe inside, just in time, I dropped my trousers, switched off the torch, and squatted there gasping with the kind of peristalsis that propels the Giant squid.

In the black dark, beneath the tree, it was eerily silent. No Sedge frogs or Bush frogs or Old World tree-frogs swore like ravens or quacked like ducks or peeped like nestlings; the cicadas had stopped their rasping. And why hadn't I noticed that the tree was covered in thorns? Its spikes stabbed my scalp; they pierced the backs of my ears, ringed my neck, stuck through my shirt. I scrabbled for the torch.

Ants, red-brown ants, about a quarter of an inch long, were running in manic bursts down my shirt-front, swinging left and right, conferring with their fellows, climbing over the hairs on my arms, pausing – and clamping themselves, head-first, into the flesh. They were falling on me from above, from the tree, from the branches of the trees. Panicking, I fumbled with the lavatory paper, pulled up my pants and trousers (a bagful of ants fastened on my genitals) and ran for the hut, stripping off my shirt, running from the pain in my back.

'Nzé! Manou!' I yelled, falling over the entrance step. 'Help me!'

'You've seen the dead man,' said Nzé. 'He was walking in the forest.'

'Ants!' I said, forcing off my boots, twisting out of my trousers and pants, jiggling about with each new cluster of bites. 'My back! Get them off my back!'

'You're nude,' observed Manou from the floor. 'You're dancing.'

'Bee ants,' said Nzé, picking one off, dropping it on the dry mud and stamping on it. 'Nothing to worry about.'

Manou, coming to my rescue, knocking them off with swipes of his hat, said, 'Maybe they really hurt the first time. Perhaps, when you're not used to them, they make you dance.'

'Bohmaaa!' said Nzé. 'He's fussing like a young girl!'

I gathered up my clothes, shook out the remaining ants, dressed, and walked gingerly out of the hut. As I made my way up through the village, in the moonless night, the heat in my skin turned to an itchy glow, the pain eased.

By the light of a paraffin lamp, placed on a table to the Chief's right (four Polaroid prints arranged beside it), Marcellin and the Chief were still talking, tin cups of palm-wine in their hands, a lidless coffee-pot, half full of palm-wine, on the floor midway between them.

Lary, red about the eyes, mournful, his palm-wine untouched, his hat in his hands, his moustache drooping at both ends, said, 'What kept you?'

'Ants!' I said, handing the Chief his painkillers (he nodded, pushed them into his pocket, and carried on talking). 'I was attacked by ants!'

'Yeah, yeah,' said Lary.

'It's true!'

'They've been at it in Kaka,' said Lary. 'All this time.'

'And you listened?' I said, sitting down beside him, 'That's the only way. The Berlitz method. Total immersion. Learn Kaka in twenty lessons.'

'Redso,' said Lary, 'go chew a chipmunk.'

The differences apparently resolved, the discussion at an end, we said goodbye to the Chief and walked slowly back past the huts, past the sounds of laughter and talking and children protesting. 'They're over-excited,' said Marcellin. 'Samalé was here. They won't go to bed.'

'That talk with the Chief,' said Lary. 'What was it all about?'

'He's not so bad,' said Marcellin, greeting a passing shadow, 'he's okay. He's promised to do something about the poachers. And he says we can take his pygmies. But we must also give work to Michel Walengué, the Chief's drummer and the Commandant of the Makao People's Militia, and also to Antoine Mokito. He owes them both a favour. We are to say yes to them, we must give them work if they ask for it, and we are to say no to everyone else. It's important not to quarrel with a Chief. Me, I don't like quarrels. It's why I'm good at my job. The best. I don't make enemies. I am not a man who likes to make enemies.'

'Marcellin, perhaps you can help me,' I said, still in that frame of mind, and falling into his rhythms of speech. 'Dokou, those little bundles of fur he wears round his neck – could you get me one? I need one. In Oxford, I have many enemies. I need a fetish, a powerful fetish for my own protection.'

Marcellin slowed his pace; he developed a slight halt in his gait.

'Redmond, I don't know. Me, I can't promise anything. But I'll try. I like you, so I'll try. But it's stupid, it's dangerous – you ought not to get involved in such things. I told you, once you start, you can't stop. But I'll see what I can do. I'll ask him. It's difficult. It takes time to prepare. There are rules . . .'

Two big fireflies were flashing in the darkness ahead of us; there was a yelping and a snickering and a swearing like a litter of fox-cubs fighting over a rabbit. 'Marcellin! Dr Marcellin!' came Nzé's voice – and, in a higher key, a yell from Manou: 'Marcellin! Help! Help us!'

Nzé and Manou, naked, hung with ants, holding their pencil torches, attempting to groom each other, were dancing with pain on the veranda.

'Driver ants!' shouted Marcellin, rolling up his hat, standing a full arm's-length away and beating first Nzé and then Manou across the back.

Manou said, 'We were asleep!'

Nzé said, 'They came right over the tarpaulins! They're in the packs! They'll eat the food!'

I said, 'I don't suppose you're fussing? Not like young girls?'

'Driver ants,' said Lary. '*Dorylus.* Jesus! According to Raignier and van Boven the moving colonies of these guys can be *twenty-two million strong*. Your Army ants in South America – a mere two million. Let's take a look.' And he strode into the hut.

'Lary! Redmond!' shouted Marcellin. 'Watch your boots! And watch your heads – they'll drop on you! From the roof!'

Five columns stretched from the lip of the square window-hole by the bamboo-clump; they were marching down and into the room, fanning out across the mud floor – three columns had mounted the inner walls, the lines disappearing into the thatch; the fourth flowed into an estuarine swarm of ants covering Nzé and Manou's tarpaulins, the mass lifting itself up and over and into the bergens and the food-sack; the fifth column led to a spiky giant football of nipped-in bodies and waving antennae and brittle legs, a ball which rocked, slightly, on its own axis. From inside it came weak, muffled, spasmodic squawks.

Lary, a yard away, kneeling on the mud floor, craning forward to look, said, 'Bye-bye, Rhode Island Red hen. Bye-bye, vicarage childhood.'

Marcellin, outside, was shouting in Kaka. Voices answered him from further off.

Lary trained his torch on the column. 'This feeder line is fifteen to twenty individuals wide – and three to four individuals *deep* in places . . . They're running forward on each other's backs!' He paused, peered closer, and then, clearly fascinated, he moved over at a half-crouch to Nzé's tarpaulin and squatted on his haunches just clear of the hyperactive swarm around the food-sack. (Biology, I thought, it's such a peaceful pursuit, so satisfying, so disengaging from the self . . .) 'Hey, Redso,' said Lary, his face a foot above an apparent chaos of ants, 'did you know? There are *three* different types of worker in a *Dorylus* column! The big guys with the black heads and pincers, they're the soldiers, *lots* more than I'd thought; the next size down, I guess they're the medium workers; and these small guys – no more than an eighth of an inch? What do you think? – they must be the minors. So altogether they can snag every animal in their path, all sizes, every bit of meat that can't get the hell out! They're blind, of course, and leaderless, it's all done by smell – if you watch' – I watched – 'the guys in front move forward and then circle back and the ones behind take over, and so on, and on and on; when they've done with a migration they make camp, dig into the ground, they construct tunnels and chambers up to three yards down, the queen spews out eggs, they tend the young, they send out columns to mince up most everything in the area and then they move on again. Awesome. All that action and lack of thought. One-third of all the animal biomass in a rainforest – it's ants. And I suspect that, at base, call it what you will, instinct, hormones, we're like everything else round here, driven by millions of years of selective evolution in this very place . . .'

Marcellin shouted, 'Lary! Redmond! Out here!'

The darkness was lit by a semi-circle of flame, fire laid along the ground, a barrier of burning palm-fronds. 'Through here!' shouted Marcellin from the other side, pointing at a gap.

'Everybody helped!' he said, gesturing at a small crowd of people, the families from the neighbouring huts, figures in the firelight, barefoot young men bringing bundles of fronds. 'Michel Walengué is here – and Muko. Muko is here!'

'The ants,' said Michel Walengué, the drummer, smiling at us, 'they eat everything but fire.'

'They clear out the chiggers, the fleas,' said Marcellin. 'They take the cockroaches from the roof.'

'They've eaten our chicken,' said Nzé.

Marcellin put his arm around the shoulders of a pygmy standing next to him, a middle-aged man of obvious authority and intelligence. Broad-chested, bandy-legged, he wore a tee-shirt that hung half-way down his thighs, and a pair of gym-shoes several sizes too large, with no laces. 'Muko!' said Marcellin. (Muko grinned, and stood still, somehow detached from the appropriating arm.) 'Muko – I've known him for ever. He's the best hunter there is. He knows all the animals, all the trees. He'll come with us – for the great walk through the forest. And tonight he will replace the chicken. He'll take the gun and kill a duiker and tomorrow we will eat well!'

The expanded, spatulate front of a column of ants, advancing out of the hut entrance, stopped a yard or so short of the ring of fire; the temporary leaders raised their antennae, circled back into the mass; the next rank followed suit; and gradually the retreat began, the army turning on itself, emptying away, back through the hut entrance, and, in half an hour, spilling out of the packs, marching down the walls, snaking up over the lip of the window and out to the forest.

Nzé, muttering some deep and private curse, threw the skeleton of the chicken after them; he rolled up his now bite-frayed, tattered rope. 'There's fou-fou,' he said. 'They don't like fou-fou.'

Not an ant was left in the bergens, just a musty, acidic smell. 'That's it for now,' said Marcellin, 'for a month or two – they'll stay in the forest. But Dokou, he was disturbed by all the fuss. He says tonight will be no use. We must meet him tomorrow, in the school hut.'

That night, safe in the tent, I inspected the ant nips, the mosquito bites, the minor sores on my legs – and hundreds of small round bumps flecked with dried blood at their centres: blackfly bites. 'Lary,' I said, 'the Makao itch – maybe we know the cause! The larvae of that worm that gives you river-blindness. You only get that in West Africa, but I've read about it, there's a forest strain – both types move about beneath the skin and drive you mad. But only in West Africa does it actually wriggle its way across your eyeballs. So here you don't go blind. You just go mad, itching.'

'Redso,' said Lary, 'will you put those disgusting legs away?'

'This morning, down at the river, did you see blackfly?'

Lary pulled *Martin Chuzzlewit* out of its bergen side-pocket.

'Nope. It must be thick with them. We were staring at that woman. Serves us right.' He opened *Chuzzlewit* at his marker (a turned-down page). 'I guess there's a simple test for your hypothesis – we'll know when we get the all-over, no-stop, no-relief itch.' He put on his head-torch and began to read. 'And another thing,' he said, looking up, 'do you really have lots of enemies in Oxford?'

'God no, I hope not,' I said, startled. 'I couldn't bear it. If I thought I had just one out there – one real enemy – that would unhinge me. I want to be loved by everyone, the milkman, everyone.'

'The milkman?' said Lary. 'You sure about that?'

'Yes.'

'Then let me break it to you,' said Lary, refocusing the beam on the head-torch, preparing to escape into Dickens. 'You have a problem.'

From our left, from Marcellin's tent, came a high-pitched, insistent murmur; and an answering sound – low, happy, female laughter.

Just after dawn, as Marcellin, Lary and I sat on the bench on the hut veranda, silently watching Manou (bright and clean, fresh back from a wash in the river) as he boiled up the breakfast manioc, Muko arrived, barefoot, wearing nothing but a pair of grey shorts, the shotgun in his right hand and two dead Blue duiker, trussed into a ball with strips of liana, slung from his left shoulder. He dropped them outside the hut, nodded to us, said something in Kaka to Marcellin, and left. Nzé, coming the other way, apparently just as tired (dressed in his Cuban Army uniform, complete with cap), passed Muko without a word and wandered on to the veranda, half-conscious, bleary with exhaustion after a night of love and music.

'Nzé!' said Marcellin, obviously a more practised manager of his own resources, chirpy after his conquest. 'You skin the duikers!'

'Ugh!' said Nzé, winded at the thought, sitting down on the end of the bench. 'Manou can do it. Today – he can do everything. He let me down! He was shy! He stayed at home! Her sister, the young one for Manou, the thin one I didn't like – she was disappointed. What could I do? I made my music – and then I had them both! It's Manou's fault. They wouldn't let me sleep. They kept me awake. All night. I couldn't sleep. I've had no sleep.'

Marcellin laughed. 'That's right, well done,' he said, 'that's how they are, the girls in this village, that's what they're like.'

'They have diseases,' said Manou, dealing out the manioc.

'Nzé and Manou,' said Marcellin, 'you two will prepare the duikers – the meat for now, and to take with us. Lary and Redmond – you will come with me to the river. We must wash all our clothes. There is nowhere to wash in the forest. We must be clean. And then – Dokou has something important to tell us, in the school hut.'

'Er, perhaps not Dokou, thanks all the same,' said Lary. 'No more Kaka, just for now, if you don't mind. I'll go kick ass with those packs. They're a mess. There's no order in there . . .'

The school hut (not much bigger than the guest-hut, but with a floor of sand, a corrugated-iron roof, and four window-holes flanking the entrance) was set slightly apart from the village, down towards the river. Inside, in the airless heat, Dokou was waiting for us, sitting at the schoolteacher's desk, dignified, dressed formally in his old black jacket, black shirt, black trousers and boots, four white plastic mugs arranged in a line in front of him.

Marcellin added the litre bottle of Cavesco red wine, and I placed my present beside it: a plastic bag containing a briar pipe from Oxford, a tin of Balkan Sobranie tobacco, a Swiss Army knife, a course of Fansidar and thirty pills of quinine. He needs iodine, I thought, mesmerized once more by the bulbous sag of his goitre, and, half-visible in the open neck of his shirt, the three little hanging bags of monkey-fur.

'The other white man,' said Dokou, pushing one mug to the edge of the desk, 'where is he?'

Marcellin and I sat down at the bench-desk in the front row, like pupils. 'Dr Shaffer,' said Marcellin, 'he has to supervise the loads for the bearers. We leave for the forest tomorrow.'

'That one, I knew he wouldn't come,' said Dokou. 'He has his own powers. Different powers. He has no need of my protection.'

'That is true,' said Marcellin, more deferential than I had ever seen him, his head slightly bowed, his speech stilted.

Dokou unscrewed the metal top of the wine-bottle and filled the three mugs. Marcellin stood up, reached across the gap, took one for himself, handed one to me, and sat down again. 'To our safety in the forest!' he said, and we took a mouthful of watery wine.

Dokou stared at me with his intense and bloodshot eyes. 'You are here to learn about Samalé,' he said, folding his hands on the desk-top. 'But soon Samalé will know that you know, and that is dangerous. You may be cut across the back, in the night. So we must make a sacrifice. For a stranger to see Samalé – death. So it cannot be an ordinary sacrifice. Samalé, for this, for a stranger to learn his secrets, even for a stranger whose friend is already close to Samalé – Samalé will demand not one chicken, but two.'

Marcellin said, '1000 CFA.'

'I'll bring the money tonight,' I said, addressing Dokou. 'At midnight, when you give me my fetish.'

Dokou glanced quickly at the window-holes. But the usual gaggle of wide-eyed children were not pressed up against the ledges. There was no one out there, nothing but the single, repeated note of a dove or a cuckoo close at hand in the forest, *hoo hoo hoo*; and a background noise, perhaps a barbet, an irregular call like a knife striking glass, *tink-tink tink-tink*.

'Here we will not talk about the other powers,' said Dokou. 'This is not the place for such a discussion.'

'You must listen,' Marcellin said to me, toying with his wine. 'We will not want to hear your opinions.'

'A white man came here once,' said Dokou. 'Long ago. He went hunting for Samalé in the forest. He used three boxes of cartridges but, every time, he missed. He had no luck. He went away.'

'Good,' I said. 'I'm glad to hear it.'

'You have heard Samalé. You are one of the very few strangers who have heard him call. That was Samalé. That was not just a man calling. Sometimes he sits down, right next to people, and they hear him. But that is the last thing they hear. From that moment they are deaf, as a man and as a spirit. You white men, in the daytime – you are kings, it is true. But at night, here in Africa, you are children, little boys. A nephew once went to study in Paris; his uncle wanted him back, so he took a friend in the night and flew to Paris in a plane. Immigration rang the nephew and said, "Your uncle is at Charles de Gaulle." So, later, the nephew went to the Congo to investigate. He arrived in his village. His uncle, in his hut, had a model aeroplane made of wood. By day it was a model aeroplane. At night, it was real.'

Marcellin (perhaps guessing that I was about to say something banal) put a restraining hand on my arm.

'Samalé calls,' said Dokou, lifting up his voice as if he was delivering a sermon, 'for the protection of the people, and for the souls of the dead. He is an animal of imagination and of mystery. He has his origins in a zone of the savanna, in the region of Ndélé, in the Central African Republic.

'A woman who was lost in the bush heard the calls of an extraordinary animal. She was frightened. She ran to alert her husband. Her husband went to the place. He succeeded in taming the animal. The animal directed him to build a shelter. This event took place around the year 1900, or a little earlier.

'It was during the period before the First World War that the tribe of the Kakas brought a similar animal, from the Central African Republic, to the area north of the Motaba river. At first, to Berandzoko, afterwards to Makao, then to Séké, and, last of all, to Lilkombo and Zingo.

'This spiritual animal was tamed to ensure the security and happiness of the people. To protect them against evil spirits and the spells of foreign sorcerers. During the World War of 1914, this animal helped the people at every turn, and it was he who gave us all the details of the enemy positions.'

Dokou paused, refilled his mug, raised it, shut his eyes (his face was wrinkled like the bark of an oak) and drank.

'The Germans came in from the Central African Republic and advanced towards the interior of the territory of the Congo, towards Makao. The people, alerted by Samalé, went to meet their enemies, and they confronted them at a site named Banga, on the path in the forest from Makao to Berandzoko. The Germans were armed with rifles, the people with crossbows and poisoned arrows, and also with a few guns – but the powder for these guns had been made in our own country. After the battle of Banga the people withdrew, and another battle took place, at Makao. After the battle of Makao the people withdrew into the forest, and the Germans occupied the village of Makao. Here they installed a camp.

'The Governor or Commandant Mosusu, an officer of the French, came to help as he was passing through Nola in the Central African Republic. He made camp at Séké, with a battalion of soldiers. He sent word to all those who had fled to the forest and he welcomed them to Séké, to his camp. Having regrouped all the inhabitants of the region of Séké, the Commandant Mosusu and his men made their way towards the land of the Kaboungas. After the passage of the Governor Mosusu the Germans withdrew from the positions they had occupied and peace came back to the region.

'During the time that the people were living in the forest, away from their villages along the rivers, not one soldier followed them, for fear of being killed by the Kaka, who, in the forest, had become very dangerous.

'The ethnic group Kaka come from Central Africa. The animal Samalé, their totem, also lives among the Bandas, where he has his origins. The two groups understand each other's language.

'The group Kaka is represented by the villages Makao, Berandzoko, Séké, Beye, Lipondza-pape. The inhabitants of the village Bangui-Motaba come from the land of the Kaboungas. There are still paths, to this day, which link the land of the Kaboungas to the north of the Motaba. And there are still Kakas in Central Africa, towards Bayanga.'

'But what,' I said, growing restless, 'does Samalé look like?'

Dokou, ignoring me, poured himself another mug of wine. Resenting the interruption, he drank without looking at either of us and, the mug emptied, fixed his gaze on the wall behind our heads, at the back of the classroom.

'The animal Samalé is always adopted by a couple who play the roles of father and mother. It is only the descendants of such a family, those who have the holy spirit, only those people have the right to claim this animal of mystery as a father.

'The name of this animal, Ngakola Samalé, comes from his origins. Ever since the ancestors knew of his existence, in the country of the Banda, in Central Africa, the name Ngakola Samalé has been the same, in the Kaka language, as Guardian of the Village.

'There is a secret sect associated with this animal and each adherent must be initiated. The baptism is effected in the following manner. No one but a descendant of the Kaka tribe may be baptized. The ceremony for the baptism is as follows. There are objects to prepare for the postulant: traditional dress, and other, secret, traditional objects. These objects help to ensure his transformation. An offering of a goat and live chickens must be made to the animal. The goat and the chickens are left in Samalé's hiding-place, in the forest, near the village. The animal kills them himself – and afterwards the bodies are recovered and cooked in the village. The food so prepared is once again taken and left in the lair of the animal. Samalé eats this food and the empty plates are then recovered.

'Before that the postulant must be taken into Samalé's hiding-place, the lair of this animal from the wilderness. Samalé sends the postulant to sleep; the boy sleeps. The boy sleeps as if struck by a poisoned arrow. Samalé then marks the postulant with the sign of the cross.'

Dokou, suddenly alert, looked straight at me. 'Samalé has three claws,' he said, breathing hard, his voice harsh and cracked. 'On each hand,' he shouted, 'Samalé has three claws! Long and curved, strong as steel, sharp as hooks!' He stood up and leaned across the desk, his pupils dilated, his lips retracted, his irregular, yellow teeth exposed. 'But he only cuts with two!' He raised his right fist as if to strike me, crooked out two bent fingers, and slashed the air in front of my face.

Dokou slumped back at the desk, poured out the last mugful of wine and drank it. 'The food is offered two days afterwards,' he intoned as if nothing had happened. 'The food is offered by the recently baptized initiate. He introduces this food into the shelter without looking at the recipient. Samalé rips his arms.' (Dokou began to gather up his own offerings on the desk-top.) 'The wounds form scars and mark the boy for life.' (He pulled back the right flap of his jacket and put the pipe, the tobacco, the knife and the pills into a bag of worn black fur, perhaps part of a Black and white colobus skin, which hung from his shoulder tight against his side.) 'During all of this ceremony the postulant knows nothing. He does not even see the animal which sets these signs upon his body. It is only after the baptism that the initiate is brought for a visit. He is presented to the animal.'

Dokou pulled his jacket across the bag, got to his feet, put the empty mugs in his jacket-pockets, picked up the empty wine-bottle and rescrewed the top. 'You two – you will wait here for a time,' he said, shuffling towards the entrance, shoulders hunched, the life gone out of him. 'We must not leave all together.'

'So what *does* Samalé look like?' I said, turning to Marcellin, as we sat side by side at the desk, like schoolboys. To my surprise, I saw that there was sweat on his forehead, that his hands were shaking. In a small voice, without looking up, apparently still studying the adze-marks on the wood in front of him, Marcellin said, 'I don't want to talk about it. Finish. No more. Okay?'

Mystified, I said, 'I'm sorry.' And, to change the subject, 'You had a good time last night.'

'And here we sit in the school!'

'How do you mean?'

'She's the schoolmaster's wife. The woman you stared at down by the river, when she was washing. The woman with the most beautiful breasts I've ever seen. Her husband – he's gone to the Central African Republic. She's alone. She's the mother of twins.'

'Twins? I thought that was a bad thing. I thought you could be banished from the village, that it meant you'd slept with a spirit, that you'd become like an animal in the forest.'

'It's a disaster. A catastrophe. But Dokou – he's powerful. He's respected by everybody, all the Kaka people, from here to Zingo. He helped her. He gave her complete protection against evil spirits and bad thoughts. Everyone knew about it. She's young, she's very poor, her husband has gone away, so Dokou did it for nothing. He refused to take her money, he wouldn't even take a present of pineapples, a chicken. And she couldn't thank him as a woman should. No one but his own wives may sleep with a sorcerer. So she came to thank me, instead; she brought me the gift of her body. She was shy at first. She'd never been inside a tent. But there was something else. To begin with, she wouldn't even let me kiss her! But she excited me. She wanted me naked, without a condom. I made love to her for an hour, maybe more. But when she had her orgasm she cried. She turned her face away and sobbed. She cried and cried.'

'I don't understand.'

'Neither do I. It's never happened to me before. Perhaps she cried because her husband has gone away; or she felt guilty, because she had an orgasm with me; or maybe she was sobbing with pleasure. I don't know. She wouldn't say. I didn't like it.'

'No – I mean, why visit you? Why think she could pay off a debt to Dokou by sleeping with you?'

Marcellin stood up without answering and we left the hut in silence. Half-way back he said, 'Again, there's something else. My wedding-ring – I'm a man of delicate feelings, an educated man. So when I'm with other women, women not my wife, I pull off my wedding-ring. It's a gesture of respect. Well, last night, the wedding-ring – I lost it. This morning, it was not in the back-pocket of my jeans. I've looked in the tent. I've looked everywhere. It's gone.'

'Maybe she took it.'

'Never. She would *never* do a thing like that,' said Marcellin, shocked, stopping in the middle of the street, waving away an approaching gallop of children. 'Never. No woman in Makao would ever treat a man like that – it just couldn't happen. No, it's much worse. I can't get the idea out of my head. Part of me knows it's a ridiculous thought – but all the same, it goes round and round, faster and faster. It's tiring. Inside, I feel a little desperate. Because something is odd and not right.'

'Don't worry – you'll find it. It's mislaid – caught in a fold of the groundsheet.'

'That's not it,' he said, with a convulsive little sideways jerk of the head, as if he was trying to free a crick in his neck. 'I know it's not there. It's just that I'm sure it went – went of its accord.'

That evening we dined on boiled duiker pieces, manioc and pineapples (a present from Antoine the drummer) and Lary said that if only he had a glass of the Macpoop, or even a double of that plain simple old Glenbraindead (because he wasn't a malt snob) or – a really wild thought, the kind of thought that drives you mad – a bacon, lettuce and tomato sandwich, life now would be perfect, but tomorrow would be one hell of a walk, bergen or no bergen, and we'd better get some sleep.

Marcellin sat on the veranda, interviewing a small crowd of would-be bearers; Nzé went to wash in the river, to prepare for his last night with the sisters; and Manou, so tired after a day of sleeping that he could barely speak, lay back down on his tarpaulin.

From the tent we could hear Marcellin asking questions, making lists.

'Bantu names!' he shouted. 'Makano, Boniface . . . Boutandzara, Pierre . . . Bilebou, Albert . . . Boyemba, Ambroise . . .'

'God damn it all to hell and back twice,' announced Lary, outwardly peaceful, lying straight out on the groundsheet. 'What's the point, that's what I want to know, what is the point of all this sorcery? What is the psychological and social function of all this fear? Why live in terror of all this magic and bullshit and spells for this and spells for that when you don't have to? Why not say to Dokou, "Dokou, old man, I'm sorry, I don't want to hurt your feelings, but with all due respect for your great age and wisdom and authority in this village, why don't you just take your mumbo-jumbo and stick it up your ass and turn it sideways?"'

'I don't know,' I said, arranging the shirt-tied ball of socks and pants under my head, turning off the torch, trying to get comfortable on the baked-hard mud. ('Babinga names!' sang Marcellin from outside. 'Muko . . . Eko . . . Bakamba . . . Djele . . .') 'The usual answer is that it gives a structure, a meaning to life, and that you certainly need one when all your thinking is pre-logical, when your idea of nature makes no distinction between subjective and objective impressions and thoughts – when your inner and outer worlds are all mixed up, when there's no obvious dividing line between your own mental reality and that of a passing leopard, or a bat over the hut, or a bamboo-clump that's holding a party for Driver ants. I imagine we all think like that for at least a fraction of each day, some more so than others, and more at some times of our life than at other times – when we've had a setback or a shock or when someone dies or when we're ill or in love – and more often at night than in the daytime. But here the nightmares never get an enclosing line drawn round them, they never get bagged up and thrown away – they just hang around out there, you meet them when you go for walks in the forest, they come at you between the trees, they get you after dark.'

'Heavy-duty tranquillizer time,' said Lary. 'Time to see your G P.'

'Exactly. So you go and get a fetish, which keeps some of the horror away, but I imagine it must bring its own fears – will it work? What if I lose it? Is it really on my side, or did that shit who wants to kill me go to the sorcerer first, with better presents?'

Lary said, 'Best to stay in Plattsburgh.'

'But the real point of it must be simple – you know the big fear is out there, waiting to bust in through your hut wall: you can be sure that two or three of your children will die as children, that you'll get ill, that you'll die young. So you give yourself lots of little fears, fears you half-know are not serious, to diffuse the big horror into the landscape. It's a bit like the psychological bargain Christians or Muslims strike with themselves: you agree to abandon for life your ability to think straight; you accept a job-lot of fairy tales, all kinds of absurdities; and in return for the effort it costs to push your intellect back into bed every time you get up in the morning, you're released from the big one, the fear of death. You can really start to tell yourself that you'll see your dead mother and father again, that your dead children are not dead, that your dead friends are still sitting drinking round the fire, and, maybe, even your favourite dog is waiting for you, fast asleep . . .'

'Put like that,' said Lary quietly, 'it's not such a bad bargain.'

At midnight, Marcellin whistled outside the tent. ('Thanks,' Lary said to me. 'But I'll stay here, if you don't mind.')

'Redmond, no torches,' Marcellin whispered through the tent-flap. 'I don't want anyone to see us.' I pulled on my boots and followed him across the street.

Marcellin tapped twice on the hut door, it slid a body-width to the left, we stepped inside, and Dokou shut it behind us.

Looking ten years younger than in the morning (he'd had a big sleep, I decided), Dokou was barefoot, but still wearing his old black jacket, black shirt and black trousers. 'Samalé,' he said, waving us to two low wooden chairs to the left of the fire, in its grate of stones, and himself perching on a three-legged stool, the white mugs and a gourd ready on a little slatted table at his side.

'Mr Redmond,' he said, pouring out the cloudy-white wine, 'tonight I will answer your question about Samalé.' His voice was unofficial, almost intimate. 'Dr Marcellin and Mr Redmond, we are here to talk about important matters, deep things. There are powers I can give you. These powers will change your lives.' Dokou replaced the gourd in its wooden stand. He gazed slowly about the smoky little room, as if reacquainting himself with something necessary and familiar in the red light of the fire, the orange-yellow glow of the palm-oil lamp, or somewhere along the slatted shelves that ran round the walls, ranged with a confusion of smoke-blackened baskets, lidded gourds, pots and pans. He studied two six-foot spears (with broad, double-barbed iron points) which rested against the back wall; he stared, for hours, it seemed, at three small bundles of fur which hung above the lintel of the door.

'Samalé is like the gorilla,' he said, reinhabiting himself, handing us the mugs of palm-wine. 'He is like the gorilla, he is like the chimpanzee, he is like a man. And he is different from all three. He is hairless. He is beardless. His arms are longer than his legs. The three cuts he makes, from left to right across a boy's back, the three cuts he makes from right to left, these cuts are longer than the wounds he leaves along the tops of that boy's arms.'

(So, I thought idly, Samalé must sometimes cut with all three claws, or with one . . .)

'Samalé is an animal of the forest. And that is why we keep the big trees close to this village. Samalé is our guardian. The trees belong to him.'

Dokou refilled Marcellin's mug. 'Drink!' he said. 'Drink, Marcellin! Tonight – you must drink my palm-wine!' Marcellin drank.

'Mr Redmond, you should know that there is another animal, for me, personally, for me and all my family, the hereditary and traditional animal of those with special powers, on land and in the water, the crocodile. You have the money?'

I took two 500 CFA notes from the plastic bag in my leg-pocket. Dokou pulled the crumpled blue notes through his fingers, laid them beside his untouched mug of wine. 'For that other matter. Your protection. You say you are going to Lake Télé. But every sorcerer from here to Senegal knows the dangers of Lake Télé. Lake Télé is a place of deserted spirits. It is peopled by spirits from villages that no longer exist. The spirits of Lake Télé never receive an offering – because all the living men they knew, and all their children, are dead. Those spirits – they are hungry, they don't know who they are. And so they have become dangerous. I, Dokou, this night in my own hut, I tell you, Marcellin and Redmond, I warn you – strong men, hunters, men in the best of health, they go to Lake Télé, they hear strange sounds, sounds they have never heard before. They walk back through the forest, they feel ill. They return to their villages, and they die.'

Marcellin stared at the floor.

'For the fetish,' I said. 'How much?'

Dokou looked straight at me. 'Ten thousand francs.'

Marcellin nodded.

I pulled out another twenty notes. Dokou picked up the other two, pushed the wad into the breast-pocket of his jacket, rose to his feet and disappeared through the dark entrance to the inner rooms.

Marcellin muttered, 'Redmond, it's your fault ... you forced me to come here ... All my life I've tried to avoid ... to be free ...'

Dokou stood in front of us, holding something wrapped in black cloth. He sat down, laid the bundle carefully on the table beside him, folded back the near edge, and drew out a small elongated bag, the size of a Field vole, a string dangling from its neck.

'Mr Redmond, this is a fetish for your protection,' he said, and gave it to me. (It fitted into my palm; it felt warm – perhaps there was another fire in the inner room; a ruff of blue cloth protruded from its bound neck; and its thick brown fur was rubbed smooth in places, revealing white skin.) 'There are no special conditions, no food conditions attached to the use of that fetish,' he said, refilling Marcellin's mug. 'You may eat whatever you wish. But it is forbidden to cross water too often. That fetish, which you must never open, the fetish which you now hold in your hand, Mr Redmond, it contains the finger of a child. The spirit of this child will protect you. The spirit will guard you from thoughts that are old and sad. The spirit will free you from disease. The fetish itself is secret. Your very closest male friends, the men who hunt with you – they may glance at it. Your wife may touch it. But if she washes her private parts with it – it will lose its power at once.'

'Yes?' I managed to say.

'Marcellin! Drink!' said Dokou.

Marcellin drank.

Dokou drew a seemingly identical bag of fur from the black cloth. 'Marcellin, this is not an ordinary fetish,' he said, leaning forward on his stool, intent, his voice suddenly uneven, parched with emotion. 'Only, I, Dokou, have protection like this. It is mine. And I wish to give it you.'

'No,' said Marcellin, drunk, pressing himself back in his chair. 'No! I don't want it!'

'This fetish,' said Dokou, his hand trembling, 'it will protect you against your enemies, misfortune, everything. This fetish – it holds the trapped breath of Samalé!'

'I've told you before,' said Marcellin, his arms tight across his chest, his neck rigid, 'I've told you a hundred times – I don't want it.'

Dokou closed his right hand over the fur; he thrust his fist into the right-hand pocket of his jacket; he stumbled to his feet and stooped forward over Marcellin, like a heron mantling a fish. 'Take it! For Lake Télé! *You need my protection.* Take it!'

Dokou's fist, palm-up, was level with Marcellin's chest. Dokou opened his fingers. In the flat of his hand, something bright and yellow lay looped to the string at the neck of the fetish.

Marcellin, barely breathing, his mouth half-open, his eyes so wide they showed the whites, stared at Dokou's palm. His right hand, stiff as the hand on a sorcerer's doll, detached itself from the edge of his seat, reached up, and took the fetish and the wedding-ring.

'Good,' said Dokou, sitting down, drinking for the first time (his goitre roused itself, bobbed up with each swallow). 'I thought so. Here in Makao we help each other. I helped her. She helped me. Her husband, the school-master, he's a stranger, he's not from here, he's a Téké, from the plateau. She wanted a son. She wanted a son for Samalé. "Marcellin is coming," I said. I sent a spirit to meet you. I knew you were coming. I knew you were coming long before you came here in the body, in bodily form. But both of you – you must go now. You have my protection. I can do no more. I must sleep.'

'Marcellin,' I said, as we walked very slowly back across the street, like old men, 'I don't understand. How can you give the schoolmaster's wife a son for Samalé? You're not initiated. You don't have the scars.'

'When I left Makao, I was too young. But that doesn't matter. Because I have a special position, a special lineage.'

'A special position?'

Marcellin turned to me. 'You really don't know, do you?'

'Know what?'

'Dokou – he's my grandfather.'

I crawled into the tent, took off my boots and lay down. Lary stirred. He said, 'That old fraud – he didn't give you a damn thing, did he?'

Guessing in the dark where Lary's face was, I took the fetish out of my pocket, leaned over, and, with the soft bag of monkey-fur, gently brushed his cheek.

Lary sat up and screamed.

22

━━━━━━━

In the grey dawn, on the narrow path into the forest, just beyond the last plantation of manioc, Muko, at the head of our small column, broke off the branch of a shrub (sparsely covered with thick and shiny, dark-green leaves like those on a laurel) and hit himself across the legs, arms and chest; he thrashed his shoulders and, with a couple of swipes, the heavy bergen which rested on his back, suspended from a loop of liana-twine across his forehead.

'They always do that,' said Marcellin, ahead of me, in answer to my question. 'He's purifying himself. He's beating off the influence of the village, clearing his head. For him, the village is a foreign place, full of bosses, humiliation. In the forest – he's a man.'

'They should *stay* in the forest,' said Lary, behind me.

'They can't,' said Marcellin, as we set off again down the little path. 'I told you – the Babinga need points for their spears, blades for their machetes. They have to catch meat in the forest, they have to work in the Bantu plantations – just for tiny bits of iron. But they like old clothes, too, and tobacco and palm-wine, the good things of life! Besides, they need starch – they go crazy for manioc.'

'Manioc!' said Lary.

'Come on,' said Marcellin, 'we must hurry. We must get ahead of the others. Muko will show us things. We must be silent. Michel Walengué and Antoine Mokito, Nzé and Manou – they're Bantu, they talk in the forest, all the time, at the top of their voices!'

'Yeah,' said Lary, 'I noticed. All the way to the pygmy camp, Nzé and Manou yelled at each other. Six hours and thirty-eight minutes. They went the distance. The energy cost! And what's so interesting all of a sudden? What do they find to talk about? What's the point?'

'Leopards, that's what they'll tell you,' said Marcellin, increasing his pace, keeping up with Muko. 'They talk to warn off leopards. But me, I think it's something else. In the forest you must never surprise a spirit. If you bump into a spirit, if you catch a spirit on the path – you go mad! You never recover!'

'Redso,' muttered Lary, closing up behind me in his big boots. 'We rely on you, okay? When you feel the first tentacle – a touch of ectoplasm on the neck – don't say squat. Just shake its claw, all formal and correct. And with the other hand – you take that goddam filthy, noisome, mangy, anthrax-ridden bag of fur – and you stroke its face. Make it *scream*. Okay?'

An hour later Muko paused, said something in Kaka to Marcellin, and, with his machete, pointed at a sapling which had been bent horizontal, the bark of its middle section peeled forward, and the leaves at its tip bound into a spiral. 'It's a pygmy sign,' said Marcellin. 'It means, "Gone to look for honey this way." And Muko – he says he wishes he'd gone to look for honey that way, too!'

And in between bursts of walking at a pace that was just short of a run, stumbling against surface roots, climbing over fallen trees, wading and slipping through small streams, we stopped to inspect anything that Muko considered to be an essential part of general knowledge (or which happened to be nearby when he wanted a rest, and a cigarette). We admired the Esolo tree, whose smooth bark, ground into a powder and mixed into a potion, cures children of diarrhoea, and whose nuts (which looked like hazelnuts) are eaten by all kinds of monkeys, and which you can use, said Marcellin, to add flavour to caterpillar or palm-maggot soup, like an onion. We ate red Bamou fruit, scattered beneath its huge trees, a fruit which has a skin like a pomegranate, a white stringy glue for pith, four nuts set in a yellow-orange flesh much prized by gorillas, and which smells like cider as it rots. We tried red fruits the size of plums, fallen in clusters like bunches of grapes, and more bitter than any grape or plum had a right to be ('We'll need that bark that stops the squits,' said Lary, lobbing his into a clump of saplings). We gathered (stuffed into our pockets) fallen *payo*, like chestnuts, because Marcellin said you could hack them open and shave them into slices, and that these slices, cooked with meat, transformed themselves into crisps, very like the kind of crisps you can make from potatoes.

'Potatoes!' said Lary.

The ground grew drier, the trees taller, the travelling easier, but the trunk of every tree was still covered with a white lichen, and from territory to territory, almost without cessation, the Red-chested cuckoo still called, as it had called to Dokou, *tok-tok-boo, tok-tok-boo* – and then we stepped into violent light, direct heat, open space. 'The sky!' said Lary, looking up at the spread of clouds.

A corridor of grassland stretched in front of us, perhaps half-a-mile wide, bounded by thick shrubs and low forest, with the occasional multi-tiered top of an emergent giant still visible from the forest proper rising on all sides further back.

'Edaphic savanna!' I said. 'I've read about them in Richards. They're little natural savannas, entirely enclosed by forests, grassland on pockets of soil too run-down to support even the smallest trees. He says you find them along old river sandbanks, sandbanks left dry when the stream changes course; but that there's another type, found only in the Oubangui region, and they're *very* interesting, because *almost nothing is known about them.*'

'I've told you before,' said Lary, kneeling down to photograph the shin-high spiky grass, like Water plantain, the off-white sand, 'no self-respecting scientist would ever come up here.' (Click.) 'No botanist would want to come all this way.' (Click.) 'No one actually wants to be burnt to a *payo* crisp by Sergeant Pepper, just to solve a little local problem' (mimicking my accent) 'in the Oubangui region.'

'Well, maybe you're right,' I said, as we followed Marcellin (in his floppy hat and olive-drab shirt, the shotgun slung across his chest, two water-bottles and his grey document-bag clipped to the back of his army belt), and, in the distance ahead of us, a fast-bobbing bergen with Muko's legs beneath it. 'There's another book that's equally impressive in its own way, Jan Vansina's *Paths in the Rainforests*. It's subtitled *Towards a history of political tradition in Equatorial Africa*, but that gives you no idea of the actual achievement. He's tried to produce a history for the different groups in the Congo basin – mostly from comparative linguistics, but also from early administrator's reports, ethnographies, memoirs by missionaries, even from a study of the current distribution of genetically distinct types of banana . . .'

'So?' said Lary, stopping to photograph a termite castle, a pinnacled mound, the central spire nine feet tall. 'What kind of history?'

'Gradual migration along the rivers, into the forests, warfare, bigger settle-ments, bigger canoes, better plantations. The pygmy as the revered ancestral teacher and then the despised, non-human serf. The gradual evolution of the idea of the Big Man, the Chief, despite the necessity of sharing all you have, staying equal, not arousing envy lest the sorcerer get you.'

'So what's new?'

'The word-histories. The Western Bantu word for hero comes from the verb meaning to enter oblivion, to be lost, to become a spirit. And he dates the start of serious trading in the south-west, for instance, by the arrival of a new verb, "to sell", derived from a derivation of "to set a trap".'

'Yeah,' said Lary, the termitary photographed to his satisfaction, 'that meat you bought, that elephant-nose . . .'

'But the real point for us is his map of the Congo basin charting all the places where observations or studies of some kind have been made, where his evidence came from, and he ranks these sources on a scale from "First-rate plus" to "Inadequate". And our whole area is simply marked "NO DATA".'

'Poor old Vansina,' said Lary. 'Sergeant Pepper torched his students.'

Marcellin waited for us to catch up. 'Ngombo!' he said, pointing at tracks across the sand (hoof-marks like a Charolais bull's). 'Forest buffalo! They're dangerous. Lary – you must never shoot at one.' ('Sure,' said Lary, crouching down, intrigued by something in the sand.) 'You may kill it. You think, "I've done it! I'm safe!" Then the others come for you. They're smaller than plains buffalo. Their horns curve up, not sideways. So they can run fast in the forest. They've got tough tongues, they eat the worst grasses. You hear them coming, you panic, you climb the wrong tree, you can't get any higher, you can't pull your legs up, you're stuck. They circle round, they lick you.'

'Lick you?' said Lary, without looking up.

'They lick the trousers off your skin; the skin off your muscles, the muscles off your bones. When they walk away – your leg-bones, they've got no flesh, they dangle from your knee-joints!'

'Sure,' said Lary, standing up, holding out a handful of sand full of tiny white and black shards of shell. 'But what are these? Bits of snail?'

'Oryctérope shit!' (Lary dropped the handful.) '*Orycteropus afer*. The aard-vark. He's like a pig, but he has a long nose, long ears and long tail, and thick front legs. And big claws! He eats ants and termites and millipedes. That's bits of millipede casing. The pygmy goes crazy for manioc, the aardvark goes crazy for millipede!'

The heat-shimmer over the sand, above the pointed tops of the grass, seemed to rise up and envelop Lary and Marcellin, blurring their outlines, oscillating their features.

Marcellin said, 'When you touch an aardvark, he screams and turns a somersault.'

Lary said, 'Have you seen one?'

'Of course not. They make burrows. They come out at night. They live alone. No one knows anything about them. Only the pygmies know how the aardvark lives.'

That's right, I thought, dizzy in the heat, as, just in time, we re-entered the forest, the filtered light, the closeness of damp, unmoving, musky air. No other mammal has little tubes radiating through its teeth, no other mammal has teeth without enamel or roots (stumbling, myself, over a double-helix of liana roots). The aardvark has no relatives. The aardvark is odder than Samalé, be-cause no one even knows where it comes from, it has no origins. The aard-vark is as rootless as its teeth. The aardvark is the sole member of its own order, family and genus: its past has entered oblivion, been lost, become a spirit, a spirit from the tunnels of the underworld which emerges after dark . . .

I stopped, fumbling with the webbing pull-release buckle on my left-hand water-bottle. 'You okay?' said Lary, behind me. 'Redso, you all right?'

'I need water,' I said, upending the black bottle, draining the last mouthful. 'I feel odd.'

Marcellin turned and walked back towards me down the path. 'You drink too much,' he said. 'A drink of water in the morning, before you start. A drink of water in the evening, before you make camp. That's the way. The more you drink, the more you sweat.' He stood over me. He'd grown thinner, I noticed, his features sharper, his eyes bigger. He said, 'You're not like Mike Fay, are you?'

'No, I suppose not.'

'You look strong, you keep up, but you're *clumsy*. Look at your shirt!' (I looked.) 'It's wet! You smell! You sweat!'

'Yes, I suppose I do.'

'Mike Fay – he walks fast with little steps. He never tires. I don't have to tell him *anything*. He never gives up. *He knows all the plants in the forest.* He's a genius!'

'Of course,' said Lary. His grin travelled to the ends of his moustache, so that the hairs stuck out, like whiskers on a cat. 'He's American.'

Marcellin took off down the path, redoubling his pace.

Lary said, *sotto voce*, in my ear, 'Most misguided piece of exercise physiology I ever heard.' And, pulling my empty water-bottle from its holder, he dropped in his full one.

Taking a swig whenever there was a clear length of path between roots and lianas and the thickets round fallen trees, the true hero, I thought, Sir Philip Shaffer, giving away his chance of a drink, dying on the battlefield (but I couldn't remember where). 'Zutphen!' I said aloud, half-an-hour later, full of water, feeling better.

We passed several aardvark holes (like the entrance to a badger sett, but twice the size); they were temporary burrows, said Marcellin, the aardvark wandered for miles every night, and when dawn came and caught him far from home he dug in for the day, covered the entrance with loose earth, leaving only a breathing-hole, and slept.

We caught up with Muko – or, rather, Muko was waiting for us, perched on his bergen under a big tree, pulling out and sucking triangular sections from a round, green-yellow fruit, half the size of his head – the *ikamou*, said Marcellin, from the same family as the pineapple, but twice as bitter as a lemon. 'And then some,' said Lary, spitting out a segment.

The ground began to undulate gently, we crossed a small stream, refilled our water-bottles – and the quality of the light changed: it was weaker, cooler, diffused through a dense and even canopy. We were walking unimpeded in a forest almost free of surface roots and lianas, with few herbs and grasses, a forest of great trees that had no buttresses or prop roots – and yet their trunks began to branch low down, the tiers of gnarled branches rising, layer on massive layer, disappearing into their own thick, dark-green crowns. And a mile or so later I realized, dimly, through the sweat, that there was something odd about the familiarity of this place, a forest that but for the size of the trees, the close heat, the dim light, might have been an English oak or beech wood.

'Marcellin! The trees – they're all the same!'

'Correct!' shouted Marcellin, as loud as Nzé, without looking round or checking his pace. 'We call them *mulapa*. Mike Fay, he calls them *Gilbertiodendron dewevrei*. They have a big root that goes deep into the earth, they live with a fungus in the soil. They get all the food there is!'

Bending down and scooping up a couple of the seeds that were scattered everywhere across the forest floor – dark-brown, wrinkled, huge flattened beans over two-and-a-half inches long and two inches broad – I thought: Marcellin, for some reason, is still angry with me, but I'll think about this problem, if it is a problem, when we stop, if we ever stop.

There was a whooshing and swishing of wings overhead, much louder, more ragged than the beat of swans; a moment of silence; a braying of donkeys; a long, single fluting note; a burbling laugh. 'Grand calao!' shouted Marcellin, unprompted. 'The big black hornbill!'

An hour or so later we crossed another small, enclosed savanna – the grass taller, waist-high, and studded with a different type of termite-mound (their air-shaft tops domed like mushrooms) – and on the far side, a few hundred yards back into normal, mixed forest, Muko decided to stop for the night. He shed his bergen, cut a sapling with his machete, sharpened it with four slicing blows, and began to dig.

'There's water here,' said Marcellin. 'Muko always knows, he never fails, he can sense it.'

'A babbling brook,' said Lary. He took off his hat, lobbed it on the ground, sat down against a tree and ran both hands through his sweat-flat hair. 'Muko the dowser. I guess there's water most any place round here. Annual rainfall two-point-something yards. What do you expect?'

'It's the dry season,' snapped Marcellin. 'It's not as simple as you think. It's complicated. There are two dry seasons.'

'Sorry I spoke,' said Lary, leaning back against the tree-trunk and shutting his eyes.

Embarrassed, I pretended to examine a nearby herb – and then looked in earnest: a nondescript plant, varying in height from around four to six feet, the most common woody herb of the forest, its straggly, elongated leaves had an odd, dark-blue and green shine to their surfaces that I had not noticed before – perhaps they contained some pigment that was hyper-sensitive to light, that enabled them to live in deep shade, to capture the last exhausted rays that had escaped the trees and climbers, the epiphytes above them? A few were in bloom – a single central spike of small purple flowers – and a few were in different stages of their fruiting, the flowers transformed into small blue swollen bags, like blood-gorged ticks, blue bags that enlarged and turned white as they ripened.

'*Matoto!*' said Marcellin, standing beside me, still holding the shotgun; he stood awkwardly, lopsided, there was sweat on his forehead, his eyes were bloodshot.

'Marcellin, what's wrong?'

'My foot hurts,' he said, sitting down next to Lary. He cradled the shotgun across his knees. 'And I'm hurt inside.' He stared at Muko, apparently mes-merized by the rise and fall of the sapling-crowbar, the flattening of Muko's breast-packs of muscle on the upstroke, the bunching forward on the downstroke, the splash of muddy water over the rim of the hole, the gurgle of Muko's pot-stirring. 'My clear head, my confidence – it's gone.'

Lary opened his eyes.

'Redmond,' said Marcellin, 'I do not want to talk. If I want to talk – I'll tell you.'

Lary said, 'Your foot?'

Marcellin unlaced his right boot, pulled the uppers wide, and eased it over his toes: he peeled off his once-white sock and rolled up the leg of his jeans. The top of his foot was swollen, a wadge of infection that puffed out from his big toe; and the ulcers on his shin were open again; dribbles of clear fluid oozed down his leg. 'It was chiggers,' he said. 'Under the nail. I dug out the eggs with a penknife. The little red penknife. The one you gave me.'

'And you walked all this way?' said Lary with admiration. 'That must hurt. That must hurt like a sonofabitch!'

Muko, the water-hole evidently working to his satisfaction, came over to look. 'Wooooo!' he said, taking the shotgun, 'Wooo!'; and he disappeared into the forest.

'There's some Floxapen left,' said Lary. 'One bottle, one complete course. I hid it. In the medicine pack. It's down the bottom of the left-hand pocket. When the pack comes, I'll fix you up. My partner Chris – she's a nurse. I know what to do. I'll bandage it just right. Like a real pro, Al.'

Marcellin managed a smile. He said, 'Just like you fixed my tooth.'

*

'*Ka-ka-ka!*' came a sudden frantic chorus. '*Ka-ka-ka!*': an explosive cacophony from behind us, at ground level. 'The Kaka bird!' said Marcellin, cheering up. 'He's a guineafowl. He's black, he lives in the forest, the hair on his head – it stands on end. He's seen a ghost! Muko can talk to them. He sticks his fingers up his nostrils' (Marcellin stuck his fingers up his nostrils); 'he callsh like thish: "*Kow-kow-kow!*"' (There was a whirring of wings, receding; and a chorus of Bantu voices, approaching.) Marcellin unplugged his nostrils. 'They answer Muko; they run towards him; they run between his legs. You must call "*Kow-kow-kow*" – never "*Kaka-kaka*". If you stick your fingers up your nostrils and call "*Kaka-kaka*", they fly away.'

'Too bad,' said Lary.

'Too bad?'

'Those Kaka guys – they went to the wrong school. You said *kow-kow-kow*: they hit the state line.'

'Nzé frightened them!'

'If you say so,' said Lary.

'Bohmaaa!' said Nzé, striding into the clearing. 'I won!'

Manou, two yards behind Nzé, said, 'You cheated.'

Michel the drummer, two yards behind Manou, slipping off his bergen, said, 'We had to come slowly. Nzé and Manou, they walk like old women. They fell so far behind we had to go back – we had to go and look for them. But for us they'd be lost in the forest. Leopard meat!'

'Bohmaaa!' said Nzé with a happy laugh. 'It's true!'

'See anything?' said Marcellin.

'Buffalo!' said Nzé. 'They charged. I stood my ground. I waited. Little Manou screamed, "Help! Help me, Nzé!" "Manou," I said, "don't you worry. Nzé is here." They bore down on us. Their hooves thundered. The dust rose. They smelt bad. Like Manou's trousers. The leader was almost on me. His horns stuck out like handlebars. Wide as my bike. He lowered his handlebars. His mouth foamed. His eyes rolled. "So what's your game?" I said, as I caught him by the horns. *Wham!* I yanked them down. *Whoosh!* Over he went. *Ker-thump!* He landed on his back. *Boom! Bang! Boom!* He bounced. I was on him in a flash. "Bohmaaa!" I said. I drew my machete. I held it to his throat. "Okay, boy," I said. "Just teaching you a lesson. I won't eat you today. We're busy. We're official. Secret mission. From the Government of the People's Republic of the Congo. The Parti Congolais du Travail. The PCT. So run along now, boy. And next time you're thinking of charging at people like that – check first. That's my advice. Pick someone your own size. Don't mess with Big Men like Nzé Oumar, a famous high-ranking officer of the People's Party Militia at Dongou. "Full-Colonel Oumar, sir," said the buffalo, "I think I'll run off." They all ran off. "Nzé," said

Manou. "You saved my life. You're a hero. I'll give you all my money. And also my wife, of course. Vivie Charlotte. That goes without saying."'

Nzé, exhausted, sat down on the edge of Antoine's bergen, slithered to the ground, leaned back and closed his eyes.

Lary and I clapped.

Nzé opened his eyes; he beamed at us; he raised his right fist into the air, and shook it.

'You liar,' said Manou, stretching flat-out on the ground. 'You're a Private, Second-class.'

'What bike?' said Marcellin, collecting our *payo* nuts and dropping them into the food-sack.

'The bike I'll buy with Redmond's money,' said Nzé, the thought providing its own energy. 'With the danger-money he'll give me for going to Lake Télé. Or maybe with the bonus I'll get because he loves my cooking, and especially my sauces. Or perhaps because he wants to hear my music. I'll go down to Brazzaville on the steamer, in a cabin, like a boss. And I'll buy a red bike with saddlebags. A red bike with saddlebags – and a hooter at the front.'

'Nzé, Manou!' said Marcellin. 'You'll put up my tent. You'll make a fire and a smoking-rack. Muko has gone hunting.'

'But he only took one cartridge,' I said. 'The one in the breech.'

'Redmond, Muko never misses. He stands behind a tree. He calls the duiker to him. Poomf!'

Antoine, barefoot, in his orange trousers and denim jacket, carrying a bergen in the approved manner, and the five pygmies, straining forward against their liana-twine headbands, packs and bundles suspended on their backs, walked into the clearing. 'We found honey!' said Antoine. 'Lots of honey!'

The accompanying bees clustered on our shirts. 'Redso,' said Lary. 'It's a bee contact. It's bee evade-and-escape time. Let's get the goddam tent up.'

'My foot!' said Marcellin.

'In a minute,' said Lary, cutting himself a bee-switch. 'It's the sweatsuckers I can't stand.' He resheathed his machete, licked the index finger of his free hand, and squashed the clusters of little black stingless bees out of the corners of his eyes. With his switch (the large-leaved top of a sapling, or perhaps of a miniature tree) he flagellated his back. He thrashed at his front. A honeybee he had not noticed, entangled in the sweaty hairs on his chest, stung him. 'Goddamit!' said Lary, dropping the bee-switch.

'You beat the *air* with it,' said Marcellin, laughing. 'Bees – you should just ignore them. Look at the pygmies. That's what they do.' He bent forward, waving his right hand to and fro over the sweat-bees drinking at the rim of his leg ulcer. '*Merde!*' he said, with a galvanic twitch of his whole body, jabbing up his elbow, flicking a honeybee out of the hairs in his armpit.

After dark, when the bees had gone, we sat on packs and kit-bags round the fire, Muko between Marcellin and the five pygmies, Nzé and Manou tending the cooking-pots, Lary to my left, Michel and Antoine to my right, our own small circle ringed by an outer circle of two tents, a smoking-rack and three shelters, one for the Bantu, two for the pygmies, roofs of sapling-poles and leaves, sloping tight down to the ground on the jungle side, open towards the fire.

'Michel! You have two wives?' said Marcellin, cutting up a slab of boiled Blue-duiker liver in his mess-tin.

Michel, the drummer, sitting beside me on the medicine-pack, dressed in his blue shorts and a white tee-shirt, eating from a leaf-plate like the pygmies, shifted uneasily to his right, away from the question. By the light of the fire the raised scars on his huge muscular back were plainly visible: three ripped lines from his left shoulder-blade, three from his right, intersecting above the centre of his spine and petering out at his loins.

'And no children!' said Marcellin, swallowing the chunk of liver.

'My wives, they're new!' said Michel, in his big bass voice. 'They're young. They're too young to have children.'

'Perhaps they fight? They fight all the time? You can't get near them?'
Everyone laughed.

'My home is peaceful,' said Michel, straightening his back. 'I share every-thing. I give this to one' – he pointed with the short, wooden-handled dagger in his right hand – 'that to the other. There's no trouble.'

'You need a son,' said Marcellin, his mouth half-full of manioc. 'Without a son, what's the purpose of life?'

'Marcellin,' said Antoine (older, quieter, gloomier than Michel), getting up, taking his leaf-plate over to Nzé for a refill from the cooking-pot, 'you yourself – how do you live? A son? I don't think you have a son!'

'My wife is pregnant. I have a daughter already, Vanessa Sweet Grace. I love my daughter. But soon I will have a son. For me, it will then be different. I will not risk my life. I will send my subordinate on these expeditions.'

'A son?' said Antoine, sitting down again. 'How do you know? Has Dokou told you? It's not easy! There are ways, but it's expensive. You may have a daughter!'

'I shall have a son. And as for you, Antoine, why did you want to come with us? After what happened? We could have gone in peace to Berandzoko. And now we must be on our guard, afraid!'

'I didn't want to come. Michel didn't want to come. Since that night, Marcellin, after what happened, we have not been back to Berandzoko. But the Chief of Makao called us to his hut, he sent for us. "You will go with young Marcellin Agnagna," he said. "You will return to Berandzoko. You will prove that we are not afraid, not of the Government, not of the men of Berandzoko, not of anything that their sorcerers can do. Our village is bigger, we are stronger, our lineage is more powerful!" That's what he said. We had no choice.'

Marcellin stood up, looked vacantly at Lary, thrust his right hand into the pocket of his jeans, withdrew it, fast, as if another bee had stung him, walked over to the cooking-fire, realized he was not holding his mess-tin, retrieved it, decided that he didn't want any more to eat, turned on his heel, kicked his pack and sat down on it. 'The Chief of Makao – he lied to me! He said he owed you a favour. He said you needed work!'

'Work! Carrying loads? For these white men?'

'So why did he say that? Why lie to me? I'm a *chef de service*. I'm an agent of the Government. I have my own Department. I work in a Ministry!'

'Not here you don't,' said Antoine quietly. 'Here you're not an agent of anything. Here we all know who you are – you're the son of Dokou's daughter, Mahonsine Mopata. We even know you in your other shape, a crocodile. The Chief of Makao does not like you, Marcellin Agnagna. He doesn't like you, and he doesn't like Dokou.'

'I've got daughters and sons and all sorts,' said Nzé, restored by his supper, collecting up the mess-tins. 'There's so many I can't count – they're all over Dongou, doctor! And there's some in Impfondo. Manou will tell you. Only my grandfather knows how many we've got – and he's dead, he's a spirit, so he goes wherever he likes. He can travel to Impfondo. For all I know he's been to Brazzaville. He goes on the steamer!'

'Of course he doesn't go to Brazzaville,' said Manou, bringing his kit-bag, placing it next to Lary. 'He's never been to Brazzaville.'

'Nzé,' said Marcellin, standing up, 'this conversation was for serious people, for men. Whereas you're a joker, a clown, a buffoon.' And he went to his tent, dropped to his knees and crawled inside.

Nzé sat down on the vacant pack, clattering the mess-tins to the ground in front of him. 'Redmond,' he said. 'Cigarettes? A new lighter?'

I found the store of cigarettes and lighters in the sack of supplies; and I handed out one disposable lighter and one packet of cigarettes to everyone. Muko and the pygmies, plainly delighted, withdrew to their shelter. Antoine and Michel, impassive, withdrew to theirs. Nzé, with his lopsided grin, buttoned the packet of cigarettes into the breast-pocket of his Cuban army fatigues, drew his Oxford pipe and his tin of Balkan Sobranie from his trouser-pocket, packed the pipe with forefinger and thumb (head on one side) and lit up with his new lighter. 'Like a *colon*,' he said. 'A white man. A boss from France.' He inhaled deeply, blew out a bonfire-top of smoke, and coughed. 'Lary,' he spluttered, 'maybe when I go to Brazzaville with all my money, I'll take my pipe to a famous restaurant, Le Soir au Village. You know it?'

'I do,' said Lary, giving me a sideways look. 'I remember it well.' And he coughed in his turn, a small dry cough that came in double bursts.

'Nzé, you're a liar,' said Manou, puffing awkwardly at a cigarette. 'You only have one son in Impfondo. I know your son. He's eight years old. He steals beer – from that old woman with a shop by the market. He gets drunk. He has no father. There's no one to tell him what to do. You don't even visit him! It's terrible. Me, I'm the only one in our family who goes to see him. No one else cares. He's thin. His mother is thin. They don't eat well.'

Nzé said, 'I saw him last year.'

Lary ground something into the earth with his boot. 'Manou, you're sensible. Perhaps you can tell me – what's going on? What is all this? Why's Marcellin so worried? Why's he gone to his tent?'

Manou rubbed out his cigarette on a tree-root and put the unsmoked half back in the packet. 'I know everything,' he said proudly. 'I make it my business.' He lowered his voice. 'The matter concerns Antoine. And also Michel. But Michel only went because he is the friend of Antoine, and to show that he is brave, and very strong, and he went, also, out of the kindness of his heart.

'The uncle of Antoine – he died suddenly in Makao, in the best of health. Now, some time before he died, as everyone will tell you, he had an argument with the old sorcerer of Berandzoko. The uncle was staying in the village of Berandzoko, where he went to buy a goat. He paid for the goat, a young girl goat. The uncle loved his goats. In Makao he bred many goats. In the night this goat disappeared from his friend's enclosure, and the uncle came to learn that a wife of the old sorcerer had stolen this goat. So he argued with the sorcerer, and the sorcerer cursed him. The uncle returned to Makao, and some time later, in the best of health, he died.

'So the Chief of Makao called Antoine to his hut and said to him, "You must avenge the death of your uncle or we will all be disgraced. The men of Berandzoko – they'll think the men of Makao are cowards. They'll think they can come to our forest and hunt our elephants. They'll steal our goats and chickens. They'll think they can marry our women and pay us almost nothing!"'

'Manou, talk *quietly*,' said Nzé, looking at the ground, his pipe in his hand.

'So Antoine and Michel took their daggers and machetes, and two special, thick poles, very hard long poles. They went to Berandzoko, walking fast.

They approached in daylight. They hid in the forest. And that night they crept into the village. They took the old sorcerer from his hut. They dragged him out of his hut and laid him on the ground. They knew the only way to kill a sorcerer. Michel held him down. Antoine broke his feet and then his ankles with the long pole. The sorcerer screamed. They had to work fast. Antoine smashed his legs, his genitals, his hips, his stomach, his chest, his neck. They drove the sorcerer's spirit up the sorcerer's body until it sought shelter in his skull. They broke his skull. They pulped his head. They drove the sorcerer's spirit out of the top of his body. The spirit went to the forest. The spirit has no home. Everyone is safe.'

'Christ,' said Lary, putting his head in his hands. 'Christ.'

'Manou, you've got it wrong,' said Nzé, almost in a whisper, still looking at the ground. 'You must ask lots of people when you want to know a secret. Not just the one girl. It's *Antoine* who's the coward. Antoine's uncle was *living* in Berandzoko. This uncle had wives in Berandzoko, and a herd of goats. He never went hunting elephants. He worked hard. He had a plantation. He was rich. The men of Berandzoko grew jealous. So when an old man in the village fell ill and died they accused Antoine's uncle. They said he was a sorcerer. They said he was a sorcerer from Makao. In the night they dragged him from his hut and killed him the way you told it, the way you kill a sorcerer. That is correct. In Makao, Antoine came to hear of it. But instead of going to Berandzoko and killing even one man, by night, in revenge, he travelled all the way to Impfondo and reported the murder to the Court. The Court! What use is that? Who's got the money to come up here? It's too far! The police never come. The army never comes. The Government sends one schoolmaster, every two years, to teach the people Communism. That's all you see – the schoolmaster.'

'Okay,' said Lary. 'So what's the problem?'

'Now the men of Berandzoko say Antoine is a coward. He had no business to report them to a Court. They have no experience of this Court. They don't know when it will attack. So they say that if Antoine himself comes to Berandzoko, they will kill him. But I myself, I think . . .'

'Nzé!' yelled Antoine in his deep voice, with tremendous force, from the darkness, from his shelter behind us, to the right. Nzé started, dropped his pipe. 'Nzé! Manou! *Petits!* Who told you such stories? Eh? One more word – and I'll kill you both. You're *petits*. Boys like you, they should stay with their mothers. But I'll tell you this – the Chief of Makao, *he thinks what he thinks.*'

'It's getting rough,' said Lary. 'It's time for bed.'

23

Marcellin woke us at four in the morning: we drank hot, sweet black coffee made by Manou, ate smoked pieces of duiker-back, broke camp and left at first light. Muko took the lead, we fell into our positions of the day before ('. . . a comfort, a routine . . .' said Lary) and gradually we drew ahead of the others.

The soil became wetter, the muddy pools and little sluggish streams more numerous, breaks in the canopy more frequent, and lianas and epiphytes more abundant. In places lianas, thick as full-grown pythons, hung in loops from tree to tree; they described slow spirals from one high branch to another; from their own roots they lay heavy along the surface of the ground, their first grip on the trunk of a tree sometimes many feet above its base, as if they had reared themselves up and struck. There were scrambling lianas (with little branches set at right-angles and sharp down-curving spines); tendril-climbers (twirling up like a clematis); and root-climbers, stuck to their hosts like ivy, their stems rising flat against a trunk – or perhaps, I thought, those are the descending roots of strangler figs, sent down from a bush high in a fork of the tree, roots that will grow thicker and stronger and intermesh with each other, caging in their host, constricting its trunk, out-foraging its roots, out-shading its crown.

So, I told myself, as the miles go by and my legs begin to develop a stiff life of their own, free of my control, I shall distract myself by looking for full-grown stranglers, towering lattice-work cages of roots, high as the highest trees in the forest . . .

Muko stopped ahead; Marcellin, half-crouched, patted an invisible ball on the path behind him, signalling to us to get down: Lary and I dropped on all-fours; and (as the thudding in my ears subsided) there came the sound of magpies chattering and pigs grunting, all at once.

A large, shaggy, black-haired monkey was walking slowly along a branch some fifty feet up; he trod carefully round a clump of ferns, his long tail held vertically behind him, the tip arched over his back. Above him smaller monkeys were feeding (perhaps ten of them, judging by the rustlings in the foliage) and, through the binoculars, I caught a glimpse of the male of the troop looking down at us, bowing his black forequarters and rapidly nodding his grey-black face from side to side; the white flash on his nose danced like a butterfly among the leaves.

Creeping forward, trying to get a better view, I put my left hand on a fallen liana-spine, and swore. The monkeys chattered, grunted, fell silent and disappeared.

'The little one,' said Marcellin, 'the *Hocheur* in French, *the shaker*, the Greater white-nosed monkey! You saw him? And the big one, the Grey-cheeked mangabey?'

'Sure did,' said Lary, with his odd, dry, double cough. 'They hate bad language.'

'Let's take a rest,' said Marcellin, moving over and lying against a buttress. Muko walked back towards us, ducked out of his bergen and sat on it, next to Marcellin. Marcellin took an unopened packet of cigarettes from his shirt-pocket, said something in Kaka, and handed it to Muko.

Muko grinned, slipped the packet under the top flap of the bergen, put his hand in the pocket of his shorts, drew out a fag-end, leaned over, plucked a leaf from a herb, wrapped it round the base of the stub, lit up with his new lighter, and, closing his eyes with the pleasure, inhaled.

'This tree's a *mukoko* or *banga*,' said Marcellin, looking up at its rose-coloured bark. 'The best wood for dugouts – soft enough to hollow out, and yet it's strong, once you've hardened it with fire, it's strong enough to last for years.'

Muko, nursing a 40,000-year-old disapproval of rivers and boats and fishing, looked bored.

'Marcellin,' said Lary, stretching out on a patch of little herbs, their leaves striped green and white. 'Why do you never call yourself a Kaka? In Brazzaville, we met people who were Batéké or Vili or whatever, and they were proud of it. They told you. What's the Kaka story? What's your take on the Kaka? Something wrong?'

'There's nothing wrong,' said Marcellin, propping himself up on his elbow. 'But me, I don't like it. Kaka, it's a bad word in French, it sounds like *caca*, a piece of shit.'

'Oh,' said Lary.

'And that's how I feel sometimes, a piece of shit.'

'Everyone feels like that,' said Lary, taking off his hat and turning the rim between his fingers. 'For a varying percentage of every day. Whisky, that's the answer. A shot or two. No more.'

'Sometimes, Lary, I even feel I'd like to leave the Congo altogether. I'd like to be a white man, an Englishman in Zimbabwe. That would be best. Great farms, whole families, big houses. It's good like that.'

A Red-chested cuckoo called nearby, and there was a sudden cawing, as if a whole chapter of ravens was cawing at once, a cawing that became faster, hysterical, died away; perhaps a Green-crested touraco . . .

'I did have a perfect job once. In France itself. I worked for Le Vicomte Paul de la Panouse. I was helping him set up a park, a zoological park. He took me to Maxim's!'

'He's got a bat named after him,' I said. 'Some kind of North African bat that lives on the edge of deserts.'

'That's right. He's famous! I like him. He's a real aristocrat. He couldn't put a teddy bear to bed.'

'So what happened?' said Lary. 'What went wrong?'

'He brought in someone else, someone who hadn't even been to university.'

'Why? Why would he do that?'

'Because I'm black!' yelled Marcellin, springing to his feet.

In mid-afternoon, some five or six troops of monkeys later (Muko wouldn't stop), we came to a series of dark, semi-stagnant shallow pools, shut away from sunlight beneath the unbroken canopy, their surfaces criss-crossed with pond-skaters, puckered with water-boatmen.

'The Ipendza river!' said Marcellin. 'We can swim!' (Lary looked dubious.) 'We can wash!'

Muko went hunting; Marcellin, Lary and I briefly covered ourselves in dilute slime from the deepest pond; and the others arrived, all together.

'I'm ill,' said Nzé.

'We saw a chimpanzee,' said Michel. 'He was rude to us. He hid behind a tree.'

'Antoine saw a Wild dog,' said Manou. 'A black one.'

Mobbed by butterflies, we put up the tents and shelters thirty yards from the pools, on a slight knoll. Bright-scarlet butterflies, the size of Speckled woods, settled on our boots (and on the inverted triangle of sweat on the back of Lary's shirt). Yellow butterflies spotted with white; butterflies like Cabbage whites; small black-and-whites; large black-and-whites (with orange roundels to the rear of their hindwings); and large butterflies with rounded, brown wings that were spotted, dashed, streaked and whorled with yellow – airborne decaying leaves complete with flecks of sunlight – fed on every patch of mud.

'It's a butterfly bar,' said Lary. 'A flutfly pub. I guess all the forest animals come to drink in those mud ponds. And then they walk up here, on to this little rise – and they feel safe, they can see a few extra feet, so they take a piss. Butterfly malt. We're camped on the town latrine.'

Muko, a smile of apology on his broad, powerful face, returned empty-handed; Manou and Nzé, subdued, shared out the last of the smoked duiker meat; Michel, Antoine and the five pygmies built their own fire, fifteen yards away from us. Muko, with a shrug, still carrying the gun, came and sat beside Marcellin.

'Muko has a son,' said Marcellin, looking straight at me with an intensity which I could not interpret. 'You think that because the Babinga have no wealth, because they're hunter-gatherers, as you call it, they have nothing to pass on to their sons – but you're wrong! You're ignorant! You're making a mistake!'

'Yes,' I said, bemused.

'Muko here' – Muko, a speaker of Kaka and Ngodi, the language to the north, looked on politely – 'he thinks he has a special power, a personal secret, something that is always on his side, that gives him success in the hunt.' ('Not tonight, he doesn't,' said Nzé, and laughed.) 'This power can reside in an object as simple, as outwardly insignificant, as laughable to you, a Westerner, as a ball of latex – the very same latex that we might sell to you, the raw material for North American chewing-gum! Or maybe it lies hidden, deep in an axe-head. Muko won't tell me where his own power lies, and now I understand, not in the way people like you and me understand, in a university – now I really understand, every minute of the day. But what happens? How can he give this power to his son? He must hand it on, all of it, as he dies – but not before; because if he gives this power to his son when he is living, full of strength – he'll die! The son, without meaning to – he'll kill the father, in the spirit way. And so there are conditions for this transfer, it's not simple – it's a matter of clear feeling. The father must love his son before all else in the forest, that's what Muko said – and the son must be a wise son, full of respect for his father, he must love his father, look up to him, give him the gift of his time, you'd say, or meat from the hunt, that's how Muko expresses it. If you're the father and you see that your son is kind and strong, generous, gentle, that he makes jokes, that he's full of life – everything a Babinga values – then you teach him, little by little, how this power works. You teach him how to release this power through the plants that it needs. You show him the plants this power needs for its own success. It's no good giving someone a present – even a gun – if they don't know how to use it!'

'What does the father do?' said Lary gently. 'When he knows? When he knows he's going to die?'

'He calls his son to him. The child enters the hut. The son holds his father's right arm, the child holds it tight, and with the father's last breath all the power passes to the son.'

Lary turned his face away, stumbled to his feet, and went to the tent.

'So it's a fetish,' I said. 'A kind of fetish.'

'Not now!' said Marcellin, standing up. 'I want to talk to you. I'm angry. But not now. Now is not the time.' And he took his mess-tin down to the pond to wash.

'Those bright-crimson butterflies,' I said in the tent that night, training my head-torch on plate 18 of John G. Williams, *A Field Guide to the Butterflies of Africa*, 'they're unmistakable. There's nothing else remotely like them. Blood-red cymothoes. Forests of West Africa and the Congo.'

'LRJs,' said Lary. 'Little Red Jobs.'

'And the Cabbage whites are Congo whites. Now, the large black-and-whites with the orange patches? They're ... here, you take a look ... go on ...'

'Oh, okay, if you insist,' said Lary, coughing, sitting up. 'Just to join in.' He turned from the plate to the key and 'Get that!' he said, absurdly pleased. '"Forests of West Africa and the Congo. Flies throughout the year. CYMOTHOE BECKERI, Schaffer."'

Around noon the next day Muko paused to inspect an expanse of rooted-up soil, tensed, walked forward a few paces, wary as a duiker, crouched down and sniffed a sapling. 'What's up?' (or something of the kind) Marcellin whispered in Kaka. Muko, his eyes big, his face alert, talked low and fast. Marcellin translated, 'A leopard, a big male. He was here this morning.' Marcellin peered at a few displaced leaves to the side of the mud – as if they meant something to him, too. (Lary gave me a wink.) 'Muko can still smell him. He says this leopard was not after the bushpig, he was tracking an antelope. He says some leopards only like bushpig, some only take antelope – but every leopard likes dog.'

We crept as quietly as we could after noiseless Muko, the twigs exploding beneath our boots like firecrackers. Fifty yards on, my nostrils picked up a rank, musty, sweetish smell, like blood – and there were tracks that even Lary and I could recognize, elephant tracks, the kind of tracks you can fall into.

'The leopard and the antelope were fighting,' whispered Marcellin, looking at the scuffed-up ground.

Muko whistled softly from behind a tree: the rear half of a Blue duiker lay on the leaves, ribs exposed, covered in bees, its left back leg chewed off, the right intact.

'We ought to eat it,' said Marcellin. 'But Muko thinks that's dangerous. He says if you want to die, if you want a leopard to drop on you out of a tree one day and rip your throat right out, then take a leopard-kill.'

'I'd be quite happy,' said Lary, glancing at the branch above our heads, 'it's okay by me, in a general way, if we leave this thing right here.'

'The leopard is close,' whispered Marcellin. 'And so are the elephants.'

We followed Muko's quick, bare feet down the invisible path into the forest, and the forest appeared markedly less like an English woodland in high summer; the lianas, the ferns, the familiar herbs and shrubs and saplings – they felt less friendly; a few yards away beneath the trees their dark places seemed soft with moving shapes . . .

'The elephants spent the night here,' hissed Marcellin, standing in a clearing, nodding at the rough circles of flattened undergrowth. We inspected several hillocks of elephant droppings (as yet there were no dung-beetles scooping fragments into balls, rolling them away); and we stopped to look at a big tree, the grooves between the raised flutings on its trunk plastered with columns of dried mud eight feet high – a *guma* tree, said Marcellin, an elephant rubbing-post. A group of Greater white-nosed monkeys and Grey-cheeked mangabeys began their magpie-chattering and pig-grunting, their turkey-gobbling and wigeon-whistling, way up, unseen, in the tree above us. Marcellin, releasing the tension, banged his machete against the bark. 'Come out!' he yelled, playing the fool. 'The white men want to see you!'

There was a silence, a swish of escaping monkeys, high up, and the thicket to our left heaved, rose, burst into splintered stems and flying leaves around a patch of grey, subsided behind a long receding crash of vegetation, and was quiet.

'We made it!' said Lary. 'We saw a certified one-inch square of the ass-end of a Forest elephant!'

'Wooo!' sang Muko. 'Wooo!' He held the shotgun level in the air above his head, and shouted at Marcellin.

We resumed the march at Muko's normal, relentless pace. 'It's not his fault,' said Marcellin over his shoulder. 'He was probably paid by the Sudanese. But Muko says he's killed four elephants and three gorillas. In his whole life. He says it's not enough.'

Muko halted to show us straggly herbs above five feet high, Wild ginger, *Afromamum*, the hot red fruits, the delight of gorillas, peeking out at the base of their stems; he inspected *bamou* fruits that had been peeled, sucked dry and cast away by chimpanzees; he pointed out small, dark-brown termite nests of dried mud, intact on boughs and tree-trunks, and, wrenched free, smashed open on the ground where the chimpanzees had eaten the grubs; and, at last, he reached his goal, one of his old hunting-camps, set up to butcher, eat and smoke the meat of a Forest elephant.

In the large clearing a rickety smoking-rack had survived; a shelter for the bachelors and four tiny half-sphere huts, their Giant phrynium leaves brown, brittle, but still intact, stood waiting; and round the open space twelve sapling-poles had been driven into the ground (for hanging up the meat, cutting it into strips, said Marcellin).

The trunks of the big trees at the edges of the clearing were exposed, the quick-growing invasive species were as yet only knee-high, and as I sat on a decayed pygmy bench I thought how odd it was that the light-brown, smooth-barked tree immediately to my right had only one liana twining up its trunk – and in coils so vertically stretched that a mere three revolutions took the liana to its crown – whereas the grey, rough-barked tree to my left was wound about with at least two species of climber. Their epiphyte loads were different, too: the tree to my right seemed almost bare of anything but mosses and lichens; the high branches of the rough-barked tree sprouted and tumbled with ferns and orchids and plants I couldn't identify, plants, I knew, with their own niches and microclimates, their own special relationships with particular species of ants or wasps or thrips or mites, their own hidden chemical war or alliance with their host tree and the competitor-plants around them. Maybe botanists live so long, I thought, because their own anxieties leach out and get lost in the intricate details of their subject – just as astronomers live for ever because no worry measures up to the universe . . . An owl, in plain view, bundled itself out of a hole half-way up the rough-barked trunk; dark-brown, barred white, medium-sized, an African wood owl, it blundered onto a neighbouring branch, ruffled itself, blinked stupidly as if roused from sleep, rotated its head through thirty degrees to squint at me, slipped off the branch and flapped awkwardly away into the shadows.

Just before dusk Muko appeared between the trees, shotgun in hand, smiling, showing his gap teeth, an antelope slung over his shoulders, its long black legs hanging down his chest, its fetlocks tied across the top of his stomach with liana-twine. He dropped it in front of the fire, sat on a kit-bag, laid the shotgun on the ground at his feet, pulled a crumpled packet of cigarettes from the back-pocket of his shorts and lit up.

The antelope was plainly a duiker, its back legs longer than its front, its body arched up, built for fast escape through the undergrowth, but it was larger than a Blue duiker, with a red-brown crest between its conical horns, a black coat, and a long triangle of coarse orange hair extending from an apex in the centre of its back to a base across its rump.

Marcellin, getting out his pipe, sat down beside Muko. 'Bemba!' he called after me, as I went to the tent to fetch Haltenorth and Diller. 'It's a Bemba!'

Inside the hot little tent Lary was straightening the tarpaulin. He knotted his shirt-pillow. He arranged his pencil-torch, his head-torch and *Martin Chuzzlewit* in their proper and comforting places relative to each other; and 'Redso,' he said, as I dug about in my bergen, 'I feel deferential about suggesting this, I don't want to interfere in your unconscious, send you barking mad like most everyone else round here, but how would it be if just for once, just for tonight, you put all that stuff away? You know – when you've found whatever the hell it is you happen to be looking for, maybe you could go right ahead and pick up the goddam sixty-three maggot-ridden black socks you bung about the tent and place them back where they belong – in that stinking grade-one public-health-hazard pack of yours? Okay? No offence?'

'Got it!' I said, holding up Haltenorth and Diller with one hand, catching socks with the other.

'And where do you keep that anthrax-bag? That fetish? Is that thing loose in here?'

'It's in my pocket. I keep it in my pocket.'

'Christ!' said Lary, scratching a roundel of mosquito-bite scabs on his right cheek. 'So you *have* blown a gasket.'

There was a burst of semi-automatic fire, close, skull-cracking, right outside.

'Poachers!' yelled Lary, ejecting himself through the tent-flap.

There came the sound of heavy canvas ripping, wood torn apart, a tree falling, a crash, silence.

'A tree!' yelled Lary.

'Wooo!' sang Muko.

The tree with the rough bark, in a long tangle of smashed branches and snapped lianas, lay to the right of the tent; a big branch, broken clear, had come to rest ten feet from the guy-ropes.

'It nearly killed us!' shouted Lary. 'Ten feet!'

'It meant to kill us,' I said. 'But it couldn't, could it? We were saved. Saved by fetish power!'

'Don't you start,' said Lary, mournful, tugging at his moustache, calming down.

'Look!' shouted Marcellin, on his feet, pointing to the trunk of the smooth tree. 'Bamakou!'

Half-way up, a squirrel with an olive-yellow back and loose, silver-grey sides clung spread-eagled on the bark, shivering with fright, its little heart pumping.

'That owl,' said Lary, craning his neck, watching the squirrel. 'It knew something. I thought that owl had bust a spring. I thought its body-clock was out of sync. But there you go. Owls are smarter than squirrels.'

I turned to plate 27, The Squirrels, in Haltenorth and Diller: 'Beecroft's flying squirrel!' – and when I glanced up again the real squirrel had gone.

'It flew!' said Lary. 'It stuck out its legs and stretched its membranes! It made a glide like you wouldn't believe!' (He pointed low into the forest.) 'Right over there!'

'Shit!'

'Redso,' said Lary, putting a hand on my arm, 'did your mother never tell you? You can't learn *everything* from books. Empiricism. Science. Careful observation. You got to look around!'

That night we ate boiled duiker (*Cephalophus sylvicultor*, the Yellow-backed duiker, but I didn't tell Lary), manioc stodge, and four palm-oil fried *payo* crisps apiece.

'Lary,' said Marcellin, sitting on a kit-bag next to Muko, 'you are a scientist. I am a scientist. We were educated in the West. But Africa is returning to Africa. Every day my people become more African.'

'Is that right?' said Lary, pushing a burnt and greasy *payo* crisp under the wadge of manioc in his mess-tin.

'All the foreigners are leaving Brazzaville. The Cubans, the Chinese, the Russians are leaving. Soon, even the French will go.'

'How so?' said Lary, still busy.

'Because, Dr Shaffer, that's the way we want it!' Marcellin struck his knife on the side of his mess-tin. 'Why should you exploit us? It's time we exploited you!'

Lary looked up.

'Yes, my friend, our time is coming! Africa is returning to Africa. We'll take the best from European thought and leave everything else. You'll be amazed!'

'I will?'

'Muko, for instance, he has his own science. The science of people who know the forest, the science of people who *live* in the forest. He has his own order, his own way of ordering life. He doesn't need your artificial system, the classification you impose on things!'

'Systematics?'

'The Bamakou, for instance – take that Flying squirrel. In Muko's world that squirrel is part-bird, part-mammal. He's a link between the birds and the rat. He connects the air to the ground. And when your wife is pregnant, you can't eat him – not until your child can walk by itself, not until you're certain that your child is safe, a creature of the ground, that he won't die, fly away, join the spirits!'

'Marcellin,' said Lary, standing up, flicking the contents of his mess-tin into the undergrowth, 'I need a big sleep.'

From inside the tent we listened to an owl hooting, a series of loud, uneven hoots from a perch somewhere low down in the forest, close at hand.

'She's calling to her dead chicks,' said Lary, laying *Martin Chuzzlewit* aside.

'Maybe she was just roosting in that tree. And anyway – how do you know it's a female?'

'Tell me, Redso, how did *you* know about Viscount Moose – whatever his name was – the man Marcellin worked for? The bat?'

'I don't. I probably got it wrong. Just a stray half-memory from reading *East African Mammals*. Jonathan Kingdon. He's the real chronicler, the Balzac for African mammals. It's the only guide you can read right through – an evolution story. He's a white African. I've met him. He's about nine feet tall, with a two-foot beard and a voice to match. He's bigger than Michel!'

'Can he shoot?'

'What?'

'Can he handle a General Purpose Heavy Machine-gun?'

'No idea.'

'Write to him. Post it tomorrow,' said Lary, taking off his head-torch, lying down, pulling his tarpaulin up to his nose, just as if he was in a bed, with sheets. 'Because, Redso, I have this nasty little hunch – when I'm gone, when you're all alone, when you're all alone at Lake Télé, you're going to need someone like this Jonathan Kingdon, someone to guard your back.'

Just after four in the morning, Nzé stuck his head through the tent-flap. 'Psst!' he said. 'Dr Lary! Let me in!'

Lary, coughing his odd, dry, rapid little cough, switched on his torch and undid the ties.

'I'm dying!' said Nzé, on all-fours, fixing Lary with his right eye and the roof of the tent with his left. 'My piss. It's full of pus.'

'The wages of sin,' said Lary, considering the idea. 'The Makao pox.'

I unzipped the map-pocket of my bergen and found the medical notes. I read out Dr Peterson's first entry. 'AMOXIL: This is a Penicillin derivative useful for any sort of bacterial infection, particularly respiratory infections, urinary infections, and even venereal infections. The dose, under most circumstances, is one capsule three times a day, but in suspected gonorrhoea it may be useful to take twelve in one go.'

Lary found the canister in the medicine-pack and counted twelve long, yellow capsules on to Nzé's palm.

Nzé, in a little voice, said, 'That's too many.'

'Too many girls,' said Lary firmly, pushing Nzé back on his haunches, unscrewing the top of my water-bottle. 'No sex for a week.'

'A week?' said Nzé, panic in both eyes.

The tops of the trees grew distinct: there came a long series of hoots in a descending scale, dying away to a single soft *hoo*, the saddest call in the forest, the lament of the Dwarf hornbill, clear, focused by the cool dawn air trapped beneath the canopy, a note of quiet misery – which was at once overwhelmed in a chorus of barks, wild staccato barks that gave out in bursts of obscene hilarity, deep dirty chuckles: a troop of Grey-cheeked mangabeys proclaiming their territory, announcing their home range, cracking jokes. And an hour later, on the march, something barked at five times the volume, a stomach-rumbling, deep, rising roar.

Marcellin swung round. 'Gorilla!' he yelled, showing the whites of his eyes.

'Wooo!' sang Muko.

'Bonzo!' said Lary.

'His nest! His bed!' said Marcellin, dropping to his knees at the base of a big tree. 'An old male! A lonely old male!' He patted the centre of a squashed-flat circle of leaves and twigs.

'How do you know?' I said, squatting beside him. 'Smell?' (It smelt rank, musty.)

Marcellin stood up. 'Of course not! What do you think I am? A pygmy?'

'Pygmies,' said Lary, taking a swig from his water-bottle. 'Great guys.'

Marcellin stepped back, peered up into the tree. 'The old male, he makes his nest on the ground. His family, the wives, the children, they build platforms to sleep on, beds in the branches. Here, there are no nests in the trees, so he has no family. He's old. He's very old. He's too old for sex!'

'Gorilla nests,' said Lary, his back towards us, taking a pee. 'I've read about it. It's a cultural thing. It's a meme, a piece of learned behaviour that's passed down, inherited through the culture. Eastern lowland gorillas – they have no manners, they urinate and defecate in their beds. Western lowland gorillas, on the other hand, are good Americans. They never mess their sheets. They have *standards*. In their considered opinion, Eastern lowland gorillas are *animals*.'

Around midday, as we walked, exhausted, in a long line, Nzé and the others close up behind us, 'Wooo!' sang a buttress in my ear.

'Don't do that!' screamed Marcellin, buckling forward as if punched in the crotch. 'Don't do that!' he gasped, regaining his pace.

The buttress heat-hazed into a pygmy. He stood preternaturally still, his spear, in line with a sapling, held vertical in front of his face: those legends, I thought, the stories about the little people, the dwarfs of the forest who can make themselves invisible, the Egyptian reports of 2000 BC, they're *true*.

'I wish they wouldn't do that,' muttered Marcellin in front of me, half to himself. 'It always makes me shake. They could kill you and you wouldn't know! They stand so still you can't see them, and then they recognize one of your own pygmies – and they make that noise, they make that *stupid* noise, right in your ear!'

Muko turned onto a thin, beaten track, and led us down a long slope to a pygmy camp, a half-abandoned settlement of ten bedraggled huts and two shelters, in one of which four naked children and three young women in dyed-red raffia skirts sat round a cooking-pot.

'The Berandzoko suburbs!' announced Marcellin, sweeping off his hat and bowing low towards the women as he passed.

We followed Muko back into the forest, down another long slope, to a small stream. Muko climbed in, up to his waist, and we filed after him, up to our thighs, wading with the current, a watery pathway through the thick jungle of a river-bank – and we emerged on to the Ibenga.

In the sudden intensity of the light, the light bouncing off the surface of the slow brown water, turning it white, we blinked like the Wood owl.

24

Marcellin took the shotgun from Muko and fired into the air. 'For the Berandzoko boatman! A signal!' He clicked open the breech, extracted the still-smoking red-plastic cartridge-case with its shiny brass cap, and put it in his pocket. 'For the son of the Berandzoko boatman!' He held the barrel up against the sky, squinted along it, blew out a puff of cordite, snapped the gun shut and shouldered it like a rifleman on parade. 'The boatman – he owns about the only dugout they possess. I told you, Redmond, Berandzoko means the village of the elephant-fighters. These people are not fishermen. This was not a good plan of yours. We may have to live here – for always. You and Lary – you can work in the plantation!'

Lary's thick blue denim shirt was stuck to his back and chest; his beard was bunched with sweat; his lower lip withdrew beneath his moustache, as if the base of his jaw had slipped back slightly into his neck. He said, 'That's fine by me.'

'Redmond,' said Marcellin, relaxing, propping the gun in a crook of liana, 'you must pay the bearers.' Antoine, Michel and the five pygmies shed their loads on a little patch of high ground. 'To each man – 15,000 francs!'

I found the correct waterproof document-bag in my bergen and handed out the little bundles of notes that Lary and I had prepared in Makao. Antoine and Michel pocketed the cash; Muko, his head on one side, pretended to count his; but the five pygmies simply looked politely at the scruffy blue slips of paper in their palms, then at me, then at each other, as if, inexplicably, I had presented them each with a packet of leaves from the forest.

'Put it away!' shouted Marcellin. 'Hide it. That's *money*!'

From behind a small island downstream a dugout appeared. The young paddler, working hard, naked but for a pair of frayed red shorts, came fast across the current towards us. Yes, he said, coughing, he'd take Dr Marcellin and the white men first; next, the two men from Makao (he looked doubtful); then the other two, the young men; and, last, in batches, the pygmies.

'You owe him one chicken and two cartridges,' said Marcellin, as he waded ashore, past the usual upturned half-dugout washing-board and one open-wickerwork basket, full of peeled white manioc-tubers, left in the shallows to soak.

'There are no dugouts here,' said Lary quietly. 'Not one.'

At the top of the slipway, a steep gully of orange-red mud, an old man stood waiting, his shoulders coat-hangering his black-and-white-check shirt, his skeletal legs cased in black drainpipe trousers. 'Welcome!' he shouted. 'You are welcome to my village!'

'Redmond,' said Marcellin in a stage-whisper, 'I forgot to warn you. This man is an old postman. He loves the French!'

Lary said, 'A postman? Here?'

'Bague! Xavier Bague!' shouted the old man, picking his way a few yards down the gully. 'You will stay with me!'

Lary said, 'That letter. You can post that letter.'

'Xavier Bague!' said the old man, shaking my hand, his finger-ends crooked like tent-pegs. 'Enchanted! I was a postman in Brazzaville. The French, they gave me a bicycle! I never missed a day. For thirty years, I never failed to deliver!' He shook Lary's hand, his tired red eyes bright with pleasure. 'You're a Frenchman? You've come from Paris?'

'I'm American.'

'Good, good,' said the old man, thinking, his right hand resting on his grizzled white hair. 'So when you return to Paris you must say to the President of France, "Come back to the Congo! Xavier Bague says you must return to Africa. Things were better in the old days, when the French were here." It was in order. Everything was in order. Now there is nothing. In Brazzaville – there was no work. I had to return here, to Berandzoko, to my own village!'

'Sure,' said Lary, taking off his hat.

Marcellin gave him a wink. 'It's okay,' he said in English. 'There are complications. Serious complications. But we'll stay at his hut.'

'Complications,' said Lary, to himself. A large blue butterfly, a shiny-blue morpho, twitched off the red mud at his feet and flicked away into the forest.

'Follow me!' said Xavier Bague. 'You'll drink my palm-wine! You'll see my wives!'

So we followed him, up the middle of the wide, hot, red laterite slope, the main street of Berandzoko, his broken trainers flapping gently over the hard ground; to either side of us, ten yards away, two twisting, five-foot-deep and fifteen-foot-wide ravines ran down the hill; forty yards beyond them, close against the forest, the parallel lines of huts ran up the hill; an eagle of some sort, too small to identify, wheeled slowly, wings spread, way up above us in a thermal; and so it is that we unwittingly join, I thought, whatever murderous faction Xavier Bague may represent.

'The erosion!' said Lary, shocked out of his inner hiding-place. 'They'll lose the street!'

'Berandzoko is old,' said Marcellin, kicking a mud-flake. 'It's been here for years.'

'Culverts! Storm-drains! That's all they need. They'll have to get together. The men will have to get together, zero-rate their time, and *do* something.'

'Of course,' said Marcellin, grinning, looking kindly at Lary as if he was dealing with a case of heat-stroke. 'The men of Berandzoko, they must forget their quarrels. They must work together. *Action, take one.* As the Americans say.'

'Simple drains! Log-drains! What's funny about that?'

'Nothing,' said Marcellin, twirling the shotgun in his right hand like a bandmaster's mace. 'They could ship in a tractor!' He snorted with laughter. 'They could paddle up an earth-grader!'

'Yes, my friends,' said the old man, looking round. 'We are all so happy! You will stay with me!' And he led us across the right-hand channel, at a point where the banks had fallen in, opposite a large, newly thatched, open-sided hut, the talking-house, in whose shade three piebald goats lay flat out, asleep.

Beyond the talking-house stood a scraggy mango tree. 'My tree!' said the old man; beyond the mango tree was a hut of red mud, much like all the others. 'My hut!' he said, beaming, exposing two broken front teeth. 'The best in Berandzoko!'

There were no windows in the front wall, and the half-open wooden door was surprisingly thick, built for defence. In a line several yards out from the hut three stout posts had been driven into the ground.

'For hanging up the elephant-meat,' I said.

'For hanging up the washing,' said Marcellin.

Xavier Bague said, 'This way, friends! I have chickens. Many chickens. I have many pygmies!'

At the back of the hut, its miniature replica in wattle and thatch hung three feet above the ground, lashed inside a stockade of thick poles, a detachable ramp of bound saplings leading to its door.

'Now, that's neat,' said Lary, setting his first seal of approval, to date, on the architecture of the villages of the northern Congo. 'That is one hell of a hen-house.'

A little further off sat the hens themselves, each in her own dust-bowl, under the bushes, out of the heat.

'Leopards,' said Marcellin. 'It's leopard-proof. The poor dogs probably creep in at night, too, when they can. There are many leopards here.'

To the right of the hen-house a small girl in a white smock, swathed in white smoke, was kneeling beside a cauldron, half a rusty oil-drum full of boiling water and manioc leaves, saka-saka in the making.

'My grand-daughter!' said Xavier Bague.

The grand-daughter looked up, wiped her shiny little forehead on the sleeve of her smock, gave us an absent-minded smile, and edged another stick into the fire.

The old man flip-flapped on past the sentry-box of a privy, to the kitchen, a shelter of slats and uprights, seeping smoke, and set slightly apart from the main hut. In front of it, protected by yard-high wickerwork dust-screens, two pygmies, an old woman and her daughter, sat on two thin logs, backs straight, thighs up, their raffia skirts tussocked behind them, pounding manioc in a trough like a child's canoe. A heavy woman in late middle-age, barefoot, wearing an old yellow dress, a blue kerchief knotted over her head, holding a white enamel bowl, stood and stared at us, aghast.

'My second wife,' said Xavier Bague his *joie de vivre* departing at the thought.

The second Madame Bague continued to stare, first at Lary, then at me. The afternoon sunlight in her eyes dimmed to dusk, to early nightfall, to black jungle night; the wrinkles round her mouth turned down decisively, like dead fronds on a palm; she raised her shoulders; she pressed her arms to her sides; the empty bowl tilted forward, slipped from her hands, hit the ground and bounced.

Maybe, I thought, as the four of us, like dogs who've sniffed a leopard, began a face-forward, one-careful-backwards-step-at-a-time retreat towards the safety of the grand-daughter's smokescreen – maybe the second Madame Bague does *not* like Frenchmen. And as, along the flaps of the old pygmy woman's breasts (which flowed up the raised incline of her stomach and on down the other side), a judder of laughter set in, the first tremor of a joke that was obviously going to last for weeks – maybe, I thought, those ghosts of Frenchmen in the collective imagination of the marital hut, those spirits which probably disrupt every conversation, invade every memory: maybe they long ago made Madame Bague feel even heavier than she really is. And to have them turn up for real, right in front of her, unannounced – it's finally released that special, domestic, internal, all-in, whole-body shake, that one long suppressed scream of yowling head-back boredom . . .

The other side of the smoke, Lary said, 'I don't think she likes us.'

We turned together, like a flock of starlings, and made for the far side of the hut.

Back on the street, Xavier Bague, his heart beginning to pump again, said, 'My second wife – very strong! A strong wife!' He brightened, spotting Muko across the street. 'Muko!' he shouted. 'Muko!' And to us, 'Friends, do not be afraid. My other wife – leave it to me – only my other wife will prepare your food.'

Lary took off his hat. 'Poison,' he said.

'Myself, I only have one wife,' said Marcellin, breathing hard, but somehow managing to suggest that women in general, and wives in particular, had never made *him* run for cover. 'Xavier Bague, you must control your wife!'

The old man, sensibly ignoring such absurd advice, beckoned Muko towards us. 'My pygmy,' he said. 'That's my pygmy.'

'Xavier Bague,' said Marcellin, bridling, his strength returning. 'That's not possible. That is not your pygmy. That is Muko, a man like you and me. In this country, it is against the law to own another man.'

Xavier Bague shrugged. 'My pygmy!' he said, clapping his hands.

Muko, breaking into an awkward run, came and stood before the old man, smiling, uncertain; he had changed into his village uniform, the long brown tee-shirt that stretched down to his thighs, the blue gym-shoes that were at least three sizes too big for him and had no laces; and he was holding his pay in his right hand.

'His father belonged to my father,' said the old man, taking the money, stuffing it into his pocket. 'His grandfather belonged to my grandfather.'

Muko, shrunk, slouched off behind the hut.

'Palm-wine!' said the old man, leading us inside; he motioned us, in the murk, towards four wooden chairs round a table, and disappeared through a double curtain at the rear of the room.

'This floor's uneven,' said Lary, as we sat down, and the chairs bucked.

'Marcellin Agnagna!' came Antoine's voice from outside. 'I must speak to you! Out here!' Marcellin stepped back into the sunlight.

Lary dropped his hat on the floor, placed his elbows on the table and his head in his hands. He said, 'I want to go to the Grand Union.'

'The canal? Yes! Wouldn't that be wonderful! Moorhens, coot, maybe a Tufted duck – we could go at night, with a big torch – there's lots of Common newts in those quiet stretches in the reeds, maybe even the odd Great crested. We might get lucky!'

'No, you bozo,' said Lary wearily. 'It's my local grocery store. GU to its friends. I'm going to go in there, buy a baguette, slice it longways, slip in and layer out sliced turkey, add a line of Dijon mustard, and on top of that I'm going to place romaine lettuce, sliced tomatoes, and Grand Union brand Cheddar cheese.'

Marcellin and Antoine, their voices lowered, were still talking, fast, just beyond the doorway.

Lary said, 'Crunchy and cool.' He bent down and picked up his hat. 'And unobtainable.' He laid his hat on the table in front of him. 'Completely, utterly,' he said.

'Palm-wine!' shouted Xavier Bague, bustling through the curtains, carrying two enamel jugs and four enamel cups on a tray. 'Alcohol of maize!'

'Everlastingly out of reach,' said Lary, staring at his hat.

Marcellin stepped back inside, and sat down. He said, 'The packs are here. They're piled against the wall.'

Xavier Bague poured a slug of clear, slightly yellow maize-alcohol into each white cup. Lary, distracted, said to Marcellin, in English, 'That was outrageous. Muko and the money. Muko's a great guy, a goddam hero, in my opinion.'

'Muko, he is not a hero,' said Marcellin, holding his cup in both hands, sniffing the fumes. 'As I said to Bague here' – the old man took his place at the head of the table – 'Muko is a man like any other, a man like you and me. In the night he chases the wives of other pygmies. He says to them, "I know about money and I've worked with Dr Marcellin and a white man. I'm a Bantu – and you, you're just pygmies."'

'Muko, Muko, Muko,' said the old man, draining his cup. With a nod of apology to Lary and me, he refilled it with palm-wine, turned to his right, to Marcellin, and, with relief and fluency, launched into Kaka.

'Here we go,' said Lary, reaching across for the maize-alcohol jug. 'Kaka. Poison. *Complications.*'

As my eyes adjusted to the shadows, the opposite wall came into focus. Nailed in pride of place, at head-height, hung an advertisement, a page torn from a French medical magazine: a plastic skull peered back at me with one eyeball and one empty socket. The eyeball, the legend informed me, was detachable, and the skull, if you so desired, would come apart, in two pieces. Beneath the skull, in smaller format, hung a line of family photographs, obviously taken, many years ago, in a Brazzaville studio: formal portraits against a white screen. A black cross in biro, on a shirt-front for the men, on both arms for the women and children, indicated that most of the family were dead.

'Lary! Redmond! Xavier here says that his senior wife, his first wife, she'll cook antelope for us, for tonight! But now we must visit the village elder, a real ancient, Pierre Welia, because now is his talking-time. His grandson lights his pipe! We must hurry!'

'Er – no thanks,' said Lary, scrabbling to his feet. 'No more Kaka. If that's okay with you. You know. I'll – I'll put up the tents. Outside!'

'Good, good,' said Marcellin, making for the door. 'Come along, Redmond. I'll bring my diary, my blue notebook. And you must bring tobacco. And 500 CFA. For one chicken.'

Against the hut wall, in the bright heat, I found a tin of Balkan Sobranie in the medicine-pack, and Marcellin and I set off down the street, to the left of the left-hand ravine, leaving Lary busy and therefore happy: 'Marcellin, the eye-holes on your tent,' he called after us, sounding like Lary, 'they're suckers! They're sub-standard!'

The goats and chickens of Berandzoko, having roused themselves for their late-afternoon walk-about, nibbled and pecked, at nothing discernible, in slow-moving groups between the huts.

A small boy, perhaps seven years old, slipped out of the doorway ahead of us, ran up to Marcellin, and stopped in front of him. 'Dr Marcellin,' he said, faltered, looked at his bare feet, hitched up his dusty red shorts, and scratched the back of his neck with one little hand.

'What is it?' said Marcellin, squatting down.

'My father, he promised . . .'

'Of course!' said Marcellin, and fumbled in his pocket. 'The cartridge-case!'

The small boy craned forward, studying, from six inches away, the red tube on Marcellin's outstretched palm, the shiny brass cap, the mysterious hieroglyphics, the blown-out, de-crimped, crenellated end.

'Go on,' said Marcellin gently. 'It's yours.'

The boy reached out with both hands, enclosed the gift against his chest, looked anxiously into Marcellin's face, as if it was obvious that anyone mad enough to part with such a treasure might want it back at any moment, burst into tears with the tension of it all, and bolted for his mother and the hut.

'He's short-sighted,' said Marcellin, picking his way, without disturbing them, through a gathering of preoccupied goats (heads down, tails wiggling). 'You don't think of simple things like that, do you? No spectacles here. He'll never have glasses like yours, things you take for granted. He'll spend his life in a mist. He can't hunt – he can't even work properly in the plantation. There's nothing he can do, no close work in an office, no watches to mend. No woman will want him.'

'So what'll happen?'

'He could become a sorcerer, or a singer, or a teller of tales, or all three. But that's difficult. Seeing the odd vision – that's not enough. It's hard. You need real talent.'

The huts towards the river were larger than the others, with bigger roofs sloping out over foot-high verandas, and resting on wooden pillars. In one of them, on the veranda, to the right of the central door, on a bench facing uphill, sat a thick-set, middle-aged man in a green tee-shirt, unmoving, his hands on his knees, staring at a small red-mud tomb, its mud headstone surmounted by a crucifix and facing downhill, towards the river, towards him.

'Marcellin?'

'Yes,' said Marcellin, when we were out of earshot. 'It's sad. He's a Christian. A missionary came here. That man was converted. Nobody liked him. He took the sacraments, and then his daughter died, ten years old. He sits there like that, every day at this time, and he asks God to tell him, please, why his daughter died, why his daughter was taken away. No answer, of course. Never will be. It would be better for him if *he* were a sorcerer, or still believed in sorcery, or witchcraft, or magic, or animism – or whatever fancy names you white men invent for it. Then at least he could be angry. He could do something. His friends would understand and they'd talk to him. People would know what to do, how to help. But now, Redmond, he just sits there, bewildered . . .'

There was a high-pitched, squawking scream from our left, from the forest, a crash of leaves and a Grey parrot, flying with all its strength, still screaming, passed low over our heads – pulling with it, at its tail, at its red rump, a long and easy shape, an African goshawk, white and rufous, un-hurried, pressing its victim, close as a mating-flight, over the opposite huts and into the forest.

'An omen,' said Marcellin, with a smile that couldn't complete itself. 'And it's your fault. We must talk. I'm angry with you. I thought all that would go away, but I'm still angry . . .'

He stepped onto the veranda of the last hut on the right before the river, the largest hut in the village. The ancient, Pierre Welia, sat in a leather chair, wearing a green woolly hat, a green shirt, black trousers to his calves, and flip-flops. He nodded at Marcellin, and with a skinny hand waved us to our places as if we were expected, and late. We took the two remaining logs, on the earth veranda, behind two young women, eight children and one dog (like a Border collie, black with a white chest and white paws).

In front of Pierre Welia's chair stood a three-legged stool, a mark of his high status, and on it lay a foot-long roll of tobacco bound with twine, and a pipe – an elaborate pipe, a pipe of state, with a bamboo mouthpiece, a long clay stem, and an intricately incised, cross-hatched clay bowl.

Pierre Welia cleared his throat and spat to his left, into the dormant fire. The grandson, about the same age as the boatman's boy, but assured, confi-dent in his movements, in the privilege of the ritual, broke off a plug from the roll of tobacco, shredded it into the bowl of the pipe, tamped it with his thumb, drew a stick from the fire, lit the pipe with one long inhalation, coughed, doubled up, spat, dropped the stick, and, wheezing, handed the pipe to his grandfather.

Pierre Welia sat back in his chair, puffed slowly, and closed his eyes. Marcellin placed his blue diary open on his knees, took a biro from his pocket, and waited. A pygmy woman passed us on her way to the river, bent forward, straining against her headband, against the wickerwork basket on her back, her towering load of manioc tubers, peeled and white.

'We Kaka,' said Pierre Welia in a querulous monotone, reclining, his eyes still shut, 'we come from the centre of Africa, from the village of Ngombilo. Hunted by the Muslims, we moved to the country of the Banda. Hunted by the Banda, we moved to the edge of their country. Our Chief, the Chief of the Kaka, Berandzoko, who had united us in the land of the Banda, met the Chief of the Banda. This Chief said to Berandzoko, "You must take my name, as a sign of friendship." Berandzoko refused this offer, and he went to war with a neighbouring people, the Ngodi, whose Chief he cut to pieces. He then decided to move south and he made his first village, Libassi, on the river Ibenga, north of here, towards the source.'

Pierre Welia opened his eyes; he sat up. 'The white men had arrived!' he shouted, pointing at me with the stem of his pipe. All the children swung round, horror in their big brown eyes. 'They were already here! They were lower down this very river, at Mimpoutou!' (The young mother in the next row, her head tied in a blue cloth with a bow at the back, gave me a reassuring smile, as if to say, 'Don't you worry. It's only a history lesson.') 'Now – these white men, *they noticed things*. They saw banana skins in the river, floating past them in the current, and "Aha!" they said. "There are human beings upstream! Human beings who like bananas!" So the white men said to each other, "We'll go upriver. We'll find these people." And that is how they discovered Libassi.'

The old man put his pipe down on the stool; with his right hand he furtively pulled on a watch-chain that ran from his belt to his trouser-pocket: a key-ring appeared, a length of string, and, briefly, between pocket and palm, a small brown oblong of fur.

'The white men! They asked Chief Berandzoko to take his people further down, where they could be reached easily, but he refused the company of these whites. He refused because – how shall I put it? The colour of their skin – it did not inspire confidence!' The children, in sympathy with Chief Berandzoko, turned eyes-front again. 'These white men, the men who discovered the Kaka of Libassi, their names were Bianzo and Kotolongo. They offered us European clothes, they asked us to abandon our traditional dress, to stop wearing cloth made from the bark of trees. Now, this offer did seem sensible and, after much discussion, the Kaka accepted it. The cloth the whites proposed was called *ndimba*, a cloth made from fibres of raffia.

'Then Chief Berandzoko delegated two emissaries, who went downriver as far as Bas, the village where the white man lived. And after that all the people went downriver and the village of Berandzoko was created. A few contacts were made with the people of Bas (Mimpoutou) and with the Bozangas, for trade, the exchange of meat from the forest, manioc and bananas from the plantation. A white man called Mamoquet came, with another white man, Mayonga Giton, and they set up the first trading-post for goods at Berandzoko. So the colonial government began to know us, and to make a register of all our names. They began to interest us in certain activities, such as the gathering of rubber, and this allowed us to make a little money, to buy white men's goods at the trading-post.

'The white men shared out the work among the people. The tribes they used were these: the Banda, Ngodi, Mbakolo and Kaka. The white men made the Kaka build a big pirogue, and the task of the Kaka was to paddle from Berandzoko to Dongou – a long way, my children! And for us this was difficult, because the Kaka are not a people of the river. But that was how we earned our money, so we could buy goods at the trading-post. We took the rubber which the white men had bought, and we journeyed with it, with our wives, all the way downriver, in the big pirogue, to Dongou, far away.' The old man paused. 'And who can tell me,' he said, looking at the little boy with the dog, in the front row, 'what happened next? What did they have to do?'

'They came back!' said the little boy in Kaka (which Marcellin, next to me, translated in a whisper). 'They came back! Because they'd left their dogs behind!' And he flung his arms round the dog's neck. The dog, wagging one end, half strangled the other, stood up, shook himself free, licked the little boy's knees apologetically, and lay down again, across the little boy's feet.

'Yes! They had to paddle all the way back, each time, against the current. But even so, the other tribes – the Banda, the Mbakolo and the Ngodi – who, for their work, had to carry the white men on their shoulders or in chairs – they saw that this division of tasks was unjust, and they decided to take action against the Kaka. So they went away to look for the fetish which is called Congoala – to fight against the white men. The Chief of the Kaka, Manzindzaki, he would not accept the plan of the Chief of the Banda, Komanda. So Komanda threatened to make war on the Kaka and the whites, equally. One party of the Kaka joined the Banda under Congoala, and the fetish was prepared.

'Exactly at this time of day!' shouted Pierre Welia, with his left hand gesturing up the slope, towards the hut with the tomb (his right hand, knobbed with arthritis, stayed clenched, on his right knee, round the oblong ball of fur). 'At the trading-post, over there, when rubber was being traded, on a day like this!' The children sat up straight, expectant: they knew the story well. 'The Banda attacked!'

'Eeeaaah!' sang the children. 'Woooosh!'

'Wooo!' sang Marcellin, and grinned at me.

'The white men grabbed their guns! Boom! One Banda dead! Boom! Two Banda dead!'

The dog, sitting on its haunches, whined, and lay down.

'The Banda thought they were safe, because of Congoala, their fetish, they thought no bullet could touch them. So after this defeat, they withdrew. The Banda, Mbakolo and Ngodi withdrew to the north forever. The Kaka rested in peace in their territory. And they were no longer the friends of the Banda.'

'And Samalé?' I said. 'Did Samalé help?'

The ancient said sharply, looking straight at me, 'Samalé is an animal of mystery.' With his left hand he pushed his green woolly hat back off his forehead. 'Samalé has his origin in the country of the Banda. This fetish was adopted for the security and protection of the people. A woman discovered the power of Samalé. She gave this power to her husband. He made a symbol of Samalé for other men, and for the protection of the people, and not for evil purposes. When your Christians arrived, your Catholics and Evangelists, they were accepted without problem, and everyone began to pray, because they understood that God was the origin of all other spirits. The Kaka were the first to colonize the forests of the Motaba and Ibenga rivers. And afterwards the pygmies came from the north, from the territories of the Bakando and the Bakota. They followed the movements of the Bantu. Berandzoko, in the language of the Kaka, means the work of the elephant. The killing, the butchering and the smoking of elephant-meat. And this is very difficult work.'

'And now?' said Marcellin.

'Now? The life of the village? Now the old men think that their children and their grandchildren will replace them and continue to guard the village, because it is here, and only here, that the spirits of the ancestors live. All the children who go to study or to work in the town – when they retire they come back to the village, to pass their last days. Then their spirits will join the spirits of their ancestors. They will talk to their fathers and their grandfathers once again, in the huts, in the talking-house, in the plantation, on the edge of the forest.'

The old man pushed the chain, the key-ring and the contents of his palm back into his pocket; he leaned forward, laid his right hand softly on his grandson's head a moment, and stood up. He closed his eyes, he stretched both arms out, palms down, over his audience, like a priest. 'The village of Berandzoko will live forever! The land of the ancestors will never be abandoned!'

Marcellin, with a happy laugh, nudged me in the ribs. 'Storm-drains,' he said in English, in Lary's accent. 'Culverts!' The old man sat down, tired, and leaned back in his worn leather chair.

School over, the children jumped up, chattered wildly, formed into two groups, girls to the left, boys to the right, and they set off up the street, the girls walking, the boys running. The little boy from the front row, running as fast as he could, sped after the three bigger boys, and the dog, adjusting its pace, lolloped along behind him, tail in the air.

The two women, laughing, talking almost as fast as the children, began to stack up the logs. History, I thought, knowledge, it takes people out of themselves, it makes them happy. 'Come on,' said Marcellin. 'No staring into space. No trances. Put the tobacco and the 500 CFA on the stool, shake his hand, and we'll go.'

Half-way to Xavier Bague's hut, to home, I plucked up courage. 'Marcellin, why are you angry?'

Marcellin glanced behind us, as if he thought that someone might be listening. He bowed his head slightly, slumped his shoulders forward, lost height. 'I used to have a clear mind, a clear conscience. There was no one I was afraid to meet. I could walk anywhere – and not be afraid.'

'Husbands?'

'Husbands!' said Marcellin, with a bitter, dismissive laugh, looking at his feet. 'Husbands!'

'So what's the problem?'

Two boys, standing at the bottom of the left-hand ditch, were kicking the mid-section of a papaya to and fro, and, with half-length spears, attempting to impale it.

'You gave me the problem. That night at my grandfather's hut. The fetish. I didn't want it. I'd always resisted it!'

'What's wrong? What's wrong with a fetish?'

'You nasty little liberal,' said Marcellin quietly, with real force, taking me aback, not lifting his eyes from the ground. 'What's wrong with a fetish?' he repeated, mocking my tone of voice. 'Everything! I keep it in my pocket. I have to have it with me. I'll go to pieces if I lose it, I know I will. I keep it in my pocket – and every time I think of Lake Télé and the fear comes, I touch it, and feel better.'

'But that's good – isn't it?'

'Good? Of course it's not good! Once you start that kind of nonsense, you can't stop. You lose your peace of mind, a bit of your reason. You can't think straight, you act without thought. You catch a spear in the night. You do stupid things. You go to Lake Télé. You get a bullet in the chest – like the Banda at the trading-post!'

'But what about your other protection? Your sacred animal? The crocodile?

You told me on the steamer. That night on the fan-deck, drinking whisky with Marie. You said I'd find out why you were studying crocodiles for your doctorate, why crocodiles were so special for you, for a man with your ancestors. You said I'd find out what crocodiles mean, that I'd find out in a place called Makao. Well, I did. Dokou told us.'

Marcellin shouted, 'You're a liar!'

A startled goat cantered off down the ravine.

'You're a liar,' he said, looking round, lowering his voice to a whisper, an emphatic hiss. 'I'm studying crocodiles, *Crocodylus cataphractus* and *Crocodylus niloticus*, for my doctorate from the Museum of Natural History in Paris. I am making a comparative study of the growth-rates of crocodiles. I am a scientist. I never said *anything* about crocodiles meaning something.' Just past the talking-house he stopped, and he yelled into my face, from two feet away, 'It's nonsense! All nonsense! You're a liar!'

'Now then, boys,' said Lary, emerging from the tent-flap. 'Having a little ding-dong, are we? Bunging ding-bats? There I was, just settling down in my favourite armchair with a bottle of fifteen-year-old Glenmorangie, the Malt of Tain, ready to watch *Dallas* – and you disturb me. We can hear you all over the village!'

'And another thing,' said Marcellin, as Lary followed us into the empty hut and we sat at the bare table. 'We've got to talk. Fast. It's Antoine. Antoine and Michel.'

Lary clattered a handful of small, black, lightly haired nuts onto the table. 'Palm kernels,' he said, holding one up between stubby finger and squared-off thumb. 'They boil the palm fruits for palm oil and then they chuck these out – they're all over the ground by the tents, everywhere. I like them. I'm collecting them. They all have these three indentations on the rind, unevenly distributed. At a rough estimate, I calculate that one in twenty of these random patterns forms a face, and, so far, each face is different. See?' (A nut with a leer.) 'So if we ever do get out of here' – he put the nut with the others, began to line them up – 'I figure I'll take a selection of faces with me. And then whenever I feel trapped – in my job, with the endless administration, with some goddam piece of construction in the house, with some chickenshit bits of pre-war gearbox which I can't quite reassemble – whatever – I'll go take a look at these goddam hopeless faces queuing on the desk in my office, and I'll say to myself, "Shaffer," I'll say, "so you think you're trapped *now*? Just you remember, Shaffer, how you felt when you were *really* trapped, in Berandzoko, with no sign of a canoe, no means of escape, nothing. Not one single sucking woodchip of a suggestion of a dugout. Not one tiny whisper of a rumour of a dugout waiting with a note from God stuck on it, just for Redso, because he's such a jolly good chap, such a pig-sticking bwana." And, in my humble opinion, there's jackshit sign of an incoming angel requesting permission to land, at least not in the immediate vicinity . . . For Chrissake, Redso, I warned you about this. I really did . . .'

'It's Antoine,' repeated Marcellin, louder, leaning forward from the head of the table. 'I must be quick. It would not do . . . it would be bad for us if Bague heard. Antoine asked me something today, outside the hut, when they brought up the packs. I didn't quite understand. He wants you, Red-mond, to buy him a goat. 12,000 CFA. He insisted. He really meant it. But this goat – it's not just for us, for food. It's for some kind of sacrifice, for use in some ritual, a secret preparation, I don't know. But we can't refuse – because we're staying with Bague, we've drunk his palm-wine, his maize-alcohol, and tonight we eat with him, after dark, we eat antelope-meat.'

Lary, tipping palm nuts from one hand to the other, said, 'I don't follow.'

'You don't know?' said Marcellin, agitated himself. 'I didn't tell you?'

'Complications,' said Lary, the nuts rattling back and forth, like dice.

'Yes, the complications. Bague, Xavier Bague – he's the one who sum-moned the young men of his family, the young men of his lineage, and that night he took them to the hut where Antoine's uncle was sleeping, and they dragged Antoine's uncle from his bed and pulled him outside, along the ground, and they beat him to death with sticks.'

There was a silence.

Lary said, 'And that involves us?'

'I don't know. I'm not sure. I don't think there'll be trouble. Not actual blood. I myself, I think that the murder, the revenge – it will be symbolic. The blood will be symbolic. Antoine and Michel, they didn't want to come here with us, the Chief of Makao ordered them to come. Besides, it's difficult, it's a matter of sorcery – so there is always a doubt. Maybe Antoine says to himself, "Perhaps my uncle *did* become a sorcerer. After all, I can't see in the dark. So how would I know?" But there again, here we are in Bague's hut, protecting him. When I knew the mind of the Chief of Makao, once Dokou had told me all that was in the Chief's mind, the blood-feud, the revenge, I had to do this. I planned it. But quite apart from this little business, visitors, in general, they're easy to blame, it's convenient. You brought bad spirits with you. *You* did it, whatever it may happen to be. You may know nothing about the matter, nothing at all. But somehow it was your fault, all along, all those years ago. You – you're a manifestation. So, in the day, poison. Or in the night, schick! schick! A machete. You're dead, everyone else is happy, the sorcerer says the problem, it's solved. Old enemies get together – for the first time in years, they speak to each other. Families are reunited. Life in the village – it gets *much* better.'

Lary said, 'Yeah. Neat.' And then, less academically, 'Thanks.'

'Me, I think we'll be okay,' said Marcellin, picking at a scab on the back of his left hand, distracted, sucking the smears of blood from the nail of his right index-finger, the ball of his thumb. 'Antoine – he's the only danger. Michel may help him. But it's this *hut* they'll have to enter. Bague is the target. But this is the strongest hut in the village, built to keep Antoine out. And we ourselves, we'll be outside, safe in our tents, off-limits.'

Lary said, 'Who's got the gun?'

'I have,' said Marcellin, standing up. 'No problem. It's hidden in my tent. And now, Redmond, you must get the money for the goat, the sacrifice. And I must take it to Antoine, before dark. I know where he is, I know where he's hiding. But if he comes with some excuse, some reason to ask for the gun – for us that will not be cheerful, for us that will be a bad sign.'

By the light of a palm-oil lamp hanging from a low rafter in the centre of the room, and two of our small white candles standing on saucers in the middle of the table, we drank palm-wine and ate boiled antelope pieces and manioc and saka-saka, waited on by the grand-daughter, still in her white smock, and by Xavier Bague's first wife. She was as old and thin as he was, but bent, almost a hunchback, her spine crumpled forward, perhaps by a simple lack of calcium – and she was certainly suffering from a simple lack of iodine, because a goitre hung from her neck, the left lobe larger than the right, the only fullness about her. The front panel of her dress, a red, Western dress, obviously bought many years ago, when she was tall and straight, now hung loose and empty; the cotton of the back panel now stretched so tight across her hump that the semi-circular seams of the arm-holes were yanked into triangles; with a posture like that, I thought, her spinal cord must be permanently squeezed, her nerves pinched, and yet, with no Western pain-killers, here she is, smiling, laughing, joking with her husband, talking, constantly, in Kaka, in a voice as deep and hoarse as Dokou's – a voice that is surprisingly vigorous. And he loves her. He laughs with her. The old couple – they're in love. No wonder the second Madame Bague . . .

'Mister Lary! My grand-daughter!' said Xavier Bague in French, handing his empty tin plate to his wife. 'She likes you!' (It was true, she stared at him, she gawped, as if Chief Berandzoko himself was sitting beside me.) 'Do you, and this is the question – do you like my grand-daughter?'

Lary turned round on his wobbly chair; he gave the small girl his biggest, kindest smile, a smile that catapulted her, overcome, straight out through the double curtain. 'She's a good kid,' he said, not sure if he'd done the right thing. 'I like her very much.'

'Good! It's time!' said Xavier Bague, looking at Lary with real affection, raising his palm-wine cup, toasting him. 'Your health! Success!'

'Yes, it's late,' said Lary, in turn raising his cup to Bague, but not, I noticed, taking so much as a sip of the drink he considered the most barfsome known to man. 'Thank you for feeding us, for your hospitality. And to Madame Bague, too, of course. You're right. We must go get some sleep.'

'No, no,' said Xavier Bague, with an ecstatic cackle. 'It's time she was married! You want to marry her? Good. I will give her to you. You may marry her, Mister Lary, but on one condition – that you stay here with me. You will stay with me while we build you a hut. A fine hut! She's my favourite! We'll build you a hut like mine – so you'll never want to leave! The best hut in Berandzoko! She's yours. You'll live in this village! You'll take care of her. You'll live out your days in Berandzoko! You'll be happy! So happy! Like me!'

'Thank you,' said Lary in a little voice, almost a squeak. He stared at Bague, pole-axed. 'Thank you,' he repeated, like a wind-up teddy bear, the eyeballs fixed.

Lary's brain, probably paralysed, the optics jammed, was plainly receiving nothing but the image of Xavier Bague, upside-down. So Lary's hypothalamus, the lowly, resentful and insubordinate controller of mere reflex-loops, of the autonomic nervous system, deficient in the educated moral sense, a stranger to long-term responsibility, ignorant of paramount social duty, void of honour, and entirely free of discriminating self-restraint, seized its chance.

Lary stared at Bague.

Lary's right hand went sleep-walking over the table, and it put out fingers, fingers which unfurled down and round the cup full of palm-wine, as slow and sure as the carnivorous leaves on a pitcher-plant.

Marcellin, hypnotized in his turn, stared, slightly cross-eyed, at Lary's right hand, which rose quietly above the table-top, the cup enclosed within it, like a chick in a talon, the milk-white wine lapping, here and there, over its brim.

'Too much happiness!' shouted Xavier Bague, hugging himself. 'A fine hut! A young wife! And all at once! I understand. Xavier Bague understands. It's a shock!'

Lary's neck stiffened backwards and locked rigid.

'Of course it is!' said Xavier Bague. 'The chance to settle down! To make a new life for yourself! And all at once, all here, just when you'd given up, when you least expected it!' Still hugging himself, for a moment he oscillated his top-half, so fast, from side to side, happy as a dancing bee at the hive (lots of nectar, near at hand), that I thought he might splinter right off at the hips. 'Yes, yes, the chance to make something of yourself! To stop travelling all the time, like an outcast!'

Lary's jaw fell open. A couple of intervertebral discs in his neck, unable to take the tension any longer, gave way at their soft cores, bulged out of line. Lary's head slipped backwards, his right hand tilted forwards, and the contents of the cup disappeared down his throat.

'Cow-crotch!' said Lary, shocked alert, sitting up straight. 'That's cow-crotch and molasses.' He looked accusingly at his cup, harbouring a grudge. 'That's what that is, and I don't mind telling you, right now . . .'

Xavier Bague, pleased to have someone to talk to, said, 'When I was your age, young Mister Lary – when I travelled, when I went on a journey, it was for a purpose. I didn't just wander about the place, like some people do. I was already a man, I *knew* what I wanted to do in life. I delivered letters!'

'Why the hell did I drink that?' said Lary, aggrieved. 'That cupful of toxins?' He eyed Marcellin, as if he might be responsible.

'You'll live,' said Marcellin, not too sure about things himself. 'It's not pasteurized. It's not filtered. But you can rest assured, here in Berandzoko it's full of whatever happens to fall in the bucket.'

'And parcels, too,' said Bague, contemplative. 'Not every day, but quite often to the houses where the Frenchmen lived. Big ones, too, sometimes.' He roused himself, remembered, perhaps, that now all the letters, the measure of his days, had gone, and that back here, in the present, his life would soon be over, and he leaned forward on the table, exhausted, angular, his thin arms folded in front of him. He said, 'My grand-daughter, Mister Lary. You'll marry her?'

'I already have a wife,' said Lary. 'I'm married.'

'Yes!' said the old man, toying with his empty cup, lifting it in his right hand, as if for a toast. 'You'll send for her? Your senior wife? You will all live . . .' And he stopped, studying the white enamel cup between his hands. 'The French, they're right,' he said quietly, as if he'd just decided on a painful change of all his opinions on the matter. 'One wife is enough. Two wives – that's one too many . . .'

'The little girl,' said Marcellin to Lary, in English, 'that child – she likes you for your blue shirt, or your jeans, or because I said you were North American. These children, if they're taught at all, they're taught by the poorest student-teachers, straight from college in Brazzaville, *real* Communists – because every teacher has to do two years' service in a village in the interior – but if they've been sent right up here, as far as you can go, and in the forest, too, where you can die of disease or get murdered or just disappear and no one cares, then believe me, Lary – those young men are *poor*: their families have no money, no influence, no relations in the Government, no one to get them a nice safe post in a village on the plateau, the savanna. They're bitter, they're our Red Guards. They tell the children that America is the enemy – you, Lary, you're cruel, ruthless, a demon, a capitalist, a colonizer, worse than the French. You're out to destroy the People's Republic, because here all men are equal, and free, and everything is shared. But don't you worry, you'll be okay – because no one believes a word of it. They all know, every child knows – America is a land where you eat as much meat as you want, and you're given blue jeans, and no one goes to a sorcerer, because every wish is granted. In America, no one dies.'

I said, 'But at least there *are* schools. It's extraordinary. A real achievement. Even to *try* to set up a school in a place like this, way out in the jungle . . .'

'So in England – you don't have a school in every village?'

'Well no, actually, the village schools are closing down, but a bus goes . . .'

'A joke! It's okay! Teasing the liberal! A joke! But all the same, perhaps you ought to know, perhaps even a man who thinks he has no politics, perhaps even a liberal ought to know that the People's Republic of the Congo was the first country in the world to send a telegram to the People's Republic of China – to congratulate them on their firm action, when they massacred the unarmed students, in Tiananmen Square.'

'The schools,' said Lary. 'What's that got to do with the village school?'

'A lot,' said Marcellin, noticing that Bague had come to the end of his reverie, and switching to French. 'It's that attitude – that's why the village schools are a disaster. And so are the schools in the towns, come to that – ever since the French left, our schools – they've been a catastrophe!'

'When the French were here,' said Bague, recovering a little energy, getting up, refilling the palm-wine jug from a black plastic bucket in the corner behind him, 'we had hospitals in every village – no schools, but hospitals, and the paths in the forest were kept open, and the rivers were kept clear all the way up to Berandzoko, and there was work for everyone – you could earn money!'

'Yes, that's true, that's very true, my old friend, you old postman,' said Marcellin, on his third or fourth pint of palm-wine. 'We're all friends here! We can admit it. No one is listening. The French are civilized, intelligent, they ran this country well – even the dregs of France, the men they sent out here from bad places in France, Marseilles, terrible cities like that – even those men, one in five of those men really cared, they fell in love with this beautiful country, they looked after us, they built houses, they treated the sick people, they set up dispensaries in every village, they organized the crops, they sent agents to buy the produce from the *paysans*, they kept the people in the villages. They understood us. They married our women!' He refilled his cup, drank half of it in one draught, and looked at Lary across the table. 'Not like the white Americans! Not like Dr Shaffer! They treat our women like ... like *pygmies*! They won't mate with them, Xavier, they don't want to touch them, they won't have sex!'

Lary, sober, but perhaps feeling a little sick, a thin residue of the bitter-sweet, stale-tasting, slightly adhesive palm-wine probably still coating his teeth, said, 'I'm married already. And your grand-daughter, Xavier, she's still a child.'

'What was I trying to say, Bague? Where were we? Yes, of course, education, our village schools. Well, I tell you again, they're a disaster, a catas-trophe. These idiots, hotheads, young Communists – they teach nothing but Marx and Lenin, and sometimes even Chairman Mao! The children leave school, and they can't write a letter. In the city, in the schools of Brazzaville, when the French were here, the children could write dissertations! And anyway, after the Revolution, there was no control, everyone went to the towns, the whole structure collapsed. But, remember, and that includes you, Lary and Redmond, we can only say such things because we are friends, and all alone, and no one is listening!'

'Armed militia!' shouted a muffled voice from outside. 'In the name of the People's Republic: Open up!'

25

Marcellin's legs kicked him up and backwards, knocking his chair over, pushing him flat up against the mud wall to the left of the door, as if, at any moment, he expected a burst of Kalashnikov fire to carry the wood away. His left cheek pressed against the wall, 'Identify yourself!' he shouted at the crack of the door-frame, pulling, with both hands, at the document-bag round his waist, trying to get a grip on the zip-tag. 'Comrade! I am an officer of the People's Republic!'

Xavier Bague, obviously used to such intrusions in the middle of the night, stood up, his old bones scraping down in their sockets; he took three stiff paces to the door; and he drew the heavy wooden bar aside.

'Comrade!' yelled Nzé, dancing across the threshold, howling with laughter, his cap in one hand, a roll of tobacco in the other. 'It's *Comrade*, is it?'

'Nzé!' said Marcellin, trying to slip his official papers unobtrusively back into his document-bag, missing the opening. 'Quiet! Don't make a noise! Where the hell have you been? Quiet!'

'Thank you,' said Nzé, tossing the roll of tobacco onto the table. 'Thank you, Comrade' – he held out his right hand – 'I'll just check those papers, if you don't mind.'

Marcellin, drunk, began, automatically, to present them, swore, I think, in Kaka, and at last managed to thrust them back into the pouch.

Xavier Bague, bemused, fastened the door and sat down.

Nzé, shuffle-dancing round the table, sang, in a good imitation of Marcellin's high-pitched voice, a little song in French, all of his own, which, roughly translated, went like this: 'I am an officer of the People's Republic! A *very* Big Man – and it makes me sick!/I'm telling you' (clapping Lary on the shoulder) 'and you' (patting my head) 'that Nzé, too/He's a high-ranking officer – from Dongou!'

'Behave yourself!' said Marcellin, sitting down. 'Nzé, what is all this? What's up?'

'Ganja, Uncle!' said Nzé, coming to rest, perching on the end of the table next to Bague. 'It's ganja! I crept up to the door, Uncle, and I listened – I listened hard – just in case the Vice-President of the People's Party Committee of Berandzoko was with you, because ganja, Uncle, it's against the law! And I heard terrible things, I heard an officer of the People's Republic saying terrible things. All about our Party schools. Things that could send him to prison. In Dongou, Uncle, they'd send you to prison!'

Marcellin, surly, said, 'I'm not your uncle. And where've you been? And where's Manou? You both agreed to report to me, on all occasions. I had to put my tent up!'

'He had to put his tent up!' sang Nzé, with a sweaty splutter of a laugh, sending his peaked Cuban Army cap twirling up into the air, and, to my surprise, managing to catch it again.

Lary said, 'I put it up.'

'I'm staying across the street. With a man that Antoine knows. A man with three daughters! One for me! One for Antoine! And an ugly one, a thin one, just for Manou! Little Manou, Uncle – he has the thin one!'

'Antoine,' said Marcellin. 'He's with you? You know where he is? Right now?'

Old Bague, abstracted, staring at a big black knot in the wood, in the centre of the table, said to himself, in a loud voice, full of anger, 'The ways of the city – they've changed. The manners of the French . . .'

'So I put my cap in my mouth, Uncle, like this' – Nzé put his cap in his mouth – 'and I shouted, "Armed militia! Open up!"'

'Yeah,' said Lary, sober. 'We clocked it, dipshit. I shot my wad.'

Nzé, his left eye focused on the palm-wine jug, his right trained on the skull with the one detachable eyeball, put his cap on his head, gathered up the jug, drained the dregs, jumped off the table, and took himself to the bucket in the corner.

'Antoine!' shouted Marcellin. 'Where is he?'

'Calm yourself!' said Nzé, filling the jug. 'It's ganja! The best! It's strong!' He lifted the jug to his lips.

'A cup!' shouted Bague, getting to his feet too fast, and swaying, dizzy, out through the curtain. There was the sound of a pot or a gourd knocked from a shelf; a slight thump; silence.

Marcellin said, 'He's passed out. He'll sleep! Old Bague – he needs his sleep.'

Nzé, carrying the jug back to the table, took another swig, in transit, and sat down in Bague's place. He filled Bague's cup, leaned back, and, his Adam's apple a yo-yo in his neck, drank the cupful in one. 'Lary,' he said with a squash-eyed grin, 'my old friend – a drink?'

'No,' said Lary. 'Thank you.'

'Antoine!' shouted Marcellin, reaching forward and seizing Nzé's arm. 'Where is he?'

'It's ganja, Uncle,' said Nzé, detaching himself. 'I've told you. The best! There's a ganja-seller from Central Africa. He's here in Berandzoko. He has a watch, a gold watch. That's the ganja there – on the table. 2500 CFA. Uncle Redmond – he'll pay. We've been smoking, Uncle – but Antoine, he smoked more than me. He's lying on the floor! Manou, he was sick. Antoine said, "Nzé, take the other stick, take it to Marcellin. The white men – they'll pay. And in return for this present, you must tell them, tell Marcellin – I need the gun for tomorrow. Tomorrow, I am going hunting, and I must have the gun. The gun – and lots of cartridges!'

'Great news,' said Lary quickly, his eyes wide. 'Cheerful news.'

'Nzé,' said Marcellin, shaking his head, trying to clear away the wine, 'Antoine – he's asleep? You're sure? Good! I'll get my pipe! The pipe that Redmond gave me. The pipe from Oxford, the pipe from England.' And he went out, leaving the door open.

'That's okay,' said Lary, coughing his odd, dry, rapid little cough. 'If that's your thing, fine. But I don't smoke, and anyway I'm damn well not staying in here to watch you mush your brains with that stuff and get mystic and blow bubbles or whatever the hell else it is you do.' He stood up. 'And just in case, Redso, just in case it had escaped your notice – this hell-hole of a little room is a steam-bath. A steam-bath with half-a-million mosquitoes pumped in, *gratis*. A malaria trap.' At the open door he turned round, still coughing. 'I'm sorry, Redso, but I'm bushed. Bushed, jungled – that's where the word comes from: *bushed*. I need sleep. The brain needs sleep. And you – you look bad. Normally, I'll give it to you, I'm surprised, but you're really quite sane, that's what I'd decided. But now – look at you! Staring eyes! A serial killer! Sleep, Redso. You need sleep. Get some sleep!'

From outside, Marcellin pushed past him, back into the room. 'I've got it! The pipe! Ganja!'

'Dope,' said Lary, and left.

Nzé shut the door. He pulled the bar across all six brackets.

'Sleeep,' he said, sitting down, trying out his first word in English. 'Sleeep.' He glanced at me with a seraphic, lopsided grin, and, between right thumb and index-finger, crumbled the end of the brittle, dusky-green roll of ganja on to the table. 'Sleeep. Bluejean. Cowboy. Amourcar. Toyota! Nissan! United Hates!'

'*America*,' said Marcellin, severely, pushing shredded leaves, a few bits of stalk and five seeds into the briar pipe. 'United *States*.'

The pipe packed to his satisfaction, Marcellin lit it from the candle in front of him, careful not to drop wax into the bowl, sat back, inhaled long and hard, blew a double-lungful of smoke into the stale air, and passed the pipe to Nzé. Nzé drew in smoke with multiple, wet sucks, like a child at the nipple, and passed the pipe to me. For a discreet moment I dried the soaking mouthpiece, holding it clenched in my damp armpit, wiping off the saliva, and then I took a deep pull of the acrid, bitter-sweet, sickly smoke, a palm-wine of smokes, and passed the pipe back across the table to Marcellin.

We sat in silence, smoking, passing the pipe. Lary was right. The room was full of mosquitoes. They were feeding on my arms, whining in my ears. How come I hadn't noticed? Was there malaria in the village? Of course there was. Why didn't the smoke chase them away?

'Uncle,' said Nzé to me, still wearing his smile, 'you join in. You really do.'

'Of course he does,' said Marcellin, slumping forward a few degrees. 'Of course he joins in. He interferes, all the time. He interferes in your life. He's a nasty little liberal. Or a fat mercenary. It all depends how you look at it. It really does. But as we say in English, Nzé, there's one thing you can be sure of – Redmond, *he doesn't know his tit from his asshole.* There's no question about that. No question at all.' And he laid his head on the table, cushioned on his left arm.

Nzé knocked the pipe out against the table-leg and set about a refill. 'Seeds, Uncle,' he said, the smile no longer fresh. 'Seeds. For strength!'

Marcellin pressed his right hand over his eyes. 'I had a terrible dream last night.' His forefinger and thumb spanning his forehead, his third finger stretching from the bridge of his nose to his left cheekbone, he peered out through the gap, with his left eye, across the top of the table. 'I was at home, with my father, my wife and my father-in-law. They said, "Why? Why do you leave your wife and child? Your daughter, Vanessa Sweet Grace, she cries for you. She cries out for you in her sleep. She must have a guardian. A man who stays at home. So we have given her away. Because you – you are in the forest!" Redmond, it's your fault – and that is why I needed a smoke. But it's no good. I've drunk too much. I've drunk too much – and so the ganja cannot help me.'

Nzé said, 'Don't you worry, Uncle. Don't you worry. Your pipe – I'll look after it.'

'Antoine!' said Marcellin suddenly, getting to his feet. 'Antoine! I'm not staying in here!'

Tipping from side to side, he tilted at the door and got it open. 'Redmond!' he shouted. 'Fasten this behind me! As tight as you can! Redmond! I'm warning you now! In Africa – *you must shut your door at night.*'

He leaned back into the room, one hand on the outer edge of the open door, one on the door-jamb. 'You think you understand me,' he said, his speech a little slurred. 'I think I understand you. So some people – they might say we were friends. And I've discovered what you're after – you want

239

to know everything, don't you? All about Africa? The secret of life?'

'Yes,' I said, fuddled. 'I suppose I do. Everybody does. But there isn't one.'

'Oh yes there is, my ignorant friend! My white friend! Mr Know-nothing-at-all! I'll *tell* you the secret – because you've earned it! Nzé, Redmond, – are you listening?'

Nzé hiccuped.

Marcellin, standing in the doorway, chanted, 'Du vin/Du pain/Et du boursin/On ne jamais fait mieux.' And he disappeared into the night.

Nzé and I smoked in silence, passing the pipe back and forth. His eyes, I thought, staring at him. Manou's words came back to me: 'With eyes like that – of course Nzé makes beautiful music. He has special powers. With eyes like that, he can see – he can see into the spirit-world. And that,' said Manou, 'is how he hypnotizes all the young women in every single village where we spend the night . . .'

In a minute, I said to myself, I'll close that door, I really will.

The pipe went out; I laid it down; I felt in my pockets, without success, for a lighter – no luck – so, very slowly, I transferred the contents of my pockets to the table-top; and when I looked up, triumphant, Nzé had vanished.

I felt calm, and entirely free, for once, from low-level background pain, from the two small ulcers on my right foot, from the all-over blackfly and mosquito and tsetse fly itch. But otherwise – nothing. So I reloaded the pipe.

'Forget it,' I said to myself as I lit up. 'You're too old. It's different, that first smoke, when you're young. Besides, this ganja business, it's not really your thing – is it? No wonder it has no effect. Whisky now, that's different, Lary's right. Lary's always right. Routine, that's what you need. Discipline. Not this ganja that sends everyone to sleep. Sleep's not your problem. Never has been. No, you need a decent stimulant. Coffee, even. Something to stop you sogging the days away until death comes, and you hardly notice he's in the room, that he's arrived. A little refuse sinks gently in the dull canal. The odd rat's turd. You must hold the mind in, that's the trick, refuse to release it into the empty cosmos, the outsweeping nothingness, indifferent immensities – an absurdity that is to be by-passed in contemplation of the Shaggy ink-cap; the dabchick diving in the river. And when did death arrive? Necessary death? Maybe one thousand million years ago . . .'

And I myself was back in the biology laboratory at school, a mere twenty-five years ago: the smell of formalin, the acid-marked bench-tops, the bunsen-burner taps; the microscopes with their brass lens-tubes, their black slide-holder plates, shiny in their glass cabinets, ranged along a shelf at the far end of the room; the freshness of it all, the excitement, the study of life, the browns and purples and greens of an opened frog in the dissecting dish. 'Let us take the green algae,' said the almost spherical biology master in his horn-rimmed glasses, gobbing into his handkerchief, wiping the blackboard clean, thrusting his left hand down between the belt of his trousers and his coccyx, scratching his buttocks as he concentrated, and, with his right hand, chalk-drawing almost spherical colonies of algae. 'Boys! Here we have the green algae – the free-living plants of ponds and horse-troughs and puddles! Let us take a series!' (He paused, but his right hand continued the drawing, his left the scratching.) 'Or rather – let us take a series if O'Hanlon and Winchester will be good enough to stop gossiping like fishwives and permit the rest of us to think. *Pandorina! Pleodorina! Volvox!* Now – here is *Pandorina*' (which was growing, the while, a work of art under his short and chubby fingers, fingers which were clumped with black hairs in their middles, between the joints). '*Pandorina*, boys, a colony of sixteen cells – cells that all reproduce when they reach the right size, cells which can multiply indefinitely, which don't die of old age. If the pond stays healthy – they're immortal! But poor *Pleodorina*, of *Pleodorina* we might say – as Winchester might say of me, or, indeed, of O'Hanlon – *Pleodorina*, boys, *Pleodorina* is burdened with a body, a *soma*. Here is a colony of thirty-two cells. And when this colony forms a daughter colony, four of those cells die. Urrh, boys, that is sad! Urrrrh!' – the second dredge, deep preparation for another gob – 'Boys, that is very sad! That is very sad indeed!'

And as for poor *Volvox*, I remembered: death walks right in on *Volvox*, carrying a suitcase; death hangs up its jacket, comes to stay. *Volvox* is a colony of 250,000 cells – and when it reproduces, only one in a thousand of those cells survives. And for us? Nothing but the occasional egg, the odd sperm . . .

From outside, an owl called, close, coming closer. And, nearer still, something called like a Whistling duck, a small flock of wigeon, so close, in fact, that they might have been in the room with me, practically under the table. Holding on to the table itself, so as not to fall off my chair, I bent sideways and took a look.

Nzé, curled like a foetus, his head towards me, lay under the table. As he breathed in, he snored gently; and as he breathed out, he whistled like a duck. A cockroach, a very big cockroach, antennae lifted, palps working, was sampling the sweat on Nzé's neck, not sure, as yet, if it was a matter for celebration or disgust.

'Koko!' said someone, from above me, from the open doorway. 'May I come in?'

Upright on my chair again, too surprised to speak, I stared at the visitor.

'I smelt the ganja,' he said, looming over me. 'It's dark out there.'

He was huge, taller than the mad sergeant at Manfouété, twice as broad across the shoulders, and wearing black boots, black trousers, a black tee-shirt and a shabby, torn black jacket with shiny, black lapels, like a dinner-jacket.

'It's dark out there, and lonely,' he said, taking off his jacket. The sleeves, sticking on his massive biceps, pulled themselves inside-out. They were extraordinarily long sleeves, I noticed, as he tugged them back through the arm-holes, jerked them straight. 'I work at night,' he said, his back to me, hanging his jacket from the top right-hand nail, the rusty nail that pinned the picture of the skull and its eye to the wall. 'So I get lonely. I suffer from loneliness. In fact – I don't mind admitting it, straight away, I see I can talk to you – sometimes I think I have so few friends I'm really not sure if I exist or not.' He grasped Marcellin's chair, opposite me. 'May I?' he said, sitting down. I pushed my own chair back a little. The skin on his face was pale in the candle-light, knobbly and blotched on his cheeks, flaking round his nose, almost white. I thought: perhaps he's an albino? But his eyes were dark, intense. He said, 'You offered me a smoke?'

He sat back in his chair, his left hand under the table, his right holding the pipe. He held it by the stem as he inhaled, two fingers hooked over the top, one underneath; his fingernails were long, thick, and crusted with black dirt or with dried blood, I couldn't decide. His little finger and thumb were missing.

He said affably, 'You're looking at my fingers,' and sent a jet of smoke out of the corner of his mouth. 'People do. It's nothing to worry about. You could say I lost them in a fight. It was careless of me. You know, the usual thing – machetes. But I won't lie to you. There's no point. Let's face it, you're a visitor, so you don't matter, do you? The soul goes on a journey every night, in every dream, and when you wake in the morning and the soul tells you all about it – where it travelled, what it saw – well, you forget most of that at once, don't you? Of course you do. So how could you matter? The only real question for you is this: am I in your dream and are you in mine? But yes! This ganja of yours is good! It's strong! And I'm beginning to like you, despite myself. So don't let's waste time. Don't let's waste time on banalities. I don't know when, but the dawn is sure to come. So I'll tell you, my friend, my new friend – I was an orphan, and that is a sad thing to be. My mother gave birth to twins, like the animals in the forest, so she was killed, strangled, and my brother with her. My father, he was chased from the village, as custom demanded.'

'And you?' I said, finding my voice.

'You can speak!' he shouted, leaning forward, showing his front teeth, his face close to mine. 'That helps. I find that helps no end – when a man needs someone to talk to.' His teeth were a dark yellow, blackish at the roots, but strong, unbroken. His breath smelt bad; it smelt of rotten meat. He should brush his teeth, I thought. ('Toothpaste!' said a mocking inner voice. 'Nonsense,' I replied. 'Sheer laziness. He should pick the old meat out with a liana-thorn, like everyone else.')

'And you?' I said. 'What happened to you?'

'Me? As is usual in such cases – me, I was given to the sorcerer. And a little later he needed a finger, and some while after that, a thumb. And so when I was old enough, when I still had three fingers on each hand, I ran away. I ran away to the forest. And one day, in the far north, I was found by a young woman, a kind young woman, a brave young woman! She brought food to my shelter after dark. But one night her husband, he noticed the loss of this food, and he followed her, he trailed her through the forest. He found me in my shelter! But he, too, he was a kind man, a brave man! And because I was all alone – no one here, as you already understand, my good, kind, new friend, no one here is ever alone; we all know each other's business, just as I know yours! – because I was all alone in the forest, after dark, with no one, no family, no friends, no one to speak for me – that kind man knew, he knew at once, he knew I was a spirit. And because of his wife, the bravest, most beautiful woman I ever hope to meet, he adopted me, and he made of me a symbol, an animal of mystery, a symbol to protect this people, the Kaka!'

'And what do you want of me? You want me to believe you!'

'Believe me? You flatter yourself! Who cares? Why should I need your belief? The belief of someone like you? This pipe – it's finished.' He handed it to me. 'Would you be so kind? Fill it for me? And pack it a little better this time, would you? Loose at the bottom, please, packed well down, firm at the top. That's how I like it. It draws better. You – you're an amateur, I can see that, you've a wild look about the eyes, you ought to take a sleep, a long, long sleep.'

'Thank you,' I said, crumbling, like Nzé, the end of the diminishing roll of ganja. 'That's kind of you.'

'And this?' he said, staring with his intense dark eyes at the contents of my pockets – the contents of my pockets which were still laid out, I realized with a twinge of fear, right there on the table in front of me, right there, for all to see. 'A cloth!' (my mould-and-worse-covered handkerchief). 'Western medicines!' (a half-tube of Savlon; a pressed-flat relic of a tube of Anthisan). 'A biro! Paper!' (scrumpled). 'Nuts!' (two palm-kernel faces, sneering, rabid as gargoyles, stolen from Lary's collection).

'And this,' he said, raising his claw, like a crab, above the fetish. 'This *really* interests me.'

I dropped the pipe to the table, the ganja to the floor – and my right hand was too quick for him, grabbing it, thrusting it deep in my pocket, closing round the warm, the comforting fur.

'Aha!' he said, half-standing up, both hands on the table, leaning over me, his bad breath on my face. 'So you don't believe in me? Well then, that fetish – give it to me! Watch me! I'll rip it to bits! I'll rip it to bits with these fingers of mine!' He slashed them past my eyes. 'Go on! Let me tear it to pieces! With these fingers! These fingers! The fingers you find so distasteful!'

He sat down, his gigantic chest heaving, the scaly skin on his forehead, like ringworm, red with sweat. 'You people, you white people – I thought you were realists. I thought you believed in reason.'

'White people? You're white yourself!'

'Yes, yes, of course. But that's because I'm dead. How ignorant you are! All the spirits of the dead are white. There's a little bush that grows here, you know, a bush with flowers like tiny bells, pure white. *Doh* – that's what it's called. You put the leaves in the water, in the reeds near the shore. The fish can't breathe. So they come to the surface and you cut them with machetes. Schick! Schick! You can kill people with it, too, sometimes.'

I was silent.

'But where were we? I'm wandering. And that won't do. Because there's no time to waste. I'm here to help you. To give you a word of advice. But where were we?' He wiped his forehead with the back of his right hand. 'Ah yes, of course, the fetish.'

'The fetish?' I said, alarmed.

'Don't upset yourself! My dear friend – I'm not going to take it from you. I'm not going to twitch my left hand under here, I won't spike it from your pocket! The power, I see, the power is working already. But it's not just my trapped breath in there, you know. Hasn't it ever occurred to you? Not for one moment? Not for one half of one moment? You – you could be holding one of my fingers wrapped in there, one of my thumbs! It's disgusting, carrying that thing about in your pocket. Disgusting. What about your own origins? Aren't you true to your childhood? Aren't you faithful to anything?'

I picked up the pipe. I bent down and recovered the ganja. I said, 'Isn't there a continuum, a continuum from the fetish to objects you like to have round you in a cave, a hut, a home? Comforting, familiar things?'

'Continuum! Relativism! We're so fashionable tonight! But that's right, get on with it! Pack my pipe! I'd do it myself. I'd make a proper job of it. But it's difficult for me, you understand – delicate tasks like that. I could cut my fingernails, of course. But then I'd lose my job.'

I handed him the pipe. He lit it from the candle, which was guttering low, and almost obscured in a swirl of tiny white moths, all the same species, some stuck in the wax, dead on the table.

I said, 'When you don't know what to do, when you're anxious, confused – you go and look at your cave-paintings before the hunt, or you visit the spirit-house, the church, you pray, you hold your fetish. It helps you concentrate, that's all. It gives you a sense of direction, a purpose. It has survival value. It helps you decide what you really want to do in life, a moment of quiet – and that helps.'

'What do you want to do?' he said, enjoying a quiet smoke himself. 'Finally?'

'Finally?' I said, thinking about it, taking a mouthful of palm-wine, half-gargling, trying to clear the smoked and acrid dryness from my throat. 'I just hope that of all the friends I have now, three or four will make it through with me, to eighty, say, and that we'll all sit together, round the fire, and that everything will become clear. Yes, we'll remember the past. The future will fall into place. We'll take life straight.'

'My poor innocent!' He turned his intense, dark, worrying eyes on me. 'Nobody does that. Nobody *could* do that.'

'What?'

'And I don't mean the absurd dream itself – that you'll live to be properly old, let alone eighty – and that even if you did, somehow you and these friends would still have the energy you have now, the energy even to *think* of inviting each other to come and sit round the fire when your joints ache, you're cold all the time, you have no teeth! And late-life depression, have you heard of that?' (I said, 'Please! Don't tell me!') 'No – I mean *take life straight*. What a mad idea! No one does that. We all need something – drink, smoke, religion, illusion, books.'

'Books?'

'Books. Oh yes. I'm very fond of books myself. I often fly to Paris. There are *excellent* libraries in Paris. I fly by night, in a wooden plane. But you know that of course.'

'Of course.'

'Only the other night I was there, warm in my usual place, right at the end, hidden away in the last bay on the right – and my shaded lamp was the only one burning in that whole long hall! That hall of kinsmen, of tribal memories, I like it like that! Well, as I say, this thought occurred to me – I thought of people like you – and I understood why white people find this kind of Africa so apparently familiar, whereas in reality it's something you'll never understand, not for a moment. You've all read your Freud . . .'

'Freud!' I shouted, startling myself, but happy, released for a moment from fear. 'I know what you're going to say! That's my thought! You're in *my* dream! You don't exist! Freud – he read a lot of West African ethnography.' ('Ethnography!' he said, and chuckled to himself, a dry sound, like cockroaches moving in the thatch.) 'All the usual nineteenth-century stuff. So when he came to invent or discover or create the unconscious he upended the line of late-Darwinian evolution, all the drives and desires of the past, selected and preserved by use and disuse, habit – because Darwin in his later years, of course, was a Lamarckian, just like Freud himself – he turned that vertically and pushed it down, loose at the bottom, tight at the top, like ganja in a pipe, down in the deep bowl, and on top of that, to liven it up, a burning glow, just beneath the layer of consciousness – he added life in an African village, at night.'

'The screams, the beatings, the sex, the fear – bumps in the night? That sort of thing?'

'Absolutely. All mixed up.'

'Yes, but not so fast. Not so fast, my good, kind, new friend. Refill my pipe, will you? And concentrate, please. Please concentrate. By all means have your thought. Please do – if it means so much to you. If you really want to own a banal little *aperçu* like that, go ahead. But my pipe, that's important – I told you, tight on *top*, loose at the *bottom*. And let me explain something else – I know your thoughts. It's really very tiring, but there you are, there's nothing to be done about it, we can all read the thoughts of the living. Believe me, it's a torment. It really is. Sometimes it can even drive a sensitive soul, like myself, to thoughts of suicide. Why, just tonight, Antoine there, across the street, he was thinking of firing the thatch on this very hut, just above us, where we sit.' (I looked up at the dry, brown, overlapping undersides of the fronds.) 'He was going to shoot you all as you ran out – or as many of you as he could, he was worried about that – whether you'd all run out together, or one by one, how fast he could reload, because it's old, that gun, a single-shot twelve-bore, not really the right weapon, not a Kalashnikov. But he swore to himself, "I'll get Lary and Redmond, because they don't matter, and Marcellin, because he does – and Bague, and all his family, especially the little girl. I'll avenge my uncle! I'll clear my name! (But I'll spare Nzé, because his eyes, they frighten me . . .)" So there you are. Horrible. There are times when I could hang myself. There are even times when I could burn myself to death!'

'You're the devil,' I said, with a stupid careless smile, ashamed of myself even as I said it.

'Am I?' Not at all annoyed, he gestured for the pipe, clacking his fingernails together. 'I hardly think so. Your angels and devils, your spirits, they're so limited. Such stereotypes. Such a clear division between good and evil. Affairs of the nursery. And to a grown man, so boring, so very boring. On the other hand, we ourselves, we're so interesting, so alive, so unpredictable. How do you know, for example? How do you know if we're here to help? Or to scar you for life?' And he laughed outright. 'But exist? Of course not. No spirits exist. But that's not the point, is it? Not at all! Come now – it's not me, here, now, me in the body' – with his left hand he scratched the table from beneath, like a cat at a chair – 'that's not why you've begun to shake. That's not why you're trembling like a duiker! No, no, it's what I represent. Madness. Clinical madness. And that, my friend, that's as real as real can be.' He sighed. 'And my dear, good, kind new friend, there's *such* a lot of it about. Especially round here. Nothing to be done. No treatment.' He lit the pipe from the last inch of candle. 'No treatment for anything much, as it happens.'

The dawn, I thought, looking at the cold square of darkness in the doorway, it *must* come soon . . .

'Very well,' he said, sitting back, smoking hard, his left arm hanging down the side of his chair, his curved fingernails resting on the mud floor. 'If that's how you want it. Let's talk about the dawn, daylight things, health, exercise, reason, running in the wood. But especially about the comfort of memories. And as you think you're such a realist' – he pronounced it ree-al-ist, and coughed once, from the smoke, deep as a leopard – 'let us contrast those memories with daylight reality, now. Your childhood home, for instance, you know – the one you bore people with – the vicarage, the mellow Bath stone, the walled garden, the enchanted gazebo, the birds, the river and all the rest of it – finished. Gone. That blue door in the wall, the one to the road outside – well, it says on it, "KEEP OUT – THIS MEANS YOU". Very Proustian, don't you think? There are gipsies living in the house; the chimney's fallen through the roof; the drawing-room's a workshop, hung with tools; they've knocked down most of the garden wall; the finial, the stone ball on top of the gazebo – it's gone; the glebe, the church field – that's a housing estate; and the little stream, the stream where you caught your minnows and kept your ducks, the banks of your stream – they're straight, and concrete. So how's that? What do you think of that?'

'I've got nothing against gipsies. Nothing at all.'

'Of course not. So how about this? You remember the day the Mistle-thrush flew over your head from her nest in the beech tree, and dropped half an eggshell at your feet, on the lawn, by the sundial?'

'Yes.'

'So how would it be if I told you that most of the people you saw that day, and every one, every single one of the birds that sang to you that day – they're dead?'

'You bastard!' I shouted, lurching to my feet, about to punch him, seeing

247

his chest, his massive chest, and collapsing, abject, back into my chair.

'That's better,' I heard him say softly, as I stared down at the table-top directly in front of me, unable, it seemed, to raise my head. 'That's much better . . .' I stared at the ganja dust on the wood, at two shiny seeds and one shred of stalk. 'A little emotion, at last . . .'

I said as clearly as I could, 'You dirty, embittered, suffering jerk. There's no logic in any of this. Not a scrap. Memory and present fact – there's no connection. None at all. So what's your problem?'

'I am your problem,' he said, horribly quiet. 'From now on I will be the problem you carry with you everywhere, like your fetish. And logic? My dear new friend, it's logic all right, oh yes – it's just not your logic. It's African logic. The emotions connect, perfectly. As you've discovered.'

'Go away. *Leave me alone.*'

He banged the pipe down hard on the table, breaking the stem clean off. 'Look at me!' he shouted. 'I come to help – and what happens? It's as I say! You're scarred for life!'

'The advice?' I said, mesmerized, staring at him. 'The message you brought?'

'You're going to die.' His eyes were wide, his face white, his mouth skewed sideways. 'You'll die at Lake Télé. A long, messy, mutilated death. And no one's fault but your own!'

He got up, lithe as a big cat, and hooked his jacket off the wall, pulling out the nail. 'So I won't say goodbye, because you'll soon be joining me.' He paused, spanning the doorway. 'See you!' he said, louder. And from outside, in the lifting darkness, he shouted: 'I'll-see-you-later!'

The blast of his breath, following the sound, blowing out the candles, warmed me as it passed across the table-top.

'All the same,' I said to myself, defiant as a child, 'all the same,' I said as I slumped forward, passing out, 'there's bound to be an Aquatic genet at Lake Télé, and perhaps, even . . . a Flying . . . mouse.'

Never stare at a gorilla. Magne, a four-year-old in Madame Yvette Leroy's orphanage, Brazzaville, corrects my manners, bites my ears

The bow of the town-ship *Impfondo*. 3,000 people, mostly on open barges, travel upriver. Islands of water-hyacinth float past; fishermen in dugout canoes wait ahead. To sell their cargoes of smoked fish they must dock alongside, a dangerous way to go to market

(*opposite top*) Disaster

(*opposite bottom*) Babinga pygmies in the forest, west of the Motaba river

(*above*) Two species of bee suck sweat from my hat

(*left*) The centrifuge, the remains of the French palm-oil factory at Manfouété

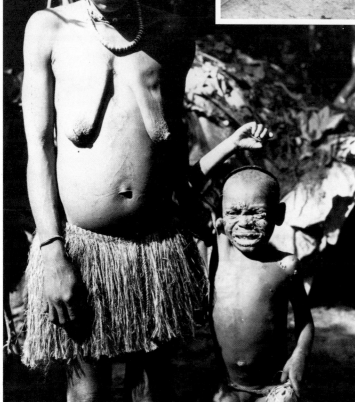

(*above*) A young Babinga at Manfouété

(*left*) Yaws

(*opposite*) Babinga woman in the forest

(*opposite*) The Babinga boy carrying his hunting-net and spear

(*above*) Lary Shaffer

(*left*) Marcellin Agnagna

(*opposite*) Babinga pygmy huts in the forest

(*above*) The beginning of the dance

(*left*) The entry of the Spirit of the Dead, in gorilla-skull mask

(*left*) The principal drummer, with hunting-net

(*below*) Waiting for the hunt to begin

(*opposite*) Parcelling out the meat

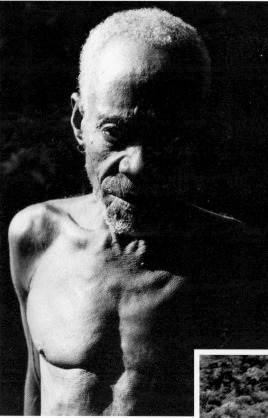

(*left*) Bakolo, the healer

(*below*) With Muko, our pygmy tracker.
Makao village, Motaba river

(*above*) An abandoned pygmy camp. On the walk across the watershed

(*right*) Tropical ulcer

(*left*) Word-carrier to the Chief of Boha

(*below*) Nzé with pineapples, gifts from his mistresses

(*above*) Lake Télé, the supposed home of Mokélé-mbembe, the Congo dinosaur. In swamp forest, twenty-five miles north-west of Boha village, Likouala aux Herbes

(*left*) Vicky, the Chief's favourite

Reunited with Redmondo, my rescued gorilla, safe in John Aspinall's orphanage at Brazzaville

(*inset*) Redmondo

26

There was a hand on my shoulder. A familiar voice said, 'You slept in my hut!' I raised my head, and set a spasm of pain travelling down my spine. The spinal nerves, I thought, sitting up, rubbing the right side of my face where it had been lying on the table. 'Cervical,' I said, trying to get a grip on something, on anything that was really there, indisputable: 'Thoracic.' Words like that – they were comforting all the way through to the object. 'Lumbar.' They didn't let you down, dissolve, disappear into the forest before you got to them: 'Sacral.' ... Antoine ... the goat ... the sacrifice!

Old Bague, still holding my shoulder, said, 'Don't worry! Xavier Bague – he is used to the ways of white men! They often go to sleep in chairs! And when they wake up, they pray to their Spirit, their Holy Spirit!' 'Jesus!' I said. 'Yes!' said Bague, his wizened old face as fresh as a wizened old face can get. 'Jesus, that's his name!' I glanced at the nail on the wall. Bague had hammered it back into place. 'You are welcome in my hut! Tonight – you will sleep here again! In your chair, your favourite chair!' With his left hand he held a white enamel plate under my nose. He said, 'Breakfast? Manioc? Fou-fou?' And on the plate was a grey, congealed, tapered cylinder of manioc, the same shape as the roll of ganja. The ganja? Where was it? Gone! And Nzé? I listened. No Whistling ducks. I looked under the table. I said, 'Gone!' Bague raised his eyebrows, sparse and bristly. He said, 'Are you in good health this morning?' He waggled my shoulder. 'Are you well disposed?' I stood up, feeling sick, my feet numb – but I managed to reverse from the manioc on its plate. 'Of course!' said Bague, as if he'd been foolish not to have thought of it before, going to the bucket. 'Palm-wine?'

Bumping into the corner of the table, knocking against Bague's chair, I got through the door.

Lary, back from a wash in the river, spreading his towel out to dry on the top of the tent, said, 'Had a good time?'

Feeling empty in the head, empty and cold, cold right down to the small of my back, I crawled inside and fell asleep.

*

'It's midday!' shouted Marcellin from outside, shaking the tent-frame. 'Come on! Get up! Antoine's here! Money! He needs money!'

'What?' I said, waking up, gasping in the desert heat of the close little tent, grabbing a water-bottle, gulping the warm water. 'What for?'

'The goat!' shouted Marcellin, his voice rising. 'You must buy a goat! 4000 CFA. The goat!'

I discovered my glasses in a fold of the sweaty tarpaulin, reached for my boots, found they were still on my feet, fumbled with the tent-flaps and hatched myself, unwillingly, into the sunlight.

Lary and Antoine (in his orange trousers and denim shirt, his bare, blistered feet covered with the sticking-plasters I'd given him) were standing outside with Marcellin, in the sun, on the hard red ground. Lary said in English, 'I told them not to screw you over. I told them you need to sleep. To sleep for a week. But they wouldn't have it.'

I got four of the blue-and-purple 1000-CFA notes out of the waterproof wallet in my leg-pocket, but somehow the numbers on them made no sense, and I found myself staring at the big bull elephant on the back of each one. Surely the curve of the tusks was excessive? Why draw tusks like scythes? Maybe the artist . . .

'Cabbage,' said Lary unaccountably. 'Cabbage in the head. Broccoli in the brains.' He yanked the money out of my hand and gave it to Marcellin, who passed it to Antoine, who gawped at me. Antoine was almost bald. The top of his head shone in the sun, I thought, exactly like the surface of my *Gilbertiodendron* seed when I'd rubbed it across the sweat on my forehead and polished it on my trousers. Which reminded me. 'Lary,' I said, digging in my right trouser-pocket, beneath the fetish. 'I'm sorry. I really am. But . . .' ('Uh?' said Lary, tipping his hat back.) 'I stole these from your collection.'

'You did?' He took the palm-kernel faces and put them in his pocket, much as a man in a white coat might accept a gift from a patient. Antoine, still staring at me, backed away. His moustache had grown bushier in the middle, but droopier at the ends. That's probably what happens, I thought, physiologically speaking, when you're technically innocent, but *want* to be a murderer . . .

Marcellin said, in a tone of voice I had not heard him use before, 'Redmond, has something happened to you?'

Antoine, walking off, jumping slightly in the heat-haze, shouted, 'Sick! He has a fever!'

Lary said to Marcellin, 'I'm sorry. We'll sort this out. It's okay.' He took me by the arm. 'Down by the river,' he said gently, his hand like a manacle, 'it's cooler, let's go for a walk.'

'Ten minutes,' said Marcellin, turning smartly in his white trainers, follow-ing Antoine. 'For the goat, you must be here! Fever or no fever!'

'That tee-shirt,' I said to Lary, 'Marcellin's tee-shirt. It says AFRICA on the front!'

'Yes,' said Lary, steering me over the ravine. 'So your eyes are functioning? Hundred per cent?'

'What's up?' I said, the sun setting fire to the hairs on the back of my neck. 'What's wrong with you?'

'No,' said Lary. 'Reversal error. It's you, Redso, what's wrong with you?'

Half the village, women and children, pygmies, they seemed to be passing us, dead souls, journeying in the other direction. But I could trust Lary. You could rely on Lary, even if it was you who was dead. No matter how busy he happened to be, praying to the ancestors before a hunt, preparing a lecture upon which his entire career, his own future, depended – if you were in real trouble Lary would abandon his concerns, at once, and he'd help you. He'd swear, but he'd help you. He was that kind of man. 'Lary,' I said, nodding at these passing people, 'tell me. Are we in their dream or are they in ours?' I was aware, as I said it, that something, out there on the edges, was not quite right, and that the centre had slipped away, not too far, perhaps, but gone; the soul had gone to fetch water, or merely to check something in the library, to check the past against a memory, something trivial . . .

'Yes,' said Lary, letting go of my arm, quickening his pace, getting half a yard ahead, looking into my face. 'Two days. You'll be okay in two days.' And you yourself, Lary, I thought, you want to be back on Walney Island, don't you? Studying those gulls and crabs of yours, to the sound of the sea, in the north – because there are wrinkles like starfish round your eyes, and those parallel, straight but oscillating lines one sees preserved along the sand at low tide, tide-marks, that's right – they're running across your forehead . . .

'Word's got round,' said Lary. 'Marcellin told me. Everyone's off to the show. Antoine sticks a goat. That uncle, the one that Bague and friends murdered, Antoine's uncle, he kept goats in his yard. So Antoine sticks a goat – and Makao and Berandzoko can start over. Makes no sense to me. There's no logic in it, legal or otherwise, but there you are – Kaka justice, or maybe just Antoine's idea of justice. Bague's house-guest – you – bought the goat, so Bague kinda pays for it, I guess. Marcellin says they knock the goat about a bit. You know – relax slaughterhouse regulations. I suppose it's better than killing that old pervert Bague. But it's bad luck on the goat.'

'So why are we going the wrong way? Let's get back!'

'No sweat. We'll wash our faces. Before the show. Eh? Cold water?'

'Cold water.'

'And by the way, Redso,' he said quietly, 'don't talk if it's a drag – but what happened last night? After I left? What happened to you? You smoke that stuff?'

'Just between us,' I said, looking round – Pierre Welia, the ancient, his grandson, and the dog, waved two hands and, I thought, one white paw at me – 'I never want to smoke again. In fact if we ever get out of here I'll give my pipes away. And if I ever see fingernails like that . . .'

'Fingernails?'

'Truth is – I've never been so frightened in my life.'

'You think *you* were frightened! You take that goddam filthy stuff, at source, grown in this heat, this humidity, packed with enough chemicals to blow your balls right off – and you tell me you were frightened! It's this *place* that's frightening. Get your long nose out of a book! Look about! Take a look! I tell you, Redso, the *reality* here – I've never been so frightened by real events in my whole goddam life. That mad sergeant, Sergeant Pepper of the People's Something-or-other, the Manfouété Sergeant – if it hadn't been for the hooch . . .'

We walked down the empty slipway in silence. A Blue plantain-eater called, '*Ko ko ko ko.*' I thought: he wants to come in . . . he's knocking on the door . . .

We took off our boots, rolled up our trousers, and waded into the river, up to our knees.

'I'll tell you for nothing,' said Lary, cupping his hands, splashing water over his face. 'The different groups round here, they sure as hell hate each other – and one day they'll get their machetes out for real. They'll cut each other down to size. And that, Redso, is a prediction based on careful, sustained, close observation. And if it comes to that, I don't like this village much either, there's a nasty feel to it. Marcellin says it's because the men don't lead a regular life – they don't work much in the plantations, they spend their time hunting elephants.'

Realizing that no, I wasn't going blind, that the world had turned opaque because my glasses were still on my face, covered in water, I took them off and put them in my pocket.

'And we're trapped here, did you know that? Just like I predicted? Marcellin said to me, like a lord, "I've sent messengers downriver." "Have you?" I said. "In dugouts? So why can't we climb aboard? And if there's only room for one, you can count me in . . ." "No, no," he said. "Overland. They've gone overland. All the way to the next village downstream." So I said, "Marcellin, we can walk. If they can walk it, so can we." But there's no chance, apparently, it's swamp all the way. Only the pygmies can do it.'

Lary, exasperated, ducked his head entirely underwater. 'Aaaah!' he shouted, re-emerging, as if he'd been struck from behind, with a machete. 'My ring! My graduation ring!'

'Your ring?'

'Don't move! Stay where you are!'

'What happened?'

'My ring! It's gone!' He took off his shirt, threw it at me. 'There's a current!' he said, his chin on the surface of the muddy water, his face furrowed with concentration, his hands feeling about on the river-bed. 'This goddam diet – I've gotten so thin my ring's come off! If I lose my ring, Redso, I'll crack like you, I really will . . . barfsome manioc, palm-wine . . . for Chrissake, we'll soon be nothing but sets of bones . . .' (A leaf-lattice, a leaf-skeleton, rippling on the current, came to rest on his beard.) 'Like Old Bague . . . buck-naked sets of bones . . .'

Jumping up, triumphant, the leaf still stuck on his beard, his right arm in the air, the wide gold ring catching the sun, he shouted: 'Got it!'

'Your fetish,' I said.

Lary, affronted, said, 'Of course it's not a sucking fetish.' He put the ring in his right-hand pocket. He squeezed out his beard (pulping the leaf). 'It just means a lot to me. It's precious,' he said, as we waded ashore. 'Redso, you forget, you're a privileged Englishman. But where I was raised, in my house – if you fell down in the yard at dinner-time you went hungry. I worked my butt off to get this ring! I put myself through school, university to you, I worked in a tannery, I humped skins from the trucks to the factory-floor – and believe me, those skins were cold in winter, so cold they stuck to you, and heavy, heavy with ice, heavy as sheets of corrugated iron. And in summer? They stank, the rotten flesh still on them, flies, clouds of flies, and the maggots crawled down your neck.'

A small group of people stood round the mango tree, beside Bague's hut. As we approached, Lary, expanding his chest, said, 'Tonight! Goat T-bone, goat porterhouse, goat tournedos . . .'

'Goat rump,' I said, joining in, beginning to feel re-natured, returned to myself, pressed by ordinary need, real hunger. 'Goat silverside.'

But the goat itself, waiting patiently, tethered by a length of liana-twine to the bole of the tree, was a little grey kid, looking straight at us, flicking its ears.

'Lary, we should stick to manioc.'

'Yup,' said Lary, turning away.

Antoine, sharpening his machete on a stone, seeing us, his audience apparently complete, affected a laugh, and waved his machete in the kid's face. The kid raised its head and bleated. Antoine, ashamed, turned himself about, straddled it with his knees, and, in one clean, sideways cut, slit its throat.

The crowd drifted away, in silence. Only the black dog with the white paws looked back, mouth open, tongue lolled out, and the black fur of its lower jaw-line specked with white saliva. Marcellin, standing next to us, in full uniform, jungle hat on his head, earphones and binoculars round his neck, the Sony Walkman, the Birmingham machete, the document-bag and two water-bottles on the belt at his waist, whispered, 'That won't do. Not at all.'

'Won't do?' said Lary, worried.

Marcellin shook his head. He pointed with his lips at Antoine, who was stooping over the dead kid, trussing its back legs with the tether. He said, 'I'll tell you later.'

Antoine, slinging the kid from a bough of the mango tree, began to flay it with his machete.

'Doctors!' shouted Bague, appearing round the far end of his hut. 'My pygmy! One of my pygmies! Can you help him?'

'Malaria pills,' said Lary, as we walked across, away from Antoine. 'Head-ache, bad back, cut on toe.'

A dignified, middle-aged man, with a thin moustache and beard, stood behind Bague, wearing nothing but a once-white loincloth, encrusted with dirt – two filthy squares of cotton, front and back, tied to a string round his waist. Bague said, 'He's been working in my plantation! He works in my plantation – but he doesn't feel well.' The man's eyes were red, there was sweat on his forehead. Bague said something to him in Kaka, and he pulled down the front panel of his loincloth.

Just above his pubis was an open ulcer, a raised, black, shiny mound of infection, four inches across. The pink inner sides of the pit, one-and-a-half inches deep, moved slightly as he breathed.

'Oh God,' said Lary, stepping backwards. 'He's had it. I'll get the Floxapen. I hid some Floxapen.' And he stumbled off to the tent.

'Xavier Bague,' said Marcellin, 'this man, this pygmy – he should not be working!'

'He wants to work,' said Bague, and shrugged. 'He needs manioc. He has a family.'

Lary, handing the small black bottle to Marcellin, looking away, his lips twitching, said, 'An hour before meals. Or last thing at night.' Marcellin translated. The pygmy, expressionless, still, all his energy absorbed in denying the pain, took the bottle.

Lary drew a tube of Savlon, a bandage and a safety-pin from his pocket. 'We're out of dressings,' he said, his voice constricted. 'You gave them all away, in Manfouété. Yaws.' And, 'Here, you do it,' he said. Lary was crying. He was silently crying: big, real tears ran down his cheeks, into his beard. 'It's not just him,' he said, choking. 'It's those children. Pygmy children. The ones with yaws. Dying, disfigured – all so miserable. And for nothing . . . a spirochaete . . . a spirochaete you can kill for 40p . . . forty goddam pennies! I'm not sure, Redso, I'm not sure I can take it. I had an inkling of what it might be like to . . . to see people dying all over the place. You'd think *someone* would get off their butt and come and . . .' And he walked off towards the river.

The hole smelt of rotten fish. I filled it with Savlon, unrolled the bandage round the man's waist and fastened it with the already rusted pin.

Pulling up his dirty loincloth, holding the bottle and the tube of Savlon, he strode off, short, quick pygmy strides, back towards the plantation.

Bague followed him.

'He'll die,' said Marcellin. 'He'll die in three weeks.'

That night, at supper, looking at his plate, Lary said, 'What's this?'

A length of large intestine, neatly corded and knotted around a flap of stomach-lining (inside-out, bobbled with yellow tubercles), lying against a dropping of manioc, with one end turned up, like an eye, winked at him.

Marcellin said, 'It's a delicacy. Offal. We have offal of the goat.'

'Tripe,' I said, helpful.

'You never know,' said Lary, trying a piece, purplish-grey, and bendy. 'Here you never know, do you? Life is full of those little surprises. Will your food, for instance, to take a randomized example – will it travel up or down your throat?'

The probable direction decided, Lary pushed away his plate. Obviously thinking of washing out his mouth with palm-wine, he made another calculation, and folded his arms. 'Where is Antoine, anyway? Who got the meat? And Manou? Where's Manou? I miss him. I like Manou.'

'Antoine,' said Marcellin, 'he did something with the meat, for his own special purposes, I don't know, a ceremony – and now he's gone. The people here, they didn't believe his story of the goat, the sacrifice. They thought he was waiting to kill Bague.' (Hearing his name, Old Bague looked up from his plate, nodded, and smiled at each of us, in turn.) 'Pierre Welia warned him, he said, "Antoine, one more night here, and your own village – you will never see it again." But I myself, I don't think Antoine *could* revenge his uncle. Antoine, he's a weak man. He comes here – he's sent here by the Chief of Makao – and what does he do? He smokes himself stupid on ganja – with Manou! With Manou, who couldn't kill a chicken! And then what? The goat! He didn't even like killing that goat! Anyone could see that. No, Antoine – he'll never clear his name, not now. He's finished.'

*

That night, reading by torchlight in the tent, Lary, looking up from *Martin Chuzzlewit*, said, 'How you feeling?'

'Much better,' I said, laying *Butterflies of Africa* aside. 'Thank you.'

'That stuff, ganja, it's probably not chronically harmful. No more than mildly psychomimetic, I'd guess – mimics a gentle, short-term psychosis. But knowing you, I suspect you took a critical dose? About equivalent to drinking neat whisky all day every day for a week, and then stopping? Enough to give anyone the odd vision? The occasional peripheral vision disturbance? And a personal ghost, of course, a ghost just for you?'

'No idea.'

'I'm worried, too, as it happens.'

'You are?' I said, over-responsive. 'Someone called? In the night? They did?'

'Don't be ridiculous,' said Lary, annoyed. 'Of course not. I'm not the type. No – I'm worried – it's this cough. Redso, I think I have TB. I can't shift this cough. I've tried a course of your Amoxil. No effect. Any guy with a TB cavity in the lung can spit four billion bacilli in twenty-four hours – each one potent, capable of producing a new infection. Impressive, don't you think, from the bacterium's point of view? The spit-droplets dry out, they're blown around on dust particles – and this red soil, I'd guess, it's optimal. "The Captain of all these men of Death," as Bunyan says, *Mycobacterium tuberculosis*. Eskimos, Indians and Africans have the least resistance, for some genetic reason. So it probably first got a grip in Europe. Natural selection just hasn't had time to get going here. TB's endemic. And there's one type I *really* don't want. It gets in through the lungs, you cough, a dry little cough, a touch of fever, no more – and it goes to roost in the kidneys. No real symptoms. Just quiet malaise, just enough to take the top off your performance, to stop you producing good work. "Poor old Shaffer," that's what they'll say. "Poor old Shaffer – he's just not been the same since he went to the Congo. Everyone told him not to go. And now look at him! His nerves are gone. Let's ask that new young guy, the one who's just got tenure, you know – what's-his-sucking-name – he can sucking well run the Department. And he can teach the nurses, too." And then you get run down and the bacilli, they get happy. They wake up, they break out, they make it to the bladder, they burst into your balls, they erupt down your dick. Grade A pain in the penis. You piss a little blood and pus, every ten minutes or so. You shake, like a mechanical sieve, one of those things on a combine-harvester . . .'

'Hey, Lary,' I said, starting to shake myself, 'knock it off, will you? Let's try and sleep. Let's get some sleep. Okay?'

*

256

In the morning, Lary, convinced that we would have to live in Berandzoko for a month, if not for ever, faced the prospect like a man, and set about constructing a routine.

'Swim!' he said, as I watched a huge black and banded-white bee, almost an inch long, a Carpenter bee (solitary bees that rasp out burrows with their jaws into dead branches and tree-trunks), patrolling over a straggly clump of pink flowers, just outside the tent. 'First off, a wash, a swim! Second off, breakfast – barfsome manioc.' And third was a walk, at Lary's fast pace, through the plantations, past the thin manioc bushes, the small patches of pineapple and maize, the banana, orange and papaya trees.

Fourth, after lunch (manioc and chicken, in the hut, with Bague and Marcellin – Nzé and Manou had disappeared, deserted, been murdered, spirited away) we took a siesta, in the shade of the open-sided talking-house, in two of Bague's leather-aproned deck-chairs, eyes shut, in the real or pretended state of sleep, when the soul goes wandering, and the waiting and empty shell of body must not be touched. On waking (with Marcellin as translator from the Kaka), we treated the minor wounds and cuts of the small group of people who had gathered, waiting; we handed out quinine pills and vitamins and listened to complex accounts of diseases we were ill-equipped to diagnose. After supper – manioc and chicken – in the hut, with Bague and Marcellin, we retired to the dark tent, strapped on our head-torches, and read for the prescribed half-hour. On that first night: 'Jesus God,' said Lary, 'To think where I could be – *right now!*'

'Where?' I said, dutiful.

'At the State-operated Performing Arts Center! At Saratoga Springs, New York! Where we sit on a lawn, with real grass. We sit on a proper lawn – and we hear the Philadelphia Orchestra or we snag the NYC Ballet, because they both have their summer quarters, right there, at Saratoga Springs. Think of that – I could be watching one of their standard offerings – I could be watching *The Firebird*, with costumes and sets by Chagall . . .'

On the second morning, regularity established, Lary was happier, but in the afternoon, during the hour supposedly set aside for the siesta, I watched him, out of the corner of my eye, as he gave up all pretence of sleep and opened, for the first time, his best, five-by-three quadruple-ring-file black notebook which, in less difficult times, lived unmolested in the right-hand side-pocket of his bergen. What had he discovered? That one essential fact? Some all-explaining secret? Some unifying principle, the key to animism? Agitated, I eased myself off the hot leather, the squeaky chair, as quietly as I could, and I crept up on him.

Lary was drawing: uprights, laterals, criss-crossing lines. 'Wire cables,' he said, without looking up. 'Air-strung wire rope. John Augustus Roebling,

1806 to 1869. A hero. He's a hero of mine. German-American, born at Mühlhausen, made it to a great school, the Berlin polytechnic, then to America. Set up a wire-rope factory near Pittsburgh, built the long-span wire suspension bridge at Niagara Falls. They laughed at him. Chain cables, that was the accepted method, but his wire rope – it worked! So his design won the competition for the big bridge over the Hudson, Manhattan to Brooklyn. Some guy. And that bridge – the men who built it, they had to go down here, into these massive boxes' (two boxes, at the bottom of the page) 'each the size of two football fields, caissons, with roofs of yellow pine, thirty-foot thick. The air, the air they had to breathe – primitive pumps pushed it in from the surface' (two long lines, looping down from the top of the page). 'And remember – no one had ever done it before, no one had worked at that depth and that pressure. Brave guys. Imagine it – the heat, the fear! Comforting, don't you think? I find that comforting, *very* comforting.'

'What happened?'

'They went ahead and died, lots of them. Breathing compressed air, down there on the river-bed, digging out foundations for the main supports, the towers, they got terrible pains in the joints, pain in the stomach, headaches, dizziness, paralysis. No one knew what was wrong. The doctors gave it a name, of course – "Oh yes," they said. "Caisson disease." Those were the first cases of the bends – their bodies were pumped with nitrogen bubbles, they were walking bubble-baths, bubble-baths of nitrogen. David McCollough, *The Great Bridge* – you should read it.'

'So it's Bernd Heinrich and the mechanics of the bumble-bee, John Augustus Roebling and the Brooklyn Bridge. Anyone else?'

'Brunel,' said Lary, drawing something very like the open end of the goat intestine. 'Isambard Kingdom Brunel. You know about him?'

'Of course, we all know about him. He's a Brit hero. It's tribal history. At twenty-seven – Chief Engineer of the Great Western Railway. He proposed and built an extension to the line – the Great Western steam-train put into Bristol and his *Great Western* steam-ship put out into the Atlantic and took you to New York. Then the much bigger iron steam-ship, the *Great Britain*, with a screw propeller, and the gigantic *Great Eastern*, 1858. But he broke down with the stress of it, cracked up, died before her maiden voyage ...'

'Yeah,' said Lary, adding half a hub, with attendant spokes, to the right of the black, open end of goat intestine. 'But did you know he was a poet?'

'A poet?'

'The Box Tunnel, he lined it up – so the sun shone right through it on his birthday.'

*

258

On the third day, a boatman, three paddlers and the largest dugout we had yet seen put in to the slipway. And on the fourth, at dawn, we left, seen off, as we had arrived, by the lone figure of Xavier Bague.

27

'Don't forget!' Old Bague called after us, waving, in his left hand, the notes I'd given him for our board (a rate of four chickens a day) and, in his right, the three promised cartridges. 'Don't forget!' he shouted. 'You tell the President! The President of all France! Xavier Bague says – the French, they must come back!'

His shout died out behind us, lost in the trees, the lianas, the enclosing reeds.

The boatman, perhaps in his late thirties, lithe, taciturn, wearing a brown cotton shirt and shorts, stood with his long-handled paddle in the stern of the dugout. Two of his sons, teenagers, dressed likewise but with strips of brown cloth wound round their heads, half-turbans against the open sun-light of the river, stood in front of him, port and starboard. His third son, the youngest, worked his paddle in the bow, keeping the canoe straight in the current, watching for snags, silent. Behind him, Manou lay half-asleep on the duckboards, his head propped on the almost empty kit-bag of medicines.

'That Manou,' said Lary, beside me in the middle of the boat, leaning back against his bergen, pulling the rim of his hat down over his eyes, 'the ganja he must have smoked! Right now, I guess – if he wasn't black, he'd be green.' Lary closed his eyes. 'His brain – it must be scaled, skinned ... flayed like that goat.' Lary worked his shoulders, slumped down a bit, got comfortable. 'Tripe,' he muttered. 'Tripe.' And he fell asleep.

'Marcellin,' I said, twisting round, looking over the top of my bergen. 'The paddlers – do they know any songs?'

Marcellin, lying against the food-sack, raised his head. (Nzé, eyes shut, mouth open, both hands on the fly of his army trousers, lay beside him.) 'Songs? No. They can paddle, these people, but they're not fishermen, they're not *paddlers*. They're farmers. Farmers and hunters. And besides, they speak Botanga.' Marcellin turned on to his side, pillowed his head on his arm and closed his eyes. 'I speak French, I speak Spanish and English ... I speak Kaka ... but no, I do not speak Botanga ... and the truth is ... I never ...

ever . . . want to speak Botanga.' And he, too, began to breathe slowly, deep, regular, peaceful breaths.

Berandzoko, I thought, village life for the intruder – it's exhausting, anxious-making, full of demands, unknowables. It's not just me – look at them, the moment we escape, everyone collapses. So I, too, lay back on my bergen and half-shut my eyes – but a passing streak of cobalt blue and chestnut whipped me awake: that was a kingfisher, I muttered to myself, a kingfisher we have not seen before, a new, rare, unrecorded, unknown . . . So I pulled Serle and Morel's *Birds of West Africa* (now held together with army tape) out of its bergen side-pocket and I turned its scrawled-over, annotated, mould-filmed pages. 'The Grey-headed kingfisher . . . a common, widespread savanna species' – an insect-eating kingfisher that migrates south to the forest for the wet season. I thought, you can't sleep now, because this river will be special: no one comes here, there are no fishermen, and besides, for once our journeying is almost silent: there's no outboard, no constant shouted talk to ward off spirits, no sound to disturb the life all around us, nothing but the dip of the four paddles, Nzé's ragged snore, and Lary, coughing in his half-sleep.

The beds of water-hyacinth and reeds became no more than a fringe along the banks; in places the great trees, heavy with lianas, crowded right down to the edge of the water; and, as the day wore on, we slid quietly past – almost beneath – troops of chatter-grunting mangabeys. In one big, sparsely creepered tree a group of Red colobus were resting after their early-morning feed, fluffy as cocker spaniels, thoughtful as old men. Two sat astride a high thin branch, legs dangling; and on the thicker branches lower down, in plain view through the binoculars, one lay on his side, half-asleep, head pillowed on his right arm, like Marcellin, and an old male sat apart among the epiphytes, his chin on his chest, his elbows on his knees, and he stared down at us, pouting.

The birds of the Motaba were here, too – the River eagles, the Palm-nut vultures, the flocks of Grey parrots, the darters, the kingfishers, the Hartlaub's ducks – but in greater numbers; and there were birds I had not noticed before. A pair of Pigmy geese, smaller than Tufted duck, sat snug on the water in a bed of water-lilies. The white face and throat of the male, the metallic green of his head, shot with violet and blue, the sea-green of his ear-muffs, the green of his back, his tawny and white flanks, the bright-yellow stub of his bill – far from making him, as I had imagined, the most conspicuous little goose on the inland waters of the earth, actually camouflaged him so effectively against the green metallic shine of the wet lily-pads, their bright-white open flowers, the white light flashing obliquely off the ripples, that it was the dull green-and-brown female, her rounded outline undisrupted, that I noticed first.

Further downstream we passed another barely studied bird, a Yellowbill coucal, the size of a jackdaw, perched on a low twig above the bank, ten yards away, curtained to either side by lianas. He held his long, stepped, blue-green tail straight down, his purple-blue body stiff and upright; he turned his thick, curved, chrome-yellow bill, a hawk's bill, to one side, and watched us with one scarlet eye.

In a stretch of near-swamp, the banks straggled with raffia palms, a small weaver, the Congo crested, a gloss of black with a crimson throat and head, crossed in front of us, itself absurdly visible against the green and brown of the palm trees, the thin blue of the sky. And back in the tall forest, up in the high canopy on the right bank, on the bare branch of a dead tree, there perched a cinnamon-brown bird with a broad yellow bill and a blue throat – the Blue-throated roller, a true forest roller with a Lary-like sense of routine: it mounts guard all day, every day, in the centre of its territory, seeing off intruders – other rollers, hawks, hornbills, parrots – and subsisting on no more than three to ten passing insects. At five o'clock every afternoon it leaves its perch, joins rollers from the surrounding territories, and the flock, two or three hundred strong, begins a communal search above the canopy for the newly hatched rising swarms of winged ants and termites. The rollers feed until nightfall – in buoyant, erratic, wheeling flights over the tree-tops, in long, fast, silent, curving glides.

And so at last, I thought, stretching back against my bergen, pulling my hat over my face, closing my eyes, I've seen a roller . . . not a beautiful roller, perhaps, not like the roller of childhood that I waited for lying on the wide slabs of Bath stone, the secret way along the top of the kitchen-garden wall. No, it was not the bird I'd longed for, the European roller that my father said was brighter than all the blues in the sky in summer, the roller that I knew was bound to land between the lines of apple trees down the centre path . . . but someone was coming up the path, a visitor, a big man in a black jacket.

On all-fours I scrambled back along the top of the wall, on to the bough of the conker tree; I jumped to the ground, ran past the pond, through the bicycle shed, the lean-to, the back door; I turned right past the locked entrance to the cellar, down the dark corridor and, tight with fear, I scrabbled with both hands at the stiff black door-knob of my father's study – where that other goal and comfort, the Pennant-winged nightjar, trailed its plumes across the moon on page 173 of volume three of Bannerman. But a stranger sat in my father's chair, the visitor, hunched forward towards the sash-window which looked out on the lawn, the lawn where the Green woodpecker came to drill holes, to lick up ants. The visitor was big, so big he half-blocked the light, and as he turned in his chair and held out his hand to me and I saw his fingernails, my small world went dark, and I lost consciousness.

'Mimpoutou!' yelled Marcellin, waking me up. 'Women, Lary! Chickens!' And then, as a brown mud beach came into view and, anchored off it, a plank-built boat with an awning amidships and a forty-horsepower outboard-motor at the stern, 'Pastor Thomas,' he said quietly, libido ebbing from his voice. 'That's the motorboat from the mission, from Impfondo. What's he doing here?'

'An American,' said Lary, *sotto voce*, as we carried the packs ashore. 'I'm going to talk to an American!'

The boatman and his sons stowed the baggage in a small wattle-and-daub hut, perhaps the guest-hut, at the head of the path from the river, and we pitched the tents beside it, watched by six small boys, one of whom held the smoked head of a Black-casqued hornbill with both hands and clacked the great bill at us, like a pair of castanets.

'Nzé, Manou!' said Marcellin. 'You will make a fire and prepare our food. Chicken and fou-fou and pineapple! Tonight you will stay here, with us, in the guest-hut. We leave in the morning.'

'Chickens?' said Nzé. 'Pineapples?'

'You will find a chicken and a pineapple. Redmond, he will give you 1000 CFA. You will buy a chicken and a pineapple. You will not buy ganja!'

Nzé, grumpy, took the money.

'And you, Lary and Redmond,' said Marcellin, unaccountably tense, his voice rising, 'you will come with me. We will visit Pastor Thomas, Pastor Gene Thomas.'

So as the boatman and his sons went to spend the night with their families, we set off through the village, in the dusk, past a settlement of pygmies – small, crumbling, half-collapsed copies of the large rectangular huts of the Bantu, the odd conical shelter – through a series of rough squares, and past a hut with projecting rafters, on one of which hung a loose figure of liana-twine, a round hole for the face, a rough cylinder of chest, a long skirt of strands.

'A mask!' I said, delighted. 'A costume for the dance!'

'Idiot!' said Marcellin with a staccato laugh, relaxing. 'A fish-trap! They're making a fish-trap!'

'Fish-dance,' said Lary.

'Pastor Thomas,' said Marcellin, 'he worked in a canning-factory in North America, he got religion, he came here – and now he's a king! Pastor Thomas is a Big Man in Impfondo. He deals in diamonds, he saves souls, he runs the mission. He's an Evangelist, he's famous!'

'He's American,' said Lary, with a happy grin, pulling down the sleeves of his denim shirt, buttoning the cuffs.

A small brown hunting-dog with a curled-over tail, white as a rabbit-scut, trotted in front of us for twenty yards, smelt something cooking off to the left, and followed his nose up a side-path.

'But it's true,' said Marcellin, as we heard the hum of a generator ahead. 'Pastor Thomas has been here for thirty-four years. He speaks Lingala and Sango and several dialects. He's got will-power!'

Pastor Thomas looked like a determined man. Big-chested, fit, tanned, wearing a spotless white singlet and pink trousers, a comb protruding from his right pocket, he stood talking to a group of Bantu women outside a long hut by the school football-pitch.

'Hey!' he called, dismissing the women, walking towards us. 'Visitors! We don't get visitors!' He shook Marcellin's hand. 'Where you from?' he said, turning to Lary.

'Plattsburgh,' said Lary.

'Petersburg, Florida!' said Pastor Thomas, clapping Lary on the shoulder. 'United World Mission, Pastor Gene Thomas!' Pastor Thomas looked at Lary as if he, Lary, was a diamond-strike.

'Hey, Sandy!' he shouted. 'An American!'

Sandy Thomas, in a pink top, pink skirt and flip-flops, sorting something in a green metal trunk, beneath the overhang of the hut, straightened up, put both hands to the small of her back, rubbed it, and pushed her dark glasses up over her forehead. 'Hi!' she said. 'We'd ask you in. But we're awful tired.' We introduced ourselves. The green trunk, and a black trunk, were full of medicines in big black bottles and white cartons. Ampoules, used syringes, dressings and plastic bags lay on a folding-table. I glanced through the hut door – an electric light dangling from the roof, a small red generator, a portable fridge, a table laid for supper. 'We gotta clear this lot away,' said Sandy, one hand gesturing at the medical debris, the other on her hips. 'We start again tomorrow.'

'What are you doing?' said Lary. 'Treating everyone?'

'Yaws,' said Pastor Thomas. 'You know about yaws?'

'Sure do,' said Lary, wiping a hand across his moustache.

'It's a curse! The pygmies get it. Terrible! So we appealed to the Lions' Club in Brazzaville. They donated all these medicines, everything.'

'It's the only way,' said Sandy, putting bottles back in the trunk. Her bare arms and legs, I noticed, were covered in mosquito and tsetse fly bites, red swellings. 'We go upriver. It's hard. I'm exhausted. But we inject as many pygmies as we can. On the first day you have to do what you can for the villagers, all their diseases, accident wounds, fractures, that sort of thing, or the Chief won't let the pygmies come to the surgery at all. It's hard work! But the Government medical teams – when they come up from Brazzaville they sell the medicines at the pharmacy in Impfondo, and get drunk. Or if you give them money, it disappears.'

'Honest to God, Marcellin,' said Pastor Thomas, 'it's true! The French, now – sleeping sickness, leprosy, TB, yaws – they wiped it out! The Chief had to produce *everyone* in his village or they beat him terribly, but it did mean they eradicated it. Honest to God, Marcellin, they wiped it out!'

'Sleeping sickness,' said Marcellin, looking at the ground, 'TB, yaws, cholera – they're back.'

Pastor Thomas said to Lary, 'And what are you doing?'

Lary explained.

'Birds! Mokélé-mbembé! Boy, do I know a thing or two about Mokélé-mbembé! One was killed in Lake Télé seventy-five years ago. People should have listened, Lary. I'm telling you – no one took that monster seriously till Roy Mackal came out here. No one took any interest. I tell you, Marcellin, boy, if you find that monster – now, that'd be really something, wouldn't it? You know I went with Mackal. There was a great wave in a *moliba*, a deep pool in the river. We didn't see anything. But what was it? Eh? What was it? They say that when that monster stands up there's a great whooshing noise and the river runs backwards! And the pygmies round Lake Télé – people say that if you give them a stick and ask them to draw you Mokélé-mbembé they go right ahead and draw you a dinosaur in the sand. And they didn't learn *that* in school, did they? You try and draw me an okapi, Marcellin! Go on! Try! It's difficult. And the pygmies right here say there are big, striped antelopes in the north, in the forest. Antelopes they've never seen before. A group of five. They *must* be okapi. Now, Marcellin, if there are okapis in the Congo, that would be really something, eh?'

'Honey,' said Sandy, 'where's the lock for the black trunk?'

'Right here, honey,' said Pastor Thomas, reaching in his right-hand pocket and handing her a small padlock and key. 'My wife's a nurse,' he said to Lary. 'Fully trained.'

'And I guess you do everything?' Lary said to her. 'Way beyond the nursing course. Right?'

'We've got an operating theatre in Impfondo. One of the best in all Congo. Our own embassy gave us 10,000 dollars. The British and French gave us the theatre equipment. And the town back home gave us the lights.'

'You operate?' said Lary, taking off his hat.

'Oh, nothing much,' said Sandy, grimacing with pain, rubbing the small of her back. 'I perform minor operations, you know, amputations, that sort of thing . . .'

'We also deal with the dead,' said Pastor Thomas. 'Sandy and I, we hook them out of the river. Lots of naked pygmies in raffia skirts. Horrible. The fishermen come and tell us where the corpses are. They won't go near them twice. They spook themselves! We go get the bodies in the boat. A few years ago, we found a young blonde girl. Floating in the river. Throat slit. We buried her. We never found out, you know. We never did find out who she was.'

'Dead white people,' said Marcellin. 'That's serious.'

'I'm sorry, Marcellin, I really am,' said Pastor Thomas quickly, laying a hand briefly on Marcellin's arm. 'But it's like you find a member of your own tribe, you know?' And he turned to me. 'Redmond, I'm forgetting. I'm forgetting your birds! There's an eagle here, vast – it carries off antelopes. It's got claws on its elbows' – he raised his elbows – 'and that's how it finishes off its prey' – he squeezed his elbows together. 'So it's got to be big, believe me, Redmond, people used to bring its feet to me to sell. They were huge – talons as thick as your thumb. I saw it. It flew over me, darkened the sky. People say it makes its nest on great trees. Isolated trees. And don't you go near the nest, Redmond, or it'll carry you off too. You could get a pygmy to point it out. But there are few eagles like that left now, you know, very few. And leopards – when I first came I could get any amount at 300 francs a skin. Now no one brings them – or if they do, they ask *ridiculous* prices.'

Marcellin said, 'It's against the law.'

'And Marcellin – of course, I'm forgetting your Mokélé-mbembé! Marcellin, Redmond, he's the only man I believe actually saw Mokélé-mbembé. But that monster's out there all right, just waiting for you people. You should look at a map! Boy! Those swamps go on for ever! They're unexplored!'

'Honey,' said Sandy. 'It's late. I'm tired.'

'There's yaws upriver,' said Lary. 'We've seen terrible cases. And there's a pygmy in Berandzoko with a hole right into his upper pubis. A burst ulcer. You can almost see the gut-lining. You could save him.'

'Oh, Sandy, honey,' said Pastor Thomas, turning to his wife. 'We should go up there. You rest up well, honey – and if you can make it and you can find the strength, honey, we'll go.'

I woke at three in the morning, cold down my back.

'A trench,' muttered Lary, turning on his torch. 'We should have dug a trench.'

'Eh?'

'It's raining.' (A violent steady drumming on the canvas.) 'There's an inch of water in here! Your clothes, the socks, the mess you make! Soaked!'

'Lary, you're such a Kraut.'

'Bach,' said Lary, trying to sop up the deepest corner of the tarpaulin with his mouldy towel. 'Beethoven, Schubert, Schumann' (opening the tent flap with his free hand), 'Robert Koch, Paul Ehrlich' (squeezing out the towel), 'Gottlieb Daimler, Karl Benz, Rudolf Diesel' (reapplying the wet ball to the internal puddle), 'Karl von Frisch, Ernst Mayr, and come to that – Pastor Thomas, he's probably a German-American. And Sandy. Those guys are heroes.'

'They're missionaries.'

'Look,' said Lary, rounding on me, 'what does that matter? They can believe in fairies at the bottom of the garden, for all I care. They're *doing* something. They're focused. They're motivated. They're the only people in this goddam country focused enough to be doing something. They're curing yaws!'

We strapped on our head-torches, crawled outside into the stinging onslaught of cold water, and dug channels with our machetes in the mud.

At first light, sheltering in the little guest-hut, we drank chicken-bone soup and swallowed wadges of manioc. 'We're stuck here,' said Marcellin. 'The boatmen won't paddle in this.' But at noon the storm cleared, the sun came out, our clothes began to steam, the rivulets of mud slowed, the goats emerged from under the eaves, and two small birds arrived in the low bush by the tent. A Didric cuckoo, smaller than a thrush, with a white stomach, a very wet green tail, a bronze-green back and russet head, a cuckoo which lays its eggs in weavers' nests, perched on the topmost twig; and lower down, almost close enough to touch, sat Fraser's forest flycatcher, slate-grey above, barred white below, tame and wet.

The water had risen two or three feet in the night, and for hours we dropped downriver in the gathering current, stopping only to axe a way round the crowns of fallen trees, and, at a small village, to buy three chickens, four pineapples, and a bunch of plantains.

Late in the afternoon, a bird the size of a buzzard, slate-grey above, chestnut beneath, with a long, grey, white-spotted, white-tipped streamer of a tail, crossed in front of us fast and low – the Long-tailed hawk, the easiest to identify of all the jungle hawks, a bird whose habits are entirely unknown, a bird whose nest no one has ever seen.

The trees edged back, gave way to reed-beds, and at dusk we turned into a side-stream, a short cut, said Marcellin, a maze of interconnecting channels between meanders.

Well after dark, back on the main river, we reached the village of Mimbéli, put up the tents and awnings on a rough patch of cleared ground above the slipway, watched Marcellin bargain outside the nearest hut with the head of the family, in Lingala (because in Mimbéli they speak Membéli), for hours, or so it felt, over three chickens, four pineapples, four sticks of sugarcane and a bunch of bananas, and we went to bed exhausted.

As we left at dawn – the spider's webs on overhanging branches bright silver in the mist – the great shaggy shapes of a pair of Black-casqued hornbills planed overhead, braying. And cutting across a bend, close in to the bank, we surprised a green-backed, white-bellied water-snake, looped in the reeds, watching for frogs.

Small groups of Black-and-white colobus, sitting close together in their feeding-trees, slow and dignified, sixty feet above the banks, looked up from their breakfast leaves to contemplate our passing, but occasionally an individual of nervous disposition, a neurasthenic colobus, would spread-eagle himself into space, his white mane and tail billowing up behind him, dropping in a long arc to safety and the undergrowth.

Lary and I decided that Grey-cheeked mangabeys (long-tailed, leggy and black) feed low down in the trees and lianas at dawn, barking, chuckling, whooping and twittering. As the morning progresses they climb into the canopy, still barking and chuckling to themselves, or at the sight of us, but bored with whooping, and too high up for us to hear a twitter. At noon, worn out with cracking nuts and seeds, tired of chewing bark, sick of soft-centred larvae, they sit close together in a single tree (and through the binoculars I saw that one mother, apparently asleep, held her infant on a leash, her tail bound round his). Between two and three in the afternoon they find the energy to groom each other, but at four in the afternoon – the boatman put in to a small abandoned settlement on the left bank, and so the night-life of the Grey-cheeked mangabey, we agreed, would have to remain a mystery.

Four long huts, arranged in a half-square, open towards the river, stood on a patch of cleared ground. Here and there shrubs and saplings had grown up, knee-high, and the palm-fronds on the hut roofs had weathered to a uniform grey.

Nzé and Manou collected wood for our fire, Marcellin, Lary and I put up our tents and a shelter strung from old sapling-poles, and the boatman and his sons made their own camp with army tarpaulins thirty yards away.

'Why go to all that trouble?' said Lary to Marcellin. 'Why don't they just go sleep in the huts?'

'It's not safe,' said Marcellin, pushing a tent-peg into the wet earth. 'They'll tell you those huts are haunted. No one here sleeps in abandoned huts. It's taboo. But me, I think the real reason is simple, whether they know it or not – disease. Maybe people began to die here, perhaps the place is cursed – bugs in the thatch, fevers, who knows?'

'That's what Jonathan Kingdon thinks,' I said, helping Lary dig his trench round the tent. 'Places full of restless spirits, areas like Lake Télé – he says they're really homes to some undiscovered virus, a virus with a local reservoir in bushbabies, say, or in some species of bat that has a restricted range . . .'

'Yeah,' said Lary, excavating a run-off channel (with a sink-hole). 'That's how we got our bed-bug. All other bed-bugs live on bats. We spent too long in caves. One bed-bug hitched a ride.' He looked up and grinned. 'Redso, if you think how many insects here are undiscovered, and how much smaller a virus is – just imagine the number of retroviruses waiting for you, coiled like threadworms, perched round that lake!'

'Bohmaaa!' yelled Nzé at Manou, who was crouched two feet away from him, puffing life into the hesitant fire. Nzé, energetic and talkative after his days of post-ganja silence, and Manou, restored to his normal shy good humour, were in dispute. 'Uncle!' called Nzé to Marcellin. 'You decide!'

'Decide what?' said Marcellin, selecting one of the scattered logs to sit on and carrying it to the fire. Lary and I followed suit. 'Fried plantains!' said Lary. 'Luxury!' 'Boiled chicken,' said Marcellin, sitting down. 'Boiled manioc, boiled plantains. No waste.'

'Manou here,' said Nzé, 'little Manou – he wants to live in the Central African Republic! He wants to live in Bangui because Bokassa is his hero. Manou calls him The Emperor Jean Bedel Bokassa the First! He says Bokassa is a Big Man, a strong man. Whereas me, Uncle, I wouldn't live there – those people, they don't know how to dress!'

Lary said, 'Bokassa's a cannibal. He eats schoolchildren.'

'Okay,' said Manou, hanging the pot over the fire. 'So he ate a few schoolchildren. But he gave the people clear government – that's what he did. He ran the country well. Besides, lots of people ate schoolchildren – and now they're free, watching television.'

'He's under house-arrest,' said Marcellin. 'He lives in his own house. He watches television.'

'TV dinners,' said Lary.

'I knew a biologist in Oxford,' I said. 'Wilma George. She studied a little rodent, the gundi, in the Sahara and in Ethiopia. She said they sit on rock outcrops in the desert and whistle and look like powder puffs. Anyway, on this occasion she was writing a cookery book, a book of African recipes. I went to a dinner she gave for her students after their Finals, their exams. She'd spent the vacation in the Central African Republic and with her husband she'd been to supper with Bokassa. She asked him how his chefs prepared the pork – it was so tender, she wanted the recipe. So Bokassa led all the guests downstairs to a big freezer. He opened the door and pulled out a tray and on it lay one of his ministers.'

'Whoaaaa!' groaned something from the forest.

'What's that?' said Lary.

'Spirits,' said Nzé.

'The Forest crocodile,' said Marcellin. 'The male Forest crocodile calling to his mate.'

'That noise,' said Lary thoughtfully, putting a hand up under his hat. 'It's raised the hairs on the back of my neck. In fact, it's raised the hairs in my armpit.'

Marcellin said, 'Wilma George. Her students – what did they think of Bokassa?'

'She told the story as a casual anecdote. No one seemed to think it remarkable. The students were all young zoologists, and they said, "Yes, well, if you're going to kill your ministers and there's a shortage of protein, it makes sense to eat them. Why not?"'

'They're right!' shouted Marcellin with startling conviction, slapping his knee. 'Those were good students! Oxford students! The best! They're right!'

'The Emperor Jean Bedel Bokassa the First,' said Manou with dignity, as if the conversation had got out of hand, 'he is as strong as ten men. A hundred men! All the men he's eaten!'

'I see,' said Lary, apparently disappointed with Manou, with students in general, and glumly watching Nzé, who with his fingers was ripping bits off a very old, dead, half-starved, half-gutted, half-plucked chicken and lobbing them into the pot.

'Djo Ballard!' said Nzé, dropping in the parson's nose and the feet and wiping his hands on his trousers. 'He's my hero. Bohmaaa! There's a Congolese for you. He knows how to dress. You should see him! He lives in Paris!'

Lary said, 'Djo Ballard? A mass murderer?'

'He's a model,' said Marcellin with a laugh, touching Lary on the shoulder. 'He's famous here. He lives in Paris. We in the Congo, we've left the old ways. We're more advanced. We know how to dress.'

And he got up and walked off into the failing light, towards the huts.

28

In the early afternoon of the following day the river metamorphosed into a narrow channel to the left of several square miles of reed-bed, a small hill appeared on the near bank ahead, and we arrived at the little frontier town of Enyélé. I paid off the boatman, and Marcellin, Lary, Nzé, Manou and I carried the bergens and half-empty kit-bags up to the People's Office of Public Security, a low building with concrete walls, a corrugated-iron roof, and a small concrete extension to the right, the prison. Two young men in yellow tee-shirts, pressing their faces against the bars of the window, shouted at Nzé.

To judge by his gestures, and the laughter, Nzé launched his habitual barrage of greetings, jokes and insults, but the language sounded unfamiliar.

'Sango,' said Marcellin. 'A language from Central Africa, the language of Dongou, Nzé's language, but here they also speak Enyélé, from south of the river, from Zaïre.'

'Nzé,' I said, as we waited in a concrete corridor, 'why are they in prison?'

'Nothing serious,' said Nzé with a big, lopsided grin. 'They killed an old woman. They'll be out in a week.'

The Commissar was large, middle-aged, washed shiny, sitting at an ordered desk in a bare little concrete office and wearing newly pressed fatigues. A broom and a Kalashnikov stood against the back wall. In the left-hand corner a knotted rope hung from a meat-hook in the ceiling.

Marcellin pulled out one of the two metal chairs in front of the desk. 'Dr Agnagna,' said the Commissar, 'please don't sit! You're dirty!'

'We've been in the forest,' said Marcellin, twisting to look at the seat of his jeans. 'We've been in the forest for months!'

'I don't care,' said the Commissar, opening his desk drawer and, in his agitation, pulling out a pair of steel handcuffs. 'You're not staying here! You can sleep in the Government Building. It's empty. There are hornets in there!'

'The stamp,' said Marcellin, looking uneasily at the handcuffs. 'You need the rubber stamp.'

*

The date of our entry into the Political District of Enyélé safely recorded in our passports and passes, we transferred the packs and bags across the mud to the concrete-walled, high-roofed Government Building. One small, pale, paper nest, a collection of concentric circles of stuck-together, downward-opening tubes, hung from each of the two light-sockets, ten feet apart, in the centre of the ceiling. On each nest five brown, delicate, inch-long hornets with nipped-in waists sat head-down, poised.

'Don't go near them!' said Marcellin. 'Keep to the sides of the room. Their sting – it's terrible.'

'Heigh-ho,' said Lary. 'And hello concrete bed.'

'We're not staying in here!' said Nzé, cocking his head to one side, looking up at the nearest nest. The hornet in his line of vision lifted its front legs and preened its antennae. 'We're staying with friends!'

'You're staying here,' said Marcellin, with an exasperated sigh. 'You'll guard the bags.'

Lary began to arrange his tarpaulin on the dusty concrete floor, up against the right-hand wall.

'No time for that!' said Marcellin. 'We must go and find Gérard. Gérard Burlion. We'll need his truck – and his speedboat. He's French. He's white. He works for FNC. He's a forester. He owes me a favour. He likes me. We get on!' He turned to Manou. 'You'll be okay. No one comes in here.'

'Haunted,' Lary muttered to me, as we set off up the mud street. 'Fevers. Hornets in the roof.'

At the top of the town we turned left on to a yellow laterite machine-made road, a cutting through the forest which led down, past a big generator and water-pump, to a hollow spread with bungalows, outside each one of which there sat a Toyota Land Cruiser Truck.

'Yes!' said Lary.

Gérard Burlion came to his steel-grille glass door. Perhaps in his late thirties, he was fit, blond, quick in his movements, and wore a trimmed beard and moustache, a sweat-shirt with *Courier pour une fleur* printed on the front, blue ski-trousers and blue-and-white trainers. We felt the cool, clean breeze from an air-conditioner; and I caught a glimpse of real armchairs, books on shelves in a bookcase, a varnished table with newspapers and magazines . . . 'Marcellin! My old friend! Monsieur Eléphant! How are you? And who are your friends?'

Marcellin explained.

'*Enchanté!*' said Gérard, with a handshake that cracked the knuckles. 'No problem! I'm off to see my foreman. I'll walk you back to town. And tomorrow I go to Impfondo. You're in luck! I'll collect you in the morning. Four o'clock sharp.'

We set off up the hill at an athlete's pace, Lary's pace. Three small brown doves, pecking about on the track, whirred off low into the forest.

'Marcellin,' said Gérard, 'I've carried out instructions. I've been spying for you. I now estimate that two or three tonnes of bush-meat pass through Enyélé every week, minimum. Mostly from Zaïre. It's madness. Soon there won't be an antelope or an elephant left. When I was a forester in Gabon, you know, I used to see leopards and chimps and gorillas every day. But then there are fewer pygmies in the Gabon. Here there are too many pygmies – the merchants lend them guns and pay them a few packets of cigarettes and they bring in the meat!'

'How long have you been here?' I said, trying to keep up.

'Me? In Africa? Twenty-four years! I like it here. I'm an African. It gives me pleasure. It may sound banal, but I'm a practical man. Intensely practical. I'm a forester first, an engineer second. In France you have machines for everything – and experts to fix them. But here I'm the man who does *everything*.' He gestured at the water-pump and generator. 'See that? I set it up! And if the taps don't work, it's my fault, there's no one else to blame. I like that.' ('Yes!' said Lary, increasing speed.) 'But Marcellin, how's your elephant survey? Eh?'

'It's almost done,' said Marcellin, sweating with the exertion in the close evening heat. 'Dr R. F. W. Barnes of Wildlife Conservation International and of the Department of Applied Biology, Pembroke Street, Cambridge – he'll publish the results. And take the credit.'

'I've been thinking about it. Marcellin – you've got one big problem. There's a pygmy I know here. A good friend of mine. He works in my timber camp. He can take the shape of an elephant whenever he wants, for hunting. Well, one day he transformed himself into an elephant and went hunting and killed a mother and son elephant – and when he returned to my camp he found that two pygmies had died.' Gérard snapped his fingers. 'Just like that! So this pygmy became disgusted with it all. He changed into an elephant to revenge himself on the Bantu – the poacher who'd lent him the gun. He went to the Bantu's plantation and trampled on the manioc bushes and rolled in the maize and he pushed over the plantain and banana trees. So what does that do to your computer? Eh? What happens with your computer?'

'How do you mean?'

'Marcellin, it's obvious! The animal left tracks everywhere. So you count that in your survey. Everyone saw elephant tracks, but all the time it was a pygmy.'

I said, 'You really believe that?'

Gérard stopped. 'That's your quickest way back,' he said, pointing to a path off the track. 'I must get on. I'm busy.' He looked at me with a sudden disdain. He reached into his shirt-pocket, took out a pair of dark glasses and put them on. 'You – you're new in Africa. I can see that. If you'd lived here for a year even, one year – you'd understand enough never to ask such a stupid question.' And he strode on up the road he'd built.

At three in the morning we got up stiff from the concrete floor, finished the chicken and manioc, packed the bags and waited on the concrete veranda from four until seven (Lary very quiet, his head in his hands) when Gérard arrived in his truck. Marcellin and Nzé sat in the cab, Lary and I and Manou on the bergens on the open flatbed – and Gérard, to make up for lost time or because he had once been a racing driver, or both, drove at stomach-curdling speed down the narrow dirt road through the forest, kicking up dust, hurtling into blind spots, lifting wheels off the corners, throwing us and bags and fear about the back of the truck.

We came to rest, still on board, in front of a pile of sawn tree-trunks beside a small wharf, beside the Oubangui river.

'Just when you think you're safe . . .' said Lary, retrieving his hat and the contents of his pockets from the steel plates. 'Just when you think you've met the one person round here who's still in his tree . . .'

We carried the packs past black tanks of diesel, a hoist-tractor, a winch-tractor, a battered lorry, and down to a big pirogue tied up beside a small white speedboat. Three men, one in blue overalls, emerged from behind a shed, Gérard issued instructions, and they carried a petrol-drum into the pirogue, refuelled the big outboard, took our baggage and loaded it.

The man in the blue overalls sat in the stern; Manou, Nzé and Lary filed in amidships; Marcellin and I squatted on the next cross-plank, and Gérard, pushing off, hopped into the bow and sat facing us.

Gérard, dressed in town clothes (green-striped shirt, green linen jacket, wallet and sheathed Mauser knife on the belt of his fawn cotton trousers) glanced at his watch. 'Late!' he said. 'Problems this morning. Domestic.' Marcellin nodded, as if he knew all about it.

The boatman pulled the string of the outboard, turned up the throttle, and we swung into the wide brown Oubangui, turning south, downriver, towards Dongou. 'Bohmaaa!' yelled Nzé, raising his fist.

'Redmond,' said Gérard, leaning forward, 'I'm sorry I was rude to you yesterday.'

'You weren't rude,' I said, still indignant. 'Not at all.'

'You must understand – there are three types of white men here. There are schoolteachers who make no money. They're here because they love the work. They're called to it, a vocation. Then there are resident, industrious individuals, people who've chosen to live here, expatriates who work hard. And then there are the *petits blancs* – white men who are just here for the money, men who are desperate, or who've been sent here by some company. They have no imagination. They hate it all. They hate the climate. They hate the Congolese. You can't talk to such people – it's impossible.'

'White trash,' said Marcellin, in English, with a happy grin.

On a distant yellow sandbar, under the vast dull grey sky, four black-and-white geese, perhaps Knob-billed geese, were resting at the water's edge.

'I belong to the second type of white man,' said Gérard, hunched, talking fast. 'My father was a teacher. He taught law. He spent twelve years in Brazzaville. He wrote a thesis, he won a doctorate – he became a magistrate in Madagascar. Those were happy years for us in Brazzaville, for the children – we had a little boat, we swam in the river! I have six sisters and a brother – and we've all stayed in Africa! They were formative years. But then I spent thirteen years in France. I was lost. I didn't know what to do. At fifteen I earned my money washing up in hotels; I worked on building sites – and it was there I discovered carpentry. I found I loved wood.' He stroked the worn-smooth gunwale of the dugout. 'So I went to the School of Forestry in Bordeaux. I got my practical experience in the Gabon, driving big machines. I became Director of Roadbuilding – and then of Exploitation. I'd found my interest in life. A trade I loved! A consuming interest! So now I'm happy. I work from four in the morning till ten at night. Every day.'

'That's like Cuba!' said Marcellin, excited. 'Cuba in the early days! We worked for sixteen hours a day. We had our meals at work. The house – that was only for sleep. If you were a good worker you earned the right to buy a car or a washing-machine. If you wanted an apartment you had to work in construction. So there was money for hospitals and schools – and for mothers like mine, a woman with nine children: in Cuba in the old days she'd have won a medal from the State, a medal as a Great Mother, and the Government would have supported her.'

Gérard said, 'Would it work here?'

'No, you know it wouldn't, you know yourself – the Congolese people do not like to work. Some people work until eleven at night, but not many.'

'That's one trouble. And then there's no industrial base. Besides, when an African makes money, he takes lots of wives. Whereas a European or a North American – he founds a business and a family dynasty . . .'

'Gérard,' I said, 'how about you? Do you have a wife?'

'Redmond, in 1979 I cocked up my life. It was difficult. My wife is from Zaïre and we had a child – but in 1979 I sent them to live in France, in Nice, because I wanted my child to have a proper education. We tried here with a correspondence course but that's difficult, very difficult. In fact –

unless the mother's a schoolmistress – it's impossible! I send them money. And I get leave, you know, every ten months or so . . .'

'And for the rest of the time,' said Marcellin, with a wink at me, 'you live like an African.'

'Perhaps.'

'In some ways,' said Marcellin, intense, his voice rising, 'I, too – I belong to your second type! I work until eleven at night! I work hard! And in Impfondo, Redmond, I'll show you, we won't rest! We'll resupply this Government Expedition in one day. That's all we need. One day! In two days from now we'll be moving to the west.'

'Where are you going?' said Gérard.

'Djéké, Boha, Lake Télé.'

'Lake Télé? Marcellin – you're crazy! You can't go back there!'

'I know,' muttered Marcellin, staring at the duckboards. 'They'll murder us.'

On the track above the Dongou landing-stage Gérard's Impfondo driver was waiting in a red Land Cruiser.

Nzé helped us load the bags and then set off to visit his wife and family, a small figure with a brown holdall walking up a path between the cactus hedges. Marcellin called after him, 'Hôtel du Parti! Two days from now! Six in the morning!'

Gérard climbed into the driving-seat; Marcellin and the driver sat beside him; Lary, Manou and I wedged ourselves well down between the bergens in the back; and Gérard made the heavy-tread tyres howl all the way down the smooth tarmac surface of the Brazilian-built road to Impfondo, the road we had once thought so commonplace.

At the Hôtel du Parti we said goodbye to Gérard, Marcellin found the *patron* (still drunk), and we took our old rooms in the annexe behind the concrete pillars, the iron-fretwork rails of the concrete veranda, rooms which, in our absence, had grown bigger, drier, luxurious – and there was glass in the windows and curtains you could draw behind the glass, and a lock on the door, and a diesel-drum water-tank outside with attendant buckets which you could fill and carry inside to the back and tip over your head as you stood naked in the concrete pen: you could take a cold shower.

So we took a shower, and Lary, I noticed, had grown thin, and the lines of his face were deeper, sharply defined, as if some sorcerer had drawn patterns with a knife across his forehead and about his eyes.

We bought a bottle of Johnny Walker Red Label in Madame Langlois' little shop (the same shopkeeper, the same bottles of Gintonic), took a slug all round, locked up, and walked with Marcellin to Yvette's restaurant, past the Brazilians' abandoned rusting yellow lorries and bulldozer, along the path through the elephant grass and up the rutted mud road.

Over the fish soup, the chunks of manioc and the bottles of Primus beer at our table in the little hut with the slatted walls, Marcellin, full of Gérard's energy, said, 'Tomorrow we work! We get Lary's ticket – they say the airstrip is working, there's fuel for the plane and it comes from Brazzaville at the end of the week. We go to the market in Joseph's Toyota and buy stores: manioc, cooking-oil, sardines, coffee, oats, powdered milk, sugar, salt, soap, lighters, tobacco – and cigarettes, two bottle of wine, two bottles of whisky and shoes, shoes and cloth for the Chief of Boha. They have problems with their feet round Lake Télé. It's a swamp! Their feet rot!'

'And candles,' I said. 'And lavatory paper. And peanut butter.'

'The pharmacy,' said Marcellin. 'Antibiotics for gonorrhoea and syphilis.'

'Extencilline for yaws,' said Lary. 'And syringes.'

'At six the following morning we say goodbye to you, Lary. And Joseph will drive Redmond and me, Nzé and Manou to Epéna, where I know the Commissar, and a *pinacier* who will take us in his dugout to Djéké. From Djéké we will walk through the swamp-forest to a hidden village. A village of women sorcerers. This village is beside a lake. A lake unmarked on any map!'

Marcellin drained his third bottle of Primus.

'And then, Redmond, if you insist, and because I made you that promise in Brazzaville, we will go to Boha, and walk to Lake Télé. But I warn you – Boha is a village unlike any other. It is full of strange people. Wicked people. Violent men. There are problems at Boha, far worse than the problems of Manfouété.' He scraped back his chair and stood up. 'At Boha I cannot answer for your safety – or mine. But now I must say farewell to my mother. And after that, Redmond, I shall spend the night with Florence. Florence will comfort me! Florence will give me courage!'

That night, as we lay wrapped in our tarpaulins beneath the mosquito-net, the bottle of whisky finished, Lary, turning off his torch, mumbled, 'It's odd to be going home. I've been counting the days, you know, for years and years. Or so it seems. My whole life – it's changed. I'm worried, Redso, I can't express it, I'm disturbed, deep down inside. But I say to myself, "Shaffer, you're going home. You've done your stint. You've kept your word. Period." And I get this terrible rush of adrenalin. Kennedy Airport! America! Chris! I can't believe it. And that's followed by these gut-wrenching moments of fear – like just now when I thought we'd be stuck in Enyélé, and then again when I thought we'd never live to see the end of the road . . .'

'Couldn't you stay a little longer? A month? Two months? Three?'

'Nope!' Lary sat bolt upright and snapped on the torch. 'Nope!' A small brown cockroach, caught in the circle of light on the left-hand wall, flattened itself and froze. 'I have to get back! I have to teach! I'll lose my job! I've told you a hundred times. The journey to the north-east. That's enough. Lake Télé – that's your affair. You'll need someone . . .'

'I'll miss you.'

'Yeah, well, I'll miss you,' he said, turning off the torch, lying down again, breathing heavily. 'But it can't be helped. You see, on another planet, in another life, a million miles away, I dimly remember that I have a job. I'm a Professor, you know. Or I think I was . . . But don't get me wrong. From the perspective of learning, Redso, this has been an enormously rich experience. It's given me stories for a lifetime. It's not always been fun . . . in fact I'm not sure it's ever been fun . . . and I've never been so frightened in my whole life, but . . .' He stretched out slowly, sighed, and fell asleep.

With a warm glow inside, a mix of Johnny Walker Red Label, gratitude and affection, I, too, fell asleep.

The following day, in the hot, still, clammy air, under the grey Impfondo sky, we drove about the little town in the People's Ministry for the Preservation of Fauna's yellow Toyota truck, working through the list of stores, adding cartridges (two boxes), white basketball boots for Marcellin, trainers for Nzé and Manou, a notebook for Manou, biros, and a sack of rice. (But there were no antibiotics in the pharmacy, no ampoules of penicillin, no syringes.) We bought Lary's ticket from the little hut of an airline office (and I gave him an extra 80,000 CFA to see him out of the country). The following morning, Manou arrived at four, Nzé at five, and Joseph, still worried, shaking slightly, as if he had a fever, his lower lip still sagging, arrived with the truck at six.

'Lary!' said Marcellin, as we loaded the bergens and the kit-bags full of new stores. 'Don't worry! Joseph will look after you. Stay close to Joseph. It's not easy. It's not like North America. Soldiers may check your papers. They'll turn out your pack. Without Joseph you're lost! And you must *run* to the plane. You must *fight* for a seat!'

'I see,' said Lary. 'No problem. Thanks.'

Lary and I gave each other a tight, awkward, Anglo-Saxon hug.

'Here,' he said, releasing me, tense, his eyes watery. 'Sign this.' He drew his best black, quadruple-ring-file notebook from his right-hand pocket and held out a biro. 'Sign this, please.' On the page next to the drawing of the entrance to Box tunnel he had written: 'I, Redmond, declare that I am going to the Lake Télé deathtrap of my own free will and I hereby forgive Lary his escape.'

BOOK III

29

The boy lay stretched out on a low wooden platform beside the hut, under an orange tree. A strip of white rag ran tight across his chin to a log beneath his neck, holding his head straight. His father sat on a stool beside him, bending forward, caressing the air above the boy's forehead and chanting at the top of his voice, over and over again, 'I've lost my child. My poor son. My son is dead.' Whenever he paused, twenty or so women and children, sitting on mats behind him, rocked back and forth, wailing in chorus.

Marcellin, Nzé, Manou and I squatted on the roots of a mango tree near the entrance of the cactus-hedged compound, with our temporary translator from Bomitaba into French, Léonard Bongou-Lami, Commandant of the People's Militia of Djéké.

Djéké was by far the largest, best-ordered village we had seen: you could walk for almost two kilometres through its plantations of manioc and bananas, cacao and plantains; it even had a little shop. And having bought coffee and sugar for the mourners, a goat for the father and a winding-sheet for the corpse, I felt I had a right to ask questions.

'What happened? How did the boy die?'

The Commandant got to his feet, folded his arms and looked away, silent. Marcellin put a finger to his lips and shook his head at me.

Fresh mourners continued to arrive. I stood up next to the Commandant.

'This is the right way to do things,' I said lamely, wishing to make amends for whatever offence I had committed. 'It's right – to share your grief with everyone. We don't deal with death like this in England.'

The Commandant turned to me. 'That father,' he said, pausing to spit, 'he killed his own children. He did it himself.'

'What do you mean?'

'Everybody knows. He's a great sorcerer here. We're all frightened of him. He killed his wife, *and then all five children.*'

Without looking back, he walked off to the far end of the compound and joined another crowd of onlookers. A group of men pushed past us bearing a huge drum, at least eight feet tall, followed by a gaggle of boys carrying chopped wood; I expected them to build a funeral pyre, but instead they made three small fires round the centre of the enclosure. In the dusk Leaf-nosed bats, the bats as big as blackbirds, appeared, quartering the air above the mud huts, the banana and safou trees: their wings creaked as they laboured over us. The fire to our right burst into life; the men picked up the drum from its place of honour by the corpse and laid it with its top towards the flames, to warm its skin.

Night fell. Marcellin took his pipe out of his trouser-pocket, filled it from the last tin of Balkan Sobranie, lit up and inhaled deeply. Despite myself, in the firelight I stared at the stem of Marcellin's pipe ... it seemed to be unbroken ... but perhaps he'd found some glue ... or, more likely, he'd unscrewed his snapped stem and replaced it with Nzé's or Manou's or ...

Marcellin's mistress of two nights, young, eager and beautiful, came and sat between us; she gazed at him, ran her hands rapidly down the inside of her thighs, and giggled.

An old man walked towards the entrance of the compound, put his head back, held out his arms, and shouted into the darkness towards the forest.

'Who's he calling?' said Marcellin to the girl.

'He says that his grandson loved to dance,' she whispered. 'So we must show God or the spirits how much we miss him by dancing. And he calls to the ghosts in the forest. "If God took young Kotela, whose sobriquet was Mourgas, then God took him; but if he died because of sorcery, then, spirits, search out the sorcerer and kill him *now*."'

'Redmond,' said Marcellin, 'I think it is different here. The sorcerers of the Bomitaba – they're organized. They have secret conventions. Families have to give a son or daughter to the sorcerer – and when the child dies, sometimes the body disappears. *Ils bouffent les enfants.* They eat children.'

'In the imagination you mean. In the spirit way.'

'Well,' said Marcellin, cupping his pipe in his hands, 'I've thought about it a lot. People say that when you bury someone killed by sorcerers you always know: they're eaten away inside. Sorcerers here don't get rich. But they must get something for their work as sorcerers. I don't think they do it for nothing. I think sometimes they take the meat.'

The drum, judged to be ready for playing, was set up in the centre of the compound, and a platform brought for the drummer; men formed one half of an enclosing circle, women the other, and laughter and the dance began. The drummer produced a massive sound, accompanied by the sharper notes of another man beating the wooden trunk of the drum with two short sticks. Nzé and Manou drifted away to find their girls for the night, and Marcellin, his mistress and I joined the dance, five steps forward, a half-turn to the left, a half-turn to the right, five steps back, and on round the circle. After two or three hours, when according to Marcellin we'd danced the mozambique, the mobenga and the ekogo, he said a temporary goodbye to the girl and we made our way back in the moonlight towards the guest-hut, via the intersecting paths between the compounds of cactus hedge, the bare mud gardens shaded by breadfruit or mandarin or safou, avocado or lemon or mango trees. Children ran past us, carrying lemons to their parents at the dance, or merely engaged in their secret games, up late with the licence of the fiesta, wide-eyed and quick with excitement. And under the moon and the unfamiliar stars, beneath the tiny orange glow of the Russian observation satellite hanging stationary in space above the Marxist People's Republic of the Congo, and, perhaps, still euphoric after the dancing and the laughter, I felt for a moment that Djéké itself was a village in an idyll, a place where nothing bad could happen.

In the guest-hut Marcellin lit a candle and I took out the gourdful of palm-wine I had bought that afternoon. Nzé and Manou slid back the corrugated-iron sheet that served as a door and joined us.

'Redmond! Uncle!' said Nzé, pleased with himself, skew-eyed and sweaty, standing four-square in the Cuban Army fatigues and peaked cloth cap of the People's Militia of Dongou. 'I need 500 CFA!'

'Not yet you don't,' said Marcellin. 'You'll make our supper first.'

'Little Manou here,' said Nzé, putting an arm round his shoulders, 'he is cheaper than me, Redmond. Tonight, no one wanted him. He is too young.'

'Djéké is full of diseases,' said Manou, sitting on one of the rough chairs. 'All the girls have diseases.'

I got the 500 CFA (one pound) from my bergen. In Djéké a pound a night was the going rate. 'But Nzé – the gonorrhoea you caught in Makao. That was the last twelve Amoxil.'

'Your Western medicine didn't help at all,' said Nzé, swilling down the palm-wine in one gulp. He picked up our pot of left-over mangabey stew from the table and took it outside to place on the fire. 'I was discharging for three days afterwards' – he turned round for greater emphasis, flicking his free hand down his crotch to mime a stream of falling pus – 'and then when I drank the bottle of bark-water the sorcerer gave me, the sorcerer in Berandzoko, it went at once. He made it in the way our grandfather taught me! That's what did it. That's why I'm cured.' He squatted down, arranging the fire, shouting back over his shoulder into the hut, 'My grandfather was the greatest sorcerer in Dongou, Uncle. Everybody knows. They all know the story. The Chief of Dongou, now, he also was powerful in the spirit way, and in the night, every night, he would kiss all the men, all the boys in the town. Yes. Everybody knew. And when you woke up in the morning and you found sperm in your turds when you went to make a shit you said, "Aha! The Chief of Dongou has been here!"'

We laughed.

'Wait,' said Nzé, getting to his feet and holding up his hand theatrically, 'I haven't finished. He visited my grandfather once, but my grandfather won the battle in the night and he took away the Chief of Dongou's clothes – and in the morning he made the Chief of Dongou walk in his sleep from one end of Dougou to the other and back again, in the nude, with his dick standing up. *That* taught him a lesson.'

'It's not as funny as you think,' said Manou, 'all this. Take that poor father – all he did wrong was at his uncle's wedding, long ago. He arrived without a present of drink or money, so his uncle the sorcerer said, "Right, when you get married and have children of your own, I'll kill them all. I'll wait until they're fourteen or fifteen years old, each one, and then, when you love them more than anything on earth, they'll die slowly in front of you."'

'That's not what I heard,' said Marcellin. 'He certainly killed his own children, but he didn't mean to do it. He visited a féticheur to get a fetish for his own protection, and that was all right; but then he asked for a fetish that would make him a great fisherman, and that was his mistake. "Put so-and-so in a bottle," said the féticheur, "something that you really value, and then throw it in the river." When his first child died he went to a second féticheur, who said, "Yes, well what did you expect? When you cut those locks of hair from all your children's heads and put them in that bottle and threw it in the river you threw away their futures. It's simple. All you have to do is get your bottle back at once, or all your children will die." But it wasn't simple. The river here is a blackwater river and you can't see into it, and he spent three months trailing the mud with his nets and he found nothing. And now his last child is dead.'

'So what do you think it is really?' I said. 'Hereditary leukaemia? Haemophilia? Something like that?'

'You and your white man's questions,' said Marcellin, pouring himself another mug of palm-wine. 'That's not what we're talking about. You yourself – you know very well. That's just the mechanism. *That's not what really matters.*'

Nzé doled out the monkey-stew and manioc.

'So, Marcellin – why don't you want to go to Boha and Lake Télé? Is that a matter of sorcery?'

'You don't understand, Redmond. You don't understand the risk I'm taking. They'll murder me. I told you – Boha is a village unlike anywhere else. They hunt the gorilla and the chimpanzee. They prefer gorilla and chimpanzee to all other meat. They hunt with special spears. Twelve feet long. The young men provoke the male gorilla until it charges on to their points.' He put down his mess-tin. 'Yes. There are all kinds of problems. The young men loyal to the traditional Chief kill the men loyal to the President of the People's Village Committee, the men who want to join the Party. They kill each other with short two-sided knives. Almost all the men of Boha have been put in prison for murder at one time or another. Whenever the police at Epéna have enough petrol they go with the army and arrest another batch of killers.'

'And then what?'

'They take them to the prison at Epéna and lock them up for five days. Five days is the punishment for a murder that is domestic or a matter of sorcery. And it's always domestic or a matter of sorcery. The Political Commissar of the People's District of Epéna put a policeman at Boha once, but he ran away.'

'I'm not surprised.'

'And we also, we will run away.'

'Why? Why should they go for you?'

'Because they think I put their *Chief* in prison. And that is the most terrible of all insults to them, to them as men, that someone should capture their Chief. They've taken a blood-oath to kill me if I ever set foot in Boha again. I have one friend there – the mother of a young man who works for me in the Department in Brazzaville. She was sent to warn my mother in Impfondo.'

'How come you put the Chief in prison?'

'I didn't. I swear it was nothing to do with me. It was after my last expedition, the all-Congolese expedition, when we saw the dinosaur. All I did was write it in my report that the Chief made us pay 75,000 CFA to enter his forests. I had to, Redmond; I had to account for all the money I spent to our Minister in Brazzaville. And when the Political Commissar of the People's District of Epéna saw the report he said it was illegal – the Chief of Boha did not own those forests, the forests belong to the Party. He said the Chief of Boha must be taught that he does not run an independent state. So he called in the army and they went downriver with big outboards and forty soldiers and they captured the Chief at dawn when he was still asleep with his wives and they took him back to Epéna and locked him in the People's Prison for three whole days.'

'But Marcellin – it's ridiculous. You're the Head of Conservation for all the People's Republic of the Congo. You're very important in your own right. You can't pretend to be in charge and then have areas you're too frightened to visit. It doesn't make sense. We've *got* to see your dinosaur...'

'I've had enough,' said Marcellin, jumping to his feet and knocking over his mug of palm-wine. He was rigid with anger; for a moment I thought he was going to hit me. 'I'm leaving,' he said. 'I'm going to see my girl.'

Nzé, looking shocked, drew the corrugated-iron door aside, but Marcellin, even in his rage, remembering his essential preparation for a night of passion, reached into the side-pocket of his pack, pulled out the bottle of aftershave, pushed it down inside the front of his shirt, sprayed himself, replaced the bottle, and, in a cloud of scent, disappeared into the night.

'You shouldn't upset him,' said Nzé. He peered round the door, his head tilted slightly to the right and up a bit so that, with his best eye, he was looking straight and left. Satisfied that Marcellin really had gone, he lunged at the pack, snatched the magic bottle, sprayed himself so hard he sneezed, tucked it back, mimed a few practice thrusts up against the wall, announced, 'He's not the only one who has a woman!' and followed Marcellin into the darkness.

Manou sat with his head in his hands, his palm-wine untouched.

'What's the matter?' I said. 'You don't believe it, do you? You don't think there's any danger?'

'Of course it's dangerous,' said Manou, unusually quiet, even for him. 'They'll kill you too.'

'Why me? It's nothing to do with me.'

'It's everything to do with you. It's a white man's problem. It's white people like you who cause all the trouble.'

'I don't understand.'

'It's simple. Marcellin wants white people to come here to see Lake Télé. He says his Minister will set up a National Park and make him rich. He told the men of Boha that if they didn't like it he'd call in the army and have the village moved somewhere else. But the men of Boha can't move – the lake is three days' walk away in the forest, it's true, but that is where the spirits of their ancestors live. If the villagers are moved any further everyone will die. The ancestors will no longer protect them.'

At that moment, underneath the waves of drumming and singing, there came a new sound, half-groan and half-scream, repeated in short bursts, a sound of uncontrolled pain.

'It's nothing to worry about,' said Manou, nodding towards the noise and drinking his wine again. 'They say he calls like that whenever he's awake. I heard him this morning when you were out in the forest. They've put him in a hut at the edge of the village by the plantation here. He can't move. They've shut him in and only his wife may visit him. He's barricaded in the hut. He killed someone, a friend, and that friend's son said, "You killed my father – and for that you are going to suffer before you die. For years before you die you will suffer in your house. You will not be able to pee. You will cry night and day." So now he has boils down his thighs and over his dick and balls and on his stomach and his joints are all swollen up and he can't move and he cries, for example, "I killed Manou! I killed Redmond! Forgive me, Manou! Forgive me, Redmond! I didn't know I was a sorcerer! I never knew I was a sorcerer!"'

'But that's terrible,' I said. 'It just sounds like a bad case of untreated gonorrhoea. All he needs is penicillin. We'll take him back with us. We'll take him to hospital.'

'He's been to the hospital at Impfondo three times, three times Redmond, but it's no good, *because it's a problem of sorcery*. Don't you understand? Don't you understand at all?'

'No, I don't,' I said, as the screams battered round my head. 'I've got one canister of Trimethoprim left. That might help. I'll give it to him. I'll give it to his wife in the morning.'

'That's a waste of medicine,' said Manou, getting up and going into the side-room where he'd spread his tarpaulin and rigged his mosquito-net. 'He'll be dead in a day or two. Far better to give me the pills. I'll keep them for my little girl. What if something happened to her?'

Deciding to escape from everything, to go to bed myself, I blew out the candle and lay down on the mud floor.

The drumming and singing seemed to be gathering strength, but the screams grew less frequent and then stopped; I put on my sweater against the sudden cold of the night, placed a shirt under my hips as a mattress and another in a pair of pants as a pillow; I pulled a tarpaulin over me; and I fell asleep to the just discernible chorus of the mobenga, the protest of the male without his 500 CFAs: *Oyo mama oyo mama/Oyo/Alouka mbogo ya ofe le*: woman, woman, you ask for money for nothing.

30

At first light our tethered cockerel crowed five feet from my head. His challenge was at once answered by the local champion, a burst of outrage from the other side of the door. But the drumming had stopped, and so had the screams. I rubbed some feeling back into my hips, put on my boots and binoculars, stole a few spoonfuls of manioc and monkey-stew (it smelt and tasted of unwashed crotch), clattered back the door, eased the cockerel aside with my foot and took a deep breath of the morning mist. Some madwoman laughed at me. Startled, I traced the hysterical whistling chuckle to the top of a straggly tree. It was a kingfisher. A small blaze of iridescent azure in the grey dawn, he had a red-orange bill, a grey head and black upper wings, and I decided he must be the Congo blue-breasted, a freak of a kingfisher that never goes fishing, lives in the forest, makes his hole in termite nests in high trees, and eats only frogs, scorpions, crabs, whip-scorpions, cockroaches, beetles, mantises, toads, spiders and millipedes. Deciding, in his turn, that I was too big to be interesting, he gave a final descending laugh of disappointment, dropped sharply out of the tree, and flew off fast and low.

Crouching behind a bush by the manioc plantation, I looked up from a spasm of diarrhoea in time to see the great black and white moth of a bird, the Palm-nut vulture, curve overhead towards the river. And walking back across a patch of waste ground, I disrupted the sex life of the Pin-tailed whydah, a bird the size of a sparrow with a white stomach, a dark-blue back, a bright-red beak – and a tail of two long black plumes, each double his own length, which he held vertically beneath him and jerked rapidly to and fro, fluttering his wings, a little bundle of feathers in the last stages of ejaculatory passion. Three dull-brown females (which, like the Common cuckoo, sneak their egg into the nests of other birds) pecked about on the ground beneath him, unimpressed by the frantic adulation a yard above their heads. Seeing me, the females flew up into the straggly tree and the male followed them, twitching his tail along behind him.

Back in the hut, Marcellin, happy again after his night of love-making, was helping Nzé and Manou pack the bergens with six days' worth of stores.

'Redmond!' he said, testing the weight of my bergen. 'Léonard says he'll come with us. Mboukou's only a day's walk. Easy. We'll carry our own packs. Light ones for Nzé and Manou, because they're *petits*, they're always ill. Heavy ones for you and me. And Léonard – he's strong! I like him. Something *crippling* for Léonard!'

We took the packs outside and lined them up against the hut wall. Léonard, off-duty, arrived wearing a red cotton shirt with white diagonal stripes, black cotton trousers and gym-shoes; we transferred the cockerel and the remaining sacks of stores to his hut for safe keeping; helping each other into the bergens, we set off for the hidden village beside the unmapped lake.

'Redmond,' said Marcellin as we passed the last cacao plantation, 'African women – they really move. They're not like white women! I had an air hostess in Brazzaville once – she cradled me all night, like a black doll. Horrible!'

Powered by the thought of such indignity, or perhaps still inspired by Gérard Burlion, Marcellin matched Léonard's Militia Commandant's pace; Nzé, Manou and I, too desperate to speak, kept them more or less in sight and, stopping only to listen to the urgent commanding whistle of a Crowned eagle in the canopy (the chatter-grunting replies of Greater white-nosed mangabeys, a crash in the leaves, a scream, silence), six hours later we arrived at Mboukou.

Seven huts stood in a clearing at the head of a small lake – huts that themselves seemed part of the undergrowth, built of sapling-poles and wattles and covered with palm-fronds. In the rough centre of the little settlement, under an old mango tree, the curved side of a dugout had been fixed flat on four short poles as a bench; and to the left an upturned hull with its bow cut off, resting on a higher platform, served as a chicken-coop. Beyond a lone papaya, its green fruits hanging down in seven circles of increasing size, as though filling with milk, a path, winding towards the untouched forest, led to a hut that was even smaller than the others. The walls of the hut were tight-slatted, closed to the light, and a door of sapling-poles, bound together with liana-twine, stood fast across the entrance. Outside the door, on the trodden ground, two white enamel bowls were waiting.

The village was quiet, peaceful in the evening light, a light that was somehow translucent despite the grey of the sky, the effect, perhaps, of reflection from the lake; the huts were irregular, the paths all curved, there were no hard edges or straight lines or squares or rectangles anywhere; tall red flowers, like wild poppies, hung above the jungle grasses. No one mobbed us, no one demanded anything. Two naked little boys, squatting over a hole scooped in the dry mud, were taking turns to throw a handful of palm kernels into the air: he who caught all the nuts above the scoop, who kept it empty, won. Nuts outside the scoop didn't count. The boys' tiny hands moved so fast that the catching was almost invisible, and the game was far too serious a matter for them to look up and see us.

We offloaded the packs to the left of the communal bench and began to put up the tents. A young man, barefoot, bare-chested, wearing a pair of dirty white trousers tied with twine and carrying a three-foot catfish by the gills, wandered up the path from the river.

'Jean!' said Marcellin. 'Jean Molengui! You'll come with us tomorrow? To the forest?'

Jean Molengui nodded, as if he saw Marcellin every day of the week.

'And the fish? How much? 1000 CFA?'

Jean Molengui smiled, I paid up, and Marcellin took the fish. Léonard and Jean Molengui walked silently off together. 'Here!' Marcellin shouted at Nzé. 'Supper and breakfast! Fish and rice!'

'Quiet, Uncle,' said Nzé to Marcellin, taking the thick, brown-grey, slimy fish with its long whiskers and small flat tail like a lance-head. 'Not too much noise.'

'Why not?' I said. 'What's up?'

'Quiet,' said Nzé, slopping the fish on to the mud. 'Or you'll wake them.'

'Wake who?'

Manou, busy preparing a fire, stood up and whispered into my ear, 'The spirits.'

'Eh?'

'Over there,' said Manou softly: his right arm flat against his side, he pointed with his index finger towards the little hut set apart. 'They sleep *there* . . . They're in their house. They're asleep.'

'How do you know?' I whispered. 'Who told you?'

'The girls in Djéké told us. Everyone knows. The girls, they warned us.'

'It's true,' said Marcellin (and even he lowered his voice). 'All the people here really believe it. Everyone in Djéké. Mouadanka, Thérèse Mouadanka the Elder, the grandmother – she's a sorceress. She's powerful. She has seven daughters. These seven daughters share her powers. And these seven daughters' – he made a sweeping gesture – 'they live in these seven huts!' ('Quiet!' hissed Nzé, stepping back, looking, boss-eyed, over his shoulder.)

'The Elder,' said Manou, his big brown eyes wide open. 'If you go into the forest, Redmond, you must ask her permission first, or you'll be lost, completely lost, lost for ever.'

'And the lake,' said Nzé, 'that's worse. If even I, Nzé Oumar, went out to fish on Lake Mboukou, all by myself, without permission, without her blessing – splash! I'd disappear. You'd never find me. You could fish for me with nets night and day – and you'd never find me. Not a trace. Not even' – he thought about it – 'not even a shoe!' And Nzé looked mournfully at his new blue trainers. 'This village, it's *run by women.*'

I said, 'Then it's a job for you.'

'No, Uncle, no jokes. Not here. Here they cut men to bits. They make no noise. If you're out in the forest and you see beautiful women, Uncle, you must be careful. You must look at their feet. Check their feet, that's what Glossina said – when they walk towards you, if their feet never touch the ground, run! Run as fast as you can! There are lots and lots of them here, the spirits of women, far more than in Djéké, because this place, this is where they have their origin.'

'Glossina!' said Marcellin. 'That's a tsetse fly!'

'She's big, Uncle,' said Nzé, forgetting the spirits, clapping his upper arm to his side. 'She's fat! She likes me!'

'True or not,' said Marcellin to me, as we continued to stand in a tight little circle, as if we were frightened, or guilty, or planning a murder, 'don't you go near that spirit-house – don't look at it, don't talk about it – and don't even *think* of taking its photograph! Tonight we'll go to Mouadanka's hut. We'll pay our respects. We'll give her one bottle of wine, a carton of cigarettes – and I've brought seven tins of sardines ... But we can't stand here all evening. Come on! Gather wood! A fire! And then we'll swim in the lake.'

'Not me,' said Nzé, reapplying his mind to his shoes. 'And not Manou. We'll wait. We'll swim in the river at Djéké.'

Fifty yards or so into the forest behind the tents, searching vaguely beneath the trees for bits of fallen branches, I saw something dull-white and brown half buried in the mud and the leaf-scatter. I knelt down, gave it a tug – and an elephant's tooth came away in my hand. Six-and-a-half inches long, three deep at its deepest, the surface of the tooth was criss-crossed with twelve squiggly white enamel strips; on the underside the openings of the four visible root-canals were large enough for me to push in the tip of my little finger. Searching in earnest, I found another tooth (smaller, with five enamel strips) and, nearer the tents, the empty, whorled shell of a snail five inches long.

'The men here are good hunters,' said Marcellin, sitting on the bench, inspecting the teeth. 'They know the forest – they live from the forest. They're not farmers, they're hunters. People in Djéké and Boha call them pygmies. But they're Bantu. Anyone can see that – you only have to look at their noses! They're as Bantu as I am. Pygmies – that's just an insult. People call them pygmies because they think they're primitive – because they live in the forest. Maybe they moved here when the French arrived, to escape – they hid in the forest, and then never came out, or maybe, perhaps, I don't know, perhaps they're descended from slaves who ran away, slaves of other Bantu groups, people captured in battle. We'll have to ask, Redmond – ask your old men!'

'The teeth,' I said. 'What happened?'

'They killed and ate a couple of elephants and threw the bits away . . .' Marcellin counted the enamel strips. 'This one – twelve lines, so – an elephant grows three sets of milk teeth; then the first adult teeth, with four white lines, appear when it's between twenty and twenty-five years old; the second set, with eight lines, around twenty-five to thirty; the third set, with twelve – this one – around thirty to forty; and then one more, with sixteen: and that set, that has to last, because when it's worn away, around sixty or seventy, they can't eat, they die. So at least both these elephants had a chance to breed. Here in Mboukou, these people, they're not real poachers, they prob-ably know every one of the elephants in their part of the forest, they don't overhunt, they're not like the men from the Sudan, they don't kill everything they can and then go home . . .'

'And Mouadanka keeps everyone out.'

'Fear! Terror! That's the best protection, the best there is! But I don't think it's deliberate. I don't think Mouadanka knows that's how it works. I think she really believes in her powers, every minute of the day. She has to, Redmond, because if she was just *pretending* to control the forest and the lake from the fetish house – the magic, it wouldn't work.'

Big blue dragonflies quartered the ground in front of us, flying, in fits and starts, low over the mud and the broad-leaved grasses. A little hornbill, smaller than a woodpigeon, with a high-arched bright-red bill, a brown back and tail and a stomach of pure white, the Red-billed dwarf hornbill, a hornbill with a liking for swamp-forest, perched for a moment in the papaya tree.

'*Calao pygmée,*' said Marcellin, putting the teeth down on the bench between us, beside the snail. 'It's time for a swim.'

'This village,' I said. 'I like it. It's different here. It's peaceful.'

'The men are out hunting. But you're right – it's quiet. There's never any trouble. Mboukou is run by women. It really is. You take anything that worries you to the Elder, and she keeps it for you, she decides. She collects up all the problems and she looks after them herself. You can take your life and give it to her if you want to: you can say, "Here, Thérèse Mouadanka, please keep my life." And then you can forget all about it. So it's peaceful for everyone but her. You'll see tonight – she's a wreck. And there again, all her daughters are married – they all found a man. But those men are frightened. They're too frightened to have sex with anyone but their wives.

Because those wives, all the Elder's daughters – they're sorcerers too. Those men don't even have girls in Djéké! Because the Elder – she can see all the way to Djéké!'

Marcellin looked absently at Manou who was rigging the cooking-pot on a pole over the fire, and then at Nzé, who with his machete had finished a perfunctory gutting of the catfish and was now (the backbone still in place) hacking the body into cylindrical blocks.

'Jean Molengui,' said Marcellin, staring at the disintegrating fish, 'he's quiet, and he's probably happy. He makes music. He can make music with anything. All the men here make music. The women like it.'

'Art, music, science, men only do it to please the women. That's the point. The peacock's tail. Every achievement . . .'

'Imagine it!' shouted Marcellin, springing off the bench. 'No sex! No trouble! I'd rather be dead!'

We went, as I thought, for a swim, stripping, jumping into the deep black water from the end of a fallen tree, striking out in the cool . . . 'Come back!' I heard through the gurgle in my ears. 'Come back!' It was Marcellin's highest shout, frantic. 'Redmond! Crocodiles!' He was standing on the tree, waving both arms. 'The biggest crocodile I've ever seen! He lives around the corner! Crocodile! Crocodile!'

I was conscious of my white, unprotected genitals, dangling like a fish-lure. The bark of the tree was one long, black opaque twenty yards away.

'Don't you learn?' said Marcellin, too angry to swear, as I hauled myself to safety, shaking. 'Don't you learn? You never swim. You wash. Swim means wash. And if the water's black and deep – you wash one pace from the bank. No more.' He wet his hair, rubbed our bar of soap over it, and submerged at my feet. 'Idiot!' he yelled, breaking surface. He cares, I thought, he really does, we must be friends . . . 'Idiot!' he said, pulling himself out, grabbing his mouldy towel. 'Idiot!'

After the catfish-soup, Marcellin and I walked across to the little hut, the Elder's hut, which stood opposite the tents, its back wall towards us.

Round the other side Thérèse Mouadanka was waiting for us, squatting in her doorway, the light of the cooking-fire behind her. In front of her, on three raffia mats arranged in a semi-circle, three women and ten or so babies, toddlers and young children sat, sucked, cuddled, lay, and (in the case of one small boy) rolled about on their backs, giggled, and kicked their legs in the air. Jean Molengui, Léonard and three other men sat on their own, further back, only just visible in the darkness.

Marcellin knelt down; he laid the bottle of Cavesco red wine and the carton of Marlboro cigarettes at the Elder's feet; emptying his shirt- and trouser-pockets he stacked up the seven tins of sardines; he withdrew backwards, half-crouched, and sat on the mud between the nearest mats. I took the empty place beside him.

Thérèse Mouadanka, wearing nothing but a raffia skirt, was old, bald, skeletal, and impressive. Her breasts long, flat and wrinkled, her sharp elbows on her sharp knees, her long, expressive fingers folded under her strong chin, she scrutinized us. The little boy stopped kicking his legs in the air, rolled on to his stomach, and covered his head with both arms. Everyone was silent.

She nodded towards Marcellin.

Marcellin explained that we wished to pay our respects, that the doyenne, the Elder, Thérèse Mouadanka, was officially requested by the Party to kill all foreigners, all poachers found trespassing in her forest. That he, Marcellin Agnagna, Head of the Department for the Preservation of the Fauna of the People's Republic, begged permission to go with his assistants, Nzé Oumar, Manou Burond, the Commandant of the Djéké Militia, Léonard Bongou-Lami – and the white man here – to the far end of her lake and to visit her forest. And that the white man wished to know the history of her people.

Thérèse Mouadanka looked at me, or rather she turned her head a fraction towards me – the light of the fire cast her face into shadow, and it was impossible to make out her eyes; her deep voice seemed disembodied. 'The founder of the village of Mboukou was called Tokoméné,' she said with a dismissive wave of her fingers. 'Having created the village of Mboukou, he moved in the forest to a village that had been abandoned, Moukendenda. The people of Mboukou come from the village of Moukendenda. The people of Mboukou belong to the group Bokolou. All the languages which are spoken by this group resemble each other and the different peoples can understand one another.

'Manbenguela, who is the Chief of the village of Mokala, which is now the Mokala quarter in the village of Djéké – he also directs the affairs of the other tribes in Djéké. He is not a pygmy but a Bokolou.

'The people of Mboukou did not come out of the forest – because they were afraid of the whites, the *colons*. They fled deep into the forest and did not show themselves until very late. During past times there existed a kind of slavery, the result of the power of certain groups, a power which enabled them to make servants of tribes which were weaker than themselves. During the time of battles, the victorious tribes took the losers hostage and turned them into slaves.

'Since the creation of this village Lake Mboukou has always been as it is now. Its shape has not changed.

'If the other Bantu who live in Djéké think of us as pygmies, that is because of our attachment to the forest. We love the forest because our ancestors lived in the forest. They never lived in camps, like pygmies, with the spirits of the forest, but in proper villages. They lived like civilized people, in villages that were well organized. Therefore we are not pygmies.'

Thérèse Mouadanka fell silent, fingers folded, still.

'Is that all?' I whispered to Marcellin.

'Quiet,' hissed Marcellin, and: 'Thérèse Mouadanka, Elder of Mboukou,' he said, 'do we have your blessing – to visit your lake and your forest?'

'Marcellin Agnagna, you have my permission. But not my blessing. You, Jean Molengui and the white man may visit the lake and the forest. No harm will come to you by day. But to stay in the forest at night – that, Marcellin Agnagna, is dangerous. You and the white man – I will not protect you. You will be troubled by a strong spirit. I will not tell you the name of this spirit. So you cannot command it. This spirit will take the shape of a leopard. For protection, you must trust to the power of your own ancestors. You, Marcellin Agnagna, and you, the white man – you will be alone!'

'And the others?' said Marcellin, his voice not quite so firm.

'The others will stay here, with me, in Mboukou. If the *petits* go to the forest they will cease to exist, for ever.'

Thérèse Mouadanka stood up. She waved her hands at her audience, as if dispersing a flock of chickens, and withdrew into her hut, leaving the presents on the mud.

Early the next morning Jean Molengui, standing in the stern of the village dugout, barefoot, bare-chested, wearing his muddy white trousers, took Marcellin and me and a bergen apiece across the thick black water of the little lake, a trail of slow white bubbles rising behind the blade of his paddle.

'Marcellin,' I said, as we squatted facing each other, holding on to the gunwales in the centre of the fishing-canoe, 'did you hear that shouting last night? The women yelled like banshees from one hut to another – until two in the morning! What happened to your quiet? What about the spirits?'

'The women were not shouting. They were not yelling. They were talking. And don't be stupid – how can you wake the spirits at night? They're awake already. They're out with your soul in the forest, they're in your dreams, they're changing shape, they're hunting, they're far away ... And besides – when you'd gone to bed, Jean came and sat by the fire. "Those women," I said, "what are they talking about? What's so funny?" Jean listened, and he translated the Bomitaba. And guess what? What was so funny?'

'No idea.'

'You.'

'Me?'

'You, Redmond. They said your beard's too long. And you smell bad.'

'Smell? Like a white man?'

'No,' said Marcellin, starting to shake. 'They just said you smell. They said you must be lazy. You should wash your clothes more often.'

'Oh,' I said, abashed, sniffing an armpit. 'I see.'

'Women, Redmond – they like men washed. You know, not stuck with dirt.'

'Yes. I'm sure. I mean I'm sorry. Bad manners.'

'Bad manners!' Marcellin doubled up. 'Bad manners! But it's true!'

'What's true?' I said, testy.

'You do smell!' spluttered Marcellin, letting go of the gunwales. 'You do smell like a white man! You always have! You stink like a bushpig!'

Jean let out a low burble, missed his footing at the stern, howled with laughter, and shot the dugout into the low mud of the bank between two big, twisted, prop-rooted trees.

'Let's go!' shouted Marcellin. 'Let's go hunting bushpig! They won't know. They won't smell us coming!'

Jean, carrying the shotgun in his right hand like a short spear, led us fast for an hour through the wet forest (too fast to watch anything but my feet, the prop-roots, the sudden patches of deep mud) across one small edaphic savanna (buffalo tracks), back into the forest, on to higher ground, to his hunting camp.

'We're here,' he said, as if we'd arrived in paradise, a shy smile beneath his wispy moustache. 'This is my camp. I made it myself.'

Collapsing onto my bergen, I took a swig from my water-bottle, removed my hat, squeezed out my sweat-band and wiped my glasses on my shirt-tail; I replaced the bottle, the hat, the band and the glasses, and, gradually, the interest of life once more became apparent.

To my right, beneath the high buttressed trees of the knoll, was an open sloping roof of Giant phrynium-leaf thatch supported on sapling-poles and, beneath it, a low sleeping-platform of poles bound with liana-twine. In front of me stood a smoking-rack, a pile of rotting wood ready beside it.

'It's my camp,' repeated Jean, still standing up, pleased as a small boy, not a trace of sweat on his forehead. 'I made it myself.'

'Well done,' said Marcellin, who, like me, was half-slumped on his pack, breathing heavily. 'It's remarkable.' He gave me a sweaty wink. 'It's the best camp I've seen – and Jean, you can believe me, I've seen plenty.'

We lit a fire to keep off the leopards, spread our tarpaulins on the pole-bed, pushed the packs underneath it and set off, slowly, for the hunt. We paused to inspect deep elephant tracks all over the mud, just outside the camp ('They're heavy,' said Marcellin. 'Full-grown animals. A big herd. But no young.') We stopped for Jean and Marcellin to discuss in whispers the fresh knuckle-prints, heel-marks and three-lobed fibrous droppings of a family of gorillas, a family which had spent the night in and beside two small trees (one broad round nest of flattened leaves on the ground, three smaller nests of intertwined branches, twigs and leaves thirty feet above us). Greater white-nosed monkeys began their honk-grunting call, somewhere to our left. Jean dropped his machete, propped the gun against a sapling, broke off a leaf, gripped it between his thumbs, cupped his hands around it, raised his thumbs to his lips and whistled like a Monkey eagle. Silence. He put two fingers in his nostrils and grunted like a Greater white-nosed monkey. Silence. He picked up his machete, swiped off a small branch and beat the ground with it. High up, the invisible monkeys chattered and honked and grunted from three different trees, but came no closer. Jean shrugged.

Behind us the sapling-tops shook. Jean snatched up the shotgun and swung round. Something big was moving towards us, on the ground.

'The leopard!' shouted Jean, dropping to one knee, the gun to his shoulder. 'Gorilla! Gorilla!' yelled Marcellin. 'Look! Look!'

I looked hard enough, but I saw nothing among the leaves, spotted with bright sunlight, full of black shadows and odd shapes of prop-roots and bushes and puddles of water. 'He stood up!' yelled Marcellin. 'He looked me in the face!' Marcellin was shaking, as if someone had him by the shoulders.

'They're curious,' said Jean, standing up, sheepish. 'They come to see what you're doing.' He picked up his machete. 'I thought it was the leopard . . . the one the grandmother . . .'

Half-an-hour later Jean stopped; he squatted down beside the prop-roots and hanging fibres of a small tree; he cut a sapling, trimmed it, and worked the end of the pole into a dark hollow – the top of an entrance just visible above the mush of water and brown and yellow leaves at the base of the tree. The tree itself, like all the others round us, was patched up its trunk with a white lichen; delicate ferns, and plants with dark-green, glaucous leaves held on a single stem and shaped like flattened arrow-heads, hung down from crevices in the brown-grey bark. Jean gently pushed the pole further in; a deep growl rose out of the water.

'He's at home!' whispered Marcellin, intent. 'They're in there!'

'Who's in there?' I said, staring. (That growl, I thought, it's too big for that hole.)

'A Forest crocodile, of course,' said Marcellin, his head cocked to one side, listening. 'What else? The Congo dwarf crocodile, *Osteolacmus tetraspis*. Maybe two. Sometimes you find the male and the female!'

With their machetes Jean and Marcellin severed a semi-circle of prop-roots; the tree fell; Marcellin cut himself a sapling and helped Jean enlarge the entrance; Jean worked in his pole; the growling intensified, the pole jerked sideways: 'Got him!' said Jean. 'He's bitten it!'

Jean and Marcellin, leaning backwards in the mud, pulled – and out came three-and-a-half feet of crocodile, jaws clamped on the end of the pole. He was dark brown, with a red tinge to his head, and widely spaced, surprisingly white teeth.

'The little one!' said Marcellin. 'There are two sub-species. Two Forest crocodiles. The other one's much bigger – and black.'

'What do they eat?'

'Frogs, millipedes, insects, birds – anything they can catch. They come out at night. They run about the place.'

'They taste good,' said Jean, trussing its front legs up over its back with a length of liana. 'We'll eat him tonight.' He lashed the jaws shut over a crosswise stick.

'No!' said Marcellin. 'I'll carry him. I want him. I want him alive – for my collection.'

Jean stood up, and, his mouth open an eighth of an inch, he looked at Marcellin, hard.

With a crackle and roar like escaping steam, a swarm of bees passed overhead.

'In Europe and North America,' said Marcellin, glancing up, 'the white men – they make little huts for bees. They keep bees in little huts.'

'Marcellin!' said Jean, relieved. 'The lies you tell! A hut for bees!' He laughed, and laid the heavy, bound crocodile in Marcellin's arms. 'A hut for bees!' Picking up his machete and the shotgun, he walked on ahead of us, humming a tune to himself.

'Hoo hoo-oo hoo-oo,' came the loud mellow sound we heard every day in the deep forest, some fifteen to twenty notes, starting high, falling in pitch and volume, trailing away . . . And a higher, monotonous note, toork-toork-toork, sustained, evenly spaced, metallic, haunting, from the same place, whose exact direction was yet impossible to determine. It's definitely a bird, I said to myself with no evidence whatever, no sighting of anything (and if crocodiles can growl . . .) and on this late afternoon, I decided, for the sake of the argument with myself, to keep it simple, *both* calls are the Red-billed dwarf hornbill. 'Yow wow wow' came a different cry, fainter, a sound of people cheering, or of women and children shouting to each other, in a village, a long way off . . .

'Chimpanzees!' said Marcellin, stopping, listening, his mouth wide open. 'Redmond – chimps!'

'They're far away,' said Jean, stepping into the thin undergrowth. 'Too far away to hunt. It's late.' And 'Look!' he said, stooping down. 'I thought so! I heard him!'

A big brown tortoise, caught biting chunks from the top of a purple-white fungus, withdrew its leathery head and flattened itself on the ground. Jean cut a length of liana, bound the tortoise tight, and handed it to me to carry. About eighteen inches long and twelve across, the top of the shell was torn in the middle and squashed down level with the surrounding ridge. The right front foot was missing. 'Yes,' said Marcellin. 'I've seen that before. Elephants! An elephant trod on him, down came the shell – and off came his foot.'

Back on the dry, almost hard ground of the knoll, Marcellin laid the crocodile alongside the sleeping-platform. Jean killed the tortoise with one blow of his machete; he gutted it and lobbed it upside-down into the fire, to roast in its shell.

'Jean,' said Marcellin, pulling up a log beside me. 'This forest, it's full of animals. Packed with big animals – elephant, gorillas, chimpanzees; and I heard three different species of monkey: the Red colobus, the Crested manga-bey and the White-nosed monkey. So how do you explain that? Half a day from a village! Don't you hunt here? That gorilla – he came to *look* at me!'

Jean took a stick and drew the tortoise nearer to the edge of the fire. 'It's our forest,' he said, without looking up. 'We look after it. The forest belongs to us.'

'But don't you come here?'

'The women and children do. Twice in the year. The men come too. We laugh. We have a party. We go fishing, everyone together. All the women – the families, everyone together.'

'Fishing?'

'We scoop water from the ponds. But we only kill the big fish. We eat lots of fish and smoke the rest and carry them in baskets back to the village. It's good that way.'

'But the hunt?'

'Marcellin,' said Jean, pulling the quarter-cooked, charred tortoise out of the flames. 'We live well here. Our mothers lived well. Our grandmothers lived well. They taught us what to do. We know what to do. We obey the spirits. We respect this place. It belongs to us. It belongs to our ancestors. And to no one else. *No one at all.*'

I fetched the mess-tins from my pack.

'Yes, but the hunt. How does that change the hunt?'

'It's obvious,' said Jean, taking his machete and dismembering the carcass. 'We're not like the men in Djéké. We don't just go out and shoot arrows at the first thing we see. We wait. We're civilized. We kill the old animals. We kill the sick and the injured animals – like this tortoise.' (He chewed a piece.) 'Marcellin, you saw it yourself – this tortoise was a present from the spirits, a present from the ancestors! We weren't even looking for him. We weren't even hunting him!'

'And chimpanzees,' said Marcellin, holding a burnt leg and claw between his fingers. 'Gorillas. Do you kill them? With special spears?'

'Chimps? Gorillas? Special spears? Of course not! Why? They're difficult. They're dangerous. They attack you! We've got antelopes and monkeys and fish and bushpig – bushpig, Marcellin, that's the best!'

'Chimp. Have you eaten chimp?'

'Yes. It's good. You want one? You want to hunt a chimp?'

'No, Jean Molengui. I don't. It's against the law. And besides, they're like us. You eat a chimp – you're a cannibal.'

'They're not a bit like us! They're not even like pygmies. They live in trees!'

'They're like us. All of us – we're apes.'

Jean laughed. 'Marcellin! Marcellin! The lies you tell!' He shook his head. A thought struck him; he stared at me; the laugh withered, and then the smile. 'Cannibals,' he said, looking at his mess-tin. 'We all know – every white man is a cannibal. Every single white man.'

'Eh?' I said, feeling guilty at once.

'How do you mean?' said Marcellin.

'You find them in tins. You often find fingers in tins. You find sausages and fingers.'

'That's a mistake,' said Marcellin. 'A mistake in the factory.'

Jean put down his mess-tin and stood up. 'Marcellin, that's no mistake.' He picked up his machete, walked to the edge of the clearing, and appeared to test the strength of the saplings, pulling one towards him, releasing it and trying another. Watching him from my log beside the fire, I thought of Roger Casement's report on the routine practices a hundred years ago in Leopold of the Belgians' personal kingdom to the south of the river – of the punishment if you failed to bring your quota of rubber to the trading station, of the pile of severed hands . . .

'Cheer up!' whispered Marcellin. 'So you're a cannibal. So what? I think Jean's going to make you a bow and arrow. Would you like that? Are you good with a bow? Shot a few students in Oxford? The odd girl? Tasty? Perhaps a young child? Just to eat?'

300

'I did have a bow and arrow once, and a quiver. I shot a chicken. A running chicken.'

'A chicken!' yelled Marcellin. 'You're crazy!'

'Wait!' said Jean, returning with a short coil of liana and a thin, trimmed sapling, six or seven feet long. 'Wait!' He moved his log back from the fire. 'I'll talk to you properly. In your own language. White man's language. Everybody's language.' Sitting down, he tied one end of the liana tightly to one end of the sapling. 'Gorillas and chimps – they like it too. They understand. They come and listen. They come here, Marcellin, and they listen to my music.'

Jean placed the knotted end of the sapling on the ground. His biceps bunched up like papayas, he bent the wood into a bow. Maintaining the pressure with his right hand, with his left he bound the free end of the liana three-quarters of the way along the arc. He picked up his stick; he reached in his pocket and pulled out a wood-chip; he sat back on his log, half-stretched out his legs and crossed his ankles (his bare toes tense and straight). He took the knotted end of the bow in his left hand (in which he also held the wood-chip); he rested the centre of the arc on his left knee, so that the extra length of sapling projected above his right shoulder; he leant the lashed end of the string against his right ear.

Tapping the string with his stick, plucking it with his teeth, stopping it with the wood-chip in his left palm, strumming it with his right thumb and index-finger, Jean Molengui played the saddest songs I had ever heard: quiet, delicate, lilting melodies full of sadness.

Night came and we still listened. A Wood owl called, and there was an odd rasping purr close at hand, like a nightjar. 'That's enough,' said Marcellin abruptly, his voice clogged. 'Jean, that's enough. Please – it's the dead. It's all about the dead. You're playing with death!' Marcellin stumbled across to the sleeping-platform; he pulled his tarpaulin over his face and turned away from us.

I was woken at dawn by a loud and discordant chorus of alarm, the *ka-ka-ka* of a flock of Plumed guineafowl disturbed at their scratching through the leaf-litter, somewhere off to the left. You're ancient birds, I thought, and you sound like it, you cackling old aunts in a tizzy, you fossils, you date from forty-five million years ago. I sat up, shaking the platform. Jean stirred to the left of me, Marcellin to the right. I realized that I was cold and stiff, that the poles had ridged my back into temporary welts, and that my hands and face were swollen with mosquito bites. Still, I thought, you auntie-fowl out there, compared with *Archaeopteryx*, that 150-million-year-old flattened feathery fossil who may or may not be the ancestor of modern birds, you're spring chickens. Marcellin raised his head. His eyes were gummed together. My eyes, too, I discovered with a finger – they were crusted with stick: it's dust from the dry leaves of the roof, I muttered to myself, or termite droppings, or fungus spores or . . . I concentrated on my legs, rubbing hard, and began to feel a reassuring tingle in my feet. But if birds think they're old, how about the closest surviving reptilian relatives of the dinosaurs, of Mokélé-mbembé – the freshwater crocodiles, our crocodile? He's hardly changed in 230 million years, he's only five million years younger than the very earliest and smallest dinosaurs, and he's got a brain and heart more advanced than any other reptile. His heart has ventricles that are completely divided, he doesn't mix his arterial and venous blood; and his brain has a true cerebral cortex, so he can learn things, he's not just a prey to his instincts, he could go to school. But if he's so smart, I thought, relieved to find that I could now move my toes, how come he lives in such a shallow hole? And he should learn not to growl when he's at home, and someone should teach him not to bite bits of wood quite so hard when they come through the letter-box. Comforted that the deep dull pain of the ulcer on the top of my right foot and of the two open sores below my left ankle had begun to reassert itself, that despite everything my central nervous system had decided to function for another day, and that I was fully awake, I eased my body off the two-foot-high platform and stood up. Jean and Marcellin, no longer trying to stir, were obviously paralysed.

But at least no one had stuck a stick in my mouth and tied my arms and legs up over my back and left me on the ground. There must be a better way to keep a crocodile . . . Maybe I could simply tether him to a stake. I looked on the dried mud beside Marcellin. Perhaps I'd got the sides the wrong way round. So I looked on the ground at Jean's end of the platform. He wasn't there either. So he *was* smart. He'd got away!

'Marcellin! The crocodile! He's got away!'

Marcellin sat up. 'Crocodile?'

Jean sat up. 'Got away?'

'The crocodile! He's gone! Escaped!'

'Crocodile,' said Marcellin. He peered over the edge of the platform. 'He's gone,' he said, slow and bleary. 'He's got away.'

With one convulsive movement, as if hit by a scorpion, Jean was on his feet, the tarpaulin sailing sideways. He dropped down beside me, on all-fours. He felt the ground where the crocodile had been, a yard away from Marcellin. 'No tracks,' he said in an odd, wavering little voice, hardly a breath.

'Of course not,' said Marcellin, still peering. 'The mud – it's dry.'

Jean sat back on his haunches and shut his eyes. He bent slowly forward until his forehead touched the ground.

'Eh?' said Marcellin. 'Jean?'

Jean stood up. Staring at the spot, he clasped his arms across his chest, gripped his shoulders and rocked from side to side.

'It's okay,' said Marcellin, his eyes wide. 'He's gone. He got away.'

Jean stepped to the other end of the platform. He picked up his machete and the gun. 'Got away?' he said quietly. 'Took the wood with him? Left no mark?'

I said, 'So what happened? Someone came? In the night?'

'Yes,' said Jean, agitated, putting the gun and machete down again and folding his tarpaulin. 'That was no ordinary leopard. She left no tracks. We must go. We must leave this place. We must go.'

'Go?' said Marcellin, standing up, stretching. 'Leave? We've only just come! Another day? Two? Three?'

'No,' said Jean, pushing the tarpaulin into my bergen. 'We must go. Now. The grandmother – she told me not to come. We must leave this place. I should never have brought you here. And a white man, Marcellin, that's bad, very bad. And she also sent me a dream, a bad dream, a terrible dream.'

Jean twitched my tarpaulin to the ground. 'A dream?' I said, picking it up.

'I dreamed I had a baby son.' He reached across and pulled Marcellin's tarpaulin off the platform. 'The baby son I've always wanted. That's what I want! Well – in my dream he smiled at me and died. It's bad, Marcellin, it's bad.'

'What did you do?' said Marcellin, hastily folding his tarpaulin.

'I stayed calm.' He stuffed the greasy mess-tins into Marcellin's pack. 'I stayed calm. If you shout and scream and cry you wear yourself out. You die too.'

'Redmond,' said Marcellin, something deep and personal presenting itself to him as he helped me into my pack, fumbling with the webbing. 'If that was a leopard he was a metre away. A bite to the head! I could have died!'

Nzé and Manou, looking subdued, were sitting together, alone, on the bench beside the tents. 'Marcellin!' shouted Nzé, catching sight of us, jumping off the bench, waving both hands in the air with an obvious onrush of adrenalin, joy and relief. 'Marcellin! Uncle! Doctor! Marcellin, we must go!'

I said, 'I must have a wash. I must wash my clothes.'

'In Djéké,' said Marcellin, his face set. 'We must take down the tents, find Léonard, and go.'

Jean gave Marcellin the gun and touched him quickly on the shoulder. I said goodbye and thanked him; he gave me a sad little smile; he wandered off towards the straggle of huts.

As we packed up the tents a young girl, wearing a faded pink dress several sizes too big for her, carrying a gourd, walked across the small open space from the grandmother's hut. She gave the gourd to Marcellin, and, looking not into our faces but at the fruit on the papaya tree above us, concentrated hard. Her skin was extraordinarily smooth, undamaged. 'Thérèse Mouadanka,' she half-chanted, 'she has seen your mothers and grandmothers, and their mothers and grandmothers. She says they are good, kind, strong women, well-meaning women. Or the leopard – she would have eaten you.'

She walked back with care across the dried mud, as if following her own tracks.

'This gourd,' said Marcellin. 'It's full of honey.'

31

Early in the morning of the following day, back in the Djéké guest-hut, Manou was listlessly packing the cooking-pot and mess-tins into an old manioc sack; and I had almost finished rearranging the loads in the bergens when 'Koko!' came the usual greeting from outside, accompanied by the usual shattering bang on whatever was near enough and strong enough to take a Herculean blow – in this case the corrugated-iron door; and then the usual shouted demands filled the hut. Almost every Bantu man I met, I thought, in a puff of exasperation, had a voice like Muddy Waters, a headache, a boil that needed dressing, and at least one wife with malaria. Our paddlers arrived – Léonard and three of his young relatives – and I handed out Paracetamol, plasters, and fifteen glossy white quinine pills to everyone. Léonard swore, on the honour of the People's Militia, to go and give the canister of Trimethoprim to the wife of the dying man; and when he returned we carried the baggage down to the combined landing-stage and washing-area in the creek that let on to the main stream of the Likouala aux Herbes river.

Léonard stowed our packs in the middle of his dugout, Manou placed the wickerwork cage containing the cockerel in the bow, and we settled down on the short scuffed grass of the bank to wait for Nzé and Marcellin. A little way downstream, a young mother was sitting on the upturned hull of a half-submerged dugout, its grey wood worn smooth with the scrubbing and pounding of clothes. Her indigo cotton dress, wrapped round tight just above her nipples, dipped low across her muscled back; her hair twirled out in two spikes to either side of her head. Washed pots and pans lay stacked to her right, clothes to her left, and between her knees she gripped her toddler son. She cuddled him with one voluptuous arm and, with the other, she scooped up a saucepanful of water and dumped it on his head. He howled as if his world had disappeared for ever; he screamed as the soap ran into his eyes; he gurgled for air in the final rinse; and then, the moment it was over and she kissed him, he opened his eyes, beamed at us and clapped his hands. We all clapped back – and, overcome with such success, he dived for cover, sinking his head between her breasts. The mother smiled, said something to Léonard, and launched her son for a swim in the shallows.

Much laughter and bantering in Bomitaba took place. 'She thinks you don't know how to dance,' said Léonard. 'She says you just shake yourself all over, like a dog fresh out of water. You must learn to use your legs, Redmond, like a man of good manners. You must not tread on people with those big boots of yours.'

'It's true,' said Manou drowsily, lying on his back and sucking on a grass stem. 'And you're not supposed to wave your arms around.'

There was a shout from the top of the path. It was Nzé. 'Five times!' he yelled. 'Five times for 500 CFA! 100 CFA a time! And just look what she gave me!'

He raised his arms in triumph, and in each hand he held a pineapple.

Marcellin arrived and the laughter ceased. He was not his usual self.

He came down the path barking questions like a Nazi. Why had we left the hut so early? Where was his breakfast? And why, he wanted to know, stepping into the dugout, was his pack at the bottom of the pile? Why were there no duckboards? What if his shirts got wet? Who had done this to him?

'It's Manou. Manou did all of it,' said Nzé, winking his good eye at me.

Marcellin, I thought, does not want to leave his young girl, or perhaps I've done something to offend him – and then it gradually dawned on me, as I watched him yank his pack to the top of the pile, scrabble at a pocket, pull out his Walkman, ferociously snap in a Bob Marley tape, cover his ears with the headphones, sink back against the baggage and close his eyes: Marcellin was afraid. He really did think there would be trouble at Boha.

Manou and Nzé got in behind the packs, the three paddlers stood in a line in the stern, and Léonard took up his position just in front of me and just behind the cockerel. The young mother picked her little son out of the water to wave goodbye to us and we made our way out to the main river.

The flood-plain of the Likouala was a narrow savanna, the high forest beginning again a mile or so to either side of us. For half-an-hour we were all as silent as Marcellin, but then the three boys began the first of their paddling songs, the rhythm dropping in time to their half-crouch at the knees as the long blades cut down and thrust back in the water, rising as they straightened sharply for the next stroke. 'We burn the grass during the dry season,' said Léonard, 'not to hunt the animals, and not to make plantations for manioc, but just to keep open the paths to the forest.' He let his paddle rest against the gunwale for a moment and gestured out across the high grass, the lone trees beside the river, the patches of water-lilies. 'I like it here,' he said. 'When I was in Brazzaville, I missed all this.'

'Why were you in Brazzaville?'

'I wanted to be rich. I found work on a building site. But poor men like me can't get rich in the city – everything costs money. You even have to pay to live in a house! So then I realized that it was in my own village that I was rich. Here you make your home from the earth, you can grow manioc wherever you choose, you can make a boat and nets and fish in the river – me, I'm happy here. I came back at once.'

'And now you're the Commandant of the People's Militia.'

'Oh, *that*,' he said, laughing. 'In Djéké that's just a joke. That's just an excuse to get a pair of trousers from the Government. Gilbert Badiledi is the Commandant d'Honneur but I'm the Commandant Actif, so I can tell the Chef d'Etat Major, the Chargé and the Adjudant de Compagnie what to do, and I can argue with the Adjoint Politique, who is supposed to know what the Party wants, and I can see the Hereditary Chief and the President of the People's Village Committee whenever I feel like it, and then we have lots of militiamen who are almost as useless as Nzé – and I'm allowed to *shout* at them.'

'You should come to Dongou and say that,' said Nzé, from behind the baggage. 'You just bring that bunch of women and say that in Dongou. We'd soon sort you out. We've got proper uniforms and proper houses and a bar – and all sorts of things,' he said, turning over and going back to sleep.

'In Boha,' said Léonard, 'it is not a joke. In Boha they killed the officers. There are no militiamen in Boha.'

'Léonard Bongou-Lami,' said Marcellin, who must have been listening all the time, 'in Boha you and your three nephews will stay with us for the first night.'

'No, Marcellin Agnagna, not for all the money you've got in your pack. Not for all the young girls you care to give me. I'm a sensible man. And besides, I have a baby son. Soon he will need a father.'

'I am the official representative of the Government here,' said Marcellin, sitting up, 'and I order you to stay for one night.'

'You can order all you like,' said the Commandant, paddling with renewed vigour. 'One hour will be enough for me. And even then you must watch your back. They've been taking oaths in Boha.'

We passed a long beach of white sand, almost too bright to look at in the sunlight – perhaps part of that friable white sandstone that formed beneath the great lake which filled the Congo basin some 225 million years ago, when you could see dinosaurs every day of the week. And upriver we came to a low overhang of dark-grey soil, and a stretch of scrubby trees. Small blue-green birds with tails tapering to two long streamers, Blue-cheeked bee-eaters, perched on its branches, fussing over their feathers, or they flew out fast like swallows low across the water or over the rough grass of the savanna margin above us, when their undersides glowed orange in the reflected light; gliding and twisting, they would return to their perch to rub their bills against the wood, probably forcing the wasp or the bee they held to eject its venom before they swallowed it. Lower in the same trees sat occasional pairs of a scaled-down, more neurotic species, with a green back and a yellow throat, the Little bee-eater: through the binoculars I watched one stick his leg over his wing and scratch the back of his head with his foot, and then, having obviously resolved the problem, like a flycatcher he looped out after a passing insect, flashing buff underwings, and dropped back on his perch. And on the branch of a dead tree, its trunk blackened from a savanna burning, I noticed a tiny roundel of scarlet that I at first took to be the flower of some parasitic plant, but which resolved itself through the glasses into the throat of a small bird, a Black bee-eater, as black as the charred wood on which it sat, flicking its tail as we approached and then dashing away out of sight beyond the high fringe of grasses. Nesting holes, larger ones in irregular clusters and smaller ones widely spaced, pocked the bank at intervals for several hundred yards.

Léonard nodded his head towards a tall tree with thin branches and small leaves which hung out over the water to our left.

'That's a fishing tree,' he said. 'When the fruits are ripe they turn yellow and drop into the river and the fish gather: there's one little fruit for each fish. That's the time to bring your nets.'

We passed a small village hidden behind its oil-palms on a piece of high ground, which Léonard said was called Ypongui; and whenever there was the slightest hint of another human being in the landscape, the splash of a paddle up a creek, smoke from the roof of one of the lone huts on the bank where families came for bouts of catching and drying fish – then Léonard and his three paddlers would shout greetings in Bomitaba and, if anyone replied, news would be exchanged for a good hundred yards or more at an ever-increasing volume until the power of sound required was too much effort, even for a Bantu.

In a stretch of comparative quiet, by a shore of white sand, a bird I recognized at once was wading carefully in the shallows: rook-size, it was brown all over, but its head was remarkable: a big broad bill balanced by a triangle of crest projecting from the back gave it the shape of an anvil: a hammerkop. It walked slowly, concentrating on the water surface as it shuffled its feet, stirring up the sand to flush out small fish, molluscs and beetles, letting us come very close before it rose jerkily into the air on surprisingly broad wings, its head stretched out, and flew past us, light and silent as an owl. A bird with a genus all its own, its place in science almost as mysterious as its role in myth, at one time or another it was thought to be related to the herons or the flamingos or the shoebill; recent egg-white protein analysis puts it closest to the storks, but the parasites on its skin and in its feathers relate it to the plovers, snipes and sandpipers. And its behaviour is all its own.

We rounded a long bend, and it was at once easy to understand why the bird has a special place in an older African natural history. In the fork of a tree about thirty feet from the ground was an extraordinary structure: a huge rough ball of sticks and debris with a hole at the side beneath an overhang of roof: the hammerkop nest. Everywhere in Africa men leave the hammerkop alone; its very name is often taboo; it is a sorcerer among the birds. There can be no ordinary explanation for spending that amount of effort on such a nest when you're no bigger than a Pied crow: the hammerkop compels all the other birds to come and build its nest for it, summoning the swallow from the air for the finishing touch, a plaster of mud round the entrance.

But then, according to the observations of Wilson and Wilson in Mali, both sexes build it with no help from anyone. Out all day fishing and hunting for frogs, they are such high achievers by dint of an exemplary Lary-like routine: they build from dawn until ten o'clock every morning and then put in more time when they come home in the evening, from four o'clock sharp until six. It takes a week to construct a mass of sticks, reeds, grass and mud with a central bowl in the fork – and at this stage the pair are sometimes driven away and the nest purloined by the Milky eagle-owl, which is enormous, a great peeler of hedgehogs, and also good at ripping up young monkeys, warthog piglets, polecats, herons, ducks and even other owls, including the Spotted eagle owl. But if all goes well the next stage takes a month or more: the sides are built up by weaving small sticks together and the roof gradually added using long ones (up to three-and-a-half feet long) which are pushed upright into the wickerwork edge, slanted towards the centre, and intertwined with others placed longitudinally. The pair work their way across the nest, one bird inside, one on top, and when the roof is complete (now so strong that a man can stand on it), it is heaped up with more reeds and grass and sticks; the last job is to plaster the entrance and the nest-chamber smooth with lots of mud. Now is the time for any passing Barn owl to move in; or a Monitor lizard to heave itself through the hallway; or a genet to curl up inside; or a large snake, particularly the Spitting cobra, to wind in and take a siesta. But if the hammerkops manage to keep their now highly desirable nest (so well insulated that it remains at an even temperature inside) they roost in it together, gaining the entrance by flying low and then swooping up to close their wings at the last moment, in a so-called upward dive.

But all that work is a terrible strain; and quite apart from the relief, as the nest is being built, of copulating eight or ten times a morning, the birds throw some spectacularly open-minded parties. Eight to ten hammerkops are invited, some unattached, some married, some divorced. They turn up near the nest on a sandbank or a slab of rock or a flat piece of grass at any time of day. Everyone pairs off and the male runs up to the female with his wings drooped but the feathers at the back of his head alternately standing on end and falling flat with excitement. The pairs then run in circles side by side and an orgy of (technically speaking) false mounting takes place. No actual rubbing together of his everting and her receiving opposable vent is allowed in public, but you can't complain. The soliciting bird crouches down, the other mounts and balances on top with open wings, and then, shivering with the erotic charge of it all, the lower bird raises its tail, the upper bird curves its tail down – and they press their tails together. They even like a little soixante-neuf, turning round and facing in opposite directions; and the whole party is accompanied by loud duets or a whole chorus of the calls known as *yip-purring*. Males mount females, females mount males, males mount males, and only lesbians are disadvantaged.

So despite all that grinding routine and disappointment (they sometimes build three nests a season and not one succeeds), hammerkops keep up their hobbies and live to a great age: average breeding success (according to Urban, Fry and Keith, 1986) is probably as low as 0.13 young per adult per year which, as the population seems to be increasing, means that the average hammerkop must live for at least twenty years.

Just as I was thinking about all that sex, and wondering why, as far as I could remember, among birds only the ostrich, the rhea, the emu and the cassowary, the tinamous, ducks and screamers have a penis; and what it would be like to be a hammerkop taking an upward dive head-first towards the cool soft sheets of the nest-chamber straight into the coils of a Spitting cobra, Léonard swung the bow of the dugout left into a small tributary and I realized that we were about to arrive at Boha.

32

The slack little river bent round to the right to disclose the palm trees of Boha on a bluff to our left; two fishermen were cleaning a net by the first path that led down to the water: one of them waved at us, but his companion turned and ran back up the bank, fast.

We put in to a landing-stage further up the shore.

'Quick!' said Marcellin, grabbing the gun from the bottom of the dugout and bounding past me. 'Get up into the village and in amongst some women and children. And don't get separated.' His white basketball boots sprayed pebbles off the sandstone path up ahead. 'Nzé! Manou!' he shouted over his shoulder. 'Stay right by me! Léonard! You and the paddlers. You follow with the packs. You stay for one hour. Just one hour. Redmond will pay you in one hour. I promise he will.'

Nzé, Manou and I caught up with him at the top of the path. He had his arm round an old man, outside the open lean-to of a cooking-hut. 'Bobé!' he shouted, not letting go. 'Bobé! My old friend!'

Bobé, bemused but happy, smiled, showing his gums. Barefoot, he wore torn, dirty white cotton trousers rolled up his shins and a red and white-striped pyjama-top open down his bony chest and wizened stomach; he gestured absent-mindedly at the main beam of the lean-to roof, from which two hunting nets were slung, one with large mesh for bushpig, one with small mesh for little forest antelope.

'Yes, Bobé! You used to be a great hunter!' yelled Marcellin, showing the whites of his eyes as he tried to watch the doors of the two huts opposite, the blind space between them, the path in front and behind him, all at once. 'You have one net for bushpig! And one net for antelope!' He pulled Bobé closer, gripping him so hard across the shoulders with his left arm that the old man's vague and toothless smile set into a grin of pain, and with his other hand he held the shotgun like a pistol, his palm over the neck of the stock, his fingers over the trigger-guard. The muzzle swung back and forth from the doors and window-holes of the huts to the path in front and behind us, following Marcellin's gaze, and, on its random tour, passing at short but irregular intervals within a foot of Nzé's nose. Nzé, mesmerized, tracked it out to the right with his best eye, and then, as the barrel ranged back and briefly transformed itself into a steel-rimmed black hole in front of his face, he dipped his chin, half-rolled his head to one side like a duck, locked on with his other eye, and tracked it out to the left.

A group of children, attracted by the noise, appeared in the blind space between the huts.

'Mondélé!' they shouted. 'Mondélé! Mondélé!'

Nzé, with a sudden stamp of his right foot, reached out and pulled the gun from Marcellin's hand.

'Yes,' said Marcellin in his normal voice, as if released from a trance, 'that's right, Nzé. You take the gun. And stay by me.'

He let go of Bobé, who stumbled against a lean-to post and began to rub his left shoulder.

The children pressed round us, and the boldest, a boy of five or six, held up a grasshopper for my inspection. He was pinching it across its back legs, between his index-finger and thumb, and as I bent down, admiring the light green of its rear end, the yellow on its back beneath a slight all-over froth, the white spots on its red, black and yellow head, he jammed it against my nostrils. I leaped backwards, my sinuses full of acrid musk like the pong of a dead stoat. Warning colours, I thought ruefully, in between sneezes, that must be one of those forest grasshoppers that processes plant chemicals and has made such a stink of itself that no sensible predator will go near it. The children jumped up and down with delight, the boy turned away with one of those half-private smiles which only personal triumph produces – and suddenly they all scattered away between the huts.

Four broad-shouldered young men were swaggering towards us down the right-hand path; I walked up to shake their hands; but they brushed past me and surrounded Marcellin. Nzé swung the gun off his shoulder, pointed the barrel at their feet, and patted the stock. Marcellin did not look reassured. No one smiled.

'You will come with us,' said the leader in French. 'We will talk at the table of the Vice-President of the People's Village Committee.'

In the silence, while Marcellin apparently considered the offer, I found myself staring at their tee-shirts. The leader, heavy-faced, wore a plea from the World Wildlife Fund across his massive chest: 'Ne tuez pas les gorilles et les chimpanzés'; a string round his cotton trousers held a dagger at his side, about fifteen inches long, with a wooden handle and a crude wooden scabbard bound together with wire. His lieutenants sported respectively a blue vest with 'Woods Hole Oceanographic Institution' emblazoned on the front; 'Harley-Davidson' on a green background; and, most bizarre of all, a cartoon of a man eating pop-corn, his eyes on stalks, ogling a big-breasted woman flopped beside a swimming-pool with her husband approaching stage left, the whole bearing the legend IT'S A NICE AFTERNOON FOR BILL, BUT BE CAREFUL, FIGHT MAYBE COME.

Despondent that Boha was obviously so visited, I was just matching up previous intruders to the tee-shirts – the first three to the American Philip Lobel of Woods Hole, who, according to Marcellin, claimed to have discovered forty-five new species of fish in Lake Télé, and the last perhaps to the Japanese dinosaur-hunting expedition of 1988 – when the Commandant and his nephews appeared laden with the baggage, Marcellin gave a nod of the head, and we followed the man with the knife into the village.

It was much smaller than Djéké, with winding paths leading away from one short broad street, fewer gardens, and only the occasional hut of grey and white clay bricks amongst the mud and thatch.

I paused for a moment to watch a middle-aged man, his head shaved bald, working at his kiln. He was updating his mud home, building a new house in his enclosure; sweating, barefoot, wearing nothing but a pair of ragged shorts, he was feeding logs into two tunnels of fire in a rectangle of clay blocks about a quarter the size of a hut, the whole plastered with mud to contain the heat. He looked round, wiped a hand across his eyes and gave me a friendly flash of gappy white teeth from the smoke. Simultaneously I felt a little hand creep into mine from behind.

The bold boy, now without his grasshopper, beamed up at me. He looked new, ready for life, as yet untouched by disease of any kind, and he talked fast in Bomitaba about something so special and pressing that my inability to reply seemed not to matter. Marcellin and the others had disappeared, so I allowed my new guide to pull me along a path branching off to the right. His gang, now swollen to a band of twenty or so, followed at a respectful distance, still chanting 'Mondélé! Mondélé!' and pointing at me, to prove it.

We stopped while the boy, intent but still talking and holding my hand, examined the ground beneath a colony of Village weavers in an oil palm, but whether for grasshoppers or nestlings or beetles or snakes among the fallen nests I could not tell; above us, the male birds, sparrow-sized with black heads, saffron chests and bright-yellow bellies, were wheezing and chattering and fussing in a mania of nest-building and displaying and quarrelling. They flew off across the river to a patch of sedge and came back with trails of grass to weave into their hanging nest-baskets; they fought off the neighbours who tried to rob them by tugging at the loose ends; or they set about attracting a dull little olive-brown female by clinging to the downward-projecting entrances of their nests and fanning their wings as if they were humming-birds sucking nectar at a flower.

A little further on, we came, I think, to the object of our quest – the boy tugged at my hand and we all processed into a small enclosure and up to the entrance of a hut where, suspended beneath the shelter of the overhanging thatch, a Green fruit-pigeon sat bedraggled in a cage. The boy talked to it and the pigeon cocked its head and listened. One of the children eased a piece of papaya through the bars. Green all over but for a purple shoulder patch, black on the wings, a blue tail, and yellow legs, its most surprising feature was its bill, the upper mandible slightly hooked over the lower, blue at the tip and glossy scarlet right up to the bird's forehead. Quiet, mating for life, a pigeon so sensitive that it is reputed to die of shock at the sound of a gun, I was just beginning to feel sorry for it when the boy yanked at my hand again and we were off round the corner and down a little incline to another hut. Five young children and two women, one with a baby on her lap, sat on a raffia mat beside it, as if on display. The women looked up and smiled. Behind them stood Marcellin, Nzé, Manou, Léonard and his paddlers.

'Where the hell have you been?' said Marcellin.

The boy let go of my hand and he and all the children bunched themselves off in a rush up the track behind us.

Marcellin moved forward and stood over me. 'I thought I told you not to get separated,' he shouted in my ear. 'Just do what I say, will you? You do not understand. *You are now out of your depth.*'

And *you* are out of your mind, I thought crossly – until a piece of genuine fear moved in my stomach like the first warning of oncoming dysentery. Four young men in odd-looking ripped-up camouflage fatigues were standing motionless under a safou tree twenty paces further down the incline. They held outrageously long spears in their right hands, the beaten-iron blades tilted at the ground, the shafts stretching way up and back over their shoulders.

'Where did they get those uniforms?'

'From the Japanese,' said Marcellin without looking round. 'On my last expedition. But please, Redmond, *no more questions.*'

A thin, nervous, middle-aged man stepped out of the hut. In the kitchen lean-to opposite his hut door, I noticed, were gourds, metal pots and pans, a large wooden mortar-and-pestle, and a manioc grating-board with stones set into the wood in intricate patterns.

'Are you ready?' said the thin man, raising his hands and rubbing them back and forth through his hair, as if his head hurt.

'Yes, Monsieur le Vice-Président,' said Marcellin. 'Now we can talk.'

Nzé, looking uncharacteristically serious, cocked the gun and stood guard by the door. The Commandant and the paddlers sat down in the shade of the lean-to kitchen; and the spearmen stayed still and silent under the safou tree.

Marcellin, Manou and I filed into the hut behind the Vice-President. A short passage led past two sleeping-rooms and into the main chamber, which contained a table and eight chairs, a curtain pinned across an entrance to another room off to the left – and an open back door.

Along the inner wall pieces of raffia matting were nailed at head-height, and on them, held in place with raffia-loop corners, were faded family photographs obscured by mould and the white tracks of some kind of burrowing worm or termite; but one colour Polaroid picture was more recent than the others, the image still distinct. A young Boha man with a moustache, whom I thought I recognized as one of the warriors under the safou tree, stared out of the picture holding a machete gobbed with blood in his right hand and the severed head of a chimpanzee in his left. The head, slightly larger than his own, was pressed against his chest, the face very pale, the mouth open, a flick of blood about the nostrils, and its open eyes looking up at us.

'If you can do that to a chimpanzee,' said Marcellin, 'you can do that to a man.'

'Of course,' said the Vice-President.

I took a chair by the middle of the table opposite the open door, the sunlight bright and hard on the baked ground outside, the view obscured by the trunk of a mango tree fifteen yards away. On the wall to my left was a solitary picture torn from a magazine, a portrait of the President of the People's Republic of the Congo (and of all the People's Village Committees), Colonel Denis Sassou-Nguesso, wearing a red parachute-regiment beret, dark glasses and fatigues, and leaning with both hands firmly on a balcony rail, a big pistol at his belt. I wondered idly if that was the same service revolver that was rumoured to have got him the job – by exploding the head of the previous incumbent all over the wall of the Presidential dining-room. It was mysterious, people said with a touch of admiration; two men went in to breakfast and only one came out: somehow Captain Marien Ngouabi had got himself assassinated. Behind me was a less perplexing picture, also torn from a magazine: an advertisement for a company called Socicom who made a lavatory paper called Lotus: a pink baby sat on top of a large roll of it, back to camera, and in the potty position.

Marcellin sat down beside me and told Manou to stand by the door; the men in the exotic tee-shirts appeared in the entrance, walked in without looking at Manou and arranged themselves on the chairs facing us. Their leader, the giant wearing the plea for gorillas and chimpanzees across his chest and the dagger at his waist, placed himself at the head of the table to Marcellin's left, and the Vice-President at the other end to my right. The giant, leaning forward with his elbows on the table, his arms crossed, each big hand stroking an even bigger bicep, demanded to see our papers. Marcellin unzipped the money and document-pouch on the front of his belt and produced our Ordre de Service from the Secrétariat Général de L'Economie Forestière and our laissez-passer from the Ministère de la Recherche Scientifique et de L'Environnement; they were passed from hand to hand around the table.

There was a scuffling noise in the passage; an old woman rushed into the room, seized Marcellin's right arm, pulled him from his chair, and bundled him out of the door behind us.

The giant turned his heavily lidded eyes on me. 'Your papers are in order,' he said, as if nothing else was.

'It's an honour to be here,' I said.

Marcellin returned and sat down, the wild look back in his eyes.

'It's all your fault,' he hissed at me in English. 'That's the mother of my friend in Brazzaville. They are going to murder me. She says we must run away right now. I should have brought my Kalashnikov. I didn't know we were coming here. You said we need not go to Boha. You lied to me. What about my little daughter? What about her? You should have brought me a pistol. A pistol would be better. I would be safe with a pistol.'

'Marcellin,' said the Vice-President, returning the papers, 'the People's Village Committee demand to know one thing. Why did you put our Chief in prison? He has now hidden himself. It is a great disgrace. Because you have come again to our village the Chief has taken his wives and he has hidden himself in the forest.'

'Why? What for?' said Marcellin, looking startled, his words rising to a high shout. 'What's he going to gain by that?'

Manou slid down the wall, slumped to a sitting position and put his head between his knees.

'Why did you put our Chief in prison?' said the giant, in his preternaturally deep voice.

'It wasn't me,' said Marcellin, turning, bizarrely, to look at me, his eyes blankly searching my face.

'Marcellin Agnagna,' said the giant, 'when you reply to the questions of the People's Village Committee you will address yourself to the Vice-President of the People's Village Committee, and not to a white man.'

'It wasn't me,' repeated Marcellin, focusing on the Vice-President. 'I am not a soldier. I am not a politician. I am under the power of the Political Commissar of the District of Epéna. I am a man of science. Whatever happened at Epéna, it was nothing to do with me.'

'You are a man of science,' said the giant, pointing a calloused finger at Marcellin's head, 'and that is why you came here with a bomb to kill all the fish in our lake and to starve us to death.'

'That was not a bomb. That was a sonar. That was a machine to measure the depth of the water.'

'That's your story,' said the giant, swatting a mosquito on his arm with a clap like a pistol-shot.

'There are men in the Party here who are jealous of me,' said Marcellin, his eyes flicking from one Committee Member to the next. 'They make a great noise and accuse me unjustly. You said nothing to me – and then you told the Commissar that Agnagna traffics in gorillas. It is not true. I have never been involved in anything louche. I work within the law. I have to be strong. The truth is that we have different mentalities, you and I. I do not belong to your world. And that is why you are jealous of me. I asked a hunter to find me an infant gorilla. I needed a gorilla for the zoo in Brazzaville so that people from the city may go and look at it. Every great country has a zoo. And now I wish to speak to your Chief. But he has hidden himself. And that is where the problem lies.'

'You killed a gorilla,' said the giant. 'You tell us not to hunt the chimpanzees and the gorillas that belong to us and our ancestors – and then you kill a gorilla.'

'It was an old male. He was in a tree right over our canoe. He was going to attack us' – Marcellin began to get excited again, in spite of himself – 'He was going to jump into our boat and upset us into the water. So I fired at him' – Marcellin raised an imaginary gun – 'He just hung there in the tree with his blood dripping down. It was dripping into the water. You wouldn't believe the amount of blood that was in him. So I fired again. It was self-defence.'

'I don't believe you,' said the giant, leaning forward across the table, his chest half-blocking my view of the open door. 'We found dead turtles in the lake when you came with the small yellow men. We found dead antelope in the forest. The antelope and the turtles, they belong to us.'

'I have brought three expeditions here,' said Marcellin, raising his voice again. 'I have given many presents to the Chief. I have given many presents to the People's Village Committee. You should thank me. I bring fame to your village. They know your name in distant lands. And I ask you, can I help it – *is it my fault if the men with me transform themselves into animals in the night and go hunting where I cannot see them?* Eh? Am I responsible for that?'

'That is possible,' said the giant, seeming to contract backwards into his chair, as if the argument had suddenly swung against him. 'But our Chief hides in the forest. He has nothing to say.'

'The white man has presents for him,' said Marcellin. 'He has a pipe from England, a knife, cloth for his wives, and two pairs of shoes.'

There was a pause. 'You will stay where you are,' said the giant at last.

'We will decide what to do with you.' He picked up his chair and carried it outside. The other young men and the Vice-President followed him, setting their chairs in a circle just beyond the door. The spearmen quietly appeared and ranged themselves on the far side of the circle.

'Get up, Manou,' said Marcellin. 'We share a mother. You must be a man.'

'I've got malaria,' said Manou, rising unsteadily to his feet, one hand against the wall. 'I'm shaking all over.'

'You shake because you are afraid,' said Marcellin, staring at the table-top in front of him. 'I promised our mother I'd make a man of you.' And then, without shifting his gaze, 'You've failed me, Redmond,' he said. 'I should have come with soldiers. You should not have refused the soldiers the Government offered you. Here we need Kalashnikovs. These are not educated men. They kill gorillas and chimps and each other and tonight they will probably kill us too. Do you know there is a village in the south that made trouble when we announced the National Park in the Mayombe? Well, we went with soldiers and we moved the whole village. We should do that here. If I live I shall say so in my report. We must move these murderers. Lake Télé is too precious to be left to such people. We must move them and bring in tourists and make money and protect the animals. I have drawn up plans. The Ministry of Economic Forestry has approved my plans.'

A little boy with a snuffly nose peered round the door behind us, holding a yellow plastic football. He wiped his nose with one hand and lobbed the ball at me with the other. I patted it back.

'Don't talk to him,' said Marcellin. 'He's a spy.'

The giant leaned through the other door, in front of us, shutting out the light. 'We have decided,' he boomed. 'We will talk to the Chief. He will know what to do. The Vice-President – he will take you to the schoolmaster's house.'

Outside, the Commandant and his paddlers were eating lumps of fou-fou stodge from a bowl in the lean-to and Nzé was sitting on the raffia mat, laughing with the two women, making faces at the children and showing them how the gun worked: as we watched he pushed the lever across with his thumb, clicked open the breech, took out the cartridge, replaced it, put the stock to his shoulder, squinted with his right eye along the top of the barrel at a palm tree, shouted 'Pouff!' – and with his free hand mimed whole armies blown flat by the blast. The children shrieked, jumped up on the mat, fell over backwards in line, gurgled, death-rattled, twitched, lay still, and sat up for more.

Marcellin lurched forward and caught Nzé by the collar of his combat jacket. 'I told you to stand guard,' he said. 'I'm sick of your laughing. You're always laughing!'

'I'm recruiting,' said Nzé, with a laugh, twisting himself free.

We picked up our packs and followed the Vice-President down past the safou tree to a large open space clear of weeds, the school playground, bounded on its far side by a low line of white and brown clay-brick school-rooms roofed with thatch and backing on to the high forest. The school-master's hut, likewise made of brick but with a corrugated-iron roof, lay to our right, by a hut for goats and a conical shelter over a latrine-pit.

'So, Marcellin,' I said, 'where shall we pitch the tents?'

'No, Redmond, I'm not going to be axed through the canvas in the night. Not even for you. I know how you hate mosquitoes and chiggers, but tonight we sleep in a brick hut with only one door. Nzé and Manou will sleep across the door.'

'Remember Djéké, my friend,' said Léonard, twisting his shoulders side-ways and downwards to shed one of our bergens against the hut wall. 'Remember Djéké where you were happy, Redmond, because – you mark my words well – one way or another the men of Boha will make you wish you'd never come to the Likouala' – he put his hand on my arm and looked anxiously into my eyes – 'you'll wish you'd never heard the name of our river, my friend.'

Shaken, I fumbled about in the transparent plastic bag full of small notes in my leg-pocket and paid him his 12,000 CFA; he and the paddlers turned and left without another word and without looking back; the Vice-President, smiling nervously, gestured us into the communal room with a hesitant wave and left too; the hut suddenly seemed isolated, and ominously quiet.

Marcellin and I piled the baggage on the earth floor behind the usual rough table and chairs and Nzé and Manou took down the boards which served as shutters across the window-holes. Each of the three bedrooms, one to the left of the door and two at the back, contained a large plank bed; there was no space in which to set up a tent.

'Real beds!' shouted Nzé. '*We can do it on real beds!*'

'You're not doing it anywhere,' said Marcellin. 'You're going to sleep by the door. And Redmond is going to sleep with me.' He gave the bed in the right-hand back room a tremendous kick. There was a small rustling noise, like the movement of dry leaves. 'Bugs,' he said.

I dropped to my knees and inspected the dry mud floor under the planks. Dark-brown insects about a fifth of an inch long, thin and flat, were scuttling towards two long cracks in the ground. Marcellin kicked the bed again and another brittle dusting fell to the floor. 'Bed-bugs,' he said. 'Their bites don't bother me. Some people hardly feel them.'

So this is it, I thought, my own secret fear, much more real than the idea of a Boha dagger in a kidney, and I tried to remember just where I had read that bed-bugs carry HIV for exactly one hour in their blood-sacs: it explains how three-year-olds and grandmothers pick up the virus: the bugs, sick with disappointment when their host gets out of bed, exude a drop of blood from the hypodermic needles, the proboscides on the end of their noses, and then, sick with excitement, they throw up another drop as they re-insert their bloodsuckers into whoever is left between the sheets. The words of the consultant in tropical medicine at the Radcliffe Hospital in Oxford came back to me: 'The Congo is *very* interesting,' he had said, with a dreamy look in his eyes. 'Very interesting indeed. It's the HIV 1 and HIV 2 overlap zone. If only you could send me some fresh blood samples. I'd be most grateful. I really would.'

'Marcellin,' I said unsteadily, wondering how many women he had slept with in his hyperactive life – five hundred? A thousand plus? – 'Why don't you sleep in here? I'll sleep in the other back room. And Manou and Nzé can sleep together as usual.'

Marcellin shouted as if I was fifty yards away, 'I don't want to die alone! Only a coward would let me die alone!

'And besides,' he said, calming down, 'it's all your fault. But for you I wouldn't be here. They'll push a spear through the window in the night. But for you I would never have returned to Boha. Never.'

'You'll thank me,' I said, momentarily hating the sight of him, and wondering why his weeping leg ulcers had never quite healed despite the two courses of Floxapen. 'This is the expedition when we find your dinosaur. We'll take its portrait.'

Marcellin sat down on the edge of the bed and held his knees. He rocked gently back and forth. 'Not even Doubla,' he mumbled, half to himself. And then, still rocking like a child in distress, but fingering his sprout of beard with both hands, 'Maybe not even Doubla would spear a white man. Maybe even Doubla knows there's terrible trouble when you kill a white man. It's not just. It's not right. But there it is.' He shrugged his shoulders and looked up at me with a helpless smile.

'Of course I'll sleep next to you,' I said, ashamed of myself. 'I'll sleep nearest the window.' But I couldn't stop the fear speaking. 'Is there a lot of AIDS here?'

'Le Sida?' he said, forceful again. 'In my country? In the Congo? Of course not. You're safe here. Everybody knows that. It's a white American capitalist disease. At Pointe-Noire, at the port on the coast, I don't know, but they say there may be three or four cases. When the white American ships put in – you won't believe this, Redmond, but there are one or two African boys who will do it for money. It's the Vili. The Vili people live on the coast.'

Well, I thought, bed-bugs feed just before dawn. I must get up as if we were in the jungle. I must get up at four in the morning. 'Who's Doubla?'

'He's the most dangerous man in Boha. He's called Doubla because you have to pay him double for everything. And also because he has a double character – he's strong, he's the best fisherman there is, he's a great hunter, you'll think he's your friend – and then he loses his temper. He's killed three men here. Maybe more.'

'Will we meet him?'

'Of course. We must take him with us. It's better that way. You must give him a job or he'll get his revenge. We'll take Doubla because he's dangerous, Vicky because he's the Chief's favourite son, and two others. Everyone will want to come. They all want the money.'

'What do they do with it?'

'They paddle downriver and buy beer in Epéna.'

There was a bang on the door. Marcellin jumped to his feet.

'Fuck off!' sang Nzé and Manou in unison from the front bedroom.

'Koko!' said a thick-set young man wearing a gold tee-shirt, blue bathing-trunks, and a pair of sunglasses so impenetrably dark that I was surprised he could see well enough to walk. 'Chief,' he said to me, standing in the doorway, 'I've hurt my neck.'

Thinking he just wanted some pills, as usual, I went to the medicine-pack to get the Paracetamol. 'Here,' he said, following, pulling down his tee-shirt and bending towards me: the whole of the back of his neck was bubbled with blisters; it was ridged and trenched with oozing yellow scabs as though he had fallen into a bonfire.

'What happened?'

He held his hands up in front of his chest, palms forward, pushing my question away.

I smeared Savlon across the wound and gave him the tube, feeling useless. He sidled out of the door.

Manou and Nzé had made a nest for themselves in the front bedroom, Nzé on the bed in his tarpaulin, Manou on the floor. They lay smoking their way through a carton of cigarettes I had bought for the bearers. 'Go buy us some palm-wine,' said Nzé with a lopsided grin.

'You'll get bitten. The beds are full of bugs.'

'I get bitten at home,' said Nzé proudly, blowing smoke rings. 'We've got beds at home.'

The Vice-President appeared in the doorway, self-effacing. 'My sister has malaria,' he said. I counted fifteen quinine pills into his palm. 'The Chief is waiting,' he said. 'He will see you now. You will follow me.'

'Nzé, bring the gun,' said Marcellin. 'Manou, you stay here and guard the packs.'

'I'm sick,' said Manou, from the floor. 'Don't leave me alone.'

'Be a man,' said Marcellin automatically, clipping his portable cassette-player to his belt and arranging the headphones around his neck, his badge of wealth and office.

He rummaged in the presents bag and found the two pairs of canvas shoes I had bought in Impfondo, one for the Chief and one for the Chief's senior wife; I put the bolt of red cloth under my arm and pocketed the Swiss Army knife, the last pipe from Savory's in Oxford and the last tin of Balkan Sobranie.

Crossing the playground in the early afternoon heat, we passed a shrub with spikes of orange flowers which spread like the arms of a starfish just above the rough grasses at the margin of the weeded area; sunbirds played about the blooms, curves and circles and zig-zags of metallic greens and purples in the air, a flash of scarlet, a speck of blue. There were two species, I decided, and the equally tiny but brown and white and olive birds, a flitter of wrens, were their mates.

'Stop it,' said Marcellin, pulling me away by my shirt. 'It's no time for one of your trances.'

The Vice-President, silent, set off down a small track, his shoulders stooped.

'What's wrong with him?' I said.

'I've told you a hundred times,' said Marcellin. 'It's the same everywhere here: the People's Political Commissar picks a low-born man who's been to school and calls himself a Communist and makes him a Vice-President in his village. The Government want to break the power of the Chiefs. Other low-born men side with the Vice-President, and so every village is divided.'

The path led past a circular pit about twenty feet across and eight feet deep; half-way down the blackish soil changed to yellow clay; two women were up to their knees in the mud at the bottom, their wraparound skirts hitched up to their thighs, one of them puddling to and fro, the other throwing up the clay with a wooden spade on to a pile at the rim. Further back in the compound a roofed-over frame of posts and closely set lateral sticks awaited its infill of mud; when that was finished the pit would be planked over, a hole cut in the middle, a thatch screen put up, and the family would have a new latrine.

'The men here talk and drink palm-wine and fight,' said Marcellin. 'The women work.'

We entered the village proper, the huts likewise almost all made of wattle-and-daub and palm-thatch, more ragged than Djéké – except one, which was much larger than the others, the mud smoothed over its walls like plaster, and, on the wall facing the path, big white-painted letters proclaimed: BOHA PILOTE DINOSAURE.

'Who lives there? Was he with you when you saw Mokélé-mbembé?'

'He is not a serious man,' snapped Marcellin. 'And we must now be quiet. We must prepare ourselves. We must be ready in our minds. We must be strong when we meet the Chief.'

We walked up the wide main street and stopped at a rough square on the right. In front of us was a long, windowless, dilapidated hut of wattle-and-daub and palm-thatch; in its doorway, on a three-legged stool, sat the Chief of Boha.

He was much younger than I had expected, perhaps in his late thirties, a handsome man of strong and regular features, with a small moustache neatly cut to the line of his upper lip. He wore a thick red band of paint across his forehead and in two curves beneath the pectoral muscles of his hairless chest; a baggy ochre loincloth embroidered with red, yellow and blue-green flowers on the patch over his genitals; and a pair of Adidas running-shoes.

In his right hand he gripped a spear against the inside of his right thigh, its end on the ground and its winged blade high above his head. His left hand lay on his left thigh, and from his right shoulder there hung a large liana-twine bag full, I presumed, of the royal fetishes. He looked at us, solemn, without moving. A yellow dog with black ears, eyebrows and muzzle lay asleep at his feet.

Twelve spearmen stood at intervals in a circle before him, enclosing a line of three chairs; an old man in a brown shirt, torn grey trousers and red plastic sandals, standing on the Chief's left, tilted his spear towards us and then at the waiting seats. Dropping his spear further, he pointed it at Nzé, motioning him away to a group of women and children who stood watching at the far side of the square. We took our places, the Vice-President on the left, Marcellin in the middle and myself nearest the old man; the circle of spearmen moved in close behind us.

The Chief inclined his head to his left: the old man, his *porte-parole*, his word-carrier, bent down until his right ear was close to the royal lips; the Chief spoke softly. The audience over, the old man straightened his back, held his spear upright, strode into the centre of the circle, filled his lungs, and sang out a speech in Bomitaba.

The dog woke up, snapped at a fly, pushed itself back on its haunches, scratched maniacally at its side with a back leg, rooted at the spot with its teeth, felt better, lost interest, lay down again and closed its eyes.

At the end of the pronouncement there were shouts from some of the spearmen and from other warriors around the square: when the old man decided to allow anyone to speak he lowered his spear towards them; and when he wanted them to stop he held it horizontal, to bar their words. The debate concluded, he returned to the Chief's side, took his instructions, and stepped back into the centre of the circle.

'The white man will pay 75,000 francs to the Chief of Boha,' he shouted in French, 'and 20,000 francs to the Vice-President of the People's Committee. Then if the Government come with soldiers to take our Chief to prison in Epéna they must take their Vice-President away too. The white man will keep faith with our Customary Rights.'

'It's far too much!' I said.

The old man nodded. The warrior to the right and behind me lowered his spear and picked me gently between the shoulder-blades.

'It's a bargain!' I said.

The old man smiled, bowed his head to the assembled company, and waved two spearmen forward to collect the presents. All three then turned about, bowed again towards the Chief and advanced the few yards into the royal presence. The two spearmen, dropping to their knees, laid the presents on the ground before him. The Chief bent forward without ceremony and with his left hand put the knife, the pipe and the tobacco into his shoulder bag. He stood up, placed his spear against the thatch overhang of the roof of the hut, stooped down to gather up the shoes and the bolt of cloth and disappeared through the dark doorway. The old man picked up the stool and followed him inside. The royal dog lay undisturbed, his tail twitching in irregular waves from base to tip as he hunted bushpig through his dreams.

'Bring your chair,' said Marcellin, smiling for the first time since Djéké. '*It's going to be all right*. You will pay up and we will now be safe.'

'Why the chair?'

He took off his floppy hat and reset the rim at a jaunty angle. 'You'll need it. We have two more palavers. When the French left and the people here moved out of the forest to make Boha they came from three different villages and so there are three traditional Chiefs. But the other two are not dangerous. They have no power. We let them talk because we have good manners. We will not give presents. You will not need to pay.'

There was a whoop at my elbow. 'But you must pay me, Uncle!' said Nzé, whooping again, the gun in one hand and his other outstretched, palm upwards. 'Now it's safe! They won't kill Nzé!' He puffed out his chest. 'No one can kill Nzé. My grandfather was the greatest sorcerer in Dongou. That's what saved you! That's why we're still alive!'

'Of course.'

His face distorted itself into his outsize grin, a mix of broken teeth, wrinkled scars, dilated nostrils and skewed eyes bright with happiness. 'You're my uncle – and you must give me some money. I'll buy pineapples and I'll find an old woman to cook for us and I'll get two, three, four buckets of palm-wine.'

I gave him far too many small notes.

He clattered the gun down on the ground, closed his eyes, put his right hand under his left armpit, clapped his biceps down on it with a thwack, and hugged himself.

'What *is* that for?' I said, bending down to slip on the safety catch, a nervous tic I had developed. 'When you flap like that? Flap a wing?'

'I don't need to carry a fetish,' he said, skipping about from side to side in front of me. 'My grandfather sewed one into me right here' – he pointed at the scar on his left wrist – 'and another one here' – the larger scar, down his left bicep – 'and when I do that' – thwack – 'I make a wish and it's *sure* to be granted' – he clicked his fingers. 'My grandfather gave it to me. He said, "Little Nzé, whenever you do that you'll have enough pleasure for ten men, and all to yourself."'

'So what's the wish?'

'A young girl,' he said, still skipping, 'with huge tits and a big bum. The prettiest youngest bum in all of Boha. That's what I want, Uncle.'

I gave him 500 CFA.

'*Come on,*' said Marcellin. 'Follow me.'

'And one for little Manou,' said Nzé, expanding with the generosity of such a thought, breaking into a proper dance and circling round me. 'I'll find him something shy and gentle. With tiny tits and long legs, that's what he likes.' He held an imaginary partner. 'The kind of girl who never looks you in the face. The kind of girl who looks at her feet and laughs.'

I gave him another 500 CFA.

He picked up the gun and my chair and cavorted along beside me.

'There aren't two of you,' he said, in between gyrations. 'You share everything. You talk to the workers. You joke with the workers. And in the forest you fall down all day long but you always get up again. You don't know where to put your feet but you always get up again. I've decided to call you Uncle. You're my uncle!'

I looked at him closely. I thought: these are the first kind words I've heard in months.

'So, Uncle,' he said, as we stumbled through a group of retreating goats and entered another dilapidated compound, 'Uncle, if I name my baby son after you – if I call him Nzé Jean Félix Nkombe Marcellin Manou Redmond

Oumar, would you give me 75,000 francs and 20,000 for my two wives? Eh? Would you?'

Back at the hut Manou had roused himself; he sat smoking at the table with two young men of about his own age, wearing the head-torch I had given him, the lamp turned off and pointing at the roof, perched on top of his hair like a fez. 'Marcellin,' he said grandly, 'here are the junior porters you wanted, Nicholas and Jean Poulain. They say that Monsieur Victor Embingui and Monsieur Ange Moutaboungou, also known as Doubla, will visit us after dark.'

We shook hands; and Marcellin sat down to start the long bargaining over rates of pay. I picked up my bergen and sidled into the back room, wondering how I was going to peel off the camouflage tape from the last bundle of notes hidden in the waterproof bag under the top flap, count out 75,000 CFA for the Chief and 20,000 for the Vice-President – and reseal the secret store without being knifed, robbed, speared, and then decapitated like the Vice-President's chimpanzee.

Manou crept in after me.

'Go away!' I said.

'Sssh,' said Manou, pulling my shirt-sleeve, 'come outside. I have something to tell you.' He announced loudly: 'I'm going to show Redmond the school,' and eased me out of the hut door.

The sun had lost its heat, and from somewhere in the great trees beyond the school huts came the sound of African grey parrots gathering to roost; whistles and shrieks and high-pitched laughter filled the playground, as if the holidays had not begun and the children were still at their games.

Manou, conspiratorial, took a last look round, and motioned me into the right-hand schoolroom. We sat down at one of the rough bench-desks cut from forest trees, in the centre of the front row, furthest from the window-holes; the last lesson was still laid out on the blackboard, a set of equations which I could not understand.

He put the pocket-book and biro I had given him on the desk-top, his face even more anxious than usual. 'I have been talking to the two boys Nicolas and Jean Poulain,' he whispered, 'they say that this affair of Lake Télé is traditional. The Chief of Boha – he knows, in the spirit way, all that goes on at the lake, but during the season of mounting waters or if we go fishing, ordinary people, you and me, we also, we may see the monster which is called Mokélé-mbembé. The Chief, he says that in the years that are gone there were two monsters living in the lake. The pygmies who lived in the forest by the lake killed one of these beasts. That is to say there was one

326

male and one female and all the pygmies who helped in the attack on the beast died. Except one who refused to eat from the carcass, and some say, Redmond, that he is still alive.

'The first inhabitants by the lake, they were pygmies – and whenever they went fishing, each time they set their hoop-nets they heard strange cries and the earth shook and great waves came from the centre of the lake – and that is how they came to know of the existence of a monster in the middle of Lake Télé. Even now, as we live now, once each year the monster turns and turns, he walks round the edge of his lake and all the area as far as the village of Boha hears the trembling of the ground and the strange cries; and this is very like the roar in the ground and the screams in the air when you hear a tornado walking towards you.'

He wiped a piece of spit from the edge of his small moustache, got up, leant over the sill of the window nearest the forest, looked left and right, and sat down again. 'In 1982, Dr Marcellin, he saw the monster standing in the water by the shore opposite him, but he had nothing but a little Nikon camera – and in his great shock he dropped it, and when he found it again, under the mud, the monster had disappeared.

'In the beginning, this affair of the monster, it became known when the pygmies went fishing in the ponds, the ponds in the forest which you empty of water in the dry season and where you pick the fish out of the mud – the pygmies, they heard the trees falling, bang! bang! The waters rose and the little ponds where they fished began to join together to form a lake. Mokélé-mbembé, he walked round and round, and where he walked the trees fell down behind him, and so he made Lake Télé. And the water rose over the manioc that the pygmies had planted round the village, so they decided to fight for their country, and where the monster walked to and from the lake, where he made a boulevard as he went to work in the morning and where he walked back at night, there they made a barricade to kill the monster, six barricades, one after the other.

'Now, when the monster had finished his work in the lake below he walked back to where he usually slept – and he saw the six barricades. He walked straight through the first five, he destroyed them all, but at the sixth barricade the pygmies put their spears into his flesh and he began to bleed and he saw his wife behind him and he cried out to her and she ran away and then he died.'

I could no longer make out the equations on the blackboard; the parrots had fallen silent; cicadas began whirring and rasping – and something screamed like a baby being knifed.

Perhaps that's what it is, I thought – that's how it got its name – it's a bushbaby. And in my mind's eye I saw what I secretly wanted to see: an animal like a heavily furred squirrel, with a long curly tail, big ears like a bat, huge eyes like an owl, a wet snout, and its hands a spidery version of our own. Had a Dwarf bushbaby been surprised high in the canopy by a civet, say, or an Eagle owl, as it urinated on its little palms, getting ready to mark its trail for the night, out from some communal sleeping-hole and across the tree-crowns in search of moths and beetles, caterpillars and birds' eggs?

Manou nudged me, interrupting my rêverie. He turned on his head-torch and opened his notebook. 'Look,' he whispered in my ear, 'I made a map.'

A small red beetle like a cockchafer locked into the torch-beam, crashed into the middle of Lake Télé, tucked its wings into their shiny cases, fussed north-east to inspect the dinosaur, re-opened its back and zig-zagged off into the darkness.

'You see?' said Manou, excited, his breath on my face, 'I have marked it at the side. Here. No aeroplane can fly over Lake Télé. No pilot would ever survive. A satellite would fall out of the sky. Nothing can withstand such power.'

He got up and put the notebook and biro back in his pocket. 'Even a white man may *see* Mokélé-mbembé,' he said with a newly found authority.

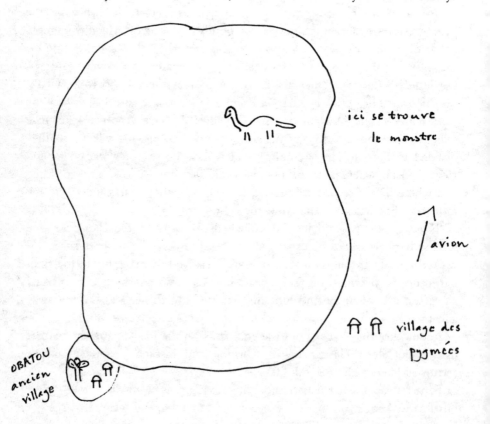

'It is not a sacred animal. It is an animal of mystery. But there is another lake, a sacred lake, much smaller than Lake Télé, but close by – it is there that the spirits of the ancestors go to sleep. No one must disturb them by fishing. If you eat the fish of that lake, if you take one small bite, you will die. Dr Marcellin, on his last expedition, he went there with the guide Dokombo. Nicolas and Jean Poulain told me. They told me – that is another of his crimes and that is why, sometime soon, the men of Boha must kill him. They must avenge the ancestors. They banished Dokombo from Boha. He will never see his village again.'

We walked back across the playground in the moonlight. 'Redmond,' he said, 'Nzé is frightened to go to Lake Télé. He is frightened, and I, too, I am frightened.'

'It will be a great adventure.'

'Yes,' he said slowly, 'I will tell my wives. And then perhaps they will think better of me.'

He stood still. 'The man whose neck you treated . . .'

'Yes?'

'He has a powerful fetish.'

'So?'

'Nobody likes him. He sided with the Vice-President. The sorcerer here tried to kill him, in the spirit way, by night. But he refused to die – before the sun came up he went away in his canoe and he paddled to Epéna and he bought those dark glasses and now the eyes of the sorcerer can't see him. He hides his glasses in a gourd when he shuts his eyes to sleep. So Nicolas and Jean Poulain grabbed him – when he was sleeping in his hut, without his glasses. They took him and tied him and they hanged him by his neck from a tree. But he wouldn't die. So they were afraid. They took him down and they undid him and they ran away.'

Manou held my arm and looked into my face from six inches away; absurdly, I thought of Mary Kingsley's remark in *Travels in West Africa*, 'Human eyeballs, particularly of white men . . . are a great charm.'

'Redmond,' he said, 'they wanted me to ask you, as a white man – do you think machetes would work?'

'Jesus!' I said.

'They don't believe in Jesus,' said Manou. 'He's the spirit of the French.'

The hut was full of candle-light and laughter, women and food.

'Uncle!' shouted Nzé, happy and sweating, standing by the table. 'Palm-wine!' (He tilted a zinc bucket and passed me a mugful.) 'Saka-saka!' (He nodded imperiously at an old woman to his left, who began to ladle mashed manioc leaves and scraps of fish from her cooking-pot into our mess-tins.)

'Pineapples!' (There were four piled on the table, and two ripe papayas.) 'Women!' (He put his arm round an enormous girl sitting on his right. She looked up at me and giggled, her bright yellow and green wraparound barely restraining her breasts, her buttocks overflowing the chair.) 'She's rich!' he yelled, over-excited, his wink a chaotic squash-down of his right eyebrow. 'Her father's a boatman! He goes to Epéna! She's well fed, Uncle' – he squeezed the flesh of her upper arm – 'When I take her, I'll have two women at once!'

'Stop shouting!' shouted Marcellin from the far end of the table. He turned to a man sitting on his left, a man with a long head, his eyes deep in their sockets, his hollowed face straggled with sideboards, a moustache and a thin growth of hair on his chin. 'This, Redmond, is Monsieur Ange Moutaboungou, also known as Doubla. Tomorrow he will take us towards Lake Télé. At Lake Télé anything may happen to us. So now we have a party.'

'Manou!' shouted Nzé with redoubled force, as I shook hands with Doubla and sat down beside him. 'Manou! I almost forgot – I found you a woman. Look!' He pointed into the far corner – where a young girl sat clutching a mug of palm-wine and staring at her knees. She half-glanced at Manou, smiled, and looked away. Manou, taken aback, sat down by the door, embarrassed. Everybody laughed.

Nzé drained his mug in one go, refilled it, and joined his large new love by the wall. 'I want to be Fela Anikulapo Kuti,' he said, calming down, abstracted, as if hit by some overwhelming thought, sudden and profound.

'Who's that?' I said.

'He's a Nigerian singer,' said Marcellin with a grin. 'He lives in Lagos with twenty-seven official wives – and he has 250 more in a special settlement next to his house. But then he's very rich, and I don't suppose he walks about the streets all day, laughing over nothing.'

'I wouldn't *need* to walk the streets,' said Nzé testily. 'They'd have to queue at my house. And I'd have a shower and a proper washbasin, too, and all the palm-wine I wanted.'

'You'd have whisky,' said Marcellin. 'You'd have Johnny Walker Black Label.'

A big, broad-chested, shambling man entered the hut, punching the door as he came, hard. 'Koko!' he said.

'Vicky!' said Marcellin. 'Have some wine! Sit by me! Vicky! You've been beating your wife again! Haven't you? We heard her screaming. She made a terrible noise. She frightened everybody. Tell me – why do you do it? It's not right. You shouldn't do that all the time. Tell me – why do you do it?'

'She's young,' said Vicky with an outsize, winning smile. 'I do it for correction.'

*

'Come on, Redmond,' said Marcellin after supper, 'you always want to talk to old men. Let's go and see Bobé. He knows the history of Boha. And it was he who sent us the food tonight. This is his wife. It will be good manners.'

So we left Doubla and Vicky and Nzé and Manou and their new girlfriends smoking the cigarettes meant for the bearers and getting drunk, and we walked slowly up through the village, the old woman between us. Her hair, grey and thin, grew only at the back of her head, and she wore a dress with a flounce round the shoulders, a party dress which she must once have filled, but which now hung empty across her chest. She refused to let me carry her cooking-pot; she waved the beam of my torch from the path in front of her; she wanted no help from anyone; and she muttered to herself in Bomitaba, a low, staccato complaint that mixed itself away into the night with the scolding of cicadas.

'Tell her that was the best saka-saka I've ever had.'

'She can't speak Lingala or French,' said Marcellin, apologetic. And I thought again how separate and obsessive your world might become – how enclosed and overwhelming your ideas and your dreams might be when a mere two or three villages away in every direction people spoke mutually incomprehensible languages.

Bobé, still wearing his red and white-striped pyjama top, a lantern at his feet, was sitting waiting for us in his lean-to, beneath his hunting-nets, his cylindrical wickerwork fish-traps, his carrying-baskets, and his bundles of large and small gourd water-containers slung from the beams.

'Welcome!' he said, jumping to his feet and shaking hands. 'You are welcome to my house.'

'Bobé, your wife is annoyed with us,' said Marcellin.

'I don't suppose she is annoyed with you in particular,' said Bobé, stooping low with the lantern and showing us into the hut. 'She is often annoyed. She complains that she is old. When I married her she was the most beautiful girl in Boha, but now she is old. Now I am the only man who still looks at her like a man. She worries about our son, Doubla. But I tell her that Doubla is a man with sons of his own. He is strong and fierce and I am proud to be his father. But she worries. She worries that the soldiers will come and take him to Epéna.'

He put his arm round her and said something in Bomitaba. Her tetchy face cracked into a smile and she disappeared through a curtain into a back room. Bobé ushered us into carved armchairs grouped round a low table and sat down himself. Spiral horns of the Swamp antelope, the sitatunga, were stuck into the plaster round the walls. A tall drum stood on its three legs in the corner next to Marcellin.

'Bobé made this,' he said, running a finger down its side, over the joins where the different cylinders of hollowed-out tree-trunks had been fitted together.

'I made everything here,' said Bobé with a slow smile, showing a full set of front teeth. 'The chairs, the table, everything.'

The old woman returned, put three empty cans labelled NORWEGIAN MACKEREL on the table, handed Bobé a gourd of palm-wine, and withdrew. Bobé filled the cans in silence; we picked the odd drowned bee, fly and caterpillar out of the white froth on top, dabbed them on to the floor, and drank.

'Me, I like to be old,' said Bobé, sitting back in his chair. 'I have always been happy. I used to be the greatest hunter in all Boha and I knew the best places to sink my fish-traps, too – but now I am old and wise and proud of different things, I am proud that I understand the history of my people. I know all our stories. My grandchildren come to see me, all the boys in Boha come to see me, and I tell them how it used to be, I tell them about the *colons*, the French people, and how the Communists helped us to build our school, and I tell them where to hunt and where to put their fish-traps in every month of the year. They like old Bobé. If you go to see the sorcerer you must pay. If you go to see old Bobé he asks for nothing but your friendship. Yes, I am always happy, except when my children and my grand-children die; then I am as sad as my wife. Then we are sad together. There are many deaths in Boha.'

'Perhaps you could tell us about the history of your people.'

Marcellin said to Bobé, 'You may talk properly. He is a white man, but he respects the old ways. He has agreed to pay the traditional dues. In full.'

'So I have heard,' said Bobé, turning to me, 'and you have entrusted yourself to my son Doubla. Well, we have a long history.'

He refocused his eyes to a point somewhere on the floor just behind the drum; and his voice changed, the hesitant old man's voice became a low incantation. 'The origin of the first people of Boha lies in the village of Bongoye,' he intoned, 'which is near the plain of Sakoua. The path Nguelo connects the village to Lake Télé. The people of Bongoye moved to make the village of Bombolo. After Bombolo they made the village of Ngouamoun-kale. The village of Ngouamounkale was also known as Old Boha. The path which leads to the lake comes out at the creek Marawa. The first Chief was called Mountelola.'

'These abandoned villages,' I said quickly, breaking into the list, 'do they have holy places near them?'

Bobé readjusted with an obvious effort, and for the first time he looked at me with genuine interest. 'In former times,' he said, his voice returned to normal, 'the people of Boha had a sacred place called Etoho. It was well known for increasing the fertility of women, this place, the people went there to make speeches, they made speeches to demand children, to demand an increase in the size of the village.'

'So where do we all come from?' I said, pleased with myself. 'That's what I want to know. What's the origin of life?'

'That's very simple,' he said, leaning forward, refilling our ex-mackerel cans, and relaxing back into his chair. 'I can put your mind at rest. The origin of life reposes in a symbol whose name is Bolo. Bolo incarnates all creative power. It is a unique symbol. This symbol embodies all the spirits, good or bad. The origin of sorcery comes from the symbol Bolo. This symbol endows certain people with a power, a power which is generally transmitted through dreams. And, concerning dreams, a meaning is always given, because certain dreams are always messages. This power of dreams is held by a few people who are very gifted, people of the village like the Chiefs and certain of the sorcerers. In our tradition, there is no system of explanation for each dream, as I have heard is the case in other tribes. But it is normal for the Chiefs to let everyone in the village know about their dreams – good or bad. In certain cases the other villagers come to tell their dreams to the Chief, who interprets them, and he spreads this knowledge by our form of newspaper. A man takes the Chief's words into his head and he cries out their message through the village, in every corner of the village.'

Bobé drained his second can of palm-wine, refilled it – and stopped with the can in his right hand, half-way to his lips, apparently mesmerized by the something or someone just behind the drum.

'Bobé, my old friend,' said Marcellin softly. 'We're here. Are you all right?'

'Yes, Marcellin,' he said slowly, confused, as if coming back from a journey. He put his can down unsteadily on the edge of the table, slopping wine on to the floor. 'I am all right. I was listening. I am directed to help you with your researches. There is something new I must tell you, the most important event in the recent history of our people. I am told it is good that our history be written down, so that other men may share our knowledge. And it is not the knowledge that the Government sends us from Epéna with the young men, a different young man every two years, it is not like the Government knowledge that fills the air in the school.'

It'll be a move of the village, I thought, or the making of a new plantation, or a scheme for a communal cash crop, as I took the gourd in my hands, feeling its smooth skin, its skin stained as black as everything else stored in the rafters, where the smoke from the hut fire weaved its way out through the thatch.

'We have come to know,' announced Bobé, intoning again, his eyes glazed over, fixed on the drum. 'We have come to know that a sacred animal, Yombé, lives in the forest of Boha. This animal, which resembles the chimpanzee and the gorilla but whose upper limbs are very elongated, is vegetarian, and it eats above all else two species of plants which are present in our forest. This animal has already been seen on many occasions, but its mystery lies in this – you must never look into its eyes. Ten years ago two hunters from the village shot at one of these animals, not with an arrow but with a gun. The animal, which was sitting in a tree, fell – and it disappeared. It disappeared leaving not the slightest trace. The two hunters returned to the village. They told their story. And as they finished speaking of this phenomenon, they died.

'I, the Bobé who sits before you, I affirm, now, as I sit here, that I too have seen this animal. I, also, met it when it was sitting in a tree. The animal began to turn its head. But the spirits of the two hunters saved my life. They called to me gently, inside my skull, and I remembered how they told their story and how they died. I lowered my eyes to the path. I returned to my wife and to my children. So I, Bobé, I am still alive. And now I have warned you in my own house, Mr Redmond, because you are said to respect our traditions, and also because you are well known to my friend Dr Marcellin. I warn you, on pain of death, do not meet the eye of this animal when you come across it in the forest.'

He pressed the palms of his loose-skinned old hands into his eyes, as if to shut something from view, and then looked at us with his slow smile again, his voice its usual self. 'I am tired,' he said. 'It takes courage to talk of such things. And now I am very tired. We will speak again. Perhaps you will visit me again.'

I was surprised to see that I was still holding the gourd.

'What did you make of that?' I said, as we walked back to our hut.

A stray dog, a bit like the Chief's but with a patch of mange on its yellow back, appeared out of the shadows and trotted along behind us. Whenever I looked round and said 'Pheasants!' it wagged its tail and cocked its ears. Why can't you just nose out the only pheasant in Africa for me, I thought, the Congo peacock? – so rare it was not discovered until 1913 (by the great ornithologist of the Belgian Congo, the American James P. Chapin, and then only from a single feather, a 'barred secondary quill of a female ... taken from the hat of a native at Avakubi in the Ituri', a feather which tantalized Chapin for twenty-three years until he finally found and named the bird in 1936). 'If you could just do that,' I said aloud, 'what a very clever pooch you would be.'

'I think you ought to know,' said Marcellin, 'that in Lingala Bolo means vagina.'

I laughed.

'So why is that funny?' he said, rounding on me.

'I'm sorry,' I said, shocked at the real venom in his voice. The happy pace of my walk involuntarily changed to a shuffle. 'I thought you meant that Old Bobé was making a fool of me.'

'Oh no you didn't,' snapped Marcellin, slowing his stride to match mine, 'that's not why you laughed. Why the hell should Old Bobé want to make a fool of you? Didn't you see how tired it made him? *It's dangerous for him to talk like that.* Didn't you see how afraid he was? And then you laugh. How dare you laugh at Old Bobé!

'And anyway,' he shouted, kicking a lump of mud off the path, 'it all makes just as much sense as your white man's superstitions! What about the fetish you all wear round your neck? Your little crosses? What about those beads you all finger in your pockets and mumble spells over? Eh? And what about your unspeakable rites? What about your cannibal symbols? Tell me – do you or do you not eat and drink the body and blood of the big white Chief of your tribe once every seven days just as if it's a proper and reasonable thing to do? Oh no – you've no right to laugh at us, at Old Bobé, at Africans. No right at all.'

'I apologize. And anyway, I've told you, I'm not a Christian. I don't believe it. I don't wear a crucifix and I've never said a rosary in my life.'

'Said a rosary!' mimicked Marcellin with a yap of laughter himself. 'You have your little words to disguise it all, don't you? For us you say it's a fetish or a ju-ju or a gris-gris – but for you, oh yes, it's very dignified, it's quite different. It's a *rosary*, is it? It's a *crucifix*. So that's all right, is it? That makes everything okay?'

'I've told you. I don't believe it.'

'Believe it or not, my friend – it's in your head. I've been thinking about it, I've been thinking about it ever since that night with Dokou. You tell me it's normal. You call it a part of your culture and you think you're perfectly reasonable. You think you're a people of reason and science, that the daylight belongs to the white man and the night to the African. And I agree, you make motorcars and outboards and aeroplanes, and we don't. But what about your three gods in one, your big holy ghost that can go anywhere, your thousands of spirits with wings and with lights shining straight out of their heads? What about your evil animal with feet like a goat and a long tail that divides into two at the end? Tell me, why sneer at the African? How is all that superior to Bolo? What's scientific about that? And what about your other god who became a man and let himself be stuck on a piece of wood and speared so that he could save you all – what could it possibly mean? Where's the sense in it?'

'There is no sense in it. It's a matter of faith. Faith means saying goodbye to reason and science, that's what faith is. When you get faith you throw the switches, you blow a gasket, you deliberately go soft in the head. It's more comfortable that way.'

Marcellin ignored me.

'No wonder we were frightened of the white man when he came here with his guns and killed us, and talked about eating his god all day long. No wonder we thought you were cannibals. And there's another thing – your god who never had a woman. Look – no one could be blacker than me' – he shone the torch on his arm – 'I'm the blackest African I know – and I have the strongest need for sex of anyone I know. It's genetic, it's in the skin. I think about it all the time. All the time. If I don't have a woman every night I get ill. I'm ill now. You should pay me double for making me risk my life for you in these forests with these people. And then you should pay me double again for making me walk all day and then sleep in a tent all alone without a woman at night. And for months on end! You white men – we don't know how you breed. You have a god born without any sex! And then he never had a woman! And what about the god's mother – in those fetish statues you have everywhere – a woman who'd never had a man, with that idiot smile on her face and a baby in her arms? If that's not just plain silly, if that's not stupid, I don't know what is.'

A fierce drumming began suddenly, fully fledged, from the far end of the village.

Marcellin was silent. Then: 'Love your neighbour as yourself,' he said, his torch-beam waving wildly off the path and into the cactus hedges to either side of us.

'Love your neighbour as yourself! What hypocrites you are!' His voice rose to its highest pitch, a falsetto shriek of indignation, of real temper. The dog turned and bolted.

'Love your neighbour! And you come here with guns and break up our families and sell us into slavery, husbands and wives and little children. It made no odds to you! You white men burned all the Jews, just in a year or two, a mere six million. You say that was a great crime, and so it was, but what about us? What about our holocaust? From the Congo alone you sold thirteen million of us into slavery. What about that? It went on for centuries. For centuries no man knew if he'd live to see his children grow up, to see his sons learn to hunt, to make new gardens with his sons. Tell me, will you – what had we done to deserve it? You white men say sorcery's a great evil,

336

and so it may be, but tell me sometime – what kind of god let you torture us like that?'

We entered the hut in silence. Doubla and Vicky had gone; the candles had guttered out on the table; there was nothing left in the mess-tins or the bucket of palm-wine; cigarette butts were strewn all over the mud floor. Nzé and Manou had hung tarpaulins flat across the doorways of the two small bedrooms.

'I can't stand it here!' said Marcellin, spinning round where he stood, flinging himself right round on his own axis, a movement I had not seen him make before. 'I am angry with you and your kind. I'm going to sleep at Bobé's hut.' And he picked up his pack and went.

'Psst!' said Nzé, from behind his curtain. 'Has he gone?'

'Yes, he has. He's not happy with me.'

'Well, I'm *very* happy with you,' came the whisper. 'That was the best 500 francs you ever spent on me.'

'How's that?'

'Put your head round the new bedroom door, Uncle. Just take a look at this. But don't fall over or make a noise or anything. Please, Uncle, try and control yourself.'

I put my head round the curtain.

'Isn't she . . . oomph?' said Nzé, full of pride, putting the tips of his fingers to his lips, kissing them, beaming, sitting on the bed naked, his towel over his genitals. 'I tell you, Uncle, she's as juicy as a ripe papaya. *She's better than a whole bottle of whisky.*'

The girl was asleep on the bed beneath a tarpaulin, her head on a pillow of Nzé's tee-shirts, her yellow and green wraparound discarded on the floor.

'There's no end of her,' he said, gently drawing back the tarpaulin. 'Just look at that!'

She lay on her right side, her breasts flopped forward, her left arm across her nipples, her hand dangling over the edge of the bed. The light of the candle on a log by the wall gave a sheen to the film of sweat on her young and flawless skin; her face was the most peaceful I had seen, it seemed, in many years.

'I had her first in the school,' said Nzé, the triumph of it swivelling his eyeballs like a chameleon's. 'We had to go there because of Vicky and Doubla. She got so excited! "Calm yourself!" I had to say. "Calm yourself!"'

'Then what?'

'I brought her back here and I had her on the bed. And I'll tell you something – she says I'm the best! It's the gift my grandfather gave me!

She's exhausted. I *am* the best. I tire them all out. There's nothing like it, Uncle.'

'I'm sure there isn't.'

'I'm going to wake her up in a minute. We're going to the dance. And then I'll have her again! Are you coming, Uncle? Are you coming to the dance?'

'No, I'm not. Not tonight. Today's gone on for several months. I'm going for a swim, and then I'm going to bed.'

'Well, don't disturb Manou, Uncle, with your crashing about and your searching for things in that big pack of yours. Don't disturb him. They've been talking. Talking! It takes him a long time to get his courage up. He's not like me. Not a bit. He's as nervous as a thief in there!'

I went to the back room, cast the torchlight over the bug-ridden bed, dug about in my bergen, trying not to rustle the slimy mass of waterproof plastic bags too badly, found my mould-covered towel and the remains of a bar of soap, and walked down to the river by the nearest path.

Frogs quacked like mallard all along the bank. I found the washing place, by the usual upturned hull of a broken dugout, took off my boots, placed my glasses gently in the left boot and my head-torch in the right, stripped, laid my clothes on top of the boots and waded in; the mud squirmed up to my ankles with every step, and then the water round my genitals pricked like a gorse-bush. I decided I was alarmed, retrieved my glasses, strapped on the head-torch and walked back to investigate.

Small catfish, about six inches long, were asleep near the surface, floating straight out in the pool of calm water formed by the wooden hull, their barbels whiskering out stiff from their lips, their gills and dorsal and pectoral fins presumably equipped with spines. Leaving them in peace, I replaced the torch and glasses and washed off the smell of the day's fear a few yards downriver. To see a dinosaur suddenly seemed such a sensible, Western achievement; how scientific it would be to record a small sauropod from the Cretaceous: whereas to catch a glimpse of two long arms up in the lianas, to meet the gaze of Yombé, the unknown ape of Boha – that might be startling; you might well register mild surprise just before your brain burst open, the white tubes of your eye-sockets turned inside-out, and your eyeballs rose up over the forest in perfect twin parabolas to drop softly down through the palm-leaves of the sorcerer's hut and into his open fetish bag.

But there must be *something* odd about the lake, I thought, as I smeared myself with mould from the towel, dressed, and walked slowly back to the hut, in the warm night, the drumming reaching me as a soft reverberation through the river water in my ears. Mackal really thought it was home to a dinosaur, partly because he supposed this to be the oldest undisturbed jungle on earth, and partly because he was sure the dinosaur was the subject of pygmy reports – and pygmy reports (unless they are designed to frighten the Bantu) are reliable. It was persistent Bambuti pygmy descriptions, after all, that set the English colonial officer and naturalist Sir Harry Johnston on to the search that became the greatest triumph of his career, the eventual discovery of the forest giraffe, the okapi (or rather of two strips of its skin which pygmies were wearing as belts). Johnston, like Mackal, was obsessed with finding an extinct animal, and he decided that his strips of skin belonged to the ancestor of the horse, *Hipparion*: he sent them to P. L. Sclater, the Secretary of the Zoological Society of London, who in the Proceedings for 10 February 1901 obligingly named it *Equus (?) johnstoni*. But a Swedish officer working for the Congo Free State, Lieutenant Eriksson, then obtained two skulls and a complete skin – the animal was cloven-hoofed and its skull related it to the giraffe; and on 10 June 1901, Sir Ray Lankester placed it in a new genus which he called *Okapia*, after its pygmy name, okapi. Johnston, determined to be the discoverer of an extinct something, immediately renamed it *Helladotherium tigrinum* (well, there is a fossil giraffe named *Helladotherium*, but its skull and teeth are different from the living okapi – and although the okapi does have white stripes on its velvety reddish-brown hide around the fetlocks and foreknees and up on to its haunches they are not much like a tiger's. And anyway, no one took him seriously).

But as I now knew, the story of the Congo dinosaur had nothing whatever to do with the pygmies. Their country lay well to the north of Lake Télé. Here 'pygmy' was just the derogatory term for those Bantu who had fled to the forest when the French came and had taken too long to come out again – the men of Boha and Djéké knew that no self-respecting Bantu lived in the jungle: real Bantu built proper huts and big plantations near rivers; they lived in the sunlight; only pygmies and animals skulked in the perpetual twilight beneath the great trees. And I thought of the recent ruling of the Dictator of the Central African Republic, General André Kolingba: pygmies, he had decreed, are henceforth to be considered as people rather than animals.

Nzé and his girl had gone to the dance or the school and Manou and his shy love had disappeared too; I was alone in the hut. Too tired to take off my boots, I spread one tarpaulin on the planks, pulled the other one over me, and tried to sleep. It was no use. The voice of Léonard at Djéké echoed in my head, telling us again to stay clear of the lake, not just because we might see Mokélé-mbembé but because we would certainly hear his cry, a long-drawn-out, high-pitched, echoing cry, a sound which, once heard, would deprive you of your mental balance for ever.

So thinking, I remembered the bed-bugs, and, annoyed that I seemed to have lost my balance already, I felt for the torch, got up, took the tarpaulins off the bed and laid them down on the mud floor. Resettled in the darkness, a stray remark of C. D. Darlington's in *The Evolution of Man and Society* rose out of my unconscious like a fish on a line: 'Africa, the oldest home of man, is the home of the most dangerous of man's diseases.' And he was only thinking of polio, diphtheria, encephalitis I and II, leprosy, yellow fever, pneumonia, bilharzia, sleeping sickness, gonorrhoea and malaria. Which put me in mind of the Congo floor maggot.

Now, the Tumbu fly is *quite* closely adapted to man's habits. The female lays her eggs in sandy soil contaminated with urine or excreta, and sometimes on clothes hung up to dry and on bedclothes spread to air: when the tiny larvae hatch out they burrow into the skin and produce boil-like swellings with a small, dark, moist opening near the top, their air-hole; they especially like babies, and, in particular, the necks of babies. But they also go for rats, cats, dogs and monkeys. Its nearest relative, the Congo floor maggot, on the other hand, is a loyal maggot, attentive only to ourselves. The female fly (very like a bluebottle, but brown) lays her eggs in the dust on hut floors; by day the larvae lurk in cracks in the mud – and at night they wriggle out and suck your blood.

As far as I knew, Congo floor maggots carried no disease; they were blameless as leeches. But what, I thought, sitting up, switching on the torch and inspecting my bare arms for dangling white larvae clamped in between the hairs – what if no one had bothered to look?

You're a fraud, I told myself, you've been suppressing your fear all day, that's why you're going mad. If you'd done the sensible thing when you first saw that giant with the knife who wanted to kill Marcellin – if you'd just sat down on the path and howled, you'd be sleeping like a bushpig. So if, I saw myself writing on the blackboard in the school, if there is a small chance that HIV can be spread in the malaria parasite (because in a study of 520 hospital patients in Zaïre the incidence of HIV antibody correlated strongly with antibody against *Plasmodium falciparum*), and if there is a very big chance that it is carried by bed-bugs (which are known to transmit hepatitis B), what 100 per cent hunk of a chance is there that it is fairly stuffed inside a Congo floor maggot?

'In any case,' I said aloud, as I got up and spread the tarpaulins back on the bed again, 'I'd rather be bitten by a bug than sucked by a maggot. And there's nothing mad about that. In fact it's perfectly normal.' (I took off my boots.) 'No sane man wants a maggot in his bed. But bugs – there's nothing you can do about it.'

So I lay on the planks and tried to think of something peaceful: of the little bedroom in the vicarage of childhood; of the blackbird which used to perch each summer evening on the roof of the bicycle shed below my window and sing me to sleep; of the woodpigeons in the conker tree; but it didn't work. Nothing held for long enough; my brain was too disturbed to be directed in its dreams; my imagination obstinately filled with thoughts of Bruce Chatwin, the only person I knew who had died of AIDS.

'Redders!' would come a familiar voice down the phone far too early in the morning. 'Not even Bunin' (for example) 'was interesting yesterday. I can't stand it a moment longer.'

'I'm sick of writing. I'm tired! tired! tired!' (said with enough energy to crack your eardrum). 'And when a man is sick of writing he must walk.' (Oh God.) 'I'm coming to get you.' (Panic.) 'What are you doing?'

'I'm in bed.'

'Up you get! Two glasses of green tea. See you in half-an-hour.'

I would begin wondering who or what Bunin was: with Bruce you could never be sure. The new Stravinsky from Albania? The nickname of the last slave in Central Mali? A lighthouse-keeper from Patagonia? Scroll 238B from a cave in the Negev? Or just the *émigré* King of Tomsk who'd dropped in for tea? Still vaguely wondering, I lurched out of the house.

A white 2CV puttered into the drive. There was a sailboard strapped to the roof. Chatwin got out, his wife Elizabeth's two dogs wagging about his feet.

'Come on! It's almost dawn! I'm taking these brutes to a hill-farm in Wales. We'll look at the tree of life on the south door of St Mary and St David at Kilpeck; we'll deliver the dogs; we'll call in on my old friend Lady Betjeman; and then I'll walk you over the Black Hill.'

'So what's the sailboard for?' I said, suspicious.

'Oh, that. That's my new hobby. You bring your car and make your own way back tonight, and I'll go sailing in the Bristol Channel in the morning.'

And you'll probably be in Dublin for supper, I thought.

Beneath the first ridge of the Black Mountains we parked by a track and got out our boots: mine, black wellingtons; his, a pair of such fine leather that Hermes would have done a swap. I put on my bergen (with nothing in it but a loaf of bread and two bottles of wine) and he put on his small haversack of dark maroon calfskin (with nothing in it but a Montblanc pen, a black, oilcloth-bound, *vrai moleskin* notebook, a copy of Aylmer Maude's translation of *War and Peace*, Strindberg's *By the Open Sea* and the most elegant pair of binoculars that I had ever seen).

'Werner Herzog gave them to me,' said Bruce, his eyes blue and bright and eager. 'He wants to film *The Viceroy of Ouidah*. And Jean-Louis Barrault had this pack designed just for me. But you *could* get some decent boots,

341

Redders. The Canadian Moccasin Company. Just say you're a friend of mine.'

He took off up the hill with a strong, loping stride through the heather and the whinberries, a real nomad's stride. In a few minutes I fell behind, trying not to pant like an engine shed.

'The twins I wrote about lived there,' he said, turning without slackening his pace and pointing to a long slate-roofed farmhouse set back from the road in the diminishing valley below us.

'And . . . that's . . . where!!!' His words whipped past me, split up and lost to sense in the wind. The speed of ascent was effort enough, replying to the wild and ceaseless monologue an impossibility – which was just as well, because it was far too late in our friendship to admit that, much as I admired *In Patagonia*, what with one siesta and another I had just not quite read *On the Black Hill*.

'There's a hippy camp down there,' he called, nodding north-west at the clouds pulling their dark fringe of falling rain towards us. He shouted with laughter. 'All the locals are terrified of them. They think they'll be strangled in their beds! When I was staying with the King of Afghanistan he had an old English colonel about the court. "Your Royal Highness," said the colonel, "you must let me remove all the hips from your country. You must let me put all the hips in trucks and take them to the border."'

Down on the Llanthony road, we walked through the hail, and Bruce talked about a female albatross that had wandered northwards to the wrong hemisphere and built a nest in Shetland, waiting for the mate that never came, and about the train he caught from King's Cross on his way to see her – and how the only other passenger in his sleeper compartment was a Tierra del Fuegian ('on his way to the North Sea oil-rigs – they're the only men who can throw a boat's painter through a ring on a buoy') whose settlement Bruce had visited on the journey that became *In Patagonia*.

He talked about his love for the herdspeople of the Sudan; about smuggling Roman coins out of Turkey; about the design of a prehistoric wheel which linked the Irish to an ethnic sub-group in the Caucasus (I think); and about his real dream – the Russian novel he would write one day.

There was the noise of an engine shaking itself to bits, three violent backfires, and a rust-holed van lurched up the road towards us. I jumped onto the bank at the base of the hedge; but Bruce, engrossed, was still walking in the road. Surprisingly slowly, it seemed, the van nudged the Jean-Louis Barrault haversack. Equally slowly, Bruce, still talking ('Just tell the story straight as Tolstoy. No tricks!'), turned a full somersault in the air. 'No tricks!' he said, as he windmilled into the ditch.

'You stupid bastards!' he shouted, getting to his feet. 'That was unnecessary.'

A young boy, his hair in a pony-tail, jumped down from the cab. 'Sorry, Squire,' he said. 'I'm sorry. Honest. What more can I say? It's like this – my wheels hasn't got no brakes.'

'I say,' said Bruce. 'How exciting. Can we have a lift!'

Just back from months in the jungle between the Orinoco and the Amazon, I thought I'd celebrate with warm scallops in a London restaurant and got a six-month dose of hepatitis A. Half-asleep, eyes shut in the isolation wing of the Churchill Hospital in Oxford, I heard a familiar voice.

'Shush,' it said. 'Don't tell anyone. I'm not here.'

I opened one eye. So it was true. Hepatitis A induced delirium. You saw visions on it.

'Shush, I'm in France. Bill Buford's after me. I'm meant to be writing a piece for *Granta*. I'm not here. But with you here too I might just as well phone Reuters and be done with it.

'I've brought you some liver pills. They're from Elizabeth's guru in India. I'm having Aboriginal warts removed from my face. I'm in the room next door. Look – I'll do the same for you if you die first. Will you be my literary executor?'

'I'll do anything you say. I want to go to sleep.'

'You know – there's something else I want you to know. When I first came in here they told me I was mortally ill. They said I had a fungus of the bone-marrow which I must have picked up in a cave in China. It's exclusive! It's so rare that I'm only the tenth recorded case in the medical literature! And they also let me know why I got it, Redders – I got it because I have AIDS. They told me I had six months or a year to live. So I thought, right, Bruce is a dog's name and I'm not going to stand for this. I can't get on with my big nomad book as it is – I can't see how I can pull material out of my notebooks and onto the page; and I'm not going to waste away and go feeble in the head and defecate all over the place.

'So I went to Geneva – there's a place in the Alps that haunts me, a ravishing cliff near Jungfrau – and I wanted to jump off it. Or, failing that, I thought I'd go to Niger and simply take off my clothes, put on my loincloth, walk out into the desert and let the sun bleach me away.

'But the bone-marrow got me first. I fainted on the pavement; someone took me to hospital in a taxi; and Elizabeth came and rescued me and brought me back here. I was so weak I couldn't whisper. I came in on a Friday and they thought I'd be dead by Monday. Then Juel-Jensen put me on his anti-fungal drip and Elizabeth nursed me night and day and I pulled through: I owe it all to them.

'I've almost finished my big book – there's a terrible old character with a twisted gut called Hanlon – and now I have a whole novel growing in the notebooks, too. I can see almost all of it. It's set in Prague and I shall call it *Utz* – *Utz!* Anyway, one day you must tell people, Redders, but not now. It's a fable. It's all there, ready-made. And the moral is simple: never kill yourself. Not under any circumstances. Not even when you're told you have AIDS.'

I last saw Bruce in Elizabeth's light-filled house which looks south down an Oxfordshire valley; he was in his second bedroom, books on the counterpane, the manuscript of a young novelist he had befriended and encouraged stacked in a box by the bed, cassettes of young musicians he had supported piled on the bedside table, his newly bought Russian icons on the walls.

Though he was very weak and so thin you could see the white bones in his arms, his telephone was still plugged into its socket. He was making and receiving calls, talking to his friends all over the world.

'Just for now, Redders, I can't hold a pen. It would be ridiculous to start yet, and I hate dictation. But the moment I'm better I'll begin that Russian novel. It's going to work. I can see almost all of it. No tricks!'

His grin gave out in a burst of coughing. As I left, the sun bright on the walls, I took his hands in both of mine. A thought struck him, and he gave a snort of laughter.

'Redders! Your hands – they're so soft I don't believe you ever go anywhere. You just lie in bed and make it all up.'

They were his last words to me. And quite right too, I thought. I must read Bunin. And get a sailboard.

But it won't be the same.

A loud clank up under the corrugated-iron roof brought me back to full consciousness. With disbelief I remembered exactly where I was – and then someone screamed outside. Something hit the bed and scratched against my arm. Jesus, I thought, sliding sideways and grabbing the torch from the top of the bergen. *It's a spear through the shutter.* And I snapped on the light.

From the head of the bed, an enormous, fluffy, white-bellied, grey-backed rat looked at me, frozen, his eyes as wide as mine, his cheeks puffed out, his ears forward, shaped like spoons, his tail white at the end and much too long. We stared at each other, both of us hyper-ventilating; the fur over his rib-cage pumped in and out; my heart twitched like a dislodged ball of maggots in my chest.

'It's okay,' I said, shaking. 'You're a rat.'

The rat, appalled by such obviousness in the middle of the night, jumped at the wall, scrabbled, fell off again, and scuttered out of the door.

'He's so clean,' I said; and then, 'You must look him up'; and then, 'You must stop talking to yourself.'

I got Haltenorth and Diller out of my bergen: there he sat, on plate 26, still startled, but with one paw up like a boxer: the Giant Gambian rat.

In Africa apparently, it was not just dinosaurs that had strange habits; rats did odd things, too, even for rats. The Giant Gambian rat, for instance, liked to defecate when upside-down.

His habitat, according to Haltenorth and Diller, is 'woodland to dry savanna, in mountains to 3500m upwards, frequently in settlements and buildings'; and his home range consists of 'self-excavated or adopted holes in ground or in termite mounds, many-chambered and with several entrances, under fallen or in hollow trees, in rock crevices, buildings, etc., as central homes. From their tracks to feeding places, ♂ marks tracks with drops of urine, deposits faecal pellets in handstand, and rubs the upturned buttocks on adjoining objects as marking.'

My Giant Gambian rat had obviously miscalculated his handstand on top of the bedroom wall, banged his upturned buttocks on the corrugated-iron roof and taken a header on to the bed. Unless, of course, his face looked so puffed out because he was already thinking of the 'subsidiary use of cheek pouches to collect unpalatable objects (nails, coins, bottle tops, ballpoint pens, etc.) for storing in a chamber below ground'.

I was just restraining myself from checking the ballpoint pens in my bergen when someone screamed again, from the same place, maybe a hundred yards out from the window – Vicky's hut. It was Vicky's wife, enduring her late-night correction. So, by association, I looked up the Dwarf bushbaby.

She stared out at me from plate 48, as did the angwantibo, bigger, heavier, more thickly furred, with smaller ears and no tail. Lines from a poem by James Fenton, the companion of my Borneo journey, ran through my mind:

> Here come the capybaras on their bikes.
> They swerve into the friendly, leafy square
> Knocking the angwantibos off their trikes,
> Giving the age-old coypus a bad scare.
> They specialize in nasty, lightning strikes.
> They leave the banks and grocers' shops quite bare
> Then swagger through the bardoors for a shot
> Of anything the barman hasn't got.

And in their own way, parts of the scientific description of the real angwantibo were just as pleasing: 'Penis with bone, prepuce without horny spines, with papillae only, scrotum hairy as far as the small glandular horny surface at base. Clitoris long and thick, root-thickened and turnip-shaped; in corner of vulva a small horny plate holding a scent gland.'

The angwantibo is a relative of our ancestors, so why had we lost our penis bone? Was Richard Dawkins right, that it was as a result of so-called honest signalling, a response to selection pressure from females, the result of a woman's need to find the best possible father for her offspring? In the same way that the Ribbon-tail bird of paradise (for instance) displays his absurdly long white tail (a real handicap in normal life) to show the girls (perhaps) that he is not suffering from diarrhoea and so is free of parasites, a man who can pump up his penis with blood demonstrates that he is well fed, free of stress and disease and only mildly kinky. Whereas any old male can wave a bone about. I thought it was an ingenious, a thoroughly pleasing idea – until I also thought what a disadvantage it would be to have a long white tail round here, given the speed with which manioc went through the system, and that if I was to do a spot of honest signalling myself right then there would be no doubt about the message: abject fear.

It was all too much at last. I fell asleep.

33

I woke well after dawn, covered in small red bites. I sorted the CFA for the Chief and the Vice-President and then went for a swim to calm the all-over itch; when I returned Manou was up, moving at twice his normal speed, his eyes bright.

'She likes me,' he said.

'Of course she does. She knows how strong you are, how fast you're going to walk in the forest.'

'It wasn't like that,' said Manou with a proud little smile. 'She said she loved my body. And my hat.'

Nzé emerged from behind his curtain; he held briefly to the edge of the table, as though he had just suffered a mild blow to the back of the head. 'Mine's gone to her mother,' he mumbled, stuffing fou-fou from the common bowl into his mouth with one hand and rubbing a finger across his gummy eyelids with the other. 'She's gone to sleep at her mother's house. She kept screaming, Uncle. Every time. She begged me to stop. She said, "Nzé, that was the best night of my life," and I said, "Yes, you big bag of happiness, for me – that was the best time I've ever had at a school desk."'

Marcellin, looking grim, arrived with Doubla, Vicky, the two brothers Nicolas and Jean Poulain and the Vice-President. 'What are you doing?' he shouted at Manou and Nzé. 'Why aren't you ready? Why aren't the loads ready outside the hut? The Chief's waiting! The bearers are here!'

We pushed everything into the sacks and bergens and lined them up against the hut wall. Vicky, Doubla and the brothers, I noticed, had all come barefoot. 'Shoes are precious here,' said Marcellin. 'No one wears them in the forest.' Vicky swung the smallest pack onto his shoulders. 'Doubla, this is the heaviest – I swear to you,' he said, drawing his right index-finger across his throat, snapping his hand down to his side and clicking his finger. Doubla grinned, grabbed Vicky by the shoulder-straps, slid the bag off his back and harnessed him into one of the big bergens. I gave the Vice-President his money and the bearers half their wages in advance. Nzé picked up the gun, sloped it smartly on his shoulder like a good militiaman, and we followed the Vice-President up through the village to the royal compound.

The Chief was standing outside his hut, informally dressed, without his red paint and fetish-bag, wearing a frayed pair of brown cotton trousers and his new running-shoes, a spear in his right hand, his word-carrier in attendance to his left. Vicky arranged us in a line on the Chief's right. A crowd of children stood corralled by three spearmen against the dilapidated hut on the far side of the compound; the boy who had jammed the grasshopper into my nostrils pushed to the front and waved at me. I waved back. 'Don't do that,' hissed Marcellin.

The Chief made a half-turn to face the forest behind him, stood to attention with his spear held vertical, and shouted towards the trees. Vicky, Doubla and the two brothers bowed their heads. The Chief stopped, cupped his left hand to his ear and listened, his mouth open. A Tinker bird called, loud in the silence, as if someone deep in the forest was tapping a bottle with a knife. The Chief, apparently satisfied with whatever it was he had heard, turned back into line, relaxed, and nodded at his word-carrier. The old man lowered his spear at me, and, well versed in such matters by now, I put the money into his free hand. Walking back down the line, he gave the notes to the Chief (who stuffed them into his left trouser-pocket and disappeared back into his hut) and led us slowly off towards the forest. A line of spears leaned against the corner of the royal roof and each bearer, as he passed, took one in his right hand, holding it at an angle of 45 degrees in front of his body, the blade pointing at the ground to his left.

Opposite our hut, on the far side of the cleared space by a gap in the bushes, the old man held his own spear horizontal, blocking our way, and re-arranged us in a different order, more to his liking: Vicky in the lead with me behind him, followed by Marcellin, Doubla and the brothers, Manou and, last of all, Nzé.

'Nzé will fire two shots,' he said.

'That's crazy,' I said without thinking, 'that's a terrible waste of cartridges.'

'The Chief has agreed!' he shouted. 'The Chief has agreed to see and control everything that happens to you at the lake!' – he rotated the shaft of the spear in his hands, very fast, so that the blade sparked in the sunlight – 'You must now tell the spirits that you come with his blessing. You need his protection, my friend! You need his help more than you need your cartridges!'

Nzé fired into the air; the African grey parrots shrieked and swore some-where off to our right; he reloaded and fired again. We were off at last.

We passed a scrappy crop of manioc to our right, the path wound through the thick bushes and saplings of low secondary growth on an abandoned plantation, and then we were in the forest proper. We were on the move again, beneath the familiar trees, away from the insistent press of village life: every time we entered the jungle, I thought, it seemed like an escape; whereas Marcellin, I knew, felt it very differently – for him, as he wrote and underlined in his diary which I was secretly reading whenever I got the chance, '*Setting out into the forest is like a soldier going to war, the return is never certain.*'

What was he so afraid of – a leopard? disease? snakebite? breaking a leg? Or was it more interesting than that, I wondered – was there, underneath all that Cuban Marxist education in Havana, all that French pharmacy and biology at Montpellier, was there just a trace of suppressed terror? Did he really half-share his grandfather's belief in the power of fetish? Was he so tense, even now that we were supposedly safe from the avenging men of Boha, simply because he thought this is a particularly malign stretch of forest, haunted by spirit animals, by Yombé? Or was he even, perhaps, plagued by an obsessive thought or two about someone like the Sasabonsum who stars in Mary Kingsley's *West African Studies* (1899):

> You see what we object to in this spirit is that one side of him is rotting and putrefying, the other sound and healthy, and it all depends on which side of him you touch whether you see the dawn again or no. Such being the case, and African bush paths being narrow, this spirit helps to make evening walks unpopular . . .

Or maybe, I thought (not quite so excited by the possibility), Marcellin just suspects that Doubla, Vicky and the brothers have secret instructions to murder us in the forest.

Vicky led the way and I followed, trying not to be mesmerized by the sight of his fifteen-inch dagger in its wooden scabbard, tied to his left-hand side with string. He was loose-limbed in his torn camouflage fatigues, the bergen shoving at his back; with his machete in his right hand he now held his twelve-foot spear in his left, blade-down along the narrow path, and the shaft, passing under his arm, swung wildly out behind him, snagged on lianas, thwacked across sapling-stems, and threatened to flick out an eye every time I came too close.

I slipped my left-hand water-bottle from its holder on my belt, took a swig, replaced it, and tried to match Vicky's stride: his bare feet slapped easily over the ground with fast, small steps.

The sweat began to ooze down my face from the band under my hat, and in the humid, unmoving air, I fell into a trance.

It was only really possible to be alone in Africa, it occurred to me, to be free of shouted conversation, when walking like this, or when awake on a tarpaulin in the middle of the night – anyone on their own was in danger, loneliness led to madness, an isolated man was an easy prey for wandering spirits, friends must keep together always, and talk. But, I thought disjointedly, my eyes on the path, fetish did have one theoretical advantage when you tried to fit its other world onto the world you knew, and perhaps that was why Christianity and Islam had made so little progress in all the villages we had visited upriver in the interior – Christianity had no answer to the simplest of questions: why did a god who loved everyone and had made everything and could do anything and was everywhere at once, why did he let your child die? And, come to that, did there really have to be 2000 different diseases of the skin? If you believed in fetish, yes, there did; suffering was no surprise; children would always die; because the gods, such as they are, love no one but themselves: the best you can do in life is simply to try and protect yourself, to give them things, to buy them off, to avoid them whenever possible. They only care about you when you are behind with your offerings; and then like Tando, for instance, the high god of Ashantee, they come in storms and famines to punish whole villages, or, when more precision is needed (according to Mary Kingsley, whose report did not seem in the least outdated), they visit you in the shape of a small and helpless boy, a desolate orphan crying for help, who, when taken in and comforted, kills off his adoptive family with a wasting disease.

So I decided to stop that line of thought too, and look about: some of the smaller trees had prop-roots; there were very few bushes and herbs in the understorey; and even the broad-leaved grasses were sparse. We were well on our way towards swamp-jungle.

Vicky suddenly stopped, leaned his spear against a sapling, eased himself out of the bergen and bent down to pick up yellow, cooking-apple-sized fruits which were scattered over the path and for twenty yards around, fruits which my eyes had been too sweat-filled to notice.

'Gorillas and chimpanzees like them,' he said, grinning at me, a super-signal of white teeth across his wide, brown, sweaty, happy face. 'You try one.'

He took his machete, cut the top off the fruit like an egg, gave it to me, and selected another for himself; under the wrinkled yellow skin a cup of orange flesh enclosed a ball of white fluff. Vicky scooped it out, discarding a cluster of big brown seeds, and I copied him, gathering a mouthful of sweetish floss.

'Mokélé-mbembé,' said Vicky mysteriously, and winked.

'Malombo,' said Marcellin, coming up behind me. The others arrived and everyone began to eat.

'From now on, Nzé,' said Marcellin, 'you walk at my back, with the gun.'

Malombo, I thought – according to Mackal this is the main food plant of Mokélé-mbembé: and I half-expected a brown, skin-flappy sauropod head on its giraffe-length neck to come slithering over my shoulder and muzzle up my fruit. (Would its lips be cold, I wondered, or were the dinosaurs really warm-blooded?) Or at the very least we might hear the high-pitched, ululating cry that would drive us all berserk. But at that moment, instead, there came the usual sound of pigs grunting and magpies chattering, the alarm call of the Greater white-nosed monkey: they were in the trees right over us, a troop of ten or so, judging by the various rustlings in the leaves, and one old male, in plain view, appeared to be eating the malombo fruit still on its vine high above our heads.

Doubla lunged forward to take the gun from Nzé, grabbing it by the stock; Nzé held on to the barrel with both hands; the Great white-nosed monkey turned smartly round on his branch, spread his immensely long black tail behind him, jumped into the next tree, and disappeared.

'That's right, Nzé,' said Marcellin, 'you hang on to the gun.'

'But he's cross-eyed,' said Doubla, aggrieved. 'Anyone can see that – he couldn't shoot a monkey if you tied it to a stake!'

'You wait,' said Nzé, without conviction.

The forest grew wetter, prop-rooted trees more common, and we heard the alarm-calls of several more troops of Greater white-nosed monkeys, but the men of Boha shouted gossip to each other in Bomitaba, and Nzé shouted tales of Dongou in Lingala to Marcellin and to Manou (who was too busy conserving his strength to say anything at all). So we saw little but the occasional pile of fibrous grey gorilla droppings beside the path, usually on our way through clumps of Wild ginger or stands of Giant phrynium. And we stopped to examine a fresh line of elongated rat-like faeces which Doubla said were mongoose turds – so I got Haltenorth and Diller's *Mammals of Africa* from the side-pocket of Vicky's bergen, and Doubla, out of all the busy snouts and trotting feet and thick coats and long furry tails of the twenty-seven mongooses illustrated on plates 33 to 37, chose the Marsh mongoose. It was plainly an emotional mongoose ('VOICE: purrs when content; in threat or defence growls, nasal snorting and spitting, in excitement a staccato rising bark, with fluffing up of fur expressing rage'), but the details of its breeding and development were not known. And (apart from the lack of a light-yellow rim to its ears) it looked exactly like the Long-nosed mongoose, also reported from the northern Congo swamp-forest – a mongoose whose 'Number of teats, glands and penis bone' were still undescribed; and of whom 'Up to now only thirty specimens known ... HABITAT: lives entirely in rain-forests. No details of habits.'

'So why not this one?' I said, getting excited. 'Look – *only thirty specimens known.*'

'Why not?' said Doubla, shrugging his shoulders. 'If that's what you want.'

'But Redmond,' said Marcellin, bristling, 'I am a scientist and I tell you – it's not likely, is it? *All we have here is a piece of shit!*'

Okay, I just stopped myself saying, as I put the book back in its pocket and we resumed our march, so as far as your Mokélé-mbembé is concerned you don't even have a piece of shit, do you? And, come to that, I'll bet a decent dinosaur turd is something we could really feast our eyes on – in fact I'd settle for one-eighth of a dingleberry hanging off its bum. Or an absolutely genuine sauropod snot. Or a toenail-clipping. Or even a discarded fag-butt. If it's not too much to ask.

And thinking of the Greater white-nosed monkeys all around us, I reminded myself of the hard time that Mokélé-mbembé must have had in the last sixty-seven million years.

Mackal tells us:

One of the most exciting things about Africa is that, at least since the end of the Cretaceous period, 65 million years ago, the Congo basin has not undergone further climatic and geophysical changes . . . Animals evolve and survive because they adapt to changing environments. Conversely, when conditions remain stable for extended periods, some well-adapted species continue to survive and even flourish with very little physical and behavioural alteration. And that is what we find in the central West African jungle-swamps where, for example, crocodiles have persisted unchanged over the past 65 million years. What other ancient creatures might still lurk in this vast expanse of seemingly changeless, ageless, largely unexplored primeval forest?

But the Greater white-nosed monkey is a guenon, and chromosome analysis tells us that the guenons broke into separate species very recently: during the last main glaciation, at its maximum some 18,000 years ago, Africa was colder and much drier and the main forests shrank away to a few scattered areas along the equatorial coasts, and around Mount Cameroon far to the west of us and the Ruwenzori range far to the east. The ancestral guenon population retreated with the forest in its different directions and so was split up and isolated – long enough to evolve into some twenty-seven species (with white, yellow, red or blue noses; with long black moustaches or full white beards, or beards like goats; with orange ear-muffs, or yellow or green sideboards; and all bright as the plumage of birds). When the rains returned and the forests spread, the guenons met up again, now equipped with their different facial signals and with slightly different feeding habits and body sizes, so that on a good day in some areas of the jungle it is possible to come across six different species foraging in a single tree.

And the evolution of other animals in the forest is just as various – in ten million years over the basin as a whole savanna and jungle may have alternated at least twenty times. But the great rivers themselves, fed by rain on the far highland rims, never ceased to flow; not even when, much reduced, they made their way across the Kalahari sands that stretched up to meet the Sahara desert encroaching from the north.

And the great central swamp-forest had always been exactly where we were now. In fact if we go back to the beginning, from Mokélé-mbembé's point of view, I thought, getting excited again, taking a sleepwalker's swig from my water-bottle and almost running into the back of Vicky's spear, then Mackal's case becomes even more convincing. The sauropods evolved 225 million years ago – and if our Mokélé-mbembé's ancestors were in Lake Télé or thereabouts for the next few million years they might have had the odd minor, nasty surprise over their breakfast malombo (except that the malombo had not yet itself evolved) as the sea came rolling in, once or twice. But we can picture them in the late Cretaceous, seventy-two million years ago, say, basking with their Loch Ness necks and little heads and humpbacks out of the water, surrounded by recognizable plants – oaks, hickories, magnolias, or, more likely round Lake Télé, swamp cypresses, giant sequoias and china firs – and by recognizable birds: gulls, ducks, waders and herons. There were snakes about, and frogs, and salamanders. And of course the place was open-jawed with freshwater crocodiles – although it was not all completely familiar: the gulls and ducks and waders and herons, for instance, must have squee-geed out a dropping or two every time the Quetzalcoatlus came over, a soaring dinosaur with the wingspan of a Spitfire.

But for Mokélé-mbembé life went peacefully by until about six million years ago, when the edges of the Congo basin were uplifted and the Congo river filled into a giant lake, a lake which lapped at its various shorelines (and produced those dazzling white sands) for five million years before that coastal river cut back into the rock, just below the present Stanley pool, and drained its waters down thirty-two rapids to the sea. And the relics of the vast lake were all about us: the swamp-forest round the confluence of the Oubangui and the Congo rivers; the shallow lakes, Tumba and Maindombe, directly to the south; and, perhaps, Lake Télé itself, just one day's walk away.

It was bad luck, though, I thought (at once losing my inner glow, realizing that I was tired and sweat-soaked and that the tsetse-bite ulcers on my feet and ankles were becoming inflamed again) – it was slightly disappointing to be arriving just too late, sixty-seven million years too late. It was a pity about that big flash when a piece of rock six miles across smacked into the Yucatan

Peninsula, dusted the earth with its tell-tale signature of other-worldly iridium, blasted moisture and pulverized rock into the atmosphere, darkened the sky for months, froze everything, and then heated it up horribly (the particles settled but the moisture in the sky produced a greenhouse effect, stopping the sun's rays from escaping) and so killed the pterosaurs, the dinosaurs, and Mokélé-mbembé's grandparents (heat-stress, probably).

Still, I cheered myself up, in terms of grand extinctions the end of the dinosaurs was not the worst of the cosmic impact disasters – then only all land animals weighing more than twenty-five kilos were corpsed; and only major groups of marine animals such as the ammonites were terminated with extreme prejudice; and life only disappeared from the surface waters of the oceans for 10,000 years. On Raup and Sepkoski's scale of mass extinctions (a percentage of marine animal families lost in a sample of 3800 in the fossil record) the end of the dinosaurs measures a mere 11 per cent. Which is not at all impressive if you compare it with the damage done by another of God's little incoming bricks at the end of the Permian, for example, 245 million years ago, when 96 per cent of all species of marine animals were killed.

There was a swish of wings like a Quetzacoatlus overhead, a call like the braying of dinosaurs – and a pair of Black-casqued hornbills returned me to the present. As big as cormorants, black all over but for a white tip to the edge of their tails, they perched high up on a branch to our right and swayed their great bills from side to side, peering down at us; through the glasses I could see the dark-blue wattles at their throats which wobbled like clusters of Adam's apples, and their casques, which appeared as though a mollusc of some kind, a Pod shell, had unaccountably sprouted on top of their upper mandibles.

'Bushpig!' called Vicky, bending over tracks further up the path. 'Lots of them! With babies!' He rubbed his stomach. 'Nothing tastes better than bushpig. Not even gorilla!'

The prints looked suspiciously big to me. Maybe, I thought, they were made not by the Red river hog (with its reddish-brown coat, a white mane along its back, and white plumes of hair streaming from its ears) but by the Giant forest hog, which is much less exotic to look at, black all over, but nearly twice as big – and the Giant forest hog was not described until 1904, three years after the okapi (and in much the same way: Colonel Richard Meinertzhagen obtained a few pieces of skin and a skull in East Africa and sent them to the Zoological Society in London). But no, I decided, Mokélé-mbembé is getting to me, everything in this forest is becoming enchanted, turning into a rarity. Any more of this and I'll be squinting up at Yombé. I must stop this sliding into dream . . .

'They were here yesterday,' said Doubla, coming up behind us with Marcellin and inspecting the rootled mud. 'There's no point going after bushpig with that Nzé blabbering like a woman all day. Anyone can see he's not a hunter. Anyone can see he couldn't shoot a goat in his own garden.' He pulled my right-hand water-bottle from its pouch, unscrewed the cap, took a huge draught, put the cap back on with a vicious turn of the wrist, replaced the bottle, wiped his mouth with the back of his hand, and spat a piece of phlegm with tremendous force and accuracy on to the laces of Marcellin's left boot. 'Marcellin Agnagna,' he said, 'I'm warning you, if you don't let me have the gun there'll be trouble – the men of Boha, we don't like to go hungry.'

Three hours later we made camp in a tiny clearing off the path, beside the black patch of an old cooking-fire whose ashes glinted with mother-of-pearl, the undersides of Forest crocodile scales. Hundreds of bees and four species of butterfly were feeding round its edge, the butterflies flicking their wings open and shut, fluttering from place to place, jostling each other: Coppery swallowtails, their black wings bright with flashes of an iridescent green; a smaller species, perhaps the Acraea swallowtail, brown with roundels of scarlet; and a large butterfly, brown-black with bands and dashes of yellow, perhaps a nymphalid, which was so intent on sucking up its soup of mud and crocodile juice that for a moment I held its closed wings between my thumb and index-finger. Its abdomen looked painfully distended, and it flew off in a slow zig-zag, vanishing in the patches of shade, flashing back into life each time it crossed a scatter of sunlight, until it finally disappeared behind a buttress.

Vicky, Doubla and the brothers cut poles and cross-pieces from saplings and set up a shelter with our tarpaulins on one side of the clearing, Marcellin and I pitched our tents on the other, Nzé hacked up a rotten log with his machete, Manou arranged the pieces for his fresh cooking-fire – and the feeding bees transferred their attentions to us.

Doubla and Vicky sharpened two heavy saplings into stakes, enlarged the muddy pit of a water-hole, and filled the water-bottles and Nzé's cooking-pot. The light failed; the bees left; and the trunk of the tree beside my tent lit up with little points of green, a scatter of female glow-worms giving the green light to their big-eyed, night-flying mates.

Nzé slopped sour manioc stodge and two sardines apiece into our mess-tins, and we sat on our different tree-roots round the fire. 'Nicolas! Jean!' he said, with his lopsided grin. 'Your girls of Boha had never had such a lover! They weren't used to it! That's what they said! Look what they gave me!' And he thrust an arm into the food-sack and pulled out a small gourd of palm-wine, stoppered with leaves. 'Even you, Doubla, you can have some too – if you promise to treat Nzé like the Chief of Boha.'

'I'm not promising anything,' said Doubla, morose.

'Cheer up!' said Nzé, pouring the wine into our mugs. 'Let's have a last drink – because in a day or two, when we get to Lake Télé, anything may happen. I'll tell you what I'm going to do – I'm going to shoot myself a Mokélé-mbembé. In fact' – he paused a moment and inclined his head to one side, as if in deep deliberation – 'maybe I'll shoot more than one. And then – Nzé will be the hero of Dongou!'

'You shouldn't talk about it,' said Manou quietly. 'It's not good to make jokes like that. You don't know anything about it.'

'Oh yes I do,' said Nzé, 'and what's more I can make you laugh whenever I want to. I've got the power – so you can't help yourselves.'

He put his mug down, stood up, turned to me with a flourish, fixed me with his right eye, and tried to square his sloping shoulders. 'I'm teaching Redmond here to speak like a man,' he said. 'I'm teaching him Lingala.' He leaned forward and wagged a finger in my face, as though I were a child in the schoolroom. 'I-WANT-SOME-FOOD,' he shouted. 'MAKATA-ELLOKO-MOLOMOU.'

'Makata,' I repeated dutifully, 'elloko molomou.'

Everyone howled with laughter. Even Doubla laughed, a bark of horrible energy. Vicky slapped his thigh, spilt his wine, and stamped his feet in the mud.

'Nzé, that's enough,' said Marcellin. 'What if he said that in a village? Eh? What would people think of me?'

'That he's not okay in the head,' said Nzé, with a grotesque wink at me, 'and they'd be quite right.'

'Redmond,' said Marcellin, 'if you really want to learn, I'll teach you Lingala myself. You can believe me. You can trust me. "I want some food" is *Na liki ko liya biliya. Makata elloko molomou*, on the other hand' – he began to shout – 'is what Nzé tells all the girls in all the villages. It means MY-COCK-IS-BEAUTIFUL.'

I stretched out luxuriously on the tarpaulin in the safety of the little tent, moved my strained ankle-joints this way and that, wiggled my bruised toes, flexed the ache in my calf-muscles and, deciding that I must have lost at least three stone since coming to the Congo, that I was probably fitter than I'd ever been in my life, that I was unreasonably happy, I shifted my position slightly to avoid a couple of roots under my right shoulder-blade, and was immediately injected in the back with two small syringes of boiling water.

Cursing myself for forgetting the insect-check routine, I switched on the torch, found my glasses, and squashed the two bees in the bed with Haltenorth and Diller's *Mammals of Africa*. I killed another one crawling across the sweaty webbing of my bergen and three more resting, surfeited, on the socks in my left boot. I eased off my shirt and with my arms half-nelson'd behind me I picked about with the tweezers from my Swiss Army knife, hoping to remove the barbs; I rubbed Anthisan into the swellings, put a fresh dressing over the main ulcer on my right foot which the day's march had re-opened, and, still waiting for the immediate pain in my back to subside, I flicked the dead bees off the cover of Haltenorth and Diller and turned to their entry for the Giant forest hog.

You'll know if you hear one, I thought, because apart from grunting like any well-adjusted pig, they growl, so you'll be sure it's a leopard; and they keep in touch with a high-pitched bark, so you'll be certain it's a bushbuck; and the very loud call of fighting males swells to a full-blown trumpeting, so you'll assume it's a Forest elephant – and that call ends in a low grunting roar, so there'll be no doubt it's a brain-damaged lion lost in the jungle. But by then it might be too late, because Giant fighting hogs get so angry they 'foam at corner of eyes', and not even a leopard has the nerve to go near them.

A soft but persistent rain began to patter on the canvas. I turned off the precious batteries, lay on my side with two mould-rotted shirts under my hip and a pair of pants for a pillow, and half-dreamed about Darwin's cousin, Francis Galton, pioneer geneticist and statistician, father of the anti-cyclone and finger-printing, and anticipator of the Freudian unconscious. Using the technique he invented, the word-association test, he would take a dictionary, write out 100 words all beginning with 'a' on separate slips of paper, hide them under a book so that only their edges peeped out, draw one at random, start a stopwatch, and give himself four seconds to produce as many responses as he could. He found it a surprisingly difficult, repugnant process – and when he published his results in the journal *Brain*, in 1879, he excused himself from detailing his actual associations, from describing images that no gentleman could disclose, because they 'lay bare the foundation of a man's thought with curious distinctness, and exhibit his mental anatomy with more vividness and truth than he would probably care to publish to the world'. He concluded that perhaps

the strongest impression left by these experiments regards the multifariousness of the work done by the mind in a state of half-unconsciousness, and the valid reason they afford for believing in the existence of still deeper strata of mental operations, sunk wholly below

the level of consciousness, which may account for such mental pheno-
mena as cannot otherwise be explained.

This was a good ten years before Freud used free association to discover or
create or invent his version of the unconscious (Freud subscribed to *Brain*
and he refers to papers by the neurologist Hughlings Jackson in the January
and October issues of 1879, although perhaps he missed Galton's article and
he certainly never acknowledged his priority).

But it was one of Galton's outwardly most trivial experiments which filled
my mind as I fell asleep. Fascinated by the so-called worship of idols, he
decided to investigate its mechanism, so he cast around for an entirely
inappropriate image and settled on Mr Punch. He pinned a cover of the
journal up in his study and forced himself to make obeisance every morning,
detailing his fears, whispering his hopes, until the experiment began to work
so well he had to stop. Each time he entered his club and caught a glimpse
of Mr Punch lying in state on the periodicals table his mouth went dry, his
legs became unsteady, and a sweat broke out across his shoulders. Here in
the forest, I thought, there seemed no mystery at all about the power of Mr
Punch.

To avoid the bees we broke camp at four-thirty and left at first light. The
rain had stopped, but cloud hung over the trees and the forest seemed
subdued. We heard little but the odd troop of mangabeys chatter-grunting;
the sound (about once an hour) of an electric train passing overhead, a
swarm of bees late for some appointment; and the usual background calls:
a prolonged and mournful *hoo-hoo-hoo* of sometimes fifteen or more evenly
spaced notes, which seemed to echo slightly as if reaching us from far away,
a spirit cry, which I had now decided was no more than the voice of the
Grey woodpigeon, a large pigeon which lives high up in the canopy of the
tallest trees; and the same sounds, equally loud, but arranged in a descending
scale, a spectral laugh, whose notes started high and then lengthened as
they fell in pitch, which I thought probably really *were* just the calls of the
Red-billed dwarf hornbill (he likes his forest wet to swampy); and then
something which, for the sake of ornithological argument, was undoubtedly
the following spirit of one of our forebears, and made a noise like a tran-
quillized nightjar.

Around midday we came to a small clearing which had been clear-cut
with a machete; everyone stopped and slid off their loads.

'What's this?' I said.

'It's nothing,' said Marcellin. 'It's a piece of superstition. You stay here
with us.'

Doubla stuck his spear upright in the soft ground and the men of Boha moved off in single file beyond it, up a path to our right. I followed.

'Come back!' shouted Marcellin. 'It's forbidden! You're not allowed beyond the spear!'

I stuck close behind Nicholas at the back of the line, and we walked fast up the well-cut little path through thick bushes, secondary growth, for 500 yards or so, and stopped in a ring of cleared ground under a safou tree: it was the site of an old village.

Vicky, Doubla and the brothers arranged themselves in a semi-circle, the tree at its centre, and bowed their heads. I stood beside Vicky, took off my hat, bowed my head likewise, and held my hands behind my back.

Vicky stood to attention, his spear gripped vertically in front of him and, as if holding a conversation with people two or three huts away, he shouted into the bushes, the Umbrella trees, pausing occasionally as he listened to the short replies of the dead.

A thin trail of dark-red ants, I noticed, led out from the waxy leaves of the forest grasses to the left of my boots, crossed the clearing in a straight line, and disappeared under the grasses on the far side.

Vicky took me by the arm. 'We can go now,' he said, with a real smile. 'It is good you were here. We are pleased.'

'What did you say to them?'

'I told them that we have come here to take a white man to Lake Télé and I asked them to give us food and to look after us and to protect us from seeing something.'

'Mokélé-mbembé?'

Vicky laughed.

'No,' said Doubla, giving the air in front of him a rabbit-chop, as if to break the neck of the question. 'You might think it was a chimpanzee or a gorilla, this something, but it's dangerous. It is not good to name names.'

'Was this your old village?'

'My father's father played here,' said Vicky. 'He played with his brothers and his sisters. This is where he grew up and became a man. He was a great Chief.'

'So why did they move to the river?'

'They became frightened. They were frightened of strange things in this forest.' He slapped at a mosquito on his arm. 'There are strange sounds in this forest.'

'No more questions,' said Doubla. 'That's enough. We must not disturb them any longer.'

*

In the clearing Marcellin was sitting on one of the surface-roots of a forest giant, a root which, where he waited (disgruntled, legs apart, his hands on his knees), was as big as the trunk of a medium-sized tree, buried to half its width, and nosing itself down at a slight angle into the leaf-litter, until it finally disappeared underground a good twenty-five feet away. The stems of perhaps four different species of liana, one thick and single-stranded, the others spindly double-helixes, descended behind his head, lowered themselves gently to earth, and twisted away across the forest floor.

'Redmond!' he shouted in English as we appeared. 'I have been thinking. If we ever get out of here alive – if the Chief of Boha really has forgiven us – then you owe me a great deal.' He began to swing his feet, kicking the heels of his boots against the rounded side of the root. Little pieces of a pale-grey lichen fragmented off the bark at every blow. 'This is the longest expedition I have made in the forest.' (Kick.) 'And before this I made eight others.' (Kick.) 'I have conducted a survey of the Forest elephant populations in this country. I am well known in England and North America for my work on Mokélé-mbembé. I am a scientist. I do not belong here. I do not wish to spend any more of my time in the Congo. What future is there? And how about my daughter? How will she get an education? Eh? You, Redmond – you must pay your debt. You must get me a job in Oxford. I want to be an Oxford Professor.'

'But that's not how it works,' I said, taken aback. I suddenly felt for him; perhaps *this* was Marcellin's guiding secret, his sustaining fantasy. 'I don't have the slightest influence in Oxford,' I said. 'None at all. And even if I did – it's not as easy as you think. There aren't any jobs in England. There are two million people looking for jobs.'

'I don't believe you. I don't believe you, Redmond. You just say that – you say it because I am a black man. I understand you, my friend. Two million people! That's – that's more than the entire population of the Congo! I don't believe a word you say.'

He stopped drumming his heels on the side of the root; he stared out beyond me, over my head, at some point in the dark tangle of shade on the far side of the clearing; he looked wistful, and then sadder than I had ever seen him; his shoulders seemed to collapse in on themselves, shrinking his chest; his hands hung limp over his knees. 'You could try,' he said in a voice so small it was almost a whisper.

'There are bound to be scholarships,' I said, without conviction. 'You could probably get a grant. You could finish your doctorate.'

Marcellin looked at his feet, and then: 'I am not a student!' he shouted, swinging off the root, drawing his machete. (My own legs kicked out and I found myself standing two paces back, feeling foolish.) With one blow he severed the loop of the thick liana a foot above his head. An initial gush of water adjusted itself to an even flow as wide as a finger; he pulled the liana over his upturned mouth and drank. When he had finished Doubla followed suit, splashing the water over his head and neck, and we each took a turn. 'You see,' said Marcellin gently, 'I know about little things, too. I know which vines to drink from, and which vines will kill you.'

Vicky thrust his spear into the ground (to bar the way behind us? To tell the ancestors we wished to return?) and we set off again, with Marcellin in the lead. A little snakebite of shame spread up from the path and into my skull with the rising sweat and the rhythm of his absurdly fast pace. 'You're bloated, aren't you?' went the usual refrain in my head. 'You're fat with all the unearned privilege that has come your way, with all the gross advantages that were yours for the taking just because of the country you were born in' – and I thought of the light on the ochre stone of the Bodleian quadrangle in Oxford on a summer morning, of the tall mullioned windows, and of the books, every book a man could possibly need, ascending row on row to the high ceilings, or standing in the stacks underground, beneath the ancient paving-stones and the manicured gravel, shelf-mile after mile, and of Marcellin's hut of an office in Brazzaville with nothing in it but two issues of the *Journal of Cryptozoology*. I thought of the young Marcellin and his father, who had deserted his mother upriver in Impfondo and moved to the capital, living in the poorest part of the poorest quarter of the city with an open drain outside their shack; and I imagined the boy walking uptown every evening to do his homework under a street-lamp, intent on winning the scholarship that would take him to Cuba. And then the path plunged waist-deep into black water and I rapidly ceased to think of anything except the invisible submerged roots which trapped my feet and cracked my shins and toppled me on to my back (if they were unexpectedly high) and forwards (the rest of the time).

Marcellin, upset, was flailing ahead of me, hardly slackening his pace, but as I was spitting out another mouthful of leaf-rot, retrieving my hat, and wedging the ear-pieces of my glasses more securely under my sweat-band, Vicky churned past me, grinning. 'We don't swim here,' he said. 'We swim in the river. It's cleaner.' He hauled himself up on to a big fallen tree and, his bare feet gripping the smooth bark, pulled me up after him.

We waded together, slowly, from one fallen tree to another – some of which, I now saw, had been felled to make a causeway – until eventually the water-level dropped to knee-height, the ground rose slightly, we were ankle-deep in mud, a recognizable path appeared, and I had time to look about once more. There were fewer forest giants and fewer buttresses, I

decided, ground herbs were rare, the main bulk of trees seemed smaller –
and almost as if they were all of the same species, planted in stands. Many of
them sprouted prop-roots from three or four feet up their trunks, misplaced
branches which curved down into the soil like the struts of inverted wicker
baskets; and about one in twenty of these trees was hoisted completely clear
of the jungle floor, held up by a mass of stilt-roots about a yard high, some
of them flattened or twisted or growing into one another, roots which looked
as if they might at any moment straighten slightly, lift their trees higher on
to their backs, and move off crabwise across the mud.

Loops of a different kind of root sprang up every now and then across
the leaf-litter like sections of constricted intestine: aerial-roots or breathing-
roots or pneumatophores or knee-roots, and they were called knee-roots, I
told myself, because they coiled up at you without warning when you were
distracted, say, by clusters of pale fleshy flowers bursting straight out of the
stem of some liana to solicit passing bats – and fetched you a blow across
the knees, hard as a cricket bat. Flying bats, fruit bats, cricket bats, old bats,
airborne batwing aunties hunting babies for high tea along Brighton beach:
Galton's word-associations fluttered in my empty mind, hour after hour –
and suddenly there were flashes of light as if someone was holding mirrors
up among the trees ahead, flashes which gradually grew together, became
consistent, turned into a layer of light head-high between the trunks; and
there in front of us was a stretch of water three or four kilometres across,
a rest for the eyes, open water, a real horizon for the first time in months.
We had reached Lake Télé.

34

'What kept you?' said Marcellin, re-ensconced on a giant root.

'Redmond,' said Vicky. 'He falls over.'

'He's just a fat mercenary,' said Marcellin, and laughed. 'But all the same – I kept my promise, Redmond, didn't I? What do you think?'

A pair of African fish eagles, perhaps 200 yards out, were soaring over the lake on their black wings, their stubs of tails spread, their heads and necks a startling white; they were calling to each other, a duet of high-pitched ringing screams, extraordinarily clear; beneath them the sunlight lay across the water in bands, along the direction of ripple; and, after the closeness of the forest, the lake seemed numinous, so miraculously different, so open a space that for a moment I thought anything might happen in the apparently perfect circle between us and the far shore where the great trees and their hanging vegetation had shrunk to a line of moss. 'It's beautiful,' I said vaguely, my attention caught by a group of eight Long-tailed cormorants crossing from left to right in front of us and looking as large as pelicans, although I knew their bodies to be no bigger than a wigeon's: there were no islands, no marker-posts, no buoys, no floating logs: it was impossible to judge distance: it was easy to imagine how an otter's tail flipped up in a dive might transform itself into the neck of a dinosaur.

Doubla and the others arrived, and Nzé, bedraggled, ran straight for the low bank as if to hurl himself into the water. Doubla, with fearsome energy, lunged out and gripped his arm – so hard that Nzé yelped like a hit dog. 'Wait!' said Doubla. 'You'll harm us all. You'll kill our children.'

Vicky took a step forward, bowed his head, and shouted towards the lake. A pair of Violet-backed sunbirds, the male a small flurry of plum-violet and white, the female white and brown-blue, flew fast and low out of a bush to his left, curved behind him as if caught in a sudden gust of wind, disappeared into a tangle of lianas to his right, evidently discussed the matter, decided that they had panicked without reason, and flew back the way they had come.

Vicky turned to face us. 'The spirits of the lake tell me we are welcome here,' he intoned – and then broke the solemnity with one of his outsize grins. Nzé, released, laid his gun down, lurched forward, stretched himself full-length on the low bank, cupped his hands in the water and drank like a Giant Log.

We walked a little way along the shore, behind the palms and prop-rooted trees and lianas, to a promontory where four trees had been cut down and a space cleared: Marcellin's old camp. One tree had been felled into the lake as a makeshift jetty and two small fishing canoes lay wedged against it, half-submerged.

'I made these here,' said Doubla, suddenly friendly. 'I made them here.'

'Doubla! You take the gun!' shouted Marcellin imperiously, as if there had never been any dispute about it, as if there was a danger that Doubla might refuse the offer. 'We need meat.'

Nzé, too tired to protest, handed it over without a word, barrel first, and even produced a couple of cartridges from the top pocket of his Cuban Army jacket. Doubla gave a smile of real pleasure, slapped me on the back without once looking at Marcellin, and slipped away into the jungle behind us.

Vicky and the brothers began to set up a shelter with the tarpaulins in the centre of the promontory, and Manou and Nzé to build a fire. Marcellin pitched his tent in the only other available space, within three yards of the bank, and I put mine up beside his. No one would do this in the forests of the Amazon, I thought idly; no one would want to sleep so close to the water, not with all those anacondas about: and just suppose you were an anaconda – you'd need about two feet of body-length to anchor your tail firmly to a tree-root underwater, one foot to rear silently over the bank, nine feet to reach that warm, rank, mammalian smell of the tent entrance, an extra foot (at most) to slide in your rat-brown head, and then all you had to do was get a good grip into my face with your fifty or so backward-slanting pointed teeth, retract those massive muscles of yours for a second or two – and I'm safely coiled up underwater. So if you're as long as the longest anaconda recorded, at thirty-seven feet, that leaves you a good twenty-four feet to play with; and even if you're just a stolidly average sort of anaconda at around twenty feet, that still leaves you a seven-foot leeway, and as you've been documented swallowing a six-foot cayman, then you'd have no trouble swallowing me, complete with boots, glasses, camera, binoculars and a pocket full of Savlon tubes. And then, how much, I wondered, does Marcellin know about pythons?

'Marcellin!' I shouted. 'Are there any pythons here?'

'Pythons!' Marcellin shouted back, sticking his head out of his tent-flap, coming alive. 'I should say so! This is the best place in all Congo for pythons!

Last time I was here I saw them all around the lake – just wrapped up in the trees, hanging down over the water – maybe one every 500 yards. They were *big*, Redmond – twenty? Twenty-five? – the record is thirty-two feet! They swallow leopards! They swallow *crocodiles*!'

Doubla, triumphant, returned with a Blue duiker slung over his shoulders, its legs linked across his chest, its front hooves spliced between the thigh-bones and tendons of its back legs.

'There you are,' he said, dumping it down in front of Nzé. 'One cartridge! One mboloko!'

'So what?' said Nzé, hurt. 'My grandfather didn't need cartridges. He used to change himself into a leopard at night – and in the morning we'd have bushpig to eat, whenever we wanted.'

To my surprise, nobody laughed.

Nzé and Manou butchered the duiker, the men of Boha made desultory talk in Bomitaba around the fire, Marcellin sat apart on a log, his head in his hands, staring at the ground; and the layer of darkness resting among the roots of the trees on the forest side of us stretched itself gradually up their straight stems to the first high forks, engulfed the canopy, rolled down past the jagged stump of the jetty-tree, along its broken trunk, over its dead branches, and out across the lake. 'It's not good,' said Marcellin suddenly. 'We've been in this forest too long. Redmond – I had a terrible dream last night. I'd just got home, and as I entered my house, my fridge – it blew up. It blew up and my baby daughter was covered in blood and my wife was screaming and I held my daughter in my arms until she died – and now there's nothing in my life worth doing and nothing will ever replace her and there's no point in anything. It's not worth it, all this.'

'I don't think fridges blow up.'

'This one did. I have a very good fridge. I have the very latest fridge. It's made in France.'

'I had a bad dream too,' said Nzé, squatting on his haunches, the roughly skinned, ripped-up carcass at his feet, his head-torch on, his machete held in his right hand while he chucked bits of muscle, heart, spleen, liver and gut indiscriminately into the pot with his left, his inner paradise obviously regained at the sight of such abundance, his squint reset at its perkiest angle. 'I dreamt my cock blew up.'

'Not before time,' said Doubla.

'I got that disease again, Uncle, and your medicine was no good, and my cock couldn't stand the strain any more and so it just blew up with a whacking great bang in the middle of the night. They heard it all over Dongou. And every girl in Dongou said to herself, *"There goes my last chance of happiness."'*

We cheered.

'It's easy to cure diseases like yours,' said Doubla. 'All you need is a very young girl. You must fuck a virgin. It costs a lot of money but it's worth it.'

'It's terrible,' said Marcellin to me in English. 'That's what these people really believe. There are girls here – eight, nine, ten years old – and they have syphilis and gonorrhoea and they are wounded down there, too. These are not educated men.'

After supper I went to my tent to get my head-torch, strapped it on, stood up again outside, and was amazed to see that the canvas roof had turned white: thousands of small moths, translucent white, were crowding over it, their eyes glowing red in the torch-beam like tiny cigarette-ends. As I watched them, wondering why they liked the tent-top and what they were doing there – feeding? Mating? Migrating? – and why you'd want to be white and visible at night if you were a moth (maybe they were poisonous, and white was their warning signal?) and whether they could simply be one of Africa's oddest butterflies going to roost, *Pseudopontia paradoxa* (long thought to be a moth and now in a subfamily of its own), and why I was so ignorant about everything, and becoming miserable at the thought, and why I felt suddenly terribly tired and old and altogether past it, Manou, in his silent way, appeared at my elbow.

'I have something to tell you,' he whispered. 'Let's sit by the water. No one here must hear us. I have something important to tell you.'

'What is it?' I said with excessive eagerness, feeling cheered up at once, as we sat on a branch of the jetty-tree, turning off our torches.

'I also had a dream,' he said quietly. 'It was a snake or a dream or a fetish. But it means the same thing.'

'A fetish?'

'It went on all last night. During the rain. Right beside us. Just where Nzé and I were sleeping. Only Doubla and Vicky and the young brothers Nicolas and Jean Poulain, on the other side of it, they talked too much about the rain.'

'But what was it?'

'The fetish of the rain, or a real snake. We don't know. It was asleep under the leaves. They made so much noise, Doubla and the rest, they kept talking so we couldn't question it. You can only ask its name at night, in the silence.'

'So what happened?'

'We felt it after that, later on, right under the tarpaulins you gave us. It was really there, or it was a dream, and it kept moving in the dark.' He straightened his shoulders and arched his spine as if something was shoving him in the small of the back. He looked up at the moon across the lake, his eyes big as an antelope's. 'Nzé prayed to his grandfather. But his grandfather said he couldn't help us. This fetish of the rain – it was too strong.'

'A Burrowing python! That's what it was! They live underground in the Congo forest and they hunt rats and mice and shrews down their tunnels.'

'Whatever it was, real or not, it was sent to warn us.'

'Warn us?'

'Not to come here. Not to come to this place. And have you seen the waves?'

'Waves?'

'They come from the centre of the lake. Everyone noticed. Marcellin saw it. There's something at the centre of the lake which lifts the water from below, *exactly in the way that the fetish of the rain lifted our backs in the night.* Those waves, my friend, they have nothing to do with the wind.'

I was silent.

'Nzé and I – we are frightened. It's a great honour to be here, Redmond. No one in my family except Marcellin has ever been to this holy place. I will tell my children that I went to Lake Télé, and they will tell their children and their children's children. But this is enough. We must leave tomorrow.'

'I had a dream,' I lied, pleased with myself, feeling that I was getting the hang of things. 'We saw Mokélé-mbembé and he made our fortunes.'

Manou stood up. 'You must be serious with me,' he said, disgusted. 'You can fool Marcellin, my friend, but not me. I can see the spirits in your face.' And he walked sharply back towards the fire.

I crawled into my tent, tied the flap securely, took off my boots, torch and glasses, lay down and wrapped myself in a tarpaulin; there were no roots or Burrowing pythons beneath me, the ground squelched as I turned over: for the first time in months it was as soft as a mattress. The talk from the fire reached me as a murmur, the lake lapped gently at its bank, and from among the chorus of frogs I picked out a note that was new to me, a double call like the bark of a vixen on a November night in Wiltshire.

Someone began to snore, but with a resonance of such sustained depth and volume that not even the giant of Boha could have produced it. I was forming a vision of Mokélé-mbembé hung with testicles as big as beer barrels, when the reverberation signed itself off with a deep hoot, followed by three more, shorter and higher, and I realized that it was just a pair of Pel's fishing owls (huge and brown with great round heads) hidden in the canopy and agreeing that it was time to stop their marital cuddling on a high branch (they mate for life and sleep close together), proclaim their territory, get up and go fishing (they watch for ripples on the surface in shallow water and snatch fish with their feet).

As the male called again (his snore is said to be audible for a mile-and-a-half) I wondered whether I would live long enough to hear a Congo bay owl, which is known only from one specimen collected in 1951, told myself it was statistically improbable, and then wondered what kind of life Mr Pel had had: he was the Governor of the Dutch Gold Coast for ten years in the mid-nineteenth century and was presumably the same Pel who had given his name to Pel's flying squirrel, a pretty brownish-black squirrel, two-and-a-half feet long from the blaze of white on its nose to the end of its white tail, a squirrel which comes out of its nest in a hole in a trunk after dark, spreads its furry membranes and glides for up to fifty yards from tree to tree.

Maybe, on cloudless nights, after a hard day's administration, His Excellency the Governor of the Dutch Gold Coast just liked to slip off to the forest with his catapult, lie on his back in a clearing, and let fly at anything that moved overhead: airborne squirrels big as cats; owls airlifting catfish; batwing aunties with cats on broomsticks; Flying Dutchmen in catamarans – and Quetzalcoatlus, the Lake Télé soaring dinosaur with the wingspan of a Hellcat.

But no. He would never have stayed alive in West Africa for those ten whole years: a hobby protected you, but too much enthusiasm led to fever: the mortality rate for white officials in the Belgian Congo was 77 per cent, and, as I remembered warning Lary in Brazzaville (where was he now? Was he okay? Did he get out? Was he with his Chris in Plattsburgh? And you'd better not think like this . . .), 85 per cent of all British traders and Government employees on the West Coast died or were invalided home permanently debilitated. Far more likely, I decided, that on a late afternoon Mr Pel would be found sitting at his table on the wide veranda of the Residency, writing up his monograph on the strange new owl with the small spiny scales on its feet like an osprey's, smoking a foot-long Dutch Sumatran cigar, one of those tall brown stone bottles of very old geneva at his elbow, too absorbed to waste one moment in homesick longing even for the leather volume-lined library of works of natural history (illustrated with hand-coloured lithographs) in his comfortable rooms at Number 22, Kromme Waal, in Amsterdam (I had given him a *very* desirable address) or even to think of a day's skating on the quiet canal, outside his window, across the quay. At sundown he would lock up his pen and notebook in the ebony chest, stub out his cigar in the sand-tray and retire to the official bedroom – where at least two of his young black mistresses with their high breasts and delicate clavicles and thin wrists and that certain thrust to the buttocks were waiting for him, wearing nothing but tight white wet silk Government-issue tennis-shirts. And with the thought of all that owl-fishing and squirrel-flying, all that happiness, I blew a fuse in my own brain and fell asleep.

In the half-light just before dawn, after a breakfast of boiled duiker bits and rice, Marcellin and I and Doubla (wearing his army shirt and a pair of frayed brown shorts) sat on the jetty-tree, bailing out the fishing canoe with the mess-tins. A thick mist hung over the lake, unmoving.

I said, 'So where did you see the dinosaur?'

Marcellin paused, as if I had been impolite. 'Over there,' he said, pointing with his mess-tin off to the left. 'Three hundred yards out. But who knows? Perhaps it was a manifestation ...' His voice trailed off; he looked intently at the now-emptied bottom of the dugout, as if the pattern of adze marks in the wood held some meaning. 'And anyway,' he said, 'I'm not coming with you. *I hate this place.* I don't feel well. I've had enough. I have malaria. I'm going to stay in my tent. I'm going to stay in my tent all day long.'

He eased himself slowly back along the tree-trunk like an old man, lowered himself to the ground, dropped his mess-tin in the mud, crawled into his tent, and closed the flap behind him.

Doubla winked at me, touched the side of his nose with his right forefinger, and gave me a smile that was almost as big as one of Vicky's. His teeth, I noticed, were all in place. If anyone gets punched in the mouth round here, I thought, it isn't Doubla.

'Our Chief is a powerful man,' he said, shaking his head with admiration. 'He is making Marcellin suffer. He'll take his revenge – you watch. Marcellin sent our Chief to prison at Epéna. Our Chief is now sending Marcellin to prison in his own tent. And the prison at Epéna is much bigger and cooler than Marcellin's tent. Our Chief oversees everything that happens at this lake. This is our lake. It belongs to us, the *paysans*.'

I collected my hat, binoculars and water-bottle belt from my bergen, and then, inspired, transferred the last plastic bag of new 1000-CFA notes from the top flap to my leg-pocket, and joined Vicky and Doubla at the jetty. Nzé, Manou and the brothers came to watch.

Vicky pulled two long-handled paddles from their hiding-place in a stilt-rooted bush at the edge of the promontory; Doubla laid his spear down the starboard side of the dugout and climbed in after it with such ease and agility that I followed at once, without thinking. The little boat rolled to port, gulped a gallon of water, and righted itself; I took another step; the bow lifted, bucked, and the little boat drank two more. 'Sit down!' yelled Doubla, his body tilted, one leg raised, his arms outstretched, gyrating, and at the same time pointing with his lips to a small block of wood amidships.

I managed to perch on the log, my knees up to my ears.

'But I want to paddle!'

'Paddle?' Doubla bent his wiry body down in an arc, taut as Jean's bow-harp, and caught a mess-tin floating at his feet. He reached out and handed it to me. 'Stay where you are! Bail! If you move we'll sink! It's my boat. I made it. Bail!' On the bank Nzé brayed with laughter, snapped to attention and saluted. 'Bail, Uncle! Bail or you'll sink! Mokélé-mbembé – he's hungry!' Manou looked concerned. 'Keep still!' he shouted as Vicky pushed off. 'You fall over all the time! There's something wrong with your legs!'

No sound came from Marcellin's tent, no hint of movement. He's slit his throat in there, I thought, as we travelled surprisingly fast over the water and the promontory fell behind us in the mist. Trying to deny brain-space to such an image, I concentrated half on the bailing and half on Doubla standing in the bows in front of me: with a ragged splash he would thrust his paddle into the lake, push back with a quick dip of the knees, churn brown water and white bubbles past me, swing the long paddle forward again, straighten his spine, reposition his hands, and repeat the process. The hairs on the backs of his legs grew in little disparate clumps, as if they had been newly planted out and given room to spread. Of course, I said to myself, as my buttocks began to go numb on the block of wood, he's bound to be annoyed with me, he *made* this tiny certified piece of rolling log that wouldn't be safe in a bath. He's *proud* of it.

Doubla and Vicky began to talk in Bomitaba – or rather, they began to shout to each other as if they were standing at either end of Boha, instead of a yard fore and aft of my head. I thought: they don't want to see anything: they want Mokélé-mbembe to dive to the bottom of the lake. 'Please!' I shouted, desperate, seizing a second's break in the blast and counter-blast of the bass duet above me. 'If we see a gorilla, I'll give you 5000 francs! And the same goes for a python – a really big python. And a chimp – any chimp!'

Doubla's paddle stopped in mid-air. He turned his head. '*Five thousand?*' From behind, the wet blade of Vicky's paddle batted me on the right arm. 'Me too?'

Doubla and Vicky stopped shouting. They slid their paddles into the water without a splash; they muffled the backward push; they withdrew the blades with a sideways flick that left the surface almost undisturbed. They began to whisper.

'Five thousand CFA,' I thought, bailing as quickly as I could, appalled. 'But that's ten chickens!'

As the sun rose the mist grew whiter, thinned, dispersed and evaporated. Three tsetse flies arrived over the canoe, buzzed Doubla's legs in a series of fast zig-zags, and landed in the open spaces between the clumps of hairs on his right calf-muscle. Brown with big heads and about half an inch long, they folded their wings like the blades of scissors and bit him. His leg twitched forward, he detached his right hand from his paddle as it swung past and, without looking round or interrupting his rhythm, slapped at them, hard, killing two. Inspecting my own legs, I counted six on my trousers – the sharp edge of this log, I thought: I'm anaesthetized from the waist down: there's nothing I can do about it: I won't be able to feel the proboscides pierce my trousers: in an hour or two I'll start to swell. How odd it is, I thought, that an insect with a reproduction-rate slower than that of a rabbit is so successful; and that this fly is the best conservationist in Africa: both sexes live exclusively on blood (riverine mammals, crocodiles, Monitor lizards) and the female hatches her eggs (only about twelve in a lifespan of six months) one at a time inside her body. She feeds her growing maggot from organs like milk glands via a nipple near its mouth, and it breathes through two black knobs on its rear end which stick out from her oviduct. When the larva is fully grown the mother finds somewhere damp and dark on the forest floor and gives birth – the maggot buries itself, turns into a brown pupa, and one month later the adult fly emerges.

Behind the thick screen of direct-sunlight-loving bushes and lianas along the lake-shore the species of riverine trees, hung with lianas and ferns and orchids adapted to the glare, crowded upwards, rising to a surprisingly uniform height, and were overshadowed only by the occasional climbing palm whose stem stuck straight up above the crown of its host, or by the odd group of emergent trees, evenly spaced, whose high branches (seemingly free of any clinging plants) spread out across the canopy like the limbs of pines.

And it's the tsetse fly, I thought, carrying the trypanosome for sleeping sickness, killing people and cattle, which has preserved this vast jungle for so long. But then the trypanosome itself, a single-celled animal with a whiplash tail (perhaps a captured bacterium) might have been here from the beginning of the Proterozoic, 'the era of pioneering life', 2500 million years ago: 2075 million years before the plants themselves, evolving in freshwater lakes like this, developed heat-resistant seeds, tough skins, stems strong enough to take their weight – and stepped ashore.

And yes, I said to myself, momentarily glad I couldn't feel their bites, in the long term you have a lot to thank these flies for. But, a little voice said, you'll change your view of things, won't you, if you actually get the disease? And then, come to that, how do you know you haven't caught it already? After all, the symptoms listed in Elaine Jong's *The Travel and Tropical Medicine Manual* fit you rather well, don't they? The western form of sleeping sickness, endemic here in the forest, starts with a tender papula within five to ten days of the tsetse bite and then ulcerates and disappears over two or three weeks (*and you've had plenty of those*). Next come intermittent fever, headaches and irregular heartbeat (*often*); then transient skin rash (*not so transient round here*). Which is superseded by increasing indifference, somnolence, and a reversal of the sleep cycle (*somnolent for years*). Which is in turn succeeded by incoordination, rigidity and Parkinsonian effect (*every night in Oxford, drinking too much*), followed by irritability and periods of mania (*afraid so*), stupor and indifference (*most mornings*) and finally death (*any minute now*).

Treatment is possible, if you can be bothered to get to a hospital, but then would you really want it when you get there? Suramin is fine, except that it's not particularly effective, and produces proteinuria, fever and shock. So maybe Melarsoprol is better, because it's just a friendly little arsenic compound which at least penetrates the central nervous system and may leave you with nothing worse than optic atrophy and acute encephalitis. But, all in all, I suggest that perhaps you go for Pentamidine, because that will simply give you abdominal cramps, a sterile abscess and a spontaneous abortion.

'Quiet!' hissed Doubla, as I began to clap at my legs like a Lewis gun.

He crouched low, slid his paddle gently to the floor, reached back with his right hand for his spear, whispered to Vicky, and the canoe moved silently forward. A brown hump, like the roundel of a shield, lay on the flat surface of the lake ahead. In one unbroken movement Doubla rose to his full height, arched his back, pitched forward, and threw the spear with a force which would have been impressive even if his feet had been planted on the ground.

Two small waves collided where the turtle had been, and spread out in concentric ripples. The shaft of the spear, sticking out of the water a yard off-centre, vibrated slightly. About seven feet of it was visible. So, I thought: let's assume that the point of the spear is buried one foot deep in the mud; that makes the lake, 100 yards out from the shore, around four feet deep. So maybe there are deeper pools in the middle. Or perhaps Mokélé-mbembé is a very small dinosaur. Or perhaps he is just a very flat dinosaur.

Doubla ran the canoe into a clump of huge arrow-plants, lopped a big green seed-pod from its stalk, cut it in half, cleaned out the seeds and handed both halves to me. 'Bail with those,' he said, pushing off again, keeping the canoe close in to the shore and rounding every little promontory.

Scooping out the water slopping round my ankles, I disturbed a Tiger bittern in a reed-bed beside me. He rose into the air, a rustle of dark brown and reds like autumn leaves in a beech wood, and banked into the forest, his long yellow legs dangling behind him.

The Tiger bittern, I thought, is very rare indeed (the great James P. Chapin only saw two on all his travels up the Congo river and explorations to the east), and if you heard its call for the first time, a deep single or double boom repeated for several minutes at dusk or in the middle of the night, a fog-horn of a note, it would be much more reasonable to think of monsters than of a shy brown bird. But then Doubla and Vicky, local fishermen, would have heard it all the time. I'll show them its picture in Serle and Morel, I told myself pedantically, and see if they can imitate its call.

I counted five Fish eagles at various points in the air above us; the comfortingly familiar honk-grunting alarm-call of Greater white-nosed monkeys reached us from the forest; and as we passed a bush like a rhododendron with clusters of small-petalled, pale-pink flowers, a Ball python, black with yellow splotches and about three feet long, curled up on the lower twigs, slid into the water like honey from a gourd.

I decided that I was almost happy, that I would forget about my numb buttocks and lost legs and the tsetse flies I couldn't swat when, rounding the tangle of a fallen tree, Doubla saw something that galvanized him into his hunting-crouch, his spear in his right hand. He had seen a sitatunga.

The Swamp antelope, much bigger than a duiker, stood up to its knees in the water about fifty yards away, as if suspended above the surface of the lake, lifted up by the reflected light which caught its soft-brown stomach and the white patch at its throat.

We drew closer; Vicky inadvertently splashed his paddle; the sitatunga turned its head, the long ears flicked towards us, the big brown eyes dilated. With a jerk-back of the spiral horns, the shoulder muscles flattening and bunching under the fur, thin legs throwing up water, its tail flashing white through the spray, like the scut on a rabbit, the sitatunga reached an opening up the bank and disappeared.

Doubla swore some terrible oath in Bomitaba, slid his spear back in place behind him, spat on his hands, rubbed them together, and picked up his paddle. I was simply glad that Lake Télé sitatungas had changed their usual defences: living in marshland, with oily, water-repellent coats and splayed-out hooves specially adapted for running over mud (the female builds a hidden platform of trodden-down vegetation in the reeds, a nest where her new-born calf lies for a month or so), the sitatunga normally escapes from leopards and men by submerging in the water with only its nose showing – which, once you have picked out the tell-tale ripples, makes it easy to spear from a canoe – but our sitatunga was a wise old male: he obviously knew that when men took to a floating log they were akin to crocodiles and pythons.

We passed many more bushes in bloom, a rare sight in the forest: the shrub with the pink flowers, and, almost equally common, a tall bush with orange flowers arranged in spikes; both species were speckled with dark-red splashes which I at first took to be the flowers of something else, a climber or a parasite, but which, as we moved quietly closer in to the shore, resolved themselves into leaves: fresh new leaves. I was wondering whether the red was a defence against caterpillars – maybe female butterflies were programmed to lay their eggs on green? – when there was a deep roar, a reverberation which seemed to shake the reeds beside us, the threat call of a male gorilla.

Vicky and Doubla shot the canoe in under a clump of arrow-plants and we crept ashore, half on our knees (which was just as well, because my legs were not yet receiving messages and my eyes, in the gloom, were still full of the fierce light of the lake). Nothing moved; and then there was the sound of breaking vegetation in a patch of Wild ginger to our right and 'Look! Look!' yelled Vicky, pointing into the branches above us. 'One of his wives! The husband – he runs! But look! One of his wives!'

She sat in a high fork of the tree, plainly visible, and through the binoculars I looked straight into her shiny black face – at her averted eyes beneath the big protruding brow, her squat nose, the two linked horseshoes of her nostrils, her wide thin lips – she seemed extraordinarily human; I was seized with an absurd desire to hold her hand, to tell her that it was all right.

She appeared reluctant to move, unsure what to do. She stood up, one hand grasping the branch above her, the other wrapped across her body, and sat down again. She was carrying something. There were two small black arms tight up round her chest: she was holding an infant.

'We need a gun,' said Doubla in my ear. 'Poof!'

'She's got a child,' I said, lowering my binoculars, afraid they might be a threat signal, an enlarged stare. 'We must leave her alone.'

'They're good to eat,' said Doubla, gesturing a thrust with his spear at her. 'They make you strong.'

'You shouldn't eat them,' I said, over-emotional, taking his arm, pulling him back towards the dugout. 'They're protected.'

'Protected! You white men. The ideas you have. Don't you eat gorillas in England? I bet you do. You're rich. Your forests must be *full* of gorillas.'

'There are no gorillas in England or anywhere else. They live only here and to the east. You should protect them.'

'Huh!' said Doubla, twitching his tendon-hard arm out of my grasp.

Vicky broke off a sprig of pink flowers from the bush by the canoe, sniffed them, kissed them, and cast them into the water. 'You must pay up,' he said.

I took the plastic bag of new 1000-CFA notes out of my leg-pocket and gave them five each. Back in the dugout even the reflex slapping at tsetse flies stopped; the fast paddling, the whispered discussion, the regular drifting pauses while they listened for chimpanzees – it was exhausting just to look at such intensity, such focused concentration.

Another big sitatunga – but at least 200 yards away – kicked up arcs of water, half-catherine-wheels of light, as it made for the bank and safety. Eight Long-tailed cormorants, perhaps the same flock which we had seen yesterday, straggled past us; their outstretched necks and stiff wedge-shaped tails and black wings blurred slightly at the edges as they flapped through the heat-haze, a dancing migraine of heat above the lake, a sweat-running, skin-crackling heat, painful on the back of the hands.

We landed beside a raffia palm which had pitched forward from the bank, its crown appearing to rise straight from the surface like some gigantic water-plant.

Vicky, impassive, studied my face for several moments, as if coming to a decision, making some judgment. (I thought: the nap of his hair is at least three inches deep, and his eyes – they're as big and brown and liquid as a bushbaby's.) 'Pygmies lived here,' he said quietly. 'This was a pygmy village. The pygmies lived here, and then they died – all of them together. We need their protection. We must ask them to help us.'

I took off my hat, bowed my head, and clasped my hands behind my back. At the upper right-hand curve of my field of vision I saw Vicky's combat-jacket swell – and the shout was so unexpectedly loud that I lost my balance, as if the sound-wave itself had knocked me backwards. So it's more important to pray, I thought – even to other people's ancestors – than it is to earn ten chickens for finding a chimpanzee: it's obvious that the laws of nature really are suspended at Lake Télé: they're as bent as the light in the heat-waves over the water: this is the only place in Africa where bribes don't work.

The passionate invocation over, we re-embarked and – having seen nothing but a lone sandpiper on a floating tree-trunk bobbing his head and flicking up his tail at our approach, flying off low with shallow fussy wing-beats and short glides, just as if he was in Poole harbour and not a visitor in the land of dinosaurs – we stopped again.

'It's good, Redmond!' Vicky yelled two feet from my face as we went ashore, clapping me on the back, flashing his enormous teeth. 'It's good to pray to the ancients! I told the spirits we'd come with a white man who *respects the tradition* and they said that was *good*. You would see gorillas and chimpanzees. You would see our animals. It's good that you respect the tradition! That's what the ancients say!'

We walked a few yards through the bushes and into a patch of open ground, where a small tree had been felled. 'This place – it belongs to

Doubla's ancestors,' said Vicky, holding a big broad thumb up in front of his nose, as if including me in some conspiracy. 'They came here to go fishing.'

Doubla ran a hand across his stubbled chin and short moustache, pulled at his scraggy sideboards, reset his eyes and mouth into a mask even more implacable than his usual expression, shouted, listened, replied, listened, shook his head, and sat down on the trunk of the tree. We joined him. I took my water-bottle out of its belt-pouch and passed it to Vicky. 'So who,' he said, taking a swig, 'loves you more than your father and your grandfather?'

'Your mother and your grandmother?' I said, mistaking the nature of the question.

Doubla and Vicky laughed.

'White men!' said Doubla, reaching for the water-bottle. 'Mothers love you for what you are. Fathers love you for what you *do*.'

'Look,' I said, feeling like some nineteenth-century ethnographer, 'I'm sure you can tell me the truth in this holy place. There's something I'd really like to know. Have you seen Mokélé-mbembé?'

'What a stupid question,' said Doubla, looking genuinely surprised, stopping with the water-bottle half-way to his lips. 'Mokélé-mbembé is not an animal like a gorilla or a python. And Mokélé-mbembé is not a sacred animal. It doesn't appear to people. It is an animal of mystery. It exists because we imagine it. But to see it – never. You don't *see* it.'

Half-an-hour later, at a place marked by two crossed sapling-poles driven into the mud, we put into the bank. More prayers, I thought, exasperated.

'Doubla found it,' said Vicky. 'She'll be finished by now. Crocodile eggs! Tonight we eat well!'

We struggled through the reeds, on to the wet bank, up a narrow flattened trail – to a pile of leaves and twigs and loose soil about a yard high and six feet across. But something had got there before us. The nest-mound was open and fragments of brittle white shell lay strewn about the leaf-litter. Judging by the bigger pieces, the eggs must have been around three inches long and oval, perhaps those of the African slender-snouted crocodile. Doubla dug down with his hands. Nothing.

'The zoko's had our supper,' said Vicky.

'What's that? A Marsh mongoose?' I said, excited. Or better still: perhaps the eggs were eaten by that Long-nosed mongoose ('Up to now only thirty specimens known ... lives entirely in rain-forests. No details of habits').

Vicky shook his head.

'A Servaline genet?' (Cat-sized, low-slung, black spots on ochre, long bushy black-ringed tail – 'HABITAT: dense woodlands and primeval forests. HABITS: details not known.')

Doubla inflated his chest and cheeks like a bullfrog.

Vicky hissed like a snake.

'A Congo clawless otter?' ('HABITS: little known'.)

Vicky put his right arm behind his buttocks and lashed it from side to side; he opened his mouth, displayed his thirty-two teeth, and came at me with his fingers crooked rigid like claws.

'Mokélé-mbembé?'

'Much worse than Mokélé-mbembé,' said Doubla with one of his short dry laughs (like the first warning bark of a dog that intends to take your leg off). 'The zoko is a *real* monster. He's bigger and faster than a man. And if you annoy him – he attacks!'

Vicky held his arms bent inwards at the elbow-joint and imitated something heavy trundling across the forest floor. He flicked out his tongue.

'A Monitor lizard!' I yelled. 'It's a Nile monitor!' (Six feet long, and having the good sense to lay its own eggs somewhere safe: by digging a hole in the side of a self-sealing termite's nest).

A faint hooting call reached us.

Vicky hissed like a Monitor, 'What did I tell you? Chimpanzees!'

Vicky and Doubla paddled with ferocity towards the intermittent calls until we turned into a creek; an inlet sheltered from the lake, secluded and still, its surface covered in water-lilies.

Doubla, using his paddle as a punt-pole, pushed the dugout into the reeds, beside a bush heavy with dense white flowers, a cross between hawthorn and cow-parsley; and we sank up to our knees in mud.

We floundered ashore in silence; the bursts of chimpanzee conversation increasing in volume and coming from straight ahead. I scooped up handfuls of black mud and plastered my shirt and face.

We crossed two swampy streams (by pushing down saplings for our feet and using the twelve-foot spear as a handhold). We crawled on all-fours across a patch of firmer ground and slithered on our stomachs to the base of a tree in which an old male sat, half-way up on a big bough, slowly pulling twigs towards his surprisingly mobile lips, fastidiously biting off selected leaves, munching, deep in thought. He was almost bald, with big ears, deep-set brown eyes and a black face.

We lay prone on the mud; Doubla put a finger in each nostril and made a high-pitched nasal grunting, as if he was calling up a duiker. The old chimpanzee stopped munching, bent forward to look down, swung his head from side to side to get a view through the branches, saw us, and urinated.

He then put his elbow against the tree-trunk and ran a hand over his bald head and face and thought a bit, looking away.

'Waaaa!' he said.

Other chimpanzees immediately began to appear in the trees around us, all of them, as far as I could see from my kneeling position in the mud, with black ears and faces and with black palms to their hands and black skin on the soles of their feet – adult tschegos, I thought reassuringly, giving them a name. They're the western lowland rainforest variety in which only the very young have faces like white men.

They swung lower, crowding down towards us, until one was about thirty feet away, another directly above us, and two more, I noticed, were edging round and down behind us.

The old male stood up on his bough, opened his mouth wide – transforming his peaceful face into a shocking display of Dracula canines – and screamed short, fast, eardrum-cracking screams. He stamped on the bough. He slapped the trunk of the tree. He gripped a small branch in each hand and shook them with an appalling singleness of purpose.

All the others joined in, their throat sacs distended with air and indignation, their hair erect with rage. They whooped together, a *whoo-whooo-whooo* which grew louder and faster and burst into a frenzy of screaming and branch-shaking. The male above us let fly an explosion of small round faeces on our heads, a shotgun-blast of droppings. It was unnerving to be the object of such concentrated dislike; no wonder even socially insensitive leopards turned and ran. This is a very effective display, I thought patronizingly. Then I thought (less patronizingly) these apes are *big*. And then I remembered Jane Goodall's account of the chimpanzee's idea of maximum excitement, a really good day out: you grab a young baboon or colobus by the foot, bash its brains out on a tree, rip it to bits and eat it. There was a stamping and beating on the ground behind us. I had a sudden twinge of fear, and in the maelstrom of whirling sound-waves it was not amenable to reason.

Doubla and Vicky, obviously sharing my thoughts, jumped to their feet, shouted, and banged the flat of their machete-blades as hard as they could against the tree-trunk.

The chimpanzees dropped to the ground and fled.

We reached camp well after dark. Nzé and Manou and the brothers came to greet us but Marcellin remained sitting in silence by the fire.

'Did you hear it?' whispered Manou, taking me by the arm the moment I stepped ashore, staring into my face, as anxious as I had ever seen him.

'Hear what? What's the matter?'

'It called this afternoon. We all heard it.' He made a thin, high-pitched cry, *ooo-ooo-oooo*. 'Nzé is frightened, too. Maybe things will not go well with us. Maybe we will not live to buy our bicycles with the money you will give us. If you hear Mokélé-mbembe – you die.'

'It's the chimpanzees!' I shouted like a Bantu, feeling I had made a great discovery, my one contribution to science to date. 'It's the sound of chimpanzees! You're just not used to sound carrying across open spaces! You can't be. This is the biggest stretch of open water for hundreds of miles!'

'We heard Mokélé-mbembé,' said Manou, completely unaffected by my logic. 'We're going to die.'

After supper, the Southern Cross bright above the lake, Doubla and I happened to be alone together, washing our mess-tins by the dugout.

'So, Doubla,' I said softly, 'why did Marcellin swear he saw the dinosaur?'

'Don't you know?' said Doubla, giving me his first real smile. 'It's to bring idiots like you here. And make a lot of money.'

Pel's fishing owl began to call.

35

The following morning, leaving Marcellin to sleep in his tent, the brothers to go hunting with the shotgun, and Nzé and Manou to nurse their fears, Doubla, Vicky and I set off south in the dugout, through the dawn mist, to find a python.

Doubla and Vicky paddled in silence, three yards out from the shore, beside the drooping palm-fronds, the overhanging bushes with their dark-green glaucous leaves, the clumps of papyrus, the patches of Giant phrynium leaves hoisted seven feet high on their single stalks: and on many of the stems and leaves, all the way along the water-margin, the inch-and-a-quarter-long, squat and jointed, brittle black-brown exoskeletons of dragonfly larvae still clung, hooked into the plant tissues where they'd crawled out of the lake, found their final resting-places, cracked open (a triangular hole in each thorax) and released their Sky-blue dragonflies.

And fossils of dragonflies, I thought, as Doubla swung the canoe out round the top of a fallen tree, its bare dead branches sticking out of the water, bleached white by the sun – the fossils of dragonflies first appear in rocks that are 330 million years old, and that's 105 million years before the sauropods evolved. So the ancestors of these larvae could certainly have shot out their extendable jaws to grab worms and insects disturbed in the mud by Mokélé-mbembé's five-toed, long-clawed, leathery feet (perhaps set with bony studs) as he waded along the Lake Télé shore-line, browsing on the vegetation. But to judge by Marcellin's sighting, Mokélé-mbembé was a small dinosaur, perhaps small enough, in Marcellin's case, to have been a Forest elephant characteristically crossing the lake by walking on the bottom, its trunk held curving up and forward as a breathing tube (Mokélé-mbembé's neck) and only the hump of its back showing above the surface. And anyway, if you're going to see a sauropod, why not pick something really memorable? How about *Breviparopus* – named from tracks left by a sauropod 157 feet long? But these spiders' webs, I thought, trying to estimate the diameter of the biggest sheet-web stretched silver-white in the mist between two of the upright branches of the dead tree – they really are memorable. And, looking closer, I noticed that a hundred or more spiders sat waiting on each web.

So they were social spiders – a great rarity, an aberrant way of life if you're a spider: only four species out of a possible 30,000 are known to be truly social. And when did spiders evolve? . . . Perhaps 395 million years ago . . .

The mist lifted and cleared, we passed under a fruiting tree (fruits like greengages) and five huge brown therapsids elbowed out of its branches, spread the leathery skin of their bony membranes and laboured away over the tree-tops. . . . But as all therapsids – the mammal-like reptiles – were annihilated by that incoming comet of 245 million years ago, the comet which killed 96 per cent of all species of marine animals, ended the Paleozoic (the era of 'old life') and started the Mesozoic (the era of Mokélé-mbembé) – then, I told myself, I have to suppose that even here on the prehistoric lake where all the laws of nature are suspended those were not therapsids but Hammer bats, monster bats, the biggest bats in Africa, *Hypsignathus monstrosus*. Fruit bats with a three-foot wingspan, they mate in leks: thirty to 150 males space themselves forty feet apart along a river or lake, hanging in the foliage at the edge of the canopy – and with their massive larynges, enlarged cheek-pouches, inflated nasal cavities and mouths like funnels, they compete for the visiting females with their calls (a braying *kwok* close-up, a metallic chink if heard from far away). The females, who are half the size of the males and have normal, elegant flying-fox heads and chests, are deeply stirred by the music of their species. Musical connoisseurs, they fly for several nights up and down the line of singers and finally select the male who has, presumably, and in their careful opinion, the biggest voice-box. And the females are almost unanimous in their choices: two or three males do all the mating. So sexual selection produces heavier males with bigger in-built trumpets, larger amplifiers and, because of the energy such music-making demands, shorter lives . . .

The canoe rocked as Doubla threw his spear. There was a swirl, a thrashing in the water ahead; Vicky thrust the boat forward, Doubla grabbed the floating shaft – and lifted in a four-foot-long catfish, transfixed through the flank. 'Two fish!' he said, feeling the distended stomach. 'One throw – two fish! He couldn't dive – he'd swallowed a fish!'

Vicky pushed the canoe into a little island five yards out from the bank. On it stood one big raffia palm, a straggly bush with pink flowers, and an open-sided shelter built with stout poles and a palm-frond roof. Doubla shouted a prayer or an address towards the lake, and 'Welcome!' he said to me with half a smile. 'This is Doubla's island. It's mine.' He sat down on a log beside the smoking-rack, I sat beside him, and Vicky, barefoot, in his combat fatigues, perched on the exposed root-clump of the leaning raffia palm. Doubla said, 'Redmond, there are no pythons. We came here to get away. To get away from Marcellin. Marcellin is not easy in himself. The

Chief of Boha is taking his revenge. And when the Chief of Boha takes his revenge you can believe me, Ange Moutaboungou – it is not safe to be near the victim. Even if he's your friend – you must ignore him.'

I said, 'No pythons?'

'January, February, March, April – when it's dry, when the rivers and ponds in the forest are dry. That's when the bushpig, the antelope, buffalo, elephants – everything, they all come here to drink. And that's when the pythons, really big pythons – they come here to eat well, and to make babies. Today, if it was the dry season, just in that little distance we've paddled, you'd see fifty, maybe sixty pythons. That's when it's dangerous! But now' – he looked out at the heavy grey sky – 'now the rains are coming. The wet season. Me – I think they'll come tonight. So we'll collect my turtle eggs; and tonight we'll capture crocodiles for Marcellin; and tomorrow, if the rains start, we'll go. Because if you stay here when the rain's come you'll never get out, the water rises, the forest – it's a swamp! You must live in the trees!'

'Vicky,' I said, 'who *does* love you more than your father and grandfather?'

'The ancients!' shouted Vicky, standing up. 'The spirits, the ancients!' Curling the fingers of his left hand into a funnel, he smacked the top, hard, with the flat of his right, making a sharp popping sound. 'They love you lots!' (Pop.) 'Lots and lots!' (Pop, pop.)

'But not always, not all of them,' said Doubla, grim. 'There's another lake near here. A small lake, a forbidden lake. The spirits of that place are not ours, they don't belong to us. All the people in that village died. They died for ever. And if you eat the fish in that lake' – he drew the index-finger of his right hand across his throat, snapped his arm to his side and clicked his fingers – 'you die, just like that!'

On the way back we stopped by a crossed-stick marker, dug out the small, round, white and leathery turtle eggs from their nest of heaped leaves, bit into and sucked out two apiece (like chicken's eggs, but oily) and carried the rest, wrapped in our shirt and jacket-fronts, to the boat.

Marcellin, shaky, his eyes bloodshot, complaining of fever, emerged from his tent; and after an almost silent supper (turtle eggs and catfish soup) Vicky cut and trimmed a long sapling, Doubla made a noose of liana-twine, Marcellin took his torch, Vicky poled off the canoe, and they left to hunt for crocodiles along the shore-line.

In the dusk, looking out through my open tent-flap at the lake, I watched five falcons – short necks, long tapered wings, their tails slightly forked, their flight quick and fluttery as a small bat's – as they dipped down fast across the still surface of the water, drinking. With the binoculars I could see that on each bird the back of the head (the apex), the upperwing-coverts and scapulars (the sides) and the rumps and uppertail-coverts (the base) formed a triangle of cinnamon. So they weren't falcons: they were rollers, they were my almost-childhood rollers, they were Broad-billed rollers. And then I thought, absurdly, with a deep and reflex rush of happiness: the rollers have come to see me: so there are places where the visitor in the black jacket, the night-visitor, Samalé, the presence with the long arms – there *are* places where you can be free of him, safe. . . . But I don't want to be compelled to think like this, I thought, compulsively thrusting my right hand into my pocket, checking that the small bundle of fur and bone and string, the fetish, was still there (and what if I lost it?). I hate this nonsense, I thought, I won't have it, this is magical thinking. 'And so it is,' came the deep, soft voice of the man in the black jacket, from just behind the tent in the gathering darkness. 'And there's nothing you can do about it,' he said, from behind me, through the canvas. 'Because even now, my dear good innocent friend, my new friend, even now, this magical thinking, as you call it – it's breeding in your subconscious. You're infected. You're marked for ever. Why, I might just as well have ripped your back!' And he laughed, that dry sound, the cockroaches moving in the thatch. 'But why be anxious? Why so disturbed? My dear new friend, it's the language of fetish. Or perhaps I should put it another way?' There was a soft, dull, regular thump on the ground outside, as if he was raising himself up on the balls of his feet where he stood, lifting the heels of his boots, exercising his foot and calf-muscles . . . 'Perhaps I should put it in other terms – terms you white men will understand. As you know, I go to Paris – by night of course – and in a wooden plane. I go to the library. I read books. I love to read books! So let me tell you – this language of fetish, it's like the language of marriage as Tolstoy describes it. Marriage of many years. A language that has no use for your logic, no need for your premises and deductions and conclusions. It's the language of dream, my friend, unreal and incoherent. It contradicts itself, all the time, and in everything except the emotion that underlies the dream – and that feeling is powerful, and clear, and true. Only now of course, my friend, because you've come here uninvited, you're married to me, like everyone else.'

I heard his feet move off over the leaf-litter; they brushed through the broad-leaved grasses and 'Redmond!' shouted Nzé from behind me. 'A monkey!' It's okay, I thought, as I crawled out of the tent. A fever . . . a touch of fever . . . I have Marcellin's fever. The brothers were walking into camp, returning from the hunt, their bare feet swishing through the undergrowth, Jean carrying the gun, Nicolas a dead monkey.

Jean handed the gun and two unused cartridges to Nzé, Nicolas gave the monkey to me; and, obviously exhausted, without a word they lay down on the sleeping-platform, flat on their backs, side by side, their right arms over their eyes.

'It's a De Brazza!' I said, looking into the monkey's eyes, not yet dull, eyes that were framed by the black crown of his head, his orange brow, his white nose and moustache and the long white beard which looked as if it had just been brushed.

'Don't touch it, Uncle,' said Nzé, propping the shotgun, barrel to the ground, against a stilt-root. 'They're dirty, monkeys. They give you fleas, they give you diseases.' Sitting down beside Manou on their joint log in front of the fire, Nzé unbuttoned the breast-pocket of his now-torn militia jacket, pulled out a new packet of cigarettes, peeled off the wrapper, tossed it in the fire, watched the crinkle and flare, plucked two clean white cigarettes, gave one to Manou, and lit up. 'It's horrible, Uncle, the way you touch things.'

I laid the monkey (his fur soft as a kitten's) on the smoking-rack. His body was olive, his tail black, his penis pink, his scrotum blue. He was an adult male in full breeding colours – a dominant male with his own small troop of females and young (they live in swamp-forest, like water and swim well) – and if there are any other males in his troop they're subordinate, their physical development is psychologically retarded: no matter how old they are they retain the brown coats of infancy, the brown that mimics the colour of the female's perineum. So now, I thought, stroking his back, at least someone else will have a chance to show his true colours and breed.

'Stop that, Uncle!' said Nzé. 'Wash your hands in the lake! That's dirty!'

I sat on the end of their log.

'I've decided,' said Nzé, taking a long drag on his cigarette, 'I've decided, Uncle, that I, Nzé Oumar – just to give people pleasure, to do good to other people as you white men, you Christians say we should . . .'

'Do unto others,' said Manou, 'as you would they do unto you.'

'Exactly,' said Nzé. 'I couldn't have put it better if I'd thought for a week – so I do unto all the girls in all the villages. I do unto for the good of this Government Expedition. I do unto for the sake of the Party! For the sake of the Government of the People's Republic! And so I get more diseases than anyone else. And that's not right. Why should I, Nzé Oumar, be the only one to suffer? That's what I want to know!' He blew a puff of smoke in Manou's face. 'Whereas, Uncle, little Manou here, he is not a Christian. He keeps his cock to himself.'

'I did unto a girl in Boha,' said Manou, affronted. 'I really did!'

'No, no, Manou. I do unto all the time. You listen to someone older and wiser than you – Nzé Oumar, a man the whole family holds in admiration and respect.'

'No one respects you. Not even Staline!'

'Staline? She's far too young! How could she form an opinion on that kind of thing, a really important matter like that?'

Manou looked at me, cast up his eyes, and shrugged.

'Yes, Uncle, it's time Manou made a sacrifice for the good of this Government Expedition, for the sake of the Party – so he can go and catch a disease for us. Even if it's just a small one. He can skin the monkey.'

'We won't skin it,' said Manou, sullen, looking at the ground. 'We'll singe it. We'll burn its fur off in the fire. We'll cook it whole.'

'Yes,' said Nzé, lighting another cigarette from the stub. 'I sacrifice myself all the time. And what do I get for it?'

'Pineapples,' I said.

'Yes, Uncle!' Nzé shouted, the grievance forgotten, clapping his right arm to his side. 'And saka-saka! And smoked fish! Papayas! Fou-fou! After a night with me, Uncle – they're so pleased, they're so happy. Bohmaaa! They give me more food than I can eat!'

'Crocodiles!' yelled Marcellin from the jetty-tree, wading ashore. 'The big ones swam away, but we've got a young one, *Crocodylus cataphractus*, Redmond – and a baby!' He walked into the circle of firelight, holding a four-foot-long crocodile in his arms, its thin straight jaws bound with twine. He lowered it on to the mud, a restraining hand on its black spine. 'The African slender-snouted! A beauty! We caught him with the noose!' Its flanks were olive-brown, flecked with black; its back feet were webbed and clawed: and along the top of its vertically flattened two-foot-long tail, black on creamy white, a line of cream-and-black scales stuck up like the backward-sloping, triangular plates on a stegosaurus. Making no movement, it watched us with its raised-up, roundel eyes. Vicky laid a nine-inch baby beside it. 'The young one eats fish,' said Marcellin, flicking his head left and right. 'He swipes his snout from side to side – because he can't see straight ahead. And the little one – he eats mosquito larvae!'

'Marcellin,' said Doubla, 'I'll make a basket tonight – and tomorrow, Jean can carry them. The rains are coming. We must leave tomorrow.'

I said, 'But Mokélé-mbembé?'

There was a silence.

'I don't know about that,' said Marcellin, running a hand along the crocodile's flank, not looking up. 'I've been thinking. Maybe Mokélé-mbembé only comes here now and then. Maybe he lives in the Sangha river.'

I went to my tent, strapped on the head-torch, unsealed the plastic bag of notes taped into the top map-pocket of the bergen and counted out the remaining half of the pay I owed Doubla, Vicky and the brothers. But however I tried to work it out there were not enough small notes left to produce the exact amounts – Jean would have to take an extra 10,000-CFA note to share with his brother, and Doubla an extra 10,000 to share between all four of them. Surely they'd be able to find the change? Of course they would – the boatman brought beer to sell from Epéna once a fortnight; and in any case, there was that shop at Djéké ... The temperature dropped; it grew noticeably colder; a wind got up, the leaves above the tent began to rustle and talk to each other; there was the sound of distant thunder, Mokélé-mbembé strolling across the far end of the lake ... I fell asleep.

We left at dawn in heavy, purposeful rain; and in the late afternoon two days later it was still raining as, wet and silent, exhausted with wading through filling ponds and watercourses, struggling across the deepening mud, just outside the Boha plantations we caught up with the Chief's word-carrier. Barefoot, the old man was walking slowly, head down against the rain, wearing nothing but a loincloth of freshly plaited green leaves. In his right hand he held his long spear, in his left a short two-edged iron sword, the hilt of wood. Slung low on his back he carried a basket of liana and bark-strips lined with leaves: inside lay one fish like a perch and an axe – the head, of stone, bound to the handle with liana-twine.

'A stone axe – and a leaf loincloth!' I said to Marcellin in English, without thinking, delighted. 'Pity about the iron sword and the spear-blade – but he's *almost* from the Stone Age!'

'Stone Age my ass,' said Marcellin, annoyed, squeezing water out of his hat. 'Poor man, his balls hurt. His balls hurt him when he wears trousers. He has swollen balls. Huge balls. A hydrocele. Elephantiasis. He's old, Redmond – and soon his balls will kill him.'

And all from a mosquito-bite, I thought, as the old man, to announce our return, made Nzé fire two shots into the air. The tiny larval worms of *Wuchereria bancrofti* are injected down the mosquito's proboscis (the old man arranged us in line, in the order in which we'd left) and as adult worms, white and slender, the female four inches long, the male one and a half, they may lodge in the lymph-ducts draining the limbs and genitals. (We processed, behind the old man, towards the Chief's hut.) The legs and scrotum are most commonly affected: elephantiasis sets in, an overgrowth of subcutaneous tissue and skin, creased and folded, so that the scrotum may eventually weigh more than the rest of the victim. (The spearmen assembled, the Chief appeared in his doorway and Vicky, his royal blood giving him precedence, sang out the story of our journey in Bomitaba.) Lymph is exuded from the scrotal skin – and between the warm wet folds bacteria, usually streptococci, settle in for a well-fed life. I remembered one particularly upsetting sentence from the standard textbook, Dion R. Bell's *Lecture Notes on Tropical Medicine*. Established elephantiasis can only be treated surgically, and even then, if your limbs are affected, you might as well not bother; but surgery on the scrotum is very pleasing – it should be possible to save your testes and: 'The penis, even if completely buried, will be found to be normal when excision of the redundant scrotal tissue reveals it.'

Vicky, his account finished, stood at ease.

The Chief, unpainted, but sitting on the royal stool, the wing-bladed spear held vertically in his right hand, muttered his reply into the inclined ear of his word-carrier. 'The Chief of Boha!' shouted the old man in French. 'He saw it all! He saw everything at the lake, exactly as you describe it. He held off the rains! It was hard work! He dismisses you!'

We piled the packs against the wall of our hut, the empty schoolmaster's hut which now felt as familiar, as friendly as a home, shook hands with Doubla, Vicky and the brothers and said our temporary goodbyes.

'How are you feeling?' said Nzé at my elbow, as we carried the packs inside.

'A bit sick.'

'Sick, Uncle? Me – I'm hurt.' And he lifted up his combat jacket. The skin over both sets of ribs was rubbed raw, bleeding in places. Two days' march, I thought, however hard, one wet night – surely it couldn't produce *that* unaided? Maybe gonorrhoea made your skin especially sensitive? And anyway (I gave him a tube of Savlon from the medicines pack) it's all very well reading medical textbooks, and trying to learn the advice in manuals like Werner's *Where There Is No Doctor*, but round here you ought to be the real thing – or at the very least you should have known about yaws and Extencilline . . .

'Look!' said Manou, lifting his shirt. 'I'm hurt too! It's just as bad! Only I don't make a noise. I don't complain!'

'But what is it? Why are you raw like that? Gonorrhoea?'

'Me? Gonorrhoea? I've *never* had anything disgusting like that. We're not like you! We're civilized. Me and Nzé – we don't go marching in the forest for fun! And in rain like that! That's for pygmies! We're not used to it. We live in a town. We've got homes!'

Nzé set about a remake of the seduction chamber to the right of the door, hanging a damp tarpaulin as a curtain, lighting a candle, humming a happy little tune to himself; Manou found the three-legged camping-stove in the bottom of the rice-sack, emptied my water-bottles into the cooking-pot and began to boil up the fou-fou; Marcellin, undoing the liana-twine knots on Doubla's carrying-basket, lifted out the large crocodile and laid it on the table. I held the long, cold, scaly jaws shut, and Marcellin, with our parachute cord, made a crocodile harness: one loop round the body behind the front legs, one in front of the back legs, a double length between the two, and a lead running from the rear knot. He placed one of the wooden chairs in the corner furthest from the door, weighted it with a pack, and the crocodile, peaceful, thinking its ancient thoughts, allowed us to tether it to the chair-leg.

Nzé waxed two candles onto the middle of the rough table, Manou filled the mess-tins, and we sat down to a supper of fou-fou and the last of the sardines.

'The pinacier Mombété,' said Marcellin, pouring the remains of his water-bottle into a mug, 'the boatman from Epéna – he's supposed to be here a week from now. That's his day. He brings beer from Epéna. He's got a big pirogue and a little engine. We'll go back with him.'

'Epéna!' said Nzé. 'A town! We'll have a fiesta! Uncle Redmond, you'll buy beer and we'll dance and get drunk and have a fiesta – because we're alive. No one died! No one died in the jungle!'

Marcellin, mashing a sardine into his fou-fou, looked at the door. He said, 'It's not over yet. We're not free yet. You wait – now we're all supposed to be friends Vicky or Doubla will come here and ask to borrow the gun. And then the Chief of Boha – he'll take his revenge.' Marcellin stared at his mess-tin. 'Yes,' he said slowly. 'Yes . . . that's what I'd do.' And then, 'Nzé!' he snapped. 'Stop that noise! I've told you, I'm sick of it – don't eat with your mouth open. When you eat – shut your mouth.'

'I can't,' said Nzé, startled, mouth open, the tail-fin of a sardine wedged between his top front teeth. 'Uncle, if I eat with my mouth shut – I can't breathe!'

'Of course you can breathe. And stop calling everyone Uncle. And you two – Nzé, Manou, I forbid you to go and sleep with girls in other huts. You're my responsibility. I said I'd bring you back. I promised your mothers. Those girls of yours – they'll open the door to someone.'

'Not with me, Uncle!' said Nzé, dislodging the fin with a smacking suck, punching the air with his right fist. 'Bohmaaa! They love me!'

'Marcellin,' I said, 'now we're here, couldn't we take a chance? Go north? To Mboua? You said there's a path from there. From Bene Toukou lake. A path the pygmies use. That's what you said. A path we might be able to follow – from Bene Toukou lake to the Ndoki river! All the way through the jungle! And on to Ouesso! How about it? A month? Two months? What do you think? Back down the Sangha. What do you say?'

'I say you're crazy,' said Marcellin, looking up, mouth open, chewing his manioc.

'Uncle,' said Nzé. 'Not me. Not now. I'm hurt. I'm ill inside. I've had enough.'

'I have a wife,' said Manou. 'I have a little son.'

'Come on – what's a month? After all this time? What's the difference?'

'Redmond,' said Marcellin, licking his fingers, 'you're exhausted. We're all exhausted. And you – you've gone crazy. You ask me what I think – and I'll tell you. I've seen it before. White men like you – something happens out there in the forest. Every time. They get a kind of madness in there. They can't leave. They never want to come out!'

'It's not like that.'

'Another month? You're crazy. Two months? That's swamp-forest! The wet season's coming. Maybe it's arrived.'

I was silent.

'And anyway – Redmond, have you got the money?'

'Well – no ... But I'll send it! I'll send the money, and presents. Lots of presents!'

'Send it?' said Marcellin, and laughed. 'What if the Government's changed? What if we get back to Brazzaville and they think you're a spy? A capitalist spy? They'll put you in the prison – the Brazzaville prison!'

'Koko!' shouted someone from outside, pushing the door open.

The man in the dark glasses stepped into the candle-light, something small and black clinging to his tee-shirt.

'Doctor,' he said to me, 'my neck – it's healed. So I've come here. I've come to thank you.' And he thrust the bundle of black hard against my chest.

Two little arms hugged me tight.

'A baby gorilla,' he said, turning to Marcellin. 'A boy.'

The infant pushed his small, sad, black face into the hollow of my neck; I kissed the top of his head; he smelt of fresh leaves.

'Marcellin Agnagna, your white man – he's cured me; it's true. But he's also made trouble in Boha. The Chief of Boha – he's angry. Everyone knows. In the forest, Marcellin Agnagna, your white man gave Ange Moutaboungou, whose sobriquet is Doubla, 10,000 francs, to share with Victor Embingui and the brothers Nicolas and Jean Poulain. But now Doubla is walking through the village. He carries his spear and his knife. He shouts, "If anyone wants my money, the money that belongs to me, Ange Moutaboungou – they must fight me for it!"'

'We'll get small notes,' I said. 'When the boatman comes. Next week. The boatman from Epéna.'

'Your white man also gave 10,000 francs to Nicolas Poulain, to share with his younger brother, Jean. But Nicolas Poulain – he refused to give 5000 francs to Jean Poulain. So Jean attacked him. He beat him up. He knocked him down! Some say that Nicolas is dead. Others say that he sleeps, that he's lost his senses. He lies in his hut.'

I said, 'That's horrible. I'm sorry, I really didn't . . .'

'Comrade Agnagna, this is your affair. You are from the Government of the People's Republic. You are a Communist. I am a Communist. So now – you give me the 20,000 francs. You can trust me. I'll share it equally. And this little problem will be solved.'

'You,' said Marcellin, pushing his chair back, standing up. 'You? A Communist? You're not even on the People's Party Village Committee. You're a nobody! You kill gorillas – and you come here and ask *me* for money! I could send you to prison! Out! Out! Get out!'

The man in the dark glasses, stepping backwards, turning too fast, banged his head on the edge of the door and escaped.

The little gorilla, upset by the noise, nipped me on the chest.

'Well done, Uncle!' said Nzé, awestruck, mouth open. And then, the admiration ebbing from his voice, 'He'll be back! He'll bring his friends. Perhaps he has a gun?'

'There are no guns in Boha. These men are too dangerous. The army took the guns away.'

'He has no friends,' said Manou, clearing away the mess-tins. 'Everyone wants to kill him.'

'But it's not good,' said Marcellin, sitting down, his elbows on the table, his head in his hands. 'You don't get gorilla babies without killing the mother – and that's bad. Because if they're hunting gorilla, if they're eating gorilla meat, they're getting ready for something. They're making themselves strong.'

Nzé pointed at the gorilla in my arms. 'Then we'd better eat that,' he said. 'Then we'll be strong, too.'

I held the gorilla closer, in case he'd understood.

Marcellin laughed. 'You don't get strong by eating babies! You need the big male! A silverback! He's ten times stronger than any man, even in Boha. But the females – there are lots of men in Boha bigger than a female gorilla. But that doesn't stop these people. They still eat females, mother gorillas – and they kick the infants about the village till they die.' He stroked the back of the gorilla's small round head (and it nipped me again). 'Redmond, you don't have to keep it. It's terrible, looking after a baby gorilla. Even worse than a chimp. They won't let you go. They scream! There's no point. That's the truth. There is no point trying to save it. You'll wear yourself out. For nothing.'

'I'm keeping him.'

'You are?' Marcellin smiled. 'So what about the extra months? One month? Two months? Lake Bene Toukou? The Ndoki river? Ouesso? The Sangha?'

'Forget it.'

'Well, Redmond, we wouldn't come with you anyway. We'd never make it. And look at you! Your face! There's nothing left of you. You've shrunk away. You're all in. Finished! You're ill. I'm ill. And you don't have to look after a gorilla.'

'We'll save him. We'll get him out. We'll take him to Madame Leroy. To the orphanage.'

'What's the point? They don't survive. Her survival rate – it's 7 per cent!'

'Then it's worth it.'

Marcellin ran his right hand over his scrub of beard. He pulled at the hairs on his chin. 'Okay. I'll go and see Bobé. Bobé will make us a box. A little cage.'

'He's not going in a cage.'

'No cage? What do you mean? Where'll he sleep?'

'With me.'

'Sleep with that?' said Manou, pushing his chair back. 'Sleep with you?'

'Of course.'

'But Redmond,' said Marcellin gently, and paused. 'He'll shit. He'll shit in the bed. He'll shit all over you!'

'I don't care.'

'That's an animal,' said Nzé. 'It's dirty. It smells.'

'I'm dirty, too. I smell.'

'That's not a person,' said Nzé, scratching his chest. 'If you were lost in the jungle – would it look after you? Would it wash your shirts? No. Then kill it. Throw it away.'

'Redmond, you've gone crazy,' said Marcellin. 'I don't know. Just a little crazy. But I'll go and see Bobé. Bobé will know what to do. He'll know why they've given us a gorilla. I don't understand. But Bobé, he'll tell me what to do.'

'The crocodiles?' said Manou.

'You, Manou – you go and fill the water-bottles in the river. You're safe now. They won't do anything tonight. Doubla will be drunk. And fighting. So wet the skin of the big crocodile; and for the little one – put some water in the cooking-pot. Take him out of the basket and slip him in the cooking-pot. He'll be fine. No trouble at all. He can spend the night in there! And in the morning I'll pay a boy to catch a cockroach – grasshoppers, millipedes, palm-maggots. That's what he likes!'

Nzé said to me, 'That's an animal. Uncle – we must kill it. How can we bring girls here, Manou and me? They won't come here. Not to a hut with a gorilla. They won't come near us! Kill it!'

'No one's going to kill it.'

'White men,' said Marcellin, standing up, his voice hard. 'Really the whites are terrible. They brought the guns here and now they say don't kill your wildlife. They're cruel one minute, sentimental the next. And it makes me sick.' He stopped in the doorway. 'If you're going to be sentimental, if you're going to sleep with that gorilla – then I'll sleep on the floor, in Nzé's room.' He gave the door a violent yank, pulling it wide open, came back into the hut, snatched up his blue pack, and turned to leave. 'In fact, I'll sleep in Bobé's hut. So you – you can look out for yourself!'

'Find some milk!' I yelled after him. 'Some powdered milk! And fruit!'

I stood up (the gorilla clasped me with his little black feet as well as his hands), got my torch, switched it on, held it between my teeth, picked up my bergen and went to the small right-hand back room, my old bedroom: the window-hole, with its half-open wooden shutter, and the plank bed, with its thousand bed-bugs waiting hidden crabwise in the cracks, no longer seemed quite so threatening. I dumped the bergen beside the bed, put the torch on the planks, undid the top flap of the bergen with my left hand, pulled out the two tarpaulins and a shirt, and, still holding the gorilla with my right arm, with my left hand I managed to spread one of the tarpaulins as a sheet and place the shirt as a pillow; I lay gently back on the bed, too tired to take off my boots, and, half expecting the gorilla to climb off my chest and scoot for the door, I released my grip.

He wriggled higher and pushed his head under my chin. I took off my glasses, placed them on the bergen, and laid both hands on his back, on his rough dense fur. He was shivering, but whether from fright or cold I couldn't tell. A gecko began to chirp up under the corrugated-iron roof. Or was it one of those outsize forest grasshoppers? I couldn't decide. Of course you can't, I thought, everyone knows: when you first become a mother you can't think straight about anything. You start nesting everywhere. That's all you want to do. So I pulled up the second tarpaulin. The gorilla raised his head; he scrutinized me with his brown-black pupils; his dark-brown eyes were milky-white at the edges; the black skin in the middle of his low forehead was furrowed with three vertically curved worry-lines, a fan of anxiety. 'It's okay,' I said. 'We call this a tarpaulin. It's a big leaf.' His quarter-open mouth was pink inside, and his breath smelt sweet, like the breath of a day-old calf. Black wrinkles ran across the top and down the sides of his flattened nose: I rubbed the end of my own ape's nose (long and sharp) against the end of his big broad nostrils: the skin was warm and dry. 'Your nose – it's dry.

Shouldn't it be cold and wet? You okay?' Bored with talk, he put his head down again. Between finger and thumb I tweaked his little, flat, black ear. 'But how are we going to sleep?' I said, and fell asleep.

A torch-beam in my face woke me. 'You slept with your torch on,' came Marcellin's voice. 'You'll waste the batteries.' He sat on the edge of the bed. My chest felt heavy, and hot, and wet. I turned over, reaching for my glasses, and something nipped me. 'A gorilla!' I said. 'I slept with a gorilla!'

Marcellin inspected my shirt. 'It's pissed on you,' he said, and handed me my glasses. The gorilla opened his eyes, looked at me, pouted with annoyance, and yawned.

'It's nearly dawn,' said Marcellin, lowering his voice. 'You awake? You listening?'

'Yes.'

'Last night – I had a long talk to Bobé. And Doubla came. I'm in trouble.'

'We're always in trouble.'

'Only here. Only in Boha. Everywhere else in this country – it's safe. It's not like Zaïre. It's well governed.'

'I'm sure it is.'

'But listen. There's not much time. We must be quick. I'm leaving.'

'Leaving?' I sat up. I put my right arm round the gorilla. Marcellin's blue pack was on the floor at his feet.

'Last night Bobé sent to another village. For a fisherman, a friend of his. This fisherman will take me to Djéké. We're meeting him in an hour – further up the bank, on the main river, out of sight. The Chief of Boha has taken an oath. The Chief has sworn to kill anyone who helps me escape. But you're okay. Because Doubla says that he, too, he'll kill anyone – he'll spear anyone who touches you or your gorilla. Because you're a friend of Bobé, his father. You drank palm-wine in his father's house. Besides, he says he likes you.'

'He does?'

'Yes, he says he likes you – because you're mad. And everyone knows, they all say you have a powerful fetish. You talk to it. In your tent.'

'I do? In my sleep? I talk in my sleep?'

'No, in daylight. At Lake Télé. The brothers Nicolas and Jean Poulain – they heard two voices from your tent. But there was no one there but you. You were alone!'

'But what about Manou? Nzé?'

'They're *petits*! They're useless – Nzé, he can't even cook. They're useless. No one's going to bother with them!'

'The crocodiles? How do I look after the crocodiles?'

'I'll take them. Nzé will help me. He'll carry them to the dugout. He'll walk back the long way round. You and Manou will stay here. I'll take the crocodiles and the gun. If a man owns crocodiles it's difficult to kill him. If you have crocodiles, Redmond, it means something.'

'So you said.'

'Here – I've got things for you. From Bobé.' He unzipped his pack, drew out two small, battered, shiny tins and put them on the bergen. 'Powdered milk. The best we could do. All his old wife could find. And you Redmond, you'll owe me 40,000 CFA. Here, I've brought you 20,000, in small notes.' (He slipped them under a milk tin.) 'My own money, for you to buy fruit and manioc in the village, papayas and pineapples – for you three and the gorilla. And the other 20,000 you owe me – I've paid Madame Bobé in advance: she'll bring you manioc and fish-soup and saka once a day, after dark. You like saka-saka!' (He touched me quickly on the shoulder.) 'I remembered! And the rest of the money – too bad. It's your fault we're here at all. But for you I would never have returned. Not to Boha. Not without soldiers. Not in a hundred years! So that's for the fisherman, and for me, to keep me in Djéké – for food and palm-wine.'

'Palm-wine?'

'Irene – she loves palm-wine.'

'Irene?'

'The young girl. My girl in Djéké. The one you met. She wants a job with me in Brazzaville. In the Ministry. But she's too young. And there's no money. It's impossible!'

'Let's square it now,' I said, leaning gently over to the bergen. 'I've got four 10,000s.'

'No!' Marcellin switched off the torch and stood up. 'Keep it for me! It's safer here. Redmond, I'm afraid. I don't know. I don't know what's going to happen. Bobé's old. His plans – they're not always good. You've seen for yourself – the men of Boha are big. Really big. They're strong. They're used to fighting. What if they come after us? What if they chase us? In their long canoes? I may have to swim! Swim to the bank! Run away in the forest!'

'Uncle,' hissed Nzé from the front room. 'Come on! Hurry!'

'Wait!' I said, turning the torch back on. 'When do we see you? Where do we meet?'

'Six days' time! Early morning! The landing-stage!'

In the front room of the hut, in the half-light, Manou, hunched over the camping-stove on the mud floor, was boiling rice for our breakfast; I got my mug, squatted beside him, and, the gorilla hanging to my chest (one arm round my neck), I mixed the milk powder with sugar and water – until it began to approach my idea of the perfect offering of the breast from paradise (thick as tapioca, rich as Belgian chocolate).

Manou, peering in, disgusted, said. 'He'll be sick.'

So I oozed half the mixture into Marcellin's big blue plastic mug, added water to both mugs and placed them on the table. I sat the baby on my knee, as you should. Like any good new mother I picked up the blue mug with tentative care, and, making encouraging noises, I tilted it gently towards the baby's mouth.

The baby's short legs and long arms struck forward. The baby's little fingers and toes gripped the blue plastic, top and bottom, with shocking force: he sucked and splashed; he gurgled; he spouted like a geyser.

My trousers sticky and wet, I said, 'We should do this with a tarpaulin.'

Manou, wiping milk from his face, said, 'You should do it outside.'

The mug three-quarters empty, the baby unclamped his feet from its bottom rim; he repositioned his feet on my thigh; he lifted up the mug; and he chucked the rest of the milk backwards over his head.

Manou laughed.

The baby slid round on his buttocks, on his little tuft of white hairs, to check out the target. He looked at my splattered glasses, at my dripping face, and then, his eyes bright, his mouth open pink, his body jigging up and down, he laughed, too, a fast and rasping pant. 'Hah-hah-hah-hah!' he said.

'Ha ha yourself,' I said, taking off my glasses, putting them on the table, and starting him on the second mug.

Manou, helpless, shrieked, 'He'll do it again!'

'Stop it, Manou! Stop laughing! Don't encourage him. Discipline – that's all we need. Besides,' I said, holding the mug tight, 'I'm ready for him.'

The mug half-empty, the baby, quick and strong, flexed his arms and caught me in the chest.

'Right!' I spluttered. 'That's it! We're going to the river. We're going to wash.' The baby, on my lap, bouncing about in the slush, said, 'Hah-hah-hah-hah-hah!'

'Wash!' howled Manou, bent double, collapsing onto a chair. 'He won't let you wash! They hate water! They're dirty! They smell! And so will you!'

My clothes were now, presumably, by gorilla standards, tasting good, the stench of alien sweat pasted well in with milk and sugar, and he sucked my shirt as I carried him, in the grey dawn, across the school playground with its straggly grasses, past the bamboo-clump, past the low shrubs with their spikes of orange flowers, past the safou tree with its dark-green leaves and small pink fruits, and on to the narrow mud path through the reed-grass which led down to the river.

The Vice-President, thin and nervous, was coming up the other way. Seeing the gorilla, he at once lost his hesitant air, his anxieties left him. 'Koko!' he shouted, as at a door, and knocked twice, hard, on top of the gorilla's head. With a convulsion, a spasm of pain that shook his whole body, the gorilla nipped me.

I shouted into the Vice-President's face: 'Don't do that! What the hell was that for? Why do that?'

'They like it!' he said with a smile, and shrugged. 'You have gorillas at home? In your village?'

'No I don't,' I said, angry, pushing past him.

'That Vice-President,' I thought, sitting down on a charred tree-trunk beside the path, to recover. 'He's a sadist. But then they so often are, those nervous types, those murderous loners . . .'

A young man I hadn't met, barefoot, bare-chested, wearing a pair of khaki trousers, a length of red cloth over his shoulder, coming down to wash, stopped beside me. *'Gorillon!'* he said and, leaning forward – but I was just in time, whipping my right hand over the gorilla's head – 'Koko!' he shouted. His knuckles struck the top of my hand like the forks on a claw-hammer.

'Jesus!' I said, shaking my damaged right hand, capping the gorilla's head with my left. 'Why do that? What's that for?'

'They like it,' he said, surprised. 'You don't have gorillas? In your village? No gorillas?'

'No.'

'They like it! That's what you do! That's how you say: "Hello, Monsieur le Gorille, good morning."' And 'No gorillas,' he said to himself, shaking his uncracked head, walking off to wash.

'That swine,' I said to the gorilla, cautiously moving each finger on my right hand in turn. 'That young swine. I think he's bust my hand. Metacarpals, that's what these bones are called. You've got them too. These five bones' – I spread his leathery little hand in mine – 'between your wrist and your fingers, see?' The gorilla looked up at me, boss-eyed. 'That's what that swine's done. He's mashed my metacarpals.' The gorilla transferred his right hand to the top of his head. 'Yes. Poor you. A terrible headache? Concussed, probably. A blood clot in there? I wouldn't be surprised. I don't think we'll come this way again, do you? Not until we leave. We'll wash at night, by torchlight. What do you think? And for our walks together – we'll go to your forest. Okay?'

I followed the young man, at a safe distance, but when the river itself came in sight, the gorilla clung to me hard and began to whimper, a pitiful low rising cry, a hint of a scream ... I turned round and walked back, fast, towards the hut.

Manou and Nzé were sitting at the table, intent, close together, eating rice. A full mess-tin, and a spoon, waited in my place.

'I'm telling Manou, Uncle. I've done it!'

'You have?' I said, sitting down, wondering whether gorillas liked half-boiled rice.

'I've save us!' (I offered the gorilla a spoonful. He wrinkled up his wrinkled nose.) 'We're safe!'

'I'm glad to hear it.'

'Yes, Uncle. You should be. I've been talking to people. All the way back. All over the village. "Nzé Oumar," I said to myself, "remember your grandfather. Be a man!" He used to say to me, Uncle, "Little Nzé," he'd say, "if you have a problem with a friend – hit him in the chest. Never in the back. Be a man!" So I said to everyone in the village, Uncle, I said, "Our white, you know. Perhaps I ought to warn you. He has a fetish. A powerful fetish. He talks to it. And this fetish of his – he got it from Dokou. From Dokou, in the north. Far away. From the great, the famous Dokou!"'

'They've heard of Dokou? Down here?'

'Of course not, Uncle! But I said to myself, "Nzé Oumar, you're from Dongou. You're not like these people. You're *clever*." So I'd start like this, straight away, I'd get close up, like you do with a secret, and I'd say, "This fetish – it's not an ordinary fetish. Not at all. Our white, this fetish of his – he got it from Dokou. And you know who I mean – Dokou, the most powerful sorcerer in the north. There's nobody can match Dokou. No one's got powers like Dokou. If you don't know about Dokou – why, you must be a real country person!" And they'd say, "Dokou! Of course!"'

'Well done!'

'But I kept quiet about some things, Uncle. I didn't tell them. Because I'm *clever*. I didn't say, "You won't believe this – but in the north, they use palm-oil in their lamps!"'

'Why? What do they use here?'

'Palm-oil! But they pretend it's kerosene. That's what civilized people use – kerosene. We've got kerosene at home.'

'So what do you mean, we're safe? How are we safe?'

'The fetish, Uncle! I said to everyone I met, I said, "Look, I like it here in Boha. You've been good to me. Especially your girls! Your beautiful big girls! So I'll do you a favour. I'll tell you a secret. It's dangerous – but you've been good to me! Listen. A word of advice. A secret. If you have evil thoughts about our white, if you harm our white – and that goes for me and Manou too, because we look after him, but it especially goes for me, Nzé Oumar, because I do all the work, and it's frightening, believe me, especially at night, in the forest, when he changes shape – where was I? Oh yes. A warning. If you're thinking of harming our white, then I'm sorry for you. Because the moment you touch him – you'll turn white. Like the dead. Like him."'

'Well done!'

'Yes, Uncle, no one wants to look like you. That's – that's horrible!'

Manou and Nzé, laughing, restored by rice and intrigue, went off to find their girls.

Six days, I thought, sitting on the plank-bed, stuffed with rice, the gorilla at my chest, what are we going to do? 'What are we going to do?' I said. 'How do we get through six days? We can't swim. We can't wash. We can't even walk through the village without you getting cracked on the head. They'll fracture your skull. Right now, I suppose, we could play round-and-round-the garden . . .' I opened his right hand and ran my finger round his broad, black, wrinkled palm. 'Went the teddy bear,' I said. Studying the circle traced by my finger, the gorilla's face expressed extreme concentration, that arduous pre-understanding phase. 'This way, that way,' I said, and (his upper arm was much longer than his forearm), 'tickly under there!'

At the third routine he looked up at me, his eyes twinkling, his mouth open (but not far enough to show his teeth), his lips stretched back: he was smiling.

'Yes,' I said, despondent. 'But I'm a rotten mother. I'm bored with this already!'

His thumb was so short it couldn't touch the base of his index finger; his fingers were short and stubby, like Lary's. 'In fact,' I said, 'I wish Lary was here. He'd help. Wouldn't he? Eh? What would he do?' The little gorilla smiled again. 'Of course! A routine!'

'Read, walk,' I said. 'Sleep, eat. I know – it sounds feeble, but there you are, it's the best we can do. There's nothing else on offer.'

So from the bergen I got the last surviving paperback, a now mould-decayed copy of the Penguin edition of Goncharov's *Oblomov* – on whose front cover Chagall's giant, green-faced fiddler plays by night above the wooden huts and stone church of a Russian village – and I put it in my leg-pocket. 'First off,' I said, as I carried the gorilla out of the hut, 'to the school! A1 quality-time leisure facilities! And a goddam yard, outside. Second off – a bike ride in the forest. Third, to the Grand Union (it's not a canal, you know, you should know that) for a Dijon-mustard something sandwich. Fourth off, we construct a house – to the State Whatsit Standard, only I guess we'll go Higher Grade. You know – we'll utilize that eight by twenty-five timber for the main support joists. (Okay, so that doesn't sound quite right.) And we'll have a cantilevered roof. Or was that a bridge? Or a wall?'

'Snush,' said the gorilla, with a sneeze. 'Hah-hah!'

At the edge of the open space, close to the school-hut, two small, earth-brown doves, perhaps Red-billed wood doves, were feeding in the grasses, criss-crossing the ground, heads nodding; as we approached they took to the air with a sharp double clap, a flash of rufous wings, and flew low, fast and silent, into the forest.

We sat at the first bench-desk to the right of the door, in front of the large, rectangular window-opening. Was this where Nzé's girl, better than a whole bottle of whisky, had cried with pleasure? Probably not. More likely over there, in the dark corner at the back. *'Calme-toi!'* I said to the gorilla. 'Snush,' he said, and sneezed.

'I hope that's just dust. I hope that's not pneumonia.' I took out my book. 'Because you get all our diseases, you know, and we get yours: all kinds of parasitic worms, malaria, yellow fever, hepatitis, yaws, even arthritis, heart disease – cirrhosis of the liver! And talking of cirrhosis of the liver,' I whispered in his ear, 'that poor Lary,' I comforted myself, 'I don't suppose he's having a carwash with the young nurse Chris in a real shower, with proper soap, and shampoo, and sex, and hot water, do you? And fluffy towels? Not a chance! I don't suppose he's altogether free of bites and sores and tropical ulcers? Of mould and slime and the pee of gorillas? Of course not!' The gorilla shook his small round head; he faced away; he stared out of the window-space. 'No, we don't think that, do we? You and me, we're not subject to fits of manic jealousy. Are we? Of course we're not! So I agree with you. He's probably lying in a bed in the university hospital – if Plattsburgh State has one – and he's got some minor Congo illness or other, you know, nothing to worry about, just the new drug-resistant tuberculosis. Jolly interesting. A gift for the medical dons, if they have them. A real present from us. And maybe he's got the odd microscopic parasitic blood-worm, too, a new species. Entirely undescribed. Not even *imagined* before. Eh?' I turned his furry head round. 'What do you think?'

The gorilla raised the tubular ridges of his eyebrows; he pursed his lips; he whimpered.

'I'm sorry. That was in bad taste. I apologize. I forgot – you gorillas have a deep moral sense. You really do.' So I opened Goncharov. I'm fond of *Oblomov*, I thought, because it's about a man, like me, who finds it difficult to get out of bed.

The gorilla whined, so I lifted him off my chest and set him facing me, on top of the desk. He sucked in his lips and closed his mouth; he tipped back his head; he looked uneasily about the room; he hooked his feet into my shirt; he put both arms round my neck. 'I know, I'll read to you – that's what mothers do!

'Now listen, I haven't got very far this time – the young Oblomov, the boy Oblomov, is in the nursery, like you, and his old nurse, like me, is telling stories. She "filled the boy's memory and imagination with the *Iliad* of Russian life, created by our Homers in the far-off days when man was not yet able to stand up to the dangers and mysteries of life and nature" … We still can't, can we? The more you know, the more frightening death is. Don't you find that? You and me – we're the product of the primordial soup plus 4000 million years of accumulated random mutations (and the theft of the odd bacterium), a development directed by nothing more than natural and sexual selection. Tragic, don't you think? Or the most interesting story there is, or both, depends on how you look at it. But – look at me – when you grow up I want you to realize, as early as possible, before *and* after all those sex hormones render you temporarily insane, that everything else – science and art, literature and music, even the history of religions, if you must – it's all a bonus, so you must enjoy it, every minute you've got. Will you promise – promise me that?'

The gorilla stared at me, his eyes fixed and hard; he looked down at the desk; he gave a little broken growl, like a puppy.

'You're upset! You're scowling, aren't you? A good sulk? Of course. You're right. You didn't come to school to hear your mother burble away. You hear that all the time. Drives you crazy. Yes – I understand – you want to get on with the story!

'Where were we? That's right. Here: "the mysteries of life and nature, when he" – *he* means man, or gorillas, you know, apes in general – "when he trembled at the thought of werewolves and wood-demons and sought Alyosha Popovich's help against the adversities threatening him on all sides, and when the air, water, forests, and plains were full of marvels. Man's life in those days was insecure and terrible; it was dangerous for him to go beyond his own threshold; a wild beast might fall upon him any moment"' – the black hand of a wild beast took hold of the top right-hand corner of the page – '"or a robber might kill him, or a wicked Tartar rob him of all his possessions, or he might disappear without a trace. Or else signs from heaven might appear, pillars or balls of fire" – that's lightning, that's what frightens you in the forest – "or a light might glimmer above a new grave" – methane gas, we release it when we rot – "or some creature might walk about in the forest as though swinging a lantern, laughing terribly and flashing its eyes in the dark"' – the brown, close-haired head of some creature began to obscure my field of view – 'Stop it! How can I read? With your head in the way? "And so many mysterious things happened to people, too: a man might live for years happily without mishap, and all of a sudden"' – the wild beast bit the top of the page – '"he would begin to talk strangely or scream in a wild voice, or walk in his sleep..."' The wild beast screamed in a wild voice. He picked up Goncharov's *Oblomov* and back-flipped it over my shoulder. The small, flimsy, brown-mouldy pages, flapping like panic in a weaver tree, landed on the mud floor twenty feet away.

'Okay,' I said, annoyed, putting him down on the mud floor too. 'You can amuse yourself! Play! Go on! Play!'

He slapped the flats of his hands on the dried mud; he screwed up his eyes; he curled back his lips; he displayed his white teeth; he opened his mouth pink and wide; and he screamed – a loud, shrill, three-second shriek.

I picked him up and held him close, my right arm across his back, my left hand pressing his head under my chin. He hugged me tight with his legs and arms, stopped screaming, tensed, and defecated in a steady stream down my shirt and trousers.

'So that's it!' I said, pleased to have solved a local mystery in infant gorilla behaviour. 'That's why you were so upset! You needed a shit!'

'Oooh!'

'And you can only manage it when you feel secure, when you're clamped to your mother. Of course you can't go behind a bush. Not when there are leopards about!' I considered my waistcoat of yellow and pungent diarrhoea. 'What does your mother do? Ignore it? Wipe it off with a roll of leaves? Because there's no doubt about it, is there? I don't suppose it's a matter for discussion? You intend to shit all over me, don't you, night and day?'

'Snush,' he said, smiling. 'Hah-hah!'

'You like it, don't you? You like to be talked to!' (He detached his right hand from my neck and scratched himself below the left armpit.) 'But I'm not sure I can keep it up. Not all day. And I'm forgetting – your mother's worked it out. She doesn't walk around standing up. Not for more than a few yards. Too risky. She's learnt. She makes sure you're hanging on beneath her, directly above the ground...'

He half-rose on all-fours against my chest, urging me on somewhere.

'Our walk!' I said, kissing him on top of his head (where he still smelt of fresh leaves). I retrieved my book, slipped it in my pocket, and carried him outside.

I glanced across at the hut. That's odd, I thought, there's no one waiting by the door for medicines, no press of children peering through the window-holes: it's deserted, there's no one in sight.

We entered the forest beneath a tall lone tree with a straight trunk of white bark, whiter than the bark on a Silver birch; its crown was deep but diaphanous against the grey sky, and on its lowest branch sat a small hornbill with a blue-black breast and back, a white stomach and a patch of yellow on its bill. I said, 'That's a Piping hornbill.' But the hornbill, far from piping, cocked its head, looked down at us – and barked. It dropped out of the tree with a laugh and a cackle, a manic burst of white-flashing wing-beats (eerily silent for a hornbill – no whoosh of ragged feathers) and, in one long glide half-way across the playground, another bout of flapping, another glide, it disappeared fast, direct and undulating, high into the forest towards the Lake Télé path.

'Today we have naming of plants,' I said, as we pushed through the bushes of the forest edge. 'You know them all, of course. But we call that an Umbrella tree, and that's a young oil palm and that's . . . well, you know . . . and anyway, it's probably only got a Latin name . . . and besides, five minutes in a library would set you right – that's what my old tutor used to say when things got tough. But you can tell it's secondary forest, can't you? Forest that's been cleared for a plantation, maybe twenty years ago? Or some of the big trees felled – for huts or canoes or those school desks?' He belched in my ear. 'What's that? How do I know? Because apart from one or two massive trees – like that one with the grey bark and the tall buttresses – it's almost uniformly low, isn't it? And all the leaves are a paler shade of green, and it's irregular – there are sudden tangles of liana' – I stopped to disconnect my trouser-leg from a curving line of Wait-awhile thorns – 'and then patches of deep shade beneath close stands of trees, where you can walk easily, just like you can in virgin forest. But you're right, let's tell the truth – you must always tell the truth as you see it, to the best of your ability, will you promise me that? – I'm half-cheating, because you can safely assume that anything this close to a reasonably old village is going to be secondary forest. But it's interesting – all the trees here will have something in common: they grow very fast, they don't live long, twenty to fifty years, and they put all their energy into – what?'

'Hah!'

'That's right! Well done!' (I hugged him.) 'You got it! Seed dispersal!' (He burped.) 'They produce a vast amount of seeds; they wrap them up in fruits that birds and bats find irresistible – and they spread their genes right across the forest. Because until the Bantu arrived (yesterday, from the tree's point of view) and began to clear larger patches of forest for a village and plantations, these light-loving trees and shrubs had to wait for a natural gap to form – the fall of a big tree, the path of a tornado, Mokélé-mbembé strolling about the place, Forest elephants tracking from one seasonal feeding-ground to another, tramping out their boulevards . . .'

He nipped me on the chest.

'What was that for?'

'Hah-hah!'

'No, that's not funny. Listen – you find the seeds of these trees right out in primary forest. If you take a sample of soil almost anywhere, even in forest that's never been disturbed, you'll find their seeds; whereas the giants of primary forest glow slowly and live for hundreds of years and don't trouble their old heads with dispersal – they mostly produce huge seeds that simply fall to the ground and bounce or roll for a yard or two. A few make fruits that people like you, and bushpigs, eat, and you leave them in droppings maybe half-a-mile away, but that's about it.'

A flock of African grey parrots whistled to each other overhead.

'Hah!' he said, and nipped me again.

'Don't do that! I don't like it. It hurts.' I bent down and bit him, gently, on his right ear.

He looked at me, astonished, his brow raised, the milky-whites of his eyes showing; he made some fundamental reassessment of the nature of our friendship, rubbed his ear, and buried his face in my neck.

'Perhaps you want something? What is it? Eh? Am I being stupid?'

He made an odd little noise, half-croon, half-whimper.

'What would you normally do? At this time of day?'

He clung on tighter and flattened himself against me.

'I know! A siesta! The whole group lies down around now. Is that it? Your mother might even build a rough nest; you sleep for a couple of hours and then feed again in the late afternoon. Is that right?'

'Snush.'

'Okay. Let's find a peaceful-looking tree. I can't go building nests, you know, not at my age. So we'll pretend we're big males, shall we? We'll flatten a circle of herbs and grasses at the base of a tree and lie on that. Okay? Will that do?'

'Ooof.'

So I trod the vegetation flat beneath a medium-sized tree with no buttresses or surface-roots, a tree whose dark-brown bark was crusted with grey lichen and from whose trunk clumps of small green fruits sprouted, ten to fifteen a cluster, one or two beginning to turn orange on top. 'See that?' I said, gathering a handful of leaves from a five-foot herb (or was it a Dwarf tree?). 'That's called Cauliflory, or at least I think it is – when flowers and fruits grow straight out of the trunk like that, or on very short shoots, or maybe that's Trunciflory?' I wiped away at the diarrhoea. 'Anyway, you get the point – it's no use depending on wind-dispersal near the forest floor where the air's as close and still as this.' I lay down on my back. We looked up at the trunk, at the low, closed canopy above us. 'And if those fruits are turning orange they must be for birds – if you're after bats there's no need to be coloured. All you have to do is smell, the stronger the better. You have to stink, like us.'

He grunted, like a small and contented pig.

'What does your mother do now? Nod off? I suppose so. But now can be a dangerous time if you're a big male, the silverback, especially if your females are in oestrus – you know, ready to make babies – Dian Fossey watched a silverback Mountain gorilla (and it's probably the same for you) when two females in his harem were in oestrus, on heat, feeling sexy, however you like to put it, and just around now, when the silverback was down on his knees with exhaustion, done in, desperate for a sleep, another big male appeared. Because the noise of all that love-making, the female's pulsating whimper, the male's long grumbling and panting and hooting, the howl of triumph when it's over – that drives any roaming young silverback crazy. Any mature male within earshot, every silverback wandering all alone through the forest, dreaming of a harem – they go berserk. And that's when you really get tested, just when all you want to do is roll over and go to sleep.'

'Hah,' he said, half-asleep, face-down on my chest.

A black swallowtail with a bright-green band on its wings flicked haphazardly past, low to the ground, as if in a trance, or lost, or with nothing in particular that it had to do.

'No, it's not even half a joke. Most of the time you're allowed to be kind and peaceful: you slow your walking pace if one of your harem is injured or old or ill, you let the infants romp all over you, tweak your nose, stick their fingers in your ears, even when you're taking your siesta. But when the intruder arrives – you have to get right out of bed. You have to strut in front of him, with short, abrupt steps, your arms held stiff, bent outwards at the elbows. Your coat must bristle. You must not let on that really you've had it for the day, you're asleep on all-fours. You must show him how big and alert and confident you are. You turn your head away. You present your flank. You steal the odd glance. Because he's displaying too, matching you step for step – only he's fresh and vigorous, he's powered by years of frustration, he's foaming with desire.'

'Ooof.'

'Yes, horrible! Because if that doesn't work you've got to find real energy. You stare straight at him. You open your mouth as wide as you can – you let him know that your enormous canines are still sharp, unbroken. You drum on your barrel of a chest. And then, I'm afraid, you have to produce, as George Schaller said of the Mountain gorilla, "the most explosive sound in nature" – your roar. And then, well, then you charge – and if he stands his ground you must fight. As viciously as you can. Somehow or other you must get close enough to bite him in the head.

'And it really matters. Because if you fail, if the younger intruder in his prime drives you away from your harem, he'll kill all your babies (and attack any mother who attempts to save her child) – because he wants to bring all the females into oestrus, into breeding condition, for himself, and as soon as possible.'

(A big black Ground beetle with white spots on its wing-cases, its jaws a pair of black hooks, the biggest beetle I'd seen, was hunting something, running, pausing, raising its antennae, running through the grasses beside me.)

'And you? You nurse your wounds a safe distance away; you try and hang around to get a glimpse of your loved ones; but it's all too much, your confidence has gone, your serotonin levels drop away to nothing, you become depressed, incapable of anything much – you become an old male that no one will ever be kind to again, wandering through the forest, all alone, for the rest of your days.'

'Ooof,' he said, and grunted.

'What should you do? The solution – is that what you mean?'

'Ooof.'

'I'm sorry, but you have to pick the right mother – that's the only sure way, to be the first-born son of the first female to attach herself to a young silverback, to be the first male offspring of a honeymoon couple, when your mother will always remain the dominant, the favourite female in the silverback's group. And you'll get lots of privileges, and your confidence will grow – because apparently that's what it all depends on, self-assurance. Your view of yourself will determine whether you build a harem at all, and for how long you manage to keep it. As Freud told us, "If a man has been his mother's undisputed darling he retains throughout life the triumphant feeling, the confidence in success . . ." He'll conquer the world. Still, how many men can say that? And anyway, who in their right mind wants to conquer the world? Still, you're right again – I'm not sure, correct me if I'm wrong, but I don't think Freud has much to say about sons who've seen their mothers speared in front of them and then cut up into steaks.'

'*Hoo hoo hoo*,' called a Red-billed dwarf hornbill, very close, or was it a Red-eyed dove, or a Red-chested cuckoo? A flicker of red receding through the forest, red spots under my eyelids, dancing away from me . . .

'Yes, you'll have to internalize your mother – turn her into the perfect mother, deep in your growing mind, someone who'll support you always, whatever you do. Maybe that'll make normal sex impossible for you, but I don't think so – it's how Darwin coped, I'm sure of it. His actual mother died when he was eight, and all he remembered of her was her black velvet gown, and her "curiously constructed work-table", so he said, but I don't think his ideal mother ever abandoned him, not for a moment...'

A small, black, gentle hand crept up under my right ear, across my beard and cheek, and fastened itself over my mouth.

I woke up, covered in big blue-black flies and the little black sweat-bees, feeding on my shirt and trousers, on the slime of diarrhoea. The gorilla was still asleep, his breathing fast and shallow under my right ear. 'Go on,' I whispered to the flies and bees, lying as still as I could. 'Keep at it. Eat all you can. And one of you – go fetch a few dung-beetles.' I stared up at the grey-green lichens on the trunk of the tree. I tried and failed to remember who had first discovered that lichens were really composites of a fungus and an alga in symbiosis, living together, or a fungus and cyanobacteria – blue-green algae, closely related to bacteria, whose fossils have been found in rocks 3000 million years old, and which, given air and light, photosynthesize, releasing oxygen. So it's thanks to you, I thought, and the oxygen you first produced, that we're here at all. And how peaceful it would be to devote one's life to the study of lichens. Or would it? Maybe even in the history of the science of lichens you'd find rivalries, jealousies, murderous disputes – indeed perhaps they're a necessity, part of the motivation for the study of anything. Maybe if you examined the skeletons of all those botanists who'd studied lichens you'd find that 74 per cent of the males had suffered severe head wounds...

The light appeared to be failing. How long had we been asleep? Or was a storm coming? 'Wake up!' I said, giving the gorilla a little shake. 'It's almost dark!'

He lifted his head, opened his eyes, rubbed them with the backs of his hands, and looked at me, hard, as if trying to remember what had happened to him, where he was.

'It's okay. We'll go back. Maybe Old Bobé's wife has brought the food. Who knows? Perhaps there'll be bananas for you. Maybe even – papayas!'

He yawned, stretched himself against my chest, sniffled, and sighed, an intense little sigh, as if, yes, now he'd remembered, it was all over, pointless, life was nothing but confusion and pain.

'Look – people do survive without their mothers. It's not quite all empty space, you know, it's not all austere as death . . . It can be done . . . Bananas! Papayas!'

I kissed the broad, soft oval of skin on the top of his nostrils.

'Oooh!'

'That's right! Courage!'

I stood up, and we set off for home, my right arm supporting him under the white-furred infant-tuft on his rump. 'What's this for, your white scut? What's the point? Or to be pedantic – what's the selective advantage? So everyone knows you're little? So your mother can find you, when you're face-down, sniffing a beetle in a thicket?'

He whined.

'Yes, I know – you're hungry. You must be very hungry. But it's okay. We're nearly there. And this nose of yours' – with my left hand I stroked the soft stub – 'the shape of the nostrils, the pattern of the creases, it's unique to you apparently, unique as our fingerprints – and yet we only have to check out the noses of the women in your dad's harem to tell who your mother is. Still, I suppose it's much the same with us.'

He whined in earnest.

'Forgive me, I'm sorry, I forgot, I mustn't keep talking about your mother. A few more minutes and it's – papayas! Except . . . hang on . . . that's a joke . . . how far in did we walk? Not far, was it? A hundred, two hundred yards? . . . And if I manage to get you out to the orphanage in Brazzaville, there may be other infant gorillas, friends your own age, people to play with . . .'

I stopped to disentangle my shirt-sleeve from a liana; it was close-set with short thorns, not the Wait-awhile – in fact I didn't recognize any of the trees or bushes or lianas, but then, I told myself, you wouldn't, would you? 'Yes, friends your own age.' And I thought of the wasted white faces of those orphanage children in nineteenth-century photographs, those faces with big sad eyes, eyes that were too old for the blurry little figures in their ill-fitting clothes – perhaps the very same children who had had to colour in, by rote, many of the lithographic plates in my favourite bird-books . . . 'Where are we? Do you know?' He whimpered. 'Of course not. We're lost. But don't you panic. Because I've got something. You'll like it. You can play with it.' And I reached into my belt-pouch for the compass.

I felt a half-spent tube of Savlon; a wet leaf; a little mud, by the brass eye of the water-exit hole, at the bottom. The fear rising from my fingers, I scrabbled at the rubberized inner panels front and back, at the canvas-webbing, on the sides. 'It's not there! It's fallen out!' I held the gorilla against me with one arm and then the other and I searched my pockets, knowing very well that it couldn't be in any of them. 'That stupid fast walk back from the lake! Through the forest. The swamp-forest! The compass – it's tipped out! It's gone!'

I must think, I thought, I must stay calm; and I started to shake. 'It's okay. We've got water' – and looking down at my belt I saw that the canvas holders were slack, that I'd left my water-bottles in the hut. 'We've broken the rules! All the rules! It's your fault. It really is. This mother business! They're right – you lose your head, you lose your own life – you can't think. You can't even think straight!'

The gorilla cried, a loud wailing cry; he pressed his face into my shirt.

'Christ, I'm sorry.' I hugged him close with both arms. 'It's absurd, blaming this on you. So let's be sensible. It's all right. Boha lies to the east of us. And the sun is . . .' But above us the very few visible, tiny, serrated patches of sky were a uniform dark grey. 'If this was a temperate northern forest we could guide ourselves by the mosses and lichens, because most of the growth is on the wetter, the shadier side of the trees, towards the north. But here it won't work – see for youself' – but he wouldn't look – 'here the lichens – the lichens grow everywhere, all the way round!

'It's obvious, isn't it? We must go back to our tree with the fruits sticking straight out of its trunk – and we'll know it's the right tree, won't we? – because of our own gorilla-nest, the flattened herbs and grasses at its base. Easy!' But even as I said it we passed another tree with green and orange fruits growing, in irregular clusters, straight out of its trunk.

We came to a clearing, a clearing I didn't recognize: the trunk of a large buttressed tree had cracked off twenty feet above the ground, snapping lianas and shearing boughs along its line of fall. We sat down, on the low end of a shattered branch. A pair of trees, no more than four feet apart, trussed together with lianas, stood opposite, the one on the left with smooth, light-brown bark patched with a white lichen, the one on the right with rough, red-brown bark covered with a green lichen. This piece of sky, I thought, is darker than the others. Night is coming.

'I don't even have a machete. I left that behind, too! I don't have a machete to cut saplings, to mark our way. It's shaming. It's embarrassing – and that's the very feeling that puts people in danger. They're too proud, you see, they're too embarrassed to stand and shout to their companions in camp. So they think, "Don't panic. Keep calm. This can't be happening to me. It's easy. Camp must be over there. I'll walk." So they walk, they try one way, that doesn't work, they imagine they're retracing their steps, they try another, they think it's systematic, this search of theirs, but already they're out of earshot, they're curving and zig-zagging and circling deeper into the forest. And it's welcoming, this forest, it's hospitable, there's plenty of room for a man and his problems to lose themselves, there's 50,000 square miles of it, 50,000 square miles of unheard-of opportunity.'

A bushbaby screamed, some way off; a Wood owl hooted, a *hoo-hoo-hoo* that seemed to come from several directions at once; 'Ooh,' said the gorilla, into my shirt.

'I agree. We'll make a nest. We'll stay here. A night in the forest won't do us any harm, will it? As long as a leopard doesn't scent us – and you have to admit, we certainly smell. We can't light a fire, you understand, because I don't have a match, and I'm not going to make a block and drill. We'd need Lary for that. But then Lary would never get lost. He's not stupid. He'd never walk out without a compass. And if he did he wouldn't be too embarrassed to shout, would he?'

Nzé's words came back to me: 'That gorilla, it's an animal, Uncle. Would it help you? Would it wash your shirts? Throw it away! Would it help you? Would it help you if you were lost in the forest?'

The bushbaby screamed, from the same place, some way off.

'On the other hand – this staying the night. You're hungry, aren't you? And you're traumatized, and you won't get off my chest, and I don't know which leaves your mother lets you eat, and which will kill you, and I haven't seen any Wild ginger ... But that bushbaby, it's not moving, is it? What do you think? Impossible! I know, but it sounds like ... Perhaps it really is ... But no luck, it's behind us. The wrong direction. I'm sure of it. Altogether wrong. Forget it. Impossible ... but it is ... it's Vicky's wife!'

I held him hard and ran, stumbling over the loose curls of liana, the surface roots, ripping my shirt on the hanging lines of liana-thorns, and 'Vicky,' I panted with the effort, 'please. Just this once. Keep at it. Keep beating her ...' and we were pushing through thick vegetation, bushes and shrubs and small trees and lianas, and there was a dull and flat, long and low reflection of light, the river, to the left, and ahead a dark block of shadow, a hut, all on its own, and a last long desperate scream, Vicky's hut. And silence.

'Aieeee!' screamed Nzé, as I scraped back the door of our own hut, home. 'Aieeee!' he screamed, jumping up and back from the table with its bright candles and warmth and food and mess-tins – and a big zinc bucket and a big shiny black gourd and two papayas and a whole hunch of green bananas. 'Don't do that!' he shouted. 'Don't do that!' He thrust his right hand under his left armpit, thwacked down his biceps, hugged himself, rocked from side to side where he stood, sat down again, and faced away, at the black and empty window-hole.

'I'm sorry,' said Manou, who was sitting in my place, with my mug, at the near end of the table, his left hand fiddling with the handle of my mug, his right pulling at his wisp of a moustache. 'I'm sorry,' he said, trying to smile. 'I was calling you back. We were frightened. We were telling stories in the village, Redmond, and we heard other stories, and we frightened ourselves.'

Manou, I thought, has a broad, deep forehead, or is it just the candlelight?

'I didn't hear you call. Not a sound.' I pulled up a chair between them and sat down, my back to the door.

'No, not like that,' said Manou, embarrassed, looking at the table-top in front of him. 'You know, calling to you, with your things, to a spirit.'

I split the skin of the nearest papaya and fed a piece of the flesh, over-ripe, half-rotten, to the gorilla. 'A spirit? What's up? Manou, look at me, what are you talking about?'

Manou stared at the same patch of table, at my mess-tin, at the green residue of saka-saka stuck inside it. 'They say your gorilla . . . they call it Redmondo. Like Impfondo.' Manou tried to laugh, a strangled little laugh. Nzé, looking into the night beyond the window, sat perfectly still, something I had never seen him do. Manou tried again, the same half-laugh, half-choke. 'In the village, the country people, we don't listen, Redmond, we don't care, because we're not like them, we're clever, we don't believe it, we really don't, but they said, "Nzé Oumar, Manou Burond," they said, "that gorilla – do you know why it likes your white so much? Can you tell us? Can you? No? Because at night, in the spirit way, your white takes his fetish and he talks to it in a horrible voice and he changes into a gorilla and he goes to the forest. That's why it likes him. And that's why your white likes the forest. That's why he likes to walk through the forest. Doubla told us, "That white," he said, "that white makes people walk through the forest – right through the swamp, in the rain!"' '

Nzé swung round on his chair, both eyes wide, both eyes trying, and failing, to focus on me, all at once. 'Only you're a *white* gorilla! So you can only stay with other gorillas in the forest at night – when they can't see you! Because if they knew you were a white gorilla, those black gorillas, they'd hate you – they'd think you were dead, white, a spirit, and they'd attack! Yes! They'd charge, they'd run after you, they'd catch you, they'd bite you. They'd bite you! They'd bite the meat off your legs!'

The gorilla in my arms, ignoring Nzé, stretched out a long right arm, a set of stubby fingers, grabbed the other papaya, and bit it.

'And when we got back,' said Manou, looking straight at me, into my face, 'it was dark. And Madame Bobé had been here. And left all this food and palm-wine. And Nzé said it was an offering. And Madame Bobé had run away. And you'd gone. Gone to the forest. In the night!'

'Your face,' said Nzé. 'It's not just white. It's not like normal, in the day, dirty white. It's *really* white.'

'And the back of your hand,' said Manou, 'it's black!'

'That's a bruise.'

'And what's this?' said Manou, standing up, bending over me. 'Your back! Your shirt! It's bleeding! Blood!'

'Uncle,' said Nzé, craning his neck. 'Blood. You're bleeding. And on your arms. Look! They've ripped you!'

'Don't be silly!' I said, catching the fear. 'It's thorns. Calm down! Liana-thorns.'

'So you *were* in the forest!' said Manou, not sitting down, edging towards the door.

'Manou, don't be silly.'

'Silly,' said Manou, one hand on the edge of the corrugated iron.

Nzé stood up. 'They say you're a sorcerer. A white sorcerer. And they're . . . they're really difficult to kill. That's not thorns. Everybody knows. If you get a thorn – you stop. You pull it out. That's like . . . that's like – Samalé!'

'Don't be ridiculous. Samalé doesn't live here. He doesn't come here.'

'So? You were walking in the forest? At night? And you didn't get lost!'

'Of course not. I never get lost. I have a special sense. A strong sense of direction. We've all got it. Like pigeons. Magnetite. Magnetite in the brain. Some have more than others, of course.'

'Right,' said Nzé, leaving his half-full mess-tin, sidling towards Manou, by the door. 'It's late. You know . . . we've got to go now, haven't we, Manou? We . . . we can't stay any longer, can we? I'm sorry, Uncle, but we promised . . . we promised . . . to see our girls!'

And they went.

I woke in the dark, conscious of a weight off my chest; I turned on the torch: the gorilla had rolled off my chest. He lay on his back, his arms and legs stretched out, his left hand resting against my shirt, his eyes shut: he was fast asleep. I felt his little stomach: tight with two papayas, milk and two-and-a-half bananas. 'That's better, isn't it?' I whispered, my own stomach full of most of the rest of the fish saka-saka in Madame Bobé's bucket – but not, and the thought still annoyed me, with palm-wine, because Nzé and Manou, despite all their dedicated spiritual devotions summoning the shape-changer, the spirit, me, from the jungle, had still found time to empty the gourd.

Itching and smarting all over (but whether from bed-bugs, mosquitoes and liana-thorns or simply from the slime of diarrhoea, milk and papaya no longer seemed to matter), I lifted his little hand off my shirt, turned towards him, and lay my head beside his on the shirt-pillow. 'Your fingers,' I said, 'they're asleep too, you know, relaxed and floppy. You've got hairs on the top here, all the way down . . . to the half-way mark on the second joint. But then' – with my left hand I pulled the torch closer – 'so have I, if I look hard enough . . . Hanno, I suppose, he was the first human in recent history to see hands like yours. 2500 years ago – yesterday, in real history – he sailed (or rowed, if the wind was awkward) out of Carthage, west through the straits, and southwards, keeping the land in sight, and he certainly reached the stretch of country we now call Cameroon and he probably got as far as Gabon. But I'm misleading you, aren't I? Because he wasn't exactly alone, any more than I am, with you here.'

The rhythm of his breathing changed, a faster, shallower panting, and in the torchlight (I turned the beam away) I thought I saw his eyelids flicker: the rapid eye movements of a dream. 'Go ahead,' I whispered (and 'Sentimental,' said the inner Marcellin) 'you dream all you can. Try and sort it out. Oyster-shell that suffering, if you can . . .' He snorted in his sleep. 'Yes, that's probably the best you can do, because gorillas can't snore. You can't snore! Okay, so I don't know why that's funny. Hanno, that's right, well, he wasn't exactly alone, because he had 30,000 soldiers, sailors and rowers with him, a fleet of sixty ships. But that's hardly the point – the interest, as far as you're concerned, is this: somewhere near present-day Gabon, way to the west of us in the forest, he came across giants, a giant people, hairy and black, a people who refused to be taken into slavery, a people who threatened and fought and bit rather than surrender, even when surrounded, obviously outnumbered, a hundred to one. They weren't sensible. Invariably they chose to die rather than opt for a life of servitude. Heroes, you see. You. Your ancestors.'

He rolled over in his sleep, put his right hand on my left shoulder, pulled himself against my chest, and sighed. I edged gently on to my back, on the sweaty tarpaulin, in the close, airless, clay-dusty little room, and I held him tight.

'Hanno had your people skinned,' I whispered at the top of his head, and so much for all this manic talking being for your benefit, I thought, unable to stop, much less sleep – anyone can see you're not interested, you're not even listening! So perhaps I really did panic out there in the forest, or maybe Marcellin's right, perhaps I am going crazy, I've certainly fallen in love with a baby gorilla – and that can't be normal. 'But I'm wandering. And that will never do. We must stick to the subject. So Hanno took the skins back to Carthage and they were hung in the temple: five hundred years later the Roman conquerors saw them: Pliny the Elder described them. And I wish I had some of those hormones that young mothers get without asking, hormones that come with the baby, an all-in package, hormones that make them look at their baby, you, with real passion, and at all other people with a vacant disinterest, as if no other adult understands anything about anything that matters . . . And after that the men in the north gave you a break for 2000 years – until the sixteenth century, when an English sailor, Andrew

Battel, taken captive by the Portuguese in West Africa, gave us the first decent descriptions of your way of life.'

He snuffled, his eyes shut, and he wiped his big nostrils on my shirt. 'Bored? Of course you are. You were in the forest all the time. You knew who you were. You didn't need to be discovered.

'And anyway, five million years ago – not that long here, even if we're only thinking of Mokélé-mbembé – you and I shared the same ancestors, the same parents, and you could have been my kid brother, and we could have held hands for real. But then I suppose the weather altered for some reason, for a time the rainfall changed, here the great forest shrunk into patches, our people got separated and we went our different ways: you, chimpanzees, pygmy chimpanzees and apemen, me. Not that long ago. We've got around 100,000 genes, a finite number, you see, and humans differ from chimpanzees in a mere one-and-a-half per cent of the total DNA sequences. I don't know about you. Maybe I'll find out some day. But you can't be so very different, can you? Dawkins, who does know about such things – he says that if we humans held hands, generation to generation, say a line of fathers and sons or mothers and daughters, or mix them up if you like, and we started at the coast and the line stretched into the interior, then we'd be holding hands with a chimpanzee long before we ever reached the centre of Africa, here.'

A big brown drowsy fly, disturbed by the torchlight, was crawling unsteadily across the dried mud floor by the base of the bergen, beside the bed. (I hope that's not a Congo floor maggot fly laying eggs, I thought, those eggs that turn into hiding and creeping white maggots, the maggots that suck your blood in the dark . . .)

'But the men of Boha probably don't agree that we're close relatives, you and me – so let's hope they don't think like the men in the north, in Berandzoko, shall we? Because if I'm a sorcerer and you're Redmondo, my apprentice, or the other way about, and something bad happens in the village – what if the Chief dies while we're here? – then it would be logical for them to take action, to protect themselves, wouldn't it? Let's hope they do the usual, the decent thing, and make us drink poison in the square outside the Chief's hut, while they stand around, and watch. Because if they're as thuggish as Marcellin says, if they decide to dispense with the formalities and simply come here at night with the special poles and drag us out and smash our feet, our legs, our hips, our ribs, our shoulders and our skulls, we wouldn't like it, would we?'

I turned off the torch. 'Lay me down like stone,' I said. 'And raise me up like new bread.' The gorilla felt warm and soft and furry, his breath on my neck. 'But I don't suppose anyone will come anywhere near us. No visitors. Just Madame Bobé, muttering to herself, dropping in the bucket after dark . . . Five nights and days! Or is it four? I don't suppose we'll make it . . .'

But we did.

36

Early in the morning of the fourth day we met Marcellin, in the mist, at the slipway: the thin Epéna boatman, wearing the same brown cotton trousers, brown sleeveless shirt and black Homburg hat, was standing in the stern with the end of his long paddle lodged in the mud, ready to punt us off. 'Quick!' said Marcellin, agitated, catching the now almost-empty bergens and kit-bags as Nzé and Manou threw them on board. 'We had to wait! I've been hiding! You're late! Late!'

'It's okay Uncle! No one's been near us!' shouted Nzé, just as though (apart from collecting his helping of Madame Bobé's saka-saka every night) he'd been anywhere near the hut himself. 'Manou and me – we fooled them all! Everyone! They're afraid!'

'Quiet!' yelled Marcellin, alternately stowing the bags and scanning the rise of the bank behind us. 'Quick! It's easy now. Now's the time. We're easy targets. Quick!'

'Bohmaaa!' shouted Nzé, raising his fist in the air. 'Uncle – I did it! My idea!'

'Quick! Quick!' Marcellin beckoned to us, a frantic gesture. 'Nzé, Manou – here! Redmond – the bow!'

I waded in after Nzé and Manou, my right arm round the gorilla against my chest, my left hand across his eyes, blinkering all that water away, and I took my position in the bow – behind one long cylindrical wicker cage full of chickens and, on the narrow upward-sloping wooden triangle of the prow itself, one tethered black-and-white goat.

The boatman poled us off. The crowns of the oil palms came into view; the roof of Old Bobé's hut; the Umbrella trees; the bushes that hid the path along the rise – and from the top of the bank Marcellin's fear swept down: as we sat there, cramped together, dead on the water.

The boatman pulled the starter-cord. The engine fired twice, and died.

'The beer? What about the beer?' I jabbered at Marcellin, swivelling round on my log. 'The beer from Epéna?'

'All done,' whispered Marcellin, staring at the bushes that hid the path.

'Bobé's got it. They have an arrangement. Old Bobé – everyone trusts Old Bobé.'

The boatman bent over the engine, fiddling with some delicate adjustment. The boat began to drift, side-on, towards the shore.

'No one's going to kill Old Bobé,' whispered Marcellin. 'No one's going to rob Old Bobé. Not while Doubla's alive. And out of prison. Doubla . . .' The boatman pulled again. A muffled stutter. Silence. 'Nzé! Manou!' yelled Marcellin, wrenching a duckboard out from under the bergens, standing up too fast, rocking the boat, shipping water. 'Paddle! Paddle!'

The boatman, with one strong, clean pull, started the motor.

Marcellin sat down, replaced the duckboard, and huddled back into the pile of kit-bags.

I kissed the gorilla on top of his head. 'Goodbye, Boha,' I said, like a child. 'And goodbye,' I said, mesmerized by the slow, muddy, opaque surface of the water as it gathered speed beside us, 'goodbye, all you catfish with prickly whiskers . . .' A small purple-blue swallow with a white throat and a stub of a tail flew fast across the bow. To my intense irritation, an irrational surge of anger ('Extraneous thought,' I mumbled to myself and, into the little flat black ear under my chin: 'But you haven't let me sleep much, have you?'). I again heard the deep harsh chant that, over the past few days, had begun to bother me: the voice of the man in the black jacket. 'So I won't say goodbye, because you'll soon be joining me . . . See you! I'll see you later!'

'I may have lost my grip on time,' I said to the gorilla, hugging him tighter, 'but not on you. I've got a grip on you. So don't you worry – eight hours downriver . . . A plane for you, maybe, from Impfondo. And – friends your own age!'

'What's that?' shouted Marcellin, against the sound of the motor, as we swung into the main river. 'What's that you said?'

The boatman opened up the throttle.

'Nothing! Nothing at all!'

The goat stretched his black neck to port; he tilted his black horns and lowered his black head until his white nose and white beard were almost level with the white curl of water beside his hooves, water that was troubled, that wouldn't stay still, that was trying to tell him something.

'Don't panic,' I said. 'It's okay. It's because we've got a motor. It's a bow-wave. You'll get used to it. I know. You're not a Mountain goat. Of course you're not. But all the same – think of that as a waterfall. A flat waterfall.'

He raised his head and with his big, soft brown eyes he looked at me inquiringly; he tipped up his long white nose and whiffled his white nostrils as if to say, 'Look, I'll be frank with you, flat waterfalls are not the real problem, there are worse things round here – in the air, for instance.' He flicked his black ears forward; he lowered his head five degrees; and he stared at the gorilla.

The gorilla gripped me hard with his left hand, swelled his little chest, opened his mouth wide, attempted, in staccato treble, a roar, gave up, in despair, and buried his head in my chest.

'Don't you worry either. It's okay. That – that's just the biggest Water chevrotain you've ever seen.'

'Ooof!'

'I know. Horrible. But wait a bit. Wait until you weigh in at a hundred pounds . . .'

'Redmond!' came Marcellin's voice from behind me. 'That gorilla – you don't *talk* to it, do you?'

'What? Me?' I turned round to glare at him. 'Talk to it? Me? What's your problem, anyway? You – you think I've gone crazy?'

'Yes.' Marcellin pulled the rim of his floppy hat over his forehead and closed his eyes. 'And I have one other question,' he said with deliberation, eyes shut, hands folded on his white tee-shirt, on his flat stomach. 'Your shirt, even on the back, all the way down the back – it's caked with shit. I can't bear to look at you. Disgusting. Tell me – how come you got shit on the *back* of your shirt?'

'I don't know! How would I know? I haven't looked. I haven't washed. I don't know – turning over, maybe. You know – at night. Sleeping. In the tarpaulin. The tarpaulin – it was full of shit. The gorilla – he won't let me wash!'

'Six days? You haven't washed? And you think you're civilized?'

'I never . . .'

'My problem,' said Marcellin, as if he'd now considered the question, 'is this. You stink.' Eyes shut, he reached into the pocket of his blue jeans. 'You look disgusting – and you stink.' He pulled out a washed, folded, clean, white handkerchief and placed it, gently, over his nose. 'Irene – I'll miss her. She washed *everything* for me. She washed me too, you know. In the river. At night. Just us . . . But she wouldn't let me sleep. You know how it is. She's young . . . So wake me, will you? Wake me when we reach Epéna . . . if you'd be so kind. As the English say . . . gentlemen, that is. Not – what's the word in English? Poor people, you know, mad people, *merdaux*, the people who sleep in shit . . .'

'You – you hunk,' I said, outraged by everything, unable to think of an insult, unable to think at all. 'You hunk – *you hunk of something-or-other*! That's what you are! You, you're – and anyway, I bet you've had more sleep than I have! I'm more tired than you are! I – you – I've had no . . .'

'Hah hah hah!' said the gorilla, perking up, looking about, regretting it – and biting me on the right nipple.

'Shit! You . . .'

'Now now,' said Marcellin dreamily. 'No tantrums. Not at your age. Irene – she wouldn't like it. Besides, when you've washed, and showered, and scrubbed, and when you've gone and swum across the Oubangui twice, both ways – I'll tell you about it, about Irene . . . I promise I will . . . all about her . . .' And slowly, holding his handkerchief in place, he turned on his side, on to the soft, yielding, half-empty rice-sack.

Sitting on my small log on the duckboards, hunched over the gorilla to protect him from the open sunlight of the river, the heat, the reflected glare, I stared at the goat, at the three hens and a cockerel squashed to their feathery haunches in the cylindrical cage, at the narrow reed-beds, at the low banks with their occasional stunted trees and bushes – some almost bare of leaves, their boughs misshapen, as if from some congenital disease of the bones, others branching so low to the ground that they seemed to have sprung into life fully formed, without trunks – and I stared at the flat floodplain of savanna; at the distant uneven lines of forest; at the dark-purple bases of the huge clouds that hung above the forest, at their white peaks, at the storm that never seemed to break; and I tried to doze, like a cat; and six hours later I was staring at the Epéna wharf, a quarter of a mile ahead.

Marcellin was still asleep, lying on his back, his legs stretched out, his white trainers twitching, a tremor in his eyelids.

I leaned forward and eased a loose length of stick from the wicker cage. The chickens, beaks open, eyes psychotic, were too hot, too dehydrated, too near death to squawk.

Holding the gorilla, I turned on my log as quietly as I could; and with the stick I gave Marcellin a sharp poke in the stomach.

'Redmond!' he squealed, eyes shut, in that eerie ventriloquist's voice that the sleeping use, the sound from another world. 'Redmond! Help me!'

Feeling guilty – and surprised that sticking Marcellin in the stomach had not immediately improved my spirits – I dropped the weapon overboard.

'I'm shot,' echoed Marcellin's voice, rising from a well. 'I'm speared! They've speared me!'

His white trainers kicked against the gunwales, port and starboard. Holding his stomach, opening his eyes, he sat up – so fast that I forgot to turn round.

'A dream! A terrible dream! They got me – they got me in the stomach!'

He pulled up his bright-white tee-shirt. 'Doubla . . .' He looked at his stomach, as if it was new to him. He felt it, as if it shouldn't be there. 'But I'm marked! Redmond! Wounded!'

'Don't be silly.'

'Look! Look! I'm marked!' And he looked at the scratch on his stomach, as if thirty feet of intestine, including one foot of rectum, were spilling out. 'Explain that! Explain it!'

'Crazy. You've gone crazy.'

'Crazy?'

'Spirits,' I said, morose. 'The spirit world. Your soul – it went on a journey. Someone speared it. By mistake, probably.'

'No!' said Marcellin. 'No!' And he thrust his right hand into his pocket. 'It's . . .'

'That's it. That's right. Go on – feel your fetish.'

'Fetish,' mumbled Marcellin, his hand quiet in his pocket. 'Redmond. You . . . yours. Where do you keep yours?'

'Same place.'

'It's bad. It's not good.'

I muttered, half to the gorilla, 'Marcellin deserves to be shot.'

'Snush.'

'Shot?'

'Yes, shot – and anyway, what's the point?'

Marcellin withdrew his hand, adjusted his tee-shirt, recovered his legs, looked about, and saw the Epéna wharf twenty yards in front of us.

'Oh dear, oh dear,' he said, perky, mimicking my accent. 'What's the point? Still in a mood, are we?'

The boatman cut the engine.

'Someone in this town,' said Marcellin, mimicking Lary's accent, 'could utilize a sleep. A goddam sleep. A sleep like you wouldn't believe. Strange but true. The kinda sleep he hasn't had since God was a boy. Goddamit. Suck.'

The bow of the dugout slid silently on to the mud of the slipway, below the wooden piles of the wharf.

'But don't worry,' said Marcellin, in his own voice. 'I'll tuck you up myself. Tight as Le Vicomte Paul de la Panouse. He used to take a teddy bear to bed you know. Every night.'

'Epéna!' yelled Nzé, from the stern. 'Bohmaaa!'

'Epéna!' shouted Manou, trying to join in, like a man. 'Fiesta!'

'Impfondo!' yelled Marcellin, springing ashore in a white flash of tee-shirt and trainers and handkerchief. 'Impfondo!' he yelled, full of energy, expectation, six hours' sleep and Irene's cooking. 'Florence!' Twirling the handkerchief in the air above his head, he danced up the steep zig-zag of path. 'I'll see the Commissar! Florence! I'll steal his big red car! Florence!'

'Florence,' said Nzé, wading past me. 'She's a snob.'

'Nzé, Manou!' Marcellin shouted from the platform of the wharf above us. 'Unload the bags! And Redmond – you're in charge! Make sure they're careful – with my chickens, and my goat. And my crocodiles – they're in the stern! I'm coming! I'll be back!'

'She's a snob,' repeated Nzé. He stood motionless, crushed by the thought, screwed into the mud. 'She works in a bank.'

Nzé and Manou carried ashore the goat, the chickens, the crocodiles (the little one in a rusty Djéké cooking-pot, the big one harnessed to a short log), the kit-bags, the bergens – and the leaving-presents from their girls in Boha: five pineapples and a gourd of palm-wine for Nzé, one pineapple and a small bunch of green bananas for Manou.

I gave the boatman the second half of his money.

'Manou, Manou, Little Manou!' sang Nzé, retying the goat's liana-lead to the chicken-coop. 'One night, one of them – she'll tell you what to do! You've got to mean it, Manou. Be brave! Be bold! Like me! And then – Bohmaaa!'

The boatman secured the bow-rope of the dugout to the trunk of an Umbrella tree, took a thick pad of oily red cloth from the duckboards, positioned it on his shoulder, swung up the heavy motor, steadied the shaft with his right hand, half-knelt, back straight, to pick up the paddle and a small tight sack with his left, cast a last glance along the empty canoe, turned without saying goodbye, laboured up the incline and disappeared over the top.

My right arm round the gorilla (who at the sight of the Umbrella tree, the straggled bushes, the long grass of the high bank, awoke from his catatonic trance), I carried up the kit-bags, one at a time. Nzé and Manou relayed the crocodiles, the chickens, the bergens; and, on the end of his liana-lead, the goat, who, happy to be on a sensible surface that didn't wobble in that worrying way, by turns pranced forward up the path and stopped, legs locked, ears flicking, resisting every tug – to nibble only at particular, thoughtfully selected, very special blades of grass, which looked just like all the others.

Sitting on the bergens under a line of three dusty palm trees, we waited for Marcellin, in the heat, on the edge of the desolate square of ground beside the wharf. To our right stood a padlocked, flat-roofed, corrugated-iron cabin, whose corrugated-iron sides were painted white along the base, red along the top. To our left stood three battered diesel-drums (red); and beyond them lay eight battered diesel-drums (blue).

At our backs, thirty yards away, under a lone mango tree, beside the dirt road, a boy in a striped brown tee-shirt and torn brown shorts sat in the dust, watching us.

Catching my feelings, the gorilla whimpered, but I was too exhausted, too dulled, too miserable to care.

From the reeds somewhere below us came a long liquid call, the *boooop boooop boooop* of a male Black crake (a bird like a small moorhen), the most common of the Congo rails – a call full of life, redolent of toad-spawn (in strings) and newts' eggs (wrapped in leaves), of aquatic worms and dragon-fly-nymphs, of water-spiders and water-beetles, a song of sex, a boast about his territory, his familiar skulking pathways through the water-plants, the food in his own patch of river – and the female responded, she replied, she agreed, she laughed at his jokes, and *dre-dee-dah daaak-daaak-daaak* she sang, in precise time with him, in one long, antiphonal, married-for-life duet.

The boy under the mango tree stood up and hobbled towards us.

'That noise,' said Nzé, wiping his forehead on the sleeve of his militia jacket. 'That bird. It lives on dead men. Drowned men. It pecks your eyes out. My father ... he was ill! You hear that sound – someone you know is dead. It's been too long, all this, we've been away too long. It's bad. That noise. He was ill when I left...'

The boy stood beside me, silent, his arms limp, his knees half-bent and knobbled with scar-tissue, as if warts had sprung up in ridges down and across his knee-caps.

'It's true,' said Manou, tipping back his now half-disintegrated wide-brimmed bush-hat, but smart in clean khaki militia fatigues, the top of his notebook and clipped biro protruding from his right breast-pocket, not a button missing, a uniform he must have carried in his pack all those months, folded, unused, ready for this very day, the triumphant, the final return to his home town, the great welcome in Impfondo ... 'You hear it – that's bad. "There goes a little black bird" – that's what you'd say, Redmond, if you saw it. You'd never guess. It's clever like that – you'd never guess that it likes to eat dead everything – dead rats, dead people. You hear it – that's bad.'

'But it calls all the time!'

'Mister...' said the boy, his eyes unnaturally large in his thin little face.

'People,' said Nzé, managing a meagre but decisive spit into the dust between his gym-shoes, 'they die all the time.'

'Mister,' said the boy. 'Mister white man.' He paused, lowered his eyes, twined his small fingers together, and lurched half a pace forward, as if his bent knees were not quite a part of him. 'Will you help me, Mister?' he said in halting French, in a voice that was half-lisp, half-breathy whistle, as if he had a cleft palate. 'I need help. Will you help me?'

'Of course,' I said, shaken. 'If I can.'

'I need something. Just one big thing.' He looked at me with his huge eyes in his thin, sad, shrunken little face; his lower lip sagged. 'But it costs money. Lots of money.'

'What is it?'

'It costs – lots and lots of money.'

'What is it you want?'

'A football,' he said, staring straight at me. 'With my friends. To play football.'

'How much?' I said, standing up, not knowing where to look, scrabbling in my pocket. 'How much?'

'Mister, it's okay.' He studied the cracks in the mud. He twisted his small fingers together as though to split the skin, to dislocate them. 'It's okay. I didn't mean it. We'll manage,' he said, like an old man. 'You – I can see, you're dirty, very dirty – you're poor, like us. I'm sorry. That's what my mother said. "Jacques," she said. "Your football. It's not good. White men? In Epéna? There are poor people," she said. "Even in America."'

'How much? How much is a football?'

'Five hundred CFA.'

I gave him the note in my hand, a crumpled, water-stained 1000 CFA (two pounds), the one that was purple and blue with a map of the Congo on the front and an elephant on the back.

The boy glanced up at me, pleasure in his eyes, anxiety across his forehead, as if I'd just passed him a gold bar.

'Uncle!' said Nzé. 'You've got to pay us, too! Pay us here. Now. In Epéna.'

The boy, dragging, swinging forward, dragging his right leg, set off down the dirt road towards the town, scrub to his right, the occasional abandoned-looking hut to his left.

'Pay us now, Uncle! And we'll come on later. Manou – fiesta! We'll drink, Manou, we'll dance – women! There's a big truck, Uncle, a lorry, from Epéna to Impfondo. We'll come on that – later! Much later! A week!'

Manou said, 'I want to go home. I want to see my family.'

'Manou, Manou!' sang Nzé. He raised his right fist in the air and shook it. 'Little Manou!'

'I want to see my son. I want to see Rocka Prince. He's two years old. I don't know how he is. I want to see my wife.'

Nzé laughed. 'Wife!' he said. 'You've got no money, Manou! A wife – you have to pay for a wife! She's not your wife. And Manou, if you go home, your family, our family – they'll take all your money. You know they will.

Everything. Even your torch! There'll be nothing left. Nothing for us. No beer. Nothing!'

'I want to go home,' said Manou, looking vacantly out over the river, the belt of savanna, the distant forest. 'Rocka Prince ... my son ... he's two years old.' With a sharp movement he sat up straight, fully alert, and turned to Nzé. 'And you – what about your son in Impfondo? He's hungry. He's always hungry. And your family, your children in Dongou, your wife – and Lary Oumar, he's a baby!'

Nzé was silent.

Manou said, 'Don't pay us here. It's not right.'

'Okay,' I said, resting my chin on the soft brown top of the gorilla's head. 'Impfondo. Tonight, in the Hôtel du Parti. Besides, it's safer.'

The official Government car of the People's Political District of Epéna, a red Toyota truck, pulled up beside us. The Commissar himself, and Marcellin, got out; they slammed their doors shut with an upward flourish of the arm, as officials do.

'Right then, Uncle,' said Nzé hurriedly, under his breath, annoyed, getting to his feet. 'Then I'll tell you what I think of you – you're crazy. And you smell.'

The Commissar, thick-set, brusque, aware of his power, directed the loading of the bags and animals on to the brushed-clean floor of the flatbed, climbed back into his cab and slammed the door. Marcellin, getting in the other side, sticking his head above the red roof a moment, gave me a happy grin, a white arc of even teeth: 'Official orders, Redmond! From the Political Commissar. You and your gorilla. Right in the back – by the tailgate. Downwind. Because – you smell!'

'Cheer up, Uncle!' shouted Nzé, lodged between kit-bags, his back against the cab, as we pulled up on to the Brazilian-made road, the strip of tarmac from Epéna to Impfondo. 'Uncle, you look so old! So old and thin!'

'It's your sauces!' I shouted against the slipstream, managing a joke; but I don't think he heard.

The goat, lying at Nzé's feet, rested his white beard on the chicken-coop, something familiar; breathing fast, almost panting, he closed his eyes. His black eyelids, his long black eyelashes, moved in spasms, little tremors.

'I didn't mean it!' shouted Nzé. 'Not really. You do smell – but it's no worse than the big pit, is it, Manou?' He turned to consult Manou, beside him. 'You know, Manou – the smell when you go in there. The big pit, the one at your place?'

'Worse!' shouted Manou, holding his hat on, as the trees with their lianas, not one by one, but all together, were hurled past and away from us, not falling, but standing, just as they were, such was the terror, the force of the tornado – and the little gorilla took his face away and hid it in my shirt, for safe-keeping, in case there was a future.

'Much worse!' shouted Manou. 'But we can't smell you now!'

And twenty minutes later the truck slowed to the official pace, past the elephant grass by the dirt chute to the port, past wattle-and-daub thatched huts, breeze-block huts with corrugated-iron roofs, the huge compound of the Protestant mission with the mown lawns, the modern church, the bar, the petrol pump – and the Hôtel du Parti.

The Commissar turned in at the back entrance, stopped outside the annexe, and blasted the horn. The door of the watchman's wooden shed slewed open and the *patron*, as if a small grenade had burst inside, at his back, fell out across the driveway.

'Drunk!' roared the Commissar, slamming his door. 'Drunk again!'

The *patron* picked himself up, retrieved his red baseball cap, dusted it off, placed it, carefully, on his head, and walked, with dignity, towards us.

'Monsieur le Patron,' said the Commissar. 'What is the name of this hotel?'

'Hôtel du Parti,' said the *patron*, after a moment's thought.

'Correct! This hotel ... this hotel ... it's a Party hotel! A political hotel! A serious matter! And you – you're a disgrace!' The Commissar unclipped the keys from the *patron*'s belt and handed them to Marcellin. 'A serious matter. And this – it's your last chance.'

The *patron* fixed a mental bearing on his shed and made for it, in a line that was nearly straight. Almost home again, and safe, he grasped the big black bolt on the inside of the open door, tripped on the sill, took a header inside – and the door slammed shut behind him.

'Bravo!' shouted the Commissar, clapping his strong hands. 'Bravo!'

'Last chance?' said Marcellin.

The Commissar laughed. 'That's his two-thousandth and thirty-first last chance,' he said, helping us unload the bags. 'I've no authority here. None at all. And anyway, it's not his fault. It's bad planning – bad town planning. By the French, not us. This hotel, Marcellin – it's too close to the bar!'

We piled the bags into our old rooms, Marcellin locked the doors and, 'See you tonight,' he said to Nzé (who was standing on the veranda with his brown hold-all in his hand). 'And you!' he shouted after Manou (who was already walking towards the front entrance, gym-bag over his shoulder). 'Dismissed! Tonight – Redmond will pay you! If he can! If he still has any money!' Marcellin opened the cab door. 'You, Redmond – in the back. With the goat!'

The Commissar drove up the rutted track past Yvette's, turned left on to a broader mud street and right through the gate of the high wire fence, on to the concrete apron of the Regional Headquarters (Impfondo) of the

Ministry of Water and Forests, a large cream-yellow bungalow with diamond-lattice steel grilles across the windows. The yellow Land Cruiser was parked outside the front door.

'Joseph's at home,' said Marcellin with a genuine smile, lifting out the four-foot crocodile and the short log. 'He's counting his money. He keeps it under his mattress, he really does. But then what do you expect? It's like me – sometimes he gets his Government salary, sometimes he doesn't. You people, white men, Westerners – if you care so much about the gorillas, the forests, the elephants – you must pay for it!'

Marcellin and the Commissar carried the goat and the chicken-coop to the strip of shade against the wall. Straightening up, putting both hands to the small of his back, 'Comrade!' said the Commissar, with a wink. 'Goodbye! And good luck! And I'll bear it in mind. Everything you said.' He stepped up into the driving seat. 'Boha!' he said, and slammed the door. He wound down the window: 'But soldiers? And fuel? And boats?' He revved the engine, in bursts: 'Trouble? My men killed? Not again! No thank you!' Reversing fast off the concrete, he turned outside the gates, the truck pitching across the ruts, and pulled up level with the fence. 'For *gorillas*?' he shouted. 'I hardly think so! For a *park*?' And he drove off up the street.

The Commissar gone, Joseph unlocked the door to his living-quarters and emerged into the late-afternoon light. Presumably off-duty, he was dressed not in the dark-green paramilitary fatigues and badged beret and black boots of the Department for the Conservation of the Fauna of the People's Republic, champion of the animals in the lakes and rivers and forests, but in a pink tee-shirt, white cotton trousers and flip-flops.

Seeing the gorilla in my arms, he paused on the doorstep, frowned, cleared his throat as if something had stuck in it, raised his pink shoulders, pressed his arms to his sides, mastered himself, and smiled. 'Marcellin – at last! We've been waiting!' he said, as if he almost meant it. 'We were worried. So long – it's been so long! . . . And Redmond, you have a *gorillon*, a little gorilla!'

He advanced towards me, his lips wet, his mouth half-open, as if he was finding it difficult to breathe through his nose. 'Hello!' he shouted, raising his knuckles for a rap on a door. 'Hello, *gorillon*!'

With a convulsive twist I turned sideways, my right hand over the small soft brown head. 'Don't do it! Don't! Don't do that!'

Joseph stepped backwards. 'But Redmond! You don't understand! That's how you say . . .'

'No! No! It's not!' I shouted, over-tired, over-emotional, sick of everything. 'It's not how you say hello to a gorilla! Would you like it? A bang on the head? Would you?'

'Hey!' snapped Marcellin, standing up beside the chicken-coop, the goat's lead in his hand. 'Steady, Redmond! Steady! You, you – don't you speak to my staff like that . . .' He stopped, looked at me hard, and changed his tone of voice, as if he was speaking to a ten-year-old. 'Now, Redmond, you wouldn't shout like that if Lary was here, would you? So – as Lary would say, "You guys – cool it. Dingbats! Suck!"'

'Lary!' said Joseph, reining in the muscles round his mouth, forcing a smile; for a moment he stared at a head-high space a yard off my right shoulder; he relaxed; he smiled a real smile. 'The Professor! Professor Lary! Lary – I looked after him! We had lunches. No beer. Nothing but water! We talked! Yes. I took him to the aeroplane. I looked after him! He was kind to me. I got him a place. And that big bag – like a soldier's bag. Marcellin, it was difficult. Believe me – the army, you know, and then we had to run, we had to fight for a place!'

'Well done,' said Marcellin. 'Well done, Joseph!'

'Yes, Professor Lary – a kind man,' said Joseph, shaking his head, as if the fact was still a mystery to him. 'Your friend,' he said, half-turning to me, but abstracted again, staring at the same head-size space a yard off my right shoulder, his neck skewed, his right hand pushing slowly up through his hair as if the knuckles, bent, were being pulled, against his will, towards the back of his head, ploughing his skull. 'A kind man,' he murmured. 'A very kind man. A good man.'

'He certainly is,' I said, mollified.

'Your *gorillon*!' said Joseph in his normal voice, coming to himself; he walked off, past the rectangular windows with their diamond-lattice steel grilles, to the far corner of the building – where he about-turned, raised his right hand as if to salute, and shouted: 'I've just the place for it!'

'Wait. I'm coming,' said Marcellin, retying the quiet black-and-white goat to the chicken-coop. 'Joseph! My goat and my chickens – we'll do it later. You'll keep them for me! You'll look after them – on the grass at the back. And Redmond,' he said, as Joseph let us in by a side door, 'I want to buy a pig. A female pig. A sow.'

'You go ahead,' I muttered, holding the gorilla close against my chest as Joseph led us along a passage to the right, past two closed doors. 'You buy a pig.'

'For breeding, Redmond. Science, genetics! You take animals from different places.'

'Different places.'

At the end of the passage, to the left of three clean concrete shower-rooms, in each of which stood a bright zinc bucket, we followed Joseph down two concrete steps and out on to a lawn; and there, immediately to our left, against the wall, was a four-foot-square iron cage with a sheet of corrugated iron as a roof, and inside, on its floor of mud, dung and banana-skins, sat two sharp empty tins, one tin water-bowl, one broken, jagged glass bowl, and one little chimpanzee, its arms over its head.

'Joseph!' said Marcellin, squatting down beside the cage. 'How could you?'

'How could I?' said Joseph, raising his eyebrows. 'How could I what?'

'This! This chimp! Keep a chimp in a cage like this!'

'But he's happy! He likes it in there. I gave him tins. Tins to play with. And Marcellin, I buy him bananas. With my own money!'

The chimpanzee looked up, saw the gorilla on my chest, dropped his arms to his sides, and stared. His little face, freckled with brown, was yellowish-white (he's got hepatitis, I thought, or perhaps that's the right colour for the young of the eastern sub-species . . .)

The gorilla craned his neck; he stared back at the chimpanzee; he averted his eyes; he took another peep; he turned his head away. The chimpanzee looked steadily up with his deep-set, light-brown eyes, and he waggled his big, brownish-white, sticking-out ears.

'They want to play!' said Marcellin, unbolting the door of the cage. 'The meeting-room, that's the place for them.'

'The meeting-room?' said Joseph. 'But it's clean in there!'

'Exactly.' Marcellin reached into the cage and took the little chimpanzee into his arms. 'They can spend the night in there. They can play together – they can chase each other over the desks! And in the morning, Joseph, you can find a couple of boxes. You'll punch holes in the lids. And you'll add these two to your cargo, your freight for the plane. Because the plane, Joseph, it comes tomorrow, doesn't it?'

'Yes, but . . .'

'You've got too many other bundles? To send to Brazzaville? But Joseph, you know everyone, don't you? The soldiers at the airport, the police – you even know the pilot, the white, the Frenchman!'

'Yes, but . . .'

'And those bundles, Joseph, you know, sometimes – not very often, it's true – but every now and then when I'm in the office in Brazzaville and there's not much going on, not a lot for my officers to do, I catch myself thinking, "I just wonder, I wonder what's in those big bundles, the ones that Joseph wraps in sacking?"'

'Okay,' said Joseph, looking at his flip-flops. 'I'll do it.'

'But my gorilla!' I said, hugging him too hard. ('Ooof!' he said.) 'I'm not leaving him! No, I'm not!'

Marcellin ignored me, leading the way up the steps, resolute, the little chimpanzee peering over his shoulder, at the gorilla.

'He'll sleep with me, in the hotel,' I said, pushing past Joseph. 'I'll take him on the steamer. I'll take him to Madame Leroy. I'll take him in person.'

'In person!' Marcellin stopped in the dark passage and laughed, a mocking laugh. 'In person! You think you're so special, don't you? What's special about you?'

'I don't think I'm special!'

'Steady,' said Marcellin, quietly. 'You pull yourself together. Okay? And don't shout like that. Not in here. This building – it's an official building. It belongs to my Ministry. And I'm in charge.'

Joseph, uneasy, mouth sagging open, flattened his back against the wall.

'I don't care. He's not staying here. He's coming with me. To the hotel.'

'I see. And in England, the hotels – they let gorillas into hotels?'

'I don't know. I never . . .'

'So where do you think you are? What's different about our hotels? Not good enough for you? Eh? And come to that,' he said, opening a door to his left, into a big room, like a classroom, full of desks, with a blackboard at one end, 'they shouldn't let *you* into a hotel – look at you! Your shirt, your trousers, you're covered in shit!'

'I'll camp outside. I'll camp by the river.'

'You'll do no such thing. They'd put you in prison. No foreign vagrants and spies. Not in District towns. The army. Security.' He set the chimpanzee on the floor. 'And as for taking a gorilla on the steamer, Redmond – I won't allow it. It's against the law.' (The little chimpanzee wrapped himself tight round my right leg. His black fur was long and rough and sparse.) 'People will say, "That Agnagna – look at him! He's corrupt like all the others. He sells gorillas to white men!"' – and with sudden agility Marcellin snatched the gorilla from my chest, dumped the gorilla on a desk-top, pulled the chimpanzee off my leg, pushed me with him through the door and closed it behind us. 'Joseph! Lock it!'

As Joseph turned the key there came a scream from inside, the little gorilla's full distress call, a three-second shriek of disbelief, hurt and fear.

'But I didn't say goodbye! I didn't kiss him!'

'Say goodbye?' said Marcellin, shoving me down the passage. 'Kiss him? You're crazy! Go away! Get some sleep! And besides,' he said, opening the front door, pushing me through, stepping out into the dusk, 'you're not the only one who's tired. I'm tired, too, you know – I get ill. Half that time in the forest and I get ill. Fevers, odd little fevers, back in Brazzaville. No one knows what they are. I'm ill for weeks. It takes weeks to recover. Not even the French doctor – not even he knows what they are. And now, because I made a mistake, because I came with you, I'll be ill for months, I can feel it, I know I will.'

I stood on the concrete, in the dusk, not sure what to do, not quite sure who I was.

'Come on, Joseph! Redmond's gone to pieces. You help me. We must tether the goat. We must pen out the chickens. And the crocodiles – you must find somewhere. We must feed them all. We must give them water!'

I said, 'Let me help you.'

'No! No!' Marcellin shouted, exasperated, waving his right arm. 'Go away! Get some sleep! Go to the hotel! Go away!

'Wait!' he shouted, as I reached the gate, and he threw me the room-key. 'There are fevers!' His shout followed me down the road. 'There are fevers out there! Unknown fevers!'

The slanted evening light pricked out the spines on the cactus, the blades of reeds and elephant-grass, and the occasional corrugated-iron roof of a hut set back from the road, half-hidden in the grass; it caught the tops of the palm trees and the long steel poles and bright dishes of the wireless masts – and something flying towards me, fifty feet up, a bird with a white stomach, a long tail ... two long tails ... and the outer half of its wings – they seemed to be detached, cut off from the rest of the bird, loose in space, parallel escorts to either side, trailing the two tails, not tails at all, but streamers ... and, 'Yes,' I said aloud, 'it really is, there's no doubt about it, they're pennants – it is; it's a Pennant-winged nightjar!' And the buoyant ghostly presence of the bird itself disappeared over the elephant-grass.

That was a male, in full breeding plumage, I thought, as I found the little short-cut of a track through the elephant-grass, the track that led to the football-field, the abandoned Brazillian roadmakers' depot, the Catholic Mission, the Hôtel du Parti and, over the road, the wide Oubangui river. And it was flying with such energy because it was stuffed with the termites of the northern savanna that swarm in the early part of the rains, and now it was on its way across the great forest again, to catch the termites on their mating flights from the soil of the southern savannas, in the early months of the southern rains, and to breed – a Lary-like story first published by the great Chapin in 1916, and quoted by Bannerman in volume three of his *Birds of Tropical West Africa*, where, in a drawing by Josef Wolf, a Pennant-winged nightjar trails its plumes across the moon.

And that gap in its wings (I came out on to the football-field), the gaps between the brown inner coverts and the outermost black finger-feathers of the primaries, they weren't gaps at all, but the broad white bands, the pure white bands that only the Pennant-winged nightjar possesses, the white bases of the plumes that are sometimes twenty-eight inches long.

And if I've got the story right, I thought (I passed the broken yellow lorries and bulldozer of the depot) then the male's pennants grow longer with each moult (in the north) that he survives – so the older he gets, the more desirable, the sexier he becomes. And it's a great pity that you can't say the same about us. 'Still,' I said aloud, punching the air, turning into the deserted compound of the Hôtel du Parti, past the annexe to my right, the concrete veranda, the cast-iron railings, the water-tanker with its mix of water and diesel residue that had once, long ago, made me so ill, 'I've seen it! The bird of birds!'

And so, I thought, why not? – already past the watchman's hut – death's not actually in the room with me yet, at least I don't think he is, so why shouldn't I celebrate the evening, at last, of the Pennant-winged nightjar, the crepuscular, the twilight bird? And so I will, and I'll pretend that Lary's still here, and I'll go right on in there (I went right on in there) to Madame Langlois' little store, and I'll buy a goddam tin of peanut-butter (I pointed across the wooden counter, past the same surly storekeeper, at the lonely little isolated groups of precious tins upon the wooden shelves) and a whole bottle of Johnny Walker Red Label, even if, strange but true, however you process your calculations it comes to £30 sterling at estimated current exchange rates (it did); and, just for me, I'll get a special compound luxury: a packet of Quaker Oats, a tin of powdered milk, and a block of brown sugar.

From my leg-pocket I found the right number of creased, sweaty, slightly mouldy notes. The storekeeper, staring at me as if Samalé had walked into his shop, took the money; he dropped it in the till, wiped his hands, thoroughly, on his trousers, selected the change, and pushed it to the extreme edge of the counter.

Back in our old room everything seemed close and familiar: the chair, the chest of drawers, the ragged curtains, the bed, the dusty mosquito-net hanging from its hook in the ceiling: switching on the lamp (it worked) I even thought I could see Lary's stubby fingerprints preserved in the layer of dust on the desk: and in the shower-room at the back the same ancient, black, insoluble turd still lay in the far left-hand corner of the square lip of concrete. Lary was right: there was not much call for hotels, official or otherwise, round here: in Lary's opinion, no market research was needed: the prospects were not good.

I took the shower-room bucket, found two more near the diesel-drum water-tank outside, filled them, carried them into the room, and locked the door behind me. I'm alone, I thought, sitting on the edge of the bed; a locked door – I can't remember when I last had real privacy: in Oxford I suppose, in a previous life, a thousand years ago . . . 'And now,' I said aloud,

'I must not start talking aloud to myself. It was bad enough, all that talking night and day, to a gorilla – but then he seemed to enjoy it, and I enjoyed him – and I wonder how he is; that scream, that terrible scream, but I suppose it's for the best, and I mustn't think about it . . . In fact here you are,' I said, putting my hands on my knees, staring at my stiff, diarrhoea-caked SAS trousers (DPM Tropical, lad), 'here you are, on your chinstrap, throwing an eppie scoppie, and all because you've had six nights without much sleep, being a mother. It's ridiculous: it's not right. It's a good thing I'm not in the Regiment. It's a good thing I only borrow the kit. Because they'd snap my sword for this, if I had one, right out there in front of everyone. They'd stamp on my water-bottles. They'd bung a flash-bang at me. They'd whip off my trousers and cut them in half. They'd certainly do whatever they do. I'd be RTU'd, Returned to Unit. The Catering Corps, probably. For dereliction of duty. For the inability to take a shower . . .'

So I got out of my stiff, stinking clothes, found a piece of soap and my slimy towel in the bergen, carried the buckets through to the shower-room and, soaping everything, I poured each bucket, slowly, over my head – and ten minutes later, dressed in the shirt and pants I used as a pillow, my thin cotton, olive-drab town trousers, and a clean pair of my black, green-moulded socks, even the room began to look fresh and interesting. There was, I noticed, an entirely new generation of young, shiny, unsquashed cockroaches randomly dispersed about the walls, cockroaches that had not yet reached their final moult. And big, slender mosquitoes, of course, but no friends, no geckos.

I hid the bottle of whisky in my bergen; I counted the notes for Manou and Nzé into two piles on the desk – and, when I'd finished, there seemed to be very few left in the final reserve, in the small cache taped in its waterproof plastic bag to the bottom of the map-pocket. 'But no,' I said. 'Not now. I'll think about that later. I'll face up to that tomorrow.' And I opened the outsize tin of peanut-butter, and, as Lary wasn't there, I scooped it out with my fingers; half-way down I began to feel sick, so I stopped, just in time, and got my mug and water-bottle and mixed up a half-pint rough paste of raw oats, powdered milk and brown sugar and sucked it all in, and mixed another, and then one more and, just in time, there was a knock on the door.

'There's no peace,' I said, not meaning it. 'There's no solitude,' I said, too disturbed to be alone, delighted to have a visitor. But whoever it is, I thought, picking up the key, how embarrassing, I hope I don't disgrace myself, I hope I don't explode, blow up in front of them, a star-burst of oats, puffed oats, a geyser of peanut-butter, oil-slicks of peanut-butter, dripping off the walls . . . Manou stood in the dark outside, the dull light of the room illuminating his big bush-hat, his smart, triumphal-return dress-uniform of the Impfondo Militia. He stood there, apparently unable to speak, unwilling to move.

'Manou!' I said, taking him by the arm. 'What's up? Come in! What's wrong? I've got your money – and I bought a bottle of whisky. Johnny Walker, your favourite!'

'From Wales!' said Manou, trying to look pleased. 'Wales!'

'Well, not quite, Scotland. But Lary says it's counterfeit – from the People's Republic of China. That's what he thinks.'

'Lary,' said Manou, managing a smile, sitting on the bed. 'America. Lary is North American. Lary is the kindest man I've ever met.'

'Yes, yes, but you, how are you?' I said, worried, pulling the bottle out of the bergen, fetching two mugs from the food-sack. 'Manou, you look bad. What's wrong?'

'It's not true.'

'What?'

'The bad things the Party says. Terrible things. About North America. The North Americans.'

'No, but . . .'

'Lary, he cares about people. Not the People's Party. But real people, single people, individuals. That's the difference. He cared about me.'

'Yes, he did. He said you ought to go to –' (but I stopped myself). 'Europe went to America, and got young again. They have ideals, they have hopes in America. They believe in the future.'

'Africans went to America. Perhaps people from here went, too.'

'Yes,' I said, abashed. I doubled the size of his slug of whisky. 'Here, drink this. All of it. Lary would. But only at night, Manou. Lary never drank in the daytime. Not like Nzé . . .'

Manou took a sip, grimaced, and put the mug on the floor at his feet. I handed him his money.

'Nzé, I've been thinking,' he said, dividing the pile of notes into two without counting it, stuffing one half into each trouser-pocket. 'Nzé – his friends are not my friends. They dance, they get drunk, they take women. Any women. They don't care. Whereas me, I'm not like that.'

'No.'

'But the women like it, Redmond. It's his eyes. He has special powers. And his grandfather, his grandfather was a great sorcerer. His uncle, my uncle, Manou Emmanuel, the one we saw in the forest, by the river, where Lary took my picture – he's the greatest hunter in all Congo. Everybody knows. They say he can call the elephants. They say he sings, he makes music in the forest, and the elephants – they come to him. And it's the same, Redmond, it's the same with Nzé. He makes music. You yourself, you've heard him. He makes music and the women – they come to him. He makes gentle music, unexpected ... deep things, you'd never think ... Redmond, it's beautiful. And all the women, each one who listens, she thinks, "Aha, I know him now. This music, it's just for me. I know it is. For me, and me alone. Only I, only I know the real Nzé." They fall in love. They really do. I've seen it many, many times. They want the music, Redmond, they want it inside them.'

I took a gulp of whisky.

'And just now, as I came here in the dark, as I came away from somewhere and walked here in the dark, I thought, but it's the truth, Manou, there's nothing you can do about it, nothing.' He took off his hat, and, turning it slowly in front of him, he kneaded the brim with both hands, as Lary used to do.

His eyes, unshaded, were red and puffy, as if he'd been crying – but that can't be right, I thought, because I've never seen Manou cry, and as Lary said, he could and should have cried, many times ...

'Because Redmond, they're right, you see. That *is* the real Nzé. Everything else about him – all the rest of him, everything that I hate, the other Nzé, the evil Nzé, the Nzé that his stupid friends copy, the bits they see, the drinking, the dancing, the stealing and shouting, the stealing other people's women, the noise they make, the way they shout and pretend to hate every-thing, all gentle things, that's what they hate – well, Redmond, all that's a lie, a deliberate lie, that's what I think.'

'Manou!' I said, bemused, feeling stupid, unable to work it out. 'Look at me!' (He wouldn't.) 'Maybe I can help?' (He shook his head.)

'It's all a lie, that's what I thought just now, as I walked on here from somewhere, in the dark, all alone, and it was quiet – it's all a lie, but he needs that lie. He made it himself – a deliberate lie – and he made it to keep the real Nzé safe, the one that plays the beautiful, the gentle music, the Nzé you saw in Makao – the Nzé who goes into a sleep when he's awake, whose soul goes on a journey, a journey to the forest, to collect that music – and if something happens, if you stop him as he plays that music, before it's come to an end – then he looks like someone else, he doesn't know where he is, he's afraid, he's really afraid. So that's why he needs that lie, you see, that's what I told myself – so I shouldn't have done what I did, but it's too late now – and I feel bad, Redmond, because the lie keeps ordinary people away, it keeps them out, away from him, so he can make that journey in peace, and come home safe.'

'I see,' I said, but I didn't, so I took another scorch of whisky, tipping my head back (and as I did so I saw a gecko, stalking, upside-down, on its suction pads, very slowly, across the crack in the ceiling above the shower-room entrance – and swivelling its gecko-eyes, upside-down, back-left, at a young carefree cockroach following its antennae high along the wall behind the mosquito-net. So where had it come from, the gecko? The drain in the shower? The cess-pit?) 'Manou,' I said. 'I don't understand. What's up? What's troubling you? What do *you* want to do in life? A bicycle? A business? Take parcels to Dongou and back? Delivery?'

'Nzé!' said Manou, jamming his hat back on, twisting his hands together, crossing and then uncrossing his legs. 'A lie! A stupid lie! That was his idea. A lie! For me, no, it's simple. I want to go to university. I want to go to America. I want to win a scholarship. I want to go to Plattsburgh, in North America, to study with Dr Lary.' He looked straight at me, a fierce look, a Manou I didn't recognize. 'I like gentle things. And Dr Lary – he likes gentle things. We like books. We agreed on that, just the two of us, without Nzé. Books are good. They really are. But what hope is there? What hope is there for people like me? There's no money. No money for books. And our powerful teachers, the Big Men – they go to learn in Cuba, and in Russia, and some – they even go to China! So you see, don't you? It's a dream, a stupid dream – a lie, a stupid lie! Nothing, nothing at all, nothing but a lie!'

Lary's words came back to me, as if I was drinking with him: 'That kid. I like him. He's bright. He should come to Plattsburgh. I could teach him.' And the Marxist-Leninist People's Republic . . . yes, it was impossible. Of course it was. And I was silent. And I couldn't look Manou in the face.

'But Redmond, I want to thank you. Thank you – for bringing Dr Lary here. And for the greatest adventure, the greatest journey of my life. I'll tell my children, and my children's children. Because you took me to Lake Télé – and I heard the monster, and anyone who hears the monster is changed for ever, and for the better, that's what I think, because Redmond, once you've heard the great fear, and you've thought, "I'm going to die," and you've known, for certain, that you're about to die – and then you don't die at all but you're still alive, well, after that, you're not so afraid, are you? You're not so afraid of all the other things. At least, you shouldn't be.' He clasped himself across the chest and rocked, very gently, from side to side. 'But most of all,' he said, looking at the floor, rocking, 'I want to thank you – for bringing Dr Lary here. Because I'm going to model myself on Dr Lary – for ever! I won't complain, I'll never tell lies, I'll never lose my temper – and I'll be faithful to my wife!'

'Manou,' I said, leaning forward, 'how is she? How was it? The home-coming? How's your mother? Were they pleased to see you? Of course they were! Your brothers and sisters? All the *petits*? And your wife? How is she? And little Rocka, Rocka Prince?'

Manou stared at me; his lower lip trembled, and tears, big tears, slow as the gecko, crept silently down, up and over his cheekbones and, gathering speed, fell off the line of his jaw. 'She's gone. She's left. She's gone to Brazzaville. She's taken him. My little son.'

'Gone?'

'With Nzé – his best friend. With Nzé's best friend!'

'And your son?'

'I've done it. I've cursed him – Nzé. I did it properly, just now. I cursed him, Redmond – before I came to see you.'

'But Nzé? Why Nzé?'

'Because he knew. Of course he knew. He knew all about it – and he never told me. He did nothing. He did nothing to stop it.'

'But how could he? He was with us! He was at Lake Télé – with us.'

'That's nothing to do with it! What's the point – what's the point talking to people like you? You don't understand! What's the point? Nzé – it doesn't matter where he is! He can talk to people – whoever he wants. You don't understand. He visits people. He visits people, in the night – in the night, whenever he wants, wherever he wants!'

'I see.' And I did, for a second or two, until the glimpse of Manou's other world, so close to me – all its spaceless and timeless and unlimited and unstoppable reasons for hatred and recrimination – overwhelmed me, and at once I pulled down the inner blind, and I shut the vision out ... 'Manou, come on the steamer with us. To Brazzaville. Go and see them. Your wife. Rocka Prince.'

'I can't,' he said, walking over to the pile of kit against the front wall. 'I can't. I've got a fever. I can feel it.' He picked up one of his pineapples. 'And anyway, perhaps they don't want me ... not at all?'

'Of course they do! Your son ...'

'No! You're wrong! Wrong! I can't dance, I don't like to dance. Not like Nzé's friend. He never reads a book. He hates books! Nzé's best friend – he loves to dance! He dances!'

'Couldn't you read books *and* dance?'

Manou, holding the pineapple, thought about it. 'No, Redmond ... no ... I, I don't think that's possible.'

'Here,' I said, holding open the neck of the half-empty rice-sack, 'put it in here. And the other one, and your bananas. And we must collect your things.'

We scattered the kit-bag contents about the room (because Lary wasn't there to stop it) and we found Manou's mosquito-net, his two tarpaulins, his head-torch, his Maglite torch, his machete – and his mug. We stuffed everything on top of the remaining rice, I retied the neck of the sack with parachute-cord, and Manou hoisted it onto his shoulder.

'Manou,' I said, opening the door for him. 'About Brazzaville' (thinking that perhaps he had misunderstood), 'if I paid for your passage to Brazzaville – couldn't you get a job? Any job? Then – you could at least see your son. Otherwise, well, you – you may never see him again . . . You could visit him, surely you could? They'd let you do that? You could see him again, watch him grow up. Help him. Little Rocka. Rocka Prince . . .'

Manou stopped outside, in the light from the doorway. 'There are no jobs!' he shouted, swinging round to face me, shaking. 'For people like me? In Brazzaville? There are no jobs! And tell me – you tell me! Where would I stay? Where would I go? To Marcellin? To Marcellin's house? No! He's mean, Marcellin. He won't have his family. He won't have his family in the house!'

'But Nzé's friend – doesn't he have a job?'

'No! No! Nzé's friend – he does not have a job!' Manou paused. 'But he has money, Redmond. Lots of money. He finds it, you know, this and that, here and there.' And he turned; he began to walk off.

'Manou! You're bright . . . you're special . . . I – could write you a reference!'

He stepped back into the light, and he appeared to have aged, to be much older than the Manou I thought I knew. 'A reference! A reference? From you?' He laughed, his first laugh of the evening. 'No, Redmond – you have to be a Big Man, you have to be in the Party.' With his free hand he squeezed my arm. 'But thank you.' And he walked off into the dark.

'Yes, of course,' I said, sitting on the edge of the bed, Manou's untouched mug of whisky in my hands. 'Nzé himself will be next – he'll come for his money. If he can walk, if he can still walk. So . . .' The town generator, and the lamp, shut down for the night. 'Damn,' I said, standing up in the darkness, sitting down again, placing the whisky, very carefully, on the floor, to my right. 'I'm losing it, I'm on my chinstrap here . . .' 'Yes, lad,' said the voice of the Major down in deep memory, in the training wing at Stirling Lines, on automatic, issuing his fiftieth set of identical instructions that year to date: 'You *sleep* with your rifle. Beside you on the pole-bed. And your torch. The right-angle torch. You and your rifle, *never forget*, you stick together – like mating toads, lad, like mating toads . . .'

Oh well, maybe, I thought, as I scrabbled about in the bergen, and found the right-angle torch (olive-drab), just maybe I added that bit about the toads, amplexus in deep memory – it happens, you know, down in the subconscious, in the primordial soup – and with the help of the right-angle torch I found the head-torch, and I strapped it on, freeing my hands, and for a moment or two I couldn't work it out – why were the kit-bags so empty? Burglars!

And I turned round and remembered that no more than ten minutes ago Manou and I had strewn their contents all over the floor, and I found Nzé's mosquito-net and one tarpaulin slung under the bed, and the other tarpaulin thrown almost into the shower-room ('Manou!' I said. 'And no wonder. You can't blame him. But this curse of his. A *proper* curse? A real sorcerer's curse?') ... Nzé's Maglite and machete and Swiss Army knife were dusty-white, but safe, down in the bottom of the empty manioc-sack. So I added the mosquito-net, the two tarpaulins, the cooking-pot (because Nzé was the cook), the spare knives, forks and spoons, two enamel plates, his mug, and one stray chicken-stock cube, still more or less in its yellow wrapper, which had bounced across the filthy floor and come to rest just in front of the offside-rear bedleg (because Nzé's only sauces – 'You must try my sauces!' – were chicken-stock cubes, and because, even I could tell, Nzé was a very bad cook indeed).

But no one came, so in the quiet I lay on the bed and, trying not to fall asleep, I trained both my torches on the ceiling. The little grey-green gecko was still there, but closer, stuck upside-down, almost directly above my head. 'But you're not actually *stuck*, are you?' I said quietly, half to the gecko (it didn't seem to mind). 'There's nothing *sticky* about you, is there?' No, I thought, you're *much* more sophisticated – 240 million years of random mutations, a thousand thousand deaths for each little change in your structure, a change that happened to fit the way you happened to be at the time, a tiny alteration (and maybe one or two big ones): and all that mating, all those generations – because every one of your lizardly ancestors must have been a triumph of a lizard, because he or she, despite everything, lived long enough to breed: and there you are, now, two feet from the join of the back wall and the ceiling, two feet from the hook for the mosquito-net: you're upside-down on this particular damp-stained patch of ceiling. And if you're anything like *Gekko gecko*, who, I'm prepared to admit, must seem a bit of an absurd little artificial nonsense to you – because he's only made it to *Gekko gecko* because he's big, and he lives in houses, and he's common as chopsticks all over South-East Asia – then you, you funny little gecko, you're hanging up there with the help of some 150,000 tiny supple outgrowths on each of the rows of scales on the undersides of your fingers and toes, and the end of each outgrowth branches into hundreds of bristles, and on the end of most of your bristles you have a minute spatulate plate, and in each plate there are sinuses that fill with blood and push it between and around microscopic irregularities in any climbing surface that takes your fancy.

'Sheeee-it!' said the gecko, like a sparrow. 'Sheeee-it sheeee-it sheeee-it!'

'You didn't know? You didn't know about your toes? Well, just enjoy it while you can, you on your grip-toes up there, you're a star, a Darwinian star. But go on,' I said, louder, 'I'm getting bored, holding this torch. And I've got a pain, a crick in my neck, it's this head-torch. So go on – *do* something. Show me!'

The gecko, an intelligent, sympathetic gecko, extended its pink tongue and licked, first, its left eye, and, second, its right eye.

'That's fine,' I said, switching off the right-angle torch, turning off the head-torch, laying both torches beside me on the bed. 'That was clever. That really was impressive. How, if you don't mind me asking – how the hell did you do that? Yes, it really has, you clever gecko you, that's knocked me out,' I said, turning over, moving my left knee over and down over my right, pressing into the U-shaped valley of the horsehair – or was it bushpig? – mattress, flexing my ankles, arching my back, wiggling my shoulders (a bed! a real bed!) ... But I'm sorry, you were saying, you Darwinian star, you gecko you ... No you weren't ... That's right, it was me. Well, it's important, all the same, an important point ... because I wish I could do that – you know, curl up my tongue and clean my glasses ... although I suppose it might be off-putting, for other people I mean ... one look at you, doing that ...'

And I dreamed that I was with the little gorilla, in the iron cage, against the wall – and it was the pre-moment, the personal, spatially vast moment when you understand that before the very next moment is out, you and all your memories will come to an end. But scratch ... scratch ... There was a friend outside, the six-inch grey-green gecko. His feet were fastened on the backplate of the bolt, his hands were grasping the knob, and his million blood-filled spatulae were swelling into every crack and crevice, over every hillock and ridge; and he pulled and pulled, and the bolt scratched back, rust on rust.

Marcellin, standing outside the cage, shouted: 'Redmond! Redmond! You okay? Okay? Let me in! In! In!' And with the butt of the shotgun he struck the side of the cage; the gecko fell to the ground; the gorilla covered his head with his arms. Marcellin, raising the butt high above his right shoulder, brought it down in an arc, and he cracked apart the bars of the cage, the door of the cage, the front of the door, the bars of the front door. 'Marcellin!' I shouted, turning on the right-angle torch, jumping off the bed. 'Hang on! Steady! You'll break the door!'

'Redmond! You need a sleep!' he yelled as I let him in. 'You need a sleep! I didn't want to wake you! So I scratched! With the knife you gave me! I scratched on the glass! But you didn't wake up. So I knocked!'

'Yes.'

'You okay? You had a sleep? You okay now?'

'Well, not much of a sleep ...'

'You will! You will! Two or three days. Four days! You can sleep – you can sleep till the steamer comes. Maybe tomorrow. Maybe next week!'

'Marcellin,' I said, sitting on the edge of the bed, turning on the head-torch, handing it to him. 'Take a seat. Calm down.'

'Yes, yes!' He sat on the chair. 'A little beer! And palm-wine! I took a little beer . . . to my mother,' and his voice dropped away to a whisper. 'But Redmond,' he said, the volume rising, 'it's dark in here. You okay? You're sitting in the dark!'

'I was asleep.'

'Asleep? Why? This is no time to sleep. I want to talk!'

'Marcellin, eat something. I think you should eat something.'

Marcellin pointed the head-torch at me. 'You're clean! Clean clothes!' The beam travelled to my feet, to the left, to the right. 'But what's this?' He half-knelt, stretched forward, and grabbed Manou's mug. 'Whisky! You – you've been drinking! Whisky!' He took a double gulp; his Adam's apple bobbed, twice. 'Johnny Walker! Red Label!'

'It was Manou's. He only had a sip. He was upset.'

'He told you? About Rocka?'

'Yes.'

'Come on Redmond! We can't drink Johnny Walker! Not like this. Not in the dark!' Marcellin got up and dug about in the food-sack. 'Candles! Here we are. Candles – and plates!' He set one full candle, and three stubs, on top of the plates, on the desk, and lit them with his lighter. 'Eat something?' He turned off the head-torch, laid it on the floor and sat down, back-lit by the candles. He peered round at the illuminated desk-top, into the outsize tin of peanut-butter. 'This? Eat this?'

'Do you good. Feel free. Peanut-butter – the best!'

'But . . .'

'But what?'

'Someone – someone's stuck their fingers in here!'

'Don't be silly. Only me. Feel free. Go ahead!'

'Silly? Only you? . . . Only you! Before you washed?'

'Well . . .'

'Forget it! You – your diseases! That's *dirty*.'

'Diseases? I don't have diseases!'

'Huh!'

'Well, there's oats. Try the oats. And powdered milk. And there's a block of sugar.'

'A mug,' said Marcellin, agitated. 'A *clean* mug.' And switching on the torch he went to the food-sack and pulled out, I was glad to see, the blue mug, the big blue one, the gorilla's mug. 'So Manou told you,' he said, mixing up a paste. 'Wife! That's not his wife! That's not even his girlfriend. Not really. The child's his. The little boy. There's no doubt about that. But she's beautiful, Redmond, she's beautiful – so what do you expect? Just what, in your opinion, is she supposed to do? She has to live! And Manou – Manou has no money. No job. Nothing.' He sat down; he took a swig at his oats. 'Manou has no job, Redmond, so he's miserable, so he doesn't eat properly, so he gets malaria, fevers, all kinds of fevers. He's ill, he's always ill, you saw for yourself! This job, this job with you – I thought it would solve things. You know, the money. But now? I thought Manou could set himself up, make a little business. He could deal in something, manioc even! But now – I don't know. She's gone. And our uncle, the one you saw upriver, Manou Emmanuel, the head of the family, people say he's here, in Impfondo. And if that's true – if he really is here – then he's here for a reason. And Redmond – I don't trust him!'

'Why not?' I said, getting up, unscrewing the bottle, pouring us each another quarter-mug. 'Why not?'

'He's the worst. They all come to me, my family. But he's the worst. When I got my job, Redmond' (he smoothed a smear of milk and oats from his moustache), 'the moment I got my job, Manou Emmanuel put in for licences from my Department – far more than anyone's allowed – enough for him to kill every elephant, every Forest elephant between the Motaba and Ibenga! He thought, "Marcellin's in the Government! I'm rich. I'll export all the ivory – I'll send it out myself." And when I said, "No. I'm sorry. I'm not like that," he was angry, Redmond. He made trouble. He was very angry. He said I was corrupt. He said someone else must have paid me. He said other poachers, richer poachers, middlemen – they must have offered me more. More money. It was bad. Very bad. It was difficult.'

'Yes. I understand.'

'I do my best, Redmond, you know I do, but I can't look after all of them. You understand – it's impossible. There's my true brothers and sisters' (he began to count off his fingers), 'my half-brothers, my half-sisters, all the uncles – the aunts – and all the children of all the husbands and all the wives of my true mother and father . . . A hundred people! Maybe more. And that's just the immediate family! Could you? Would you look after a hundred people? In your family?' He twisted forward in his chair, his right hand on the small of his back, as if the question was turning his spine. 'Go on! Tell me! It's hard to believe, I know – look at you! And the way you behave! – but you, you're supposed to be a Westerner: so tell me! Tell me now! Could you? Could you do that? Would even Lary do that? I ask you – would Lary, the Lary that everyone admires – would he? Would you have all those people in the house, in relays, all year round? No rest, no peace? Taking everything? All you earn? Would you? Would Lary?'

'I'm not sure,' I said, jumping up, facing away from the emotion, and emptying, without thinking, the whole of the rest of the bottle into our mugs. 'I'm not sure about Lary – he only sleeps four hours a night, as it is, but he'd probably cut that to three – you know, not a word, no fuss – and goddam well go ahead all by himself and build another house, triple-plus timbers, all that, whatever the word is, just for them. But I wouldn't. No, of course not.' And I sat down again, determined.

'Of course not! Of course you wouldn't. North Americans – they're different. But me – oh yes! – I'm a Big Man. I must be rich, because I won a scholarship to Cuba, and now – I'm in the Government! It doesn't matter, they don't believe it, it doesn't matter that I only get sixty dollars a day – and that's if I'm paid at all! Sometimes, for months, Redmond, the Party says, "I'm sorry, Comrades, we must make sacrifices. For the good of the Party and the People. This month, the country has no money. We can't afford to pay you." But what can I do? It's my job. There's nothing else!'

'Could Manou . . . could Manou get to university, in Brazzaville?'

'Hah!' said Marcellin, waving a small brown moth away from his face, picking up his mug of whisky. 'He should have worked harder. He should have worked harder at school.'

'But he wants to go to university. He really does. Lary inspired him. Isn't there some way . . .'

'Where do you think you are? North America? Here, Redmond, there are no second chances.' He took a sip of whisky, swilled it round his mouth, as if he was cleaning his teeth, and swallowed. 'And very few first chances – if you'd care to look around.'

The little brown moth, now flying round the candles, appeared to have at least five pairs of wings, narrow membranous wisps, its fore- and hindwings divided into streamers, plumes, so maybe, I thought, it's some kind of African Plume moth . . . 'Marcellin,' I said, 'when I walked back here today I saw something special – a bird with long plumes streaming out from its wings, pennants – the Pennant-winged nightjar!'

'Nightjar? A drink! A whisky? I know – it's a whisky, a whisky that puts you to sleep! It knocks you out!'

'The bird I really wanted to see, the one I asked you about in Brazzaville, you remember, at the place with the hippo – the Pennant-winged nightjar!'

'Of course I know! *Engoulevent! Engoulevent porte-étendard!* But Redmond – you see them everywhere! Round here, in Impfondo, at this time of year – they're all over the place. You don't have to go to the forest. They don't even like the forest! They like roads. They rest on the roads. To see a bird like that – all you have to do is drive around in a truck!'

'Okay, but . . .'

'But let's talk. I want to talk! I want to thank you. Just for one thing. One important thing.'

'Thank me? That's twice in one evening!'

'Eh? Listen! We'll talk about it right now – and then that's it, okay? Never again!'

Marcellin put his mug on the floor and leant forward, his elbows on his knees, his hands in front of him, palms together, his fingertips pointing at me. 'Okay?'

'Okay.'

'It's the fetish. The fetish, the ones that Dokou gave us. My fetish. I think – I think it saved my life. In Boha. There's – there's no other explanation.'

'How do you mean?'

He glanced at the door and lowered his voice. 'However you look at it – everyone in Djéké thought the men of Boha would kill us. All those men, everyone except Doubla – because of Bobé – they'd taken an oath. And to take an oath, Redmond, in front of the Chief, that's a very serious matter. And what was there to stop it? The killing? I might have shot one of them. But no more. That gun' – he nodded at it, leaning against the wall – 'one shot! Useless! And can you imagine it – Manou with a machete?'

Marcellin laughed, paused, stared at me, grew quiet, pushed both palms up over his face, shook his head, and took a mouthful of whisky. 'They're killers. The men in Boha. Doubla, all of them – they fight all the time! . . . Nzé and Doubla? With machetes? Nzé! There'd be nothing left. Little bits, Redmond, little bits. Bits for my chickens . . .'

'In Djéké – what happened? When you ran away? When you left us?'

'Ran away? Left you? Is that what you think?'

'No, of course not,' I said, trying to sober up, wondering if there was any water left in the bottles. 'No, I'm sorry. I didn't mean . . . to say that.'

'But you did! You did! Look, Redmond – it wasn't you they'd sworn to kill. They weren't after *you*. It was me. And if we'd all gone to Djéké – they'd have followed. Killed us. For sure. Whereas with you there, still in Boha, they thought, "We'll wait. Because Marcellin – he'll return."'

'I see.'

'Irene – she found the fetish in my pocket. You know, she's young, she liked to put her hand in my pocket! And she said, "So that's it! Now I know. *That's* why you came back to me! *That's* why you're still alive!" So I swore her to secrecy, and I told her all about my grandfather, about Dokou, and about our night with Dokou, the wedding-ring, everything, and how he saved my life – in Boha. So she told her parents. And they told everyone in Djéké. And everyone said, "Aha! So that's why Marcellin Agnagna is still alive! Now we know, we know for sure – there are sorcerers in the north, sorcerers who are even more powerful, sorcerers who know secrets that are hidden even from the sorcerers in Boha! Who is this Dokou? We must find him! We must send someone to him – Badiledi, he'll go – we must send to Dokou, all the way to the far north, and get a fetish, and then we won't be afraid. Never again need we fear the men of Boha!'

'Well done!'

'And that night, Irene – she did things to me. She did things no other girl has ever done to me. And her hands, Redmond, all over me, her little breasts, her orgasms – she exhausted me!'

'What kind of things?' I said, emptying my mug. 'Things? What things?'

'I'm not telling you! What things? I'm not telling you! No – I'm not! I can't tell you everything! Why should I? I'm sick of your questions! It's questions, questions, all day long with you – yes it is, you can't deny it, and I've had enough. I have. I'm squeezed dry. I'm squeezed dry by your questions. Like manioc – that's what I am! A bag of manioc in the press – squeezed, squeezed dry by questions! You know, sometimes, Redmond, I think you're a little boy. And sometimes – not so often – you're like my teachers, the French teachers, the Frenchmen at the lycée in Brazzaville. But you won't find men like that any more! Not in the Congo! Oh no – and now I think about it, no, you're not like them, not at all, because they were good, strict, terrible men! They cared. They taught us. They made us learn. They cared, they cared about us . . .'

'I know. You told me.'

'I did? Did I? . . . Well, you're just as bad. Yes, you are. You repeat yourself. On and on! It's not just me! And besides, of course you repeat yourself – because you're old! It's okay, it's normal. We young men – we expect it. But look at you! You're grey. Pink and grey. Or white – pink and white! Your hair – it's white! You're old!'

'Old yourself!' I said, nettled, too old to think of a rejoinder. 'And I don't repeat myself! And I do care!'

'This bird, that bird,' said Marcellin with a big grin, showing his even white teeth. 'That bird, this bird – who cares?'

'Open up!' came a muffled voice from outside. 'Open up! In the name of the People's Militia!'

'Nzé,' said Marcellin, going to the door. 'He repeats himself. But that's because he's stupid. And he's always laughing. Laughing at nothing . . .'

'He's not stupid,' I said, as Nzé, his cap in his mouth, fell across the threshold. 'Nzé is many things,' I said, like an old man in his chair, 'but he's certainly not stupid.'

'He's drunk,' said Marcellin. 'Nzé – you're drunk!'

'Yes,' said Nzé, picking himself off a kit-bag, focusing on Marcellin with his right, terrestrial eye. 'And so are you.'

'What do you want?' said Marcellin, sitting down. 'What do you want? You're disturbing us. What is it?'

'My money. Quick! There's a girl. Where is it? My money?'

'No idea,' said Marcellin, shrugging his shoulders. 'Who knows? Ask Redmond. Maybe he's got it. Who knows?'

'Your room – it's a mess!' said Nzé, kicking the kit-bag at me. 'It's a mess in here!'

'It's waiting for you,' I said, standing up, reaching behind Marcellin, taking the pile off the desk (the top note was sticky with candle-grease). 'And thank you. Thanks for everything.'

'Yes!' said Nzé, dropping a see-saw of notes to the floor, following them down, ramming them into his right trouser-pocket. 'A girl!' Getting to his feet, he swayed out of the door, banging it shut behind him.

'In Djéké,' said Marcellin, as if Nzé had ceased to exist, 'I felt bad. About deserting you. So I thought – what would Redmond want, what would he ask me to do? The old men! Of course! So I went to see Old Emmanuel. Emmanuel Mangouméla! Emmanuel has a big armchair in his hut, and his wife was there, too. I'm not sure, but I think she's his senior wife, the most important, and perhaps she's not quite right in the head, I don't know, but she wears a crown of leaves. Fresh leaves, every day. Irene says Emmanuel was cursed, long ago, by a sorcerer in Boha. The sorcerer's dead now, but Emmanuel Mangouméla's first wife still wears the crown of leaves, just in case – because it keeps the curse off, and besides, it shows she loves him. Anyway, Redmond, you'll thank me, you'll be pleased with me – you'll forgive me – because Emmanuel told me many things and I made a real effort, hard work, I wrote it down, I remembered it all for you!' Marcellin pulled a minutely folded sheet of paper out of his shirt-pocket, opened it up, and smoothed it flat on his knees.

'Thank you,' I said, trying to keep my eyes open, to stay upright on the edge of the bed. 'Thank you very much.'

'Emmanuel says the true name of the village of Mboukou is Mounpaela and the path that leads there is called Paela or Bassimounpaela.' ('Shee-it!' said the gecko, softly, above me.) 'Mogua's younger brother, Ekoka, bought the pygmy Tokoméné, and, setting himself up in Djéké, gave his slave Tokoméné the neighbouring territory – and it was Tokoméné who created the present village beside Lake Mboukou. On his death Tokoméné was succeeded by his sons Loma, Mouandapa, Mouboussé, and so on, I forget. His children were then joined by other pygmies from the villages of Ebolé, Mokala, Dilé, etcetera. Mogua's sisters were called Boléla, Bandinga, and Momkoumaka, and they lived with Dgomoko. He brought two children into the world, with Boléla. Boléla, in her turn, had two more children, and two are still alive. Their names are Emmanuel Moungouméla and Albert Mouassitea. Mboukou is a village owned by these Bantu and not by the pygmies and its real name is Mounpaela. Mboukou is the name of the lake. The present inhabitants of Mounpaela say the village belongs to them, but that is not correct, they are not the true owners.'

'So Old Emmanuel thinks it's his.'

'Yes, he does. But they're not pygmies in Mboukou. They're slaves. Bantu slaves.'

'Marcellin,' I said, relieved, stretching back on the bed. 'Is that all? Is that it? Could we knock off? Get some sleep?'

'Sleep? No, wait. Of course not. And Redmond, I still have my Johnny Walker! I haven't finished. Sit up! That's rude, lying down. I want to talk. I want to talk to you! Sit up!'

I sat up.

'Emmanuel told me about the coming of the French, the *colons*!'

'Oh dear.'

'The *colons* arrived in the country of the Bomitaba on the first of January 1910. They came up the Likouala aux Herbes river. They installed the first staging-post at Embambé, the chief *colon* was Monsieur Marqueti. The second post was called Elondi, the chief was called Sergeant Major Georges. The third and central post was Djéké whose chief was Joro Joro Gabriel, the second chief was Piala, Honoré, the third was Mouzoromba. The fourth post was Botoumayo with an African in command, Sergeant-Chief Kaïba. The fifth post was Mitoubou whose chief was Jean-Jules Aureli. The sixth post was at Kakasengué with a true Frenchman as chief, Kassimata Omer. The seventh post was Moumbelou with Captain Jean-Marie in charge . . .'

'Marcellin, what about the morning? Eh? Sleep? Couldn't we get some sleep?'

'Sleep? No. Wait – it gets better, much better. History, Redmond, history! You like it. You'll be pleased. You'll want to thank me!'

'But the morning . . . What's wrong with the morning?'

'The *colons* began the war with a massacre in the village of Edzama in the valley of Djéké. Edzama was too small and weak to fight the *colons* and the people fled to Djéké. On learning the news Djéké decided to imprison its *colons* and make war. Two soldiers were killed (Africans who worked for the *colons*). The first soldier to be killed was called Kobôlé, a Yakomadu from

Central Africa. The second was Kande, a Yalomaldé from Central Africa. The leader of the war was a Bomitaba, by the name of Minéngué, from the village of Embambé.

'The second battle took place at Botoumouana. One morning, in front of the vegetable market, the people of Ibolo formed an attack platoon. This platoon had no spears or guns. The combat was at close quarters with double-sided knives. The villagers surprised the unarmed soldiers in the vegetable market. The soldiers were killed like goats by the people of the village of Ibolo on the twenty-fifth of July 1914, at eight o'clock in the morning. Afterwards the news reached Captain Jean-Marie, as well as our headquarters at Djéké, by way of a priest. Father Leon of Liranga came to help, to give advice to the villagers. He was the only one who was able to intervene and he brought the battle to an end on the first of October 1914.

'The name Likouala is the third which the region has held.' (Marcellin took a very small sip of whisky. What's up? I thought. What's going on? . . . And whatever it is, when it comes, I'll be too sleepy to do anything about it . . .) 'From 1910 to 1916 this region was called Oubangui Alima. The taxes were paid at Port-Rousset (Owando). Because the Gabon was the least populated of all the French region in the territory of the Congo that area was given to the Gabon and this area again became Moyen Congo. The Moyen Congo was once more part of Oubangui Chari. The name became Bas-Oubangui and the taxes were paid at Mbaïki. On the thirtieth of July of the same year the *colons* realized that the Oubangui was three times less populated than Moyen Congo, and Bas-Oubangui once more became part of Moyen Congo.'

'Marcellin . . .'

'The most important place became Impfondo and the administrator in charge of the region, Honoré Bédalet, reunited all the Chiefs under him before he allowed them to go back to their villages. He made them the following request: "I am holding you here for a matter of administration. Your region has been called Oubangui-Alima and after that Bas-Oubangui. Before the day is out you will find me another name for your region." This request was put to two Hereditary Chiefs, Evongo from Impfondo and Mondaye from Epéna. The interpreter was Mawengué. Evongo replied as follows: "The first names were given by the *colons*. We must now find a new name for the region."

'The administrator Bédalet took as his example the French Indies where there is a river and the French asked the Indians what they called that river in the Indian language. The Indians replied that the river was called Liné because it was bordered with stones. "And what do you call the stones?"

"We call the stones roes." And the French nicknamed the river Linesroe.

'At Epéna you have a river bordered with savanna and osiers. "I give a name to your region," and Honoré Bédalet. "This is the Region of the Likouala aux Herbes." This is the third name, which has lasted from the twenty-sixth of August 1926, until now. The taxes are paid at Epéna. And Redmond, guess what?'

'Uh?'

'Guess what he wanted, Old Emmanuel? Guess what he asked for, in payment!'

'No idea.'

'Pills, Redmond. Pills for *la faiblesse sexuelle*, sexual weakness, what do they call that? In England?'

'Impotence.'

'Impotence! Horrible! Imagine it! Redmond – I hope I don't grow old.'

'You won't.'

'So I gave him some of your vitamin pills. The orange ones. And the yeast, the ones that are brown and powdery.'

'He'll get wind.'

'But they'll work – if he thinks they'll work.'

'Maybe.'

'And now, Redmond, you must pay me.'

'Pay you? What for?'

'The information, of course, the history. Because you're pleased. You want to thank me!'

'Thank you.'

'That's 50,000 CFA.'

'Fifty thousand? For that?'

'Okay,' said Marcellin, upending his mug, draining his whisky, 'I'll tell you. Redmond – it's my mother. The husband, he's moved out. He wanted to take a young wife, to bring her home. He asked my mother. It's normal, after all. It's sensible. You know, for him – for the sex. And for my mother – because the new wife, the junior wife, she has to help about the house, do all the heavy jobs. She helps them when they're old, and with all the children, too, lots of children. Besides, he can afford it, Redmond, because he's rich, he has a job, he works up the road, at the diesel depot, Hydro-Congo. He moves oil-drums around, something like that, and he never gets drunk. He's okay. I'm all for it. Just one more wife – it's not much to ask – and then he'll stay and look after my mother, too. And anyway – think of Bague, Xavier Bague! – after a time they always like the first wife best. Because of the memories, that's what you say, but I think it's because the first wife's learnt – she doesn't make demands, she's no longer rude to her husband all day. She's just there, by his side. So they start to love each other. All over again. They really love each other.'

'Yeah.'

'Yeah? You don't agree? Well, it's civilized, Redmond, and ancient, and in any case, in every case, it's better than your way – your horrible way, with your divorces and courts and misery and all the different houses that everyone moves into – the expense, the waste! The money!'

'So what went wrong?'

'It's my fault. I think it's my fault. My mother – she's caught your Western ways. She caught them from me. Because I went to Cuba, and France. She wouldn't have it. She wouldn't have them in the house. She threw them out.'

'So now what?'

'Now? Now she's starving, Redmond. The children. She has no food. And the moneylender, he's in the house. He won't go away. He asks for sex.'

'I'd better face it,' I said, getting off the bed. 'I'd better face it. I'd better count the money. I'd better see what's left.'

I unpeeled the top of the taped-in bag in the bergen map-pocket, pulled out the small bundle of notes and laid them on the desk-top. We counted and recounted, and however hard we tried it came to 99,000 CFA, just under £200. I gave Marcellin the 50,000.

'Redmond, it's okay. Don't worry. You've got enough for the hotel – I'll live with Florence! And the steamer, that's okay, you've paid our passage. And food. And in Brazzaville – you can send for money, more money, from the post office, the big one, in the square!'

'Well, no, I can't actually.' I felt a little stab of panic in the guts. 'Not exactly, because, you see – I brought it all here, everything I could, everything I had.'

'You did?' He opened the door. 'Everything? Then welcome to Africa, my friend. Now you really are an African! It's what you wanted! In Brazzaville – you'll have to live like an African!'

Pulling the door to behind him with uncharacteristic gentleness, he paused. He looked back at me. 'You'll have to trust to your fetish,' he said, with no hint of irony. 'Your fetish will protect you.' And he closed the door, quietly.

37

For the next two days I had no need to invoke Lary and invent a routine: I slept, and ate peanut-butter, and shuffled out to Madame Langlois' little store to buy more peanut-butter and oats and powdered milk and sugar, and shuffled back, to sleep. Early in the morning of the third day I managed to gather up my stiff and crusty clothes, find my mould-covered towel, the last half-bar of red soap, and walk down to the river. The far shore was invisible in the white dawn mist, and there was no one about but a pair of fishermen a hundred yards upstream, standing in their long dugout, bending down, checking their basket-traps, close in to the bank. I stripped to my shirt and pants, soaked my clothes, soaped them on the upturned hull of the broken dugout, rinsed them, scrubbed them with the scrubbing-stone, repeated the whole process, washed myself with the clothes-soap, waded out in my wet shirt and pants, took off my pants, put on my dry trousers and boots, waved at the fishermen (they waved back) and walked home, up the bank, across the tarmac road, up the track to the left of the Catholic mission and left into the hotel garden.

I spread the cleanish wet clothes and towel along the veranda railings, locked the quarter-bar of soap in the room, and sat under the tree with the multiple stems (or were they aerial roots?) in the early morning sun, to dry my shirt. As I watched a black lizard of about, I thought, the body-weight of one and a half rats, with an orange head and a tempting, orange end to its tail, plodding sluggishly, four-square, lizard-fashion, through the grass beneath a little tree opposite, Manou, slipping silently through the entrance from the track, came and sat beside me. His gym-bag over his shoulder, he was still wearing his militia uniform and his big hat. His movements over-emphatic, slightly manic, he looked bedraggled, frayed, as if, unlike me, he'd had very little sleep.

'It's bad,' he said. 'It's bad at home.'

'I know. Marcellin told me.'

'My uncle, Manou Emmanuel, the head of the family, the hunter, he's there.'

'Yes, Marcellin said – he said he was in Impfondo. That's good. He came to help.'

'To help? Manou Emmanuel? No! Of course not! He came – he came because he thought I'd be back by now, back from Lake Télé. He asked for money. He took my torch.'

'Your torch?'

'My two tarpaulins, my mosquito-net, my machete, my head-torch – everything.'

'But why?'

'I said to him, "Please. Don't do this. Redmond – he gave them to me. They're precious. They're mine. They went to Lake Télé. I've never owned such things, not in all my life! I'll give them to my children, to little Rocka, and he'll give them to his children, to his children's children." Manou Emmanuel laughed at me, in front of everyone. "Rocka!" he said. "Who's that? Forget him, Manou! He's gone. You'll never see Rocka again! So why do you want these? What use are they to you? It's a waste. Give them to me. I command you, as Head of the Family! The tarpaulins – just right, they're camouflaged. And the mosquito-net. I need one. I need it all, for hunting. So give it to me, and I'll go hunting with my pygmies, and kill elephants – lots of elephants!"'

'The bastard.'

'Then Marcellin came, late at night, and he gave my mother money – and she gave it to the moneylender and the moneylender went away. Then Marcellin said, "Manou, I know exactly how much Redmond paid you. So now you must give that money to our mother. All of it. For her and for the children." So I did. All of it. So, Redmond, that's it, isn't it?' He looked at me, and tried to smile, but his lips set askew, half-way. 'So . . . no books. No books! Not one!' And he tried to laugh.

'Manou . . .'

'It's okay! That's normal! That's right – when you have money you *should* give it to your family. All of it! That's correct. No, Redmond, no – that's not why I came here. It's something else. Something bad. Something I've done, something I did.'

The lizard, who was now round the other side of the tree, reared his orange head on its scaly black wrinkled neck, above the grass, and stared at us, like a dinosaur.

'Nzé's father – I killed him.'

'You what?'

'The curse, Redmond, the curse I made. I killed him – but I didn't mean to, I didn't mean to do that! Nzé was in the vegetable market, and he was boasting about his journey, the journey to Lake Télé, about the monster. He was boasting to this girl, and the girl said, "Nzé, your father at Dongou – he was ill, and now he's dead." And the girl ran, Redmond, the girl ran away.

And Nzé, he's been drunk for two days and nights, with all his friends, and a lot of people who aren't his friends, and he's spent almost all his money. On beer! On beer Redmond! They've had more beer than any of them have ever had in all their lives. And they're all drunk. And Nzé's sick. He's lying in the hut of his first woman, the mother of his first child, the one with the thin little boy, the boy with the bent legs – she's looking after him. And Nzé screams, Redmond, he screams, "My father! My father is dead!"'

'Manou, listen. Even if it's true – even if it's true that Nzé's father really is dead – the two events, your curse and his death, they're not related. Impossible. Nature – it's not arranged that way.'

'But Redmond . . .'

'You didn't do it!'

'Steady,' said Manou, like Marcellin. 'Steady, Redmond. I know you now. And you don't have to be polite. Not with me. Not any more.'

'Polite?'

'Lary told me, in Makao.'

'Makao? Lary? Manou – what are you talking about?'

'You don't know? He didn't tell you? Not once?'

'What? Tell me what?'

'Dr Lary,' said Manou, slipping his gym-bag off his shoulder and placing it carefully on the ground beside him, to his right. 'Dr Lary – he can keep a secret!' Manou leant back against the tree; he stretched out his legs on the grass – and I noticed that somehow, despite everything, he'd found time to wash his gym-shoes. 'It was in Makao, when I was ill, and Marcellin said I could leave – I could go all the way back home, all the way back down the Motaba to Rocka, for free, because the boatman, he was waiting.'

'Yes, I remember.'

'And you didn't care! You didn't care if I went or stayed!'

'I did care. Manou, I . . .'

'But when you were out the back, in the bushes, and Marcellin and Nzé were in the village somewhere, looking for women, Dr Lary came and sat beside me where I was lying, you remember – on your tarpaulin – against the wall. And that was before the ants came, several days before the ants came.'

'Yes.'

'I didn't feel well. I was ill. I was missing Rocka. I was sad. I looked at Dr Lary's big brown boots – with all those laces. "Manou," he said, "don't you worry. Redmond, he's English. In England – they're *polite*. They don't tell you what they're thinking. They don't tell you how they feel. They can't. They're *polite*. But that doesn't mean he doesn't like you, Manou – he just can't tell you, that's all. It's a rule, you know, a tribal rule. Manou," he said, 'before we met you, I got to know a Batéké, a great guy, Nicholas, in Brazzaville, and he's quite different from these people – and not just to look at!" So Redmond, then I understood, and I wasn't upset about you, I wasn't miserable about you – about what you thought of me. Not any more. Not after that.'

'Manou, I'd no . . .'

'He said, "Manou! In America! Stateside, in the US of A, we're straight-forward people – or we try to be! If we like someone, we tell them. And Manou, by the way," he said, "I like you." That's what he said. Dr Lary said to me: "I like you."'

'But Manou, I do care, I did care. I just didn't know what was for the best, that's all, I thought you were ill . . .'

'You never talked! You didn't say. You – you never talked to me!'

'No, I suppose . . . no, I didn't. I never did.'

'Dr Lary, he talked to me, not for long, you know, but often, all the time. He said to me one day, after a march, in the forest, when you'd all gone with Muko to see how he dug a hole for water – to watch Muko dig a hole! – Dr Lary told me, he told me about the people in America. He said they're not like us in America, Redmond, not like you and me, the English and the Africans – they have no Hereditary Chiefs, none at all! In America it's different – there are very few Big Men. And the people in America, they think well of a man not for what he is, but for what he's done! So they're the real Communists, aren't they? Not like here!'

'Well, yes, put like that . . .'

'So Redmond! Now you understand! I want to do something so people will think well of me – and then I'll go to America!'

'Yes, let's hope. Maybe something . . .'

'That's my plan! And Rocka – I'll find him! I'll take him, too. I'll hold him. All the way. I'll hold his hand!'

'Manou, you . . .'

'Yes! I know! It won't be long! Redmond – you're right! And Dr Lary, that's when it started, in the hut in Makao – when you, you were in the bushes!'

'I was? But I thought I was quick. You know – at that sort of thing.'

'You? In the bushes? You take forever!'

'Oh.'

'He said to me, "Manou," he said, "listen. I'm a teacher. I know about this. It's okay. You're okay. It happens to us all. Listen – if you go back now you'll never forgive yourself. A month of release, happiness; and – misery. You'll think less of yourself. You'll have to live with it, for the rest of your life, because there it was, the one great opportunity, right in front of you, and you didn't take it. I see it with my students when they drop out of school – and I don't mean the ones who leave for something else they want to do, something they know they can do, something better. No, Manou, I mean the ones like you, now, the ones who leave because they're frightened, because they can't face it, because they're afraid they may fail; and most common of all, Manou, are the ones who leave just because there's the usual dirty little swaggering jerk in their year, and they see this jerk, this untested, bragging little bag of syphilis swaggering all about the place, and they say to themselves, 'There's no point! I'll fail! Because he's better than me, that Nzé!' So they leave."'

'Lary? He said that?'

'I sat up!' said Manou, and sat up. 'I sat up! I felt better! "And Manou, you'd better believe me," he said. "Don't do it! Because, Manou, I won't tell anyone, I promise, you can trust me, but Manou – me, I don't think you have a fever. You shake, yes, and you look ill – but you don't sweat and shiver and toss about and bang your teeth around and groan and talk to yourself all night like Redmond did when he had a fever, in Brazzaville, before I knew you. No, I think you're frightened, Manou. I think you're frightened of the goddam jungle, something like that – and quite right, too, it can be frightening, very frightening, I don't deny it. And it's not comfortable – but you promise me: you won't go back! Trust me. Stay close to me. I'll look after you, I promise. Because your spirits – all that goddam crazy bullshit. The sucks. They won't get me!"'

'Suckers.'

'So Redmond – I came with you. And I lasted – and I didn't let you down – and I went to Lake Télé!'

'Well done!'

'Dr Lary – how he sweated! He sweated under his hat – where the hair had fallen out! All wet! And the bees – you remember? – how he hated the bees!'

'The bees!' I said, and laughed, the first laugh, it seemed, in a long time, and the laugh travelled down my spine, and all my muscles went limp, and they sank into the grass, and I could feel my toes in my boots. 'The bees! But not the ones that sting you – he didn't mind that. It was the sweat-bees, mopani, the ones that do you no harm at all, that's what he couldn't stand. The ones that crawl into your eyes and up your nose for a suck. The suckers! He'd swear. And get angry. And thrash about! And then the real bees, the honeybees – they'd get annoyed and sting him!'

'He'd swear! Terrible things! He taught me words, Redmond, lots of words. But tell me, truly, I wondered – in America, do people do things like that to their mothers? And to chickens?'

'I don't know!' I said, stretching out in the gathering heat, my shirt steamed dry, long ago. 'How would I know? Don't ask me – but no more than anywhere else, I suspect. Although in England, it's true, I don't know *anyone* who does things to their mother, or to chickens, come to that, but sheep – now that's a different matter.'

'Sheep?'

'Yeah – you stuff their back legs down your wellies.'

'Wellies?'

'Wellington boots. Special boots. Rubber. For knocking up sheep.'

'Dr Lary – he worked with sheep!'

'Yes. He liked it.'

'And he has boots like that? Special boots?'

'Several pairs.'

'So Dr Lary,' said Manou slowly, with a grin, as if some thought was giving him great happiness. 'Dr Lary – he's not perfect!'

'Perfect? The hell he is!'

Manou, quiet and earnest, plucked at a grass stem. 'So what, in your opinion, are the faults of Dr Lary?'

'Uh? I don't know!' I said, trying, and failing, to think of something damning. 'Maybe – maybe he doesn't have any! Because there must be at least one or two people on earth who've missed out on faults, mustn't there? If you think about it – if we're all so various, and everything's distributed on a graph, then Lary's banged up one end, that's all. Law of averages, or something. Statistics, Manou, that's what it's called.'

'I know what it's called! You forget! I went to school! You're not the only one who went to school! Here in the Congo Redmond – we're the best-educated people in all Africa, because the whites in South Africa, they don't count, because they're Nazis, like the war, the war when Brazzaville was the capital of France. And I learnt that, too, you see, in school! Statistics! I know you now, Redmond, you forget, you can't fool me. It's no good, being polite. It won't work! Not any more! Because I know what you really think – yes, "Manou," you say, "that Manou, he's *primitive*, he believes in spirits, he's a *savage*." And that's what Dr Lary thought, too – he said to me, that very day in Makao he said, "Manou," he said to me. "You're bright. I can tell. I'd take you as a student, no problem. But tell me, there's one thing I don't understand. Not at all. This spirit stuff – why not dump on it? Manou," he said to me, "how could you believe in sheepshit like that?" Sheepshit!' And Manou gave one of his odd, constrained little laughs.

'*Savage*,' I said, sitting up, plucking at the grass myself. 'Manou, for Christ sake!'

'"Christ!" – that's what you all say. That's what Dr Lary said: "Christ!"

Who's that? The spirit of the French, the *colons*. The spirit of the Portuguese. The spirit of slavery. The spirit of the slavers! An evil spirit, Redmond, really evil, a vicious spirit. Yes, and your Allah, he's younger, I know, but he's just as bad, he's worse, I don't care – he's the same – the spirit of the Arabs!' Manou leant forward and waved his right hand towards the Oubangui, towards the east. 'The spirit of slavery, but that way! Another vicious spirit, with no mercy, who told the slavers what to do, who visited them, by night, in the spirit way, but he lives over there! And that's the only difference! They're shits, Redmond, your Allah and your Christ, vicious evil spirits, slavers, spirits that murdered us, and our little children, too, like Rocka – they're *caca*, Redmond, your spirits, they're sheepshit!'

'Yes, Manou, they are, they're thoroughly immoral, primitive, *savages*, with no mercy – and if you don't believe in them they pack you off to hell, to the everlasting gas-chamber, except, of course, that you're never quite allowed to die, you scream for ever. Because the followers of those spirits, Manou, they think they're special, the chosen – like a leopard-sect!'

'African spirits – they're not like that! No! Not at all! The worst – the very worst they do – you must wander through the forest, all alone, for ever.'

'I know. And Manou – there are botanists who *pay* to do that – so come on, why not do as Lary said? Why not dump all of it, all the spirits? Say goodbye? Get free? Lary's right, isn't he? It's wrecking your life. Because Nzé – for instance – he doesn't wish you ill. He doesn't visit people in the night, in the spirit way, any more than you do. He's talented, like you said, and he plays all those instruments – and he's a human being, like you and me. And Manou – you didn't kill his father!'

'You whites,' said Manou, staring at me. 'You really don't understand, do you? You're children in such things. Nothing but children. You're too young to understand. And to think – I came here to ask for your help. And you've given me no help. Because you're no good. You're no good at all!' And he turned away.

'Manou, I'm not sure I *can* help you,' I muttered, feeling dizzy in the gathering heat, 'I'm not sure what you want. Not at all. And I'm sorry, I seem to be tired, very tired – and the worst of it is . . . I don't know why. There's no excuse, none. But there you are, I shake a bit, you see – inside. It's not physical. It's not a *physical* shake.' And I held up my right hand, to show him.

Manou looked at me for a moment; he smiled, as if everything had become plain; he put his left arm across my shoulders, and pulled me to him. 'Of course you're tired! Of course you shake! Look – I'll help you. Because you can't help me! And now that you shake, too, Redmond, you'll listen to me, I know you will. Because I can explain it all to you, I like you, I can help you.' (He released me.) 'Of course you're tired! Because your spirit – it's been fighting! Inside, fighting all the time, fighting off the spirits in the forest. Yes. They're the worst, Redmond, there's no spirit stronger, and the sorcerers, the really powerful sorcerers in the forest – they control those spirits. You don't know anything about it, not at the time, you just feel tired, and you just feel ill, as if you had a fever – and you do have a fever, all night long, every night, because your spirit is fighting for you. And Redmond, that's why you need to sleep, why you sleep so long!'

'I see.'

'But you don't. Not yet. So I'll tell you Redmond – take Boha, for instance, just the one village. Statistics! It happens in every village in the forest, and you, you never knew! Nzé's girl, she told him in secret, the most powerful sorcerer in Boha, he wanted to pay Madame Bobé – a chicken would do it, or even less – he wanted to pay her to leave her hut, her kitchen hut, just for a short while, when she was cooking, and in the darkness, so no one could see. It's easy, it really is – you just take a skull, the head of someone who loved you, your mother or father or brother, or maybe just someone who liked you, that'll do – and, when no one is about, you scrape up a potful of that white sand beside the river. Back in your hut, when it's dark and in secret – you tell no one but your wives – you light your lamp, or a candle, and you turn the head up the other way, throat-downwards, and you rest the head on the white sand: and you leave it looking at you there, Redmond – you must look at it all the time, for hours and hours, without moving, and you must meet its eyes, you must talk to it – until all the insides of the head you love have dripped into that new white sand in your own pot. And that sand in your pot, it lasts a lifetime – because whenever you ask it to help you, whenever you're in trouble or you want something, you only take a very little bit – just a smear, Redmond, but on all ten fingers. It smells, it smells for a time, Nzé told me, but then the smell goes away, into the air, it leaves for the forest, and the spirit stays, and it fights for you – whenever you ask, because you must talk to it, Redmond, every night. So Redmond – you push your fingers into the food of this person, when it's warm, not too hot, the food of the person whose mind you wish to enter, by night, so his supper, the last meal, that's the best! And he eats it, the paste, and if it's fish, he says to his wives, "That fish, you caught it just in time. I'm not angry, but Natalie!" (so to speak) he shouts, "Are you deaf?" (She's out the back, Redmond, in the kitchen, she's my junior wife.) "Come here girl! At once! Do you hear? That fish I caught with my best net, in the river, under the tree in the deep pool – you throw it away, the rest of it! You hear me? It's strong. It's too strong!" But if it's meat I've caught, antelope or bushpig, in my biggest, longest, most expensive nets – nets, Redmond, that have taken me years to make – "That meat," I say. "It's good, it's strong!" Or even, Redmond, perhaps it's elephant! Because by now, of course, I'm a hunter, a proper hunter, like Manou Emmanuel – and I'm famous, and everyone knows me, and I'm rich, and I own pygmies, lots of pygmies, and very probably I've bought one or two Bantu pygmies as well, say Jean Molongui and one other Bantu pygmy from Mboukou, because they know how to hunt in the swamps, and they're not afraid of the monster, and the monster, he's not afraid of them – they're *friends* – well, if it's elephant in my saka-saka, I shout "Wives! Wives!" I shout, "Come here! At once!" And they come from the back, and stand in front of me, beside the television set, and at their backs there's my special, favourite wall, with my bookcase – made of real steel that shines – and all my books, hundreds of books, and I say, as it were, to all of them, all five, I shout, "My elephant! That big one with the thirty-kilogram points I shot last week, with my brand-new Kalashnikov, it's good! It's strong! Well done, wives. But wait a minute, don't go – I'll see you later, like my young friend Nzé, who's dead, and his spirit is dead, I'm sorry, but it's dead for ever – and we won't mention it again, will we? We won't go into it, but you know, and I know, poor Nzé, God rest his soul, as my friend Redmond, a Westerner, would say, long ago – poor Nzé, he was no good was he? He was no good at sex! But here, wives, here's a little something – here's 50,000 CFA for each of you . . ." Because you see Redmond, I'd sold all my points, all the ivory I'd shot that week – I'd taken it downriver all the way to Brazzaville to the wife of the President – and "Manou," she said. "Well done! You're rich and famous, and I'll ask my husband, Denis Sassou-Nguesso, and – if you promise not to tell anyone, not even your mother, and most certainly not your elder brother Marcellin – perhaps Denis Sassou-Nguesso, the President, will pay for you and your wives to go to North America to study with Dr Lary. But for now, Manou Jean Felix Burond, take this, a small gift," – and she gave me a soldier's bag like yours, but it was full of notes, and, Redmond, I don't mean your 1,000 CFA – and, "Goodbye for now," she said, "I'll see you later, by night," – and she flew off to Japan with my points, my elephant tusks (and these tusks were even bigger than those of Manou Emmanuel) in her own aeroplane, which is very fast, a jet.'

'Manou, please,' I said, getting up (spots like paramecium swimming across my eyeballs), feeling faint in the heat which was now intense, 'Manou, please – let's go inside. We must drink a little water.'

Manou sat on the chair in the dusty little room, the gym-bag at his feet. 'Manou,' I said, weary, handing him a water-bottle, the tin of peanut-butter – and a spoon. 'Is that really your fantasy? Is that how you see it?'

Manou bent forward; he lined up the water-bottle, the spoon, and the tin of peanut-butter, on the floor, beside the gym-bag; he took off his hat, held it between his knees, and in his long, delicate fingers he turned it slowly, like Lary, kneading the brim. 'Redmond, I knew it,' he said softly. 'I knew it – that *is* how you think of me.'

'I don't . . . It didn't . . . it didn't sound like you!'

'You know me! How could you? You know me now! You *know* what I want in life – I want my wife back; I want Rocka back. I want to go to America, to study with Dr Lary. I want to learn things; I want to learn about the world – to learn how it was made. So how? How could you think that? Because I worked for you, real work – remember? Or have you forgotten? Because I, Manou Burond, found things out for you – it wasn't easy, it wasn't even safe – but I found secrets. I wrote them down in my notebook – when no one was looking – the notebook you gave me, and I heard about Lake Télé. I drew a map. I learned where the monster walks.'

'And Madame Bobé? You wrote that down? The paste?'

'Two saka-saka! Always two!'

'Two? She brought it in a bucket!'

'On the top – fish saka-saka, for you. And under the leaf – meat saka-saka, the chickens you bought – meat, for Nzé and me! We left the fish. We took the meat!'

'But why?'

'The paste! The sorcerer's fingers. He put them in the fish!'

That diarrhoea, I thought, the diarrhoea that wouldn't go away . . . the one I blamed on the little gorilla . . .

'The sorcerer – he's good, he's powerful, it worked!'

'Worked?'

'You gave Madame Bobé double her money! You paid twice for chickens. You gave Old Bobé your penknife, the little red one! And that penknife, Redmond, that was a better penknife than the one you gave me – it had scissors, and a little bit of glass to start fires, to catch the sun.'

'Yes, I suppose I did . . . But, Manou, why didn't you *tell* me?'

'Tell you? That's dangerous! You could die like that! And Old Madame Bobé, she doesn't like white men. She complained about you, all the time, all day long. They say her father's father – he was a leader, a famous fighter, a Bomitaba from Ibolo. He fought in the great battle against the *colons* – but, Redmond, his fetish failed. He died. They killed him.'

Manou put his hat back on his head, picked up the water-bottle, unscrewed the lid and took a long drink. 'Biology! That's my fantasy! Dr Lary said, "Manou," he said, "biology – that's full of real miracles, biology *tells* you how life began, what it is, who we are, why we behave like we do, and you can take it from me, Manou, strange but true – biology is more interesting and complicated and mysterious than all your goddam spirits, however many there are – and it's more complicated, it's more fun even than physics and chemistry; it *uses* physics and chemistry, it's Number One! And Manou," he said, "you'd better believe it – biology, it tells you more than your spirits do, to the power of . . ." I didn't understand, but it was recurring, you know, a really big number. Statistics! "Your spirits!" he said. "The sucks!"'

'Suckers.'

'So that's my fantasy, Redmond, you know it is – to study with Dr Lary. He's wrong about the spirits, he knows nothing, he's like you, he's a child – but I won't tell him, because he wouldn't like it. The spirits will help me. They'll be my secret, they'll be silent, deep inside – and at night they'll help me. I'll study at night, you see, because I'll have a light, a real electric lamp, and a desk, all my own – and the spirits, they'll help me! Dr Lary' (Manou started on the peanut-butter, spooning it out), 'he's no good at night. He doesn't understand. He's afraid of the dark. In Manfouété, he was frightened.'

'So was I – and so were you.'

'In Manfouété? Me? I was asleep! Redmond – I escaped! I sent my spirit away. I came here, to Impfondo. I was safe. I escaped!'

'Manou . . . I don't know, but America, you see, that might be difficult. Because this is a Communist state, so maybe, just maybe, you ought to think about Cuba, or Moscow, or Peking. Win a scholarship. In fact I think you have to go there – to Moscow – even if you want to be a midwife.'

'Midwife?' Manou clattered the empty tin of peanut-butter and the spoon across the top of the desk. 'Girls! That's for girls! No – I'll go to America, where the people are free, and they work hard, and they're equal – because they value each other! Yes, Redmond, I'll write to you, at night, from my desk, and I'll tell you about it, in secret, all about how the spirits have helped me – and I'll ask about your fetish, too, because that fetish from Dokou, Redmond, that fetish will change your life. Yes! I'll tell you about my house! The one I built myself! And in the evenings I'll read this Dickens, and I'll watch all the films of Dr Lary and I'll eat saka-saka and I'll drink Coca-Cola – and Johnny Walker Black Label. Because by then, of course, I've passed all my exams, and by now I teach, I teach the young people how to pass their exams; I teach with Dr Lary, we're workers, co-workers, we're equal, we value each other! And, Redmond – I see Dr Lary, I see him *every day*. And perhaps, I don't know, but maybe, if I ask him personally, in the dark, then Dr Lary and his new young wife – she's called Chris – his junior wife, the most beautiful girl in America, perhaps they'd come to my hut? Redmond – tell me now, truly – would they come?'

'Of course!'

'Yes, I think so too. Because Dr Lary, you see, every night in the forest he'd say to me, "Manou," he'd say, "what wouldn't I give for a goddam bath! I'd kill for a bath!" But if Dr Lary came to my hut, my big house, he wouldn't need his machete, because I'd say, "Dr Lary, and you, Chris, the most beautiful woman in America, you are welcome! Because when I built this house – with my own hands – I built a bath inside it." (Imagine, Redmond! Imagine it! A bath! And this bath – it'll be just like your basin in the cabin, you know, First Class, on the steamer, because I'll have those taps that you just turn in your hands and the water comes out – but a bath is big, huge, on the ground, and it's big enough to lie in!

'Yes, Dr Lary and his new young wife, they'll like that, so they'll come and see me – Dr Manou Burond. I'll teach hard, Redmond, I'll really work, I'll teach and teach, all about the beginning of life and the dinosaurs and the monster I heard. I'll teach the young people everything I know about Lake Télé, and the forest, the jungle. And so because I'm in America and there are jobs – and you're paid money for what you do – I'll have a truck outside. Yes! But not a yellow Toyota like Joseph – the one that Marcellin drives when he's here. No! I want the best. An American truck – it's called a Dodge. Just like Dr Lary's. The same. Only mine, Redmond, I'll paint it red. And you know why? Can you guess?'

'No idea.'

'To remind me! To remind me of my origins, my roots – to remind me of the People's Republic of the Congo! The flag! The Parti du Travail!'

'Well done!'

'But that's not why I came. Redmond – I'm not like all the others, am I?'

'No Manou, you're not.'

'I don't ask for things – do I?'

'No, you don't.'

'So here, look, I've bought you a present. A real one.'

Manou unzipped his gym-bag and drew out its sole contents, the bronze circlet, the three fused bronze rings that I'd seen him hold, long ago, it seemed, on that night in his mother's house. He handed it to me.

It was heavy, reddish-brown, spotted with a dull green; this circlet, this ancient bracelet, I thought, this is the most organic, the most nearly-living piece of metal I've ever felt. 'Manou,' I said, placing it on the floor between us, no longer sure what it was made of, 'I can't take this. You must not give me this.'

'Why not?' he said quietly, hunching his shoulders down and forward, until his chest looked concave, and he'd shrunk into himself.

'Because it's special, Manou. It's precious. It belongs to you. It belongs to your family.'

'I know! And that's – that's why you must have it.'

'I don't understand.'

'Dr Lary told me – he gave you one of his used-up pens.'

'What?'

'But you have pens of your own!'

'Yes.'

'I saw! So when we were alone I said, "Doctor Lary, tell me, please, why did you give Redmond that used-up pen? He has pens of his own. Pens that work!"'

'And what did he say? What did Lary say?'

'You know how it is with Dr Lary!'

'I do,' I said, uneasy.

'Yes, Dr Lary, he tells you the truth! He's not like you. Not at all. Redmond, if you go to Dr Lary to ask a question, and you ask him that question, he looks at you, into your eyes, he thinks to himself, he thinks hard – and he tells you the truth!'

'I know. It's a rotten habit.'

'Dr Larry said, "Look, Manou. I'm sorry. I really am. But as you asked – I'll tell you the truth. It's not nice. So prepare yourself. Let's sit down on those logs, by the fire, and you'd better hold on to something." Well, Redmond, that great big branch that Muko cut – the dead branch, you remember, the one that he carried to the fire, all by himself? – that branch, it was waiting, right in front of us. And there was no one about, so we hung on to it.'

'And?' I said, uneasier still, shifting about on the edge of the bed.

'Dr Lary said, "It's not nice," he said. "But Manou, as you asked, I'll tell you the truth. In my opinion," he said, "and it's only my opinion – our Redso, he's not completely sane."'

'The pig!'

'"Manou," he said, "I'm sorry to have to tell you, I really am, but Redso, he has a little room in his house, in his hut at home, in his village, and this room, Manou – it's crammed with goddam junk. Old books," he said, "old pictures, that's okay, but, Manou, you wouldn't believe it, there's used-up pens and old boots in there, and goddam moth-eaten skins of foxes and bits of rabbit (they're furry things) and a stuffed stoat, like a civet, or a mongoose, and really horrible stuffed birds – you can't tell what they are – and birds' eggs, and bags of fur, and, worst of all, Manou, there's a burnt-up foot, the burnt foot of a friend of his and that, Manou, is in a coffee-jar! This room, Manou, it has no windows, and he keeps the door locked, and it's all black in there, black as his socks, but Manou, the spooky thing, the really spooky thing, is this – everything in that room belongs to someone who's dead, snuffed it, gone! And, Manou, in my opinion, and it's only an opinion, that

461

is one whole heap of goddam sheepshit that he ought to throw away!" "Dr Lary!" I said, and I held on, "I knew it! Our Redmond – he's a sorcerer! A sorcerer! He has a house for the spirits! That room, Dr Lary, that's a fetish house!"'

'"Yes," said Dr Lary. "Yes, our Redso, he's a sorcerer! I hadn't thought of it like that. But you're right. He is. He bloody well is!" And Dr Lary let go of the branch. He took off his big hat – and he laughed. We let go of the branch and we laughed! We laughed together! And when we'd finished all our laughing Dr Lary said, "That Redso," he said, "I don't know, but you can bet your bottom dollar he's got leopards' teeth in there – on a goddam necklace, I shouldn't wonder – and more than one stinking black sock he's lost, and elephant noses, for all I know, and gorilla skulls!"'

'I don't have gorilla skulls! There are no gorilla skulls!'

'So it's true! It's true!'

'The bastard!'

'But what's wrong? Why be ashamed? It's African! It's sensible! It's a fetish house!'

'It's not! It's . . . those objects . . . they're . . . *aide-mémoires*. Yes, that's what you'd say! They're *aide-mémoires*. They help me. They really matter. They tell me who I am. They help me remember the past, those objects, they mean something only to me, childhood things, and the people – yes, there are objects that belonged to people, friends, dead friends. That little room, Manou, that's not junk, that's part of the brain, the region that puts you in touch with the only bits of your past you really value, your true self, the hidden self. And you can only see the future – shape the future – when you're in touch with that real self, the deep self, the only one that matters!'

'That's it! It's true! The objects! The ancestors! A fetish house!'

'But . . .'

'Redso!' Manou paused. He stared at his clean gym-shoes. 'Redso,' he said gently, 'Redso . . . before . . . I couldn't call you Redso . . . but now, I understand. You look white – but you're an African. Your ancestors, they're really African, the old people, pygmy ancestors, the ones who love the forest. And that is why you went crazy, and why you wanted to walk in the forest, with no food, for ever and ever, all the way to Ouesso. Yes, your ancestors were the real Africans, pygmies – animals, some people say, like chimpanzees and gorillas – and they called to you, and that is why you talked to spirits, in your tent, and in Brazzaville, too, Dr Lary said, in your fever. And it's why you talked and talked, all day, all night, to that gorilla. You knew. You knew how to talk to the spirit of gorillas. Whereas us, Redso, we come from the north-west!'

'Manou, all our ancestors were African. Everyone on earth – we come from Africa.'

'Redso, Redso, you don't have to be *polite*. Not any more. I know you now. Your reason, science – it's all a pretence. Bullshit! Sucks! Sheepshit! So here' (he picked up the bronze ring) 'I want you to have it. Take it! You'll place it in the fetish house, and you'll remember. Because you know and I know – you and I will never meet again. But with this, you'll remember. I'll help you. You'll look at this and you'll remember. You'll remember your friend, your dead friend, Manou!'

Taking the circlet in my right hand, I turned away, horribly afraid that I'd burst into tears, and I found myself looking at the back wall, for the gecko. But he wasn't there. 'Manou,' I said, obeying a reflex, reaching, with my left hand, into my right pocket. 'Here,' I said, facing away, holding out two 10,000-CFA notes. 'Please. I'm sorry. It's crude. I know. But you see I don't have anything – anything special. So please. Take it!'

'I'll keep it,' he said, looping the gym-bag over his right shoulder, standing up to go. 'I'll keep it secret. And I'll buy a book. Two books! Three books! Because I saw one, Redso. Last year – I saw one in the market!'

Late that evening I was woken by a bang on the door. 'Koko!' (Bang! Bang!) 'Koko!'

'Nzé!' I shouted, switching on both torches. 'Wait!'

'Redmond!' he yelled in my ear as I let him in, 'Redmond! My father – he's dead!'

'I know,' I said, backing into the room, in front of him. 'I heard. I'm sorry.'

'My cap – my cap from Cuba. I've lost it!'

'I'm sorry.'

'And my money – I've lost it!'

'Your money? All of it?'

'Give it back! My money! I need it!'

'Give it back? I haven't got it!'

'I know. It's gone. So give it to me. Just the same. All over again. No more. I need it!'

'But I don't have it . . .'

'I know!' he said, swaying, looking round for it, catching hold of the railing at the foot of the bed. 'So where is it?'

'You don't understand,' I said, picking up the food-sack full of his gifts and belongings, trying to hand it to him. 'Twenty-nine thousand – that's all I have left.'

'That'll do. That's a start. That's not much, that's for *petits*. But for now – that'll do!'

'No. It won't do. It's all I have,' I said, forcing the neck of the sack into his right hand. 'I need it.'

'This?' said Nzé, looking at the sack, with horror, as if I'd handed him a corpse. 'What's in it?'

'You must go home, Nzé. Face your family. Tell them what's happened. About your father. Maybe – maybe they'll understand.'

Arching forward, pushing himself off the bedrail, with his right foot Nzé kicked the door wide open. 'They won't!' he shouted, high-pitched, almost a scream. Holding the sack in his arms, as if it was a child, he stumbled into the night.

Bibliography

Alexander, Lieutenant Boyd, *From the Niger to the Nile*, 2 vols, London, 1908

Alexander, Herbert, ed., *Boyd Alexander's Last Journey*, London, 1912

Alexander, R. McNeill, *Dynamics of Dinosaurs and other Extinct Giants*, New York, 1989

Allégret, Marc, *Carnets du Congo: Voyage avec Gide*, Paris, 1987

Allen, Chris, et al., eds, *Benin, The Congo, Burkina Faso: Economics, Politics and Society*, London, 1989

Andriamirado, Sennen, *Le Défi du Congo-Ocean: ou l'Épopée d'un Chemin de Fer*, Paris, 1984

Anon. By A F.R.G.S., *Wanderings in West Africa: From Liverpool to Fernando Po*, 2 vols, 2nd ed., London, 1863

Anon, ed., *Africa and its Exploration as told by its Explorers*, 6 vols, London, 1891

Arya, O. P., A. O. Osoba and F. J. Benett, *Tropical Venereology*, 2nd ed., Edinburgh, 1988

Badian, Seydon, *Congo: Terre généreuse forêt féconde*, Paris, 1983

Bahuchet, Serge, *Les Pygmées Aka et la forêt centrafricaine*, Paris, 1984

Bailey, K. V., *Connaissons nos oisaux: les oiseaux communs des alentours de Brazzaville*, Brazzaville, n.d.

Bakker, Robert T., *The Dinosaur Heresies: New Theories Unlocking the Mystery of the Dinosaurs and their Extinction*, New York, 1986

Bannerman, David Armitage, *The Birds of Tropical West Africa: With Special Reference to those of the Gambia, Sierra Leone, the Gold Coast and Nigeria*, 8 vols, London, 1930–1951

Barley, Nigel, *Smashing Pots: Feats of clay from Africa*, London, 1994

Barns, Alexander T., *The Wonderland of the Eastern Congo: The Region of the Snow-crowned Volcanoes the Pygmies the Giant Gorilla and the Okapi*, London, 1922

Bass, Thomas A., *Camping with the Prince: And Other Tales of Science in Africa*, Boston, 1990

Bates, Robert H., V. Y. Mudimbe, and Jean O'Barr, eds, *Africa and the Disciplines: The Contributions of Research in Africa to the Social Sciences and Humanities*, Chicago, 1993

Beadle, L. C., *The Inland Waters of Tropical Africa: An Introduction to Tropical Limnology*, London, 1974

Bell, Dion R., *Lecture Notes on Tropical Medicine*, 2nd ed., Oxford, 1985

Biebuyck, Daniel, *The Arts of Zaire*: vol. I: *Southwestern Zaire*, Berkeley, 1985; vol. II: *Eastern Zaire: The Ritual and Artistic Context of Voluntary Associations*, 1986

Biebuyck, Daniel, and Kahombo C. Mateene, eds and trans., *The Mwindo Epic: From the Banyanga (Congo Republic)*, Berkeley, 1969

Birmingham, David, and Phyllis M. Martin, eds, *History of Central Africa*, 2 vols, Harlow, 1923

Bishop, Walter W., and J. Desmond Clark, *Background to Evolution in Africa*, 1967

Bonnafé, Pierre, *Histoire sociale d'un peuple congolais*, Livre I: *La Terre et le Ciel*, Paris, 1987; Livre II: *Posseder et Gouverner*, 1988

Boote, Paul, and Jeremy Wade, *Somewhere down the Crazy River: Journeys in search of Giant Fish*, Swindon, 1992

Boyer, Pascal, 'Parquoi les Pygmées n'ont pas de culture?', *Gradhiva*, No. 7, Paris, 1989

Branch, Bill, *Field Guide to the Snakes and other Reptiles of Southern Africa*, Cape Town, 1988

Brown, Leslie H., Emil K. Urban, and Kenneth Newman, eds, *The Birds of Africa*, London: vol. I, 1982; Emil K. Urban, C. Hilary Fry and Stuart Keith, eds, vol. II., 1986; C. Hilary Fry, Stuart Keith and Emil K. Urban, eds, vol. III, 1988; Stuart Keith, Emil K. Urban and C. Hilary Fry, eds, vol. IV, 1992

Browne, Stanley G., 'Yaws', *International Journal of Dermatology*, 1982, pp. 220–223

Bücherl, W., E. Buckley, and V. Deulofeu, eds, *Venemous Animals and their Venoms*, vol. I, New York, 1968; W. Bücherl and E. Buckley, vol II, eds, 1971; W. Bücherl and E. Buckley, eds, vol. III, 1971

Buckland, Francis T., *Curiosities of Natural History*, London, 1857; Popular ed., 1893

Burrows, Captain Guy, *The Land of the Pigmies*, London, 1898

Canizares, Orlando, ed., *Clinical Tropical Dermatology*, London, 1975

Carter, Gwendolen M., *National Unity and Regionalism in Eight African States*, New York, 1966

Chadwick, Douglas H., *The Fate of the Elephants*, London, 1993

Chapin, James P., 'The Birds of the Belgium Congo', Part I, *Bulletin of the American Museum of Natural History*, New York: vol. LXV, 1932, pp. 1–756, Part II, vol. LXXV, 1939, pp. 1–632; Part 3, vol. 75A, pp. 1–821; Part 4, vol. 75B, 1954, pp. 1–846.

Chief, Roberto, *The Macdonald Encyclopedia of Medicinal Plants*, Milan, 1982; trans. Sylvia Mulcahy, London, 1984

Clark, J. Desmond, ed., The Cambridge History of Africa: vol. I: From the Earliest Times to *c.* 500 BC, Cambridge, 1982; vol. 2: From *c.* 500 BC to AD 1050, ed. J. D. Fage, 1978; vol. 3 From *c.* 1050 to *c.* 1600, ed. Roland Oliver, 1977; vol. 4: From *c.* 1600 to *c.* 1790, ed. Richard Gray, 1975; vol. 5: From *c.* 1790 to *c.* 1870, ed. John E. Flint, 1976; vol. 6: From 1870 to 1905, ed. Roland Oliver and G. W. Sanderson 1985; vol. 7: From 1905 to 1940, ed. A. D. Roberts, 1986; vol. 8: From *c.* 1940 to *c.* 1975, ed. Michael Crowder, 1984.

Cloud, Preston, *Oasis in Space: Earth History from the Beginning*, New York, 1928

Commission de Coopération Technique en Afrique au Sud du Sahara, *Comptes Rendues de la Troisième Conférence Internationale pour la Protection de la Faune et de la Flore en Afrique*, Bakavu, Congo belge, 1953

Connah, Graham, *African Civilizations: Precolonial Cities and States in Tropical Africa: An Archaeological Perspective*, Cambridge, 1987

Cook. G. C., *Communicable and Tropical Diseases*, London, 1988

Cousins, Don, *The Magnificent Gorilla: The Life History of a Great Ape*, Lewes, 1990

Crompton, D. W. T., *Parasites and People*, Basingstoke, 1984

Crowther, Geoff, *Africa on a Shoestring*, 2nd edn, South Yarra, 1986

Curry-Lindahl, Kai, 'Ecological Studies on Mammals, Birds, Reptiles and Amphibians in the Eastern Belgian Congo', Part II (Report No. 1 of the Swedish Congo Expeditions 1951–1952 and 1958–1959), Annalen van het Koninklijk Museum van Belgisch-Congo, Tervuren, 1960

Curry-Lindahl, Kai, *Bird Migration in Africa: Movements between Six Continents*, 2 vols, London, 1981

Darwin, Charles, *On the Origin of Species by means of Natural Selection, or the Preservation of Favoured Races in the Struggle for Life*, London, 1859

Darwin, Charles, *The Descent of Man and Selection in Relation to Sex*, 2 vols, London, 1871

Darwin, Charles, *The Expression of the Emotions in Man and Animals*, London, 1872

Davidson, Basil, *Old Africa Rediscovered: The Story of Africa's Forgotten Past*, London, 1959

Dawkins, Richard, *The Extended Phenotype: The Long Reach of the Gene*, Oxford, 1982

Dawkins, Richard, *The Blind Watchmaker*, Harlow, 1986

Dawkins, Richard, *The Selfish Gene*, 2nd edn, Oxford, 1989.

de Foy, Guy Philippart, *Les Pygmées d'Afrique Centrale*, Rocquevaire, 1984

Delaporte, François, *The History of Yellow Fever: An Essay on the Birth of Tropical Medicine*, trans. Arthur Goldhammer, Cambridge, Massachusetts, 1991

Demesse, Lucien, *Quest for the Bebingas the World's Most Primitive Tribe*, trans. E. Noel Bowman, London, 1958

Demesse, Lucien, *Techniques et économe des Pygmées Babinga*, Paris, 1980

Denham, Major, Captain Clafferton, and the late Doctor Oudney, *Narrative of Travels and Discoveries: in Northern and Central Africa, in the Years 1822, 1823 and 1824, extending across the Great Desert to the Tenth Degree of Northern Latitude, and from Kouka in Bournou, to Sackatoo, the Capital of the Felatah Empire*, 2 vols, London, 1826

Desowitz, Robert S., *The Malaria Capers: More Tales of Parasites and People, Research and Reality*, New York, 1991

Du Chaillu, Paul B., *Explorations and Adventures in Equatorial Africa: With Accounts of the Manners and Customs of the People, and of the Chace of the Gorilla, Crocodile, Leopard, Elephant, Hippopotamus, and Other Animals*, London, 1861

Du Chaillu, Paul B., *A Journey to Ashango-Land: And Further Penetration into Equatorial Africa*, London, 1867

Du Plessis, J., *Thrice through the Dark Continent: A Record of Journeyings across Africa during the Years 1913–16*, London, 1917

Eggert, Manfred K. H., 'The Central African rain forest: historical speculation and archaeological facts', *World Archaeology*, vol. 24, no. 1, *The Humid Tropics*, 1 June 1992, pp. 1–24

Ehret, Christopher, and Merrick Posnansky, eds, *The Archaeological and Linguistic Reconstruction of African History*, Berkeley, 1982

Estes, Richard Despard, *The Behaviour Guide to African Mammals: Including Hoofed Mammals, Carnivores, Primates*, Berkeley, 1991

FitzSimons, V. F. M., *A Field Guide to the Snakes of Southern Africa*, London, 1962

Foelix, Rainer F., *Biology of Spiders*, Cambridge, Massachusetts, 1982

Frank, Katherine, *A Voyager Out: The Life of Mary Kingsley*, London, 1986

Gide, André, *Voyage au Congo*, Paris, 1927; *Travels in the Congo*, trans. Dorothy Bussy, New York, 1929

Gillon, Werner, *A Short History of African Art*, London, 1984

Goodall, Jane, *The Chimpanzees of Gombe: Patterns of Behaviour*, Cambridge, Massachusetts, 1986

Gorer, Geoffrey, *Africa Dances*, London, 1935

Greenway, James C., *Extinct and Vanishing Birds of the World*, New York, 1958

Grzimek, Bernhard, ed., *Grzimek's Encyclopedia of Mammals*, 5 vols, New York, 1990

Hall, Richard, *Stanley: An Adventurer Explored*, London, 1974

Haltenorth, Theodor, and Helmut Diller, *A Field Guide to the Mammals of Africa including Madagascar*, trans. Robert W. Hayman, London, 1980

Hamilton, W. D., *Narrow Roads of Gene Land: The Collected Papers of W. D. Hamilton: Evolution of Social Behaviour*, Oxford, 1996

Happold, D. C. D., *The Mammals of Nigeria*, Oxford, 1987

Harding, Jeremy, *Small Wars, Small Mercies: Journeys in Africa's Disputed Nations*, London, 1993

Harrison, Christopher, *France and Islam in West Africa, 1860–1960*, Cambridge, 1988

Hather, John G., ed., *Tropical Archaeobotany Applications and New Developments*, London, 1994

Hatt, John, *The Tropical Traveller*, 2nd edn, London, 1985

Heinrich, Bernd, *Bumblebee Economics*, Cambridge, Massachusetts, 1979

Hill, John E., and James D. Smith, *Bats: A Natural History*, London, 1984

Hilton, Anne, *The Kingdom of Kongo*, Oxford, 1985

Hogendorn, Jan, and Marion Johnson, *The Shell Money of the Slave Trade*, Cambridge, 1986

Hölldobler, Bert, and Edward O. Wilson, *The Ants*, Berlin, 1990

Hoskyns, Catherine, *The Congo since Independence: January 1960–December 1961*, Oxford, 1965

Hutchinson J., and J. M. Dalziel, *Flora of West Tropical Africa: the British West African Territories, Liberia, the French and Portuguese Territories South of Latitude 18°N to Lake Chad, and Fernando Po*, 2nd edn, rev. R. W. J. Keay, vol. I, London, 1954; vol. II, 1958; vol. III: *The Ferns and Fern-Allies of West Tropical Africa*, A. H. G. Alston, 1959

Ingold, Tim, David Riches, and James Woodburn, *Hunters and Gatherers 1: History, evolution and social change; Hunters and Gatherers 2: Property, power and ideology*, 2 vols, Oxford, 1988

Jobling, James A., *A Dictionary of Scientific Bird Names*, Oxford, 1991

Johanson, Donald C., and Maitland A. Edey, *Lucy: The Beginnings of Humankind*, London, 1981

Johnston, H. H., *The River Congo: From its Mouth to Bólóbó; with a General Description of the Natural History and Anthropology of its Western Basin*, London, 1884

Johnston, Sir Harry H., *The Story of my Life*, Indianapolis, 1923

Jong, Elaine C., *The Travel and Tropical Medicine Manual*, Philadelphia, 1987

Kano, Takayoshi, *The Last Ape: Pygmy Chimpanzee Behaviour and Ecology*, Stanford, 1992

Kearton, Cherry, and James Barnes, *Through Central Africa from East to West*, London, 1915

Keay, R. W. J., *Trees of Nigeria*, Oxford, 1989

Kingdon, Jonathan, *East African Mammals: An Atlas of Evolution in Africa*, 7 vols, London, 1974–82

Kingdon, J. S. [Jonathan], 'The role of visual signals and face patterns in African forest monkeys (guenons) of the genus Cercopithecus', *Transactions of the Zoological Society of London*, 35, 1980, pp. 425–75

Kingdon, Jonathan, *Island Africa: The Evolution of Africa's Rare Animals and Plants*, London, 1990

Kingdon, Jonathan, *Self-Made Man and His Undoing*, London, 1993

Kingsley, Mary H., *Travels in West Africa: Congo Français, Corisco and Cameroons*, London, 1897

Kingsley, Mary H., *West African Studies*, London, 1899

Ki-Zerbo, J., ed., *General History of Africa*, vol. I: *Methodology and African Prehistory*, London, 1981; vol. II: *Ancient Civilizations of Africa*, G. Mokhtar, ed., 1981; vol. III: *Africa from the Seventh to the Eleventh Century*, M. Elfasi, I. Hrbek, eds, 1988; vol. V: *Africa from the Sixteenth to the Eighteenth Century*, B. A. Ogot, ed., 1992; vol. VI: *Africa in the Nineteenth Century until the 1880s*, J. F. Ade Ajayi, ed., 1989; vol. VIII: *Africa under Colonial Domination 1880–1935*, A. Adu Boahen, ed., 1985; vol. VIII: Africa since 1935, Ali A. Mazrui, ed., 1993

Lambert, David, *Collins Guide to Dinosaurs*, London, 1983

Lieth, L., and M. J. A. Werger, eds, *Tropical Rain Forest Ecosystems*, Amsterdam, 1989

Lloyd, A. B., *In Dwarf Land and Cannibal Country: A Record of Travel and Discovery in Central Africa*, London, 1909

Lucas, Adetokunbo O., and Herbert M. Gilles, *A Short Textbook of Preventive Medicine for the Tropics*, 2nd edn, London, 1984

Macdonald, David, ed., *The Encyclopaedia of Mammals*, 2 vols, London, 1984

McDonald, Gordon C., et al., *Area Handbook for People's Republic of the Congo (Congo Brazzaville)*, Washington, DC, 1971

McEwan, P. J. M., ed., *Nineteenth-Century Africa*, London, 1968

MacGaffey, Janet, *Entrepreneurs and Parasites: The Struggle for Indigenous Capitalism in Zaire*, Cambridge, 1988

Mack, John, *Emil Torday and the Art of the Congo, 1900–1909*, London, 1990

Mackal, Roy P., *A Living Dinosaur? In Search of Mokele-Mbembe*, Leiden, 1987

Mackworth-Praed, C. W., and Captain C. H. B. Grant, *Birds of West Central and Western Africa*, 2 vols, London, 1970–73

McLynn, Frank, *Stanley: The Making of an African Explorer*, London, 1989

McMillan, Nora, 'Robert Bruce Napoleon Walker, F.R.G.S., F.A.S., F.G.S., C.M.Z.S. (1832–1901), West African trader, explorer and collector of zoological specimens', *Archives of Natural History*, vol. 23, part 1, February 1996, pp. 125–141

Malbrant, René, *Faune du Centre Africain Français (Mammifères et Oiseaux)*, Paris, 1936

Manning, Patrick, *Francophone Sub-Saharan Africa*, Cambridge, 1988

Mason, K., ed., Naval Intelligence Division, *French Equatorial Africa and Cameroons*, London, 1942

Mattingly, P. F., *The Biology of Mosquito-Borne Disease*, London, 1969

Mecklenburg, Adolphus Frederick Duke of, *In the Heart of Africa*, trans. G. E. Maberly-Oppler, London, 1910

Mecklenburg, Adolf Friedrich Duke of, *From the Congo to the Niger and the Nile: An account of the German Central African Expedition of 1910–1911*, 2 vols, London, 1913

Meredith, Martin, *The First Dance of Freedom: Black Africa in the Postwar Era*, London, 1984

Miller, Christopher L., *Theories of Africans: Francophone Literature and Anthropology in Africa*, London, 1990

Milligan, Robert H., *The Fetish Folk of West Africa*, New York, 1912

Moffett, Mark W., *The High Frontier: Exploring the Tropical Rainforest Canopy*, Cambridge, Massachusetts, 1993

Nassau, The Rev. Robert Hamill, *Fetichism in West Africa: Forty Years' Observation of Native Customs and Superstitions*, London, 1904

Noordhock, Gerda, *Syphilis and Yaws: A Molecular Study to Detect and Differentiate Pathogenic Treponemes*, Amsterdam, 1991

Northern, Tamara, *The Art of Cameroon*, Washington, DC, 1984

Nowak, Ronald M., *Walker's Mammals of the World, Fifth Edition*, 2 vols, Baltimore, 1991

Oliver, Roland, *The African Experience*, London, 1991

Oliver, Roland, and Anthony Atmore, *The African Middle Ages 1400–1800*, Cambridge, 1981

Oliver-Bever, Bep, *Medicinal Plants in Tropical West Africa*, Cambridge, 1986

Owen, D. F., *Tropical Butterflies: The Ecology and Behaviour of Butterflies in the Tropics with Special Reference to African Species*, Oxford, 1971

Owomoyela, Oyekan, *A History of Twentieth-Century African Literatures*, Lincoln, 1993

Preston, Richard, *The Hot Zone*, London, 1994

Putnam, Anne Eisner, *Eight Years with Congo Pigmies*, London, 1955

Radin, Paul, and James Johnson Sweeney, *African Folktales and Sculpture*, New York, 1952

Richards, P. W., *The Tropical Rain Forest: An Ecological Study*, Cambridge, 1952

Ridley, Matt, *The Red Queen: Sex and the Evolution of Human Nature*, London, 1993

Ridley, Matt, *The Origins of Virtue*, London, 1996

Riemenschneider, Dieter, and Frank Schulze-Engler, *African Literatures in the Eighties*, Amsterdam, 1993

Robbins, Warren M., and Nancy Ingram Nooter, *African Art in American Collections: survey 1989*, Washington DC, 1989

Rosevear, D. R., *The Rodents of West Africa*, London, 1969

Sarno, Louis, *Song from the Forest: My Life Among the Ba-Benjellé Pygmies*, London, 1993

Schaller, George B., *The Year of the Gorilla*, London, 1965

Schebesta, Paul, *Among Congo Pigmies*, trans. from the German, Gerald Griffin, London, 1933

Schebesta, Paul, *My Pigmy and Negro Hosts*, trans. from the German, Gerald Griffin, London, 1936

Schebesta Paul, *Revisiting My Pygmy Hosts*, trans. from the German, Gerald Griffin, London, 1936

Schweinfurth, Georg, *The Heart of Africa: Three Years' Travels and Adventures in the Unexplored Regions of Central Africa. From 1868 to 1871*, 2 vols, London, 1873

Segy, Ladislas, *African Sculpture Speaks*, New York, 1951

Sénéchal, Jacques, Matuka Kabala, and Frédéric Fournier, *Revue des connaissances sur le Mayombe*, Paris, 1989

Serle, William, and Gérard J. Morel, *A Field Guide to the Birds of West Africa*, London, 1977

Shoumatoff, Alex, *In Southern Light*, London, 1986

Skaife, S. H., *African Insect Life*, Cape Town, 1953

Smuts, Barbara B., et al., eds, *Primate Societies*, London, 1987

Stanley, H. M., *Through the Dark Continent: Or the Sources of the Nile around the Great Lakes of Equatorial Africa and down the Livingstone River to the Atlantic Ocean*, 2 vols, London, 1878; 2nd edn, 1 vol., 1899

Stanley, H. M., *In Darkest Africa: Or the Quest Rescue and Retreat of Emin, Governor of Equatoria*, 2 vols, London, 1890

Stanley, Richard, and Alan Neame, eds, *The Exploration Diaries of H. M. Stanley*, London, 1961

Steentoft, Margaret, *Flowering Plants in West Africa*, Cambridge, 1988

Stoecker, Helmut, *German Imperialism in Africa*, trans. Bernd Zöllner, London, 1986

Stringer, Chris, and Robin McKie, *African Exodus*, London, 1996

Sutton, S. L., T. C. Whitmore, and A. C. Chadwick, *Tropical Rain Forest: Ecology and Management*, Oxford, 1983

Swainson, W., *Birds of Western Africa*, 2 vols, London, 1837

Swinton, W. E., *The Dinosaurs*, London, 1970

Tati-Loutard, J. B., *Anthologie de la littérature congolaise d'expression française*, Yaounde, 1977

Thompson, Virginia, and Richard Adloff, *Historical Dictionary of the People's Republic of the Congo*, Metuchen, N. J., 1974, 2nd edn, 1984

Thonner, Franz, *Dans la grande forêt de l'Afrique Centrale: mon voyage au Congo et à la Mongola en 1896*, Brussels, 1899

Torday, E., *Camp and Tramp in African Wilds: A Record of Adventure, Impressions, and Experiences during many years spent among the Savage Tribes round Lake Tanganyika and in Central Africa, with a description of Native Life, Character, and Customs*, London, 1913

Tremearne, Major A. J. N., *The Ban of the Bori: Demons and Demon-Dancing in West and North Africa*, London, 1914

Trial, Georges, *Dix ans de chasse au Gabon*, Paris, 1955

Turnbull, Colin M., *The Forest People*, New York, 1961

Vanden Bergh, Dr Leonard John, *On the Trail of the Pigmies: An Anthropological Exploration under the cooperation of the American Museum of Natural History and American Universities*, London, 1922

van Lawick-Goodall, J., *In the Shadow of Man*, London, 1971

Vansina, Jan, *Paths in the Rainforests: Towards a History of Political Tradition in Equatorial Africa*, London, 1990.

Wack, Henry Wellington, *The Story of the Congo Free State: Social, Political, and Economic Aspects of the Belgian System of Government in Central Africa*, New York, 1905

Werner, A., *The Language-Families of Africa*, London, 1915

Werner, David, *Where There Is No Doctor: A Village Health Care Notebook*, London, 1979

West, Richard, *Brazza of the Congo: Exploration and Exploitation in French Equatorial Africa*, London, 1972

Williams, John G., *A Field Guide to the Butterflies of Africa*, London, 1969

Wilson, Henry S., *The Imperial Experience in Sub-Saharan Africa since 1870*, Minneapolis, 1977

Wissmann, Hermann von, *My Second Journey Through Equatorial Africa: From the Congo to the Zambesi in the Years 1886 and 1887*, Bergmann, Minna J. A., trans., London, 1891.

Wollaston, A. F. R., *From Ruwenzori to the Congo: A Naturalist's Journey across Africa*, London, 1908

Woodruff, A. W., and S. G. Wright, *A Synopsis of Infectious and Tropical Diseases*, 3rd edn., Bristol, 1987

Worthington, S. and E. B., *Inland Waters of Africa: The Result of Two Expeditions to the Great Lakes of Kenya and Uganda, with Accounts of their Biology, Native Tribes and Development*, London, 1933

Wrangham, Richard W., et al., *Chimpanzee Cultures*, Cambridge, Massachusetts, 1994